We the Gamers

We the Gamers

How Games Teach Ethics and Civics

Karen Schrier

OXFORD
UNIVERSITY PRESS

OXFORD
UNIVERSITY PRESS

Oxford University Press is a department of the University of Oxford. It furthers the University's objective of excellence in research, scholarship, and education by publishing worldwide. Oxford is a registered trade mark of Oxford University Press in the UK and certain other countries.

Published in the United States of America by Oxford University Press
198 Madison Avenue, New York, NY 10016, United States of America.

Library of Congress Cataloging-in-Publication Data
Names: Schrier, Karen, author.
Title: We the gamers : how games teach ethics and civics / Karen Schrier.
Description: New York : Oxford University Press, [2021] |
Includes bibliographical references and index.
Identifiers: LCCN 2020049209 (print) | LCCN 2020049210 (ebook) |
ISBN 9780190926106 (hardback) | ISBN 9780190926113 (paperback) |
ISBN 9780190926137 (epub)
Subjects: LCSH: Moral education. | Games—Moral and ethical aspects. |
Civics—Study and teaching. | Ethics—Study and teaching.
Classification: LCC LC268 .S397 2021 (print) | LCC LC268 (ebook) |
DDC 370.11/4—dc23
LC record available at https://lccn.loc.gov/2020049209
LC ebook record available at https://lccn.loc.gov/2020049210

DOI: 10.1093/oso/9780190926106.001.0001

To my family

To our teachers

To us

Contents

Acknowledgments   *ix*

PART I   TEACHING ETHICS AND CIVICS

1. We the People   3

2. Why Should We Teach Ethics and Civics?   19

3. What Should We Teach?   29

PART II   USING GAMES FOR KNOWLEDGE AND ACTION

4. What Is the Knowledge We Need?   51

5. How Do We Take Real-World Action?   65

PART III   USING GAMES FOR CONNECTION AND COMMUNITY

6. How Do We Connect and Communicate?   83

7. How Do We Understand Ourselves and Our Emotions?   99

8. How Do We Cultivate Compassion and Respect for Others?   117

PART IV   USING GAMES FOR CRITICAL THINKING AND INQUIRY

9. How Do We Make and Reflect on Decisions?   141

10. How Do We Read and Evaluate Information?   157

11. How Do We Analyze Problems and Systems?   171

12. How Do We Explore and Design?   191

PART V   GAMES FOR ETHICS AND CIVICS

13. Guidelines, Questions, and Considerations   211

14. We the Gamers   224

Appendix I. Example Lesson Outline 1   231
Appendix II. Example Lesson Outline 2   235
Appendix III. Design Toolkit   239
Appendix IV. Design Principles   245
Appendix V. Recommendations   249
Notes   253
Index   385

Acknowledgments

Most of this book was written during the global COVID-19 pandemic.

I want to acknowledge the difficulty of writing, editing, and researching during a time of uncertainty, fear, loss, and grief. I also want to acknowledge the intensity of educating and learning, of caring for one's children, and of just staying home during such a time. It is complicated to be existing amid so many contradictions—of being both isolated and surrounded, silent and chaotic, and hidden and longing to be found. I cannot help but be influenced as these events unfolded around me.

And, I want to acknowledge the bittersweet joy of having a new baby, Jacob, who was born during the process of writing this book, and who grew alongside the pandemic.

I also want to acknowledge the importance of community. This book would not exist without all of my communities—my families, my friends, my colleagues, and the games community.

First, I want to thank all the amazing people I interviewed or connected with: Valencia Abbott, Morenike Alugo, Sarah Andes, Princess Anifowose, Joshua Archer, Adeola Babatunde, Janine Berger, Ikeola Bodunde, Amber Coleman-Mortley, Grace Collins, Sabrina Culyba, Caitlin Daniels, Paul Darvasi, Fiyinfunjah Dosumu, Kelli Dunlap, Cynthia Emami, Trish Everett, Matthew Farber, Marla Felton, Joshua A. Fisher, Emmanuel Guardiola, Ailsa Gilliam, Eric Gordon, Owen Gottlieb, Leigh Hallisey, Jessica Hammer, Christopher Harris, Tom Harrison, J. Tuomas Harviainen, Emma Humphries, Barry Joseph, Aparna Khanna, Thomas Kunze, Elizabeth LaPensée, Shannon Meneses, Francisco Moller, Elizabeth Newbury, Eugene Ohu, Judith Okonkwo, Scot Osterweil, Ashley Penney, Lindsay Portnoy, Nick Proctor, Susan Rivers, Susana Ruiz, Doris Rusch, Ian Schreiber, Steven Schrier, Alyssa Shaenfield, David Shaenfield, Noah Shaenfield, Mamta Shah, Vit Šisler, Sue Spiegel, Brendon Trombley, Alfred Twu, Aaron Vanek, Ralph Vituccio, Brooke Wallace, Jennifer Worth, and Neil Wrona.

Thank you to those who gave me permission to use their games' images in this book: iCivics, PolitiCraft, Inc, Numinous Games, Cogburn Research Group and Virtual Human Interaction Lab, Charles Games, FableVision Studios, Gigantic Mechanic, Common Circles, SheroHub LLC, Ndemic Creations, DROG, Avery Chenoweth, Jaehee Cho, Laura Gillespie, Owen Gottlieb, Luigi Guatieri, Jessica Hammer, Elizabeth LaPensée, Catt Small, Ziba Scott, Vit Šisler, Moyra Turkington, Alfred Twu, Ralph Vituccio, Maggie Farley, Robert Hone, American University Game Lab, and Tracy Fullerton and the *Walden* Team.

I want to thank the ADL for giving me the opportunity to serve as a Belfer Fellow for the Center for Technology & Society from 2018 to 2019. The people I met through my fellowship have inspired my thinking about games, perspective-taking, and inclusion, especially Daniel Kelley, and my advisors and colleagues on various projects and panels, including Mark Bartlet, Sharang Biswas, Seth Bleecker, Mark Chen, Grace Collins, Laquana Cooke, Osama Dorias, Dave Eng, Jason Engerman, Joan Getman, Ailsa Gilliam, Elaine Gómez, Jonathan Greenblatt, Jessica Hammer, Jess Haskins, Greg Haynes, Steven Hodas, Elizabeth LaPensée, Josh Lee, Steph Loehr, Erin Malone, Heidi McDonald, David Or, Lindsay Portnoy, Zhenzhen Qi, Johansen Quijano, Gabriela Richard, David Shaenfield, Mamta Shah, Dave Sifry, Juan Vaca, Kim Voll, and Christopher Wong. I also want to thank the Belfer Foundation.

I want to thank my current and former students for their enthusiasm for games, and for inspiring me in so many different ways. Thank you also to my Marist College colleagues.

I am appreciative of the insight, passion, and camaraderie of the learning and games community, including the Games for Change community, the Learning and Education Games Special Interest Group (LEG SIG) of the International Game Developers Association (IGDA), and the authors and contributors of the book *Learning, Education, & Games, Vol. 3: 100 Games to Use in the Classroom and Beyond*.

Thank you also to the Oxford University Press staff for their support, encouragement, and guidance in publishing this book, including Emma Hodgdon and Sarah Humphreville.

I want to thank my family, including my parents, Steven and Janet Schrier, and my brother, David, and my grandparents, Anne and Bernard, and Betty and Seymour. I also want to thank Bernard and Sandra Shaenfield.

I am in awe of the patience, love, and support provided by my husband, David Shaenfield. I am inspired and motivated by my children, Alyssa, Noah, and Jacob. They have all given me a valuable gift: time. The only reason I am able to write this book is because David spent the immense amount of time watching, playing, and caring for our three loves. I look forward to a lifetime of playing games with all of you.

* * *

Right after I turned 18 years old, my parents took me to vote in a local village election. I wasn't too excited at first: it was not a presidential election, or even held in November, but my parents made this minor election a cause for major celebration. So we walked over to the polling place, I voted, and they cheered. I felt like what I was doing mattered, and I have celebrated voting ever since. My hope is that games can help us to feel like practicing civics and ethics is an everyday celebration.

PART I

TEACHING ETHICS AND CIVICS

1

We the People

In 2020, all of the world's citizens were embroiled in a global pandemic. The virus, SARS-CoV-2, quickly spread to all continents, countries, and corners of the Earth. As the numbers of sick people increased daily, the world also started to realize how much we, the people, rely on each other. We depend on each other to stay healthy, or to stay home when not healthy. We depend on each other to make ethical decisions about how to live and work. If we are in a country that allows representative elections, we depend on each other to vote for people who will govern ethically, responsibly, and scientifically. We depend on each other to serve as first responders, essential workers, and caregivers, and to make sure that we are all fed, sheltered, and healed. And we depend on each other to help find answers and repair us—to connect and contribute to solving the world's pressing problems. Whether it is a pandemic or an environmental crisis, we are all in this life together.[1]

Yet we also realized that even though we are all human, we are not all participating in humanity equally and equitably. The pandemic further revealed a systemic "survival gap," where people differentially have access to the means to survive—such as the healthcare, social, and financial opportunities to be protected and safe. Beyond a health crisis, we started to see what was already there—a public in crisis. We collectively saw how systemic economic, social, and cultural chasms, like racism and oppression, were cracking at the façade of a shared, just world. We realized that we are in a values crisis, too.[2]

Ethics and civics have always mattered. But now, perhaps more than ever before in our lifetime, it is becoming evident how *much* they matter. We realize firsthand how much our decisions and actions affect and are affected by others in the world. Civic participation and ethical decision making have public consequences. What someone does in a mall in Idaho affects someone in a school in Bangalore, India, which affects someone in a church in Lagos, Nigeria, and so on. Who we elect, and how we govern, matters. Not only do *we* need to learn ethics and civics, but we need to teach each generation, model it for every peer, and share it with our neighbors, families, and faraway friends. Personal responsibility for ethical and civic education is a collective necessity.

Games in the Time of a Coronavirus

The COVID-19 pandemic has upended how we do almost everything—teach, work, play, socialize, connect, give care, and even civically engage. It also upended how the

We the Gamers. Karen Schrier, Oxford University Press. © Oxford University Press 2021.
DOI: 10.1093/oso/9780190926106.003.0001

public thinks about games. In 2019, the World Health Organization (WHO) added "gaming disorder" to their list of recognized psychological disorders.[3] For years, pundits, parents, and public officials denounced games for a litany of civic problems—such as addiction, gun violence, and more.[4]

It's surprising what a difference a pandemic can make.

Only one year later, in 2020, media outlets, companies, and social organizations were telling people to stay home and play games, touting playing as if it were an act of good citizenship.[5] The #PlayApartTogether movement encouraged players to avoid transmitting the virus (and social isolation) by being together virtually through games. And in March 2020, the WHO reversed their previous anti-games stance and backed the #PlayApartTogether movement. While people have always played games, and many teachers have been innovatively using games for teaching, the collective stigma around them started to dissipate.[6]

Moreover, during the pandemic, games were used as virtual civic and social spaces. When people could not be physically together in classrooms, corporate offices, and community centers, teachers and professors held classes through games, colleagues held conferences and meetings through games, friends chatted and interacted through games, and grandparents and grandkids shared time and nonphysical space together through games. People celebrated birthdays and graduations through *Minecraft*, baby showers in *Animal Crossing: New Horizons*, and weddings in *World of Warcraft*. Games have always been places where people have connected, engaged, expressed themselves, or healed, but they became *the* place.[7]

Games also were communities where civic deliberation, public demonstration, and values sharing took place. People did not only go to the streets—they also went to the games. In 2020, members of the US House of Representatives livestreamed their play of the online imposter game *Among Us* on Twitch, with over 400,000 viewers watching. The US President Joe Biden and Vice President Kamala Harris created their own islands in *Animal Crossing: New Horizons* to support their election campaign. Gamers mounted demonstrations, rallies, protests, and debates through *The Sims*, *Grand Theft Auto*, *Fortnite*, and many other games.

Games have always been places where norms and values are negotiated, and they often have their own unique cultures that players need to learn to be able to fully participate.[8] But the pandemic helped to ratify this. In the absence of physical civic spaces where ethics and values could be shared, games served as communal spaces where players could navigate the rapidly changing norms of our everyday, public lives. Through games, players were able to think and talk about how we should collectively behave beyond the game, such as whether to wear masks in public. Through games, players could practice these choices before enacting them in the real world. Or, they could enact risky behaviors in the game (like holding social events), which they could not do as safely in the physical world.

There are other ways that people were engaged in gaming during the pandemic. In-person classes were rapidly transformed to hybrid and virtual configurations. Students participated in more distance learning, online courses, and at-home activities. Simultaneously, educators of all types more frequently assigned and used games to teach. What was once perhaps an in-class bonus or side jaunt became much more central to the curriculum. Games have been used to teach everything from math facts to art history to civic institutions.[9] But they have now become more frequently adapted and modified to be used at home, virtually, and from a distance to learn, connect, and share. For instance, iCivics, an organization that creates games to teach about civics and the US government, created a remote learning toolkit to support at-home learning.[10]

Games themselves also continued to help people to understand and learn about pandemics as well as viruses and their spread.[11] *Pandemic* is a board game where players work together playing different roles related to containing a pandemic (e.g., medic, field operative, researcher). The players all play against "the board" to "save humanity" and conquer a viral illness, which rapidly and exponentially jumps from city to city. Leacock, creator of *Pandemic*, wrote that his board game teaches us that the solution to a pandemic is that we all work together "to play to our strengths, balance short-term threats against long-term goals and make sacrifices for the common good. If we can communicate, coordinate and cooperate effectively we might better overcome this uncaring, relentless and frightening opponent."[12] Likewise, the games *Plague Inc.* and *Plague Inc.: Evolved* are pathogen simulators, where players intentionally spread a virus or other pathogens such as fungi and bacteria. During the COVID-19 pandemic, the *Plague Inc.* developers created a new version of the game that flips this around. In *Plague Inc.: The Cure*, players instead "try to save the world by controlling the global pandemic response," through mitigating the outbreak, creating a vaccine, and making economic and social policies (see more in chapter 11). Moreover, Lofgren and Feffernan looked at a virtual viral outbreak in the game *World of Warcraft*, which helped them to model epidemiological responses to real-world pandemics. Researchers then used these results to better understand the COVID-19 pandemic.[13]

Games also served as a form of communication, helping to spread information on the coronavirus, and helping us to understand what we should do as a society to collectively solve the problem of its proliferation. The *Washington Post* posted simulations of the spread of the virus to help its audience visualize what would happen if we quarantine people or enforce social distancing: Would it flatten the curve?[14] Likewise, Ahuja, Huang, Kovach, and Woods created simulations of viral spread, and applied it to college classrooms.[15] Salathé and Case created "What Happens Next?," a series of playable simulations about COVID-19 and its possible epidemiological spread.[16] Kirby took a narrative approach, and used a Twine game to expose what it would feel like as a college student attending class in person in fall 2020.[17] Game players also took collective real-world action, and worked together to try to solve the problem of COVID-19 through games like *Foldit* and *EteRNA*.[18]

Games have always mattered and do not need to be legitimized, but the pandemic further showed us that games can serve as publics: as places and communities for learning, for connecting, for problem-solving, and for ethical and civic engagement.

This book acknowledges and observes all the ways that people are *already* engaging in and learning about civics and ethics through games. It explores *how* educators can make the best use of games for teaching ethics and civics, given their limitations and strengths. It shares strategies and examples of using games in educational settings. It also imagines possibilities for how we might use games to reshape, repair, and remake our world, together.[19]

Defining Ethics and Civics

The world—and humanity—is messy, and that may be why we need to learn ethics and civics. When we talk about ethics and civics, what do we mean? Ethics are typically associated with the reflective, affective, and cognitive processes related to applying moral principles to choices, decisions, and scenarios. Ethics involves thinking through possibilities and deciding how to act when it comes to questions of "what our guiding ideals should be ... what sort of life is worth living, [and] how should we treat one another."[20] This is distinct from morals or values, as morals often refer to "universal truths, or public rules or principles,"[21] while values typically refer to the guidelines on what matters to someone, their family, an organization, or a society.[22] This is also different from virtues and character. Character relates to the landscape of who we are, our traits and temperaments, and the attitudes that shape how we act, behave, and make ethical decisions. Virtues are personal traits or qualities that are intrinsically good, like generosity, courage, humility, gratitude, or respect.[23] In this book I focus less on the distinctions among these terms, and more in how we, as educators, can shape and inspire all facets of moral behavior, ethical decision-making, and the development of character. How do we help our students to grow?

Civics relates to governance and how the public participates in governance; it involves understanding how people work together to decide how a society should function. Civic participation includes all different types of necessary—though often unpaid—activities, including volunteer work, community planning, attending town halls, voting, protesting, writing letters to officials, and solving local problems.[24] It also relates to day-to-day respect and humility; the care of others; and how we treat our colleagues, neighbors, and community members. It includes all the big and little individual and collective decisions as to how we should live together.

Why put ethics and civics together in the same book? I argue that it is because they are so intertwined. To fully participate in civics, we need to be ethical thinkers and moral arbiters. We need to cultivate moral wisdom, navigate moral complexity, and excavate ethical nuances.[25] Likewise, to be living as ethical citizens in a community, we also need to be civically engaged and civically active.

Being a good citizen is not just about having necessary knowledge, "but being able to participate in affecting the policies, societal behaviors, and practices around that knowledge."[26] "Citizen," however, is a problematic word, and by citizen, I do not mean someone's legal status or role in a nation. Rather, Muñoz and El-Hani describe a citizen as someone who thinks "critically about their actions and society's actions." To them, "citizenship demands political participation, activism, cultural engagement, that is, the capacity of being a global citizen ... entails being able to engage in critical dialogue with the past, question authority ... struggle with power relationships, be active and critical in the interrelated local, national, and global public sphere, be able to recognize antidemocratic forces denying social, economic, and political justice, and to struggle for a better world."[27] Being a citizen requires engagement in our communities and a commitment to making ethical change.[28] "Just because we have knowledge and apply it to make real-world changes does not mean we know how to use it wisely, ethically, or appropriately." We need both knowledge and wisdom, civics and ethics, together, to traverse the messiness of humanity.[29]

That said, perhaps what we really need to describe this is not a noun, but a verb.[30] Is someone a "good citizen," or do they practice it? Davisson and Gehm explain that to act as a citizen is not just to embody the identity of a citizen, but to be part of a body politic acting as a citizen. "To citizen" is an act of bravery, an ongoing struggle, and a critical dialogue with the complexity of humanity. To citizen is a process we do together to repair our world.[31]

Moreover, to citizen is to live our fullest life, individually and collectively. The Jubilee Centre explains that our ultimate goal as educators is "human flourishing, [which] requires the acquisition and development of intellectual, moral, and civic virtues ... to achieve the highest potential in life." We want our students to live their best life—to contribute to the good of their own lives, while also contributing to the good of society. In East Africa they use the word *Utu*, which means "humanity and moral goodness" in Swahili. As educators, how do we encourage our children to embody the concept of *Utu*?[32] How do we inspire our students to flourish?[33]

Yet in the past few decades, the skills and topic areas related to civics and ethics have not been prioritized in US schools, and are often squeezed out. Only 39 US states require students to take a class in government or civics to graduate from high school. Globally, while ethics education programs exist in over 43 countries, most do not have any national, institutional, or systemic support.[34]

In the United States, compared to what is necessary for an engaged citizenry,

1. civic knowledge and skills are low;
2. access to civic knowledge and skills is inequitable;
3. people are not civically engaged enough;
4. access to civic engagement is inequitable;
5. political divides and distrust have grown;
6. disinformation has increased; and
7. harassment and hate have been rising.[35]

So what can we do? How do we help people become ethical thinkers and learn the "knowledge, skills, attitudes, and experience to ... be an active, informed participant in democratic life?"[36] How do games support or hinder this?

This book is for those who want to teach people to flourish, to grow, to connect, and "to citizen"—with games.

What Are Games?

The world—and humanity—is messy, and that may be why we need games.

First, what is a game? Typically, games are described as having a number of characteristics: goals, and actions that players can take to reach goals, and players, as well as a tacit agreement from players that they are playing a game, where the differential outcomes of that game matter. The definitions and uses of games vary tremendously, however. Games have been labeled as tools, media, experiences, art, and systems. They come in all different genres and styles, shapes, sizes, communities, and platforms. In this book I discuss augmented reality (AR) games, which are games that integrate virtual gameplay such as virtual objects, clues, or characters, with real-world locations, interactions, and people. I also look at analog (nondigital) games such as card games, board games, and larps (live action role-playing games). I talk about virtual reality (VR) games, in which the whole experience is virtual, the players' entire visual field is virtually generated, and the players are interacting with virtual objects, people, and locations (though some VR games may incorporate players who are not virtually participating). I also investigate digital and online games, which are games that are played using personal computers, mobile devices, game consoles, internet browsers, livestreaming platforms, or other connected devices or platforms.[37]

These games can come in all different genres, such as adventure, puzzle, first-person shooter, battle royale, or walking simulator. They can involve one person playing by themselves in their home or multiple people playing across many different locations around the world. They may be played only in a specific location, such as Lexington, Massachusetts in the United States or Karachi in Pakistan. Or they might be played anywhere, with any type of object that is available to the players.

Moreover, all different types of games are being played by all different people.[38] The latest Entertainment Software Association (ESA) statistics on game-playing explains that 75% of Americans have at least one gamer in their home, and that 57% of parents say they play video games with their kids at least once per week.[39] Since the COVID-19 pandemic, game-playing has increased even further. A report from Unity explains that there was a 46% increase in daily active users of PC and consoles and a 17% increase in mobile device use. Mobile game installations increased 84%. Video game spending overall rose 22% from 2019 to 2020.[40]

Games and Learning

Games are also being used for teaching and learning. Games are being used in remote and physical classrooms, museums, libraries, after-school programs, and other learning environments, including the home.[41] Educators are using games to teach, with 74% of K-8 educators using games at some point in their teaching and 55% of teachers using games at least once per week.[42] Games are also being designed with the intention of supporting learning in some way—whether to teach addition and subtraction, like *DragonBox Numbers*, or to teach Arabic letters, such as *Antura and the Letters*. While the mainstream games industry was at about $43.4 billion in 2018,[43] the educational games, game-based learning, or "serious games" industry is predicted to reach $24 billion by 2024 globally, and is growing in the double digits in many regions around the world, including Africa.[44]

Just as games come in many different forms and formats, there are many terms that have been used to describe their different pedagogic functions. Games that aim to teach have been called "educational games," "games for change," "games for social impact," and "serious games."[45] The intersection of games and learning typically describes teaching, instruction, and learning environments that incorporate games or playful experiences into the classroom, school, library, home, or other location. A game could even become a classroom itself, where students can meet virtually to create and experiment, or discuss and deliberate (such as when teachers hold a class in *Minecraft*). However, I am less interested in choosing the right term to describe these games and more in their possibilities. What are the circumstances where games are more or less effective? How can we reconceive what games can do (or already do)?[46] For the purposes of brevity, I will call all of these types of tools, media, art, or experiences "games," whether they are digital or nondigital, VR or AR, or fully realized or not-quite games.

Just because games are frequently used does not mean they are effective in doing what we want them to do, such as teaching skills, attitudes, behaviors, or content. So are games even beneficial for learning? Thus far, the research on whether games are suitable for education and actually enhance learning is often contradictory or inconsistent, though the potential of games has been cited frequently.[47] Frustratingly, large-scale empirical studies cannot definitively prove that games support learning. Civics games are also uneven in their effectiveness.[48] This is not surprising, however, because the success of any learning experience is highly complex and relies on its design, its audience and context, and how it is implemented or its ecology of use.[49] The same worksheet might work well with one class section in the morning, but not with the one in the late afternoon. A film may connect with one set of fifth graders in a district but not in a neighboring one, and a book reading could fall flat with a kindergarten cohort and then, reshared the following year, elicit laughs and excitement. Empirical studies on games, as well as anecdotal evidence, suggest that under certain circumstances, with particular audiences, and by meeting specific learning goals and needs, games can be quite effective and meaningful. A study by Clark et al. that was a large-scale meta-analysis of research on game-based learning, suggested that digital games can enhance cognitive learning outcomes as compared to a nongame condition, and that the "design of the game, rather than the medium of 'games' itself, was more important to whether the environment supported learning."[50] Depending on how they are designed or used, games can be beneficial and empowering at best, or they can be a waste of time and may even backfire, at worst. Games are a bit messy when it comes to learning.[51]

What Are Games for Civics and Ethics?

So what do I mean by games for ethics and civics?

Raphael et al. explain that games for learning civics "help players to develop knowledge, skills, and dispositions that players then apply to public matters in the world outside the game."[52] We could add ethics to this definition and say that these games help to support the knowledge, skills, and dispositions necessary for ethical, public, and societal matters.[53]

Games that teach ethics and civics can vary tremendously, from acting like the "President of the United States in iCivics' *Executive Command* to understanding what it's like to be the parent of a terminally ill young son in *That Dragon, Cancer*."[54] Sometimes a game is the primary part of a classroom lesson, such as deliberating and voting on historic proposals in *VoxPop*, or collaboratively crafting a historical building like the Taj Mahal in *Minecraft*.[55] Other times games may be played to support further deliberation, such as using the game *Immigration Nation* to kick off a discussion on immigration, or the digital game *Acceptance* to reflect on gender expression, identity, and belongingness.[56] Civics and ethics games could involve playing a simple rhyming game in a preschool or be "as complex as transforming an entire class module into an alternate reality game (ARG), such as Darvasi did to teach *One Flew over the Cuckoo's Nest* for his English literature students."[57] These games may aim to make real-world change in one's community, such as *Macon Money* or *Participatory Chinatown*.[58] They can also take place in real-world locations, such as *Pokémon Go*, *Time Trek*, or *Jewish Time Jump*.[59] They could be raw, unpolished games made in one night by one person (such as Kirby's *September 7, 2020* Twine game), or multimillion dollar games made and updated over the course of many years (such as *Fortnite*, *Overwatch*, or *World of Warcraft*).

There are a number of ways that games can share and express civics and ethics topics and enable the practice of relevant skills:

1. **Real-world knowledge and action.** Games can enhance knowledge of real-world issues and topics; encourage the understanding of real-world concepts, institutions, processes, and policies; and enable real-world action and change. For instance, in Abbott's high school civics course at a public school in North Carolina, she teaches concepts such as the US government's three branches and the Bill of Rights. To provide foundational knowledge she may use the iCivics game *Do I Have a Right*, in which players run their own law firm and decide whether to take on a client who may have had a constitutional right violated. Or she may have students learn about real-world concepts like the US Electoral

Figure 1.1 An image from the game *Win the White House*. Source: iCivics.

College through games such as *Win the White House*, where players campaign to win a fictional US presidential election (see Figure 1.1).[60]

2. **Community and connection.** Games are civic communities. They can help to strengthen social interactions, communication, and a sense of belongingness in a community of learners. They can help people to better understand themselves, their identities, and their roles as members of a society as well as to respect, empathize with, and have compassion for others.[61] (Just like all communities, however, they can also do the opposite and foster hate, harassment, bullying, exclusion, and toxicity.) Games like *Animal Crossing: New Horizons* can encourage community among people who are physically distanced from each other. Games may also support an in-class community more deliberately, like in *VoxPop*, where players work together to discuss and negotiate different proposals, views, and values. Moreover, games themselves are forms of human expression and as such can communicate a perspective on humanity, such as *SweetXheart,* which tells of a Black woman's experiences (see Figure 1.2), or *A Woman Goes to a Private Games Industry Party*, which expresses perspectives on harassment in the game development community.[62]

3. **Critical thinking and critical inquiry.** Games are ethical systems, and players are moral actors who engage in them. Games can help people practice

Figure 1.2 An image from the game *SweetXHeart*. Image courtesy of Catt Small.

relevant critical thinking and inquiry skills such as reasoning, decision-making, problem-solving, systems thinking and analysis, interpretation, evaluation, information gathering, and design and creation. They can pose problems and quests or act like morality tales and ethical case studies, where the player can enact part of the story to help them practice making decisions or analyzing outcomes.[63] For instance, in *Planet Planners*, a mobile ecology simulation game,[64] players practice resource management skills; in *Max*, a board game about helping creatures avoid a hungry kitty, kids learn how to collaboratively make decisions. The online digital games *Bad News* and *Harmony Square* seek to teach players how to identify disinformation and political manipulation techniques. Games can also serve as arguments about the world by enabling players to interact with systems, such as how we might learn about the oppressiveness of bureaucracy through *Papers, Please* or of systemic bias in *Parable of the Polygons*.[65]

Games have been and can continue to be used for all different parts of ethics and civics education.[66] To further give you a sense of the breadth and variety of the types of games that could be used, here are some brief examples of how games can be included in the classroom, after-school program, home, remote learning environment, or other educational context.

- In *Factitious*, a mobile and browser-based game, players decide if an article is "authentic" and based on vetted facts and interviews, or "fake" and based on made-up quotations, misinformation, or satire. Teachers can use the game to foster information literacy skills, such as reading articles, checking sources, and vetting facts.
- The VR game *Along the River of Spacetime* helps to express and communicate Anishinaabeg teachings and cultural practices related to ecology, space, and the environment (see Figure 1.3). Teachers can use the game to share Indigenous perspectives on land and place.[67]
- In *Buffalo*, a card game, players need to name characters or people who match combinations of characteristics. There is an orange deck (made up of adjectives) and a blue deck (with nouns). Players flip over one of each and have to come up with any type of figure who matches the two words. The game was designed to help players become more aware of their biases and prejudices.[68]
- *Quandary*, an online and mobile digital game, invites players to decide the best solutions to problems faced by a new society, Braxos. Players need to solicit input from Braxos citizens, mount arguments, weigh pros and cons,

Figure 1.3 An image from the game *Along the River of Spacetime*. Image courtesy of Elizabeth (Beth) LaPensée.

and iterate through choices and consequences to make the best decisions. Teachers can use this to support ethical decision-making, such as holding an in-class deliberation around the strategies and tactics used in the game. "They can also extend the lessons of *Quandary* to real-life dilemmas suggested by students."

- In *The Migrant Trail*, a browser-based game, players take on the roles of two different sides of an immigration issue. They play as a migrant who is trying to cross the border and escape the border patrol officers. Or they play as a border control agent, who is trying to find the illegal immigrants. Teachers can use this game to show multiple perspectives on an issue, and to help students explore the complexities of representing an issue like immigration through games.[69]

- Using a series of plastic (about 8 feet by 8 feet) floor games in Indian community workshops, researcher Khanna teaches issues such as electoral literacy or child rights to different audiences.[70]

- In the VR game *Keep Talking and Nobody Explodes*, players must defuse a virtual bomb. One player has the virtual headset and can see the virtual bomb, along with some tools. The other set of players has a manual but no access to the bomb, and needs to communicate with the VR headset-wearing player to figure out how to defuse the bomb before time runs out. Teachers can use this to support collaboration and dialogue, as well as cooperative problem-solving under pressure.[71]

- In the short indie digital game *Loneliness*, players move a white square piece toward other squares, and the other squares move away. Though the game is brief, players can discuss how emotion can be evoked by a game, even a game that is abstract and simple.

- In *Mission US*, players take on the role of a fictional adolescent and explore a historic moment, while making decisions for them, going on missions, and completing goals. In the *Mission US: City of Immigrants* module they play as Lena Brodsky, a Jewish immigrant who just arrived in New York City at the turn of the twentieth century.[72]

- In the online multiplayer game *Among Us*, a group of players needs to figure out who the imposter(s) are and collectively vote to remove them from the game before the imposter(s) eliminate them instead. Students could use this game to practice communication and deliberation, and to reflect on the ethics of deciding which fellow players to eject from the game.

- *Time Trek* is a series of augmented reality (AR) games played at Harpers Ferry National Historical Park in Harpers Ferry, West Virginia, a US Civil War site (see Figure 1.4). In these games players explore the physical site while interacting with virtual historic and fictional characters. They learn about personal struggles and stories related to enslavement and emancipation, and meet characters such as Joseph, a free Black person who is helping runaway slaves escape on a ferry he operates.[73]

Figure 1.4 An image of people playing *Time Trek*, a mobile game that takes place at the Harper's Ferry landmark in West Virginia in the United States. Image courtesy of Avery Chenoweth and Laura Gillespie.

What to Expect

This is a book about games, and it is a book about learning. Yet I am not trying to argue that games *should* be used for educational purposes. Games are not universally bad, nor always good, at teaching ethics and civics. This book is not going to laud games as the panacea, nor is it going to only point out their problems. And just because something is a game does not necessarily make them fun nor functional.

The reality is much more nuanced. Rather, I will question games and consider the circumstances under which they may help us to better engage with, support, and inspire each other. I will cheerlead for games, but I will also problematize them by pointing out their limitations, weaknesses, ethical challenges, and idiosyncrasies.[74] I will assert that they are often awkward worlds that embed in them their designers' and players' own biases, prejudices, heuristics, and assumptions. I will help to reveal how games matter.

First, games should not be used just because they are trendy or popular, or because they worked for one kid, one class, or one educational context. A game is complex and needs to be adapted, played, and evaluated with consideration to the complexity of the ecosystem of its use. Games need to be played with the care of the community in mind. Games are not standalone, one-stop-shopping solutions. Games, like people, are messy.

Second, games should not be used just to show kids how to do civics or how to be civically engaged. Rather, they should also be used to show *us* what civics *is*.

When discussing the use of hip hop in education, Bettina Love aptly argues that teachers do not need to bring hip hop into the classroom so that students can be creative—instead, we should include hip hop to "show [us] how creative kids already are." Love explains that "hip hop is civics, hip hop is social justice, hip hop is creativity."[75] This argument inspires my understanding of games. Games are civics, and civics is playful. Games are how students are already engaging with the world and with the public. Through games, students are designing, discovering, and deliberating. Through games, students are grappling with what it means to be human and with what it means to govern as a society. Through games, students are already "citizening."

Mirra and Garcia argue that when we are defining civic participation, we cannot just use adult perspectives on what youth *should* be doing as "civic agents," but also "asking young people what actually engages them or what kinds of civic learning opportunities they may already be experiencing."[76] As Coleman-Mortley notes, "we need to reach kids where they are."[77] Games have always been civic spaces for youth.[78] We need, as Mirra and Garcia contend, to further enable the "kinds of civic learning that youth are already doing in online games like *Minecraft* . . . leading to new disruptions of old civics."[79]

Third, games should not be used just because they may be effective or productive at making "good citizens." Rather, we need to reconsider what it means to learn civics and ethics. Is it just about being proficient on tests and doing good deeds? Is it just about maintaining civility and upholding our institutions? Or, is it also about redesigning and reenvisioning our world and its systems? Is it about questioning what it means to citizen?[80]

What, then, is the value in games? In my previous book, I wrote about what I call "knowledge games," or games that aim to collectively solve real problems and build new knowledge about humanity through the play of the game.[81] I explain that knowledge games can help us struggle with the world's problems—to make a better world not necessarily by *solving* these real-world problems, but by revealing them and helping us to see their flaws, foibles, and messiness. Or, as Bogost explains, playing games is the work, the hard stuff, of maybe not coming up with solutions but perhaps instead "troubling the idea of solutions rather than leading us toward them."[82] I explained that these knowledge games bring up age-old questions about what it means to be a good citizen, to participate in society, and to create new knowledge—questions that we may never entirely answer, but perhaps we can more fully address through games.

Bernard Suits describes play as the ultimate human act, or as a "voluntary attempt to overcome unnecessary obstacles."[83] Perhaps this is one of the greatest possibilities for games. Games may help us to collectively overcome the unnecessary obstacles of life, and the unnecessary problems in our publics, by helping us to better see all of our messiness. Who is allowed to be in the game's civic spaces, and how can they engage? Who is included and who is empowered? Who is allowed or invited "to citizen?"[84] Games may help to reveal obstacles to ethics and civics—and may show us how to overcome them. Games may help to reveal who we are, and maybe how to reimagine who we can become. This is where I situate this book: as a call to use games not necessarily to "make citizens," but to reveal citizens.

What if games don't just allow us to participate in civics and ethics? What if we *need* games *to* citizen, or to "overcome the unnecessary obstacles" that exist in our world?[85]

We should readjust what we expect of games and what we ask of teaching and learning. Teaching becomes not just about imparting facts and figures, but about helping students to connect with themselves and each other to overcome the obstacles that society has placed on us, so that we can live together more equitably.[86] Education becomes not about reinforcing social hierarchies about who should contribute and participate in the public, but about liberating them, and empowering the contributions of all. Playing becomes not about exclusion, but about ensuring we all belong so that we can rebuild our world together. And games, then, become about engaging our follies so we shall overcome.[87]

As I mentioned earlier, Raphael et al. argue that civic learning happens in games "when they help players to … apply [it] to public matters in the world outside the game."[88] Dishon and Kafai take this definition further, arguing that games should be seen as part of a learning ecosystem, with players viewed as active and cocreative participants rather than passive consumers of a predesigned, single-purpose product. They explain that we need "connected civic games," which include youth as active makers and remixers of civics, through games and play. As Dishon and Kafai argue, we need to reframe our expectations of learning in games and think about how to "enrich the spectrum of experiences players have in-and-out of games."[89]

I would adjust the definition even more. As I have started to explore, playing helps us to struggle, to wonder, to grapple, to dance, and to act. Playing helps us to overcome. Gamers engage in civics and ethics outside and beyond the game—but also inside, through, around, and between. Games, and our play of them, are part of an active conversation with the world. Games are public spheres and public matters. Games are publics. They are communities where deliberation, civic engagement, ethical decision-making, socialization and norm-sharing, and civic problem-solving take place.[90] Games are part of who we are and how we learn about the world—and how we decide the type of world in which to live. To play games *is* to citizen.

How can we, as teachers, help to empower our students to citizen in, around, and with games—equitably, and with justice for all?

Mapping the Book

With all this in mind, as teachers, we want to help our students make the most of their play. We need to meet specific educational objectives. In this book, I show teachers how to meet standards and curricular needs, and I provide practical advice, strategies, and examples for how to use games to explore the nuances and complexities of life. I delve into the research-based possibilities for empowerment and inspiration, as well as the limitations, complexities, and complications of games (which also serve as learning opportunities). This book will answer questions such as: How do games support the learning of ethical and civic skills—which games may be notable and under what conditions?[91] What types of classroom configurations and activities best support play and engagement with civics and ethics? What are the current limitations and gaps of games, and how do we wrestle with these limitations?[92] This book aims to point out the messiness of games so teachers can help students better navigate it.

To do this, in part 1, I first investigate why we need to learn ethics and civics. I then describe the types of skills, concepts, and knowledge needed for civic, public, and ethical engagement. I create a three-part set of nine driving questions for teaching ethics and civics, derived from an analysis of current standards.

In part 2, I dive into the first set of questions, which relates to using games to build real-world knowledge and to take real-world action.

In part 3, I look into the second set of questions, and consider how games may or may not support community and connection, as well as how they may encourage the practice of skills related to identity, emotion, respect, cultural humility, perspective-taking, compassion, and empathy.

In part 4, I look at questions related to critical thinking and critical inquiry. For instance, how may games help us to practice skills such as making decisions, solving problems, analyzing information, engaging in design, and thinking systemically?

In part 5, I consider logistical and practical considerations for bringing games into the classroom and other learning environments, such as online and remote ones. I delve into curricular considerations, such as how to choose the right game, how to develop activities around games, and how to handle the logistical and practical aspects of using games in a classroom or educational context. An appendix also shares information on designing games, as well as design principles and best practices for making and using games for civics and ethics.

Finally, in the concluding chapter of this book, I imagine the future of learning ethics and civics through games—and also the future of humanity, more broadly. How might we shape our future through games?

2
Why Should We Teach Ethics and Civics?

Global catastrophe. Systemic oppression. Crisis. Destruction. Turmoil. We can imagine a world where ethics and civics are not taught nor valued. In fact, many of us have lived in and experienced the consequences of such a world, first-hand. Yet, ethics and civics education is lacking.[1]

The United States went from having three civics-centered courses in the mid-twentieth century to just one for most students today—if that. And many US high schools will teach that one course in 12th grade (the final year), which means that many students may never stay in school long enough to reach the class.[2] Moreover, only three states in the United States require middle schools to include a separate civics class in their state standards,[3] and only nine states require that a student pass a social studies-related test to be able to graduate from high school.[4]

What about younger US students? Due in part to an increasing focus on reading and math, as well as other STEM fields, 80% of elementary school teachers have acknowledged making less room for social studies. As a result, only around 7% of total instruction in elementary schools is spent on social studies as a whole, which includes history, geography, cultural studies, sociology, psychology, civics, and ethics. Weekly time spent on social studies for US students in grades one to six went from three hours in 1999–2000 to 2.6 hours in 2003–04.[5]

Across the world, interest in and implementation of civics education has varied widely, country by country. In Romania, for instance, few civics education initiatives were implemented, but there were also barriers to cultural and political acceptance of these initiatives. In Poland, civics education was made a prime initiative, and the country took steps such as including a course in civics, teacher training, and teacher materials, as well as government programs for adults.[6] In a study of 21 countries (including Afghanistan, India, Ireland, Uganda, Zimbabwe, Guatemala, and Ecuador), the results suggested that around half of the country's governments were receptive to building civic education programs. Nigeria's and Burkina Faso's governments were particularly open to civics education.[7]

What about ethics education? It fares even worse. Ethics teaching may exist in a number of countries, but it's typically not formalized, and quite precarious—and it varies widely school to school or setting to setting.[8] In the United States, there are no state or national standards for ethics.[9] Ethics and character education often get shoehorned into social studies, history, or even home economics courses, without fully being seen as a discipline in its own right. Some students may not get any ethics content until they reach college—or they may never get it.

We the Gamers. Karen Schrier, Oxford University Press. © Oxford University Press 2021.
DOI: 10.1093/oso/9780190926106.003.0002

Only around seven US states actually assess civics as part of the state accountability measures, which means it may never ever get taught as it is not tied to quantifiable results or funding. No US state tests ethics, character, or ethical thinking.[10] If you don't test something, it doesn't matter, and if it isn't valued, it's not learned, developed, or practiced.

And look at the results.

Former Supreme Court Justice Sandra Day O'Connor explains, "Only one-third of Americans can name the three branches of government, but two-thirds can name a judge on American Idol."[11]

People have lost trust in government, and in each other.[12] Civic participation is low, with low volunteerism, especially among youth.[13]

Access to civic participation is also inequitable, particularly for communities of color, working class adults, and low-income students.[14]

An international study of civics knowledge found that no country's 14-year-olds scored high on all factors, and that in some countries young people seemed disinterested in and even systemically unable to participate in civic engagement.[15]

Yet historically, civics is part of why we started public schools in the first place.[16] We are all part of the public—so we need to practice being public participants. As O'Connor explains, "We started public schools in [the United States] with the thought that we had to teach ... people about our system of government ... it's complicated and it requires citizen participation."[17]

Flash forward to today. We need to prepare people for civic life by directly engaging people in it. Schools do not just serve the public, they create a public who can participate meaningfully with "civic competence," or "the knowledge, skills, and dispositions needed for active and engaged civic life."[18] Moreover, civics education *can* make a difference in building civic competence, and can raise civics learning test scores and enhance civic participation.[19] But beyond lifting scores, education can lift people so that they can *citizen*. Learning can help to lift the fears and obstacles that contribute to the inequities in civic participation and in public life.

On paper, civics and ethics education should be seen as important—even essential—but we seem to overlook it as a priority. It becomes an afterthought rather than the central mission of schools. This goes beyond the United States or any one country. We, the people of the world, all need civics and ethics to fully participate in the public life of the world.

In this chapter I delve further into why empowering people with ethics and civics is so important. Why is developing civic and ethics skills and knowledge so necessary—and why are they particularly beneficial to teach *now*?

We Are a "We"

It's not enough for us to individually practice ethics and be civically engaged—we also need everyone else to be engaged. We are all part of the public.

Our votes, values, and voices have *always* mattered, but perhaps now more than ever, it is becoming evident how *much* they matter. The COVID-19 pandemic laid bare our collective humanity and our shared systemic inhumanities. It helped us to realize that our actions and decisions affect others and have civic and ethical consequences not only for our neighbors and local communities, but even for people across the whole world. We saw first-hand, on a large scale, how much our individual and collective decisions count.[20] Yes, we are all in this world together—not equitably—but interdependently, in that we all need to speak up together, engage in dialogue, listen, learn, and teach to make the world better for humanity.

In the United States, for instance, people rely on each other to participate, be informed, and make well-reasoned decisions.[21] O'Connor explains that "our citizens need to be educated to analyze things, to make reasoned opinions, to express themselves, how to get through the political process.... How do you choose responsible leaders, how do you participate if citizens don't understand the system at all?"[22] However, we cannot just be engaged as citizens of a nation—we also need to be together as citizens of a world. We need to feel connected amid rising loneliness and isolation.[23] We need to think, care, teach, learn, and civically engage across borders. Students are "living in an increasingly interconnected world" and need global perspectives.[24] We need to figure out with each other how to behave, collectively, as a human society.[25]

Moreover, engagement in civics and ethics may also help us to feel more like we are a "we," which contributes to our well-being and feeling of belongingness. The more a person participates in their community the more connected they may feel, the more actively involved they may become, and so forth. Well-being has even been found to be enhanced in places where people are more able to be engaged in the community and the democratic process, and as a result, are more actively involved.[26]

We Live in a Diverse World

While we are one global community, we are also participants in many different types of communities, each with their own rules, norms, and challenges. A virtual classroom community may be different from a physical one. How a local group meets on Facebook may be different from how it meets in person or through Zoom. Moreover, with connective platforms such as games or social media, we may be constantly interacting with people across the globe and jumping from one micro-community to another.[27]

Thus, we need to be able to fluidly navigate different types of communities—whether offline or online, in school, at work, in our neighborhoods, or in our peer groups. We need to be globally savvy and aware of the changing norms, values, and participatory modes of the different communities we may weave in and out of.[28] We need to be able to understand how to take civic action in our local communities and our countries, our online realms and our virtual publics, as well as how to connect with others across the world to make global change.[29]

We Need to Prepare for the Future

The skills necessary for civic engagement and ethical thinking are important for responsible participation in civic life, but also for success in other domains, online, offline, in school, and in the workplace more generally. The National Council for the Social Studies's C3 framework explains that "many of the same skills that are needed for active and responsible citizenship—working effectively with other people, deliberating and reasoning quantitatively about issues, following the news, and forming and sustaining groups—are also crucial to success in the 21st century workplace and in college."[30] The Education Commission of the States talks about the 4 Cs—critical thinking, communication, creativity, and collaboration—which are taught through civics and ethics education, and also prepare students for career and life success.[31] Moreover, the skills that companies are looking for are ones that are developed, in part, by ethics and civics education. For instance, at a meeting at my kids' school district, the principal projected a list of the top skills desired by companies based on the World Economic Forum's list, and they included things like problem-solving, critical thinking, systems thinking, and judgment and decision-making.[32] Learning ethics and civics is essential for the future.

We Can Enhance Humanity

We need ethical thinkers and deliberators, action-takers, and decision-makers. We need people who can engage in informed, reasoned discourse, who seek out others' views and opinions, and who know how to navigate different types of communities, values, and norms. We need people who can help to solve the everyday problems of civic life, as well as the larger problems of global concern. Learning civics and ethics is its own reward.

But we also need to teach ethics and civics in tandem with other fields, and to show how they are foundational to all pursuits and questions. We cannot teach computer science, business, chemistry, or art without also thinking about their ethical implications, such as how data is collected or interpreted, how algorithms are programmed, how ideas are represented, or how knowledge is inequitably accessed.[33] The pendulum is starting to swing back another way, in that social studies is beginning to be reprioritized as a discipline, but civics and ethics should not be taught in isolation from other fields.[34]

We Can Raise Proficiency in Knowledge and Skills

Historically, one of the main purposes of school, at least in the United States, has been to teach civic engagement and prepare future citizens.[35] Yet proficiency in civics and ethics is lacking among youth. Only 23% of eighth graders in the United States are at the proficient level on a test of civic skills and knowledge (the NAEP (National Assessment of Educational Progress) civic assessment).[36] Students from top colleges also do poorly. Eighty percent of college senior students from the top 55 American colleges and universities scored a D or F on a test of civic and history-related knowledge. And this was only 13% higher than those students who had a high school diploma as their highest earned degree.[37] O'Connor explains that "Less than 1/5 of high school seniors can explain how civic participation benefits our system of government. Less than that can say what the purpose of the Declaration of Independence is (and it's right there in the title)."[38]

Likewise, in an ongoing, cyclical study of civics (the IEA (International Association for the Evaluation of Educational Achievement) Civic Education Study), students are tested on their civic knowledge, support for democratic values, support for government, and participation in civics-related activities. Researchers found that none of the 14-year-olds in any of the countries that give this test scored high on all of these factors.[39] Moreover, in some countries, students reported that they were not likely to vote, nor engage in civics more generally. They also had major gaps in knowledge, and did not have the social, educational, and institutional support necessary to civically engage.[40] Researchers reviewed the curricula across these countries and found that while they typically included the country's history, human rights, and discussion of issues and concerns, "civics education generally had a low, sometimes precarious, status in schools, with many teachers reporting a lack of materials and limited training."[41]

What about ethics knowledge and skills? While it is difficult to create a standardized test of ethics behavior, and specific tests of ethical thinking and decision-making are rare in K-12 in the United States, studies have suggested that students are increasing in unethical behavior, such as cheating on schoolwork, paper-writing, and tests, as well as in incivility online.[42] However, we should not conflate the practice of ethical thinking skills with what may be the changing norms and values of a society—and a possible moral panic about what is happening with kids and media. We should also not only look at test scores to understand proficiency in civics and ethics.[43]

We Can Enhance Civic Engagement

Civic engagement and participation vary greatly in different countries, depending on their rules and regulations, government systems, and culture. In the United States, citizens who are 18 or over are allowed to vote, yet youth aged 18–24 are typically less likely to vote than any other age demographic. Only around 46% of youth 18–29 voted in the 2016 US presidential election, and only 21% and 31% participated in the 2014 and 2018 midterm elections, respectively,[44] with even lower participation rates in other types of civic activities, such as town hall events or meetings.[45] (However, youth voting rates increased from 2016, with an estimated 52–55% of eligible voters 18–29 voting in the 2020 US election). Moreover, civic engagement is generally low across the world. Youth are not as involved in community service and volunteering.[46] Overall voter turnout in Organization for Economic Cooperation and Development (OECD) countries has dropped by about 8 percentage points since 1970, and turnout has decreased by 20 points in the United Kingdom and 30 points in Japan.[47]

Lerner argues that *meaningful* civic engagement is decreasing overall, with people perhaps signing more online petitions or marching in virtual marches, but not necessarily engaging in the day-to-day tedious but necessary tasks and deliberations with each other.[48] Around 58% of 15- to 25-year-olds in the United States were deemed civically "disengaged," and not participating in activities like charity-giving, volunteering, and voting.[49] Steven Schrier, a professor at a US community college, estimates that only about 10% of the students who take his local and state government course have ever participated in any type of civic activity, such as working on a campaign.[50]

One reason why college students and other youth may be disengaged from civics is because they have trouble seeing how it may personally affect them. They feel they won't be able to meaningfully impact civic processes. Many people aged 18 to 24 years old are also just starting out with families or beginning to work at jobs, and only beginning to learn about how they could participate in civic life.[51] Moreover, Lerner explains that people may be feeling distrustful and disempowered when it comes to civics and politics.[52]

In fact, civic engagement is lower than it could be across all demographic groups, as people often do not engage with civics unless it personally affects them. For instance, I did not start attending my own town's public board meetings until there were three things in place: the meetings were more *accessible* to me because they were livestreamed online, my *neighbors* encouraged me to attend, and the *issues that I care about* and that personally affect me and my family were being discussed at the meetings. I have continued to attend the meetings because I now feel I have a personal stake in our town and a sense of responsibility to engage, though I would not have attended these meetings otherwise.[53]

We Must Reduce Hate and Harassment

Has there been an increase in incivility, toxicity, and disrespect in public? Certainly, Americans think so. According to a Weber Shandwick and Powell Tate survey in 2018, 93% of those surveyed stated that they believe that "civility is a problem in society," with 69% saying that it is a major problem.[54] This is up from a decade prior.[55]

The survey also found that only half of Americans thought that the general tone of Facebook was civil. "Civility," however, is itself a problematic term and concept. It can be used and applied harmfully, such as being a way to oppress and marginalize, or socially control Black, Brown, Indigenous, and other people of color in public.[56]

We can also look at reports of harassment and hate in public spheres, including games. In an ADL study of American people on social media platforms, they found that 37% of respondents experienced severe online and digital harassment.[57] A third of the respondents also reported that they experienced harassment specifically targeting an aspect of their identity (such as race or religion). Of the participants who identified as LGBTQQA+, 63% reported being harassed due to their identity, with Muslims (35%), Hispanics (30%), African Americans (27%), women (24%), Asian Americans (20%), and Jews (16%) also reporting identity-based harassment.[58] In games, players have also experienced harassment. In another ADL survey of Americans, 81% of the people who play online multiplayer games reported that they experienced some type of harassment during their game play. In that study, they found that of the participants who identified as LGBTQQA+, 37% reported being harassed in online games due to their identity, with Muslims (25%), Hispanics (30%), African Americans (31%), women (41%), Asian Americans (26%), and Jews (18%) also reporting identity-based harassment. They also found that 25% of those who are disabled were harassed due to their ability status.[59]

Likewise, reported hate crimes overall are also on the rise for different groups in the United States, including Latinos, Blacks, Muslims, Asians, and Jewish people, with a significant increase in violence against Latinos.[60] Reports of hate crimes and violence against Asian Americans also increased in 2020, particularly following the start of the COVID-19 pandemic. Hate crimes overall have been found to disproportionately affect Blacks, Muslims, LGBTQQA+, and Jewish people.[61] Yet, we can change this. Ethics and civics education, civic engagement, and ethics practice can enhance our respect, care, and understanding of others, and can strengthen belongingness and compassion.

We Can Bridge Divides

Political divisiveness has been rising. People are often in "partisan bubbles," where they only hear (or believe) the beliefs, views, and news from those that already agree with their ideas. People are self-segregating into political clusters, where they may be less likely to interact with (or listen to) those who have different backgrounds or views than themselves. Social media may even be crystallizing this further, with algorithms that serve up, replicate, and propagate partisan takes on content and news, or even egg on conflict and discord between people who do not agree.[62]

People may even be harassed specifically because of who they are and what they believe in, including political differences. The 2017 Pew Internet Study found that for 14% of the people who were harassed online, it was due to their politics (equally

Republican and Democrat in the United States). Anonymity is often cited as a reason why people are more able to harass each other, with more than half of those who were harassed saying that they were harassed by anonymous strangers. Yet harassment is reported as not just coming from strangers, but from friends and family, too.[63]

We need to have experiences interacting with and engaging with other viewpoints so that we can better deliberate decisions collectively. Civics and ethics practice can help us to connect with others and listen to their views, and collaboratively construct well-rounded arguments.[64]

We Can Disrupt Disinformation

Along with an increase in the amount of information and news being shared offline and online, there has also been an increase in the amount of disinformation that has been created and spread.[65] False or disinformation has been called "fake news" or "fabricated information that mimics news media content in form but not in organizational process or intent."[66] A study found that Americans encountered an average of one to three stories from common publishers of fake news in the month leading up to the 2016 US presidential election. Another study found that people are more likely to retweet fake news stories than articles based on factual information. The people tweeting may not even be people, and around 9–15% of Twitter accounts are estimated to be bots or autonomous programs designed to act like a social media participant. About 60 million bots may be on Facebook.[67] A growing number of videos are deepfakes, or artificially programmed video content that is not authentic nor based on reality.[68]

Yet we need to be able to identify and counter fake news and other forms of disinformation, and these skills can be taught.[69] Just as we need to enhance how we listen and communicate with each other around our differing views, we also need to read, interpret, and vet views, news, and information. We need to learn how to assess valid and reliable information to make the best decisions on how to act as individuals and as a society. We need to learn how to be responsible for what we share and how we spread it.[70]

We Can Enhance Access to Civics

As I stated at the beginning of this chapter, "we are a we." Communities are able to solve problems more effectively when more voices and perspectives are included. Yet civic participation is not equally accessible to all people—whether it is being able to be an active volunteer, an elected official, or a student in a civics class. The ability to fully participate in public life is affected by systemic factors, such as racism and racist policies, as well as one's location, nationality, and geography, and other socioeconomic factors.[71]

For one, access to educational opportunities is inequitable. In the United States, researchers note that students who are from lower-income households, have parents without college degrees, or are English-language learners perform lower than other students on the NAEP civic assessment, which is a test of the skills and knowledge related to civic engagement.[72] They also cite a large gap in test scores on the civics assessment between white and Black students and white students and Hispanic students.[73] However, we should question whether to call this "a gap" or a more intentionally designed result of systemic inequities in civic education for low-income students and students of color. For instance, take a public school district in the United States. If there is a lack of resources overall for that district, coupled with a lack of requirements to meet civics test scores, and greater incentives for raising math and reading scores, this may mean that disproportionately more time, energy, and materials will go into teaching math and reading at the detriment of subjects like social studies.[74] We might mistakenly blame the district—or its students—for low test scores. But, the underlying issue is that there is a systemic lack of resources for certain districts, due to long-standing racist policies and systems, which will continue to be propagated as those districts and students will not have the access, knowledge, or skills to reform the policies and systems. Kahne and Middaugh note that the students in higher-income families or wealthier districts have more opportunities to engage in civics than those in less wealthy schools. This "civic empowerment gap" means that poorer students and students of color will have fewer and fewer opportunities to participate in civics and get the practice needed for this participation. Levinson explains that inequitable access to civics education, knowledge, and skills, combined with systemically less power, influence, and the ability to participate, continues to further this gap.[75]

Korbey also notes other types of inequities in civics participation in the United States, such as the so-called civic deserts. These are areas with limited opportunities for community engagement, and they lack places like cultural organizations and youth centers.[76] A study from the Center for Information and Research on Civic Learning and Engagement (CIRCLE) noted that 60% of young people in rural areas and 30% of young people in urban and suburban areas are in a civic desert of some kind.[77] Living in areas with limited opportunities for civic engagement, and lower "civic health," may contribute to feelings of alienation and disempowerment for the people living there, which only furthers a lack of access to civic participation.

Moreover, Mirra and Garcia point out that much of civic education in the United States relates to "patriotic observances" and the "virtues of the American form of government," rather than a focus on real-world problem-solving or community-building. It relies on narrow, exclusionary definitions of what a "good citizen" is. Learning civics, then, becomes not about meeting people where they are, but about promoting jingoistic tropes like "the American Dream" or about upholding white, middle-class forms of citizenship. It becomes about reinforcing social hierarchies and inequities rather than dissolving them. This furthers the chasm even more, because why should we engage with a broken system that excludes so many of us?[78]

We need to reconceive the concept of participation gaps. While we definitely need to enhance access and participation, we also need to rethink how people are already participating, including youth and people of color. Love explains that Black people are showing up and civically engaging, such as through creative works like hip hop, and through creative movements, digital formats, and grassroots communities. Likewise, youth are engaging in dialogues and creative expression, governance, and political protests such as through games and social media. Take, for instance, the teenagers who met on Twitter and organized a Black Lives Matter protest of over 10,000 people in Tennessee.[79] Or the group of K-Pop stans who collectively worked together to protect Black Lives Matter protestors in Dallas by interrupting the policing app with K-Pop Fancams (short clips of live performances by South Korean pop stars).[80] And then there are the TikTok teens and K-Pop stans who used social media to disrupt a political rally in Tulsa, Oklahoma by filling the ticket requests with false registrations.[81]

Mirra and Garcia ask us to look at how students of color are participating in ways that the traditional methodologies to measure civic engagement may not capture. They call for "a critical vision of citizenship that can counter the dominant perspective that young Americans of color are civically disengaged and instead acknowledge the innovative ways in which they are participating in civic life."[82] It is important not only to teach civics and ethics, but to find ways to equitably teach it, equitably enable access and belongingness to it, and equitably acknowledge participation in it. To do this, we need to reveal the complexity of and problematize ethics and civics systems themselves.

We need ethics and civics—even if it is messy and complex, *especially* if it is messy and complex. In the next chapter I will describe the types of specific skills, knowledge, concepts, and practices we need to learn *to citizen*, with an understanding that we should be continually reflecting on and revising what "to citizen" means.

3
What Should We Teach?

What Is Currently Being Taught?

But certainly, teachers *are* teaching ethics and civics. Educators around the world are teaching students how to think critically, solve problems, make ethical decisions, and take action in their communities. So what are teachers doing now? What should teachers teach?

In the United States, the teachers that typically teach civics and ethics are social studies teachers, history teachers, government and political science teachers, and philosophy teachers. They teach to all different types of students—including honors and AP students, as well as students in private, charter, public, and alternative middle and high schools, community colleges, universities, and four-year colleges. Beyond formal education, civics is taught in the home, after-school programs, libraries, community centers, museums, and historic sites, as well as online.[1]

US educators teach topics and themes such as states rights versus federalism, the separation of powers and branches of government, the election process, the party system, and news literacy. They teach skills such as reading comprehension, writing, critical thinking, making inferences, and argumentation, and how to read, compare, evaluate, and use documents and evidence. Teachers also have their students read and learn about current events and investigate their local communities and governments.[2]

Teachers use workbooks, picture books, worksheets, and textbooks. They use videos, films, and visual material. Many also use websites, games, and other interactive experiences.[3] They use a mix of lecture-focused classes and project-based learning. Their assignments range from multiple-choice tests, essays, and research papers to document-based questions and Socratic-style seminars. Their students are also doing real-world activities, like writing to their congressperson or taking field trips to civic spaces in their community.[4] But as Coleman-Mortley explains, time is limited to even take kids to local spaces such as city hall or the post office.[5] As a result, teachers may be "focusing more on facts and history narratives and less on activities like debate or simulation exercises" that have been shown to be effective.[6]

Despite these challenges, teachers are encouraging hands-on projects. Daniels, a teacher at a public International Baccalaureate school in the District of Columbia, has capstone community projects where students have gone "to one of the local food banks, donated time to campaigns, or worked for animal shelters. One group that was really influential created a social media campaign around raising awareness of teen anxiety and depression and what you can do about it. One girl wanted to raise

We the Gamers. Karen Schrier, Oxford University Press. © Oxford University Press 2021.
DOI: 10.1093/oso/9780190926106.003.0003

awareness to teachers on better supporting students with autism. She has an autistic brother, so she ran a professional development for teachers one afternoon for an hour."[7]

Teacher Everett, a Florida private school teacher, has students do community-focused civic engagement projects where they identify a problem and then find a way to help solve the problem, such as through a policy solution, community partnership, or creative project. For instance, one student created a series of videos for different civics-related topics, while others created adult education civics classes with a local library.[8]

Abbott, who teaches at a rural North Carolina school, has her students work on a group project where they need to call county officials and investigate the local, state, and national level branches. They sift through voting records of elected officials. Abbott also has a "current event of the day" where the students need to "break down the current event, look at how the U.S. Constitution applies to that current event, and then do an activity around the topic."[9] For example, the week I interviewed Abbott, her students looked at traffic cameras and whether they violate due process. The following week they were planning to look at affirmative action and the 2019 college admissions scandal, where celebrities and others were paying to have their children receive special privileges to help them get admitted into colleges.

And some teachers are implementing the Generation Citizen curriculum, an action civics-based curriculum that aims to take students step-by-step through how to identify problems and take action in their communities. During the 10-week unit, students practice skills related to civic engagement "through attending community meetings, through keeping abreast of current events in [their] locality, through collaborating with others to collectively solve a problem.... It gives students the opportunity to experience and practice engaging in a democratic culture within the confines of the community."[10]

While this is what may be happening in the classroom, it's not necessarily consistent across classrooms and schools, from state to state, or country to country. What is mandated by state and government standards varies. In the next section I will dive into different frameworks, standards, and curricula that explore what we should teach, such as through and with games.

Standards, Frameworks, and Tools

Why do standards matter?[11] When you are using any educational activity or experience—such as a game—you need to make sure that it fits the requirements of what should be taught in that country, state, region, or place. Coleman-Mortley explains that "you can create the best K-12 learning tools in the entire world. But if it's not aligned with the standards, teachers will say 'goodbye.' There's no value in it because they are required to adhere to their state standards."[12] In the United States,

states drive their own standards for social studies courses, which could include civics-related content but more broadly includes geography, history, and economics as well. Godsay et al. investigated all of the state standards and found some common themes, including "civic ideals and practices" in almost all of the states (50 states) and "culture and diversity" in 44 of 51 states (including the District of Columbia). Developing civics skills was included in 41 of 51 state curricula.[13] Although civics and social studies standards vary by state, there are national standards that have been developed in an effort to support state-by-state curriculum standards. The following are frameworks (mostly from the United States) to consider when thinking through what to teach and how to approach ethics and civics.[14]

College, Career, and Civic Life (C3) Framework for Social Studies State Standards

The C3 framework, created and published in 2013 by the National Council for the Social Studies (NCSS), focuses on creating standards for K-12 social studies areas including civics, geography, history, and economics. Similar to the NCSS National Standards, which explain the general concepts and content that should be covered in a social studies classroom, the C3 framework explores the pedagogical approaches for how to update and implement social studies standards. The purpose of this framework is to prepare students for becoming citizens in the twenty-first century, and to "a) enhance the rigor of the social studies disciplines; b) build critical thinking, problem solving, and participatory skills to become engaged citizens; and c) align academic programs to the Common Core State Standards for English Language Arts and Literacy in History/Social Studies."[15] The framework is focused on enhancing inquiry and curiosity, and being able to apply knowledge in real-world contexts. The framework has four different dimensions:

1. **Developing questions and planning inquiries:** This relates to the underlying foundation of social studies as being inquiry-based, with *questioning* as the key component of the learning process. Teachers are an integral part of the process by helping students compose questions.
2. **Applying disciplinary tools and concepts:** This area provides the support for *developing* these questions, in that students need disciplinary knowledge to help pose questions and begin to pursue their answers. This includes the different disciplines (civics, economics, geography, and history) and what to teach in each. The civics area includes concepts like "civic and political institutions; participation and deliberation: applying civic virtues and democratic principles; processes, rules, and laws."[16]
3. **Evaluating sources and using evidence:** This component aims to help students in *answering* questions, by building skills such as gathering, evaluating, and analyzing data; sifting through evidence; and vetting sources. Students also

need to practice using this evidence to support or counter accounts, claims, and arguments, and to deliberate possibilities.

4. **Communicating conclusions and taking informed action:** In this area students are asked to communicate their findings, whether through persuasive writing, blog posts, discussions in the classroom, group presentations, video testimonials, or even through game design. Students may work solo, as well as partner with others or work in a group to discuss, digest, communicate, and reflect on their findings. Connecting students with real-world issues and solutions as related to civic and ethical questions is also a part of taking action.[17]

Civics Assessment Framework

The National Assessment Governing Board of the US Department of Education developed and published a Civics Assessment framework in 2018, which includes the following three components:[18]

1. **Civic knowledge:** This part of the framework cites knowledge areas that are needed for an informed citizenry. It relates specifically to the US democratic system, and addresses questions such as: What are civic life, politics, and government? How does the government established by the Constitution embody the purposes, values, and principles of American democracy? What are the roles of citizens in American democracy? These questions are drawn from the National Standards for Civics and Government.

2. **Civic skills:** This part of the framework outlines the skills that citizens should have to be able to fully participate in civic life, including learning and applying civic knowledge; finding, explaining, and analyzing information, sources, perspectives, and claims; and evaluating and critiquing positions on different issues. In addition, citizens need to be aware of public needs, and should be able to communicate and work with others; organize, connect, and create coalitions; and negotiate with others and resolve conflicts.

3. **Civic dispositions:** These dispositions or inclinations are based on de Tocqueville's idea of the "habits of the heart" that underlie all of citizenship.[19] In democratic engagement, these relate to the "rights and responsibilities of individuals in society" to become "an independent member of society; respect individual worth and human dignity; assume the personal, political, and economic responsibilities of a citizen; participate in civic affairs in an informed, thoughtful, and effective manner; and promote the healthy functioning of American constitutional democracy."[20]

This framework is not meant to dictate curriculum in civics; rather, it explores what students should be able to practice as engaged citizens.

Campaign for the Civic Mission of Schools

This framework aims to answer the following question: What do people really need to be able to be informed citizens, and civically engaged, globally aware, and culturally respectful people of the world? The Campaign for the Civic Mission of Schools provides four main competencies, which are similar to the Civics Assessment framework. Their framework includes:

1. **Content knowledge:** The core relevant knowledge and ability to apply it.
2. **Intellectual skills:** Skills such as the ability to identify and analyze information and processes related to civics.
3. **Participatory skills:** Skills related to how to organize and plan, solve civic problems and make change, interact in groups and other settings, communicate with others and representatives, and share perspectives, views, and arguments.
4. **Dispositions:** These include values and responsibilities, such as caring about others, supporting equality and equity, and considering one's social and emotional responsibilities and needs.[21]

United States Common Core

In History/Social Studies and English Language Arts (ELA), for grades 6 to 12, there are some specific common core standards that may be useful to consider, including:

1. Analyzing primary and secondary sources and citing evidence to support one's analysis.
2. Determining the central ideas in a source or summarizing a source.
3. Interpreting the meaning of words in a text.
4. Interpreting and integrating both visual (e.g., charts, photographs, maps) and textual information.
5. Distinguishing facts from opinions and evaluating claims.
6. Reading and interpreting texts from social studies, and understanding how they are structured.
7. Using different types of evidence to be able to solve a problem.
8. Working with and collaborating with people who have other perspectives.
9. Participating with others in civil discussions, planning, and problem-solving.[22]

The 10 Proven Practices for Civics Education

While the previous frameworks primarily refer to student outcomes and curricular components, the 10 practices provide guidance as to how to teach civics. The

10 proven practices are derived from the report *Guardian of Democracy: The Civic Mission of Schools*, which lists six practices, the report *The Republic is (Still) at Risk*, which lists an additional four more. The practices are as follows:

1. Classroom instruction in civics, government, and history.
2. Discussion of current events.
3. Service learning.
4. Extracurricular activities.
5. Student participation in school governance.
6. Simulations of democratic processes and procedures.
7. News media literacy.
8. Action civics.
9. Social and emotional learning (SEL).
10. School climate reform.[23]

Student-Centered Approaches to Civics

The following are additional approaches to consider when thinking about what to teach, how to teach, and how to design and implement civics and ethics learning experiences.

1. **Youth Participatory Action Research (YPAR)** is not a framework but an approach to civic participation and inquiry that situates "civic learning from the perspective of young people and builds opportunities for action out of the contexts and experiences of their daily lives." This approach centers youth as the creators and curators of their civic experiences. It challenges the traditional epistemologies of what knowledge is and who can create knowledge. It is not a specific set of criteria or series of standards, but rather a new paradigm for what matters when it comes to civics and ethics, and who is empowered to decide what matters.[24]

2. **Connected civics** relates to how civic learning should aim to enhance connections among youth interests and identities and civic participation. While it recommends that students have opportunities to make social change, Ito et al. write that what counts as civic activities could be "tied to community problem-solving and social justice that do not necessarily lead to or even involve direct governmental action," like the sharing stories of discrimination via a hashtag on social media. Dishon and Kafai expand the definition further and describe a connected civic gaming approach. This invites and labels as civic activities that which is outside the traditional definition, such as game-playing and game-making. This approach also explores how games themselves may act as simulative civic spaces, where players have the opportunity

to enact civic and ethical decisions "not only within the game but also about the game."[25]

3. **Action civics** describes an approach to civics where students play a key role in creating their own learning through active participation in their communities, such as through real-world projects that help the local and national community.[26] Generation Citizen is an organization that creates an action civics curriculum for middle and high school students.[27] With the Generation Citizen curriculum, students get to choose the issues that are most meaningful to them to learn more about and act on. The students then perform real-world activities to help to solve these issues. They are "writing and publishing op-eds, testifying at meetings. They are emailing or calling elected officials. They are hosting town halls. They are meeting with decision makers and working to get their plan done."

4. **Strengthening Our Democracy: Civic Participation in the 21st Century** describes an approach to civics that stems from ADL's anti-bias framework and curricula. This approach aims to reduce obstacles to civic participation and challenge biases that perpetuate inequities. The curricula includes units like "Activism" and "Human Rights" and is guided by themes like "Power and Privilege" and "Social Justice and Human Rights."[28]

Ethics Frameworks and Curricula

What about ethics standards and curricula, specifically? Ethics education is called by a number of different names—such as moral education or character education—and sometimes it is part of social and emotional learning (SEL). Regardless of the label, the purpose is to help students grapple with ethical decisions and reflect on their own and society's values. Overall, what has been more effective is not just telling students "what moral codes to follow" or what the "right ethics are."[29] Instead, what works is also helping students to learn the skills necessary to navigate shifting ethical norms, decisions, and scenarios.[30]

There is no one framework or set of standards for ethics in the United States. There are codes of ethics for different professions and organizations.[31] There are best practices for ethics, moral, and character education. However, there are no specific standards for teaching ethics in a K-12 environment in the United States, though the Common Core standards includes some connections to ethics.[32] For instance, the Literacy/English Language core standards listed earlier mention working with others to listen to their perspectives, and to deliberate, plan, and problem-solve.[33] Although there are no ethics-only standards, ethics should not be deprioritized. Rather, ethics should be seen as a partner to civics and other content areas. It is the lens through which we can enact scientific, social scientific, and humanistic inquiry, as ethics always needs to be tied to our pursuits, insights, and applications. It is a worthy area to learn on its own, as well.

In this section I will share some frameworks that may identify which goals, skills, thought processes, and activities are useful when teaching ethics.

Collaborative for Academic, Social and Emotional Learning (CASEL) Framework

While not a civics or ethics framework, CASEL reviews skills that are related to ethical thinking and civic literacy. It covers five areas of competencies around social and emotional learning, which are meant to "enhance students' capacity to integrate skills, attitudes, and behaviors to deal effectively and ethically with daily tasks and challenges."[34] The framework focuses on how to help students manage interactions, whether in classrooms, schools, homes, or communities. While these may have initially been dismissed as unnecessary "soft" skills, there is a growing awareness that these types of skills matter in all different types of inquiries and disciplines, and areas of learning.[35]

The five areas of the CASEL framework are:

1. **Self-awareness:** This refers to the ability of a person to assess their own strengths and limitations, to recognize and identify their own emotions and values, and to understand how these may affect their behaviors. This includes skills such as identifying emotions and values, and concepts such as self-efficacy.
2. **Self-management:** This relates to the ability of someone to regulate their own emotions and behaviors depending on different contexts, and to set and meet goals and needs. This includes skills such as goal-setting, organizational skills, and executive function.
3. **Social awareness:** This area refers to the ability to take on the perspectives of others and empathize with their thoughts and feelings, as well as to recognize and be open to people from different backgrounds. It also relates to navigating different social, cultural, and ethical norms depending on the context or community. Skills include perspective-taking, empathy, and respect for others and cultural humility.
4. **Relationship skills:** This competency relates to managing healthy and beneficial relationships with different types of people. It includes skills such as clear listening and communication, conflict resolution, cooperation, and teamwork.
5. **Responsible decision-making:** This area refers to the ability to make appropriate personal, social, and ethical choices, and to understand and evaluate the consequences of these choices. This also includes knowing how and when to focus on taking care of one's own or other's needs. The skills include ethical thinking, problem-solving, evaluating, reflecting, and analyzing situations and problems.[36]

Jubilee Centre for Character & Virtues Framework

The Jubilee Centre at the University of Birmingham in the United Kingdom has created a framework for Character Education in Schools.[37] It consists of four different building blocks of virtues:

1. **Intellectual virtues:** This includes virtues such as critical thinking, reflection, and judgment.
2. **Moral virtues:** This includes compassion, justice, and respect.
3. **Civic virtues:** This includes community awareness, service, and citizenship.[38]
4. **Performance virtues:** This includes resilience, motivation, teamwork, and determination.

These building blocks form the basis of practical wisdom, or the complex set of experiences and virtues, developed over time and using critical reflection, which helps people understand how to put the four building blocks of virtues into practice. This practical wisdom then leads to what the Centre calls the flourishing of individuals and society. To develop these virtues they use a neo-Aristotelian model of moral development, which includes virtue knowledge and understanding, virtue reasoning, and virtue practice.[39]

EPIC (Ethics Practice and Implementation Categorization Framework)

As there is no vetted framework for choosing games for ethics learning, I created a novel framework. This framework, EPIC, provides educators with a series of possible educational goals, along with a list of strategies for teaching ethics through games. EPIC is useful for finding the right game for a particular ethics need, but could also be applied to other types of media, activities, and experiences. The framework is split into two different parts: (1) seven educational goals, or ethics learning needs, and (2) educational strategies, or ways to support or meet particular objectives that could be found in a game. We can use the framework's goals to help think about the types of ethics skills and processes that should be taught.[40] Goals include:

1. **Enhance ethical awareness:** This goal relates to moral sensitivity and identity, in that it helps people understand their own moral and ethical opinions, decisions, and actions.[41] Relevant questions are what a person's ethical identity is, what their own perspectives are, and their moral orientation.[42]
2. **Enhance emotional intelligence or general SEL abilities:** This is a necessary goal because ethical thinking requires the ability to think through one's emotions and use them appropriately in decision-making and action.[43] Social and

emotional intelligence includes being able to identify emotions, understand others' emotions, and manage one's emotions.[44] Those who are more aware of their own emotions and able to manage them may be more aware of how emotions affect their attitudes, biases, decisions, and behaviors.[45]

3. **Practice care or empathy-related skills:** Empathy and compassion are an integral part of ethical decision-making. Care, connectedness, and relationships are foundational to how people make ethical decisions.[46] This goal works with the others to help people to "identify, consider, care about, and integrate other's perspectives and ethical points of view."[47]

4. **Practice ethical reasoning:** This goal involves students identifying, analyzing, and evaluating ethical issues, choices, and consequences. People need to be able to think through ethical scenarios and issues.[48] "Ethical reasoning relates to a number of skills, such as prioritizing, establishing pros and cons, evaluating the issue, analyzing evidence, identifying biases, and interpreting."[49]

5. **Practice ethical reflection:** This goal relates to reflection, a critical skill in helping students reflect on their decisions and think through their actions and its consequences. With reflection, students need to interpret and reconsider their own assumptions and attitudes to more fully understand and accept one's decisions, which helps to transform one's perspectives and actions moving forward.[50]

6. **Enhance character:** This goal relates to people understanding how to better treat others with respect, value all areas of humanity and society and the world, and being engaged with civic life.[51] Character relates to many different types of elements but includes a variety of things such as "respect, responsibility, trustworthiness, caring, justice, fairness, civic virtue, and citizenship."[52]

7. **Cultivate facility with major ethics issues, approaches, and frameworks:** This goal relates to sharing and building ethics-related content and key theories, such as the Kantian approach, hedonism, or utilitarian framework.[53] While different people may access or privilege one particular framework over another, students should be able to identify the strengths and weaknesses of different approaches, be able to apply it to scenarios, and use it in different circumstances (such as a justice vs. care approach to ethics). In addition, students should be able to articulate, identify, and evaluate the key current ethical and humanistic issues, as well as historical issues, and be able to understand why they are important and apply them to future scenarios.[54]

What Skills and Concepts Should We Teach?

In this book I do not aim to reinvent civics and ethics education, or to create new local or global standards. Rather, I want to reimagine and reframe how we can use games to teach what may be useful to learn and practice. How can games support all different approaches to civics and ethics, including how youth may already be participating? How do we meet youth where they already are?

I also try not to privilege one type of ethical or civics framework over another, nor favor a particular civic configuration, governing structure, or political process. There are many different types of standards or goals an educator may need to meet, and the specific content they use often depends on the age group, location, and even the time period in which one lives.[55] Since civic processes may differ starkly across nations and even within local communities, this book instead shares possibilities—questions, themes, concepts, skills, and practices that could apply to different types of civic configurations, ethical frameworks, or social studies, rather than dictating the type of instructional content or curricular facets that should be relayed to students.[56] What works best for one teacher in one country or district is not going to be the same as what works better for another teacher in a different part of the world.

That said, the game examples and teaching strategies I describe in this book often relate to specific topics, skills, topics, or units, which could be adapted to others. Although I may mention specific frameworks to use or topics to teach, such as the electoral college, gerrymandering, the Constitution, filibuster, comparative governments, Utilitarianism, or Hedonism, the actual instructional needs and curriculum should be further developed or modified by the educator.[57]

So what should we teach? From my review of the current standards and curricula in ethics and civics, three themes have emerged (see Table 3.1). These three themes drive the structure of the rest of the book, including the nine questions, concepts, and constellations of skills that inspire the next nine chapters. These three themes are:

1. Real-world knowledge and action.
2. Community and connection.
3. Critical inquiry and critical thinking.[58]

Even though I establish nine guiding questions for the remainder of the book, our entire approach should be about questioning. We need to ask our students what they already do, what they need, and where they want to be. How can we empower our students to become critical civic participators on their own terms? How do we make a curriculum and learning experience that aims to dissolve social inequities, rather than further systemic injustices? How do we prepare our students to citizen while also revealing the messiness of citizenship? Regardless of the content we use, we should take a student-empowering, reflective approach.

Real-World Knowledge and Action

This section, and the following two sections, expand on the three themes of this book: Real-World Knowledge and Action, Connection and Community, and Critical Thinking and Inquiry.

Table 3.1 Connections to standards

Theme	Driving Question	Skills	Standards Connections	Chapter
Knowledge and action	**What is the knowledge we need?**	Knowledge-building, recalling, remembering	**C3 framework:** Applying disciplinary tools and concepts. **Civics Assessment framework:** Civic knowledge. **Campaign for the Civic Mission of Schools:** Content knowledge.	4
Knowledge and action	**How do we take real-world action?**	Applying knowledge, volunteering, serving, doing, acting, changing	**C3 framework:** Communicating conclusions and taking informed action. **Civics Assessment framework:** Civics skills, including learning and applying civic knowledge. **Campaign for the Civic Mission of Schools:** Participatory skills; organizing and planning how to solve civic problems and make change. **US Common Core:** Participating with others in civil discussions; planning and problem-solving. **Jubilee framework:** Civic virtues	5
Connection and community	**How do we connect and communicate?**	Communication, collaboration, teamwork, civil discourse, argumentation, structured thinking	**C3 framework:** Communicating conclusions and taking informed action. **Civics Assessment framework:** Civic dispositions; civic skills; organizing, connecting, and creating coalitions; negotiating with others and resolving conflict. **Campaign for the Civic Mission of Schools:** Participatory skills; interacting in groups and other settings; communicating with others and representatives; dispositions; caring about others. **US Common Core:** Participating with others in civil discussions, planning, and problem-solving; working with and collaborating with people who have other perspectives. **CASEL:** Relationship skills; social awareness. **Jubilee framework:** Civic virtues; performance virtues.	6

Connection and community	How do we understand ourselves and our emotions?	Expression, identity exploration, identifying emotions, managing emotions, emotional expression, bias identification	**C3 framework:** Communicating conclusions and taking informed action. **Civics Assessment framework:** Civic dispositions; respecting individual worth and human dignity; assuming the personal, political, and economic responsibilities of a citizen. **Campaign for the Civic Mission of Schools:** Dispositions; caring about others and equality and equity. **US Common Core:** Working with and collaborating with people who have other perspectives. **CASEL:** Self-awareness; self-management; social awareness. **Jubilee framework:** Civic virtues; performance virtues; moral virtues.	7
Connection and community	How do we cultivate compassion and respect for others?	Perspective-taking, empathy, compassion, respect, cultural awareness and cultural humility	**C3 framework:** Communicating conclusions and taking informed action. **Civics Assessment framework:** Civic dispositions; respecting individual worth and human dignity; assuming the personal, political, and economic responsibilities of a citizen. **Campaign for the Civic Mission of Schools:** Dispositions; caring about others and equality and equity. **US Common Core:** Working with and collaborating with people who have other perspectives. **CASEL:** Social awareness. **Jubilee framework:** Moral virtues.	8
Critical thinking and inquiry	How do we make and reflect on decisions?	Reasoning, questioning, decision-making, reflection, argumentation	**C3 framework:** Developing questions and planning inquiries. **Civics Assessment framework:** Civic skills. **Campaign for the Civic Mission of Schools:** Intellectual skills; participatory skills. **US Common Core:** Using different types of evidence to be able to solve a problem; participating with others in civil discussions, planning, and problem-solving. **CASEL:** Responsible decision-making; self-management. **Jubilee framework:** Intellectual virtues.	9

Continued

Table 3.1 *Continued*

Theme	Driving Question	Skills	Standards Connections	Chapter
Critical thinking and inquiry	**How do we read and evaluate information?**	Evaluation, judgment, synthesis, sourcing and locating information	**C3 framework:** Evaluating sources and using evidence. **Civics Assessment framework:** Civics skills; finding, explaining, and analyzing information, sources, perspectives, and claims; and evaluating and critiquing positions on different issues. **Campaign for the Civic Mission of Schools:** Intellectual skills; the ability to identify and analyze information. **US Common Core:** Analyzing primary and secondary sources; distinguishing facts from opinions and evaluate claims; interpreting the meaning of words in a text; interpreting and integrating both visual (e.g., charts, photographs, maps) and textual information; reading and interpreting texts from social studies, and understanding how they are structured. **CASEL:** Responsible decision-making. **Jubilee framework:** Intellectual virtues	10
Critical thinking and inquiry	**How do we analyze systems and problems?**	Systems analysis and systems thinking, problem-solving	**C3 framework:** Developing questions and planning inquiries. **Civics Assessment framework:** Civic skills. **Campaign for the Civic Mission of Schools:** Intellectual skills; participatory skills. **US Common Core:** Using different types of evidence to be able to solve a problem; participating with others in civil discussions, planning and problem-solving. **CASEL:** Responsible decision-making; self-management. **Jubilee framework:** Intellectual virtues.	11
Critical thinking and inquiry	**How do we explore and design?**	Design, creating, making, constructing, exploring, experimenting	**C3 framework:** Developing questions and planning inquiries. **Civics Assessment framework:** Civic skills. **Campaign for the Civic Mission of Schools:** Intellectual skills; participatory skills. **US Common Core:** Using different types of evidence to be able to solve a problem; participating with others in civil discussions, planning, and problem-solving. **CASEL:** Responsible decision-making; self-management; relationship skills. **Jubilee framework:** Intellectual virtues; performance virtues.	12

This table is a summary of the ethics and civics themes and driving questions discussed in this book.

We need to gain real-world knowledge and understand the ethical frameworks and civic processes and institutions of our communities. We also need the ability to apply this knowledge and engage in real-world action. Students need to build a strong foundation in civics and ethics knowledge, such as how their local, national, and global communities are governed. Some questions they need to be able to answer are: What are the key institutions and processes in a particular government? How are people able to participate in their communities? What are the rules and policies, and how are they applied? What is the historical context?

A recurring theme across many of the standards and frameworks for civics and ethics is the ability to identify, remember, and understand the major components of public life and governance, such as its policies, protocols, principles, institutions, locations, rules, frameworks, and roles. These differ by locality and national and sociocultural context. For instance, in the United States students may need to be able to be understand, describe, analyze, and compare concepts and processes such as the three branches of government, the electoral college, impeachment, town halls, voting, juries, and the US Constitution.[59]

Alongside understanding the main components of civic life in one's local, national, and global communities, students should also be conversant with the major ethical approaches and frameworks. Students need to know how they differ, and their strengths and weaknesses. Depending on age, audience, and cultural context, students might need to be able to identify a justice versus care approach to ethics, recognize the differences among Western and Eastern philosophies, or compare virtue ethics, deontological perspectives, Feminist ethics approaches, and consequentialist frameworks. Students should be able to identify current ethical, civics, and humanistic issues as well as historical issues, and their major tensions, themes, and actors.[60] Students may also be able to identify different virtues and components of character.[61]

Instead of just memorizing facts, however, students need to be able to use this knowledge, and form a personal connection with the material. Active, engaged, and empowered learning is necessary.[62] As the C3 framework states, students stay engaged when they are able to take their learning and apply it to the real world, rather than just reading textbooks and memorizing facts for exams. Knowledge needs to be relevant and meaningful to the student, and even driven by the student. Dewey writes, "Knowledge as an act is bringing some of our dispositions to consciousness with a view to straightening out a perplexity, by conceiving the connection between ourselves and the world in which we live."[63] Thus, students should be encouraged to go beyond regurgitating knowledge and instead use it meaningfully in their everyday lives.[64] To do this, students should to be able to participate in the creation of their own learning environment and have opportunities to make an impact on the communities that matter to them. They need to learn, grow, and participate in real, meaningful public spheres to build this knowledge.[65]

The Campaign for the Civic Mission of Schools' best practices for teaching civics explains that classrooms and other educational contexts should encourage deliberation and discussion of "local, national and international issues and events into the classroom, particularly those that young people view as important to their lives" and communities.[66] They explain that students should participate in their communities and engage in real-life interactions, problems, and issues outside of the classroom, such as through volunteer work or participating in town hall meetings. For instance, a high school student in my community created bat houses to place in local parks, and presented the project to the town board for approval. Schools and other educational contexts should also provide students with opportunities to directly interact with and simulate real-world democratic processes.[67] Students should be able to participate in all areas of the governance and regulation of their own schools, such as through student government. This theme will be addressed in chapters 4 and 5, as well as throughout the book.

Connection and Community

We need to connect with others and ourselves, and cultivate respect for the dignity and humanity of others.

Students need to be able to engage in respectful dialogue and discourse, show compassion, explore their identities and other's identities, care about each other, and connect with one another. Students need novel ways to practice relevant civic and ethics skills, particularly given the need to navigate, interact, and communicate in communities online and offline in our globally interconnected and culturally diverse world. These skills are vital for personal, local, and global success.[68]

Dewey explains that schools *are* communities, such that these skills are not just learned but are themselves practiced within the school-as-civic community.[69] The Campaign for the Civic Mission for Schools, for instance, recommends that students be involved in changing the climate of the school and broader community. Students need to feel like they belong, and need to be part of an inclusive, caring environment that understands and fulfills their needs—whether financial, spiritual, physical, or emotional. This relates to understanding the whole student, and how a school's environment, in addition to one's home and community environment, affects students. This may be a paradigm shift for the schools and educators, because it means they need to open themselves up to being uncomfortable and vulnerable, and receiving and acting upon the criticism given by students. It also requires not just listening to the majority of voices, but ensuring that the voices of those who are oppressed are not further marginalized within their school community.[70]

Additionally, the Campaign for the Civic Mission for Schools and CASEL recommend that social and emotional learning be a strong component of a curriculum. This involves helping students to manage and understand their emotions, connect with others and build relationships, and practice ethical decision-making and empathy, which help to cultivate civics skills and dispositions. It also may help to spur further learning overall.[71] Results from studies on the impact of SEL has suggested that these skills help to enhance reasoning, increase academic achievement, and positively affect the behavior and attitudes of learners.[72] Greater self-efficacy may positively affect one's ability to learn a variety of content areas and skills—and not just ethics and civics.[73]

Initially, when social media and other connected platforms emerged, many saw them as a potential place for the inclusion of multiple voices where people together could make, grow, learn, interact, vote, and inspire.[74] On the other hand, we have also seen that many of the inequities we face in our ability to fully participate in society, such as systemic racism, sexism, or classism, are replicated and even magnified through online and in virtual spaces (such as games).[75] We need to ensure full access to and empower participation in learning environments both online and offline, and this requires teaching a number of skills, such as identity exploration, bias reduction, inclusion, cultural awareness and cultural humility, and activist and social justice skills.[76] Our teaching and learning needs to be transformative in that it does not just build or replicate community, but in that it repairs inequities and helps to change the very institutions of our public sphere. This theme will be addressed in chapters 6, 7, and 8, as well as throughout the book.

Critical Thinking and Inquiry

We need to practice critical thinking and critical inquiry skills, and to reimagine how we can solve problems together.

As a society, we need to be able to answer critical questions about the world around us, and about how people should act, behave, and live together.[77] To do this we need to be critical thinkers and sifters, and be able to reason through information and decisions about how we should act, live, and function. Citing Dewey, Haber explains that a "democratic society requires citizens who can take a leading role in their own lives and government by, among other things, being informed and knowing how to approach problems systematically and logically."[78]

Students need to practice critical inquiry and thinking skills of all types, including reading, writing, interpretation, and analysis, as well as information, news, and media literacy, to help evaluate the reliability and accuracy of information, evidence, testimonials, and news sources. We need to teach and learn skills such as the ability to take on alternative viewpoints and consider others' perspectives; engage in thoughtful deliberation, reflection, and argumentation; and consider one's own biases, as well as make ethical decisions. We also need to be able to evaluate the greater systemic issues that make it more difficult to engage, belong, and act compassionately.[79]

Finally, students need to be creators of new tools, solutions, and policies that can better support their families, communities, and public life. Creativity and civic imagination are vital to people being able to develop and participate in the future of humanity. As we create new ways of living together, we also need to consider: What are the ethics of our designs, and how do we ensure that everyone is included and belongs? How do we redesign our current and future institutions? While we revise our designs, we also need to problematize our solutions. How do we grapple with its messiness? Students need to be problem-solvers and decision-makers who can revise, redesign, and disrupt.[80]

Critical thinking and inquiry skills are practices we need to engage in as members of our community, workers at our jobs, and students in our schools, now and in the future.[81] Critical thinking and critical inquiry involve a number of different skills.[82] While there is no one set definition of critical thinking, there are a number of different skills that could be associated with the process of deeply considering a "subject, content, or problem—in which the thinker improves the quality of [their] thinking by skillfully analyzing, assessing, and reconstructing it."[83] (Although these are the critical skills under current epistemologies, we also need to rethink *how we think*. What is the critical thinking needed for our future?[84]) The following are five areas of critical thinking skills:

1. **Structured thinking, communication, and argumentation:** This involves explaining and clearly communicating ideas, and making our thinking clear to others. It also includes identifying claims, translating language into premises and conclusions, and moving audiences through sound arguments.[85] It requires avoiding cognitive biases and decision-making, and determining whether the reasons or rationales for an argument, view, or perspective are valid.[86] Reasoning and applying logic, decision-making, deduction and induction, and argumentation and persuasive communication or rhetoric are part of this cluster of skills,[87] some of which are discussed in chapters 6 and 9.

2. **Questioning and reflecting:** This relates to the ability to develop critical questions and deliberate the answers to these questions. It also involves being able to deeply consider and reconsider one's questions, choices, and decisions, and revise future decisions based on these reflections.[88] This cluster of skills, which orthogonally crosses all other categories of skills, involves reflection and reflective practice, questioning, and deliberation. These skills will be discussed in chapter 9.

3. **Evaluation and judgment:** This refers to the ability to find and locate information and data and critically evaluate it, form judgments, and organize it. It also includes uncovering patterns, synthesizing information, and sharing it with others.[89] The critical skills associated with reading, interpreting, and evaluating information, data, and evidence, such as critique and authentication, will be discussed in chapter 10.

4. **Systems analysis and problem-solving:** This involves understanding the relationships among variables in a system, or dynamic sets of interlocking parts. This also relates to skills such as problem-solving or the ability to identify, define, and work toward solutions to problems or issues in one's environment or community.[90] This will be discussed further in chapter 11.

5. **Experimentation and creativity:** This relates to creating new knowledge through engagement in the process of making and creation, as well as exploring and iterating through possibilities.[91] It includes skills like exploration, experimentation, designing, computational thinking, planning, creating, and constructing. These will be discussed in chapter 12.

In the next nine chapters I will describe strategies to use in the classroom (and beyond) to help students engage civically and ethically in, around, and through games. Each chapter will:

1. Identify the guiding question, which will serve as the learning goal for the chapter.
2. Summarize research related to the guiding question, concept, or series of skills, as well as the complexities of using games to support it.
3. Share a number of examples of using games to meet these goals, and the strategies that teachers may apply to better support learning, engagement, and participation.

PART II

USING GAMES FOR KNOWLEDGE AND ACTION

4
What Is the Knowledge We Need?

When I was a kid, civic processes, like elections, seemed so inaccessible. There were elections that I could not participate in for people I had never heard of. There were documents and laws, like the Bill of Rights, which were written in ways I could not easily read nor apply to my own life. And, there was a president, a role that I was not allowed to play—and likely never would.[1] It made me feel like *all* aspects of civic life were also off-limits. Civics was not relatable nor personally relevant, nor did it seem to matter.

So how can we change this? Today, game players *can* be the president of the United States—through a game. In iCivic's game *Win the White House*, players act as a presidential candidate for a fictional election and need to decide how to gain enough electoral votes to win.[2] They have to balance advertising buys, choose stump speech locations, and select issues to debate. Likewise, in another iCivic's game, *Executive Command*, players make decisions and plan their agenda while acting as the commander in chief of the United States.[3] Teachers can incorporate these games into units on elections, civic processes, ethics and character, the US executive branch, or even media literacy. Coleman-Mortley, the Director of Social Engagement at iCivics, the organization that created these games, explains that "the games are a bridge to becoming engaged in civics, making it an accessible experience for all kids ... These games provide players with the first-person experience of running for the president or passing a law or balancing all three branches of government."[4]

Very few of us will ever actually get to be president. But through a game, we can imagine what it is like to make the types of decisions a president might face. As Humphries explains, in the game *Executive Command*, students "get to pass laws, ... manage the Oval Office, be the President of the United States" and put into practice the ethical choices a leader might make (see Figure 4.1).[5] This is important because even if we won't ever make these types of decisions directly, we need to reflect on these roles and processes so that we can imagine the types of people who should represent us, and how we would want them to represent us in government.

Likewise, in the Reagan Leadership Academy, a physical facility and museum in California, students can participate in presidential simulation modules. For example, there is one module where students get to practice being a commander in chief and "discuss landing on the island of Grenada," in a mock (but realistic-looking) military strategy room. There is also a module, "On the Brink of Nuclear War," where students can make decisions, and negotiate and discuss plans, which takes place in a room that is a replica of the White House Oval Office.[6] Through

We the Gamers. Karen Schrier, Oxford University Press. © Oxford University Press 2021.
DOI: 10.1093/oso/9780190926106.003.0004

Figure 4.1 An image from the game *Executive Command*. Image courtesy of iCivics.

these types of playful experiences, students can have a great deal of responsibility—even presidential responsibility—which can help make civics and ethics learning more meaningful.

In this chapter I discuss how games can help students to identify the real-world structures, institutions, and processes of government and civic life, such as the three branches of government in the United States or Nigeria, or the parliamentary procedure in India or the United Kingdom. Games may help us to understand the answers to questions like: What are the specific policies, procedures, roles, and locations that help to govern one's country, region, or local community? What are the major ethical perspectives that can help to guide our evaluations and decisions? What are the moral lenses that affect our public participation?

Why Build Civics and Ethics Knowledge?

Chapters 5 to 12 in this book center on the skills, practices, experiences, and "the arts and habits of civic life."[7] But the *knowledge* and *content* that is taught is also critically important, even if the specifics of what content is shared is place-, time-, and people- dependent.[8] This chapter focuses on how games may help to build this real-world civics and ethics *knowledge*.

Understanding civics and ethics institutions, processes, and systems is foundational, and learning it is necessary for students to fully participate in public life. In a constitutional democracy such as the United States, "productive civic engagement requires knowledge of the history, principles, and foundations of ... democracy."[9] In chapter 3, I described the types of ethics and civics content that we should teach, including the major components of public life and governance, such as its policies, protocols, principles, institutions, locations, rules, and roles.[10] For instance, in the United States, students need to understand the Constitution, state and local government structures, courts and legal systems, and institutions and governmental systems around the world. They need to understand terms like impeachment or filibuster, or processes like how to advocate for policy reform. They need to understand the concept of public participation. They need to understand and identify virtues, ethical frameworks, and components of character. Students may also need to be aware of current events and issues—local, national, and global.[11]

Knowledge is necessary for building and practicing skills like problem-solving, perspective-taking, and critical thinking; they go hand-in-hand.[12] Declarative or factual knowledge enhances cognitive processes, and vice versa.[13] Korbey argues that "thinking about any topic is bound up with background knowledge about that topic ... if a teacher asks a student to look at an issue from multiple perspectives, if [they don't] know much about an issue, [they cannot] think about it from multiple perspectives." An informed view or opinion relies on awareness of public and current issues, and an understanding of the possibilities and their historical contexts.[14]

Students do not just need civics and ethics-specific knowledge, but a foundation in all areas of humanistic pursuits, including the arts, sciences, history, literature, philosophy, culture, and media. Knowledge of history helps us to contextualize our present choices and views, and understand how civic institutions or policies came to be and how they shaped public life.[15] Economic knowledge helps us to be able to properly assess budgets or public policy changes.[16]

Yet students are still not learning the necessary knowledge to give context, nuance, and texture to their skills practice. Studies have suggested that students in the United States do not know things like the number of amendments in the Constitution, that it took a constitutional amendment to officially end slavery, or how provisions in the Constitution enabled slaveholders to have advantages. On a key civics exam, less than one-third of eighth graders knew the purpose of the Declaration of Independence or why citizen participation was integral to democracy.[17] In other recent studies, only 8% of the high school seniors surveyed could identify slavery as a cause of the Civil War; 22% of Millennials did not know what the Holocaust is; 72% of Americans could not name the 13 original states, and more than half of Americans surveyed (57%) did not know how many justices are on the US Supreme Court.[18] It's not just a recent problem. A 1943 history test of college freshmen in the United States revealed that fewer than a quarter could name two achievements of President Abraham Lincoln and only 6% could name the original 13 colonies of the United States (see more in chapter 2).[19]

Taking civics classes and engaging in civic learning works—it helps support greater civic knowledge and leads to greater civic action.[20] Students in Florida have seen higher civics test scores and civics knowledge due in part to the state's Sandra Day O'Connor Civic Education Act of 2010, which mandated a middle school course in civics and a civics test. This has also led to more engagement in their communities and homes around civics issues.[21]

How Do Games Teach Knowledge?

Games May Share Knowledge

Students in Florida are not just taking civics classes—they are playing civics games. Over 75% of Florida teachers surveyed in a 2016 study reported that their students are playing games about civics.[22] Dishon and Kafai point out that the most common way people use games to teach civics is for knowledge acquisition, as it helps to situate knowledge and enable active engagement in the development of that knowledge.[23] The *Guardian of Democracy* report discusses that one of the proven practices that support civic education are simulations of procedures and processes, which includes role-playing, mock trials, elections, debates, and specifically, games.[24]

There are a number of ways that games can represent and express civics and ethics frameworks, content, and topics. Games can convey factual and declarative knowledge about a particular government's roles and institutions, such as by showing the main branches of a government or by relaying how voting works.[25] Games can represent, simulate, and enable interaction with real-world civics and ethics processes, institutions, objects, peoples, or events.[26] The board game *1960: The Making of the President* simulates gaining support in the electoral college by using the Kennedy and Nixon presidency as its backdrop.[27] The digital card game *That's Your Right* teaches students about the first 10 amendments to the US Constitution (the Bill of Rights).[28]

In these knowledge acquisition games, players build knowledge of "how government works by ... experiencing it directly." Players may take on a role in the game's scenarios, such as president in *Executive Command*, or they may use a bird's-eye view perspective and control a town, agency, branch of government, city, or country, as in the *SimCity* or *Civilization* series.[29] Schell Games is working on a virtual reality history game, *HistoryMakerVR*,[30] in which players can choose a historic figure as their role in the game (such as Benjamin Franklin or Harriet Tubman). Players embody this person like they are a life-size digital puppet, thereby becoming that figure in the game. In *HistoryMakerVR*, players can also interact with props and write and relay speeches related to that figure and their historical time period.

So, why else might games be useful?

Games Can Be Fun

The authors of the report, *The Republic Is (Still) at Risk* talk about "excitement" as a necessary condition for the 10 proven practices for civic education to be effective. They write, "Civic action rarely brings immediate material rewards. Therefore, even if students learn civic knowledge in schools, they will not update, expand, and employ their knowledge as adults unless they want to do so. More than with subjects that bring immediate economic benefits, civics requires motivation," curiosity, and fun.[31]

Likewise, in *Making Democracy Fun*, Lerner contends that participating in civic processes,[32] such as attending public hearings or town halls, lobbying and campaigning, and even protesting and voting, can be time-intensive, tedious, and boring, making these processes unappealing. Civics involves a good deal of sitting and waiting or standing and waiting, listening, or reading through and interpreting long documents. Lerner contends that we should approach civic participation with a playful mindset, and that it should be fulfilling, satisfying, and meaningful. He argues that participants in places such as Venezuela are more engaged because their political and civic processes, such as community councils or town projects, are set up more like well-designed games. He argues that "the experience was more engaging thanks to vivid sights, sounds, and sensations (posters, music, and food)."[33]

Thus, playful approaches, such as games, may be effective in part because they can enhance excitement, motivation, curiosity, and meaningfulness in civics and ethic. A fun game may help motivate students to learn and do things they wouldn't normally do—like learn the structures of government, gain the fundamentals of virtue ethics, or read through documents like the Constitution.[34] Wrona, a teacher who works at a non-public alternative school, explains that his students "have not generally been successful [at school] . . . They're the [so-called] 'bad kids' who get into fights and yell and scream and have bad impulse control." But when he played the iCivics game *Executive Command* with his students, they loved it and began gaining the civic knowledge necessary to be able to engage in conversations with other students about the game.[35]

Fun does not mean frivolous. Koster explains that games are fun in part "*because they pose problems for the player to solve.*"[36] Or as I describe in chapter one, games may be about the work of revealing the messiness of life.[37] Play is not a diversion from work; it is the work. It's what Bogost explains is the "work of working a system . . . particularly of operating it in a way we haven't done before, that lets us discover something within it that was always there, but that we didn't notice. Or that we overlooked, or that we found before and are finding again."[38]

Fun could also relate to a person's sense of empowerment as they play, in that they are actually being called upon to pose solutions to problems (even if they cannot fully solve them).[39] Rusch talks about "deep games" or games that may be profound, where "there is more than what meets the eye and you need to dig for that meaning to own it and unpack it for yourself. And that's what makes it meaningful."[40] The fun is the search for meaning, even if that meaning is never fully found. The fun of games—and civics and ethics—then, may also be in our ability to connect with ourselves and to express our humanity, and to connect with others' humanity.[41]

Games May Enhance Motivation and Curiosity

We want our students to be engaged, curious, and motivated to learn. But the reality is that students are constantly being pulled in many different directions, and this will affect their ability to willingly participate in any learning experience. They may be managing a number of needs, like hunger and having to use the bathroom, family or work obligations, or friendship or health needs. Amid all of these competing needs, we also want to help our students to cultivate the curiosity they need to fully engage in meaningful learning.

Motivation and curiosity go hand-in-hand. Motivation refers to what someone wants to do and why they want to do it, whereas curiosity is a desire to seek knowledge and answer questions about the world. Ryan and Deci's self-determination theory maps out two different motivation types: intrinsic (driven by one's inner desires, wants, and needs, such as one's own innate interest), and extrinsic (driven by external rewards such as grades, badges, or trophies). Huck et al. describe epistemic curiosity, which is the "desire for knowledge that motivates individuals to learn new ideas, eliminate information gaps, and solve intellectual problems." This is different from perceptual curiosity, which is about a "drive to experience and feel."[42]

Games are possibly motivating and curiosity-driving experiences, which can help compel players to engage in learning new knowledge, skills, and concepts, as well as to participate and feel. Games can also help motivate players to complete difficult problems, take on tedious tasks, reach goals, find new solutions, test hypotheses, and manage systems—and to keep going whenever they meet resistance.[43] Games can help to motivate curiosity and interest in specific civics and ethics topics and themes and compel players to persist in learning new knowledge. Importantly, players can also be motivated by choosing and playing games that match their interests and play styles.[44] By building on student interests, we can better facilitate the types of meaningful connections necessary for learning and knowledge acquisition. Ultimately, however, the goal is not to use a game to artificially compel a student to engage in civics and ethics, but to spark curiosity and interest in it so that they engage in it for its own sake. We want a game to help students develop a genuine love for civics and ethics, rather than a love for the points, rewards, or badges they can earn through a game.

Many examples of games are already being used to motivate understanding of civics and ethics content. For instance, students can play games to grapple directly with common moral dilemmas, such as the trolley problem or the footbridge dilemma. Or, they could, through a game, choose outcomes in a prisoner's dilemma setup. The stakes of these moral dilemmas grow higher because the student is enacting their choices and seeing the consequences of it through the game. Actively participating in the dilemma helps the student better understand the tensions and complexities of responding to it.[45] As another example, Martin, Draper, and Lamey describe using their nondigital game *Justice* in a philosophy classroom. In the game, players role-play with goals and policy needs inspired by philosophers like John Rawls, Martha Nussbaum, and Amartya Sen. To play the game, players need to become familiar with their texts and their philosophical approaches.[46]

Limitations of Using Games for Building Knowledge

Games May Oversimplify Complex Knowledge

One of the limitations of finding and making games for specific civics and ethics processes and frameworks is that they are often needed to be just that—very specific. Given the complexity of high school and college-level goals, content, and themes, games need to rise up to that complexity. Yet, games often represent knowledge, terms, and processes in simple ways to make the game more playable and engaging. This may go too far, and oversimplify the knowledge. If a purpose of games is to reveal the messiness and complexity of knowledge, then simplifying that knowledge through a game may backfire.

This also speaks to practical concerns. The games that will get made, funded, and resourced are the ones that will reach the most people. The more specific, complex ones may have a more limited audience, even if they are effective. Trombley explains that "It's hard for a design team to justify the cost of making a game when it only addresses some small set of standards" or content needs.[47] As a result, a game may not be the right learning experience for meeting goals or standards. Humphries explains that the iCivics team once received a fantastic pitch for a very specific game about "the federal budgeting process and the role of congressional accountability" in budgeting. They declined to go ahead with making the game, however. Though this type of game may have provided a public service in that it would have shared the systemic issues around debt and congressional decision-making, it did not meet a clear-cut, prioritized pedagogical need, and was not flexible enough in how it could be used by educators.[48]

Games May Be Too Complex

On the other hand, games may also be overly complex and use up enormous amounts of resources to create and play them—so much so that there may be other, more effective ways to teach a particular topic. Library director Harris explains that some of the games they play in high school classrooms are extremely lengthy, complicated, and require expert knowledge. For instance, with the role-playing game *A Distant Plain*, players need to create campaigns against insurgencies and terror in Afghanistan. Harris explains that it takes hours to play this game, so educators need "to find ways to break it up and use it across multiple periods for multiple days."[49] It's an asynchronous game with four different sides, and different victory conditions and gameplay actions. This type of game may not only be daunting to most educators and students, but also may not fit practically in a class period, and may not be the best use of the time needed to learn about current-day issues in Afghanistan, though the game itself may be effective. Therefore, a question we should ask is whether a game is worthwhile if it helps to show the intricacies of an issue, but the game itself is overwrought, unrelatable, or tedious.

Knowledge Is Always Evolving

Furthermore, real-world ethics and civics issues are always changing, and need to be current, timely, and relatable. Games may not be able to keep up with these changes. While some games can be made and played in an expedited fashion (or can be updated regularly), it often takes many years of designing, developing, and testing games to ensure it meets standards, content needs, and knowledge goals. And, the games that are able to relay just-in-time perspectives and content around current issues may not be very fun games. They may be more raw, simplistic, or derivative, and they may not be designed in a way to be readily effective in a classroom or other type of learning environment.

Newsgames are a type of game that grapples journalistically with current events, by documenting them, satirizing them, or illustrating problems using infographic-type techniques.[50] These games can relay a viewpoint on a current event, and they do not necessarily need to be extensive, polished, or complex. An example of a newsgame is *September 12*, by Gonzalo Frasca and Newsgaming, where players need to decide whether to bomb terrorists in a village.[51] If they do, they hit some civilians as well, who then respawn in the game as terrorists. The game was very timely in 2001, as it shared the dangers of responding with violence following the 9/11 terrorist attack in the United States. Many years later it may be less viscerally timely as a warning for the future, though still useful for providing historical context to 9/11 and its aftermath. But, it also ran on Flash (an outdated browser-based interactive platform), rendering the game in its original format unplayable. Other newsgames, such as Kirby's *September 7, 2020* or Salanthé's and Case's "What Happens Next?," were made in response to the COVID-19 pandemic. These games provided of-the-moment reactions to present events and predictions for the future, which may not have the same effect in the years following the pandemic.[52]

Who Decides Which Knowledge Matters?

Which knowledge should we learn and who is allowed to create it? Is this knowledge problematic? The knowledge that is taught in K-12 civics and ethics classes is often related to dominant ideologies, such as so-called good citizenship or good character. Yet who decides what it means to be a good citizen? Davisson and Gehm argue that civics education in the United States is often about participating in ritualized narratives around the presidential election process or the American Dream, rather than reflecting on or problematizing our institutions and stories.[53] They argue that games such as *Win the White House* uphold a jingoistic story of America, and model good citizenship by facilitating participation in the election ritual. They contend that such games help to establish the dominance of and comfort in that type of knowledge or way of thinking through repetition or ritual,[54] instead of liberating us to critique this form of citizenship. Likewise, Freire talks about empowering oppressed communities to "expose and dismantle unjust power hierarchies and ideologies and imagine alternative possibilities," and to instead revisit and uphold the knowledge created by Black, Brown, Indigenous, youth, and other marginalized communities.[55]

How do we value the knowledge our students bring, and how do we overturn the norms of our knowledge-making? In my book *Knowledge Games*, I questioned the production of knowledge. Games, I argued, help us to problematize problem-solving and "lift the hood" of the machinery underlying knowledge creation. Games may help us to see the ethical issues of what it means to make, use, uphold, spread, and trust knowledge. Thus, we should also use games to liberate us—to overturn oppressive norms and revise problematic knowledge systems, rather than to further establish them.

The Fun of Games Is Also Problematic

Finally, the framing of games as "fun" is itself a limitation. There are a number of different factors to share in regard to this. First, referring to a game as fun may mislabel or even stigmatize it as not being educationally effective, and teachers, parents, librarians, and district administrators may mistakenly see games as outside of everyday instruction rather than as experiences and communities that can be used as directly part of the curriculum.[56] Even students may have misperceptions about games. Farber explains that "I found the students were often the barrier because the students were accustomed to terrible educational games."[57]

Second, the "fun" label may even affect how much students learn from a game. A study placed students into "high fun" and "low fun" groups. When their task was deemed as more important, their performance was lower in the "high fun" group, suggesting that either students expect learning to not be fun or that they expect more engagement from something that is labeled as such.[58]

Third, Stenros argues that play is not always fun, and Harviainen and Hassan point out that the goal of a game may not even be to have fun—but to engage in something more serious and meaningful. When we think of concepts like *flourishing*, *Utu*, and *eudaimonia* (humans living their best lives), do we refer to "fun" or something more like fulfillment?[59] Is fun even the purpose of play?

When designing and using games, it is also unclear whether educational effectiveness or fun should be prioritized more, and the extent to which games need to be fun and entertaining to be beneficial. Does a fun, motivating, and engaging game experience take players away from the actual learning, or does it help facilitate the learning? Are students who are more engaged in a game also more able to transfer the learning from that game world to a nongame environment?[60] Engagement and fun in a game are not static throughout an experience, but ebb and "flicker" throughout.[61] Students are also motivated by different types of interests, different types of gameplay, and different types of goals.[62] Games are not automatically motivating or fun for all students in a learning environment and may be differentially motivating for different players.[63]

In the next section, I provide strategies for using games to enhance engagement with real-world knowledge and content.

Strategies for Using Games to Build Knowledge

Use Real-World Content and Contexts, Meaningfully

Teachers should use games in ways that can help players meaningfully interact with real-world contexts and content. For example, they should ask students what motivates them or find out what types of games they already play, and match games and game goals to student interests and play styles. Teachers can help students connect with the ethics and civics practices they are already engaging with through games. For instance, students may be participating in public discourse in online game chats, or moderating social media communities. Teachers could also adapt games to help students to continue engaging in ways they already do in their everyday lives. Finally, teachers should consider how to enable students to critique games and to think about how they may be problematic representations of reality. How can we use games to enable reflection on our own civic systems and institutions, rather than just to further establish and normalize entrenched social structures?

Example in Action: *Win the White House*
It's the big US presidential election and in the iCivics game *Win the White House*, you get to be the candidate. You can decide on your political platform, and which issues matter to you. Do you stand for gun control, immigration restrictions, or LGBTQIA+ rights? Will you win the electoral college by starting in Texas, Pennsylvania, or Ohio? How will you spend your campaign money, which advertising will you buy, which states you will visit, and what types of points you will make during a speech?

By acting in the role of the presidential candidate, players may feel more personally connected to a process that often feels distant from many people, old and young. The game also may enhance the curiosity needed to deal with the complexity of social issues, and to understand that there is no one right answer and no clear-cut path to the best solution. Teacher Penney explains that one of the challenges that students have is that they will make what they think is a great decision, but then it won't have the consequences that they expect. For instance, when Penney used *Win the White House* in her middle school social studies class, she said that the students would make what they thought was an effective choice, but they then discovered through the game that they might not necessarily win over the voters or enhance their campaign. Penney said that the students started to make connections among their actions in this game and historical moments, where past public figures did what seemed like a good action at the time but it did not have good results—such as when John Adams's Alien and Sedition Act backfired with the public, or "when Andrew Jackson did something and the public got angry, and when he didn't do anything, they were still angry."[64] Historic moments and current issues are more meaningful because the students are making these choices themselves and seeing their consequences in the game.

Activities around the game also matter. Students could have mini-debates in class about the issues they chose, and can play the game individually or as a full class. Teachers can also use the game to invite students to critique American electoral institutions such as the Electoral College, or to deliberate policies like campaign finance reform. Teachers may also use this game to compare the US process to voting processes around the world, and to explore the different ways that the public can participate in the political process. Finally, teachers may use this game to critique the use of games in representing real-world knowledge. Researchers have pointed out that civics games may help us to ratify current processes rather than also encourage us to question and redesign them. Teachers may want to ask students whether this is a valid critique of a game like *Win the White House*.[65]

Use Active Learning of Real-World Content

Teachers can use games to spur students to actively use, interact with, and playfully interrogate relevant real-world ethics and civics concepts. By doing things with concepts, such as solving problems or sharing perspectives on issues, players can construct and build knowledge.[66] For instance, in Abbott's high school civics course, she uses the iCivics game *Do I Have a Right* to introduce concepts such as the US government's three branches and the Bill of Rights.[67] Likewise, Wrona, who teaches social studies at an alternative middle school in Maryland, uses *Do I Have a Right* to help explicate the rights that Americans have and the constitutional amendments. He begins the class by asking students to list all the rights that they remember are in the US Constitution. The students often list the freedom of speech and the right to bear arms, but they are less knowledgeable about the other rights that Americans have. By playing *Do I Have a Right*, the students end up learning the specific rights that American citizens have because they need to apply them to real-world scenarios through the game.[68]

Example in Action: *PolitiCraft*

In the game *PolitiCraft: An Action Civics Card Game*, players do "action civics" through the play of the game. Players actively construct civic knowledge by using real-world civic processes to meet game goals (see Figure 4.2).[69]

Here is how it is played. Each deck has different types of cards; the action cards include categories such as media and relationships, policy and practices, or campaigns and elections.[70] For example, a campaigns and elections card may be about hosting a town hall meeting or exploring options for running for a public office. Players can choose which civic activities they want to participate in and which issues to focus on (such as personal or global issues). Each card is associated with different point values, and "the goal of the game is to collect as many social impact points while working toward a solution to an issue, all while telling an interesting narrative."[71] Some cards can only be played if certain other cards have been already played. For instance, you may have to play two media and relationships cards together, like building a website or buying a billboard, before you can play them. There is an ethical component to the game as well: "integrity cards" are given to all players in the beginning of the game and players may gain or lose them depending on what they do in the game. If you help

Figure 4.2 An image of the card game *PolitiCraft: An Action Civics Card Game*. Copyright © 2014–2020 PolitiCraft, Inc. All Rights Reserved. *PolitiCraft* is a Registered Trademark of PolitiCraft, Inc.

out another player by giving them a helpful card, you would gain an integrity card. Players with the most integrity cards at the end of the game get an additional large bonus, on top of the points that each integrity card gains.

At the beginning of *Politicraft*, players decide which civics issue they want to pursue throughout the game, and all the cards they play help them to construct a narrative about how they are impacting that issue. The designers explain that "using the cards, the player develops potential solutions, which are conveyed to the other players by creating a narrative that links the various actions, [such as] I am working to get more parks in my city, so I may organize a fundraiser to fund a campaign to build a new park [based on the 'organize a fundraiser' policy and practices card]. Or, I may work with my friend on city council to pass a local ordinance to set aside land for my new park [based on the 'city council friend' media and relationships card and the 'impact local legislation' policy and practices card]."[72] Once a player collects and plays a sequence of relevant cards, and amasses enough points, they become a "public figure," which means they impact other players' activities. At the end of the game, the winning player is the one with the most impact points, coupled with integrity points.

Teachers can use the cards in a number of ways. Before playing the game, the *PolitiCraft* team recommends placing students in small groups, and having them look through the cards together. Students could find cards that serve as examples of actions made by different types of citizens, as defined in Kahne and Westheimer's "What Kind of Citizen?" Or they could pick out the cards that relate to activities they have participated in, or the ones they would like to perform in their communities. As another activity, students could first choose a social issue to research, brainstorm their "root causes," and generate possible solutions. Then, after playing the game, students could revisit their solutions, and expand upon them.[73]

Use Fantastical Contexts, Too

Games do not necessarily need to cover completely realistic content to relay relevant issues and knowledge. For instance, games such as *Do I Have a Right* and *Win the White House* may not entirely realistically simulate a presidential election or the historic events of the past, but they still can help students gain an understanding of civics content, as well as a greater appreciation for the context of the topic. In *Mission US*, for example, the player plays as a main character who is fictional, but is situated in a historic moment that is based on real-world events, themes, and peoples.[74]

Games can even be fantastical in themes and topics, and still help students to practice real-world skills or grasp new concepts. Ethical issues in games also do not need to be realistic for them to be evocative. In the *Mass Effect* game series, there is a fictional war between two constituencies: the Geth (artificially intelligent machines) and the Reapers (synthetic-organic machine race). The player plays as Commander Shephard and finds out that some Geth rebels created a virus that they want to upload so that other Geth will immediately begin following the Reapers instead. Shephard has a choice of how to stop these rebels: she can (1) destroy the rebels or (2) rewrite the rebels so they instead are loyal again to the Geth. This leads to more questions, Granshaw says, such as: Is it okay to force a belief on a machine? "Will rewriting them strengthen the entire Geth group, making them a bigger threat? Is killing them the safer route?"[75] There is no clear-cut "right" answer, though. While we may never need to decide whether to help the Geth or the Reapers in our everyday lives, the game helps players meaningfully explore real-world ethical questions related to artificial intelligence, how we treat machines, how we handle rebellions, and the responsibility of humanity to our world.

Example in Action: *Fable III*

In the role-playing digital game *Fable III*, players are playing the role of a citizen of Albion (and later, as a king or queen of Albion) in a steampunk fantasy world, which is filled with magical monsters of all kinds, such as lupine Balverines. Players go on missions and can use magic spells and special weapons, such as the Wolfsbane.[76] As a citizen or leader of Albion, players also need to make ethical and civic-related decisions such as whether to drain a lake in the town, raise the tax on the citizens, or build an orphanage. These decisions also impact whether the player can raise money for an army to protect the villagers from a "coming darkness." To make these decisions, the player needs to engage in virtual town halls, where they meet with advisors (NPCs or nonplayer characters) who give them different perspectives on the issues. After a decision is made, the fictional town changes and players experience the consequences of that decision such as in how the virtual townspeople (also NPCs) speak to the player's avatar. My research on *Fable III* found that when making these decisions players were performing ethical thinking skills, including the weighing of pros and cons, identifying of emotions, and the considering of alternate perspectives. I compared these skills with paper versions of the same scenarios and found that players were able to think more systemically about how their decisions may affect the game world, and that they were thinking of possible consequences beyond even what the game was able to simulate. Players may even connect real, personally relevant scenarios to the fantastic content. For instance, one of the players of *Fable III* explained that he was going through the process of an in-person adoption of a child, so building an orphanage and then adopting a child in the game was particularly meaningful to him.[77]

Fable III is not appropriate for younger audiences. But this research suggests that teachers can use games with fictional and fantastical content to support the practice of relevant civics and ethics skills and thought processes.[78] Thus, while using realistic cases or issues can help students practice and implement skills, fantastical and unrealistic contexts that include decisions and meaningful scenarios may help students to practice skills, too.[79]

5

How Do We Take Real-World Action?

When civics and ethics are relatable and meaningful, students feel like their voices matter. They may not just gain new knowledge, but they may also be motivated to take action in their communities and even in the broader global conversation. Consider the teens from Parkland, Florida, who survived a school shooting that killed 17 students at Marjory Stoneman Douglas High School. Some of the Parkland teens began using the knowledge they learned from a middle school civics course and an advanced placement (AP) government class to take real-world action—such as organizing student walk outs to protest gun violence, which resulted in over one million students in the United States walking out of their schools in 2018.[1]

Or, take the six teen women activists from the Southern part of the United States, calling themselves Teens 4 Equality. They used Twitter, FaceTime, TikTok, and Instagram to discuss police brutality, call for the removal of confederate statues, and organize a 10,000-person protest in Nashville, Tennessee to support Black Lives Matter in 2020. And they also have already made real-world change, such as the creation of new policies around the use of body cameras by the police in Nashville, and other reformations.[2]

Or take the game *EteRNA*, which was developed by scientists at Stanford and Carnegie Mellon and enables players from all over the world to help design new RNA molecules through the game.[3] In the spring of 2020, *EteRNA* started the OpenVaccine campaign, which included a series of game challenges to support the development of a safe mRNA vaccine, new antivirals, and better diagnostics related to the COVID-19 pandemic.[4] Although the *EteRNA* labs were shut down due to the global pandemic, the public could still take real-world action through the virtual game and help to create solutions to a crisis.[5]

This chapter describes how we can use games to inspire and take real-world action. It may initially seem surprising that games may support real-world change, particularly because they are often seen as escapes from it.[6] Yet I will show how games may be especially valuable for further strengthening connections between students and real-world civics and ethics processes and practices.

Why Engage in Real-World Action?

Ethics and Civics Require Action

As described in chapter 4, knowledge, skills, and concepts may become more relatable and memorable when connected to real-world activities, institutions, policies,

We the Gamers. Karen Schrier, Oxford University Press. © Oxford University Press 2021.
DOI: 10.1093/oso/9780190926106.003.0005

processes, applications, scenarios, and contexts.[7] Shaffer talks about "epistemic knowledge" or knowledge that relates to the real-world tools, practices, and approaches of a particular discipline, where people learn the language, jargon, terms, materials, and processes by directly performing and enacting within that field.[8] For instance, we may learn more about governance and community management by acting as a social media moderator through a game and using the typical tools, terms, and tactics that a real moderator might use (as players do in the game *NewsFeed Defenders*).

Engaging in real-world action may even be particularly beneficial to learning ethics and civics. Students need to understand that civics is not just about gaining knowledge, content, and skills, but about working with others to solve problems, address social issues, speak out, protest, influence, organize, and vote. Students need to be able to practice ethics in situ and participate in communities where they can negotiate values and norms. The C3 framework describes taking action as one of the four integral components of the framework, explaining that teachers need to teach students to act because citizens act: "They vote, serve on juries, follow the news and current events, and participate in voluntary groups and efforts."[9] As Dewey explains, the school is not just the place to learn so that a person can eventually do, act, and participate; it is also itself the place to do, act, and participate.[10] When we connect students to real-world issues, contexts, tools, problems, and topics it helps them not just to learn content, but to strengthen their roles as members of society. This is particularly important given the low engagement of people in public life, as described in chapter 2.[11]

Many researchers call for an active and engaged approach to civics and ethics. Levine and Kawashima-Ginsberg include action civics as one of the 10 proven practices in civics education, which involves "empowering young people to engage in community development and improvement."[12] Blevins, LeCompte, and Ellis explain that action civics happens "when students do civics and behave as citizens by engaging in a cycle of research, action, and reflection about problems they personally care about while learning about deeper principles of effective civic and … political action."[13] Likewise, Westheimer and Kahne created a framework for citizenship in action, which recommends that we encourage students to become directly involved in "civic affairs at the local, state, and national levels,"[14] such as by participating on campaigns, going to town halls, writing letters, starting petitions, joining protests, and making media related to civic issues.

Teachers Already Encourage Real-World Action

Teachers are already encouraging this as well. Abbott, a teacher at a rural high school in North Carolina, has her civics class look at the local, state, and national level legislative branches. Her goal is to have students learn how to access information, whether it is about their town council members or their state senator. Abbott explains that sometimes the students "don't realize that the mayor of the town or their town council member lives on their street and that they can call them. We also look at the media portrayal of them and look up the voting records. And students may be surprised that the media representation and the voting record of this representative did not match."[15]

Service learning is also one of the proven practices of civics education, too. It relates to giving students the opportunity to act in their community to help them create meaningful connections between knowledge and action.[16] When students participate in scaffolded civic engagement projects it can help them to practice communication, critical thinking, citizenship, and other relevant skills. Moreover, Arthur et al. explain that "when young people engage in meaningful acts of service, there is a 'double benefit': a contribution to the common good of society and the building of one's own character." Service itself is a virtue, which requires practice. Arthur et al. found that those participants who had a "habit of service" or started practicing service learning at a younger age, and had more opportunities for practice, better understood its importance and in turn more frequently participated in service to others. Their communities benefitted more as well.[17]

Everett teaches at a private K-12 school in Florida. In her high school advanced seminar (Post-AP) course, she has students do a civic engagement project of their choice. Students have done things like clean up a beach, attend a political rally, or contact grocery stores to get them to reduce the use of plastic bags. But after the Parkland shooting, which happened only 12 miles from their school, the students decided to change their projects. Instead, they did activities like proposing changes to the wording of the second amendment, and "contacting senators and representatives about federal and state law."[18] The students were extremely engaged in the project because they wanted to make a real-world impact, particularly considering the events that had transpired at a neighboring school.

Thus, it is not just about learning and understanding civics and ethics knowledge, but also about applying it to real-world situations and embodying and performing civics and ethics in one's own local communities and global environments. This helps to develop students' deeper understanding of civics and ethics, while also transforming real-world society and encouraging longer-term and more meaningful civic participation across the lifespan.[19]

How Do Games Engage Students in Real-World Action?

Games Can Enable Practice of Real-World Skills

How can we continue to engage students, actively and meaningfully, in ethics and civics? How might games support civics and ethics in action, and inspire the real-world applications of knowledge, skills, and practices (see also Table 5.1)?

Table 5.1 Real-world and game connections

Possible Connections to Real-World Skills and Knowledge	Brief Summary
Games can enable the practice of real skills.	Game players can practice ethics and civics-related skills through a game, such as communication, decision-making, problem-solving, and identifying emotions.
Games can enable facility with simulations and models of real-world systems.	Games can help players have access to and manipulate models and simulations of real-world processes.
Games can address relevant topics, themes, and issues.	Games can help make topics more relevant and timely, such as by tying them to issues that are of local or global concern.
Games can incorporate real-world tools, machinery, instruments, data, and evidence.	Games can enable the use of real-world, authentic tools, which can help players to participate in how experts measure, evaluate, capture, and organize our world.
Games can use real-world people, stories, perspectives, testimonials, and points of view.	Games may enable access to other real people or players that can help support learning for the player, or connect them further to the issues, views, problems, tools, and communities that relate to the topic.
Games may use real time or real money and other resources to manage.	The use of time and other limited resources, such as money, adds further authenticity and relevancy to the content of a game, as well as urgency.
Games can provide real-world goals, feedback, hints, clues, and messaging.	Games can provide nudges, messaging, and other types of feedback, and help players to progress appropriately to their goals.
Games can use real locations, physical or virtual, and incorporate them into gameplay.	Games can incorporate real-world locations and sites, which will help support learning in a relevant context, and situate learning.
Games can connect players to real communities.	Games can connect players more closely with real-world communities, and can spur action, activities, and activism beyond the game.
Game players can engage in real-world problem-solving and knowledge-making.	Games can help bring players together to solve real-world civic and ethics problems, and contribute new knowledge and understandings of humanity (see more in chapter 11).

This table shares 10 different ways that a player may connect to the real world through and around games. There may be other ways as well. (Note also that the game is part of the real world and are real-world communities and public spheres themselves.) See more about this in B. Stokes, *Locally Played* (Cambridge, MA: MIT Press, 2020) and K. Schrier, *Knowledge Games: How Playing Games Can Solve Problems, Create Insight, and Make Change* (Baltimore: Johns Hopkins University Press, 2016).

First, games can provide opportunities to develop and practice real-world skills that relate to ethical decision-making and civic engagement, such as reasoning, reflecting, communicating, building relationships, and writing. There are many ways games can motivate practice of these skills. Games can provide goals and obstacles such that players need to use these skills to overcome the challenges or solve specific problems. Games can also provide a rich storyworld where players need to use these skills while exploring and shaping that world.[20] For instance, in *Gone Home*, players need to explore a virtual home with objects and artifacts that a player can pick up and inspect, such as videotapes, notes, or locker doors. The player begins to actively reveal the story by meaningfully exploring this environment, interacting with narrative scraps, and piecing together clues about a family's past. Through interacting with the storyworld of *Gone Home*, players need to practice interpretation and reflection.[21] (See more about story in chapters 8 and 12).

Games Can Use Real-World Tools, Data, and Systems

Beyond just practicing skills, games can also provide opportunities for players to use real-world tools and enable students to actually perform how people might measure, evaluate, capture, and organize our world. Games can help players have access to and manipulate data, models, resources, and simulations of real-world processes, such as by including rulers or maps, or through visualizations, such as charts on population growth or gross national product.[22] Through a game, players may be able to adjust different factors (such as food availability, parental leave policies, or childcare support) and see how that may dynamically affect something like population growth.[23] Moreover, a game could tie these tools and models to a compelling story or fictional purpose. Suddenly, a map of the world becomes more significant because it has clues on it for where to find Carmen Sandiego, or an economic model becomes more interesting because a player wants to optimize the growth of their city as in the *SimCity* series.

A game can also embed the player in real-world social and economic systems. For example, in *Fiscal Ship*, players need to figure out how they would solve and balance a real-world budget by making priorities from among many options. Likewise, in *Budget Hero*, made by the Wilson Center, players need to balance the budget by choosing from among dozens of policy options.[24]

Finally, having access to realistic tools, terms, and problems in a game may also transfer to enhanced problem-solving outside of the game.[25] It helps players to develop the epistemic knowledge (including the right words to use) to be able to participate in conversations with other experts. Games can scaffold the practices and jargon of a particular field by situating the player in its sociocultural context, helping to make these practices more relatable and less mysterious.[26]

Games Can Use Real-World Locations

In addition to providing authentic tools, data, and systems, games can also incorporate real-world locations, which will help support and situate learning. *Where* someone learns information can help in establishing profound connections with the material, and can even help to foster further practice of a particular skill.[27] For example, a game may help players more readily to visit and learn about real-world locations, such as in the case of *Pokémon Go*. In the augmented reality game *Reliving the Revolution*, players used a mobile device to interact with the real-world location of Lexington (Massachusetts) and explore the Lexington Common, Buckman Tavern, and the bell tower, all of which are related to the actual Battle of Lexington in 1775 and are still present in the town today. By playing the game in the actual location, players can get a better sense of the scale, sights, smells, and physical landscape of the battle, even if the roads, cars, and traffic that trisect the common are anachronistic. This also may add resonance and authenticity to the historical testimonials that are part of the game, while making them easier to recall and relate to.[28]

Stokes describes how the game *Macon Money* used physical objects (pieces of game money bonds) that could be used to take action in the game and in the real-world location of Macon, Georgia. Community members each received half of the bond and they needed to find people with "the other half" by coming together in the real-world physical spaces of Macon.[29] Likewise, *Jewish Time Jump*, designed by Owen Gottlieb and Jennifer Ash, is a mobile augmented reality game to teach immigrant, Jewish, and women's history, and uses real, relevant physical locations in New York City (see Figure 5.1). The players use their phone as a time machine to go back to 1909 and act as a journalist to interview union leaders and manufacturers around labor disputes. The game and its character's stories touch upon real historic events, which led up to the Triangle Factory Shirtwaist fire in 1911 in which 147 young, mostly Jewish and Italian women died. The game takes place around the real-world Washington Square Park in the Greenwich Village area, where players learn about the factory fire, and are "literally standing next to that building" where the fire took place.[30]

Games Can Connect Real People

Games may also enable access to real people or players that can help support greater learning for the player, including community members, experts, and activists.[31] For instance, a game could help players learn stories of the Holocaust directly from a real person telling the story (such as through the VR game *Journey through the Camps*), or a game could help players interact with their local government officials and fellow constituents to learn about their needs and perspectives, such as with the board game *Bay Area Regional Planner*. A game could also encourage players in different classes, communities, or even countries, to help connect and collaborate on problems, and to better understand each other's cultural needs and interests. In *Mind Field*, players

Figure 5.1 An image of the mobile, location-based game *Jewish Time Jump*. Artist: Liza Singer. Image copyright of Owen Gottlieb, 2013.

hear authentic stories about dealing with bias directly from people who experienced bias.[32]

Games can also connect players more closely with their own communities and local places in a number of ways. First, players playing together may begin to connect and develop trust and intimacy with each other by playing together.[33] Games can also help players explore parts of their local community, such as by motivating players to do real-world actions through or outside of the game. These games encourage students to make face-to-face and virtual connections, as well as to take action and organize.[34] For instance, through *Community PlanIt*, players connect with local officials to help solve communal problems.[35] The card game *Mahalo* (which no longer exists) aimed to encourage participants to practice real-world activities, such as showing compassion to a neighbor or helping out in a community garden. Players would earn points for each good deed they did. A similar game to this is *The Good Cards*, which is like "pay it forward" in a card-digital hybrid game format. People get a paper card, scan it, and do a good deed and tell a story about, and then pass the card along for others to do their own good deed.[36] Likewise, in the game *Kind Words*, players can exchange kind letters with real people (strangers) around the world (see more in chapter 7).[37]

Creation Is a Type of Real-World Participation

Making games, collaborating on mods (game modifications), or codesigning experiences around games are also all forms of real-world civic participation, and help to connect youth further with their communities whether online, offline, or locally. Mirra and Garcia argue that youth already participate in online, digital, and gaming spaces through the creation, remixing, and redistribution of games, fan fiction around games, or the modifications of game rules and communities, and that these engagements are types of public dialogue and expressions of civic and ethical understandings of our world (see more in chapter 12).[38]

Games Can Share Real-World Issues

Games can also help make real-world issues, stories, and needs more accessible. They may help players to interact with real information, case studies, current issues, and historic objects and events. Games may spur understandings of everyday issues such as those affecting one's local community (e.g., the need for improved playgrounds, better bus schedules, or more access to affordable housing).[39] For instance, in iCivics' *Argument Wars*, players need to argue real-world cases, such as *Brown v. Board of Education*.[40] In *EteRNA*, players are submitting real-world mRNA solutions to help solve actual societal problems. Likewise, in FableVision's *Civics! An American Musical*, players get to view and (digitally) use real letters, photographs, and other artifacts that exist in the Library of Congress archive. In the Smithsonian game *Ripped Apart*, players are able to look through a photographic history collection as part of the game, such as analyzing cartes de visite.[41]

Limitations of Using Games for Real-World Action

Inequitable Access and Participation

Decision-making needs to be accessible to everyone in the community, and equitably shared among different types of people. As described in chapter 2, civic participation in the United States is inequitable, where Black, Brown, Indigenous, and people of color, and youth may be systemically less able to access civics and make social change, as well as to receive the necessary education and practice to fully participate.[42] Likewise, youth overall may have limited opportunity to participate directly in local, state, national, and global matters, particularly if they are from marginalized backgrounds, such as lower socioeconomic groups or politically underrepresented populations.[43] But as Mirra and Garcia point out, we also may be discounting how and where marginalized communities are already participating in public, because we are valuing certain types of good citizenship over others. Games further these inequities.[44]

Ethical Issues with Real-World Participation

Games with real-world participation may be tied to real-world outcomes. This could be highly beneficial to learning, as it makes the knowledge more relatable and relevant.

But, let's imagine, for instance, a future game where players are able to vote for officials, contribute suggestions for a new policy, decide how a school or community should spend money, or share views on how to better teach and model anti-racism. How are these contributions, such as personal data or perspectives, being used by the government, scientists, or game designers? One crowdsourcing website, "COVID near you,"[45] invites participants to share how they are feeling and their current health status each day. The website then provides a real-time, online map that shows all of the "hot spots" of COVID-19 activity in the United States. Certainly, there are benefits to being able to rapidly collect and widely share this type of data (in the aggregate), as we can then create localized policies or deploy public health and mitigation measures more effectively. But how is this information used and communicated? Will there be real-world consequences for participants? For instance, we can conceive of a government using the feedback from its citizens to help make changes that benefit the needs of the public (such as ensuring safer water or reducing viral outbreaks). On the other hand, we could also see how information gathered can be used to surveil citizens, apply social benefits to those who comply with governmental rules, or to control the public further.[46] Governments have toyed with the idea of using mobile device data to help to trace the contacts and locations of people who are diagnosed with a virus to help predict and mitigate a new outbreak in progress. China has used gamification-type practices (such as a social credit system) to reduce immorality and spur prosocial behaviors, such as helping others in public. But these types of practices can have dire social consequences, such as restricting one's access to everything from jobs to transportation to loans.[47]

While the intention—encouraging good behavior or maintaining public health—may seem entirely beneficial, there are some underlying problems.[48] How fair and equitable is the system? How is privacy retained?[49] What happens if a person does something wrong, such as breaking a quarantine during a pandemic lockdown? Should people trust a game or application that invites personal data of any kind? As more civic and ethics real-world games are created and used, we should continue to find ways to ensure that games and gaming communities are ethically created and maintained.

What are the best practices for using games to spur real-world interactions? In the next section I will walk through strategies on how to use games to connect players to real world issues, problems, communities, and solutions.

Strategies for Using Games for Real-World Action

Enable Practice with Realistic Tools, Locations, and Models

Teachers should find and use games that meaningfully employ realistic tools, models, locations, and instruments that are relevant to the ethics and civics concepts and processes. Games can incorporate realistic (but fictionalized) representations of tools, instruments, and locations in the game. Games can also approximate reality by using real or realistic data, models, and simulations.[50] For instance, a virtual camera enables players to take photos inside the game *Revolution 1979: Black Friday*. The measurement tools in Killer Snail's virtual reality experiences, *BioDive* and *Scuba Adventure VR*, can be used to conduct a realistic (though fictionalized) evaluation of the ecosystems of marine snails, which are recreated in the game's world.[51]

Example in Action: *Reliving the Revolution*

In *Reliving the Revolution (RTR)*, a mobile game, players re-enter an integral moment in American history, the Battle of Lexington, which was part of the American Revolution. The game takes place in real-world Lexington, Massachusetts, and uses a GPS-enabled mobile device. Depending on where the player is standing in the real-life town of Lexington, digital representations of historic people, places, and objects appear on the player's mobile device. While playing the game, players are able to explore the still-present physical monuments, houses, buildings (such as Buckman Tavern), and Lexington Green where the battle took place.

A goal of the game is to figure out who fired the first shot at the Battle of Lexington. This is a history mystery. No one knows definitively who fired the first shot—though there are multiple interpretations—so the game invites players to analyze testimonials and other evidence, build a case and decide what happened, and then reflect on the information gathered and interpretations made by fellow players.[52] To further the concept that people may have different perspectives on what may have happened, players take on one of four roles, such as Prince Estabrook, a Black freed former slave who served in the Minuteman army, or Ann Hulton, a female Loyalist.[53] I tested the game with middle school students, who, after gathering the evidence for about an hour, spent 30–45 minutes deliberating their findings with their fellow players.

During the game, the students practiced skills relevant to civic and ethical engagement, such as reasoning, argumentation, and perspective-taking skills. They started to see how the past is open to interpretation and may be written up differently, depending on the perspective, person, or country making that history. Players also began to critically question what we take for granted as knowledge, in that historical accounts are not the truth, but a version of the past. One player noted that "in America, we have American textbooks and they are written by Americans, so of course you always get that portrayal of the British as being the bad guys and I'm sure the British kids when they learn about this, it's completely different."[54]

RTR also helped show that the battle was about people—their stories, their fears, their triumphs, and their losses—and this contributed to the authentic emotional connection players felt in the game. A soldier, John Harrington, was shot during the Battle of Lexington and started to step toward his home, where his wife was at the door, watching him crawl back. This story played out during the game and is reflected on a physical plaque at the Harrington house on the Lexington Common. As one player explained, "I found out that John Harrington had been shot in the game… [first] you met someone on the street who told you that [he was dead] and then you ran into his wife who was like 'Oh my God.' And then you passed his [actual] house and you looked at the house and it has the actual plaque saying that this is where John Harrington died in his wife's arms … And then you saw John Harrington [in the game], who was dead and didn't have anything to say, and it felt like the process of discovering."[55] The game helped the battle become more meaningful to the players because they could experience the real-life stories unfold while the players were exploring the real physical environment of Lexington. Suddenly the past did not seem so far away, and knowledge of this historic moment became more relatable, understandable, and memorable.

While this game focuses on one specific location, it can serve as a model for creating and using other types of location-based games. Teachers can even work with students to create their own games based on local locations and historic events. A software program, ARIS, may be useful in designing these types of games (see more at https://fielddaylab.org/make/aris/).

Example in Action: *1979 Revolution: Black Friday*

The game *1979 Revolution: Black Friday* takes place during the time leading up to and following the Iranian Revolution of 1979. The player plays as Reza Shirazi, an 18-year-old photojournalist who lives with his family in Tehran. As Reza, the player needs to make a series of ethical choices as he interacts with friends and family throughout the city streets. In between these scenes Reza appears in a flash-forward, where he is being interrogated on his interactions related to the overthrow of the Shah. For instance, in one choice in the game, the player needs to choose whom to accuse of a crime, and in another, whom to try to save. To craft the game the creators used their own photographs, memories, and anecdotes, as well as stories based on interviews with people who lived during the Revolution. This gives the game an authentic feel, as the dialogue, in-game photos, characters, and scenarios are all based on real-life activities.

In *1979 Revolution*, players can also use an in-game camera to take photos of the game world. The photo that is created is based on the real actions of the player in the game, and how they hold the camera and what they shoot. All images taken are collected in an album that the player can refer back to and use to build evidence, share with other characters, and decide on actions in the game, such as which character to accuse of stabbing a Revolution leader.

The game may not be suitable for younger students. But teachers can use this game with other audiences in a variety of ways. They could have the students use the images they take in the game to support discussion and activities beyond the game. The images could be used to help in telling stories, writing journals, sharing ethical choices or views, collecting data or information, or deliberating actions with other students, such as through a forum or virtual breakout room.[56] Then, after playing the game, students could take their own photos of their world, and think about how they might be used to create social change, to take action, or to connect with others.

Enable Interactions with Real Data and Resources

Just as it is important to use realistic tools and models that approximate what might happen in the real world, using actual data is also beneficial for helping students make meaningful connections with social, civic, and ethical issues, and learn relevant skills. Games can encourage players to submit, analyze, and interpret real-world data, information, or perspectives. Players may conduct research in their neighborhood, classroom, or online, and then feed the results back into the game, such as one might do as part of a citizen science project (see Table 11.1).[57] These types of games could enable students to survey or collect data in their communities and then use that data to affect the game.

We can also imagine a game that provides real-world data about one's local government or community and enables players to make decisions based on the data, similar to a *SimCity* game but using local urban planning or policy needs. For instance, in *Counties Work*, players need to plan out how to serve their counties (a governmental division of a US state) and then decide on the policies, structures, and buildings that will best serve their constituency. The types of actions that the player can take are based on real-world information about what county executives actually do and run.

Example in Action: *Community PlanIt*

Community PlanIt is an online gaming platform made by the Emerson Engagement Lab, which spurs real-world deliberation and community planning among players. Through the platform, players receive missions and are asked to compete with other teams of people to "earn influence in their community to fund local projects." One of the goals of the platform is to help youth see how their participation matters and can have an impact. A consideration with many planning processes is that they are often longer-term, such as over five years, and it is hard for a young person to see how they can make a difference over such a long time period. The *Community PlanIt* platform therefore helps gather contributions from young people that can be implemented for shorter-term change as well, such as murals, a public garden, or a board game club.[58] People compete to get their projects reviewed using in-game currency. These projects then may get awarded with real money to help initiate them.

The online platform also encourages offline debate among community members as to the best course of action for real-world problems. It helps to structure the path through that problem in that it guides the players, scaffolds conversations, and provides support for players to meaningfully contribute to their own cities. In Boston, the game platform was used to support conversations among stakeholders from the Boston Public Schools and their district-wide planning (for the creation of a school performance index). It was also used in a planning process in Detroit (such as the creation of a planning document for the next 50 years). Gordon and Baldwin-Philippi found that through the game the participants engaged in critical reflection and

dialogues, enhanced trust, and formed a greater awareness of how people are connected in civic life. In particular, the game supported reciprocal communication, or
communication that fosters listening to others and valuing their viewpoints. It led
to a greater appreciation for the contributions of everyday citizens and a desire to
build consensus.[59] Gordon explains that the platform also provides playful opportunities for youth to engage in civics such as through perspective-taking, or failing and
trying again. This helped him to personally see how games may not just be designed
for civics, but how "civics can be framed through the lens of a game."[60]

Empower Students to Make Games That Express Their Real Lives

Making games is a type of real-world participation.[61] Games do not need to be digital
to be effective; they simply need to be accessible to and representative of real-world
communities and peoples.[62] Khanna, a researcher in India, creates floor mat (8 feet by
8 feet) games using flexible plastic material. She has designed and used these games
in India to teach issues such as electoral literacy, sanitation, and children's rights to a
wide range of audiences (from nine-year-olds to elderly adults). These types of games
work well because they can easily be played in schools, community workshops, and
other cooperative settings outside of school. She uses these games to help "give information, change attitudes and opinions, but also as recall, recapitulation, and evaluation tools [to create] citizens who are aware and can disseminate the messages in their
peer group and the community."[63] These types of games also help to bring together
the community through play, and they help to spread awareness through the community's networks.

Likewise, the Emerson Engagement Lab created *Workflow*, a tabletop board game
that aims to help youth in Bhutan engage in conversations around career and job possibilities. The game was designed using real anecdotes and stories from Bhutan youth.
Through the game, the players are able to practice different job-related skills, such as
networking.[64]

Empowering students to make games based in the real world also helps them to
take risks, manage real resources, and experience realistic outcomes. It helps them
to understand real-world contexts, pressures, and constraints, how to approach
problems, and what to do to solve them.[65] Teachers and students can even work together to make games. Archer worked with students in his Spanish in the workplace
course to codesign an analog role-playing game called *Game of Life*. Students in this
game needed to make resumes, conduct interviews, and balance their income and
expenses. They had to think about how to spend their time and money to make short-
term and longer-term decisions, such as whether to go to school, save for buying a
home, or make other investments. Making the game with the students had a twofold
purpose: helping the students to practice Spanish in situ, as they needed to understand it to be able to design the game, and helping the students to develop real-world

skills like career preparation and financial planning (see more about game design in chapter 12).[66]

Use Games That Connect to Real-World Issues

Teachers should use games and game content that tie into students' personal interests and motivations, as well as ones that are relevant to a community's goals or needs. Teachers may want to find or modify games such that players can choose from among a number of goals, or withdraw from a goal, particularly if a goal, story, or gameplay mechanic is personally upsetting or inappropriate in some way.[67] For instance, sometimes games can map to reality in ways that could get too close for comfort depending upon the systems of government and civic policies of a particular culture or country.

Vanek talks about a larp (live action role-playing) game made by Young called *The Road Not Taken*, which includes a number of ethical dilemmas.[68] Vanek created new dilemmas for it, and Vanek and Young submitted it for a larp writing contest in Belarus. In one of the new dilemmas, the character has to decide whether to join a protest against a corrupt government. In this larp scenario, "characters are young people in a bar and they see a crowd outside and they have to decide [whether] they are going to join their friends in a protest against a corrupt government." The game was to be run in Belarus soon after a protest against Lukashenko, the country's dictator. The group running the larp extension felt it was too politically provocative to run that scene in Belarus, and decided against playing it then.[69] Likewise, teachers may need to consider the real-world personal and political ramifications of a game, and adjust it to be more relevant to further its effectiveness for learning.

Example in Action: *Bay Area Regional Planner*
Game designer Twu created *Bay Area Regional Planner* to get players to talk about relevant local issues in the San Francisco Bay Area, such as the different systemic factors related to a housing crisis, and the need for a more complex housing solution in the Bay Area.

Bay Area Regional Planner is a cooperative game that incorporates different points of view on a housing issue, where each player may have slightly different goals, such as preserving the neighborhood or avoiding traffic. Twu explains that *Bay Area Regional Planner* has been used in real-world housing advocacy meetings, where people play the game to help understand these different perspectives, engage in real-world discourse around the issue, and work together to solve the problem and create more actionable housing policies (see Figure 5.2). For example, Twu explains that the game helps players to see the different perspectives in action, such as that "there's people that want see more housing built, people who want to make sure that there's a high percentage of affordable housing, and people who want more parking." The game has also helped to facilitate conversations among different constituents about short-term and longer-term housing consequences, and the tradeoffs involved in different

Figure 5.2 An image of the game *Bay Area Regional Planner*. Image courtesy of Alfred Twu.

policies. In fact, it helped players to become more empowered to even enter these conversations. After playing the game, they are better equipped when they go to city hall meetings because they have "learned a lot of the vocabulary around these issues."[70]

Teachers can consider playing and making board or card games with students around local or community issues. Even just the game design process can help to facilitate problem-solving and conversations around real-world issues.

Use Games That Connect Students to Real Stories

Games can provide awareness of real-world issues and help share authentic stories. McDowell and Chincilla recommend that rather than designing games for the mainstream or majority, we should design experiences for the people who are least likely to access it and are most marginalized.[71] Teachers may want to consider how the games they choose are ensuring equitable access and participation such that not only mainstream or powerful voices are being heard, but all people are empowered to participate and be heard.[72]

Example in Action: *Thunderbird Strike*
LaPensée created *Thunderbird Strike* to share Anishinaabeg stories and art, while also exploring the environmental issues that result from leaking pipelines, such as the Line 5 oil pipeline. In this 2D mobile game, LaPensée explains that "players fly from the Alberta Tar Sands to the Great Lakes as a thunderbird protecting Turtle Island with lightning against the snake that threatens to swallow the lands and waters whole.

Created with hand drawn art, stop motion animations, and music from northern territories where toxins have damaged the lands, the game exemplifies Indigenous aesthetic and the hope for passing on thunderbird stories through gameplay."[73] The game features Indigenous artworks, such as Isaac Murdoch's *Thunderbird Woman* and Dylan Miner's *No Pipelines on Indigenous Land*, as well as the stories and symbols from the Anishinaabeg and Métis Indigenous communities of which the developer is a part.[74]

LaPensée's authentic game design gives voice to Indigenous perspectives on how we can honor the environment, the land, and all living creatures. However, this game, and its creation and deployment, also had real-world consequences for the developer when the oil lobbyists began targeting the game with a coordinated media campaign that aimed to pressure the Michigan government to revoke funding on the game. LaPensée explains that this situation "offers insights into the realities and risks of self-determined Indigenous representation." It suggests that while games may be seen as imaginary or fictional worlds, and even apart from reality, we still need to be mindful of the real-world consequences of making and using games to show marginalized, nonmainstream, or even subversive perspectives.[75]

PART III

USING GAMES FOR CONNECTION AND COMMUNITY

6
How Do We Connect and Communicate?

In the online game *Way*, two strangers play the game together. I am one of the strangers, and I play as the blue character (my avatar). The other stranger, who is unknown to me, plays as the red one. The screen is split so that I can see both characters, but I am not able to speak to the other player, or write or type, and there's no mic or other way of communicating. I can only click on an emotion icon (emojis), or use my avatar to communicate nonverbally, such as by gesturing with it.[1]

And yet, though we are separated by distance, we must control our characters with collaborative synchronicity so that we can together solve puzzles and achieve goals. For instance, in one of the game's puzzles, I can see a series of platforms but the other player cannot see them. I, however, cannot jump on the platforms, only my partner can. I need to show them where the platforms are located so that they can jump up to reach the goal. We need to work together and teach, listen, and learn.[2]

The only point in *Way* where players can directly communicate with words is through a shared whiteboard at the very end of the game, where the split screen finally dissolves, and the players come together in a shared virtual space. The players can write words or draw pictures on this whiteboard. Even though the entire game is only about 20 minutes long, players often spend the most time here, happily writing to each other about where they are from or what language they speak. When I watched another person play *Way*, for instance, their anonymous partner wrote, "you are a friend."

Through the game, *Way* is able to support communication and collaboration among players—and even camaraderie, care, connection, and a sense of community. In this chapter I will discuss why and how games may teach communication and other social skills like argumentation.

Why Should We Encourage Communication?

People Learn Through Social Interactions

Learning and knowledge building are socially constructed and socially maintained.[3] Bandura explains how people learn through the modeling of behavior, or the way in which people observe how others act, behave, or speak, and learn to replicate it.[4] Likewise, Vygotsky's social constructivism theory suggests that the sociocultural context of learning matters, and interacting with adults and peers with differential

We the Gamers. Karen Schrier, Oxford University Press. © Oxford University Press 2021.
DOI: 10.1093/oso/9780190926106.003.0006

knowledge ("the knowledgeable other") helps the learner to form concepts and mental models of the world.

This also relates to learning and practicing civics and ethics. People learn by watching one other and seeing how others respond to ethical or civics issues, decisions, and actions. People can serve as role models or "moral exemplars"[5] in that they show or model values, norms, and ways of doing things, as well as how to behave or how to solve problems. They can show others how to act and treat people through the choices, behaviors, and perspectives that they perform and model. Students, then, may formulate their values in part through observations of their parents, teachers, or peers. Students may also learn by observing others' civic actions or acts of service, such as by seeing others engaged in volunteer work, which may motivate them to join in as well.[6] In *Habits of Service*, Arthur et al. explain that students are more likely to be involved in service to their communities if their parents, and particularly their friends, are involved.[7]

Moreover, people continue to learn *as* they express and communicate their views, findings, and decisions to others. The fourth component of the C3 framework includes not just taking action but communicating conclusions, which includes speaking and presenting as well as "essays, reports, and multimedia presentations [which] offer students opportunities to represent their ideas in a variety of forms and communicate their conclusions to a range of audiences."[8]

People Learn Through Relationships and Community

Learning civics and ethics is not just about being motivated to vote or engage in political acts, but it is also about developing and participating in a community. Dewey explains that democracy is not just about government but about the people, living together. Civics is about people, and about communities.

In a community, people will organically communicate norms, values, and responsibilities by how they react to and interact around various activities, goals, and topics. Just as students in a classroom need to understand and adhere to the rules and norms of that class, people in any community also need to negotiate, navigate, and share norms and values. Lave and Wenger describe the concept of "communities of practice," where people come together around a specific practice or activity, such as a local school board coming together to discuss a budget or school closure, or a Massively Multiplayer Online (MMO) guild working together on a virtual quest. Through these groups, people can learn through something called "legitimate peripheral participation" or a process by which novices or newcomers to a community learn the ropes by taking on increasingly more central tasks related to an organization. The newcomers to a community begin to gradually embody the norms, communication styles, approaches, and practices of that community, moving from the periphery of the community to becoming core members who are reinforcing its culture.[9] Schools and other learning environments are also themselves communities, where students can learn from within a socially situated context and can directly participate in and practice ethics and civics, such as by engaging in informed discourse and argumentation with others. They are civic communities where people may vote (such as for school governance) or decide on how to treat others (such as on the playground or in the classroom). Dewey explains that "the School must itself be a community life in all which that implies. . . . In place of a school set apart from life as a place for learning lessons, we have . . . incidents of present shared experience. Playgrounds, shops, workrooms, laboratories . . . involve . . . communication, and cooperation, all extending the perception of connections."[10] School is a public sphere.[11]

Thus participating in a community, and seeing oneself as part of a community, helps people to learn and share the norms and values around civics practices. It also helps students to take a step back and realize the important role of community in sharing these norms and values. This helps students better understand how ethics and civics function and get applied—it reveals the hidden social and cultural machinery behind ethics and civics systems. Researchers recommend evaluating one's community to understand power dynamics, discover new ways to solve problems, and find new ways for people to access problem-solving.[12]

Learning through community furthers ethics and civics in another way, too. It reinforces the idea that practicing civics and ethics is not just an individual endeavor, but a community effort. It emphasizes that civic engagement relies on the collective action of those in our local, national, and global communities. Mirra and Garcia note that civics requires the "'build[ing] of commonwealth' between individuals of various backgrounds, experiences, and beliefs by being 'productive and generative, not simply [through] a bitter distributive struggle over scarce resources.'"[13] Learning through community helps us to better see that if someone in the group cannot fully engage in civics, then that affects the entire community. It further shows us that we all need equitable access to education, participation in our communities, and in making change.[14] Learning civics should include the process of becoming aware of and joining a community of citizens. To citizen is to connect.

Building Community Supports Other Skills

Social interactions and the building of community interrelate to many other skills as well, including problem solving and decision-making. Social interactions can motivate further communication, dialogue, and problem-solving, such as with those who have different views, perspectives, mindsets, and needs. These interactions may help to spur more effective problem solving, as problems may be addressed differently because of how a group comes together to share expertise and solve it.[15] In fact, civic problems are often wicked problems and they are often systemic problems.[16] "Wicked" problems are problems that require information, expertise, skills, and experiences that are beyond any one individual's capabilities. Solutions need to be community-minded, evolving, and dynamic. They need to take into account how communities interact and the interdependence of people on all others. Honing skills within a community can support this mindset. However, the climate of the school or community matters in how people feel safe enough to communicate, solve problems, or engage.[17]

Discourse and Dialogue Matter, Too

People also learn through engaging in discourse, dialogues, or conversations with others, and sharing their views and beliefs. Levine and Kawashima-Ginsberg point out the effectiveness in civic education of encouraging "facilitated, planned discussions" and that "discussions across political and social differences [is] ... a habit that can be taught."[18] The *Guardian of Democracy* report refers to the need for students to participate in productive and constructive dialogues.[19] Thus, an important skill is being able to engage in discourse, particularly in the public sphere.[20]

A main component of discourse is formulating arguments or engaging in argumentation. When people hear the word "argumentation," they often think that it refers to a negative form of communication or one filled with conflict, anger, and division. Yet argumentation is also about fortifying community and enabling collective action. Argumentation involves positing arguments, such as sharing a perspective on an ethical issue, and then persuading others of the argument by providing evidence, information, data, and reasons as to why the argument is sound. This is essential to civic and moral engagement and ethical thinking, because at their core they are about making arguments about how societies should function, work together, and solve any problems that they face. As Noddings explains, in "dialogue, both parties speak, and both parties listen. They work their way sensitively toward the resolution of a problem."[21] After all, there is rarely only one correct answer when we are faced with a social, civic, or ethical conundrum, so people need to work together and solve problems by sharing their views, supporting them with evidence, and trying to persuade others that it is the right decision.

Argumentation is not just about respectfully persuading someone of one's ideas by posing arguments, though. It also involves listening to others' ideas, acknowledging their arguments, discussing the strengths and weaknesses, and perhaps even allowing one's own ideas to change. The act of listening to other people and their views helps people to evaluate, reflect on, and revise their own.[22] Thus, disagreement is not necessarily an issue, as throughout history people have always disagreed and this disagreement often leads to more creative social problem-solving, change, and growth. Rather, people learn from engaging in dialogue with those who have differing views. These types of exchanges can help people to consider other perspectives more substantively, which strengthens bonds.[23] "Even just feeling that someone else is taking our perspective may be beneficial, as it could lead to more connection with the other person and greater empathy for them."[24] In sum, having students engage in conversations and deeply listen to others' views can support communication skills, as well as perspective taking, connection, and empathy, which all help to further ethics and civics learning and practice (see more in chapter 8).[25]

How Do Games Support Communication and Connection?

Games Can Support Social Interactions

Games can enable social interactions, like playing together, as well as verbal and non-verbal communication. Some games enable team-based, community-based, or pair-based play, and some enable direct communication through the game (e.g., live voice chat, text chats, emoticons, avatar gestures).[26] Social interactions may also occur around or beyond the game (see next section).

Some games may enable social interactions among real people in the same physical space, such as in the case of *Apples to Apples* or *Werewolf*, or interactions among people in different spaces and times, such as in the case of *Words with Friends* or *Kind Words* (see more in chapter 7). Some games support interactions among different people at the same time, such as *Way*, *World of Warcraft*, *Overwatch*, or *Fortnite*. Other games have options where the players may even be able to interact socially with nonplayer characters in the world, such as in *Red Dead Redemption II* or *Fallout 4*, or with real players in the online versions of those game series (such as in *Red Dead Online* or *Fallout 76*).

The tenor of social interactions may differ depending on the game, or even may differ within the same game. Interactions can be more competitive in nature (where players or groups of players are competing for the same resources, to meet a particular goal, or to be the last one standing), or collaborative or cooperative, where players share resources and work toward similar goals.[27] For example, in *Crisis of Nations*, an iCivics game, players take on the role of different countries and compete and cooperate to solve problems. While there is a competitive element, players can earn bonuses if they also cooperate with other players. The crises in the game, in fact, are only able to be solved through the sharing of expertise and information among the four countries that are competing with each other.[28] Similarly, in the game *Among Us*, a group of players are playing together in a virtual space, while communicating through a platform like Zoom or Discord. The identity of each player is secret, but there are imposter(s) among them. Players need to figure out who the imposter(s) are, and which players to collectively vote on to be ejected from the game. Players need to both compete and collaborate to decide whom to remove from the game and ensure that their side (civilian or imposter) wins.

Games Are Communities

Like schools, games are civic communities. Games are communities where civic participation and ethical negotiation take place, such as through direct discourse, view exchanges, rule mediation, and information sharing—just like in any social media or in-person community. Likewise, games are public spheres, where people can civically participate and enact change.

Communities may emerge around games, such as through watching livestreams together on Twitch; talking and playing together on platforms like Discord or Zoom; or by sharing fanfics with other fans through online forums, hashtags, or Facebook groups.[29] Communities may also form around playing games competitively, such as esports leagues and teams. Collins created and ran a varsity esports team for students at a private all-girls' school, Hathaway Brown. The team included cis female students, nonbinary students, and trans boys, who played games like *Super Smash Bros.*, *Minecraft*, *Hearthstone*, and *Heroes of the Storm*, while also building camaraderie and friendship. Game communities may also be able to foster engagement with broader political and civic communities, such as when players can participate in protests or debates in games like *Fortnite* or *Animal Crossing: New Horizons*.

Through game communities, players can learn and engage in the culture of a community, and the shared norms of a game world.[30] Games and their communities can serve as moral exemplars, in that they can model and express the virtues and values that they want the player to embody. An avatar or character, or another player in a game, could also model behaviors, choices, perspectives, or values for the player.[31]

Players in a community can also act as mentors or coaches who can help onboard newer players and get them accustomed to a new world and its possibilities, in a type of apprenticeship arrangement.[32] In *World of Warcraft*, players develop shared practices through communities in the game, such as guilds, and engage in peer mentorship with each other.[33] By participating in a game community, players begin to epistemically learn and adapt to each other, and the tools, theories, values, and jargon of that community.[34] This helps to further foster a sense of belonging, because being able to communicate with the correct vocabulary or act by following the proper norms and values helps someone to feel more included. Novice gamers can learn from more experienced people, and more experienced people can crystallize their learning by teaching others.[35]

Games Can Support Discourse

Game communities can support discourse and the sharing of information, values, and opinions. Games may act like town squares, where "gamers may use in-game quests or in-game chatting as sources of game news."[36] Through a game, players may consider others' perspectives, argue a particular view, or provide a point and counterpoint to an argument or view. Players may also discuss ethics, rules, norms, and behavior through and around games. Kafai and Fields explored how youth discuss and create artifacts about cheating in Whyville, an online community for youth ages eight to 16.[37] Likewise, in *Win the White House*, players need to first pick issues for their platform that would be supported by the particular political party they chose, such as gun control or LBGTQIA+ issues if they are playing as the Democratic party. But players also need to choose an issue that would be typically supported by the opposing party (in this case, the Republican party), such as lowering taxes or military support.

Games can also set goals that motivate players to make statements or premises and back them up with vetted evidence. This relates to one of the trickiest parts of teaching argumentation, which is not only championing one's own argument, but listening to and debunking other's arguments. As Shaenfield explains, "When you're discussing something with someone else, the tendency is for you to put a premium on having reasons that support your positions and promoting those. However, the other side of an argumentative discourse is also critiquing the other side. Our tendency is not to do that, but to favor pushing our own reasons forward."[38] Games can scaffold argumentation, and make listening the primary action in the game.

Games can also support problem-solving through enhanced communication and discourse. Games can help players engage in constructive communication around a problem, share perspectives, talk about ideas and strategies, and deliberate next steps. Players can work together to do activities in a game (like strategizing how to solve a problem together) or even around a game (like sharing tasks with others in a forum or finding resources on how to solve a task in a game's wiki).[39] Thus, playing games is not just in service to practicing civic participation skills, playing may itself be a form of civic participation.

Games Can Support Connection

Games can help people connect and foster a sense of belonging. Games can help players build social capital, or community involvement, connectedness, and the ability to maintain social ties.[40] Games can also enhance the amount of time that people spend together, which enhances trust, connectedness, and intimacy.[41] For instance, my research on *Fable III* suggests that spending time with even a virtual character helps players develop a connection to them, and use perspective-taking, compassion, and empathy-related skills when making decisions that relate to them.

Games can also foster prosocial interactions. The ADL conducted a study of over 1,000 American gamers and found that 95% of the respondents who play online multiplayer games had some positive social experiences while playing, such as making friends (83%) or being helped by other players (86%). Eighty-three percent reported that they felt like they belonged to a game community; 56% found a mentor; and 59% found partners (romantic, teammates) through an online game.[42]

Feeling like one belongs in turn enhances learning, and can encourage greater civic engagement.[43] Inclusion in a social community may help to further communication around civic issues and collective action in public matters. Gordon and Baldwin-Philippi explain that when players were engaged in *Community PlanIt* (described in chapter 5), they developed greater trust with each other and felt more connected to their community. My research on game jams suggests that game makers may feel safer in a community after having spent time engaged in game creation with others.[44]

Molyneux et al explain that "this sense of connectedness to others can lead people to form face-to-face bonds and participate in their real-world communities. The implication is that there are now multiple pathways for people (especially young people, who have traditionally been less engaged in civic life than their older fellows) to become better citizens."[45] Thus, games are useful for strengthening friendships and communities, as well as for exchanging ideas, learning, and overcoming real-world problems—all necessary components of civics and ethics.

Games Are Also Forms of Communication

Communication is not just between people, but also between the game and the player. Game design is a form of communication or dialogue with the player, and together they are communicating to each other through play. The game designer communicates their message, purpose, and desired experience for the player in how they design the game. The player then responds through their own play, shaping the game even further.

Communication between the game designer and player includes providing explicit feedback (in the form of audio or visual cues, for instance) or representing characters and expressing stories that relay the types of relationships, themes, and topics that they want the player to experience. One integral aspect of a game's design is how the system manages communication and builds community, such as the policies, incentives, rewards, and handling of problematic communication. What are the ways the game ensures safe social interactions? How does the game moderate its communities and what does it provide to its players as tools, safety measures, or processes for remediation of any issues? How does the game represent cultures and peoples—does it inadvertently further stereotypes or strengthen belonginess through its designs?

Limitations to Using Games for Communication

Learning Together Is Not Always Beneficial

Social interaction and communication through games is not always useful. Learning is not necessarily better accomplished alongside, with, or against other people, whether those people are real or virtual, and whether the game is digital or not. Some types of deep learning need to be accomplished alone and with intensive, focused solo practice.[46] Some people are demotivated, for instance, by competitive social environments, and will mentally "check out" when in a situation where they need to compete with others. Research by Song et al. suggests that people who were driven by competition were more motivated to play an exergaming game, but those not driven by competition were less motivated overall. Some people are overwhelmed by social interactions or being on a team. Adjusting one's social behavior to suit others can get in the way of being able to focus on problem-solving or other tasks. And some people just prefer to learn on their own or to do projects by themselves, whether through a game or not.[47]

Communication and Communities Can Be Harmful

Communication does not necessarily build community. While communication is important to initiating and sustaining relationships, some types of communication can be harmful. Communication can be conflict-laden, hurtful, and insensitive, filled with ad hominem attacks, or threatening. A 2017 Pew Internet survey on online harassment found that 41% of those online (in the United States) personally experienced harassment, and 66% had witnessed others being harassed.[48] The ADL reported that 37% of Americans surveyed expressed that they had experienced severe harassment online in 2018 (as opposed to 18% in 2017), including physical threats, sexual harassment, or sustained harassment by someone else. Of those who were harassed online, 56% reported that some of the harassment happened on Facebook, with 19% on Twitter, 17% on YouTube, and 16% on Instagram.[49]

Harmful behavior and harassment is also happening in online games and gaming communities. Games such as *Fortnite, Valorant, DOTA 2 (Defense of the Ancients), League of Legends*, or *Overwatch*, or social gaming platforms such as Twitch or Discord, have their own sets of cultural norms and participatory rules, just like other social media platforms such as Facebook and Twitter.

In an ADL study, they found that 47% of all the daily users on Twitch deal with some type of harassment (Twitch is a game-streaming platform that also functions as a social media platform). The ADL also reported that 81% of respondents to a survey, of people who play online multiplayer games, experienced some type of harassment during their game (this is an increase from 2019, where it was 74%). They also reported that 68% of the surveyed online gamers experienced severe forms of harassment, including threats and stalking, which is up from 65% in 2019.

And having positive experiences in games does not protect people from also having negative ones that may drive them away from playing a game. In 2019, 43% of respondents explained that they stopped playing a game due to harassment, even if they had had positive social experiences in it. In particular, females and other marginalized populations may be targeted for harassment in online gaming, which may lead them to finding other ways to play, such as offline or in more socially supportive online environments. Ortiz describes how racist hate speech in online gaming negatively affects men of color (see also more about games, harassment, and disinformation in chapter 10).[50]

Moreover, people may not report the harassing behavior. An ADL report found that 64% of players who were harassed did not report others for the harassment. A study done by Ratan and *Wired* found that only 20% of game players stood up to bullying, harassment, or name calling done by a teammate. The culture of a community may affect how people communicate or whether they report problems. Cary et al. found that when it is culturally the norm in a game to report other players, the players are more likely to report them. (However, this study also suggests the reverse, which is that if the culture is supportive of prejudiced comments, the players will also more likely engage in making prejudiced comments). This suggests that the culture of a community matters in how willing players are to stand up for each other.

Thus some games and gaming communities may lend themselves to better supporting connectedness and more prosocial behavior. But cruelty and harm are not just problems with games and social media platforms. As Dishon and Kafai explain, all different forms of civic engagement and communication can be used for "undemocratic ends" such as the radicalization of youth, spread of disinformation, reinforcement of toxic masculinity, bullying, and further oppression of marginalized groups.[51]

Engaging in Productive Dialogue Is Difficult to Attain

Disagreement and argumentation are not always constructive. Both sides of an argument are not necessarily equal and some arguments (merely by being posited) are akin to cruelty, abuse, and even acts of violence. Moreover, finding people with different opinions with whom to engage in constructive disagreement has also become more complicated, particularly due to demographic, social, and technological changes. As described in chapters 2 and 10, we may be separating into partisan bubbles or echo chambers, and not interacting in a shared public sphere where we can engage in the productive dialogues needed to solve problems and reimagine our society. This may be due in part to political homophily, where in virtual and real-world spaces, people tend to connect with those who are more like them in terms of interests, politics, identities, and backgrounds. Social algorithms also encourage more likemindedness or groupthink, which further limits communication with those who may have differing views and those with whom they could engage in productive dialogue.[52] Games may even replicate or propagate these divides.

The Game Itself May Communicate With Harm

Game designers may not always communicate what they hope to communicate to the player. They may misrepresent cultures, such as by creating a character based on harmful stereotypes. They may create gameplay that inadvertently values negative or toxic behavior or problematic solutions. They may create a game that has a harmful community, perhaps because they did not design the necessary moderation processes and safety measures for that community. Benjamin argues that technology is not neutral; it "is not just a bystander that happens to be at the scene of the crime; it actually aids and abets the process by which carcerality penetrates social life." The fact that it is technology and "appears" neutral, or innocent, makes this even more problematic.

Benjamin calls this the new "Jim Code" in that it "hides not only the nature of domination, but allows it to penetrate every facet of social life." Gray echoes this, arguing that these digital practices are oppressive, and contribute to further isolation of Black gamers and other marginalized populations. Technology may seem like it is rising above issues of human bias, but it is in actuality "sediment[ing] existing hierarchies."[53]

Teachers should think about the types of behaviors that are incentivized by a game—not only through its rules, but also by the culture that emerges in a game. For instance, do *gemeinschaft* or *gesellschaft* communities emerge around the game? A *gemeinschaft* community, which values sharing and win-win solutions, may cultivate more respectful dialogue, whereas more individualistic *gesellschaft* communities may unwittingly lead to less listening to others' views.[54]

Strategies for Using Games to Support Communication

Choose Games that Encourage Deliberate Communication

Teachers should use games or activities around games that encourage students to practice deliberate communication and collaborative problem-solving. Teachers can look for games that use a "jigsaw method" to spread out knowledge, responsibilities, and tasks to different individuals or groups of players, who then bring that unique expertise to the table when solving a common problem.[55] A teacher might assign each player as the expert in a different country's needs, and they need to together negotiate how to solve a global problem, similar to the Model UN. Or a teacher might have each player take on the role of a community member with different perspectives (taxes are too high, buildings are too tall) to figure out next steps collaboratively, as they do in *Bay Area Regional Planner.*[56]

Teachers can also use games to help players practice deliberate communication in other ways as well, such as by setting goals that can only be achieved through constructive communication. *#BeFearless: Fear of Public Speaking* is a VR experience where players engage in conversations with different characters, listen to their recorded speeches, and get evaluated on language used, pronunciation, and other oral skills.[57]

Example in Action: *Keep Talking and Nobody Explodes*
In the VR game, *Keep Talking and Nobody Explodes*, players need to work together to defuse a virtual bomb. The catch is that only one player is actually wearing the VR headset and can see the bomb, while the rest of the players (such as people in a class) can access the manual that explains how to defuse it. The players need to communicate to be able to solve the problem together, as they each have what the other needs to meet the goal of the game. Jiménez used this game in an undergraduate

game development class. He explains that he used the game to foster teamwork and reciprocal communication to help better facilitate team-based software projects in his class.[58] Likewise, Dormer et al. used *Keep Talking and Nobody Explodes* in their English-Language Learning course to practice language use and facilitate further communication in English. Jiménez explains that teachers can modify the game and create their own units, as it has an active "modding" (game modification) community. For instance, teachers could make a module that encourages players to take different civic planning roles, or to manage relationships to ensure that the bomb is diffused ethically.[59] The game also comes in non-VR versions, like mobile.

Consider Social Interactions Around Games

To support learning, teachers may include social activities around games, such as by using pair-share groups that work together on in-game problems, or who read and reflect on each other's game play journals. Teachers can put students in pairs to play games, even if the game is a single-player game, to ensure that players talk to each other and decide on next steps. For instance, Farber puts students in pairs so that they "communicate and reflect, so they are vocalizing it out loud."[60]

Research suggests this technique is effective. For example, researchers found that players who shared a computer while playing a game were more motivated to keep playing the game and to learn, and ended up with better learning outcomes. They suggested that it was because pairs needed to say their ideas and decisions out loud, teach each other their perspectives, and plan out moves collaboratively, which help to reinforce learning and engage players in a game.[61]

Teachers can also pair students with differing abilities, such as a student who has more game-playing experience with someone else who is a novice player. Daniels teaches in a Washington, DC public school. She explains, "I put it them in pairs or maybe groups of three, where I have someone who is an early reader, and someone who is a little bit more advanced, so that they can help each other understand and critically think, so that everyone's on the same playing field."[62]

Teachers should also consider how players socially interact through a game, such as whether a game incentivizes competition or collaboration and cooperation, and the types of dialogues and conversations that could emerge from the game.

Example in Action: *Lasers*

Shaenfield worked in a series of public middle schools in New York City and taught his students how to engage in argumentation and discursive skills in a number of ways. First, he paired them together and had them talk and engage in argumentation. At first, they typically just gave their own arguments and took turns sharing their arguments. Next, he had them practice critiquing each other's arguments, and developing that skill. Finally, after a few weeks, he had his students look back at their initial arguments and reflect on what they could have done differently. This helped them to develop the metacognitive skills they needed to take a step back from their dialogues, and engage in argumentation skills, such as listening, identifying other's arguments, and critiquing them.[63]

In another exercise that Shaenfield used, he paired students together to play games. In one activity he used the physics game *Lasers*, and had students work together and communicate to each other what to do next. The purpose was to enhance metacognitive skills, such as collaborating to form a plan, test solutions, and reflect on strategies. He had the pairs first discuss their strategies before trying them in the game. Then, after playing the game, he had them discuss the outcome of these strategies. Initially, the students had trouble communicating with enough detail to share their strategies and perspectives. They would make statements like "let's move the mirror," without giving enough information for their partner to know which mirror, or where to move it. After practicing this using the game, the pairs began developing better ways of communicating. For instance, they would say something like "you see that mirror on the right side of the screen [wait for other student to nod]. Let's move it over three spaces to the left so it will bend the laser that we need to complete the game." Teachers can use activities and practices around a game, regardless of the game used, to help support communication practice, as well as other critical skills.[64]

Consider Communities Around Games

Teachers should be mindful of reviewing the types of communities that emerge within a game or beyond the game, such as in social media spaces, or in classrooms, playgrounds, homes, or school hallways. Educators who want to use a game should look at its policies, moderation processes, and observe the norms of the communities— how do people comport themselves in these spaces? To minimize problematic and harassing interactions in a game community, teachers may want to see the strategies and tips in Salen's *Raising Good Gamers*, such as advocating for policy changes that protect youth or encouraging prosocial influencers. The ADL and FairPlay Alliance put together a framework for creating inclusive communities and evaluating policies around community moderation in games (see https://fairplayalliance.org/wp-content/uploads/2020/12/FPA-Framework.pdf). See also work by Take This, AbleGamers Charity, I Need Diverse Games, Love Has No Labels, and AnyKey.[65]

An example of an online game community for kids is *Whyville*. Kafai, Fields, and Ellis looked at *Whyville*, a virtual world with over 5 million registered users that targets kids ages eight to 16. Participants can play science games in *Whyville* as well as share opinions, such as through forums or public spaces in the virtual space. Kafai et al. looked at community moderation and the nuanced ways that youth respond to cheating in the game, such as through their video creations, articles, and other artifacts. They found that this virtual world supported the practice of reflective ethical thinking and decision-making. They argue that "digital publics ... like *Whyville*, may indeed provide unique opportunities to engage children and youth in thinking about ethical issues. Because of its nuances, cheating creates not only educationally rich but also psychologically problematic experiences for children and youth. It is a complex territory which children and youth need to learn to navigate in their play, in which rules are negotiated by players, often situated within the designs of powerful media companies, and where technology itself can shape and be shaped to provide educational and community supports for safe play."[66]

Teachers need to help students learn how to engage ethically in all different circumstances—whether with a friend in the hallway, with peers in an MMO world like *Whyville*, or over Twitch or Discord. As we continue to teach students how to shape their arguments for different audiences and contexts, we also need to be mindful of teaching them how to navigate online and in-game conversations, and what to do when discourse becomes harmful.

Example in Action: *Minecraft*

Minecraft is an open environment and game where players can construct, explore, and create objects, buildings, and tools. Players can explore and decide how they want to play in the environment, based on their own interests. Bertozzi talks about how her students recreated the Taj Mahal and *Star Trek*'s Starship Enterprise within the world of *Minecraft*.[67] During the global COVID-19 pandemic, students recreated their university campuses, schools, and classrooms in virtual spaces like *Minecraft* to host graduations, classes, and other events. In this way they were rebuilding physical places so that people could come together virtually, and maintain and foster community. Importantly, in-world creations do not need to be exact replicas of places to be meaningful public spaces where friends and peers can have conversations and share views, participate in cultural rituals together (like graduation), or learn together (such as in a virtual classroom).

Players may also make things in and around the game, such as stories, drawings, websites, fan fiction, live performances, or new games. Dream, the creator of the Dream SMP *Minecraft* server, collaborates with other *Minecraft* livestreamers to script and improvise dramatic narratives while playing the game and streaming it to a live audience. In fall 2020, this included staging a controversial (fictional) election for the president of L'Manberg, in which four imaginary political parties competed. The events and conversations around the "election" included speeches, debates, political endorsements, and even voter fraud allegations. These performances in *Minecraft* have engaged thousands of viewers. During the last day of the series, Tommyinnit's livestream of the Dream SMP server had over 650,000 live viewers across Twitch and YouTube.[68]

In a game world like *Minecraft*, the students may become the mentors and guides who show the teacher what is interesting. Shah explains that the teacher may become a "pedagogical partner to help make game environments accessible to more students," whereas the students may take the lead in shaping their goals or designing the world as they want. Thus, teachers need to meet students where their interests are and let go of preconceived notions of how educators should act. One way to approach this is by "just letting students play the game, and make sense of it on their own," which may be challenging for some teachers who are used to guiding students carefully and giving them more structure than a foray into *Minecraft* might facilitate.

Shah also explains that *Minecraft* works for some groups of students but not others, depending on the context of use and how the teacher uses it. It can also depend on whether there is a toxic player in the game, which is in part why many teachers opt to set up their own *Minecraft* servers.[69] While students may set the pace and may customize the world to match their interests, teachers may still need to ensure that communication and connection is happening respectfully and compassionately, so that players do not feel excluded, bullied, or harassed. Anderson et al. point out that racial and gender representations in *Minecraft* are often stereotypical and are influenced by (and influence) representations beyond the game. Teachers should be mindful of the ways that students may be marginalized in the online and offline communities in and around a game like *Minecraft*.[70]

Reward Listening

One of the most challenging parts of argumentation is listening to each other's arguments and perspectives. Teachers can use games to support the practice of engaging in respectful dialogue and discourse. Even competitive games may be effective at this. The competitive game *PolitiCraft* rewards players for having the most points, but players also get points for helping others gain points, which requires them to listen to each other's narratives and needs. Active listening can also happen in games with no sound and no verbal communication. Students can listen to nonverbal communication such as gestures in games like *Way*, or teachers can modify games to be chat-free to help players focus on nonverbal cues and interactions. Using alternative ways to communicate and listen, beyond just text and voice, can also support communication among people who speak different languages, or connectedness among people with different abilities.[71]

Example in Action: *Argument Wars*

In *Argument Wars*, players need to argue real historic Supreme Court cases by constructing arguments and then deciding how to refute the arguments of the opposing lawyer (see Figure 6.1). For example, in the game *Brown v. Board of Education* players first get to choose which side they want to argue. If they choose *Brown*, they need to decide which amendment(s) would support their case. However, players need to listen carefully to what the other side argues, and then decide what to do next. They can play cards that either continue to solidify their own views, or they can respond more directly to what their opponent states, and put forth an argument that directly counters their opponent's views. Players also need to decide whether their opponent's argument is solid or not, so the game rewards players for fully listening to and analyzing each other's arguments.[72] Thus the game's design ensures that players do not

Figure 6.1 An image from the game *Argument Wars*. Image courtesy of iCivics.

just get stuck in their own arguments, but that they first acknowledge and affirm the presence of each other's arguments, and then use that to build their own. This is similar to improv, where you need to think about what your partner is saying, and then build on it (such as by saying "yes and . . .") rather than not responding to what they say or negating it. Teachers may want to create an improv-type exercise around the game, which elaborates on the skill of listening to and building on each other's arguments. The exercises do not necessarily need to be around court cases, but could be around anything from school lunches to local hangouts or community needs. Teachers might also consider incorporating props that students bring from home, and have students take turns arguing for the best trip souvenirs or sports team paraphernalia, to win a silly class prize.

7

How Do We Understand Ourselves and Our Emotions?

In *Fortnite*, players can do different dances, such as the Electro Shuffle, the Flapper Dance, or the Robot.[1] They can watch performers like Travis Scott and Marshmello at virtual live concerts in the game, they can mount Black Lives Matter protests, and they can engage in conversations on race and politics.[2] Yet the goal of *Fortnite* is not to dance, watch music performers, protest, or discuss, but to be the last character standing in a 100-person Battle Royale standoff. Players parachute down to an island and need to craft fortresses and weapons, avoid bad weather, and remain the last player (or group of players) to survive.

On the surface, it may seem like dancing and protesting in *Fortnite* is tangential or trivial to its gameplay. Yet players learn the dances in the game, and then perform these moves at school the next day. They post their videos of the dances on TikTok and YouTube, and share them with thousands of others. They meet friends, hang out, watch movies, and participate in events inside *Fortnite*. The personal and communal nature of the game, and ability to share remnants of the game with others outside of the game, helps to further engage players, establish its cultural norms, and enable personal expression. *Fortnite* becomes a sphere through which people can express themselves publicly. It also helps players leave their mark on a game that evaporates after each play session.

Game worlds function as their own public spaces, communities, and cultures, which intersect and interact with broader culture, as well as the identities and previous experiences of the player. Players bring in their own preconceived notions of what a game is; what their friends, an esports celebrity or a Twitch streamer, think of the game; and what they expect from a particular genre, game company, or famous designer. They also bring in their own identities and emotional responses to the game, which furthers how it is personally experienced and socially shared. For instance, when I was a kid playing the *Super Mario Brothers* series, I had names for characters that related to what I was experiencing at that time: the Boo Diddleys became Boo Radleys because I was reading *To Kill a Mockingbird*; the Lakitu's Cloud became the name of a sixth-grade teacher, which sounded just like Lakitu. I continue to use these names today. Now, whenever I play newer versions of Mario games with my kids, they call the characters these names, too. My kids have also created their own personal connections with the game, with my daughter always choosing the purple

We the Gamers. Karen Schrier, Oxford University Press. © Oxford University Press 2021.
DOI: 10.1093/oso/9780190926106.003.0007

Yoshi, because that is her favorite color, and one son deciding his first child will be called Bowser Junior, his favorite character.

In this chapter I look at how games help us to understand ourselves and others as citizens in society. It asks: who are we, how do we express ourselves, and how do we see ourselves represented in our communities? To do this, I consider how games can help students explore and experiment with aspects of their identity, as well as how they may support social and emotional learning (SEL), such as identifying one's own and others' emotions, regulating one's emotions, and expressing emotions.[3]

Why Does Identity Matter for Civics and Ethics?

Defining Identity

In the last chapter, I talked about how communicating and connecting with others helps to develop skills and knowledge related to ethics and civics. I also discussed how these skills help students "to citizen" communally, or to actively engage within a civic community. Connecting with one's own self also cultivates these skills. Expressing oneself, such as one's identity, interests, opinions, and emotions, is a form of civic participation. It helps students to better understand themselves and their roles in society, and to see themselves as ethical agents and civic actors. It also helps them to better appreciate others in these roles, and appreciate the ways in which they are already playing these roles in their everyday lives.

Identity is defined as "qualities and views of a person that makes them unique." Identity can include all different types of aspects, such as one's religion, sexual identity and orientation, race and gender identity, and also one's health status or profession. Identity can relate to one's membership in a community or a system, such as a specific game or television show (for instance, Dr. Who watchers may call themselves Whovians).[4] Likewise, people can have civic identities. Political views can be part of someone's identity, and identity can be based around how someone engages in public life (such as through volunteering or voting). People can also have moral identities, such as whether someone sees themselves, more humorously, as "chaotic good" or "lawful evil," or whether someone embodies virtues such as having resilience, gratitude, or perseverance.[5] Experiences of identities are nuanced; and need intersectional, cultural, and contextual approaches. We need to understand "how multiple intersecting identities and oppressions might shape experience and design of the digital, as well how marginalized groups might counter and transcend these incursions."[6]

Identity Matters for Learning

Part of our job as teachers is to help distill the fears and other emotion-related obstacles that students may have. Feeling secure in one's own identity can help students do better in school overall, in that it may relate to greater confidence in one's own abilities. Having greater self-efficacy enhances motivation and academic performance overall.[7] If people see themselves as the type of someone who is good at math, social studies, or writing, then they are more likely to practice those skills, and will even perform better at them.

A learning experience is also more effective when we feel like we belong, that our identities matter, and that we are in a caring, inclusive environment. It matters if our identities are included in the classroom's textbooks and whether our histories are shared, accurately and ethically. It matters if we share aspects of our identities with other people in our schools and our neighborhoods. Identity—including gender, race, ethnicity, and social class—all factor into whether we have a sense of belonging.[8] It affects our access to civic communities, and how we see our role in public life.[9] Civic engagement and public life needs to be for everyone, not just certain identities in a community.[10] We need to be able to express our full uniqueness to fully connect with others. We need to feel like we matter individually to be able "to citizen" collectively.

Identity does not just shape whether we act and feel belongingness in a community. It also shapes how we act. Our identity, including our *character*, affects the choices we make, and how we perform as citizens in a society. The Jubilee Centre for Character and Virtues describes four building blocks of character, which all form the foundation of "flourishing individuals and society." These four components are (1) intellectual virtues, such as reasoning, reflection, and critical thinking; (2) moral virtues, such as compassion, respect, and justice; (3) civic virtues, such as citizenship, service, and community awareness; and (4) performance virtues, such as motivation, resilience, and teamwork.[11] All of these virtues all work together and inform the development of civics and ethical practices, and foster character (or what the Centre calls "practical wisdom"). These shape how we can flourish or "citizen" with others (see more in chapter 3).

Moreover, we all have different beliefs and values, such as about how society should be governed, how to build communities, and how people should participate in public life. These different values matter, and should be reflected in our civic institutions, processes, and policies.[12]

Emotion Matters for Learning, Too

Likewise, being able to practice and enhance emotional skills is associated with greater academic achievement. Social and emotional skills and practices—including the ability to identify, manage, share, express, and sift through one's own and others' complex emotions—often relates to greater academic and career success.[13] Social and emotional learning (SEL) is being integrated into curricula in the United States, and seen as foundational to all different types of learning, including civics and ethics. SEL refers to skills, practices, and knowledge around how we socially connect with others, such as being emotionally aware of others and ourselves. The Collaborative for Academic, Social, and Emotional Learning (CASEL) framework includes SEL skills like developing self-awareness, self-management, relationship skills, and social awareness. The skills listed in CASEL's core competencies also all interrelate to skills associated with ethical and civics thinking, and it even situates "responsible decision-making" ("making ethical choices about personal and social behavior") as a primary component of the framework (see more in chapter 3).[14]

Emotions also factor into the development and expression of our character, and our civic and ethical identities, as well as how we perform these in public. Emotions help us to express ourselves and explore who we are as human beings in a society. For one thing, emotions are integral to being ethical thinkers and making ethical decisions as an individual or community.[15] Noddings explains that morality requires a "sentiment of natural caring. There can be no ethical sentiment without the initial, enabling sentiment."[16] Emotions also help us to understand how best to govern, protect, and care for our communities, and to make decisions on how we act in a society. Learning ethics and civics is not just about acquiring and applying information, it is about why we feel the way we feel, how we connect as a society, and how we treat others. We need to understand others, take on their perspectives, learn what motivates them, and care about what matters to them to be able to be fully civically engaged and community-minded.[17] Moreover, by expressing our own emotions and listening to others express their feelings, we are better able to form relationships and develop trust and intimacy. Emotions help us to connect to someone else, learn what matters to them, and make better decisions for us all.

On the other hand, we also need to make sure that emotions matter equitably. Who is allowed to feel and whose feelings inhabit our publics? Which emotions are more valued? We need to make sure that we are all equally welcome to express our emotions.[18]

How Do Games Enable the Expression of Identity and Emotions?

People Can Express Identities Through Games

Through games, people may explore themselves, reflect on aspects of their identities, and experiment with their interests and personal goals. This may happen through interacting with other players, through sharing game experiences in a classroom, peer group, or family, or even through playing alone. One example of this is in the game *Monster Prom*, a narrative dating simulation (dating sim) game, where players need to choose a date for the prom and choose how to interact with and build friendships with nonplayer characters (NPCs). The game allows players to express their gender identities, sexual identities, and romantic identities in different ways, such as by giving players choices of gender pronouns to use, and enabling gay, lesbian, and straight dating options.[19]

Watching games is another way that people may express their identities and interests. Anderson et al. describe how intersectional identities are constructed in the "*Minecraft* ecology," such as in the game itself, but also in the "metagame" environment or the communities surrounding the game, such as YouTube.[20] (See more about *Minecraft* in chapter 6). For instance, students may watch "Let's Play" videos on YouTube or watch other game players livestream their plays on Twitch. They may even set up their own livestreams or YouTube channels and interact with their audience and subscribers. Or they may connect with other viewers and gamers through the online chat platform Discord and talk about the latest battle royale challenges, such as in *Fortnite* or *Fall Guys: Ultimate Knockout*.[21]

Multiplayer games and team-based play may also help to connect players and help them express their identities. In one of the competitive modes of the digital online game, *Splatoon 2*, four players need to work together to spray colored ink over virtual platforms before the other team does. The game also hosts live events like Splatfest, where players pick one of two mega-teams to join, like Trick or Treat, or Stars or Mushrooms. When my daughter played, she joined the Stars team, and got a digital t-shirt with a Star icon on it for her avatar to wear. The opportunity to identify with and feel allegiance to a team enabled her to better express her personal interests (e.g., stars, *Mario* games) and helped to engage her further in the game as well.

Another way games may help foster self-expression is in how they represent different identities through their characters, storylines, relationships, objects, goals, and other elements.[22] Seeing oneself and one's identities represented in a game can help players feel like they belong and matter to the game, and can help them to feel more engaged in the skills, practices, and activities of that game.[23] For instance, some games include avatars that actually reflect those who play the game. Coleman-Mortley explains that "representation matters" and who you can select as your avatar is an "important part of [expressing] your identity ... whether students select an avatar in a wheelchair or wearing glasses or [are provided with] a variety of skin colors and hair textures ... their avatar [is] reflective of themselves."[24]

Players may also be able to customize games in ways that are meaningful to them.[25] This can be simple, such as naming a character or a place, as in the case of *Crisis of Nations*, where players can decide what to call the nation that they are running. Or it can include choosing from a set of possible languages (such as in *Zelda: Breath of the Wild*, which is available in eight languages); avatar gender identities (as in the case of *Fable* or *Mass Effect* series); races (as in the case of *Skyrim* and *Dragon Age* series); or fully formed avatar choices (as in the case of *Win the White House* and *Quandary*). Some games, such as *Mass Effect* or *Fallout*, let players sculpt an avatar to look as much as possible like themselves or someone else, by adjusting everything from eye and hair color, body type, and even the shape of one's forehead, chin, and nose.[26]

Games can also be personalized to the player's playstyle, educational needs, or identity. Personalization involves an app, game, or website altering itself to better fit the needs of the player—rather than the player actively making changes.[27] Some games incorporate a tutorial mode for new players, such as the *New Super Mario Bros.*

U Deluxe for the Nintendo Switch, which gives the player unlimited chances to complete a level and help from a computer-controlled character.[28] Other games might use advanced learning analytics and adapt to the player's specific educational gaps, or use in-game real-time data to predict whether a player is at risk of being frustrated or overwhelmed in the game, based on how they approach obstacles or answer questions. It will then adapt to the player to better support them.[29]

Making games for others to play is also a way of expressing one's identity. In *SweetxHeart*, a narrative game, you play as Kara, a Black woman. The game, made by Small, expresses how a Black woman navigates day-to-day microaggressions in school and at a workplace in the United States. Players need to make choices such as how to respond to someone calling Kara pet names at work. These interactions affect Kara's stress level, which wavers throughout the play experience, and reinforces how emotion and identity can interact.[30] Chapter 8 delves further into the complexities around games and perspective-taking.

People Can Explore New Identities through Games

Throughout this book I argue that games are civic communities, where players are producing new knowledge, contributing ideas and perspectives, and negotiating values—just as they would in any public sphere.[31] Playing a game and being part of a game community may also encourage players to explore and interact with others' identities that are not necessarily their own. One way this happens is through playing with other people or characters.[32] Research on literature suggests that readers can start to identify with a book characters' perspectives, which helps the reader to more deeply immerse themselves in the fictional world, and also to rehearse and enact, through their imagination, the perspectives of another.[33]

Games may encourage this, too. Games may motivate people to connect with others and become more open and comfortable with people who are different from themselves—such as people they may deem as being from "out-groups."[34] Games may help facilitate communication among distinct groups by enabling players to expand the types of identities with whom they would typically interact.[35] Moreover, through games, players may have the opportunity to interact with others through shared goals or cocreated stories, such as in the case of *Way* (see more in chapter 6).[36] As Aviles writes, "If one reason individuals self-segregate in the physical world is because they have no prior experience interacting with diverse individuals, the virtual world can be a safe place to gain this experience and lead to further contact in the real world. In addition, virtual contact with diverse representations of users may be enough to enact the positive qualities associated with contact in the physical world."[37]

In Geer's game *Offline*, players can experience the story of two people questioning their sexual and gender identities. Through playing the game and interacting with these two characters, players may become more accepting of identities that are different from their own, and more able to open up about and share their own identities. Chapter 8 delves into perspective-taking further.

Games may also help to reveal the biases and systemic issues that members of a particular identity group may face. Biases are an "inclination or preference either for or against an individual or group that interferes with impartial judgment." Games may help to reduce our biases by enabling us to experience stories or interactions while taking on the role of that identity (with the caveat that people cannot fully understand or embody another's identity that is different from their own). The idea is this: if we take on someone else's identity and see what they see firsthand in a virtual space, we may be more understanding and less biased toward those with that identity in the future. For instance, a goal of Nonny de la Pena's *One Dark Night* or the Special Broadcasting Service (SBS) Australia program *Is Australia Racist?* is to help people become more aware of systemic biases, as well as individual biases. Kaufman and Flanagan used the game, *Buffalo* and *Awkward Moment*, to help players reduce prejudice and confront bias, with initial results suggesting the games are effective.[38] I am working with colleagues at Lagos Business School in Nigeria to create a VR game to reduce biases and enhance compassion for different ethnic groups in Nigeria.[39] However, thus far, research is inconsistent on whether embodying an avatar or playing a game can lower biases about others, and this will be discussed further in this chapter, as well as in chapter 8.[40]

People Can Express Emotions Through Games

Emotions matter when it comes to expressing ourselves through games, and learning ethics and civics. People play games in part because they want to feel. This may seem surprising, because we often associate games with the idea of zombie-like players. But similar to other works of art like dance, opera, books, and television, games can evoke emotions through elements such as immersive storytelling techniques and dynamic characters. Through games, however, players can feel also emotions through how they perform; what they say or do; the choices they make; how they interact with other players, characters, objects, and environments; how they experience the system; and how they manage the resources in the game.[41]

Through games, players can have a range of emotions, including the six universal emotions (happiness, sadness, disgust, fear, surprise, anger) as well as jealousy, greed, love, or grief.[42] For instance, the color-changing platformer game *Gris* may evoke sadness and helplessness. The mobile game *Liyla and the Shadows* may reveal what it is like for a family living in the Gaza strip and the fear, grief, and loss of control in dealing with war and violence.[43]

Feeling strong emotions may be part of why a game engages—games are not just fun, they are also fulfilling emotionally. Feeling emotion while playing helps us feel more connected to the game, and it helps us feel more connected to ourselves. They help us to connect with our humanity.

Through games and gaming communities, players can also practice identifying and handling their own and others' emotions.[44] For instance, in the game *Nevermind*, which can be played using VR systems, players need to explore a frightening, labyrinthine world. While playing, the game is able to sense how scared the player is (using biofeedback sensors) and it may adapt by making the game even scarier. The aim of the game is to help players become more aware of their responses to stress and fear, and to manage and regulate their responses and calm themselves down.[45]

Games may also be a way to safely explore difficult or complex emotions, and to connect with others while more open, trusting, and vulnerable. Through a game, students may feel more comfortable discussing and sharing their emotions and identities with others. Take a short game called *The End of Us* by dikaffe, made in 48 hours for the 2011 Global Game Jam. In this game, players need to control a comet while it interacts with another comet. According to the designers, "*The End of Us* was designed to evoke friendship, attachment, and affinity without overt narrative. The orange comet's behaviors—introducing itself with a walloping hello, then running away can-you-catch-me style, circling around you for attention or chasing after the stars (what do those do, anyway? Do you just want them because Orange does?)—are intended to endear." At the end of the game you have one choice, which is to decide which comet will be destroyed by the asteroid belt and which will continue to float alone.[46] One student was so moved by this brief game that upon recounting what happened in it, he started crying at how sad this choice was for him. Other students then felt safer sharing their own emotions and responses to the game. Through shared emotion around a game, the students were able to connect with each other, as well as with what we were learning.

Games do not even need to be complex to evoke complex emotions. In one of my classes I have students play *Loneliness*, a simple game by Jordan Magnuson that is made of only a black screen with white boxes. As a player moves a box forward, the other boxes move away from it in all different directions. No matter how quickly or stealthily the player tries to move their box toward another group of boxes, those boxes move away, mimicking the behavior of social avoidance and rejection. While not everyone is moved by this game, some students have explained that it helps them to better understand the concept of loneliness, or that it even causes them to feel sad or lonely themselves.[47]

Expressing Through Games Can Support Learning

Games can enhance confidence in oneself and in one's identity, and this may in turn support learning. First, games can help people feel more comfortable with their own identities, which can enhance confidence in oneself and enhance self-efficacy. Greater self-efficacy, or one's belief in one's abilities, is also tied to emotion, which in turn can enhance learning, and can further curiosity and knowledge acquisition.[48]

Games can also help people stretch their identities by introducing them to new topics, new ideas, new people, and new ways of being in the world. Foster and Shah describe how students may explore science identities through a game like *Land Science*, which also helped to make knowledge acquisition more meaningful.[49] Portnoy and I looked at a science card game, *Assassins of the Sea*, to understand how it supported both enhanced self-efficacy and performance.[50] Likewise, Akkus-Caķir used game design to encourage young women's interest in computing and computer science by simultaneously enabling them to develop their identities as computer scientists.[51] Leonard et al. engaged youth in game prototypes and robotics to increase self-efficacy around STEM attitudes and strategies for middle school girls and Indigenous populations.[52]

Antura & the Letters is a mobile game created by the Cologne Game Lab of Cologne University of Applied Sciences (TH Köln), which aims to teach Arabic literacy skills to five- to ten-year-old Syrian refugees in the Middle East. The game was used in Turkey and Jordan, and research showed enhancements in Arabic literacy and well-being and social connectedness.[53] The game seeks to support not only literacy learning, but also social and emotional learning and prosocial behavior, such as through taking care of pets. Guardiola explains that "due to the Syrian conflict, nearly three million children have dropped out of school or are in precarious educational situations."[54] The social and emotional elements help to connect the players to their culture and to each other, and also help to support their language learning.

Limitations to Using Games for Expressing Identity and Emotions

Games Are Not Inclusive of the Diversity of Expression

However, games and gaming communities may not be inclusive to all types of identities, and certain identities are not equitably able to be expressed through games. As discussed in chapter 6, games are "nowhere near as inclusive and diverse as they need to be."[55] As with other communities, in game communities certain people may feel like they belong and are able to connect while others may feel excluded and marginalized, or even harassed and attacked.[56]

All games are biased. Just like any other system or designed experience, games embed the biases of their developers, and of the historic moment and culture from which they are constructed.[57] Individually, we all have biases or preconceived notions about others. People can have biases about someone's identity, such as gender or race, how someone behaves, or even about their political affiliation. People may not even be aware of their own biases, as some biases are implicit and not consciously applied, while others are more explicitly voiced and exchanged. Bias can also be systemic, as policies, designs, laws, and institutions carry with them the biases of those who created them. Policies may then continue to enact these biases and weave them into the fabric of the society they govern. Thus individual biases may become magnified and even transmogrified through a designed system like a game.[58]

Bias can affect a game's design in subtle and explicit ways, such as when Ubisoft decided not to include a female avatar in *Far Cry 4* because it would take up too many "resources." Or when designers enable only certain hair types and textures, skin tones, or gender pronouns. For instance, Martineau explains how the developers of *Valley of the Gods* appropriately represented type 4 hair texture—and that they had never experienced the choice of this hair texture before in a game.[59] Anderson et al. point to problematic and stereotypical representations of gender and race in games, such as how women may be shown as "sex objects" or racial minorities might be characterized as "criminals," and how these may further empower or marginalize certain people and affect who belongs in a community of play.[60]

Researchers such as Gray, Richard, and Shaw also critique the lack of complexity in identity representations in games, and call for more intersectional design approaches. For instance, is the design of an identity tokenistic, in that the game includes different identities without meaningfully integrating them into the game? Are identities in a game overly simplified or even inaccurate, instead of layered and complex, as real human identities would be? Are white players engaging in a "digital Blackface" by embodying a Black avatar, or are they meaningfully interacting with Black identities? Are some identities systemically allowed access to certain roles, abilities, relationships, or artifacts, while others may be excluded?[61] Benjamin argues that the mythology of technology as "neutral" belies how biased it actually is. This myth of neutrality may even further reinforce social oppression. Anderson et al.'s work in *Minecraft* supports this. They found that "despite a seemingly neutral design," the universe of *Minecraft* reflects "identity markers for gender and race" such as through avatar selections, how identities are presented in YouTube videos, or in fan events, and that diversity of identities is lacking.[62]

In any given game, players may be constrained in how they can express and reflect on their own identities depending on what the game allows or does not allow them to do. Who or what gets included ends up affecting whether a person can express their identity fully through a game. It can also affect the types of people and identities that a player comes into contact with. Thus, game communities and games are not welcoming to all identities, and not everyone equally feels like they belong or are represented through games. Access to particular games or gaming communities may also change over time and across contexts. Belonginess is ephemeral.

The concept of "citizenship" or a "civic identity" may also be too constraining. It may not fully capture how we may participate or how we are already participating in civics. What does it mean to be a good citizen? What type of person is a virtuous one? How does this play out through games? These concepts may be particularly marginalizing to communities of color and youth. Banks argues that the so-called universal conception of citizenship is problematic because it tends to "minimize and suppress the experiences" of people who are already marginalized. Game may further these constraints.[63]

Identity Interacts with Games in Complex Ways

Identity itself is also ephemeral, and can be seen as a complex, constraining, problematic concept. People express and explore aspects of their identities in all different ways, and one's identities may evolve and change throughout one's life.

Adding games to this further complicates it. The word identity is used in so many different ways, and it gets particularly complicated when we think through how games can support identity exploration. Are players playing as themselves in the game? Are they performing as a character and taking on their identity? Or is it some type of hybrid among these differing identities?[64]

In the last section, I discussed how games are biased and constraining. But what about using games to reduce biases? Even good intentions may backfire. Research suggests that a white person playing as a Black avatar can possibly lower biases about Black people. But Yang et al. explain that having white players play as a Black avatar can actually raise biases, depending on how the game is designed and its context of use. They found that in violent video games, when players played as a Black avatar (instead of a white one), this enhanced their negative attitudes toward Black people. Players also acted more aggressively in the game while playing as a Black avatar.[65] An overly strong identity with one's in-group can also get in the way of whether players can connect with those who they deem are in an out-group. Some players of *Rust* were upset when the developers decided to randomize the gender and race of the avatars in the game. These players overly identified with their own gender and race and wanted to continue to choose their avatar's identity, rather than explore another one.

People's biases and misconceptions can also affect whether a game is effective. Roussos and Dovidio found that people with preconceived but inaccurate notions about poverty (such as it being the result of one's choices, rather than systemic pressures) affected how players of the game *Spent* exhibited compassionate attitudes toward poor people.[66] To more effectively use games, we need to continually reflect on our biases and consider how they intersect with our gameplay and our learning and practice of ethics and civics (see more about perspective-taking and biases in chapter 8).[67]

Games Can Emotionally Overwhelm

Players need to be able to feel and express their emotions through games, but they may also get so overwhelmed with their own emotions that they cannot fully participate or learn. For instance, Vituccio describes his cocreated VR experience *Journey through the Camps*, which takes the player on a realistic journey to a concentration camp during the Holocaust (see Figure 7.1). In this experience, "You come into the two camps as a prisoner, you start off on the transport cars and you hear the tracks, you see the light ... the more you look around, the more people are populating the

Figure 7.1 An image from the VR experience *Journey through the Camps*. Image courtesy of Ralph Vituccio and Jaehee Cho.

car ... and you hear people crying, sobbing, and coughing. And we use live testimonials from real Holocaust survivors talking about these locations, that space.... You hear dogs barking, you hear German guards outside screaming at you in German to 'get out, get out, get out.' ... Then you transition into the showers. And you have a real Holocaust survivor talking about how we didn't know what was going to happen; if the gas was going to come up. And then the pipe starts clanking and glowing ... and it starts submitting water." Not surprising, given the authenticity of the voices and visuals, this caused some players to feel too emotionally overwhelmed, and unable to continue the experience.[68]

Too much distress may cause players to recoil or avoid experiences, rather than engaging further with them. Being in another person's shoes through a game can also raise a player's anxiety so much that they may be less willing to interact with others or show compassion. For instance, Nario-Redmond, Gospodinov, and Cobb used a VR game to show the perspectives of people with a disability, such as a mobility disability or dyslexia, and found that after the game people were more upset, ashamed, and helpless. The players did become more empathic and concerned toward people who are disabled, but they did not want to more frequently interact with people with disabilities, partly because they felt like they would not be capable of doing it well, and also because they felt so badly once they experienced their perspectives.[69]

Finally, emotions can be exploited, manipulated, and used for unethical purposes, such as to foster the spread of disinformation or to foment hate. Games may engage with one's emotions but may not necessarily be ethical in how they use those emotions to share knowledge or make change (see more in chapter 10).

Emotions Are Discounted

Emotions are useful for the decision-making, perspective-taking, and communication necessary for full engagement in civic action or ethical choices. Emotion is an integral part of decision-making, especially when it comes to decisions that affect interpersonal, social, civic, political, and societal decisions. Emotions may even help the person making the decision in getting the information they need, consider diverse perspectives, or better understand and evaluate them. Emotions also affect how people actually make decisions—how they process and navigate decisions, and how they act on and implement those decisions.[70]

But there is often a myth or stigma that civic engagement and ethical decision-making should *not* include care, compassion, empathy, or emotions. These myths may affect who can participate and how they can participate. Moreover, emotions themselves may affect whether some can even show up, be part of the conversation, or participate in a community.[71]

Emotion may also be devalued in games. Emotional expression may be constrained in games, in that players cannot emote the ways they want to. Players may be teased or marginalized by others for expressing emotions through games. *Who* gets to express and *how* they get to express it may be inequitable through a game and game community. As described earlier, technology and media are not neutral. They replicate and even propagate injustice and uphold social hierarchies, including who gets to feel, express, and act on those emotions. Games further cement this type of "sentiment" oppression and injustice.

Strategies for Using Games for Expressing Identity and Emotion

Make Belongingness and Inclusion a Priority

Educators need to make sure that all students, of all different backgrounds, feel that they can express their identities, interests, emotions, and idiosyncrasies. Does everyone feel included? Can everyone access the game? Do all students feel like they belong? Can they express all aspects of their identities, whether it is their family status, their pronouns, their skin color, their disabilities, or their sexual identity? Teachers need to lift the hood of a game and see how the system is systemically including or excluding people.

Example in Action: *Kind Words*

The game *Kind Words* designs for inclusion (see Figure 7.2). It also aims to connect strangers. In the game your role is to share and express your emotions to others, through words, and to support and heal others. A virtual deer helps you on your

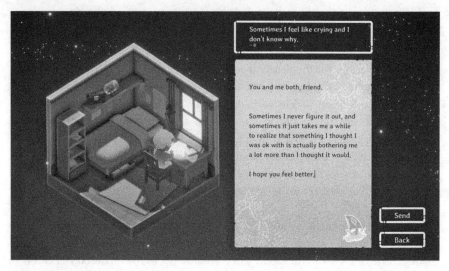

Figure 7.2 An image from the game *Kind Words*. Image courtesy of Ziba Scott and Luigi Guatieri.

journey, which involves connecting with others through anonymous letters. You have four actions you can take: you can write a letter, such as by sharing something that is worrying you; you can read others' letters and decide which ones to respond to; you can respond to others' letters; or you can send a paper airplane to the whole community by writing a few lines of encouraging words.

The words are kind, by design. The game encourages connection through emotional expression. It asks, "What are you worried about? Maybe someone else is too." Throughout, the deer gives you tips on how to write a meaningful letter, such as by providing prompts on what to write, by explaining that bullying and name-calling are not tolerated, and by reminding players that no one should share any personally identifiable information. The deer says, "You can let people know you hear them, and that they are not alone."

The letters, written by anonymous writers, express people's authentic inner fears, desires, and emotions, such as a need for acceptance, a desire for connection, or a concern that they are not enough. The responses and letters are generally supportive and caring, with most people either talking about their own interests (e.g., favorite games), giving encouraging words, or sharing personal stories to show how we are all connected. When I played *Kind Words*, I received paper airplanes with words like "I hope you all know that someone out here cares about you." I also wrote a letter about my fears in writing this book, and I received letters of support and encouragement in return.

Teachers can use *Kind Words* to practice reading, giving advice to peers, or engaging in other forms of social and emotional learning (SEL). Teachers can use the game to help students safely share stories or worries, and to practice writing letters of support for others.

One drawback of the game for learning purposes is that (by design) the letters are anonymous and personal, so the teacher should not be reading the students' letters or grading them. If teachers want to more directly scaffold letter-writing, or support emotional expression through words, they can first play the game as a class, together. Teachers can then engage the students in a discussion around the letters received in the game, such as by identifying the emotions in a letter, deliberating ways to respond to them, or analyzing the ethical choices that the letter brings up. (Note again that the letters in the game come from anonymous strangers, so teachers may want to review and choose some first before sharing them with the class.)

Another possibility is to have the students first play the game briefly, on their own. Then, teachers can support letter sharing outside of the game. Teachers can pair students to write each other letters, or two or more teachers can pair their classes to write letters to each other's classes (see more tips in the notes).[72]

Let Students Express Themselves through Games

Teachers can also use a game as a springboard for helping players to further understand, shape, and express their own identities. For instance, players can use *Animal Crossing: New Horizons* as a way of expressing their identities. In this game, players can customize their avatars, design rooms in their virtual homes, and alter their islands with different flora and digital objects such as trees, statues, or paths. Students can then discuss how these modifications reflect who they are. When I played *Animal Crossing: New Horizons*, I altered my avatar to look like me and I changed my home to look like a library, my favorite place. Through playing the game I learned what I value and how I see myself, as well as how I hope others will see me. When my daughter played the game she dressed herself in purple, and made the living room of her home into an aquarium.

Example in Action: *What Remains of Edith Finch*
Darvasi, a teacher at an all-boys' private school in Toronto, used the game *What Remains of Edith Finch* as a unit on identity in his twelfth-grade English language arts (ELA) class. In this month-long unit he used a number of different assignments to help the students share and express their identities.[73]

To play *What Remains of Edith Finch*, you visit different characters' bedrooms and learn about their personal histories through the artifacts in their room. The rooms function as cabinets of curiosity where the player can pick up, hold, and interact with the artifacts. The rooms and their objects become figurative doorways through which the player is able to explore the inner world of that character and their stories. Darvasi explains that the game helped his students express their identities because it enabled them to directly interact with in-game artifacts, and to think about how "these touch-stones of artifacts relate to yourself, which can nourish the identity work."[74]

Darvasi used a series of exercises to help students feel increasingly more comfort-able with expressing their own identities with others. In one exercise, students needed to bring in personal objects. One student brought in a hockey stick because "he found a lot of security, fulfillment and satisfaction through playing hockey."[75] Class projects included creating a "Museum of Me," which might include devising an artistic assem-blage of their personal artifacts, writing an interactive story using Twine that tours the objects, or developing an online website featuring the artifacts. Darvasi explains that one student created a suitcase that functioned as a mini-art museum, where on the outside he included all the "different destinations and places he dreams of going. And on the inside, it was the more personal stuff that relate to his internal sense of identity or internal sense of self."[76]

These types of activities helped the students reveal themselves and learn about each other. It also helped Darvasi, as the teacher, to express his own identity, such as how his relationship with his father had transformed over the years, something that he believes helped his students feel more comfortable when thinking about their own relationships with their parents. Darvasi noted that the students became increasingly more open about sharing things they would not normally share in the classroom.[77]

One of the reasons this unit worked so well was also because of the type of inclusive classroom environment that Darvasi fostered with his students. He explains that "it was a format where you enter as deeply as you feel comfortable entering."[78] Thus, a game, coupled with an appropriate context, can help a student feel more comfortable with their own identities, and safer to express them.

Acknowledge Emotions

Emotions matter, when playing, learning, and connecting with ourselves and our communities. Students are dealing with all different emotions and traumas, as are we. Teachers should consider the emotional traumas wrapped in people's identities and acknowledge that these emotions exist and matter. How can we civically engage or connect with others (and how can we teach or learn) without first acknowledging and accepting ourselves and our emotional needs? Teachers can use games—and all aspects of their own teaching—to help model for students how to identify, express, and share these emotions and reflect on how they affect us.[79]

First and foremost, teachers need to ensure that students continue to feel secure. Can students opt out of games or conversations, for instance, if they are too emo-tionally overwhelmed to participate? Is a game safe for a student? Are students being made to relive traumas of their pasts, like racial oppression, genocide, sexual assault, gun violence, or war? Teachers should weigh whether to enforce game play, and should consider giving students the active choice to find and play games that emo-tionally and constructively connect with them.[80]

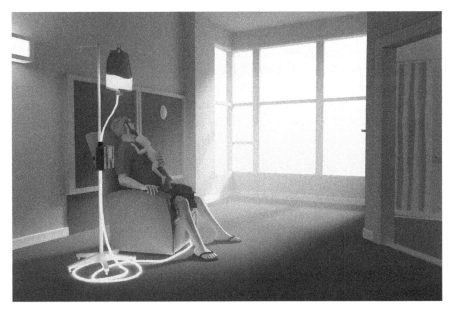

Figure 7.3 An image from the game *That Dragon, Cancer*. Image courtesy of Numinous Games.

Example in Action: *That Dragon, Cancer*

That Dragon, Cancer is a game made by two parents (Ryan and Amy Green) who were faced with the real-world cancer illness of their young son, Joel (see Figure 7.3).[81] They started to make the game when he was in remission from cancer, but while they were making the game, the cancer returned and their son died. I use this game in my class because it gives us permission to be vulnerable together, and more open to engage in a conversation about difficult topics and emotions—like loss and grief. It also helps me to feel free to talk about my own personal experience of losing a son, as well as the experience of having another son in the hospital for many months.

To ground our conversation, we use the game *That Dragon, Cancer* and we continue to go back to it whenever emotions begin to overwhelm us. We discuss how the game's design evokes emotion, represents love and loss, and shapes the expression of the family's grief. In a scene from the game, players eavesdrop on a conversation between parents (the Greens) and a doctor (an oncologist), who explains that Joel's cancer is back. As the scene unfolds and they speak, water begins to fill up in the room, and it soon overtakes the parents. We watch as Joel's father, Ryan, falls downward until he is pulled up by his wife, representing his feeling of drowning in grief. In another scene, the player, as Ryan, tries to give a thirsty Joel a beverage in a hospital room, but the wailing son is too sick to accept anything. As we try to help Joel (as Ryan) we continually fail, and we feel his sense of helplessness. The game features real voices, sounds, and interactions from Joel and his family, including a voicemail message that Amy Green leaves about her son and sounds of real crying by Joel. This adds to the authenticity of the loss and the family's grief, which in turn enhances the emotional impact of the game, as well as our ability to take on the perspective of the family, and empathize with their difficult situation.[82]

For students (and for us), however, sometimes this game is too raw or emotionally stirring, which gets in the way of learning. I give all students the option not to play. In these cases I provide an alternate assignment, such as inviting students to design their own games around an emotional state, such as serenity, helplessness, envy, or hope.

8

How Do We Cultivate Compassion and Respect for Others?

What is it like to be a cat? A dog? A bird? A taller person? A shorter person? Close your eyes and imagine for a moment. What would it be like to be an older person with limited mobility, a baby living in an orphanage, or a person on death row? Now, imagine you are a tree in the rainforest. Your body is the trunk of the tree, and as you lift up your arms, they act as tree branches. You can reach for the sunlight, feel water drip onto your leaves, and sense a bug tickle up your spine. This is what happens in *Tree*, a VR experience where players embody a tree and take on the role of what it means to be another type of living object. The project helps participants to imagine what it feels like to *not* be rooted in our everyday human experience, but to instead take on the role of something different and to see, hear, feel, and taste what the world offers when you are experiencing this type of perspective.[1]

Next, imagine you are a person, but not yourself. "You have now become Mike Sterling; look at yourself in the mirror." In the VR experience *1000 Cut Journey*, players take on the role of a Black male, Mike Sterling, and encounter racism and racist microaggressions as a child, teenager, and an adult (see Figure 8.1).[2] The scenarios are based on real-world experiences and personal accounts—such as interactions with police officers or interviews for jobs—and are meant to help players understand what it is like to walk in someone else's shoes.

These experiences tap into something human. We all have tried to imagine what it is like to be someone or something else. And perhaps we have also wanted the reverse. We have yearned for others to understand us and "get" what we have gone through or experienced. Yet one of the more frustrating things about being human is that we cannot fully step outside of ourselves and our own perspectives and put on another person's set of needs, interests, and views. Rather, human beings are bounded by their selves, making them unable to truly inhabit someone else. Since we cannot *be* someone else, how do we more fully understand others so that we can connect with them, empathize with them, and see them as part of our civic communities?

In this chapter I consider how games enable the practice of empathy, compassion, and care, as well as respect for others. At the heart of all of these practices is perspective-taking.

We the Gamers. Karen Schrier, Oxford University Press. © Oxford University Press 2021.
DOI: 10.1093/oso/9780190926106.003.0008

Figure 8.1 An image from the game *1000 Cut Journey*. Image courtesy of Cogburn Research Group and Virtual Human Interaction Lab.

Why Teach Perspective-Taking?

Perspective-Taking Can Enhance Compassion

Perspective-taking is the act of considering someone else's views. It involves thinking about issues, evidence, choices, or feelings from the point of view of another person.[3] Taking on others' perspectives helps us to better create solutions for our communities because it encourages us to consider multiple possibilities rather than just settle on one set solution. Perspective-taking can also enhance empathy and compassion, which may further civic connectedness, community building, acceptance and openness to other views and identities, and the ability to make more well-reasoned ethical choices.

Empathy relates to process of embodying someone else's views or emotions and taking on their world, whether it is filled with happiness or suffering, or something else. It is the desire to uncover what someone else believes and what led them to believe it. Empathy has been debated as being related to emotions or feeling another's suffering, and as being related to cognition or thinking about what someone might be feeling. Zaki adds a third aspect to empathy, which is related to motivation: "Does a person, after experiencing the emotional and cognitive reactions to another's suffering, have a desire to alleviate the suffering of that person?"[4]

Empathy is seen as distinct from compassion, which is typically described as also requiring some action. Compassion involves understanding and feeling what someone else is feeling, and then acting on it, such as by being nurturing, caring, or helpful, or just by joining in on someone else's joy. Practicing empathy and compassion are acts of bravery, because you need to be vulnerable enough to be open to someone else's emotions and views. You also need to be aware of and manage your own emotions to be able to meet someone else where they are, rather than where you want them to be.[5]

Taking on others' perspectives and practicing empathy and compassion may help people to better understand where someone else is coming from; to listen to their views, stories, and histories; and to learn more about what a community needs. It can help people to identify and care about the civic problems, values, or needs of another person or community.[6] This in turn can help others also care about *our* needs. In fact, simply feeling like someone may be caring about our perspectives can help us to have more empathy for them.[7]

Perspective-Taking Reduces Bias

Taking on new perspectives and practicing empathy and compassion may also support greater civic and ethical understanding by reducing our biases. First, perspective-taking helps people to stop and make sure that they understand another's arguments or views before proceeding.[8] This can help us to avoid confirmation bias, or the tendency that human beings have to believe or confirm ideas that they already believe, and reject those that they do not.[9]

Perspective-taking can also help us to see more people in our community as human beings who matter, and who deserve justice, fairness, and equitable governance, care, and civic support. This may help people to recognize their own biases, improve attitudes toward people who are marginalized, and encourage more open-mindedness, all practices also related to democratic engagement.[10] In one study, for instance, adults were provided with a story about a Moroccan immigrant and were guided through a perspective-taking exercise; the research suggested that the exercise was moderately effective for reducing stereotypes and intergroup biases.[11] In another exercise, participants were invited to take on the perspective of a Black student, and the results suggested that they had more positive, empathetic attitudes toward Black people afterward.[12]

Perspective-Taking Can Enhance Respect For Others

Perspective-taking can also help to hone cultural awareness and respect for others. Respect for others relates to expressing genuine care for and civility toward others, and recognizing their human worth and dignity. It involves valuing other cultures and ways of living. These are essential skills, as students need to be culturally literate to navigate online and offline civic communities. "Culture" does not just refer to national identities or ethnic communities, but also differences in professional realms or even in gaming communities. We are not just denizens of our own countries but also "citizens of the mediated world." With new ways of connecting with others—whether through an online forum, livestreamed game, or study abroad trip—students need to be culturally humble and able to fluidly move among different cultures and their differing norms and values.[13]

Culture also affects our civic processes and how we make decisions. On one level, we understand that there are rules and laws—such as the right of all US citizens to vote once they turn eighteen years old. But on another level, culture matters in how those rights get exercised, who gets access to those rights, and how we think of ourselves as someone who can exercise them.[14] To fully participate and make social change, we need to be able to understand the ins and outs of political structures and their differing cultures to know what types of behaviors are acceptable, and what types of resources are necessary. While we may want to start a small business or plant a tree, we also need to understand the zoning laws that regulate properties in an area. Beyond the laws, we also need to know how to find these laws, who decides and interprets them, and how they may be differently applied or enforced based on the relationships, cultural understandings, and interactions of a community. While laws may get ratified, culture often determines how they get applied and enforced, and whether they get revised in the future.[15]

Thus, we need to be culturally aware and culturally competent.[16] Cultural humility may also be what is necessary to fully shape and address civic solutions across cultural needs.[17] Tervalon and Murray-Garcia describe cultural humility as incorporating "a lifelong commitment to self-evaluation and critique, to redressing the power imbalances in the [teacher-student] dynamic, and to developing mutually beneficial and nonpaternalistic partnerships with communities on behalf of individuals and defined populations."[18] Developing this type of cultural humility—being proactively mindful of one's cultural biases, thoughtful in critiquing and addressing systemic problems, and able to navigate across different cultural norms and values—can help sustain full civic participation for one's self, as well as help to elevate it for others.[19]

How Do Games Enhance Compassion and Respect?

Games Can Encourage Role-Playing

As discussed in the last chapter, players may be able to express and explore aspects of their own and others' identities. Perspective-taking and empathy can also work together to spur players to further explore different identities, and understand others' views, needs, goals, and feelings.[20] One way that games can encourage this is through role-playing. Role-playing is the process of performing or embodying other roles, characters, mindsets, voices, or moral styles.[21] Role-playing can allow people to step outside of their everyday roles (such as that of a student), and take on a new role (such as that of a teacher).

Games encourage players to take on the role of someone or something else, perform the actions and make the decisions they would make, interact with characters and other players as someone in that role might, and begin to see the world in a new way. In the game *Lives in Balance*, players take on the role of government officials during a global pandemic. While in this role, the players need to meet with other players and decide how to reopen their states, while navigating different sources of information.[22]

Games can use also historical perspectives and roles.[23] Consider the *Reacting to the Past* series of scenarios, where students take on the role of someone from a historic moment, like the French Revolution in the 1790s. They need to enact that role's perspectives through what they say in speeches or in how they interpret documents.[24] Or consider a playful exercise described by Lim, where students take on the role of a historic character and need to write letters as if they were that person.[25] Games such as *Reliving the Revolution* center on historic moments, where students can relive past choices and events through the role of a specific person during that time period (see more in chapter 5).

Perspective-Taking Through Games May Reduce Biases

Through games, players may be able to learn about and inhabit another person's perspectives, consider how it differs from their own perspectives, and experience new views on topics and issues.[26] This type of perspective-taking through games may also help to reduce biases about others, which may affect prejudice toward certain groups. As described in the previous chapter, biases are preconceived notions about an individual or group that affects how we judge them. Prejudice is a systemically "unfavorable attitude or belief toward a specific group of people." Simonovits et al. created a game where players need to take on the perspectives of Roma and refugees. The game significantly reduced prejudice toward stigmatized groups in Hungary (Roma and refugees). This reduction in prejudice lasted at least a month, and also resulted in changes in voting behavior in Hungary.[27]

Some games may help us to embody people and through this, we become more aware of the prejudice or discrimination they may face. In the *I Am a Man* VR experience, the player is put into different 1960s Memphis-based scenes and locations related to the Civil Rights Movement in the United States, such as the Lorraine Motel where Dr. Martin Luther King Jr. was shot. In one scene, players engage in a peaceful protest and in another, they interact with a police officer, who asks the player to surrender.[28] In Thompson's analog role-playing game *&maybetheywontkillyou*, the player takes on the role of a Black man in a hoodie who needs to make choices about how to interact with others in different (imaginary) encounters, such as whether to speak or be silent while walking through a grocery store or past a police officer. Players may get frisked by police and may not even make it home, depending on their choices and the outcome of their dice rolls. In the VR experience *Injustice*, players play as a Black man, and encounter a situation involving racial profiling and police brutality, and then need to respond to it.

An open question is whether these types of experiences actually enhance perspective-taking and reduce bias, and how a player's identity may factor into this. How might these games affect us—or even harm us—if we share aspects of our identity with the person or peoples harmed in the game? The limitations section in this chapter will delve into this further.[29]

Playing with Others May Enhance Compassion

Playing with other people may help students to develop and practice skills like perspective-taking, empathy, and compassion, alongside collaborative and communication skills. Playing together supports empathy-related skills in part because you need to imagine the game *as a team*, which requires you to think about what other players are experiencing.[30] In the cooperative board game *Pandemic*, players need to work together to contain the outbreak of a disease.[31] Players need to listen to each other's strategies and work together to figure out the best course of action.

Spending time with others and working collaboratively can help to build trust, intimacy, connectedness, and perspective-taking. Research suggests that people may be more empathetic to others if they feel like they are more like them (or consider them as being part of their in-group) versus those who they believe are unlike them (or a member of an out-group).[32] People become more familiar with and more trusting of others the more time they spend with them, particularly if this time is spent meaningfully connecting. Games can enable this.[33] For example, players in *Way* voiced becoming more trusting of a stranger after playing with them and relying on them for the duration of the game.[34] In my research on *Fable III*, players did not want to sacrifice their friend in the game, a virtual character named Walter, because they had spent 10 hours prior with this character getting to know him and being mentored by him.[35]

Games do not have to be multiplayer, however, to be effective in this way. Teachers can pair or group students together to play a single-player game where they need to listen to others' views and decide on a course of action together. (See more about this in chapter 6.) In-game characters (NPCs) can also serve as partners for players, and help to share differing perspectives. In *Fable III*, players need to make ethical and civic-related decisions about the fictional town of Albion, such as whether to raise taxes or drain a lake (or whether to sacrifice Walter, as previously explained). During an in-game virtual town hall meeting, two characters (NPCs) represent the opposing sides and debate the policy with Page explaining one side, and Reaver explaining the other. Page typically wants to spend money on social supports and welfare for all the citizens, whereas Reaver wants to save and gain money to spend on military protection. The players I interviewed typically aligned themselves with Page, but also listened to the opposing view, embodied by the character Reaver, and sometimes chose to follow his advice.[36] (For more about *Fable III*, see chapter 4).

One thing to note is that players may be more able to empathize with another player in a game, or even a virtual character in a game, rather than "ourselves" in the game (the avatar that we play as). Research suggests that we empathize more readily with an avatar that is in a third-person perspective (that we "see"), rather than an avatar that is in a first-person perspective (which we "embody"). This may be because we move and control this character as if it were ourselves. We do not typically empathize with ourselves because we already embody ourselves. Rather, we empathize with others, who are distinct from us.[37]

Story in Games May Enhance Compassion

Story can also factor into the practice of perspective-taking, compassion, and empathy. I have not yet focused heavily on story in this book, but it may be an important factor in how games encourage players to take on new perspectives and practice empathy and compassion. Story can also enhance civics and ethics practice. Story "allows access into other people's lives and opens us further to practicing empathy … story provides a context to how we view ethics, which helps us further understand ethical issues, our own ethical assumptions, and makes us more ethically self-aware."[38]

Games can share stories in a number of ways. They may enable us to explore a new world and interact with its characters, places, and conflicts. They may have us take on the role of a character who is sharing their story through dialogue or narration, or through the choices we make and the actions we perform. Games may even enable players to cocreate stories together. However, games do not have to relay, tell, or share stories, and many games have no narrative components.

Games may help players feel more connected to another's story and more open to their perspectives because we can actually perform part of their story. Interacting with perspectives, through stories in games, can help players to better understand another's obstacles, emotions, and mindset. For instance, Rajaratnam's game *Go and Come Back*, explores memories of the Sri Lankan civil war while telling a story about a Tamil person and their family dealing with Alzheimer's disease. This game uses story to share a human perspective on a civil war as well as on a disease.[39] *Mind Field* is an interactive experience that helps people become more aware of different forms of microaggressions.[40] The game lets the player make dialogue choices while exploring fictionalized versions of real-life stories about experiencing bias. In one vignette players can interact with a study group, where the students are dividing up responsibilities on the project. One of the students starts to voice that her role on the project has been diminished. The player can decide how to respond to it, such as by dismissing her feelings. After the vignette is over, we also hear a longer perspective, voiced by the real person behind the character, who explains what it actually felt like when her role was diminished. The authenticity of this perspective further contributes to our ability to better understand her real-life experience. Moreover, because we are actively making choices that affect this person in the game, we feel more responsible to them, which may affect how we listen to and respond to their stories.[41]

Story can help players experience and challenge their own biases, such that they could expand their perspectives. Cragg explains that "to weaken the grip of prejudice in a society, people, particularly children have to be brought into contact with images, stories, experiences that challenge stereotypes and change perceptions."[42] The more we interact with other's stories and cultures, the more familiar they become and the less distant they seem from ourselves. Story sharing can reduce the "othering" that leads to biased attitudes and behaviors.[43] For instance, the VR and immersive journalism experience *Project Syria* puts players in the perspective of someone who is in Syria, and bearing direct witness to violent events and random acts of terror.[44] Creator de la Pena explains that "you feel like you are actual there … If we can make people think about how difficult these circumstances are, perhaps they can start to think about what kinds of changes they too can bring about."[45] Experiencing the Syria bombing first-hand through VR makes the event more real, more tangible, and more visceral. It makes what may otherwise be a far-away story seem more immediate. It is harder to dismiss this perspective because we have embodied it first-hand.

Moreover, Liu explains that embodying others' stories and telling our own stories helps to make social change because it helps to empower and organize people, and spur them to challenge the status quo. Liu explains, "This is more than stepping into someone else's shoes—it's stepping into the story of *how* someone else came to be wearing those shoes," which can also help us to visualize and solve potential problems.[46] Take for instance Kirby's viral game that tells the story of one day in the life of a student entering campus in fall 2020. This game helped people to imagine what it would be like to be on a university campus as a student amid a global pandemic, beyond the policies, rules, and regulations.[47] Story, then, can help people "to citizen" by connecting with others' lives, and connecting lives to real-world change. It helps us to collectively imagine a better future.

Games Can Enhance Respect for Others

Games can help people to navigate different cultural spaces, whether online, in a game, or in their classrooms. Students do not just need to understand their own cultures—they also need to be able to adapt rapidly to different niches, norms, and values.[48] Games can also help students to respect other cultures by showing how other cultures address social issues and humanistic questions, like how we should live together or be governed. By acknowledging and respecting other cultural views of ethics and public governance, we enable more voices to access the public and make change.

Games can also help culture persist over time, such as by helping to bring together players who are dispersed, in transit, physically distanced, or not able to access other forms of cultural transmission. For instance, LaPensée describes the VR game *Along the River of Spacetime*, which was inspired by her mother's worldview of "Indigenous futurisms" and relays Anishinaabeg teachings and stories through technology. She explains that it "shares Anishinaabeg teachings relating to land practices, star knowledge, and quantum physics in an interactive non-linear journey about restoring rivers and their ecosystems by activating Anishinaabe constellations. Coded particle systems of light, hand drawn art brought into form with copper, and 360° film of riverways running through Nkwejong in Michigan are merged into technology-empowered storytelling."[49]

In fact, engaging in a game is an act of culture. Davisson and Gehm, building on work by Bogost, argue that the repetitive ritual of play helps to reinforce norms and systems, including cultural ones. They look at how games mimic "civic rituals such as military service or campaigning for public office, [which] has a persuasive impact on player's interpretation of those activities in real life. This functions rhetorically to not only develop citizenship as a mode of engagement, but to make larger normative claims about the role a good citizen plays in the foundation of a good society."[50]

Games can also inspire players to engage in the critique of these systems, and to help challenge norms. Ruiz explains that "games (not all games, certainly!) can make arguments about a social system's structure that can help support or challenge it. A game can require that the player reflect upon her own place in the real world and its systems, as well as upon her behavior, assumptions, and societal norms. A game can require that the player work to identify social needs and design civic reform." Ruiz's *The Directing Game* helps players engage with film production and filmmaker cultures, and to create their own inclusive, collaborative-based culture. This helps to further establish an inclusive culture in the film program at the University of California-Santa Cruz, where it has been played.[51]

Limitations to Using Games for Compassion and Respect

Perspective-Taking May Further Bias

Role-playing and perspective-taking are not always effective. Nario-Redmond et al. found that perspective-taking can contribute to flawed or even stereotypical understandings of others. Work by Wang et al. suggests that perspective-taking may be more effective in Western cultures, but not as useful in East Asian cultures.[52]

Research on the effectiveness of VR and games in supporting perspective-taking and civic action is inconsistent. In one experiment looking at attitudes toward the homeless, the researchers found that players had more positive attitudes toward people who are homeless if they did a VR experience where they took on the role of someone who became homeless, than if they just did a traditional perspective-taking exercise. But a replication of the study showed no differences. In both studies they found that those who participated in the VR experience were more likely to sign a petition supporting people who are homeless.[53] Yet in another study, a VR exercise was able to enhance perspective-taking, but it did not spur prosocial behavior.[54] Likewise, as described in chapter 7, studies on games and bias have shown inconsistent results. On the one hand, some research suggests that white players may decrease their implicit bias when playing as darker-skinned avatars in a virtual space.[55] On the other hand, players may use more stereotypes and implicit bias when playing as a Black avatar than a white one in a virtual space.[56]

Moreover, Olson and Harrell's research on VR and race suggests that players' preconceived notions about race factor into how bias in a game is identified and evaluated. They designed a simulation of a racially discriminatory event between a Black student (played by the player) and a white female teacher (NPC), where the student was falsely accused of plagiarism. They found that those players who had a "color-blind racial attitude" or an attitude that they "don't see color" (i.e., they are not aware of their racial privilege) may empathize more with the racist white teacher and may not interpret the teacher's accusation as being biased against the Black student. They may blame the Black student for their incompetence rather than see the systemic and structural racial issues that underlie the interactions between the teacher and the student.[57]

Perspective-taking and role-playing in a game can also backfire when a person feels threatened or emotionally overwhelmed, which can raise their anxiety and make them less willing to interact with people who are different from them.[58] As I discussed in chapter 7, researchers found that when players took on a role of a person who is disabled, which led to more empathy, it also may have contributed to more stigma and fewer interactions with people who are disabled.[59] Just because someone has empathy and feels for those who are hurt or marginalized does not mean they will act ethically or morally.[60] In the game *Injustice*, players experience interactions as a Black man, including an event involving police brutality. Does playing *Injustice* enhance empathy for people who are dealing with police bias? Does it help us to understand police brutality better? How does it affect what we might do if we saw police brutality, or how we might make changes to reduce and deter police brutality?[61] Empathy itself is a complicated concept in that people may have empathy for others, but may feel unable or unwilling to act on it to constructively help or connect with another.[62]

Role-playing without sufficient support or consideration even risks enhancing stereotypes about groups to which the player does not belong, and may further bias and oppression.[63] For instance, the ADL explains that simulation activities to teach about historic atrocities, where players take on identities such as that of Nazis or slaveowners, may trivialize victims' experiences, reinforce negative views toward victims, encourage identification with oppressors, or be emotionally upsetting and traumatizing to the participants.[64] Thus perspective-taking and role-playing may lead to more misunderstandings, and even harm.

Moreover, story can backfire too, and can lead to further inaccuracies or misunderstandings. People can use storytelling to emotionally manipulate others and to exploit empathic concern. People can also use story to misrepresent past and current events, spread disinformation, or alter how we perceive facts, laws, or policies (see more in chapter 10). Story may be a powerful technique, but it needs to be used wisely, ethically, and humanely.

Perspective-Taking Itself Can Be Unethical

The very process of perspective-taking may itself be unethical. No game can enable a person to completely inhabit someone else's life. Playing a game cannot fully access what someone else has gone through or the steps that got them to where they currently stand. Thinking that we can accomplish this through a game is itself problematic.[65]

For one thing, players may erroneously think that they fully understand a perspective (such as what it is like to be a Black person interacting with the police, a person who is trans, or a Syrian refugee) just because they have played a game where they took on or learned about this perspective.[66] If we take on another perspective in a game, we may not be accurate in knowing what the perspective is, as it is really what *we* think the other person is thinking, rather than what *they* actually think, feel, or believe.[67] Players may *believe* they are taking on someone's views or emotions, but they may be incorrect. While we can try to imagine what someone else might feel, or what being a tree or cat might be like, it is incredibly difficult to suddenly lift outside of our own perspectives, mindsets, time periods, and contexts. So on the one hand, perspective-taking can enhance empathy, familiarity, and connection, but on the other, it can possibly enhance misunderstandings, stigma, further stereotyping, and disconnection.[68]

Antropy explains that her autobiographical game *Dys4ia* can never fully "confer an understanding of her lived experience, marginalization, and personal struggle."[69] To express this further, Antropy created a real-world exhibit called "Empathy Game," which featured one pair of furry boots in the middle of a room. The "Empathy Game" asked people to try on the boots, as if to actually emulate walking in her shoes. Each experience earned the participant one point.[70] "'You can get a high score on that game,' Antropy said, 'but you're probably not going to beat mine. You can spend hours stomping around in those boots and it will only bring you a fraction closer to knowing what it's like to be me, to be trans.'"[71]

Empathy itself is a concept and term that has been heavily critiqued. Bloom argues that empathy does not support moral reasoning, and may even hinder our ability to reason or care for others. He argues that concepts such as compassion may be more relevant. Others have critiqued the use of the term, such as being incorrectly applied to games, or inconsistently used in research. Ruberg disentangles the messiness of the term empathy, and has also argued for using more specific phrases and terms for the goals we may have for games, such as allyship, loss, or caring, rather than relying on empathy as a catch-all buzzword. In addition, Ruberg writes, "a focus on 'empathy' establishes and justifies discriminatory beliefs about how video game[s] should make players feel and who has the right to experience those feelings." The application of empathy disempowers the complexity of feelings that players and developers may have while they design, play, or grapple with a game.

Moreover, Nakamura calls perspective-taking through games a type of "virtual tourism," where a player may spend some time in a virtual space as a Black, Brown, Indigenous person, other person of color, or a different gender identity not to respect or honor their differences, but to take on and off their identities (free of any dire consequences) and pretend they understand some underlying truth about being this person (a truth that they could never fully comprehend).[72] For instance, Mortley points out that painting one's avatar's skin Black in the game *Roblox* to support Black Lives Matter is a type of digital "Blackface." Roxworthy, using work by Hartman, suggests that perspective-taking and identification with others who are not you may even be a form of violence, in that you are erasing the other's experience by taking it on yourself.[73]

The process of participating in a new perspective can be emotionally taxing or even harmful to the player, too. A person who has faced police brutality in real life may be re-harmed through a game that asks them to experience a similar type of event. A woman may be traumatized if she plays as a woman in a game who is discriminated against, bullied, or violated due to that identity. During a game, one's role in a game and one's own real-world identity may also start to affect each other. A person could be upset by something that happens within the game and then continue to feel upset even after the game is over. This is called bleed in the larp (live action role-playing) community.[74] As Vanek explains, "The advantage of live action role playing is that you can exercise emotional reactions and ethical choices because you are in a controlled safe environment and can see how you would react in the situation." However, some people can understandably have negative emotional responses that need to be addressed. So while there may be some educational merit—and emotional resonance—to perspective-taking in a game, it may also end up having unintended consequences, even if the game aims to create a safe environment for experimenting with these perspectives.

Games May Misrepresent Cultures

As mentioned in chapter 4, another limitation of games is that they often simplify their topics and themes to make them easier or more relatable to play. This often means using icons or colors to represent ideas, factions, or beliefs so that players can readily work with or manage them to reach their goals. However, these types of oversimplifications can also run the risk of distilling something as complex as culture into stereotypical representations.

When we aim to represent cultures of which we are unfamiliar, or even when we play games where we learn about different cultural beliefs, we may inadvertently engage in cultural appropriation by adopting the customs, clothing, language, and behaviors of a culture without meaningfully and respectfully engaging in its context. This ends up being exploitative rather than enriching. LaPensée explains that "there is a fine line between genuine representation and appropriation. Best approaches for inclusivity during game development involve meaningful collaboration and facilitating self-determination." This could mean ensuring that the games we play in our classes have included game developers and experts in the design process who are embedded in a culture, or who can accurately represent its voices. It means advocating for fully involving people in designing the representations of their culture, and giving interpretive control and design influence.[75] It also means avoiding relying on one person or one game to be the sole "voice" of a culture or identity, and to understand that identities and cultures are multilayered and complex.[76]

Culture can also evolve over time, and what may seem sensitive at the time of creation may not continue to be appropriate once norms and values change. For instance, two *Mission US* modules (on the Cheyenne people and slavery in the antebellum era) have been critiqued for not realistically portraying characters and cultures, and not providing enough historic context and nuance to these topics. The fact that they are animated games may also feel culturally inappropriate. Thus an overriding question is how we should represent and continue to represent cultures and complex topics through games.[77] If a game is imperfect—as they all are—is it better to have a game that expresses a flawed view of an important topic, or no game at all? (See more on *Mission US* later in the chapter).

Furthermore, if games and their developers are not inclusive, diverse, and culturally aware, this affects how those games can in turn teach these skills to others. The games industry and development culture need to change to become more inclusive for the benefit of games and for society overall. Ruiz argues that we need to prioritize inclusive practice such that "game makers (both independent and working in the industry), game scholars, and game educators ... work at making this an inclusive practice and culture."[78]

We need to critique our culture, cultural values, and systemic norms around games, such as what it means to design, to create, and to play—and what it means "to citizen" through games. Games are not neutral; they embed our cultural biases. Civics and civic institutions are also culturally constructed and constricting, such as constraining our conception of what good citizenship is.[79] We need to reinvent our cultural institutions with justice and ethics at the forefront. Benjamin explains that we need to rethink "what counts as innovation, remaining alert to the ways that race and other hierarchies of difference get embedded in the creation of new designs, and ultimately refashioning the relationship between technology and society by prioritizing justice and equity."[80]

Strategies for Using Games to Support Compassion and Respect

Use Historical Perspectives and Roles

One way teachers can encourage players to listen to others' perspectives is by having students take on a role of a person in the past and relive their historic moment. This type of role-playing could help students practice historical empathy, or taking on the view point of someone from history, inhabiting their social and historic context and using this to understand attitudes and actions from yesteryear.[81] Even if we cannot computationally or entirely recreate a moment from the past, we can still share authentic historic perspectives through a game.

Lim explains that using historic roles is effective because it gives players enough distance that they can fully embrace and empathize with this role. On the other hand, she explains that sometimes players "forget" to think from that historic figures' viewpoint and they may instead revert back to their own views. Using clear, easy-to-understand profile sheets, role cards, or even a digital character that a player could embody through a game could help to continually remind players of their historical figures' goals, needs, and fears, and can support more immersive role-playing and perspective-taking.

Using historical and real-world events and perspectives needs to be handled sensitively. We need to make sure not to harm or even traumatize students—which means designing access to historic attitudes in restorative and healing ways.[82] Teachers need to consider: How do we handle historic perspectives or roles that are distressing?

Example in Action: *Mission US*

Mission US is a series of digital games that take place in specific moments in the past where players have the opportunity to experience a new perspective on that moment, such as Revolutionary War–era Boston or Kentucky before the Civil War.[83] In one of the modules, *For Crown or Colony?*, the player plays as Nat Wheeler, a printer's apprentice, who serves as the avatar. As Nat, the player needs to interact with people who have differing views on British rule and the possible uprisings by the colonists.[84] At one point in the game, the player experiences the moments leading up to the Boston Massacre. Each player gets a unique series of randomly generated views of the massacre on King Street. Some players may get views of snowballs being thrown by colonists, while others may see the British soldiers holding threatening-looking bayonets.[85] Students then need to sift through these different perspectives, develop their own perspectives on the event, and interpret what happened at King Street in an in-game deposition.[86]

At certain points during the game (such as after the massacre event), or after the game is over, teachers may also facilitate discussions among students about their differing perspectives.[87] Teachers might ask: Why did we have different views? Why did we make different choices? This helps students to understand that the past is interpretable, and what we think happened in history is determined by how we view it through our own unique lenses. It also helps players to consider that the results of a vote or another collective action was not predetermined. It did not *need* to happen the way that it actually happened, and an outcome often relies on "who showed up, and which voices and perspectives are shared" in the moment.[88]

The example of *Mission US* also brings up a different point about cultural relevancy, and how the same game may itself be interpreted differently, culturally, at different periods of time. Some schools have banned the use of *Mission US* because of the way it portrayed Black and Indigenous people in the game, and how it did not provide enough nuance in the representation of the culture and historic time period. They also felt that it was culturally inappropriate to use an animated game to share complex and challenging topics such as racism and slavery. However, the designers intended, in making these games, to share the perspectives of people throughout history—including those of marginalized people—a complex goal that is challenging to fully achieve through a game, let alone any experience.

So what do we do with imperfect cultural representations? Do we remove them from our curricula outright, or do we contextualize them in a way that better serves our learning purposes? Teachers should consider how to ethically navigate and share games that portray challenging topics like genocide and slavery, with particular thought to avoiding cause harm and misconceptions. We also need to move beyond moral panic and fear responses to games. How do we balance accuracy with the importance of representing uncomfortable but important topics through games? How do we handle evolving cultural notions around games and gaming?[89]

Example in Action: *Attentat 1942*

Attentat 1942 is a game that uses real footage and interviews, researched by historians, to tell the "the story of Nazi occupation of the Czech lands from the perspective of those who experienced it first-hand (see Figure 8.2). Players speak to eyewitnesses, listen to their memories, and discover the untold story of their family." While many World War II and other war games focus on the military aspects of the event, this game focuses on the multiple perspectives of civilians and "the impact that the war and the totalitarian regime had on the lives and minds of ordinary people."[90]

The game uses eight different characters to help tell these stories. Šisler explains that "these characters include people of various ages, genders, ethnicities, and political and social backgrounds. We deliberately included voices of groups that were typically marginalized in history education in the Czech republic, like Roma. Players have the opportunity to speak to all these characters during the game and critically analyze and compare not only their different, unique personal stories, but also their oftentimes contradicting worldviews and evaluations of historical events." The game has been played in Czech schools, with approximately 15% of Czech history teachers having downloaded the game so far.

Figure 8.2 An image from *Attentat 1942*. Image courtesy of Charles Games.

The creators of *Attentat 1942* tried to approach the topic and gameplay sensitively in a number of ways. First, they rigorously researched the testimonials. They did not use the testimonials verbatim, but instead created a fictitious assemblage of "authentic testimonies" by combining real testimonies to be told through one fictional character. They also avoided "gamifying" the testimonies, especially considering their emotional nature. Finally, they did not allow players to "change the course of history" or alter the characters' stories.[91]

Teachers can use this game to highlight the human aspects of war, as well as to engage students in the act of sharing and interpreting testimonials. For instance, students can pick an event from their own lives and express their perspective on it. Or they can view real-world testimonials from an event that took place in their local area and analyze the differences and similarities among the views.

Use Games That Encourage Multiple Perspectives

While it is beneficial to have students take on roles and embody them, it may also be valuable to have players take on differing roles or switch roles so that they become more open to the notion that multiple viewpoints or perspectives could be valid. This could mean pairing students so that they each need to take turns deliberating from a perspective. It could mean a full-class discussion where students are sharing their unique viewpoints, and uncovering why so many multiple perspectives are possible. It could also mean tackling a problem collaboratively, and needing to share multiple possibilities on how to solve it, without just stopping at the first solution. The very act of seeking out other viewpoints, rather than simply sticking to one's own views, is a process that can expand someone's openness and compassion for others and can lead to better civic outcomes and ethical practices.[92]However, teachers need to handle this carefully and ethically, as taking on certain roles or having people switch roles can be problematic and harmful. We also do not want to necessarily suggest that certain perspectives are as substantive and as compelling as others. We should not tolerate perspectives that are intolerant.

Example in Action: *The Migrant Trail*

In the *The Migrant Trail,* players can play one of two mini-games. In the first, inspired by the classic game *Oregon Trail*, players take on a role as a migrant entering into the United States from Mexico. At the start of the game, the player needs to decide which types of resources and rations (e.g., food, water, clothing, supplies) to take on a trip through the harsh desert conditions along the border from Mexico to the United States. The player then embarks on their journey, which involves staying hidden from border control patrol people, staying fed and hydrated, and keeping their entire party safe and healthy. They need to make choices and decisions about whether to leave behind a member of their group or use one of their rations to help a sick person. The goal is to make it to the destination safely, with as many people in the party still alive.

In the other mini-game, however, the player plays as a totally different role. In this game they are a border control patrol person, and their mission is to find as many migrants as possible. They need to manage resources to decide where to drive, search, and find migrants. The more migrants they find, the more they are rewarded. The game thus requires the player to take on two very different perspectives on the act of migration across the Mexico-US border.

On one hand, we can argue that the inclusion of these two mini-games about the same issue from different perspectives assists in showing that there are *at least* two sides to every issue. It also personalizes each side in a way that makes it more relevant and meaningful to the student. However, we should also critique this game. The two mini-games and their playable perspectives are oversimplified and caricatured (and they are also imbalanced, as the migrant-focused game is more complex and interesting in terms of the game play). Moreover, does this game help to foster discussions on the issue of migration and illegal immigration without privileging one side or another? Or does it further stereotypes, misconceptions, and problematic assumptions? Should we be role-playing as oppressors or as those who are in power (the patrol agents)? The stakes are much higher for those who are migrating, in that they are possibly facing imprisonment, injury, loss, or death. What harms do we cause by performing actions as border patrol agents in the game, who aim to track down people who would face such dire consequences? Are these two sides just different, or is one more ethically problematic than another? Should we should give them equal weight?

Teachers could use these types of questions to jumpstart discussions in class. They can use the game to encourage the sharing of further views on complex issues such as migration, as well as to examine the ethics of representing these perspectives through games. Or, depending on the context, teachers may want to refrain from using games like this, if they think it may further harm or misconceptions.[93]

Reflect on Ethics Through Previewing and Debriefing

The use of particular roles in games needs to be carefully considered and scaffolded in light of the age group of the students, and the game's context, culture, and views. Is it appropriate to have students reenact and take on the role of slaveowners and slaves? What about Nazis and concentration camp prisoners? What about white supremacists? Apartheid supporters? Genocidal leaders? At what point and under what conditions is this unethical and deleterious to a student (or to ourselves)?[94] In fact, the ADL cautions against all of these types of role-playing simulations, as it could perpetuate stereotypes and other harm. While a game may have good intentions, such as to enable access to multiple perspectives, there may be very harmful consequences. Having players take on or play problematic perspectives in a game may tacitly (or explicitly) tell students that these are okay to embody. In these cases we should *not* have our students play these games or take on these roles. But sometimes the answer is more nuanced.

Teachers need to preview games and consider their cultural, emotional, and social ramifications. Game participants can be emotionally and negatively affected by a role, even just physically exhausted from it, and their role in a game may influence their normal, everyday role in damaging ways.

On the other hand, we may not want to write off all perspective-taking activities simply because they may be problematic, or may have unintended consequences. Whether a perspective-taking activity is pedagogically sound relies on the ecology of game use—including a nuanced relationship among the game, the teacher, and the students.

Teachers should also make sure to do a debrief or reflection with students, such as one where the students can express metacognitively how they thought through their decisions in the game, how their own viewpoints differed from those of the roles that they played, and how the experience affected them. Teachers should not expect perfection, however. Mistakes will happen, and they should together with the students learn from them. This requires trust, vulnerability, and care.

Example in Action: *The Road Not Taken*

The Game Academy uses nondigital role-playing games to support ethical decision-making and reflection, such as *The Road Not Taken*, a larp where 10 participants make ethical choices based on a scenario (such as whether to cheat on a test while role-playing as a medical student who wants to solve cancer; see more in chapter 5). In each scenario the main character sits in the center, and the nine others play out different points of view on the dilemma, such as sharing the view of the main character's mother. The players can also improvise what they think those characters would say during the dilemma. Vanek explains that if someone has a particularly emotionally trying role, they get to sit out for the next scenario and recuperate from it. "Game masters" may periodically check in with players and adapt game play before problems arise. But, sometimes issues emerge, and the players need to work together to solve them.[95]

Likewise, teachers may also discover problems once they have students play a game. They may try to make modifications when any learning activity starts to go awry, but mistakes will happen. Teachers should be open and reflective with students when they do make mistakes while running a game. As a class, teachers and students can discuss what they can all collectively learn from those mistakes, and how they might revise the game to better support student learning in the future. What was the road not taken with the deployment of the game, as well as within the game itself?

Use Games to Enhance Respect, Not Stereotypes

Teachers should use games that show how cultural norms get communicated, shared, and transmitted. For instance, in the Japanese board game *Osaki Ni Shitsurei Shimasu!* (Excuse Me for Leaving Early), players play as office workers who are taking turns performing tasks, or giving them to other players, until all their work is done. Hourdequin explains that this game could be played to show cultural differences among workers from different countries. The name of the game refers to the polite phrase that is translated to "excuse me for leaving early," which Japanese employees will say as they leave the office.[96]

Teachers should look for games that not only help students interact with cultural norms and cultural complexity, but also represent cultures appropriately. This may mean ensuring that the game they use has included authentic voices, cultural experts, and sensitivity readers (people embedded in that culture who ensure that the game is designed culturally competently).[97] However, reaching out to experts or including voices on one's development team does not necessarily mean that the game will be culturally sensitive. Teachers need to continually review and revisit the cultural representations and implications of the games that they use.[98]

Example in Action: *When Rivers Were Trails*
In *When Rivers Were Trails*,[99] players play as an Anishinaabe person during the 1890s in Minnesota (see Figure 8.3). Players first get to choose which clan they are in, such as Ajijaak/Crane or Makwa/Bear. Soon in their journey in the game, however, players find out that they are being displaced from their lands due to the allotment acts in the 1880s in the United States, historic acts that took land from Indigenous people and forced them into reservations. As players travel from Minnesota to a new home, they need to ensure that their well-being (mental, emotional, physical, and spiritual) stays high enough. They need to find food (by fishing and hunting), and trade for needs such as medicine. They can also interact with different characters they meet along

A Northern Cheyenne woman is humming nonchalantly to herself and picking chokecherries. She nods at you, then continues gathering.

Talk

Figure 8.3 An image of the game *When Rivers Were Trails*. Character art created by Weshoyot Alvitre. Image courtesy of Elizabeth (Beth) LaPensée.

their journey, and can decide whether to ask for advice, trade, honor elders, or find information about what is happening in the area to other peoples. They can make ethical decisions, such as deciding whether to feed a weak, hungry dog with one's limited food supply. LaPensée, a creative director and designer of the project, explains that "the journey can change from game to game as players randomly come across Indigenous people, animals, plants, and run-ins with Indian Agents."

LaPensée explains that "games have the potential to be self-determined spaces, where Indigenous people (meaning First Nations, Inuit, Métis, Native American, Maori, Aboriginal and similar communities) can express themselves on their own terms."[100] Games can help to teach about different cultures by using realistic language, activities, rituals, and behaviors. In *When Rivers Were Trails*, the names, such as that of the clans, are based on Anishinaabeg (Anishinaabe people) words, adding to the authenticity of the perspectives of the Anishinaabeg during the 1890s. Anishinaabeg words are also peppered throughout the dialogue, such as "niiji" (friend), "boozhoo" (greetings), and "nokomis" (grandmother), as well as in the names of places, such as Spirit Lake or Chippewa. Other parts of the culture are woven through the experience, such as offering tobacco before the hunt, which makes shooting an arrow more successful, or stories about the jingle dress. Throughout the game historical information is also shared, grounding the player in the historical reality amid the personal stories and cultural touchstones. As LaPensée explains, "The game supports educators bringing forward Indigenous perspectives of history, cultural expression, land recovery, and land management practices in dynamic ways."

Games can more accurately express culture when including people from that culture in the development process. The game was created by using Indigenous voices throughout the design process, such as that of San Manuel Band of Mission Indians, as well as dozens of Indigenous writers, designers, musicians, and artists. LaPensée explains that "games have the potential to rectify concerns regarding education of Indigenous issues in classrooms in dynamic ways when the development process and game content deeply involve Indigenous collaboration … [it] was created with sovereignty as a model for the development process in the hopes of bringing self-determined representations into classrooms through interactive gameplay."[101]

Teachers can use games like *When Rivers Were Trails* to enhance knowledge of and curiosity for stories, perspectives, and voices from different cultures, and to help students feel more comfortable sharing their own stories and perspectives. However, teachers should look into how a game was designed, and whose voices were included during the process of creating it. Questions to ask include: What is the authenticity and accuracy of the cultural representations? How were people from that culture included? How might we ensure the authenticity of our own cultures through games?

PART IV

USING GAMES FOR CRITICAL THINKING AND INQUIRY

9

How Do We Make and Reflect on Decisions?

In *Life Is Strange*, I sit on a virtual bench and contemplate. I think back to all the ethical questions I have experienced so far in the fictional game world of Arcadia Bay. These decisions run the gamut from deciding how to help a bullied teen, to what types of relationships to cultivate with other characters, to how to support a friend contemplating suicide.

In the game, I control an avatar. In *Life Is Strange* this avatar is Max Caulfield, a teenage girl attending high school. In *Life Is Strange 2* I play as Sean Diaz, who is on the run from police with his younger brother. In all the *Life Is Strange* games, choice-making is at the core of the game experience: I need to choose what I say to other characters or what actions to take. When I make decisions as Max or Sean, I am able to experience the initial consequences of that decision. But as I continue to play, I may also observe how these decisions have rippling effects on my relationships with other characters, my interactions in the game, and even my virtual town. In the original *Life Is Strange* I can make decisions, experience their initial consequences, and then rewind my choices and make brand-new ones based on what I have learned. Throughout the *Life Is Strange* game series I can also take moments to reflect on my choices by engaging in artistic creation, whether through drawing a scene, writing graffiti, or taking photos.[1] Through this series of games, I can review and interpret evidence, ask critical questions, experiment with different choices, and make decisions and reflect on their consequences.

In this chapter (and the next three chapters) I discuss using games for critical thinking and inquiry skills such as decision-making, reasoning, questioning, reflection, experimentation, and interpretation. How can games enable us to reason through and make ethical choices, ask critical questions about our communities, or encourage us to evaluate, interpret, and use primary sources, testimonials, or evidence? How do games help us to reflect on and revise our decisions moving forward?

Why Should We Teach Decision-Making and Reflection?

Decision-Making Is Crucial

Decision-making is at the heart of civic engagement and the practice of ethics. Decision-making relates to the process of determining what to do and how to act. It

We the Gamers. Karen Schrier, Oxford University Press. © Oxford University Press 2021.
DOI: 10.1093/oso/9780190926106.003.0009

involves forming judgments and making well-reasoned choices that avoid cognitive biases, and stem from vetted information and data.

Communities and societies rely on individuals, and their leaders, to make sound ethical and civic decisions.[2] We may need to choose which civic and social issues to pursue or determine which course of action to take. We may need to decide which candidate to choose, whether to follow laws or rules, or which virtues to model for our children. These could include decisions such as whether to trust and share an article we see on Facebook or Twitter, how we monitor our kids' media use, or whether we drive above or below the speed limit.

Knowing which questions to ask, and knowing how to seek their answers is a critical component of decision-making. Students need to learn how to develop critical questions about their world, as well as a habit for engaging in the process of questioning. We need to be able to question sources, information, data, perspectives, and arguments to understand whether they are sound, valid, reliable, and replicable. Simply being able to know what to ask is often the first step in understanding what an individual, community, or society needs. We need to be purveyors of problems to pursue and the questions to pose, so that we can continually search for better ways to live together. We need to be questioners who do not just accept the status quo, but seek to make social change. However, we should not question so much that we never accept any truths. What may be more useful is to question ourselves—our biases and our limitations.[3]

We Need to Practice Reasoning Skills

Civics and ethics also are about making arguments about how we should live and function as a society. Making solid, logical, well-reasoned arguments and communicating these arguments persuasively is necessary for setting forth civic goals, making ethical choices, and deciding how to approach problems or how to convince others of what to do in one's community.

How do we devise arguments and make decisions based on information, data, and perspectives? Shaenfield cites reasoning as part of the argumentation and decision-making process. There are two different types of reasoning, including deductive and inductive reasoning. Deductive reasoning typically refers to arguments where the premise that is put forth always leads 100% to the conclusion. He gives the example that "Thanksgiving is always on a Thursday in the United States, and Fridays always follow Thursdays." Given this information, we could lead to the logical conclusion that the day after Thanksgiving is always a Friday. On the other hand, inductive reasoning relates to processes where we use evidence to support an argument, but we cannot be 100% certain of the conclusion. Shaenfield explains that this is what happens when we make inferential conclusions, such as ones based on a sampling of the population, since we cannot survey or measure everyone.[4] Social and civics problems often require inductive reasoning, as we do not always know exactly how to solve them. For instance, we might ask: Which ethical framework should we apply in a given moral conundrum? Which types of information should we prioritize to make a civic decision? Practicing reasoning skills helps us to be better equipped to answer these questions (see more in chapter 6 about argumentation and discourse).

We Need to Practice Reflection Skills

We also need to continually reflect on and review the answers we find, the consequences of our choices, and the results of our actions. Having an experience is often not enough for full transformation or engagement; rather, learning requires reflection on that experience. Reflection includes thinking through choices and their consequences and outcomes. It involves reconsidering decisions, and thinking about the evidence, information, processes, and perspectives that led to that decision. It also includes critiquing one's assumptions and engaging in discourse with others about our decisions. Dewey explains that reflective thinking requires "active, persistent, and careful consideration of any belief or supposed form of knowledge in the light of the grounds that support it and the further conclusions to which it tends."[5]

Reflection involves stopping, looking, and listening to what you did, how you did it, and whether you would do it the same way given the same or different circumstances. It also means filtering through dynamically changing relationships and outcomes to see how decisions impacted them in short-term, longer-term, and systemic ways. It requires a type of metacognition that Shaenfield describes, where students can look back and see what they have done and use this process to analyze their approaches moving forward.[6]

Reflection on ethical and civic issues and decisions is important because it asks us to interrogate ourselves, our choices, our designs, and our systems.[7] Reflection can help people reshape their worlds by taking a metacognitive pause and thinking about what they are doing, what they have done, why they have done it, and what they may do differently in the future to shape civic institutions, policies, or outcomes. It is about prioritizing time and space to look back on past ethical decisions—especially mistakes—and learn from them.[8]

How Do Games Support Decision-Making and Reflection?

Games Can Enable Decision-Making

Making decisions is central to playing games. Games establish goals that the player needs to decide how to reach, based on the constraints and rules of the game.[9] Players need to evaluate the choices that are available in a game, decide on strategies and tactics, take action, and make the choices that they believe will help them reach their goals. Decisions could involve anything from when to jump on a Koopa Troopa in *Super Mario Brothers*, which ghost to eat first when super-powered in *Pac-Man*, or which dialogue options to choose in the *Fallout* series.

Decisions can also be explicitly related to civics and ethics. The play of a game could consist of interpreting and making ethical choices, deciding on a course of action, and acting on a decision and experiencing its outcomes. Dorn et al. describe peacekeeping decision-making processes around games such as *Diplomacy*, which engages players in decisions "where trust and rational calculations play an important role, as in real politics."[10]

Games may also feature or simulate ethical and civic dilemmas. They may help people think through the possible outcomes of choices in dilemmas, and to then try them out and see if the actual results matched their expectations. Games can also pose dilemmas that do not have one single right answer, but which may have many multiple potential solutions that have varying strengths and weaknesses (similar to games themselves!). For instance, in the ethical decision-making game, *Decisions that Matter*,[11] players take on the role of a college student in a group of peers. The game poses choices that involve how assertively or diplomatically to act in different scenarios, such as how to respond to a peer in a high-pressure social situation (like whether to talk back to a person who is cat-calling a peer). There are no obvious "right" answers, though some responses may be more or less appropriate depending on the context, and the player has to navigate different social and ethical pressures to make their choices.

Games may enable players to make decisions within a world, time period, or culture that is very different from their own, which can help players to rehearse and perform how they might act given a specific unique set of circumstances. For instance, in *This War of Mine*, players take on the roles of survivors from the Bosnian war. As these survivors, players need to manage limited resources, such as food and drink, and decide who will scavenge for food, supplies, and weapons each night. Given the dire circumstances, players need to make a series of ethical decisions, both major and minor. They have to decide which character may get to sleep or be the lookout for their shelter, or who gets to make the food or eat the limited rations. Players also need to make decisions like whether to steal food from an elderly couple and take the food back to their own settlement. Players also experience the consequences of these actions, when, depending on decisions made, characters may die, the elderly couple may starve, or NPCs may break in and steal food from the settlement (such as if there are not enough weapons or lookouts to protect the settlement). The game enhances exploration and contemplation because it makes it difficult to make these decisions. Players are often deciding between two unpalatable options, and trying to minimize harm rather than making an obviously "correct" choice.[12]

We can conceive of a game as a public sphere for rehearsing decision-making skills and performing different ethical mindsets or civic pathways.[13] Players may use and enact different types of frameworks or moral perspectives to help them practice making decisions or analyzing outcomes. Sicart explains that a game itself is an ethical system, which expresses values and interacts with other systems: "This is an important distinction, because it suggests that games are not just expressing ethics content (like a book might explain ethical theories or pose ethical dilemmas), but it explores how games are ethical systems that may impact other systems, and that games and game designers are part of broader ethical, cultural and economic systems." (See more about systems in chapter 11.) Sicart explains that players are also ethical agents. They interact with the game system and they affect how values are expressed through them. Players make decisions that affect how ethics are expressed.[14] However, Dishon and Kafai caution that just because something is a game and involves decisions does not mean the decisions are meaningful: "Meaningful participation in decision-making within and about the game environment is exactly the sort of experience needed to cultivate democratic modes of civic action."[15]

Games May Show Consequences, Too

Games do not just enable players to make decisions and choices—they can also have players experience their consequences. In *Life Is Strange*, players cannot progress without making ethical decisions, seeing initial consequences, reflecting on them, and then revising their initial choices and experiencing the new result.

Other games may adapt and change based on player decisions, such as *Undertale*. *Undertale* incorporates ethical choices into its gameplay, and also uses a morality system (see more about *Undertale* later in the chapter). A morality system analyzes a players' choices in a game and provides feedback on those choices in the form of varying consequences, such as differing story outcomes, nonplayer character (NPC) interactions, or even the physical look of an avatar. Some role-playing games, such as the *Fallout*, *Fable*, *Bioshock*, *Dragon Age*, *Red Dead Redemption*, and *Mass Effect* series, have morality systems.[16] In *Mass Effect*, players are invited to make dialogue choices that are either lawful and compliant or chaotic and rebellious, leading the avatar to move along a spectrum from "Paragon" to "Renegade," respectively. Likewise, *Red Dead Redemption II* has a "honor" meter that goes up or down, depending on how one acts in the game. For instance, if players decide to help a stranded NPC and bring them back to their home, their honor may go up. If they decide to ignore the stranger or steal items from their wagon, their honor may go down (or down quite a bit, depending on the activity). *Fallout 3* functions similarly, where one's actions affect one's karma points (in that actions like giving help to those in aid may raise it, while conducting violence toward innocent victims will lower it).[17] The morality system in a game, along with a dynamically changing game environment, may help reinforce for the player the need to make careful choices.[18]

On the other hand, some games may be compelling even if there is no clear morality system, and even if the "quantifiable outcomes are the same" as to how the game progresses.[19] In the digital game *I Have No Mouth and I Must Scream* (based on the Ellison short story of the same name), the player needs to make ethical choices while solving puzzles for five different characters. Depending on one's choices, the game eventually leads to varied game endings, though the game world is basically the same until the end of the game. The game, however, still elicits moral contemplation through the use of thoughtful dialogue, missions, and characters.[20]

Playing is A Form of Reasoning

Playing a game helps to reason through its argument. Bogost explains that "games mount claims through … rule-based representations and interactions" or what he calls "procedural rhetorics."[21] Games use the rhetoric of rule-based play to make a statement about how the world is or should be. The repetition of play helps to reveal this argument. For instance, in the game *Papers, Please* the player acts as an immigration officer, and decides who to let into a made-up country. The player can decide whether and when to break the rules, such as whether to let in someone who does not have the right documentation. "Through the playing of the game and its rules, players begin to understand the game's ethical system, and experience its brutal arbitrariness, as well as the suffocating nature of the bureaucracy surrounding immigration."[22] (See more in chapter 11).

Playing a game, then, is like a ritualized working of an idea, argument, or system, such that we come to understand it better through the repeated play of it. This is akin to a ritual like voting, whereby participating it in again and again, over time, we begin to gain an understanding of the electoral system as well as the broader civic and political system where we live. (See also more in chapter 8).

Building on this, Davisson and Gehm argue that "to play games involves taking on roles in those worlds, making decisions within the constraints they impose, and then forming judgments about living in them. Video games can synthesize the raw materials of civil life and help us pose the fundamental political question: *What should be the rules by which we live?*"[23] Therefore, playing games—and designing games—can be a way of positing how we should live. When we play, explicitly or even implicitly, we need to consider questions like: What types of ethical systems should we use to guide our play? What types of values should matter? How should we govern and what rules should we enact? A game is a reflection of and argument about our public life, and it is the result of many decisions about the ethical apparatuses and civic structures of our world.

Games Can Encourage Reflection

Reflection is an important part of any learning process, and can be encouraged through and around games. It may be surprising to hear that a game can support reflective practice, as games are sometimes seen as being filled with frenetic activity and nonstop action—with no time to think, only time to act. And this is often true. But some games have reflective practices built directly into the game.

For instance, in *Way*, an online collaborative game described in chapter 6, players are finally able to communicate once they complete the game together. The final scene is a shared whiteboard where they can write to each other. This stage of the game supports reflective practice, in that the two strangers are now able to divulge who they are and how they have connected through their experience. The reflection helps solidify their trust and admiration for each other.[24]

Life Is Strange shows some of the different types of reflection that can take place within a game. First, it supports reflection-in-action. "Reflection-in-action" is reflection that happens while the action is occurring, such as when someone is making a decision. In these circumstances, the game is actively enabling the players to reflect on and revise their decisions as they are happening.[25] In *Life Is Strange*, you can see one outcome of your decision and then you need to rewind it back to do something different. To play the game, you need to continually make decisions while reflecting on your choices.

Life Is Strange also incorporates reflection after action takes place, or "reflection-on-action." In *Life Is Strange: Before the Storm*, the player (controlling their avatar, Chloe) can take a moment to sit on a virtual bench and recount the events that have happened so far. Stopping at the bench provides an opportunity to contemplate what has transpired so far while the player is removed from the main action of the game. Games that incorporate this type of contemplative practice may help further ethical awareness and civic sensitivity, because it helps players to slow down and consider their values and identities, and how to express them through future choices and decisions.[26]

Likewise, in the game *Play the Mirror*, players need to reflect on the very notion of decisions in games. In this text-based role-playing game you need to defeat different enemies, but continue to fail at your quests no matter what you choose. As you progress, the game spurs you to reflect by having you make choices that directly challenge the concept of choice.[27] *Play the Mirror* shows us that games can themselves be reflections on games. In this case, the game functions as a reflection literally (as the image and name of the game is that of a mirror), and ludically, in that it uses play to directly engage the player in a process of questioning and reflecting.

Limitations to Using Games for Decision-Making and Reflection

Some Games Are Poorly Designed for Critical Thinking

One of the key limitations of games is that many are not able to effectively prompt the practice of critical thinking skills. Good design is deceptively complex. Some games aim to teach critical thinking skills, but instead become more akin to trivia games, which reward the regurgitation of facts. Or games are designed to be like interactive worksheets, which may invite the categorization of information without the further interpretation and application of it. These games do not make use of the strengths of games—often by no fault of the enthusiastic creators but possibly due to the limited expertise, resources, or budgets that these creators may have.

What are some of the particular strengths of games? Games can provide a compelling context and interactive environment by which players can grapple with, reason through, and experience choices and consequences. They can enable players to enter into ethical choices, mindsets, and circumstances that they would not normally have access to, such as what they might do on a jury or what it is like to be a refugee from another country. But designing games that really value what games can do, and that effectively meet critical thinking goals, is difficult, complex work. Moreover, because of the stigma around games and the way they are typically discussed in the media or within peer groups, teachers and administrators may not realize the potential for critical thinking and deeper inquiry through play. This may perpetuate the use and design of games that do not enable as effective engagement in critical thinking practice.[28]

Games and Teachers Are Better Together

Games are also more effective when used in tandem with a teacher, mentor, or guide who knows how to draw out the game's strengths and use it to further critical inquiry. Games may effectively support the practice of critical inquiry skills, but teachers know how to adjust and modify the game to match their students' needs and interests, or how to ensure that the game's possible benefits are realized. In particular, reflection and reflective practice during, around, and after a game may stem in part through how a teacher uses the game. While some games design reflection to occur throughout the actions in the game, reflection can also happen beyond the game. Teachers know how to best shape the game to their curriculum, and how to incorporate reflective and metacognitive activities beyond and around the game.[29]

Choices in a Game May Not Be Meaningful

The types of choices that are presented in games, and the context by which they are presented, may also be a limitation of games. First, games may not provide realistic or relevant choices. In *The Walking Dead* (Telltale) video game, players need to make ethical decisions around who to sacrifice or spare during a zombie apocalypse. The decisions are unlikely to be ones that players will ever (hopefully) face, though the process of thinking through the decisions may be useful practice.[30] A fantastical premise in a game may even motivate students to practice decision-making more than an informational approach might. A question, however, is whether these skills will transfer out of the game context as easily if the choices are less realistic.

Simply including choices in a game is also not enough. The more effective games do not just provide choices, but provide *meaningful* choices. Game choices may be meaningful to the player, or meaningful within the game.[31] Players need to feel like what they choose matters, and that their choices affect their participation in the game—just like they should have "meaningful decision-making power within" public participation more generally.[32] People need to feel like their decisions, choices, actions, and votes matter, and can bring about social change—whether through a game or beyond.[33]

Unfortunately, some games do not provide meaningful choices. Games may provide only two overly simplistic choices. Or, they may provide two diametrically opposed choices (e.g., a good choice and a bad choice), without additional choices that are more "gray" or nuanced. In *Fallout 3* players are given a decision of whether to kill a player who is going to set off a bomb in Megaton, or diffuse the bomb. Setting it off lowers karma points drastically, hurtling the player toward a Bad Karma status in their moral system. (Not setting it off leads to a Good Karma status.) But there are not more nuanced, alternatives to this in the game, nor necessarily meaningful choices.[34] A game's morality system may be too simplistic, and feel more like "moral accounting" rather than complex and dynamic ethical arbitration.[35]

When choosing a game, a question that teachers should ask is whether a game compels their players to grapple with moral complexity, or whether it just motivates them to beat the game. Are players flourishing, or merely optimizing their game play so they reach their game goals more efficiently?

Consequences May Be Inconsequential

In addition to providing simplistic choices, games may also provide overly simplistic conclusions or outcomes to choices. In the first episode of *The Walking Dead* (Telltale) game, players make some seemingly key decisions such as whether to save one or the other character (Doug or Carley). Yet, although the choice may slightly adjust the storyline, all of the players ultimately end up at the same point in the story at the end of the episode, no matter who they choose to sacrifice or save.[36] This speaks to another limitation of games: it is difficult to computationally develop and creatively imagine all of the different permutations of possible outcomes that could occur from any given decision. Games may only have one, two, or a limited set of possible outcomes or endings, because it is so resource-heavy to have a game world dynamically respond to a player.

Let's explore this further. Say we want to fully respond to the player, and give relevant feedback based on every unique choice. To do this, developers would need to create exponentially greater numbers of consequences for every choice that is made. They would have to program all of the possibilities (or create algorithms that could procedurally generate them), develop all of the art assets, and write all of the infinitely possible paths and endings. All of this could rapidly become insurmountable.[37]

Or, let's say the consequences *are* meaningful, but the consequences only fully get experienced after a player spends time in a game. Results of choices can be cumulative or have rippling effects that only reveal themselves later in the game. In *Life Is Strange* players may make decisions in the first episode of the game, which may affect storylines and character interactions in all of the remaining chapters.[38] Beyond the creative limitations of designing consequences in games, there are also educational considerations. The length of time needed to experience meaningful consequences in games can be challenging from a practical standpoint, as students may not be able to be experience them during a class session.[39]

These challenges suggest that games may struggle to fully enable the practice of ethical and civic decision-making.[40] However, even simple games can evoke complex thinking.[41] Games like *Loneliness, Girl with the Gray Hair Awakens, Passage, Howling Dogs, Among Us, Werewolf, Trade Off, Florence, Queers in Love at the End of the World, A Woman Goes to a Private Games Industry Party*, and *Parable of the Polygons*, to name just a few, each have simple game mechanics or interactions, but can enable deep, meaningful play.[42]

In my *Fable III* research, I found that players did think critically about their ethical choices and decisions, even when choices were fictional and simplistic, and even when the outcomes were underdeveloped.[43] This is in part because players felt like their choices mattered. The game also ignited their imagination. The storyworld, characters, and interactions in the game, among other elements, helped to motivate meaningful play. This further suggests that story and emotive elements, as described in the previous section of this book, may work together with critical thinking skills, to help make games (and experiences around games) more effective. The teacher also plays an important role in motivating deeper reflection, reasoning, and inquiry.

Reflection May Not Be Meaningful, Either

Reflection is not only a part of learning—it may even be necessary for learning. We need practice making decisions and choices, but also to actively reflect on the results of our choices.[44] Staines et al. investigated whether designers are creating morally complex games that invite reflection. In looking at three games, *Firewatch, Deus Ex: Mankind Divided*, and *Darkest Dungeon*, they found that games are beginning to incorporate more meaningful everyday choices, which do invite reflection on choices. However, even the players of these games may seek to meet "ludic goals" rather than grapple with and reflect on morality. Staines et al. argue that players need to "choose to be reflective because free choice is the fundamental basis of ethical responsibility: it isn't enough to simply tell players when their choices are morally significant, or to force ethical reflectiveness with reductive metrics like morality metres and karma points."[45] Players need to purposefully and meaningfully reflect.

Likewise, Villareale et al. point out that learning games in general may not be well-positioned to effectively encourage reflection. They rightly argue that common game approaches to reflection are problematic, such as leaving reflection to only after the game (e.g., a debrief), using postgame assessments to evaluate gameplay (e.g., final scores), or using reflection features that are too general rather than individualized to the player.[46] Teachers need to ask: How should we encourage meaningful, individualized reflection around games? Which games encourage the type of reflection necessary to help students "to citizen"?

Strategies for Using Games for Decision-Making and Reflection

Enable Students to Make Meaningful Choices

It's hard to know which games will be meaningful to a person, but a teacher can help make a game more relevant to current issues and timely topics. Teachers can use games that can incorporate real-world civics or ethical decisions that are relevant to their students' families, communities, and lives. The choice of a game to play is itself meaningful. Can students choose a game that matches their own interests? Does the game help to "position youth as shapers of their (physical and virtual) environments, much like citizens in a democracy"?[47]

Example in Action: Moral Machine
When we drive we make hundreds of little and big decisions, which are based on our own judgments. Do we let a car cut us off in our lane, or press the accelerator and speed up past them? If an animal suddenly runs across the street, do we swerve, hit the brakes, or go on the shoulder?[48]

Moral Machine is a playful activity that considers these types of questions for self-driving cars. It is an online interactive activity that simulates a type of trolley problem, and asks us to think about how self-driving cars might handle deciding between two awful scenarios. Players choose between two randomly generated choices of whom to save or let die. For instance, if they were the car, should they save two older women, an active man, and a baby, or three cats, a pregnant woman, and two kids? Participants click on the group to save and then move on to the next challenging decision.[49]

The self-driving car cannot make these types of decisions on its own—it relies on designers and programmers to predetermine how the car should make these decisions before it ever gets on the road.[50] So then how do self-driving cars make life or death decisions? Moral Machine poses these questions for us to help collectively answer them.

A teacher can use this activity with older students and ask questions like: What happens when we get into a self-driving car? How does the car know when to stop or go? Speed up or slow down?[51] When in a physical classroom, I show the activity up on a projector and I ask the students to discuss which they think is the more ethically sound decision (which group to save).[52] First, I have students share their initial views and begin to construct their arguments, including which ethical frameworks they might use to approach this decision. Then, I have them take turns sharing their positions with the class, as well as listen to others' perspectives.[53] Students also spend time questioning the choices they have been given, and thinking through the types of additional evidence that they could use to help make their decisions. Finally, I have the students make their final decisions, and express their vote for which people the car should save.

I have done this activity with a wide range of students—high school students in a diverse suburban school, college students in an ethics class, and retired adults in a local course on news media. I even did it live through Discord in a course taught remotely. All the students have been engaged in the activity, as cars and driving are personally relevant to many different people, particularly in a car-centric culture such as the United States. I am able to make ethical decision-making more personally relevant and meaningful to my students by applying it to a topic that many care about.

But there's another level to this activity. What we collectively decide matters. Our decisions help the MIT researchers who made Moral Machine better understand human decision-making in general. The researchers have found individual and cultural differences in how participants vote. Some cultures greatly prefer sparing younger versus older people, or females versus males.[54] People in countries with more individualistic societies tend to have more of a preference for sparing the larger number of people, as these societies may "emphasize the distinctive value of each individual."[55] Those in countries that were more collectivist in nature are more likely to spare older people, as these societies may "emphasize the respect that is due to older members of the community."[56] Students are able participate in an ethics experience and have an impact on real-world knowledge and understanding,[57] which serves to further its relevance and meaningfulness.[58]

Use Games That Have Clear Feedback on Choices

Teachers should find games that give students clear feedback on their decisions and choices, both short- and longer-term. Students should be able to see how their choices shape the game's world, affect their relationships with other characters, or alter the story or solution to a problem. The students should understand what the outcome was, why the outcome occurred, and possibly even what they could have done differently to experience a different result. This can be implemented within a game, where a player can make a choice or take actions based on community or civic data, perspectives, or information, and then get feedback on those choices in a way that is meaningful or relevant to the game.[59] A teacher can also support this by posing questions around the game.

Teachers may also want to find games that show short-term results, as well as more systemic, longer-term consequences, so that students can have experience critically evaluating, comparing, and reflecting on these different consequences over time. However, even if a game does not show short-term and longer-term consequences, teachers can invite students to reflect on possible systemic consequences, or predict what might occur in the shorter or longer term.

Example in Action: *Undertale*

Undertale is a single-player digital role-playing game where players need to play as a human child and navigate an underworld filled with monsters. To return home, they need to journey through caverns and labs, and figure out how to handle different monsters. They may come across a frog-like creature, called Froggit, and can choose to fight, act, give an item, or practice mercy. There are a number of characters, such as Toriel, a goat, and Flowey, the flower.

In *Undertale*, players need to protect their hit points (HP) and keep from running out of lives. Defeating enemies enhances one's experience (EXP) points, which then enhances their love (LV) or their gold, which in turn affects their ability to engage in battle or perform in the game. Depending on how someone plays, which dialogue options they choose, and whether they choose to defeat or spare enemies, the dialogue, storylines, and outcomes of the game will vary greatly. Further playthroughs of the game are also affected by previous playthroughs. In other words, in *Undertale*, choices matter greatly in the shorter term and much longer term, as how a player acts in a game session has consequences for the types of gameplay they are able to experience in the future.[60]

Teachers may use the game in a number of ways. They might pair players together and have them make choices. They can also have students work together to imagine and iterate through possible outcomes to the choices as they reach each one. The use of ethical choices in the game, and the ability to see the short-term and longer-term results of the choices in action is a particular benefit of this game. Teachers may also use the game to encourage students to reflect on any consequences and see if they matched their expectations.[61] Geer and Matthews posit another possibility for *Undertale*, which is to first discuss different ethical frameworks, such as consequentialist or deontological approaches, and then have students either use a particular framework to help guide their choices, or have them play the game and then reflect on which frameworks most closely aligned with how they played the game. Geer and Matthews offer the following prompts: Would you make the same choices you did in the first run-through, knowing what you know now? If not, what would you do differently? They explain that teachers can put students in groups to discuss and play the game together, and then either journal independently or collectively deliberate what they would do in a new play through, such as how they would respond to Flowey's "kill or be killed" mentality.[62]

Use Games That Promote Meaningful Reflection

To encourage reflection, teachers may use games in a number of ways. They may have students play part of a game, and then invite students to reflect on their game play after the activity. This is reflection-on-action,[63] which typically happens after a decision is made, an activity is conducted, or even after a game is played. For instance, teachers may have students play part of a game each night, and keep a journal, write a reflection paper, or discuss what they played in class the next day. Keeping a portfolio or diary can help "students to consolidate and assess their learning of a discipline and its practices." Everett, who teaches in a private independent school in Florida, uses a metacognitive exercise in which students write Yelp-style reviews of games, such as *Executive Command*. The students need to think not only about how they learned from the game, but they have to explain how others may learn from this. This reinforces their own learning and builds empathy, Everett explains, because the students need to think about how other students may learn from it, too.[64]

Teachers can also invite students to reflect during the game and while they are making decisions (reflection-in-action). They may have students take notes while playing, or talk aloud through their decisions with another player. In *Mission US: For Crown or Colony?* (described in chapter 8) students are able to reflect inside the game on their experience of the Boston Massacre during the deposition scene, where they need to answer in-game questions about the event, and make visible their thinking of what happened.[65]

Likewise, while playing *Reliving the Revolution*, an augmented reality game, students share their collected viewpoints and testimonials about the Battle of Lexington. They deliberate with each other about who fired the first shot at the battle, which serves as a reflective activity during the game.[66]

Teachers may also want to have students pause their games and reflect on that current moment, such as before a big decision or in the middle of a problem.[67] When I investigated how participants made ethical decisions in the game, *Fable III*, one participant told me he would press pause on his game during each ethical decision and call his father to ask him what he thought he should do and how he should proceed. They would discuss the context for the decision and the choices that were possible. The social interaction and dialogue with his father helped him to reflect on the best course of action and decide which one to do next. Teachers can do something similar by having students pause games and discuss decisions with the class or with a partner.

Example in Action: *Walden*

The game *Walden* is purposefully designed to incorporate reflective practice (see Figure 9.1).[68] The game is set in 1845 New England and is an open world where players can explore, experiment, and engage. It is based on Henry David Thoreau's *Walden*, a book where he reflects on natural surroundings and living in the woods. In the game version of *Walden*, activities have a type of reflective or contemplative quality.

Figure 9.1 A screenshot from the game *Walden* (2017). Image courtesy of Tracy Fullerton and the *Walden* team.

Players can engage in different types of nature-related and survivalist activities, such as gathering seeds, finding shelter materials, or fishing. What a player decides to do each day is gently guided by the game, but also decided upon by and directed by the player. Chen and Zdeb explain that "the goal of the game is to find balance between meeting basic material needs and finding connection with nature to remain inspired." Throughout the game Thoreau's writings are also shared with the player, giving a transcendent quality to the natural surroundings.[69]

Chen and Zdeb explain that teachers can use the game to support students in reflective acts and practices beyond the game, such as through journaling, listening to texts, or collecting specimens in the natural world. The game can also be used to create prompts for writing exercises or class discussions, in that the teacher can "keep multiple save points in the game, allowing for easy reloading of specific moments or narrated passages to use during class discussion." Students can also compare the letters and documents in the game to real-world messages and communications, such as ones on current issues or public debates about the natural world.[70]

A teachers' guide suggests that educators can use the game to consider how reflective practices such as writing and creative work can inspire social changes and movements. One of their extension activities invites teachers to have students read Thoreau's "Civil Disobedience" essay and consider how he influenced historic and modern civic leaders like Martin Luther King Jr. or Emma Goldman. The guide explains: "You may also wish to give students the opportunity to discuss their ideas about whether civil disobedience is acceptable and/or useful today, with groups like Black Lives Matter, the protesters of the Dakota Access Pipeline, and sit-ins by disability activists in the halls of Congress."[71]

Not all civic engagement is public—some of it is reflective and private. The game helps to show that sometimes people need to feel connected to each other to understand their roles in society, and that at other times people need to connect with themselves and with nature to better understand their identity, and better imagine how they can make social change.[72]

10
How Do We Read and Evaluate Information?

Can you figure out if these COVID-19 articles are real or fake? The title of the first one is "He just got better and better: 104-year-old veteran beats Coronavirus in time to celebrate his birthday," and the second is "There's a connection between coronavirus and 5G." Which way will you swipe? (Swipe right if you think it is an accurate article, and left for a fake one.)

The game is *Factitious: Pandemic Edition*, which is a 2020 version of a game made by the American University Game Lab (see Figure 10.1). The game asks players to vet actual news articles and decide whether an article is an example of disinformation ("fake news") or an example of solid reporting and journalistic accuracy. To play, it presents recent articles from a variety of news sources, such as large news enterprises like the *Washington Post* and *New York Times*, online sites like The Hill or Infowars, magazines like *Fortune*, and satire sites like *Initial Reaction News* or *The Onion*. Players can read the article and look at the source, and consider the provenance of the data or information. They can also analyze it further, such as by fact-checking the article and validating its claims. After the player decides if the article is based on "real" or "fake" information, the game provides instant feedback. It explains if the player was correct or not, and then gives tips on what types of cues to look for going forward.[1]

A teacher could use the game to teach critical information literacy skills.[2] But the game also helps us to build knowledge about information literacy itself—and the gaps and biases that human beings may have. The game has been played over 1 million times, and the designers have been using the data derived from game plays to determine which types of news articles are harder for people to decipher for authenticity (which may help us to better understand how people get fooled by fake news and better able to counter this).[3] For instance, they ask: Which articles tend to trick players? Which ones take longer for people to read and interpret? Thus, *Factitious* may help to teach critical literacy skills, and it also may further support the development of policies, algorithms, strategies, or educational approaches that dissuade disinformation.

In this chapter I look at how to use games help us to find, read, evaluate, and analyze information. The skills that are involved include literacy skills (reading and writing) as well as information and media literacy skills, such as the ability to fluidly interpret information across different modalities (such as through social media or

We the Gamers. Karen Schrier, Oxford University Press. © Oxford University Press 2021.
DOI: 10.1093/oso/9780190926106.003.0010

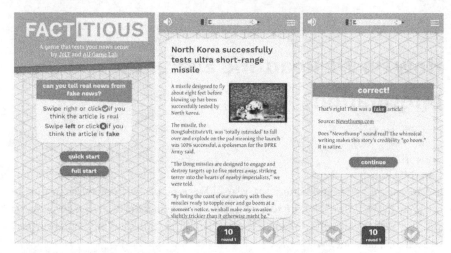

Figure 10.1 A screenshot of the game *Factitious*. Created by Maggie Farley, Bob Hone, Joyce Rice, and Chas Brown, and the American University Game Lab. Image courtesy of Maggie Farley, Robert Hone, and the American University Game Lab.

television), or how to evaluate information and data to understand whether it is valid and reliable.

Why Should We Teach Literacy Skills?

In the previous chapter, I looked at skills like decision-making, reasoning, and reflection. Critical thinking also involves reading, gathering, and evaluating information, such as primary documents, testimonials, and other data, and managing various resources to be able to critically evaluate a system, circumstance, context, or problem, and make sound decisions.

Literacy Skills Are Foundational

Literacy skills are foundational skills for ethics and civics education. To be able to participate fully in civic and ethics activities in our world, we need to be able to read and interpret documents, write arguments, peruse policies, and apply what we comprehend to real-world scenarios.[4] Social studies teachers Wrona and Penney explain that unfortunately students often do not like doing these basic skills, which could end up keeping them from doing the deeper listening, thought, and engagement necessary for full participation as a citizen of the world. Penney, a middle school teacher in Texas, explains that when students slow down and take the time to read, "to apply the reading to a situation, and practice the habits to think about what they are doing and

reading, they do better with homework, better on tests, and better in class,"[5] and retain, process, and apply the information more readily. Reading and writing are at the
core of being able to engage in ethics and civics.

Other Types of Literacies Are Essential, Too

As we consider how to support literacy skills such as reading comprehension and
writing, we should also consider how to support other types of literacies, such as
media literacy, information literacy, and news literacy.[6] Media literacy is defined
as the ability to fluidly navigate different types of media (such as memes, videos, or
games), interpret and evaluate media, and create and construct one's own media
responses. News and information literacy involve the ability to vet different sources,
differentiate between facts and opinions (and news and propaganda), evaluate information and evidence, and use it to build an argument or share a viewpoint.[7] We need
to be able to analyze information to make critical decisions such as how to vote, how
to solve civic problems, how to behave as an electorate, or how to work together on
new initiatives.

There are a number of phenomena that people need to be mindful of when interpreting information. First, people approach information differently. People may be
guided by different types of motivated reasoning, including directional motivation
and accuracy motivation. Directional motivation refers to the desire to seek and justify conclusions that align with one's own beliefs or versions of the truth. People who
are guided by directional motivation may apply a less critical eye to sources that align
with their beliefs and a more critical approach to those sources that oppose their
beliefs, even if they are presented with compelling evidence that counter their beliefs
(this is similar to confirmation bias).[8] People who are guided by accuracy motivation,
however, desire to contextualize and evaluate evidence to determine its accuracy, regardless of their beliefs or how well information aligns with them.[9] Those who are
guided by accuracy motivation may be more likely to consider evidence that runs
counter to their beliefs, but everyone needs support in engaging in this practice. How
do we encourage people who are guided by directional motivation to be more open to
evidence that does not confirm their beliefs?

Another consideration is that people may engage in political homophily, where
they are in "bubbles" surrounded by people with more similar opinions and mindsets.
They may even continue to seek relationships with those who are more alike, perpet-
uating their isolation from other opinions.[10] Nguyen calls this an epistemic bubble,
where the people inside the bubble do not get exposed to people with opposing views.
Social media may even further these perspective divides, as people may "teach" or
train their Facebook or Instagram accounts to show them material that they already
like and which does not push on their ideological boundaries. Social media algorithms may even be purposely designed to continue to serve up articles and information that are personalized to a users' already-established interests and opinions.

However, Nguyen explains that there are not really any epistemic bubbles—they argue that people *are* exposed to other views, and they know the common arguments of those with whom they disagree. Nguyen argues that the bigger problem is echo chambers. Echo chambers are not just about being isolated, but also about distrusting people who are beyond one's bubble. People in echo chambers won't even consider others' views or their compelling evidence because they do not trust people outside their bubble. This is much more difficult to disrupt because the paradigm of whom to trust has been upended. The very civic institutions we typically need to trust to get valid information and to help us make decisions—news media, medical profession-als, and scientists—may be ignored in favor of the voices inside the chamber.[11] We need to teach people how to move beyond echo chambers and validate information and value others' perspectives.

The amount of disinformation being created and shared (even by these civic institutions) may also be increasing. People can more readily make, share, and as-sert knowledge, and they have access to tools to make their information look and sound professional. In many ways this is beneficial: more people can access infor-mation and share their views. Ideally, it also means there are more people working together toward solving problems. On the other hand, it means we have overturned what it means to be an amateur or a professional scientist, journalist, or civic leader. We don't know who to trust because the markers of trustworthiness are no longer valid. Thus, the democratization of knowledge-making may simultaneously be ben-eficial *and* contributing to the erosion of trust with our knowledge institutions. We have disrupted our ability as a society to create, trust, and spread knowledge, truth, and facts to make the critical decisions we need to make.[12]

Practicing These Skills Is Lacking

What skills should we teach? We need to be able to authenticate information, weigh evidence, and cull from multiple sources to be able to make appropriate decisions, such as whether to back a policy or referendum, or whether to wear a mask during a global health crisis. Students need to be able to evaluate primary and secondary sources,[13] think about when the source was made, where and how it was shared, how credible it is, and where it derived its information or ideas.[14] Students also need to think about the ideologies and beliefs that may be driving the creation and spread of this information, and the techniques that are being used to target audi-ences and persuade them.[15] We need to be questioners, but we also need accept vetted facts and truths. We need to question our own assumptions around trust and distrust.

Yet, students are not practicing these skills as deeply as they need to. In a study of 170 high school students, less than 20% of students questioned the source of an image or the accuracy of a headline associated with it.[16] Kahne and Bowyer researched over 2,000 kids from age 15 to 27 to see how well they were able to judge the accuracy of political posts. The results suggested that the students used both directional and accuracy motivations, but that their worldview factored more in influencing them in whether they believed a post, rather than the accuracy of the information.[17] Crocco et al. looked at how students evaluated evidence. Their findings suggested that students may be good at knowing what constitutes legitimate evidence in the abstract, but when tasked to actually look at evidence, they were less able to determine whether evidence was reputable.[18]

Moreover, some of the teachers I interviewed commented that their students often just want "the right answer." They are used to taking tests with one right answer or getting "fed" information, and they want to do the minimal work required to get to the correct response. Some students do not like needing to evaluate evidence or deliberate among different possible correct answers—they just want to know which one is "correct." They do not want to spend the time to interpret information to parse out the differences among possible right answers, and they do not want to sift among multiple perspectives to provide a more nuanced argument or response.

However, ethical and civics issues need nuanced engagement. They require people to consider the differences among possible right answers and to tease out the benefits or drawbacks from among multiple solutions.

Practice can make a difference. The students with media literacy and information literacy training are more effective at assessing evidence.[19] In one study by Journell et al., students practiced assessing information and analyzing poll data, and were more able to analyze the trustworthiness of partisan news around the 2012 US presidential election.[20] Games may also be ways to help motivate students to deliberate among a number of decisions, views, or claims, and to uncover these nuances, as I will discuss in the next section.

How Do Games Teach Literacy Skills?

Games Can Encourage Reading

Games can include the reading of text—as well as the reading of images, symbols, and time-based media. It may be surprising to consider games as a way to support greater reading, but many games have a ton of reading, in the form of documents, dialogue, and even instructions. There are densely, story-rich games with an enormous amount of content to read, such as the *Elder Scrolls*, *Mass Effect*, *Animal Crossing*, and *Dragon Age* series. Beyond just reading or listening to the dialogue, in these games players can also read long letters and texts (such as a book they find in an in-game library or a letter they find in an abandoned virtual home), or they can read about magical weapons or other special objects. In the *Civilization* series, there is a lengthy "Civilopedia"—a multiple volume encyclopedia that talks about various countries, buildings, figures, and laws that show up in the game.[21] To do well in the game or learn about different strategies, players may access this resource and read one of the entries, just as they might do if they looked up an entry in a book like an encyclopedia or a website like Wikipedia.[22]

Likewise, in the game *Race to Ratify*, players need to travel back to the 1780s and try to convince each of the 13 states to ratify the newly written US Constitution.[23] To do this, students need to read different perspectives on whether to ratify the Constitution, and then consider how to convince other people of their viewpoints. Penney talks about how she uses this game because there is so much reading involved—and direct application of that reading. This is reading-in-action, where students become motivated to read so that they can achieve the goals of the game.

Games Can Encourage Interpretation Skills

Games can also motivate practice with news and information, historical evidence, political documents, testimonies, diaries, and other literature. Games can do this in a number of ways. They can make the completion of the game contingent on reading and vetting information, such as in the opening example, *Factitious*, where players need to check sources, read articles, and fact-check information to be more effective at the game. Games can also make the play contingent on investigating and interpreting real documents and information. In *Civics! An American Musical* students need to dig through archives, appraise sources, and find information that can support their viewpoints and vision of past moments (see more in chapter 12). *Jewish Time Jump, Revolution 1979*, and *Reliving the Revolution* use recreations of real historic documents, such as historic testimonials of events, images and photographs, or newspaper clippings, which may need to be reviewed, compared, assessed, and applied to reach the goals in the game.[24]

Reacting to the Past is a series of analog role-playing game modules. These modules are "college-level pedagogy that is meant to engage deeply, both with actual historical moments and real big ideas, as well as 'great texts' or the important texts that are generally offered as part of a college curriculum."[25] *Reacting to the Past* invites students to reenact and engage with different moments from history, including the Constitutional Convention of 1787 in the United States, Athens in 403 B.C., India's independence in 1945, and human rights and intervention in Rwanda in 1994. Worth used a module on the French Revolution in 1791 in her college class. Instead of just reading works by Rousseau, the students needed to deeply analyze and apply it to participate in the game.[26] They also needed to use historical documents to "build their arguments against a separation of church and state. Whereas other people are looking at those same documents but arguing for separation of church and state."[27] The students needed to practice critical literacy skills to be able to play the game; they needed to read, interpret, evaluate, compare, and apply documents to build their arguments.

The games I described in this section are civic or historical in nature, but games that are not explicitly civic-related may also be useful for practicing information interpretation skills.[28] Games may further the practice of these skills by using relevant, personally meaningful real-world topics and issues, such as ones that match student interests. For instance, a game may focus on issues that are of local, global, or community concern to students, such as a toxic dump site in a neighborhood, a rise in opioid addiction in a school district, or animal drug testing by a popular makeup company. Using relevant and meaningful issues may help to motivate students to further investigate evidence around an issue, both inside and outside of the game. *Bury Me, My Love* centers on the story of a Syrian migrant in Europe and incorporates real-world stories and testimonials, such as that of a series of text messages between one woman and her husband,[29] as well a realistic interface (that of a phone). The player needs to make real-world ethical decisions for the couple, Nour and Magd, and help them to navigate the consequences of those choices. Teachers can use this game as a springboard to have students evaluate news articles and policies about Syrian refugees (or immigration more generally), assess them for accuracy, and to discuss any discrepancies they may find.

Games Are Media, Too

Finally, games themselves are a type of media that can be analyzed. Games are often multimodal, and through their play can help to hone literacy skills across different modalities, such as oral, written, and ludic. We can analyze currently popular games like *Valorant* or *Fall Guys* by looking at their game play, system, design, moderation, and the values they express. This is a type of literacy practice called gaming literacy.[30]

Games also can be a form of "news" that can and should be evaluated and vetted. We may mistakenly conceive of journalism as only being in the format of written articles, television news shows, social media, or documentaries, but games and VR can be journalistic, too. "Newgames" are a genre of games that express current events, issues, and opinions. These games describe, persuade, mount claims, and make arguments using the rhetoric of play, rather than just words or video.[31] For instance, *Project Syria* enables participants to experience the Syrian civil war in Aleppo first hand, and feel the visceral intensity of a bomb attack. It was created using meticulously researched first-hand video and sound recordings. By participating in *Project Syria*, people become not just viewers or readers, but witnesses, too (see more in chapters 4 and 8).[32]

These types of games may be effective because they engage audiences that may not otherwise read or watch the news.[33] Newsgames may also share a perspective on a current issue or event that is not as well communicated through other forms of media, such as video or text. These games enable players to embody a perspective, perform a personal take, or explore a system in a way they cannot just by reading a newspaper article, watching television, or scrolling through tweets. Newsgames are often not polished, complex games, but instead raw, spontaneous, even feral in their attempt to balance the need for timeliness and temporality, with the need to playfully share, express, and show a point of view on an event, topic, or issue.

The *Voter Suppression Trail* game, for example, came out on the *New York Times* website just before the 2016 presidential election.[34] It aims to convey an argument about the types of obstacles that keep people from fully participating civically. Players take the role of different people trying to get to a voting booth to vote in a US election: a white male programmer in California, a Black salesman in Wisconsin, and a Latina nurse in Texas. Inspired by *Oregon Trail*, the players face many more obstacles as the Latina nurse or the Black salesman, and are continually (and often humorously) kept from voting, whereas the male programmer can just go and vote. The game posits a claim and makes it playable: it asserts that some types of communities or people may be systematically restricted from being able to fully participate in civic life in the United States. The creators of the game explain that their argument is derived from real-world interviews and data on voting, just as an article might be. And just like any article (or any game), students should be able to evaluate and vet the information used to create this game, to uncover the biases and ideologies that may be affecting how that information was used and interpreted, and to describe the techniques used by the designers to persuade the player of their interpretations.[35]

Limitations to Using Games to Teach Literacy Skills

Games May Misuse Information

Games may not include lots of text or information to read, analyze, or apply—and this is not always a bad thing. Any game needs to clearly present and organize its information, through an interface that tells the player what they need to do, how they need to do it, and when it matters to do it. Take, for instance, the *Red Dead Redemption 2* main interface. It condenses an enormous amount of data into a very small amount of real estate on the screen. It shows a map with multiple symbols on it, each representing different quests and important locations. It shows a number of different meters, such as the life force and energy level of the avatar and his horse, represented by a heart and a bolt (the horse symbols have a horseshoe in them). The player does not need to sift through enormous amounts of text to get to this information. Rather, the game distills it down into clear, concise symbols so the player can perform the game more easily.

Likewise, news, ethics, or other types of relevant information, data, documents, and evidence also need to be clearly presented to the player through the game. This may mean communicating game content through other modalities besides text or written words. Some games rely on visual or audio cues or symbolic representations, which students need to decipher. *Win the White House* uses simple icons to represent issues, such as a heart with a rainbow in it to represent marriage equality. Some games present data and information graphically, or even transform it into game activities, storylines, or characters. In the game *Play to Cure: Genes in Space*, the designers took breast cancer data collected by Cancer Research UK and transformed it into a type of space fuel that players need to collect so that they can run their spaceships. Where the players navigate their spaceships in the game, in turn, reveals to the cancer researchers where there are anomalies in the data set. Thus, instead of having players tediously look at data sets, players get to go on a space adventure and simultaneously analyze these data sets. This can be strength, because it can make data and information more approachable and accessible. It can also help to motivate media literacy skills, such as fluency across modalities, and the interpretation of symbols and signs.

However, it can also be a limitation. Transforming information in a game environment may oversimplify or even distort it. Take the *Play to Cure* example, where data is translated into space fuel. Is it ethical to represent real people's cancer data this way? Does it distort our interpretations to present it through a game like this? What is lost or gained when information gets translated into different forms, or presented through a game versus another medium?

Information in games should be organized in ways that players can easily grasp it, but also in ways that they can understand its provenance and critique it. Teachers may want to question how these types of representations may help to foster understanding (such as due to their simplicity), and how they may contribute to misunderstandings (such as by omitting the nuance and complexity necessary for a more holistic comprehension of a social issue). For more about games and oversimplifications, see chapters 4 and 8.

Even if a game does have lots of text and requires a lot of reading, this may not be useful or effective. Sometimes the amount of reading in a game may backfire, in that a player feels overwhelmed by the information and choices they have. Wrona, who teaches middle school social studies students at an alternative school in Maryland, explains that he needs to encourage his students to slow down and read the text, because often they just click through it without actively reflecting on it (see more in the *Executive Command* example later in the chapter). Teachers should consider the amount and level of reading in a game, and whether this matches students' age and experience levels.

Writing Practice May Happen Beyond the Game

While this is not a limitation per se, one consideration is that writing practice may come outside of the game. While many games require critical reading skills, they may not incorporate writing directly into the play. Sometimes writing can come after or alongside the game-playing, where the reading done in the game helps the player to formulate writing a response or essay. For instance, high school teacher Darvasi used a narrative game writing exercise to help students reflect further on their identity in light of their game experience with *What Remains of Edith Finch*.[36]

Beyond directly incorporating writing into the game itself, some games may help build skills related to writing, such as argument formation or choosing words, or they may raise self-efficacy around writing. In FableVision's *Civics: An American Musical*, players construct songs based on stanza options provided to them.[37] Finding innovative ways to marry reading and writing through the game itself is a growth area for future civics and ethics games.

Games and Gamers May Spread Disinformation

Just like any other community, games may be designed or used to spread disinformation—or even to foment hate. A 2020 ADL study reported that 9% of the online multiplayer gamers they surveyed heard discussions of white supremacist views and ideologies while playing a game. The report also looked at players' exposure to malicious disinformation and hate related to various topics, like the Holocaust being a myth. They found that 10% of players reported being exposed to conversations related to Holocaust denial. They also found that 17% of players reported being exposed to malicious disinformation about COVID-19 and the Asian community.

Games may also be used to emotionally manipulate people. The types of emotion-driving elements that engage people in games and their communities (e.g., story, sense of belongingness), may also motivate people to believe in and spread disinformation, inaccurate conspiracy theories, and harmful rhetoric. Fantastical premises in games may help players to retain factual information, but also may help them to learn and perpetuate inaccurate or false information. Teachers and designers need to be mindful of how games and their stories can be used to inspire the civic imagination, but also to proliferate lies, ratify problematic institutions, and obstruct justice.

Games like *Troll Factory*, *Harmony Square*, and *Bad News* aim to teach players the types of techniques that people may use to create and spread disinformation (see more about *Bad News* later in the chapter). In *Troll Factory*, the player takes on the role of someone who *spreads* fake news and hate speech, so that they can see first-hand how bots or memes may be used to influence emotions and behavior. Likewise, in the game *Harmony Square*, players need to purposefully "sow discord and chaos" in the fictional town of Harmony Square. By playing these games, players may get better at identifying disinformation techniques, and may gain more confidence in being able to so. These games may also particularly engage young audiences by using story elements, humor, and by having players play as the "villains." But a question is how these games may lead to change. How will players then impede or counter disinformation? Will they just be able to identify it, or will they also be able to disrupt it?[38]

Strategies to Use Games to Teach Literacy Skills

Use Games That Encourage Reading

Reading text or symbols through a game can help students learn new words, jargon, data, and technical language in context. The *Mission US* series places players in different historic moments and lets them click on and collect "smart words" that they may not understand. Players may see a word such as "tenement" during the City of Immigrants module, for instance, where they are taking on the role of Lena Brodsky, a 14-year-old Jewish immigrant who stays with family on the Lower East Side. By seeing this word in the context of Lena's journey, and through living in a tenement in the game, the students are more likely to learn and understand the definition.[39] Teachers should think about using games that fit the reading level of their audience, or that adjust to different student needs.

Example in Action: *Executive Command*

In the iCivics game *Executive Command*, players take on the role of president of the United States, where they need to accomplish different goals and decide which tasks to complete over a four-year term. As president, players need to decide which policy to focus on, such as security, health, or education. Different diplomatic issues come up during the game and the students need to decide how to act, such as whether to go to war with another nation.

The game can spur a lot of reading, as players need to look at evidence and understand its context to make more optimal decisions. However, the amount and level of the text could be overwhelming for some students. Wrona, the middle school social studies teacher in Maryland, adapts the game, *Executive Command*, to his class's needs.[40] He observed that when the students were playing on their own they would often click through all of the text bubbles without reading the relevant information. As a result, they did not end up having the foundational knowledge necessary to make informed decisions. To help the students slow down and read the necessary cues, Wrona plays the game with the full class (by projecting it on a screen in the front of the room), and reads aloud the information in each bubble. He then has students work together to collaborate and decide on the next course of action.[41]

Penney also uses *Executive Command* in her class to encourage writing. She has the students first play the game, and then has them respond to a writing prompt based on the game. In the prompt, she asks students to reflect on the difficulty of being president of the United States, using at least two details from their game experience, such as the laws they signed or the outside issues that affected their policies. Some students explained how the positive feedback on their policies might go up and down in response to their decisions in the game. The students were able to not only experience the game, but also to reflect on their decisions and its outcomes in written form.

Critique Games as Forms of Media

Teachers should use games to help students think about and critique how information is designed and presented through games, and more generally.[42] Games themselves are a type of media (or even propaganda) that can make arguments, and should be critiqued in terms of how they may oversimplify or misrepresent data or use persuasive techniques. Games can spread disinformation. The information presented through games should be validated and authenticated, just like in other forms of media, such as news articles or social media.

Teachers can also use games (and newsgames) to provide additional perspectives on current events and issues. For instance *Fake Your Own Election* was made in response to the 2020 presidential election in Belarus, which has been critiqued for being manipulated.[43] The game, which invites players to rig an election in the fictional Republic of Krakozhia, reveals the techniques that a corrupt government may take to ensure their victory in an election.[44]

Example in Action: *Thoughts and Prayers*

Thoughts and Prayers is a brief newsgame where players need use "thoughts" and "prayers" (operationalized as clickable words on the screen) to fight against gun violence.[45] During the game, players have the opportunity to try to enact a gun control policy, but they are always denied and told to just use thoughts or prayers.

Teachers can use the game with older students in a number of ways. After playing the game, students can discuss how the information about gun violence is presented through the game, as well as what arguments they think the designers are trying to posit through the design of the game (regardless of whether they agree with them). Students can critique the arguments and how they are expressed through the game and discuss whether the game was designed appropriately to reach an audience.[46]

When I showed my class *Thoughts and Prayers*, some students argued that while the game is simple and clear in its argument (which is that thoughts and prayers will not stop gun violence), the persuasive techniques that it uses are ineffective. The game may not reach the audience the designers want, because it is in a game format, which may affect its perceived validity. Also, the game uses a satirical approach, by personifying thoughts and prayers as active agents, which could further lessen its authoritativeness and authenticity. Finally, they argued that the game does not seem to help players overcome their cognitive biases, so it may not help them break out of their own beliefs and use evidence that runs contrary to it.

Likewise, teachers and students can choose other timely newsgames related to topics of interest, and critique and analyze their arguments and how they are expressed through the game's play, systems, and design. And, teachers can invite students to make their own (digital or nondigital) newsgames on current events or issues that matter to them.

Use Games That Enable Interpretation Skills

Teachers can use games that enable skills such as interpreting, validating and authenticating, and comparing and evaluating evidence, data, and other types of information. Teachers could also encourage differing interpretations of this information, so that students do not get stuck in their own interpretations, and are motivated to think beyond their own viewpoints.

In the iCivics game *Newsfeed Defenders*, players need to ensure the accuracy, transparency, trustworthiness, and impartiality of the news that appears in a newsfeed. Players can click on different articles as they enter the newsfeed and decide if they fit the rules of the game. Their integrity meter is affected depending on their decisions in the game. As Coleman-Mortley of iCivics explains, "we wanted a game that increases digital literacy by challenging students to make critical decisions about what they share online, their responsibility to pass along truthful information, and their ability to discern fact from fiction."[47]

Students also need to understand how people may try to spread false news and disinformation. Teachers may want to use games that reveal to students the techniques that are used to spread disinformation—and how to counter it. *Fake It to Make It* asks players to act as media curators who persuade an audience to believe and spread fake news or disinformation. Players need to construct a news site and manage its content, such as by deciding which article content to include, and which forums to post them in. Players need to consider which headlines or claims will attract certain groups of people, and how to use different emotions (anger, sadness) to manipulate these groups. By acting in the role of a media creator, players can see how ethical choices can impact and disrupt publics, including civic systems, institutions, and civic engagement. This game asks us to consider how disinformation is spread and what our responsibilities are as purveyors and curators of media.[48]

Example in Action: *Bad News*

In the game *Bad News*, players need to spread fake news (see Figure 10.2). To do this, players need to gain "followers" or people that like their content on social media. Players also need to raise their credibility, so that their followers will trust the content that they get. The game gives the player a series of prompts and choices on which types of tweets to send, articles to write, memes to post, and news sites to make. However, to do this, the game brings players on a journey through six different techniques that a person might use to spread disinformation. It has the player participate in these techniques, like impersonation, or the act of pretending to be a credible news source; manipulation of emotion, or playing to people's fears, anger, or compassion; and discreditation, the smearing of someone's reputation as a response to criticism. By walking the players through these problematic techniques, and applying them, the hope is that the player will then be able to identify when someone is using the techniques on them. The game creators explain that it "confers resistance against bad online information by putting players in the position of the people who create it."

In *Bad News*, players may choose to create a "fake news" campaign around climate change that attacks scientists and their credibility, or they may choose to spread a conspiracy theory around a passenger plane crash, by sharing articles that raise doubts about the validity of a safety commission's inspection of it. The game also includes

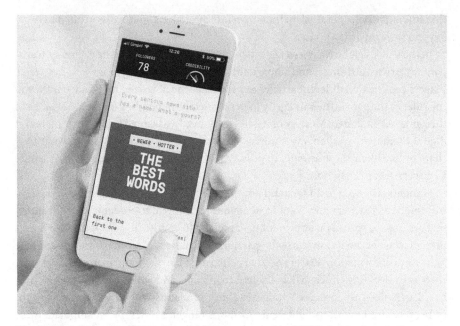

Figure 10.2 An image of the game *Bad News*, created by DROG. Design by gusmanson. Image courtesy of Rivka Otten and DROG.

some content related to the COVID-19 pandemic, and gives the player a choice of how to respond to a tweet from the World Health Organization.

The game provides a teachers' guide, which shares tips on how to use it in a class. The guide explains that teachers may have students play the game first, and then discuss the techniques that were used. The guide also recommends putting the players in teams or pairs and having them play together, while talking aloud through their choices and negotiating together what to do next. However, the content in the game is sensitive and the designers recommend it for students in high school and up, with the note that it could be uncomfortable for some players, and that it needs a teacher to support and guide the students on what to take away from the play. For instance, how do we ensure that the players come out with the idea that we should identify and overturn disinformation techniques, rather than to simply laugh at them (or employ them ourselves)?[49]

11

How Do We Analyze Problems and Systems?

You probably can't imagine ever cheering for a virus. But in the game *Plague Inc.*, you want a virus to "win." In the game, you play as bacteria, virus, or fungus and try to make it spread, infect, and mutate for as long as possible (see Figure 11.1). You begin the game by naming your plague, which starts out by infecting just one person. Soon, it begins to spread. That one person begins to infect others. Cruise ships sail and planes fly across the world, and along with them, the plague travels.[1]

Once the plague starts to spread, you can control how it spreads by evolving it, or by changing its characteristics. With enough points, you can mutate the plague, and change its transmission method (such as by having animals carry it), adjust its symptoms (such as coughing or cysts), or alter its abilities (like being able to resist heat or cold). These modifications affect how the plague is spread, or where it spreads to.

As you evolve it, you can also watch a dashboard to see how many people your plague has infected or killed, and where they live. Messages sometimes pop up, giving you updates on the spread of the plague and its containment, such as whether there are spontaneous mutations, how countries are handling it, or how infectious it is as compared to other bacteria or viruses, such as HIV.

The game play continues until one of the countries finds a cure or the plague infects and kills everyone in the world.[2] The game is fictional, but it uses real-world epidemiological concepts and variables to model a system of spread. Thus the system is realistic even if the plague is not real.

Moreover, the system is dynamic. Players can adjust variables and see how their actions affect the overall system. The game helps us to see that something like a virus is a systemic problem, rather than one that has simple causes and effects. Teachers can use a game like *Plague, Inc.* to also examine and reflect on the ethical reasoning used when thinking through systemic problems, as Kelly did in their college English class.[3]

In case the interactions in this game are not relevant *enough* to real-life events, people can even modify *Plague Inc.* As early as January 2020, people were creating and playing COVID-19 simulations of the game—so much so that Ndemic had to put out a statement that explained that their game was not a realistic replication of the spread of the coronavirus, and should not be used for real-world modeling. Later in 2020, the company created a new expansion called *Plague, Inc: The Cure*, which lets players save the world from a plague rather than spur it on. This mode included

We the Gamers. Karen Schrier, Oxford University Press. © Oxford University Press 2021.
DOI: 10.1093/oso/9780190926106.003.0011

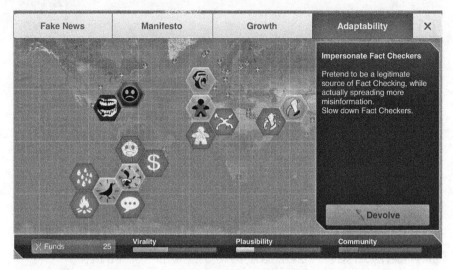

Figure 11.1 An image from the Fake News update to *Plague Inc.* Image courtesy of Ndemic. Creations, Ltd.

controlling government responses to a plague, developing a vaccine, and managing healthcare systems and public services.[4]

   In this chapter I discuss the use of games to help us to practice problem solving skills and how to better think "with systems."

Why Analyze Problems and Systems?

We Need to Solve Problems

Every society faces problems.[5] Solving these problems are a fundamental part of any society. For instance, how do we govern and structure our society? How do we live and work together, raise our families, and teach one another? How do we grow and cope amid limited resources, changing environmental conditions, and sociopolitical crises? We have so many complex and everyday questions that we need to answer as a society. Yet this is also challenging because there are so many ways to solve them, and, understandably, differing ideas on how we should live together. There are often no clear-cut answers, so we need people who can offer and construct possible solutions. Being able to generate and evaluate possible solutions to civic, ethical, and social problems is necessary for all members of a community—whether that community is local, global, or online. Briggs argues that part of our responsibility as participants in a society is to solve problems. "To citizen" is to care about problems and to solve them, or at least to act *toward* solutions. It is to wonder about how we can make solutions that help us to flourish as a society.[6]

Problems are defined as something that is unknown and for which there is no answer—yet. It also refers to something that matters, or something that has some type of societal, ethical, or civic value.[7]

We do not become aware of problems, however, until we name and identify them. "A problem is only a problem if someone [or some community] cares about it."[8] We need to identify a problem first for it to become something that we can work toward solving—such as noticing the amount of trash left in a park, or the rise in water level in a city's coasts. Problem-solving, then, is the act of trying to find a solution to something that has been designated as a problem.[9] We need to be able to ask the right questions and find out the necessary information for us to frame something as a problem, so that we can eventually try to solve it.[10]

There are a number of different types of problems, including dilemmas, decision-making, policy and case studies, design, and more. Voting could be seen as a decision-making problem, as you are choosing from among a limited set of candidates or referendum choices. A design problem may be how to create a game that teaches problem-solving, for instance. Many social, ethical, or civics problems could be described as dilemmas, or problems that are unstructured, less predictable, and more open-ended, as there is often no one obvious right answer.[11] Some dilemmas may involve deciding how to best support an aging population in town, how to spend a limited town budget, or how to incentivize prosocial behavior in a classroom.

Many civics and ethics problems could also be described as "wicked problems" or ones that require perspectives from multiple people and many disciplines to be able to begin to unravel them.[12] Things like climate change, social inequity, and global pandemics all require an all-hands-on-deck approach, with people working together to try to solve it.[13] Likewise, international relations problems require perspectives from economics, anthropology, politics, religion, and cultural studies.[14]

We Need to Approach Problems Systemically

To more effectively solve problems, we also need to be able to analyze systems. Systems are interactive and dynamic sets of interlocking parts, such as the public school system, a legal system, or an ecosystem. Lai identifies systems analysis and thinking as key components of critical thinking, and defines it as "identifying and determining the relationships between variables to understand a system."[15] Systems thinking involves seeing how different variables may interact and evolve, dynamically, over the short and longer term.[16] It also involves being able to adjust and manipulate those variables to see how they affect each other, and change the overall system.

Why think about systems? For one thing, looking at systems may show us how our individual decisions (such as letter writing or protesting) have more far-reaching impact than we may initially realize—and that different people's actions and decisions can intersect dynamically to lead to collective changes. It helps us to see that our choices do not just have direct cause-and-effect results, but that they can have an interlocking web of rippling short- and longer-term effects. Being able to solve a problem fully may also involve dismantling or recreating systems. It is not always enough to change a policy or rule; instead we may need to redesign the entire system of behavior to ensure lasting change.[17]

Thinking systemically requires multiple disciplines and lenses to understand how parts of a system all work together dynamically.[18] Worth, who used *Reacting to the Past* modules in her class, explains that she wants her students to realize that what ends up happening, such as in an election or historical event, "is not a foregone conclusion. It could have gone differently.... It can come down to literally who was in the room at the time. It matters whether you show up. It matters if you do the work. It matters if you cooperate with people that you're supposed to be collaborating with. It matters if there's a charismatic leader or there's an absence of leadership. All of these things can make a difference in how things turn out in history and how things turn out in our own lives."[19] How we solve problems and the solutions we derive—whether it is whom to vote for as a nation, or how to solve a global pandemic as a world—is not a given. It is affected by numerous cultural, social, ethical, and political factors that work together uniquely to generate the outcome that ends up happening. Every individual, however, mattered in that they each affected that collective result.

Societies can change and evolve based on the communal responses of the participants in a group in ways we cannot always imagine or predict based on our individual vantage point. Only by stepping away and seeing it systemically can we see it more fully. However, systems and simulations should not replace stories, art, and poetry as ways of knowing and learning, and expressing change. There are many ways to approach problems—and this is not the only way.

How Do Games Enable Problem-Solving and Systems-Thinking?

Games Can Pose Problems

The act of playing a game is also a form of problem-solving. Games are a manifestation of what Jonassen calls the "problem space," in that the problem emerges from (and is) the space of the game.[20] We can think of the game's goal as a type of question that needs to be answered, or problem that needs to be solved. Playing the game and meeting that goal, then, is a type of engagement in problem-solving—a working of a solution and a tinkering in a problem space.

As such, games can help players practice problem-solving skills, including making hypotheses, gathering evidence, testing out solutions, and deciding on the best course of action. "Players can test out hypotheses about how to solve a particular game's problems (e.g., avoiding enemies in *Super Mario Run*), such as through trial and error (e.g., jumping and seeing what happens), in-game tutorials (e.g., watching an example of jumping over enemies), educated strategies (e.g., trying jumping because it worked in the original *Super Mario Brothers*), or observing other players (e.g., watching videos of other people playing the game)."[21] For example, if my daughter wants to solve a problem in a game, such as how to find hidden power moons in *Super Mario Odyssey*, she will use a number of different problem-solving strategies. She will make educated guesses and try out different techniques based on her prior knowledge and experience, such as how she previously found moons. She may watch a video of someone else finding moons and then she will try out similar strategies. She may ask an in-game character (Toad) to help her with hints, and she may use in-game tools, like a map.[22] She might also ask peers or her family members (like me) to help her find and access the moons.

Games may be particularly effective for practicing problem-solving skills. They can give relevant, just-in-time feedback to the player on their progression to a solution in the game.[23] Games may also simulate, constrain, and structure problems so that they are not too overwhelming. They may break down problems into palatable chunks and manageable mini-problems. In addition, the game may help to contextualize problems by providing clear rules and boundaries so that the player knows what the problem is and what the possible solutions may be (or at least what the possible actions are that could help them to get to a solution).[24] For instance, in the game *Resilience*, you are living in a new world and need to build a camp for refugees, named Murians, who are joining your home. You have to decide what to build and where to put it, and weigh a number of factors and measures, such as hydration, nutrition, hygiene, and medicine. You also need to be continually talking to the refugees to find out how they are feeling, and what they need.[25] The game bounds your decisions and walks players through each choice. Players can even choose a shorter version with fewer options, or a longer one with more possibilities, to help support the problem-solving process.

Games Can Encourage Flexibility

Games can encourage players to expand the types of solutions they may consider and even nudge players to solve problems more flexibly. Games may help players to consider alternate paths to solutions. For instance, games may introduce players to characters that share perspectives, stories, or facts that lead a player down an unexpected path. This helps players avoid "functional fixedness" or being stuck on a typical way of doing something or solving something.[26] We can imagine that some people may get fixated on their usual ways of solving problems, such as by using their go-to political views or cognitive biases in how to approach a social issue. Games can help people move beyond knee-jerk heuristics by putting them in a new role, historic moment, or social standing.

In a *Reacting to the Past* module called the "Threshold of Democracy in Athens in 403 B.C.," players need to use sources such as Plato's *Republic* to solve civic-related problems.[27] The players have to give persuasive speeches about how to respond to civic actions, but they have to persuade from the perspective of the historic role they are given, even if they do not personally agree with that perspective. Porter, who used this in his college classroom, explains that "a Socratic is going to have a very different idea from a radical Democrat is going to have a idea again from an oligarch."[28] Sharing solutions while inhabiting a new role or perspective may help people become more open to multiple approaches to a given problem (see more in chapter 8).

Likewise, in *Branches of Power*, players can switch among different branches of US government (e.g., legislative, executive) to see how the different branches approach the passing of a particular bill. This may keep students' thinking flexible, as these different roles have different goals or constituencies to focus on.[29]

Games can also encourage players to iterate through different solutions and try them out to see how they affect the overall system. For instance, in *Life Is Strange*, players may try out a particular choice, see the short-term result, and then even rewind backward to try out a different choice. The game helps players to see that the choices are not necessarily good or bad, but that there are multiple solutions or pathways (see more in chapter 9).

Games Are Systems

Games can also support problem-solving in another way—in that they can help us to see the systemic factors that affect and underlie a problem. Games are mini-worlds where players can see a dynamic set of intersecting causes and effects, over time and space.[30] Because games themselves are systems, they can help to situate meaning and simulate the complexity of a problem or issue.[31] As I explain in my previous book, "While games cannot possibly simulate or model every corner of a dynamic system, they can realistically reimagine aspects of complex processes, skills, actions, and information within an authentic context, situate learning, and bring people together."[32]

For example, the *Lost & Found* series of games helps players to interact directly with ancient religious legal systems (see Figure 11.2). The games ask players to balance the needs of the many with the needs of the self. Playing this series of games, which models a system of rules (such as Maimonides' legal code), helps players to understand and better appreciate how values and ethics were expressed through past policies.[33]

Furthermore, games can help players to see how different solutions, choices, and actions can affect the outcome of a game and its entire system.[34] This is beneficial because to fully understand civics and ethical problems, people need to envision all of the interconnecting parts of that problem. They need to embrace the whole system around and within the problem—including the social, cultural, political, psychological, economic, and scientific systems that intersect with it.

In the mobile game *Idle Factory Tycoon*, players set up a factory system that includes a warehouse, market, and a series of workstations. After clicking on the different parts

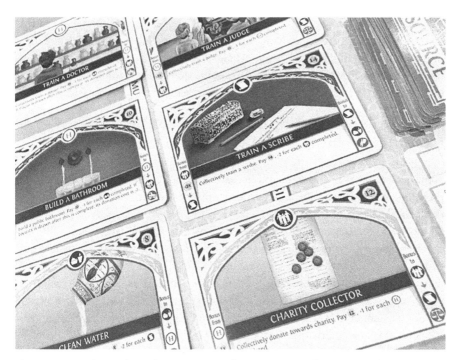

Figure 11.2 An image from the strategic card game version of *Lost & Found*. Image copyright of Owen Gottlieb, 2017.

of the factory, players can start to see how the system works, dynamically, and how each part of that system relies on the other.[35] The system can also get unbalanced. If you decide to upgrade the market component too quickly without leveling up the other components (workstations and warehouses), the system will not work as well and this could create a bottleneck. The game will give you feedback on this relationship, in that it will tell you which of the three component needs to be upgraded—or whether all three are balanced.[36]

Understanding how a system all fits together (and when in motion, where things don't fit as well) also helps us to see where further problems and issues may emerge. The *Animal Farm*-esque political game *Democratic Socialism Simulator* helps us to see the promises and pitfalls of various policies, and the larger system of trade-offs related to different forms of government. To do this, it takes you through a series of policy choices as president, within a dynamic environment, which helps the player to see the societal consequences more holistically, rather than as just a series of possible cause and effect statements.[37]

Games can also help us to develop the practice of looking at the systems that are often obscured in our everyday realities. Archer explains how games can help us to look closer at our systems, such as "systems of government or systems of society, and how those systems can create expectations for engagement and behavior."[38] In

Parable of the Polygons, a playful simulation, participants need to move blue squares and yellow triangles. But by moving these around according to rules (which relate to individual biases, in that squares and triangles do not want to live near each other), the player is able to see how over time this could lead to larger systemic issues, such as a segregated society, as "small individual bias can lead to large collective bias."[39]

Games Can Help Solve Real-World Problems

Some games may even engage people in real-world data collection, interpretation, and problem-solving. These games may encourage people to contribute data or perspectives that help elected officials or scientists make better decisions about their community. Or they may encourage constituents to identify problems in their neighborhoods. Such experiences can spur greater civic learning and action, and further engagement in one's community, as well as in the larger professional world.[40] Teachers can use these games to directly engage students in civic-related data collection, analysis, and problem-solving, which may make it more meaningful to them, especially if they are contributing data about their school, local community, or personal interests.[41] The following are types of real-world games (and other media) that may help to motivate real-world problem-solving and learning (see also the examples in Table 11.1).

1. **Crowdsourcing.** Crowdsourcing is the process of culling information from multiple people about different aspects of the world.[42] Sometimes these projects use interactive platforms and communities, such as websites, mobile applications, and games. Examples of crowdsourcing activities include collecting and submitting data on birds in one's community, sharing weather conditions, or even identifying gravesite wording.[43] In other projects, people communally review and analyze historic evidence, interpret cultural sites, collect civic data and opinions, and solve-local problems.[44] Brabham explains how people in a community used SeeClickFix to post problems and communicate issues in their local region, such as potholes or fallen trees, and in doing so helped with urban planning and government response to issues.[45]

2. **Citizen science.** Citizen science involves including citizens or nonprofessionals in scientific practices. It is similar to crowdsourcing in that citizen science may also use sociotechnical platforms, such as websites and games to invite data and perspectives from people. Examples of citizen science activities include looking at galaxies and stars in the sky above one's home, as the American Association of Variable Star Observers (AAVSO) does, or looking at shark fossils in a bunch of sand sent to a classroom. Or it could involve submitting the size of fish caught in a particular location on the Hudson River, as the Department of Environmental Conservation in New York State does each year to track the migration of eel, fish, and climate patterns. COVID.SI is a citizen science project that helps to collectively analyze molecular compound libraries to support our understanding of COVID-19.[46]

Table 11.1 Examples of problem-solving and knowledge-making games and interactive experiences

Name of Game or Experience	Website	Brief Summary
Operation War Diary	https://www.operationwardiary.org/	People annotate real-world World War I diaries that were written by soldiers from the Western front.
AnnoTate	https://anno.tate.org.uk/	People help to transcribe letters, sketchbooks, and other artist materials for the British Tate Museum.
Clean Games	https://cleangames.org/	This NGO uses games to encourage volunteers to compete with others to clean real-world locations like the Baltic Sea.
What's on the Menu	http://menus.nypl.org/	People transcribe the menus of historic New York City restaurants or inspect buildings and details on maps for the New York Public Library.
Measuring the ANZACs	https://www.zooniverse.org/projects/zooniverse/measuring-the-anzacs	People transcribe the accounts of New Zealand soldiers in World War I for the New Zealand and Auckland War Memorial Museum.
Decide Madrid/ Decide Barcelona	https://decide.madrid.es/; https://www.decidim.barcelona/	Participants engage in online debates and submit and support proposals for a city, such as supporting a more child-friendly Madrid through more playful public spaces, or by engaging in participatory budgeting.
Play the City/ Play Khayelitsha	https://stimuleringsfonds.nl/en/latest/news/play_khayelitsha_cape_town/Read	Designers used their physical game to support collaborative problem-solving in South Africa. The game activity included around 100 participants who sought to remodel a market in Khayelitsha, Cape Town.
SchoolLife	https://www.giantotter.com/schoollifelab	Players learn empathy while interacting with a virtual bully and responding to their interactions. Players are also contributing to an algorithm for understanding the complexities of bullying, such that future games can better simulate it and teach people how to reduce it.
Mapatón	https://www.oecd.org/gov/innovative-government/embracing-innovation-in-government-mexico.pdf	Participants gain prizes and points by mapping the bus routes in Mexico City.

Continued

Table 11.1 *Continued*

Name of Game or Experience	Website	Brief Summary
Stall Catchers	https://stallcatchers.com/main	A crowdsourcing or knowledge game where players aim to help understand Alzheimer's disease through the play of the game.
Movi Joven	https://www.rosario.gob.ar/web/aplicaciones/aplicaciones-moviles/movi-joven	In Argentina, youth can use the Movi Joven app to help engage them in cultural and educational spaces around Rosario. Participants can earn points to get real-world discounts.
CiviQ Platform	https://civiq.eu/about/, https://smartcitiesireland.org/projects/civiq-smart-public-engagement/	Ireland's CiviQ company created this platform for engaging with constituents to use for public planning purposes.
See Click Fix	https://seeclickfix.com/	This app encourages public participation in urban planning and governmental issues, where users can post problems in their municipality such as the presence of a pothole on a road or a broken sidewalk.
Next Stop Design	https://archiseek.com/2009/next-stop-design/	This ran in 2009–2010, and invited users to participate in a transit planning contest, such as ones to design bus stop shelters on a bus stop at the University of Utah in Salt Lake City.
Traffic Agent	https://www.theguardian.com/public-leaders-network/2016/sep/02/app-oslo-children-traffic-road-safety	This app/game helps children in Oslo, Norway to share reports on their school routes, like if there is heavy traffic.
ProPublica/ Lost Mothers	https://www.propublica.org/article/lost-mothers-maternal-health-died-childbirth-pregnancy#disqus_thread	The news organization ProPublica invited people to submit stories for their journalistic piece on Lost Mothers (mothers who died due to pregnancy or childbirth in the United States).
CovidWatcher	https://covidwatcher.dbmi.columbia.edu/	People can submit data related to COVID-19 during the global Sars-CoV-2 pandemic.
Smithsonian Transcription	https://transcription.si.edu/	People transcribe historical documents for the Smithsonian Institution, including ones related to girlhood history as part of the American Women's History Initiative.
Sensafety	https://www.sensafety.org/	This is an app in Berlin, Germany where participants contribute how safe they feel in different public spaces.

This table provides some examples of websites, applications, and games that invite the public to participate. It is not comprehensive. Some of these projects may no longer be running, or only ran for a short amount of time. Note that ethical considerations should be made for how all of these apps and games are used and applied.

3. **Knowledge games.** Knowledge games are real-world problem-solving games, where players are contributing data, interpreting information, and working with others to help find solutions to conundrums through the game itself.[47] These games use many of the same types of actions, tasks, and mechanics as crowdsourcing and citizen science. For instance, in *The Sudan Game*, a prototype made by USC's GamePipe Lab and Carnegie Mellon, players work together to devise steps to peace in the Sudan, by enacting perspectives from all the different Sudanese tribes. The players need to try out different sequences to evaluate whether they could lead to a peaceful outcome, in the hopes that one of the many permutations will lead to peace.[48] One of the classic examples of a STEM-focused knowledge game is *Foldit*, where players work together alongside powerful computers, to understand protein structures.[49] In another game, *EteRNA*, players manipulate puzzles to help create new RNA molecules that could be used as medicine.[50] During the COVID-19 pandemic, these games were also used to solve problems related to COVID-19 (see more in chapter 5).[51]

Limitations to Using Games for Problem-Solving

The Problem-Solving Process Is Biased

The problem-solving process itself can be problematic because it can rely on biases, like cognitive biases. To solve a problem, people may rely on biases, such as confirmation bias, where we tend to search for and use information that confirms our preconceived notions, rather than refutes it.[52] A reason that this happens is because, as Shaenfield explains, "your mind wants to save its resources. Following the one to two million steps is using up energy. So, your mind wants to take shortcuts. Imagine if every object you encountered, you were learning all over again from the beginning."[53] An example of a shortcut is that if you see books, you may make an assumption there will be words inside the book.[54] We often need to take shortcuts and use heuristics, or commonly held strategies, to solve problems, otherwise we would be overwhelmed by all of the resources a problem takes up. This is extremely useful because we need to navigate a complex world. The issue is that sometimes when we are solving a problem we do need to take the long way, and spend time reflecting on and revising our assumptions. Or we need to find partners who will critique our assumptions, and we need to be open to those critiques. Designers and educators need to be mindful of the way a game's design intersects with their own and players' own biases, myths, and misconceptions.[55]

Games May Misrepresent Problems

Games may not structure and constrain a problem properly—furthering more problems or faulty solutions. Sometimes games are overwhelming and do not give players the necessary skills and knowledge to solve a problem. Or games may not be able to usefully or optimally simulate or represent a given problem. In the game, *Stranded*, players need to work collaboratively to survive being stranded on an island.[56] Each player can take three turns, such as clearing a forest, harvesting food, or mining stone. At the end of the turns, players vote together on which type of building they should build. Based on what the players have done, the society may then decrease or increase in happiness.[57] This game has good intentions, which is to enhance collective problem-solving. But the game misses out on showing the complexities of balancing the needs of the individual (staying alive on an island) with the needs of the many (growing a society together). As a result, the game, and its representation of a problem, may not be as structured, relevant, or compelling as it could be. Problems should be designed in a game such that they are appropriately matched to the game play of the game, as well as matched to the audience of the game, its prior knowledge and expertise, and the educational context or classroom needs.[58]

On the other hand, no game can fully replicate or represent all the nuances of a given problem. As with any translation of a real-world issue to a designed experience or simulacrum, some parts of it may be over- or underemphasized, key parts may be left out, and complexities may be overlooked because it needs to be simple and straightforward enough to include in a game. In *Plague Inc.*, the designers cannot include every possible factor that may affect viral spread, such as all the social pressures or norms that may affect how much people physically distance themselves. But they can include a number of prioritized variables in their model to help to simulate the spread of a virus, such as travel restrictions, availability of personal protective equipment (PPE), sharing of disinformation, distribution of a vaccine, or whether schools or businesses are closed.[59]

Games May Not Consider Broader Systems

Games can help players to grapple with the complexity of ethical or civic problems, such as considering them from within dynamic social, cultural, and economic systems. But games do not necessarily enable problem-solving and choice-making from within a complex system. And games may not consider the broader systems beyond the game and how those may affect gameplay. In the game *Spent*, players need to make financial choices that enable enough money left over by the end of the month. Most of the game is text-based, and players are given a (mostly) randomly series of decisions, which affect the amount of money they have.[60] For example, players may be asked whether to spend money on their kids' sneakers or on a broken appliance. The goal of the game is seemingly to help players better empathize with people who are financially insecure by having them make the same types of difficult decisions, and see how hard it is to save money given those decisions.[61]

However, Roussos and Dovidio tested participants who played *Spent*, and their results suggested that empathy and positive attitudes toward those who are poor *did not* increase, and in fact, even *decreased* for many players.[62] This may be because of what the players brought to the game—and how they were affected by cultural, economic, and social systems. Some people who played the game came away with the attitude that people who are financially struggling could have just "made better choices."[63] The game upheld their already established beliefs, such as their belief in meritocracy: that we all have equal agency over our choices, and if we just make the right ones, we will succeed. This may be because the game further instilled the myth that people can control the choices in their own lives by letting players control the choices in the game.

When the researchers removed the player's agency over their choices in *Spent*, by having them watch a video of the game being played by someone else, this did *not* decrease empathy for people who are poor as it did in the other condition.[64] This suggests that the game's design was at odds with its intentions. Thus, although the game *meant* well, and included choices, consequences, and problem-solving, the game may not be effective in enhancing empathy for all populations.

To better support problem-solving, games may need to show short-term and longer-term outcomes and enable players to experience them within dynamic systems, and with consideration to broader systemic forces. We do not always know what myths our students bring with them, and how these will interact with and impact the system of a game.

However, designing such complex systems of choices, decisions, solutions, and consequences can be extremely difficult computationally, artistically, and even logistically through a game. Fully representing the systemic aspects of a problem in or out of a game may even not yet be fully possible given societal expertise, technical constraints, or design knowhow. This also may not be relevant to a narrative-based, story-driven game. We need to think about achieving the balance between clear, understandable gameplay, and complex, nuanced problem-solving, such that we do not mistakenly spur more misconceptions or misguided solutions.

Real-World Problem-Solving Can Be Problematic

In this chapter I have identified some of the ways that games and other experiences can function as calls-to-action to help solve real-world problems. However, games that solve real-world problems may instead create new problems. They may not be well-designed, or they may function more as a superficial gamifying of political processes or social issues, rather than being a meaningful playable experience.[65] Does this matter? Hassan suggests that less meaningful platforms may not be as effective, as many people may make contributions initially, but may not continue to do this over time.[66] However, what counts as meaningful may not have to be a fully realized game. Hassan and Hamari found that gamification can help to enhance citizen participation, which could "lead to better governmental decision-making, legitimacy, and increased trust in government."[67] Harviainen and Hassan also argue that engagement in governmental types of processes is short-term, so gamification (even shallow formats) may be appropriate, such as to encourage voting in the near future.[68]

The line between game and gamified crowdsourcing activity may be blurred—though this may not matter when it comes to civics and ethics learning. What may matter more is whether the players can meaningfully embody roles or practice the types of skills and concepts that we want them to learn. Thus depending on how it is designed and used, a gamified experience may motivate meaningful interactions. On the other hand, a fully-formed game may not activate relevant skills or make meaningful real-world change. Take two experiences: a gamified activity, *Traffic Agent*, and a game, *Free Rice*. In *Traffic Agent*, from Oslo, Norway, students report on hazards while they travel to school, and can gain rewards for doing so.[69] The platform is effective because it enables participants to actually identify and report on problems in their communities. *Free Rice* also aims to make real-world change, and help solve the issues of food shortages and hunger.[70] To do this, players answer vocabulary questions and through getting correct answers, are able to "earn" rice that will be actually shared with those in need, with the goal of helping to end world hunger. However, the game's vocabulary quizzes have little to do, operationally, with how to solve hunger issues.[71] We could imagine a more effective game—such as one that enables players to systemically explore why food shortages happen or why rice may struggle to grow in certain conditions. We can also imagine a game that explores issues such as how to better distribute the food that we do grow to all who need it. A game might even help people permutate through possible solutions to hunger issues so that we could solve a specific challenge. When choosing a game, teachers should consider whether the experience involves practice without meaningful context, or a meaningful context without relevant practice. Is it a well-designed fully realized system of decisions, goals, and obstacles, or does it have only a superficial layer of badges and rewards? If it is the latter, it may not meet longer-term pedagogical goals.

Finally, real-world games bring up other ethical and design issues. What are the privacy considerations of the game? How are students participating in it? Are participants just contributing data, or are they also interpreting and taking other types of actions that support the greater good?[72] Who benefits from this knowledge production and labor, and how will this knowledge be applied in our communities? Are the benefits equitably applied?[73] Pearlman warns that companies may weaponize our information, and our use of gaming technologies.[74] Privacy, transparency, and an ethic of care for the players should not be added features of a game, but instead basic human rights that are fully integrated into any game.[75]

Strategies for Using Games for Problem-Solving

Use Games That Help Situate Problems

Games can help players to solve problems from within a relevant context. They can also enable people to experience the problem from within a dynamic system and manage that system, including its data, resources, and various parameters. Teachers should find games where students can directly manage and adjust different variables and actions that help them to understand the complexities and nuances of a problem or system.[76]

This is useful because we are not usually solving a problem in a vacuum. Rather we are thinking about it within the context of a larger system of interlocking issues. It's never just about giving someone a problem and having them solve it, but also about them managing it alongside other competing pressures. In my research on *Fable III*, a role-playing digital game about running a fictional kingdom, I observed that when players made ethical decisions, they disliked making the so-called bad choice. But they needed to make some so-called bad decisions to earn enough money to protect their fictional citizens from a coming threat. The bad decision that was most frequently made was one on an environmental issue: whether to drain a lake.[77] I hypothesized that this is because its perceived negative consequences are longer-term and require a bigger picture understanding of the world. When faced with the shorter-term gains that are easier to see, players may deprioritize longer-term, more complex issues such as ones related to the environment. We would not have understood this, though, had we not seen the environmental question from within a system of other choices and concerns.[78]

Example in Action: *Happy Farm*

Games do not even have to model complex systems—they can also simplify systems to teach systems thinking for kids as young as kindergarten or pre-K. In *Happy Farm*, a board game, students move pieces around a board, but they also need to engage with an economic system. Harris, a library director who plays the game with students in his district, explains that "you can trade three chickens for a sheep and two sheep for a cow, and two cows trade for a tractor, and the player that gets the tractor first wins the game."[79] The game, which aligns with kindergarten economic standards, helps the students understand concepts like worth and value. By engaging in a system of resource exchanges, the players start to understand how value gets made, shared, and negotiated.

Example in Action: *Papers, Please*

It's 1982 in Arstotzka, a fictional Eastern European country in the game *Papers, Please*.[80] You are playing as an immigration officer, checking passports and other documentation to decide who you let in, and who gets denied entry. You have to balance different actions: you need to let people in to earn credits or money in the game, which you can use to house, medicate, and feed your family. But you also need to follow the very restrictive game rules, and make sure those you decide to let in are approved to be let in. You have to consider whether the country they are from is off-limits (Impor or Republia citizens are not allowed in, for instance, and Kolechians have to be searched). You also have to inspect their passports, see whether their work visa is dated properly, or check whether they are in the newspaper as a wanted criminal. Not following the rules could result in your termination as an officer (and signals the end of the game).

As the games progresses, the player needs to navigate more and more rules, documents, and constraints. The player can use two allowable transgressions per round to decide if and when they want to knowingly break the rules. Should you let in Safadi Shaddy, who is bringing in some contraband, as he will give you 10 credits for it? Should you sneak in Wilma Hoff, who hasn't seen her son in six months? In another choice, one man is able to come in, but not his wife; should you let them both in and take his bribe?[81] Players can choose whether to follow the game's (and the fictional country's) rules or break them, and can negotiate how their country's draconian regulations affect their own (in-game) needs.

Papers, Please is an example of how games can help players think through ethical and civic issues because the game represents an oppressive system that a player can explore.[82] Playing such a suffocating system helps us to better understand how this system suffocates.[83]

Moreover, even though the game is fictional, it enables us to experience civic relationships among polities and explore their tensions, and to see how these get operationalized, such as through rules around whom gets let in or shut out. Teachers can use this game and have students share the ethical choices they made, and why they made them, either in pairs or larger groups. Students can discuss how their own values and ethical mindsets (may or may not) intersect with a regime's sociopolitical system—how politics intersects with the personal. Finally, teachers can use the game to talk about different types of real-world civic and political systems.

Use Games That Encourage Multiple Solutions

Games may encourage particular types of solutions, pathways, or hypotheses. The types of solutions that get rewarded and the types of pathways that are open to the player in a game will shape how that player solves problems. Teachers may want to use games that counter this, however, and enable players to see that there may be more than one possible solution to a problem.

Games can provide enough variety and randomness to keep players lithe and mindful. This could mean having players continue to pose and retest hypotheses and possible solutions. For instance, in the virtual reality game *BioDive*, players need to make hypotheses about snails based on their observations.[84]

Observing how others approach a problem through a game can also be effective in civics and ethics learning.[85] Enabling players to take on opposing roles or even switch roles and see differing viewpoints may be useful.[86] In the card game *PolitiCraft*, players can see how other players solve a civics-related problem, and how they construct narratives using the cards they choose.[87]

Example in Action: *Quandary*

In the game *Quandary* players are tasked with building a new society on the fictional planet, Braxos, and handling the different problems that arise (see Figure 11.3).[88] Players act as a leader for the society, gathering evidence from the community members and using this to build a case for a solution to a problem. One issue is how to handle missing sheep, which may have been eaten by the Yashor, a fictional creature on Braxos. There are a number of possible solutions that are presented to the player, including using a fence, setting traps, feeding the Yashor poison, or doing nothing at all. Players need to interact with nonplayer characters (NPCs) to listen to their perspectives, gather and sort these perspectives into opinions and facts, organize the evidence into different solution buckets, and then decide on the best way forward for Braxos.

In *Quandary*, however, there are no right or wrong solutions. The player gains points based on how well they distinguish between facts and opinions, and how they use information to support the solution they decide on. The process of solving a problem, rather than the solution itself, gets rewarded. The designer, Osterweil, explains that this was intentional: "There were solutions that we thought of as better or worse. But we really tried to structure it so that a player would have more satisfactory results if they showed an ability to listen to other people regardless of what actual

Figure 11.3 An image of the game *Quandary*, created by FableVision Studios. Image courtesy of Learning Games Network.

choice they have made. We did not favor any one choice over any other one" in how the points were awarded.[89] As a result, some students may decide on the same exact solution but may earn a different number of points, because of the skills they used to reach their solution.

Teachers can use this game in a number of ways. One, they can have students work in pairs while playing the game, and discuss the actions they should take, such as which evidence to use to solve the problems posed by the game. Two, teachers can have students first individually play the game. Then, as a class, they can compare the solutions they chose, and the evidence they used to get to those solutions. Teachers could also have students engage in a class debate and use evidence from the game to support their arguments. Finally, teachers can have their students create their own new societies or new worlds. Students could work in teams to design everything from how the people in the new society eat or communicate, or the types of places where the people live, work, or play. Students should also think about the ethical problems that their new society may face, and how its citizens may approach these problems.[90]

Use Games that Solve Real-World Problems

Problems in games can be based on realistic (or at least, relevant) data, statistics, choices, or decisions. Although Braxos in *Quandary* and its inhabitants are fictional, the logic of the solutions, and the evidence and perspectives related to them, are realistic. Problems in a game could even be based on real-world problems. Games can provide opportunities for students to use real-world tools and models, interact with real people, and make a real impact. Being able to work with relevant and authentic information and choices can help the player to apply those problem-solving skills to other real-world scenarios (see more in chapter 5).

Harviainen describes two games that directly engage the public in civic processes. For example, in the Finnish game *Lykkylä* by the Association of Municipalities, players need to think about and address Nordic political processes, as well as community, budgeting, and stakeholders needs. The game "gathers information from citizens and has received initiatives and suggestions that were actually put into practice by the government."[91] This game is run in high schools, where students are able to learn about Nordic civic processes, while also proposing changes. Likewise, the City of Helsinki had more than 2,000 employees from its city departments play *The Participation Game*, which helped them to understand how to better engage citizens, such as during public meetings.[92]

Games may also help players understand the types of issues and questions that government officials, leaders, and experts may face. In the iCivics game *Represent Me!*, players need to listen to and balance the needs of their constituents to make sure they can sponsor a bill in Congress.[93] Likewise, in *The ReDistricting Game*, players learn about the issues surrounding redistricting voting districts and gerrymandering by actually playing a game where they need to redistrict real-world counties.[94] Steven

Schrier uses this game in his community college class and explains that the students learn some of questions around redistricting, such as "whether you redistrict and keep certain populations together, or whether you try not to push out the incumbent, and be fair to the political parties."

It is important for teachers to also think about whether the game they are using is meaningful and personally relevant to their player. What are the issues that matter to the students, and their friends, families, and communities? Are the actions in the game enabling the player to participate meaningfully in civics and ethics practice (such as with the skills and concepts shared in this book)? Or is the game play irrelevant to authentic civics and ethics practices, such as in the case of *Free Rice*?[95]

Example in Action: *VoxPop*

The game *VoxPop* supports learning through a series of live action role-plays, where students work together to solve a problem from the past (see Figure 11.4). To play, each student gets a role from a historical crisis or movement, like the 1960s Civil Rights movement or Shay's Rebellion. The students find out who their role or character is, as well as the character's wants and fears, and a few details about their biography. The students need to role-play with this character and work with others to solve the crisis.[96]

The game also provides context to the historic moment and crisis. It breaks down the main issues and perspectives on the problem into three smaller, more digestible chunks, so that players can start to approach the problem more systemically. Lim

Figure 11.4 An image of students playing *Vox Pop*. Image courtesy of Gigantic Mechanic.

explains that in the Shay's Rebellion role-play, the three key parts of the problem are financial, representation-related, and about the rule of law.[97]

The game uses software to support the game's interactions, such as voting and teacher controls. The software can be accessed from phones or tablets so that students can play face-to-face and socially interact more easily. *VoxPop* can also be used remotely. In a physical classroom, teachers can put students in teams to work together. The set up typically goes like this: students first work in character groups, with all the farmers, bankers, or traders working together. Next, they review specific proposals and decide whether it would be good for them. Then they engage in a compromise phase, where they work *across* the groups to find a solution that works for all the characters. Then, the whole class goes through the proposals together, and decide which proposals they want to push forward to a town hall vote. They also have a series of debates, with students giving speeches for either side of the proposal, and they even host a vote where they decide whether the proposals get passed. Finally, the groups debrief and reflect on what happened in the game.

For the debrief, Lim and Trefry suggest prompts like: "What strategies did you use to try and work together?"; "What parallels do you see with today?"; "How did your solution differ from what actually happened in the past?"; or "Was this was a solution that people would have enacted at the time, or is this a 21st century solution?" The debrief period is particularly important for students who played characters that did not have the same values and opinions as they would have shared. It gives them an opportunity to explain how their personal views differed from their character's views.

While in a remote setting, teachers can have a similar setup. The teachers can share the historic context virtually, such as through a video or online slideshow. They can also share character "cards" by assigning each student to one of the four characters, and then doing virtual breakout rooms where the students can discuss with others in their group. The students can then decide via the virtual platform which proposals to put forth. They can also use the platform (like Zoom or Seesaw) to share written statements or make speeches. Students could vote via Google forms or an online poll to determine the winning proposals. At the end, students can reflect together on what happened, such as by considering how their process may have been different in person.[98]

12
How Do We Explore and Design?

In the game *Civics! An American Musical*, students act like mini-Lin-Manuel Mirandas and make their own musicals (see Figure 12.1).[1] To do this, they need to dig into an American historical event and research a time period, just like Miranda did with *Hamilton*.

The first step in creating the musical is deciding on the topic from a pool of historical subjects. For instance, one of the topics is school desegregation in the 1950s and 1960s in the United States, and how student activists played a role. Hallisey explains that through the game, students need to decide how they want to represent the historic moment and figure out "which pieces go into the set design, the props, the costume design, and what actors to cast in the main roles." They also need to decide how to "present these historic characters in a way that expresses their emotions and points of view." The players even construct an original song for their musical, such as by selecting stanzas that capture the meaning and spirit of protest songs from the civil rights movement.[2]

To select the right elements for the musical, students work with and analyze digital versions of primary sources such as letters, testimonials, photographs, opinion pieces, essays, and other artifacts that exist in the Library of Congress archives. This means they get to hear original voices and inspect the smudges on the documents, and "really get the feel of the hand of the person who wrote it," which is different than just reading a transcription of it.[3] Because of the game's musical creation context it's not just about looking at these primary sources, but also about using them in ways that build knowledge and civic engagement. Players need to critically analyze documents, make evidence-based decisions, think about media's representation of the past, and also reflect on other's possible evaluations of their work. Through the process of creation—by making a musical in the game—players engage in civics and ethics.[4]

In this chapter I investigate how designing, making, constructing, and tinkering helps us to learn and practice civics and ethics skills. I also consider how we can help students explore and experiment with ideas, hypotheses, rules, and boundaries. By engaging in creative practices, we can exercise the "civic imagination" necessary to solve problems, devise new policies, and redesign our world.[5]

We the Gamers. Karen Schrier, Oxford University Press. © Oxford University Press 2021.
DOI: 10.1093/oso/9780190926106.003.0012

Figure 12.1 A splash screen image from the game *Civics! An American Musical*. Copyright © 2020 FableVision.

How Does Design Support Ethics and Civics?

Design is Critical Thinking

Games can help us to interrogate our worlds, but can the *process* of making games—and remaking our systems—also help to engage us in civics and ethics? According to Jonassen, "design" is a type of problem that involves understanding the best way to construct a policy, create a system, or modify a process.[6] Design often gets applied to more aesthetic questions, such as how a game looks, or the art style of a character or setting. But design is much more than that. To design is to choose from among many options, or to decide how to act. It involves how we shape a game—or any other type of experience, object, product, or place—to better fit the needs of those interacting with it. It includes developing tools and artifacts, communities, media, and experiences.[7] It's "an active process of finding the best solution to a given problem based on the available resources and constraints, designers' previous knowledge and experiences, and the desired outcomes or goals."[8] For example, teachers, when designing any type of learning experience, must first identify a gap, problem, or need. Next, they need to research that problem, the context for it, and the audience that it affects. Finally, they need to try out different solutions, and continue to refine them until they find the best solution to the problem or gap.

The same is true for making a game. Designers need to create a game that they think is the best solution for their audience. They have to keep refining their game to make sure it meets goals and engages its audience.

Like problem solving, design is also a critical thinking skill. Ventura et al. cite creation as one of the key components of critical thinking, which includes skills like synthesis, computational thinking, and planning. It involves creating strategies, theories, and methods based on a synthesis of evidence, data, and information.[9] Design is a process that helps us to think more systemically about issues, and to see how different needs and parts are interconnected.[10] Design serves as a type of argument for how we should solve a problem in our world, and how parts of our society should be, act, function, or change. Games and the way they are designed make claims about how the world is and how the world should be.[11]

Design Involves Iteration

Design involves iteration or interactive refinement. Designers need to test, retest, and iteratively refine and revise their solutions based on feedback from their constituents. They need to ensure that what they want to express through the design is expressed—including all the functions, messages, and interactions. They need to interrogate the ethical ramifications of their design and reflect on the choices they made. They need to question whether the experience is appropriate, fulfilling, useful, and humane.

Designers also need to review other's solutions—see what is already out there—and identify what's missing and what we should change about them going forward. Design can invite people to imagine, experiment, play with, and explore new possible solutions and arguments, rather than just accept the status quo. These types of skills and practices are essential for civic problem-solving, and also for addressing community needs and revising institutions, policies, and processes. Engaging in design helps us to critically interact with our current institutions, and refine or even overhaul them, so that we can more equitably lift one another up and enable more people to flourish.

Design Also Reveals

The process of designing something helps us to explore the contours of a problem, and to get to know its constraints. By creating an experience, we need to really dig into that problem. We have to figure out how to best represent it, and this requires continually prioritizing different evidence and information, making choices, and figuring out the best design solution.

Practicing design over time can help to make design processes more transparent in general—and can help us to think about the decisions that went into *others'* creations. It helps us to think about design as one possibility, rather than a predetermined result. It helps us to realize that any given policy, game, or system is one possible solution, though there could have been many other ways of expressing it. It also empowers us to think about the ways that it could have been designed differently. Benjamin explains that the sociotechnical imaginary is not just about revealing "how the technical and social components of design are intertwined, but also imagines how they might be configured differently."[12] For instance, how are systems designed to include or empower people? How are policies designed to keep out certain people? How are experiences shaped to recreate and uphold problematic social hierarchies? Engaging in civics is not just about understanding the hidden machinations of our institutions, but also about how we can reimagine our world and our understanding of the past and future.[13]

Design Helps Us Connect

Design is about people. To engage in design we need to empathize with our audience, consider their needs and perspectives, and construct the best path forward for our world. Portnoy, in her book on design thinking in education, explains that the first step in approaching any problem is to first understand and empathize with those dealing with the problem, as well as identify and research the problem from their perspectives. She asks, "Whose experiences are improved by designing a solution to this problem?"[14]

Design also helps us to externalize our knowledge and share it with others through our created artifacts and products. By engaging in the creative process and constructing representations of how we see the world, we are better able to express our views of the world and share those with other people.[15] By designing with others, we are also better able to see how *they* think through problems and solutions, and we are better able to access their perspectives and empathize with their points of view.[16]

The practice of designing with and for others has another benefit, too. By redesigning with others in mind, we can begin to reconceptualize what citizenship is, so that more voices and ways of "citizening" are included.

How Do Games Support Design and Exploration?

People Can Make Their Own Games

Having students design their own games may be an effective and meaningful way to learn about ethics and civics, and practice relevant skills. Through working together on teams or individually, students can design games that share ethical perspectives and posit arguments about current events, local issues, or community needs. They can even use design as a way of solving real-world civic and ethics problems, such as making games about their local, citywide, or regional community. Kishon and Kafai argue that making and modding games (modifying aspects of a game), particularly games related to civics issues, helps engage students in civic participation because it encourages makers to think about how to express complex civics issues, and "become aware of the values embedded in games and digital media at large." Reflecting on one's design choices and assumptions, and critiquing one's own creations, are integral parts of this process, too.[17]

Games are systems, and designing games helps to reveal systemic issues. Osterweil explains that his students often have trouble seeing problems systemically, so he has them make games about the problems to help them realize their systemic foundations. Osterweil explains that "to really look at the problems in the world, you have to look at the system that created it." For their first assignment, they need to take a system in the world and design it as a game, such as "how education funding gets apportioned in municipalities or the electoral college system. Some try to model the electoral college system and how that affects how people campaign, where people campaign, and why."[18]

Fullerton and Upton note that game design is not just about interactions and transactions between the game and player, but about designing emotional and social experiences, too. It's about designing for community and connection just as much as it is about rules, mechanics, and procedures.

The process of making a game is also about community.[19] In 2018 I co-organized a series of "game jams" (events where people come together to work in teams to make games in a short amount of time). The participants needed to make a game about identity. Regardless of the games they made, the goal was to connect them to others, connect them with themselves, and include them in a community (see more about game jams later in the chapter).[20]

Design Lets People Express

More than just sharing facts and figures, games may also change minds and hearts by empowering us to express our perspectives and tell our stories.[21]

Using stories, cases, and scenarios is a common technique in ethics and civics education, as they "provide narratives that convey real world situations and problems."[22] Games can tell stories in different ways. In *Bioshock*, the player plays as Jack (the main character), who they both play as and observe. Through this interaction with the avatar and with the choices, obstacles, and goals in the world, the player is able to engage with the game's moral system and reveal the story of Jack's origin. The game, *Hades*, builds on stories from Greek mythology and has players play as Hades's son Zagreus, who wants to escape the underworld. *Kentucky Route Zero* tells a story over multiple game episodes that were released from 2013 to 2020.[23]

Another strength of sharing and listening to stories is that it helps us to access and enter a new world, imagine its possibilities, and better process or rehearse its nuances. We may use a "willing suspension of disbelief for the moment," and accept and even engage with views and perspectives in ways we may not otherwise.[24] When people are engrossed in a narrative or story world, they may even be more open to new ideas, information, places, and peoples, as well as more open to changing behaviors, attitudes, and perspectives. Kaufman et al. explain that *ZombiePox*, a game that uses a fantastical setting to help players understand about viral spread of viruses, helped players retain more knowledge and information than the non-fantastical version of the game, *Pox*.[25]

Students can also tell their own stories and share views through games. Games are communities and public spheres, or mini-playgrounds of civic ideas, where players can test out their views, values, and virtues. In some games, players can play within a game's creative space and produce everything from stories and scripts, characters and avatars, art assets and objects, and technical modifications and programming snippets.

Players can even make their own games within some games. My daughter makes game levels in *Mario Maker 2*, a game creation environment on the Nintendo Switch, where you can use objects like bricks, items like mushrooms, and enemies like Koopa Troopas to construct a game level and then play it. By creating her own levels, she is able to craft and share her own *Mario*-world designs with the public. She is also able to tell stories *about* her creations. She told me that while making one level, she wanted to use golden mushrooms as objects in it, but *Mario Maker 2* did not have these items available. So she experimented with the design tools and was able to place the red and green mushrooms on top of each other to make an object that approximates a golden mushroom. This process engaged her creative, problem-solving, perspective-taking, and experimentation skills as well.

Likewise, players can make games, vehicles, sculptures, music, film, and characters in the online community *Dreams*. In this virtual community, participants can play and interact with others' creations and also use the in-game tools to express their own creativity. In chapter 6, I explored how people may even create and script their own dramas and improvise live-action performances through games like *Minecraft*. *Roblox* is another online multiplayer game creation community where participants can make and trade virtual items, and make games and play others' game creations. Players can create and play all different types of games—including *Adopt Me*, where players take care of digital pets or *Would You Rather?* where players decide between two humorous choices. Creating a game that is shared publicly, such as through *Roblox*, may help people to feel more empowered to participate in all of our publics, and in the broader conversations about how we should design our world.[26]

Thus designing and sharing stories through and around games can help players to reason through and reflect on their own perspectives and those of others, as well as share and learn information and views.[27] (See more about story in chapter 8.)

Players Can Explore Rules, Norms, and Ethics

Games can provide clear boundaries, rules, and constraints. Some games also let the player decide when they will follow or break rules.[28] Games like the *Fable*, *Fallout*, and *Dragon Age* series, *Undertale*, and *This War of Mine*, enable players to explore a new world and its morality system, while experimenting with who they are, their values, and their own boundaries (see more in chapter 9).

Consalvo talks about this in her book *Cheating*, where players look for ways to transgress and traverse the game's boundaries as a way of engaging meaningfully in play.[29] Deciding to break or not break rules in a game may also help players explore and reflect on their identities further (see more in chapter 7).

Games may even invite players to purposely break rules or cross boundaries so as to get out of their comfort zone, which could help in encouraging new ways of solving problems or the trying on of new perspectives, strategies, or values. Games may do this by suddenly changing the rules, goals, or even adding in new obstacles or characters. The board game *Pandemic: Legacy* takes the game *Pandemic* and lets players transgress by "ruining" the game—whether by ripping up a card or drawing an "X" over a card—each time it is played. This helps people to see that we can break conventions, like the norm of keeping a board game in its original, pristine format.

Exploration of a game world is even a type of cocreation, in that you are actively engaged in creating the experience. How you explore a game's story, gameplay, or world shapes that game. The player and designer become a type of cocreative apparatus that authors the experience together.

Critiquing Design Is Beneficial

Analyzing and critiquing a game can also be useful. By "lifting the hood" of a game or stepping back and reflecting on its design, we can start to see how the game could have been made or played other ways. We start to realize that this particular game—this one particular result—stemmed from the experiences, biases, mindsets, experiences, epistemologies, and values of the team making the game in that particular moment. We also begin to see that this game (or policy, institution, governmental system, ethical approach, or community initiative) could have been made thousands of different ways.

Likewise, with social issues, historic moments, and ethical conundrums, there are no clear-cut ways to proceed, no one right answer, and things may have progressed very differently given other options, biases, variables, and even people working together on the problem.[30] The practice of analyzing a game's design can help us engage in societal critique, as it sheds light on how our institutions and social structures are designed as well.

Limitations to Practicing Design

Designers and Design Communities Are Biased

Games embed the biases of their creators, as well as their players, just like any designed experience.[31] We cannot help this: we are products of our time and place, and we will unwittingly inscribe these biases into our own creations (see also chapters 7 and 8).

How a game is designed may even spur further biases. Yang et al. found that playing as a violent Black avatar in a mainstream game, *Saints Row 2*, may lead to more harmful attitudes toward Blacks in real life, though playing the same game as a white avatar does not.[32] Consider also the discussion of the game *Spent* in chapter 11 and how the game may have inadvertently increased negative attitudes toward people who are financially struggling, even though it was intended to enhance empathy.

The culture and systems in which we make and play games also embed biases and may further ethical issues. This includes the digital game development, livestreaming, esports, and board game communities. For instance, a number of people have expressed stories of sexual assault, harassment, and toxic culture in the game-streaming space (people who broadcast their game play live on platforms such as Twitch), as well as in the development space more broadly.[33]

Design interacts with people in other ways, too. All types of problems can arise when players interact within a game system. Players can cause harm. They can break game and community rules in ways that negatively affect others. They may use hate speech, sexually assault others, doxx, swat, or stalk. Players may harass strangers through games, as well as people who are friends. Just like any other communities or communal spaces, people may bully, threaten, and exclude. These types of transgressions need to be challenged and stopped (see also chapter 6).[34]

While games are possible places to play with new ideas and push on the boundaries of propriety, they are also potentially problematic. We should ethically analyze and critically consider others' and our own games. We need to think about the ethics of our play, the ethics of our use of the game in the classroom, and how games may themselves perpetuate harm of all types.[35]

Teachers and students should consider: What are the responsibilities of designers to their players, and to the impact of their game? If a game designer is trying to change a player, for instance, is the game changing the player without their consent?[36] Another question is whether the very institution of design—and the process of design thinking—are upholding white supremacy.[37] Likewise, Rusch challenges assumptions around games for change, and asks whether it is problematic if the player does not "get a say in whether they want change and what kind of change they want." We need to be thinking about the ethics of transformation.[38]

Games May Intentionally Foster Hate

Some games are clearly meant to be harmful, such as ones that aim to propagate hate and violence.[39] In the game *Ethnic Cleansing*, players kill stereotypes of characters who are Black, Latino, or Jewish. Likewise, *Zog's Nightmare* is a game created by white supremacists to spread inaccurate conspiracy theories such as "Jews are taking over the world." In another game, players are asked to punch a virtual representation of a real person, made by someone who disagreed with her views. Other games portray and sensationalize sexual violence, such as *Rapelay* or the more recent, *RapeDay*, where players are supposed to rape virtual characters as zombies. These games are not providing fruitful transgression; rather they are fostering misery. I need to reflect even on the inclusion of them in this book—as naming them and continuing to prop-agate the existence of these games is problematic as well.

Moreover, some games and game platforms are used purposefully by players to foster hate—such as those who use games to spread malicious disinformation or share racist ideology (see more in chapter 10). Unfortunately, design can be used to foment hate, just as it can be used to cultivate connection and care. We should stand against designs that express hate, and those people who purposefully use games to propagate hate. But we should also not engage in "moral panic" responses to games, in that we dismiss them all as being communities to be feared. How might we use de-sign to support care or constrain unethical behaviors? How might we critique games and their communities in a more nuanced way?[40]

Design May Provoke

However, the line between provocative and stirring, and damaging and immiserating, is often blurred. In these cases, the ethics of a game's design and use need to be consid-ered more contextually.

Some games may provoke. They poke and prod at our well-worn beliefs, and en-gage players in the exploration of new ideas, values, or mindsets. They may aim to overturn norms or reveal human truths in ways that may make players uncomfort-able, or even distressed. For instance, *That Dragon, Cancer* could overwhelm a player emotionally as they coexperience (with the designers of the game, or others who are playing the game) the grief of losing a son.[41] We might argue, though, that this type of discomfort is beneficent.

On the other hand, take the game *The Slaying of Sandy Hook Elementary*. In this game, players play as the Sandy Hook elementary school killer.[42] The game offers the chance to pick up a gun and kill your (virtual) mother, as well as the (virtual) kids in an elementary school, who are drawn as cowering figures in the game. After the time runs out you can replay the game, but this time with no guns and just a machete. The game aims to provide an argument about gun control, as it lets the player realize that the killer had the opportunity to murder more people with guns rather than with other weapons. The game is also disturbing to play. But does the intention matter? What are the lines of propriety given that the game represents a real-life, horrific murder of children? In actuality, the parents of the children killed tried to petition to censor this game, but we can still play it. Should we?[43]

Games may also have problematic interactions that are beyond what a de-signer may have intended. Design interacts with context in unpredictable ways. Fisher explains that when *Pokémon Go* was being played frequently, there was a poison gas Pokémon that was "instantiated at the DC Holocaust museum, which was distasteful." Likewise, Vituccio cocreated *Journey through the Camps*, a VR experience where players go on a realistic journey to the concentration camps. He explains that at first people found it problematic in that they were in essence gamifying the Holocaust.[44] Vituccio describes how some players stopped playing *Journey through the Camps* because it was too emotionally overwhelming (see more in chapter 7).[45] When choosing games, teachers need to engage with how a game's design interacts with the ecology of its play—including its players and their needs.

Design Is Complex

While it is not necessarily a limitation, the process of design has unique challenges. First off, design requires time. It can be an all-consuming practice that requires expertise, the right platforms, and access to the necessary tools. Just as we think about accessibility of playing and using games for education, we also need to think about how accessible it is to be creating and designing games. How approachable is the process of making games?

On the other hand, does design *really* need to require so much expertise? Educators and students may have preconceived ideas about games—even biases about what games can do or what constitutes good game design. For one thing, they may think that making games is intimidating. Even professional and seasoned game developers are intimidated at the prospect of making a game.[46] We can imagine that teachers, mentors, and students, most of whom have no formal training in game development, may not see themselves as possible designers, which makes the creation of one's own games even more daunting. They may imagine that they need to create high-quality, professional-level games that cost millions of dollars to create, and thousands of developers to work on. They may mistakenly think that they are not creative enough, or not capable of telling compelling stories or sharing unique views. Moreover, they may have limited experience with games, and their variety and possibility. To counter this, Farber tells his students that the games they make do not need to be "good."[47] The process of making matters—not just the final product.[48]

Strategies for Encouraging Design and Exploration

Enable Students to Transgress, Ethically

It may seem like a contradiction, but teachers can use games to help students break the rules in ways that help them to explore ethics. Games can help us to push on boundaries and provoke students' imagination and creativity. Sometimes when students are able to transgress—in nonharmful ways—they are able to enter into an exploratory mindset, where they can better imagine possibilities or step outside of their own perspectives. Through exploring and transgressing in the game, players may begin to embody roles and do things they wouldn't typically do in their everyday lives. However, this needs to be managed by a teacher to ensure it is done ethically and beneficially.

Example in Action: *Rosenstrasse*

In the analog role-playing game *Rosenstrasse*, players play in pairs to engage in ethical questions around a historic women-led protest in 1943, when non-Jewish women asked for their imprisoned Jewish husbands to be released from the Nazis—and were successful (see Figure 12.2). Hammer explains that throughout the game, players need to make difficult decisions; they need to take turns choosing one of two "terrible things to choose from and they have to decide which one to inflict on another player," such as reporting a Jewish person for going to a movie.[49]

One of the goals of the game, Hammer explains, is to "give people the chance to see themselves as people whose actions can make a difference. Meaning if the *Rosenstrasse* women in 1943 Berlin could resist the Reich and win, . . . nothing is impossible."[50] As a result of the game, the players start to push their own real-world boundaries and change their future civic decisions. Players would say things like "I'm the kind of person who wouldn't protest," but the game helped them to try out being a character who *would* protest.[51] Teachers can use this type of game to encourage students to think about times where they were more open to new activities or ideas. Or, teachers could have students design their own games that urge exploration of a new historic moment, a difficult choice, or a new mindset or perspective.

Figure 12.2 An image of the game *Rosenstrasse*, by Moyra Turkington and Jessica Hammer. Image courtesy of Jessica Hammer.

Use Hackathons, Game Jams, and Charettes

Teachers can encourage students to make games through impromptu design challenges and hands-on prototyping activities, like hackathons, game jams, or charettes. A hackathon is an intensive period of time where participants are building or designing something, such as an app (application), website, or game. A game jam is a type of hackathon where participants make a game for a specific purpose, usually over the course of a week or weekend. Likewise, charettes are hands-on, collaborative design meetings where participants come together around a common purpose or problem to solve.[52]

Game jams, charettes, and other design-focused workshops may be effective ways to practice civics and ethics skills, and help students become more comfortable with uncomfortable issues and people who are different from them. These design events often use some type of theme or topic. A theme could be related to a civic problem, or it could be more general, like a concept, saying, or feeling.[53] Games for Change hosted virtual and in-person game jams for youth with themes such as climate change and inclusivity.[54] Díez and the Devs of Personal Games hosted a virtual game jam on friendship, togetherness, emotions, and feelings. Another jam, #ResistJam, was organized to encourage people to develop games to "resist oppressive authoritarianism in all its forms." The Global Game Jam organization runs a game jam every year, which takes place at thousands of individual sites around the world.[55] These types of events can take place online or in an in-person setting (such as a classroom or after-school program). While some of the games created through game jams may themselves be effective for learning, the process of creating games may be what matters more than the final product that is created.

Example in Action: Game Jams

In 2018, with the ADL and Global Game Jam, I co-organized a series of game jams around the theme of identity.[56] The purpose of the event was twofold. First, we wanted to provide a safe, inclusive event for participants to grapple with identity through game design, to collaborate with others, and to develop more confidence in their ability to make games, particularly about social issues. Second, we also wanted to understand whether the *process* of making games was meaningful in and of itself. Regardless of the games that were made, or how effective or expressive they were—was the act of designing games edifying or transformational in some way?

We researched the game jam using three conditions.[57] Our major findings were as follows:

1. The participants felt that they had the opportunity throughout the jam to either explore their own identity or other's identities.[58] They began to open up about their own identities and connected with others through the sharing of their identities.[59]

2. Participants reported feeling safer and having more fun and enjoyment following the event.[60]

3. While 88% of the participants liked the theme, "identity," 12% did not.[61] Some wanted a more specific theme, and some did not like designing games for prosocial purposes. We need to think further about how to reach those people who may be most resistant.[62]

4. Attitudes about games also changed. Participants more frequently believed in the ability of games to enhance empathy or reduce bias, after participating in the game jam.[63]

5. Perspective-taking and empathic concern measures did not change as a result of the event.[64]

Teachers may want to incorporate game jams into their teaching, or as extracurricular opportunities. They can come up with a theme that relates more closely to their curricula or current events, such as an upcoming election, community problem, or timely ethical issue. Teachers do not have to do a game jam in 48 hours, but can spread the activities over a longer period of time. They can also just focus on one aspect of a game jam process, such as having students brainstorm and conceptualize a game without needing to then create a fully-playable prototype. Or they could have students pitch ideas to each other and vote on which games to "mock" invest in.

Finally they could also lengthen the process of a game jam so that it takes place over the course of a semester or quarter. They could have teams form mini-startups, where they conduct research, incubate ideas, build game demos, and come up with business and marketing plans for their games.

Design Using Meaningful Constraints

Constraints are necessary to design. They create the boundaries to which you need to design for or around. Having no constraints may actually stifle design. It would be unwieldy to just design something—the solutions would be infinite and not focused on a specific need. Rather, people design *for* something else, whether a place, a gap, a person, or a societal issue.

Teachers should give students meaningful constraints and seek to have students create games and engage in design about relevant topics, themes, or needs, such as social issues, community problems, or current events that personally affect them.

Example in Action: Civic Hackathons

At Brooklyn Borough Hall in Spring of 2019, teams of Brooklyn middle and high school students worked together to design a website, mobile application, or game to solve a real-world civics-related problem. They were participating in the Hack League Civic Hackathon, competing with other teams to create and present a prototype to

City Hall, for possible further development and deployment to the City of New York and general public.[65]

Most of the teams sought to solve civic problems that affected them personally. One group provided compelling data about the city buses and their unreliability. They surveyed students in their school and found that a large percentage of students are late to school because the city bus either never shows up or is incredibly delayed. They sought to create an app that informs the students on the bus schedule and collects data, which could in turn inform the public and Metropolitan Transit Authority, and propel them to make real-world changes to the bus system.[66] Other groups wanted to enhance opportunities for affordable housing and getting proper heat and hot water for residents of New York City. The students participating did not necessarily have prior knowledge or technical expertise, but they were able to grapple with the intricacies of civic issues through the hackathon.[67]

Teachers can work together with other teachers or public officials to design their own regional or district-wide civic hackathons. Teachers can also do a version of this type of hackathon in their own classes, such as by having students design something that solves a problem they collectively vote on as a class.

Engage in Critical Design

Teachers should help students engage in critical, reflective design with consideration to accessibility, equity, justice, and empathy. They should always be reflecting on their designs and the decisions they make while designing.[68] Teachers and students need to be cognizant and empathetic toward their audience and they need to think about the entire ethical ecosystem around their games. How are values expressed through the game by its players? Who can access their game? How can they ensure that everyone is physically, economically, socially, and emotionally included in a game's community?

One way to address accessibility and inclusivity is through playtesting. This involves getting and giving explicit feedback. It involves watching others play the game, observing what worked and did not work, and listening to what the players say during the game—and what they don't say. Where do they laugh? Where do they seem engaged? Where are they confused? Who seems included and who seems left out? Who was able to play the game and who was hindered? Was the news event, argument, or message of the game getting expressed appropriately, or was the game's play dissonant with the theme? Based on this feedback, designers can revise their games. Teachers need to be mindful of setting expectations for students so that they are prepared to change and adjust their games and are more open to receiving and using critical feedback.

Moreover, games need to be rigorously reflected upon for as long as the game is "living"—and even beyond. Games evolve dynamically over time. Ethical, social, and cultural aspects of a game need to be continually reviewed and reconsidered.

Designers should be continually evaluating how values are embedded in and transmitted through their games and its communities.[69]

Example in Action: Common Circles Workshops

Common Circles is a nonprofit organization that creates experiences to enhance empathy and respect, reduce bias, and improve intergroup relations. One way they have done this is by supporting collaborative design.

Common Circles ran a two-day workshop for students from seven high schools in St. Louis, Missouri in 2018. The event involved students from all different types of schools, including rural, suburban, urban, private, public, and charter schools. The participants were placed into teams, which also included local business executives and professional game designers.[70]

During the workshop, the teams were tasked with creating a game that youth would want to play, which would help them to explore their own identities and the identities of others.[71] One game that a team created was called *Common Threads*, a nondigital card game (see Figure 12.3). The purpose of this game is to help players find meaningful connections among one's own identities, other players' identities, and those of celebrities.[72]

Overall, the workshop was effective. Preliminary results of the workshop suggested that participants felt that they understood their identity better.[73] One student said that they "looked internally and externally and learned about identity and how it affects how we see the world. We also learned how we can acknowledge our unconscious biases."[74]

The event also helped students from different schools in St. Louis get to know each other, as well as to connect with professionals in the community. Through the act of sharing and collaborating on meaningful projects, the students felt more comfortable contributing their own ideas and connecting with others.[75] One student explained that "We actually didn't know each other before and so I feel like now we're all becoming really close because of the ways that we opened our minds and we're able to just share things. It was a really comfortable space that was created."[76]

Teachers should consider how the act of designing together may help disparate groups come together and feel closer to each other, as well. Game-making, then, can serve as an ice breaker or team-building exercise to help people in a class or group gain trust with others.

Example in Action: *SheroHub*

Gilliam is creating a game through her organization, SheroHub, LLC, which teaches domestic violence awareness to middle and high school students.[77] She is also adapting their game, *SheroHub*, for use in Haiti, aiming for the game to be played by workers in the garment sector (see Figure 12.4). She is targeting the Haitian population in particular because of the prevalence of domestic violence there, with more than one in three women directly affected by it. Unfortunately this violence has

Figure 12.3 An image of the game *Common Threads*. Image courtesy of Common Circles.

become normalized, such that, "17% of Haitian women think it's okay to be beaten for burning the family dinner."[78]

When revising the game for a Haitian audience, Gilliam has had to think about how to translate all different aspects of the game, even beyond just translating it from English to Haitian creole.[79] It needs culturally relevant artwork and dialogue, because "showing American scenery, or scenarios that are meaningless to the player's daily life would not be helpful. I can't show them an American locker room and think that they would identify with the game." She is working with a Haitian writer on the script to ensure the storylines meet the cultural touchstones of Haitian society today.

Figure 12.4 A scene from the SheroHub LLC's "Fi Ewo" prototype videogame on gender-based violence prevention, Haiti, by Jayda Murray, artist. Copyright © 2020 SheroHub, LLC.

Moreover, how the game is distributed is also different. She is working with a non-profit called Share Hope, which is a 200+-member peer educator network of garment factory workers in Port-au-Prince, Haiti that already teaches on a diverse curriculum of health topics. Gilliam explains that "a group of 100 of the peer educators will be trained on domestic awareness and will deploy the game to thousands of their factory-worker colleagues."[80] This creates a support system and community around the game, so players of the game can continue to be connected to the resources they need, discuss their game play, and learn more about preventing domestic violence.[81] When creating games, teachers and their students should think about how the game might be shared, and the circumstances by which it could be played. How do we design the game, but also design for the system around the game?

Design Your Own Games

Educators with all levels of game development expertise should consider designing their own games, and encouraging their students to make their own games. A game that is useful in a classroom does not need to be perfectly polished, with voice actors, an immersive story, and top-notch graphics and programming. The game does not even have to be digital. A game could be simple, focused, and use raw materials commonly found in a classroom. It could be short, people-centered, and collaborative.[82] Teachers can also codesign games with students.

Some examples: Martyniuk, a teacher in British Columbia, Canada, creates a simple but powerful trivia game using a PowerPoint template.[83] Kunze is working on a series of youth hackathons and lessons on the "4 Cs" (communication, collaboration, critical thinking, and creativity) that are based around esports, in Swedish schools.[84] Hammer worked with girls in rural Ethiopia to give them "a kit that you can use with local, freely available materials to make your own game." I created the game, *Trade Off*, which is an in-person non-digital game that uses classroom materials like paper and pens. When playing it with students, I have them play two rounds of it (the ones that I designed). Then we co-design further rounds together.[85]

To help educators and designers to create meaningful play experiences, I have included a research-based list of design principles and a toolkit of strategies for designing games for civics and ethics (see appendices III and IV).

PART V
GAMES FOR ETHICS AND CIVICS

13
Guidelines, Questions, and Considerations

How do we choose the right game? What are the configurations that best support learning? Are the students playing the game in a physical classroom, an online environment, or at home with their caretakers? Do we place students in pairs, groups, or individually? If it's a nondigital game, is our table big enough? Do we have enough copies of it? If it is digital, are there enough computers to play it on? Do we need to connect to the internet and if so, how reliable is the connection? How do we adjust the game to meet our curricular needs?

In the previous nine chapters I considered how games can support questions, concepts, and skills related to civic and ethics learning, such as problem-solving, communication, and real-world action. I shared how we might use games to engage students further in the public sphere and how to use games as public spheres themselves.

The practical and logistical considerations around using games matter, too. We need to understand how to choose the right game, and once we have that game, how to incorporate it into the (in-person or virtual) classroom so that it is most effective. While the game itself matters, we also need to consider the entire ecosystem around and within the game—such as all the practical, technical, curricular, logistical, social, cultural, and assessment needs. For as many different approaches as there are to using any type of learning activity, there are just as many possibilities for using games.[1]

In this chapter I dive into how to choose, use, and assess games for the social studies, civics, and ethics classroom, whether online or in-person, as well as how to how to match games to different audiences, standards, and other needs. This will include research and best practices on the educators' role in guiding instruction, as well as instructional strategies.

While this chapter will provide some best practices and guiding questions, educators should consider how to adapt these practices in ways to suit their own specific needs and that of their students. Games can be designed and used in multiple ways, and there may be multiple right ways (and wrong ways) to play a game. Educators may even find that the use of games needs to be adapted from year to year, or even between sections of classes.

How Do We Choose the Right Game?

All different types of games could be used for learning. Some games are designed explicitly for learning (often called serious games, educational games, or games for

We the Gamers. Karen Schrier, Oxford University Press. © Oxford University Press 2021.
DOI: 10.1093/oso/9780190926106.003.0013

change). Examples of educational games include *Quandary*, *Do I Have a Right?*, or *Bad News*. Some games are designed primarily for entertainment purposes, such as commercial off-the-shelf (COTS) games. Examples of COTs games are *Fallout*, *Call of Duty*, *Red Dead Redemption*, *Minecraft*, *Animal Crossing*, *Fortnite*, *Roblox*, and *Apex Legend*. COTS games may or may not be effective for instruction. However, games do not need to have instrumental value to be valuable to learning.[2]

How do we select the appropriate game for a particular need? Let's say we want to create a lesson around immigration, and the complexities of immigration policies and realities. We could look at personal narratives on immigration, analyze policies in our country, connect with local immigrants, review historical archives to analyze immigration documents, look at data on systemic biases against immigrants, or compare global approaches to immigration. We can use a mix of maps, charts, historical narratives, guest speakers, textbook reading, group discussions, and attendance at town hall meetings to help support this learning. How can games fit into this as well?

Different games can show different aspects of an issue, and no one game needs to show all of it. We could use games to explore American immigration policies and views, such as *The Migrant Trail* and *Immigration Nation*. Or we could use games like *Bury Me My Love*, BBC's *Syrian Journey*, and *Refugee Choices* from *The Guardian* to share perspectives on immigration from countries such as Syria into other countries such as Turkey. We could also look at imaginary immigration systems and play games like *Papers, Please*. Finally, we could invite students to choose games that fit their interests, or we could have them design their own games around immigration.[3]

Teachers need to find games that match their educational goals and the strategies they want students to use to reach those goals. Portnoy explains that you do not want to just use a game or VR experience "because it's fun shiny objects … you have to consider where it fits within the curriculum."[4] But how do we approach which games to use? Do we base it on age group? Theme? Curricular goals? Gameplay? Ease of use? Low barrier to entry? Or some combination? When do we bring students into the choice?[5]

There are a few factors to consider. One factor that determines what game to use and whether it is effective is the teacher. The relevance of a game depends in part on a teacher's beliefs and attitudes toward games, their prior experience with using games, and their facility with knowing how to use the game to support a learning goal.[6] The first time a teacher uses a game may be effective—or it could be a disaster. A game may still be useful even if it does not work in a given set of conditions. Teachers often need to tweak how they use a game, from year to year and class to class, even if it works well the first time.[7] Therefore, teachers need to take an iterative approach to *using* games. They need to try it out, see what works and what doesn't, and fix it for the next scenario or situation. They need to continually adjust their expectations, consider how new audiences, classes, sessions, and populations may respond to the game differently, and how different schools, time periods, and other conditions may influence how the game is received.[8] For instance, consider how teachers adapted to going online during the COVID-19 pandemic. They needed to keep adjusting their pedagogy, expectations, and materials to better serve their students in response to a new and challenging situation.

Another factor is student preferences. We need to ask students and find out what they want to play. By inviting students to participate in the choosing of games, we support their engagement in their own learning. It also enacts the very processes you want students to take—to be empowered to make decisions, vote, and voice their interests and needs.[9] Table 13.1 shares some questions we may want to ask when choosing and using games for ethics and civics.[10]

However, I also want to acknowledge how challenging it is to use games. It is complex, thoughtful work to take into consideration all the different factors and questions, and adapt games to different needs. We should also accept just trying games out, ethically and responsibly—even if we fail and especially if we do.

Table 13.1 Questions for teachers to ask when using games for learning

Consideration	Associated Questions
Who is the audience?	• What is the age of the students? • What previous work have they done? • What is their reading level and current skills? • What is their interest in the topic? • Which games do the students want to play and which games match their interests, values, and needs? • Is the game leveled to their age? • Will the game engage these particular students? • Will the game help to confirm their misconceptions about a topic, or will it help them to question their assumptions? • Will the game get them further excited about the topic or will it feel tedious?
What are the learning goals and curricular needs?	• What class or topic are you teaching? • What unit are you developing? • What are the standards you need to meet? • What are the ethics and civics questions, concepts, and skills you need to teach? • How does the game match the learning goals and objectives?
What is the context and ecology of play?	• Where will the game be played? • How will it be incorporated into the classroom? • Is the classroom in-person, remote, or virtual? • Is the class done asynchronously or synchronously? • Will it be played at home, with parental supervision? Or will students be playing it unsupervised? • How will players play the game? Should teachers project the game at the front of the class and have all students play together? Should students take turns at the front? Should students play on their own devices or computers, pair up and take turns, or work in teams? • What is the larger culture around the game, including the norms and values of the game's or class's community? • What are the written and unwritten laws, regulations, and policies around the use of this game? • Who has the power to shape and affect the design and play of the game? • How are educators enforcing rules beyond those that are already embedded in the game?

Continued

Table 13.1 *Continued*

Consideration	Associated Questions
What are the technological limitations?	• Why even use a game? Is this the right experience? Educators should consider whether and why this should be a game and if that is the best use of the time and space in the class. • What are the technological and networking needs of the game? • What are the technological constraints of the place where the game is played? • Is the game accessible on an iPad, or does it need a laptop? • Does everyone have the right equipment, such as enough computers, VR headsets, or mobile devices? • If the game needs to be downloaded, what is the bandwidth of the connection and how long will it take for it to be deployed? • Can the students download to the computers themselves or is there a firewall or privacy setting that needs to be changed? • If the game needs an internet connection, is it reliable? • Does the student have access to an internet connection, if it is needed? • Does the game only run using an obviated platform like Flash, or are there updated versions of the game? • Does the game require regular software updates or downloadable content (DLC)? • Does the browser have safeguards that may shut students out? • If it's a location-based game, are there spots at the location without wifi or phone service? • How might any of these connections or equipment break down? Are there backups? • Who can you access if you need to troubleshoot solutions or adaptations?
What are the logistical limitations?	• Do teachers or students need a subscription? Are there license fees? What does it cost? Are there educator discounts? Is there a fee per student, per class, or per district? • What is the physical or online space and location where the game experience will take place? • Do teachers need to share the game with other teachers or schedule sign ups? • Do you have enough game copies for a classroom, or the right license to use so it can be deployed to multiple computers or accessed from students' homes? • How much time do you have to play the game? • Can the game be broken up into smaller chunks to ensure it works well in a session? • Can it be saved? Can it be shared? • How many people can play it at once? • Does it have a long tutorial that may affect how much progress students can make? • Do students need to make accounts and if so, how will they remember their passwords and usernames? • Is the space large enough for the game? Like, is the table or desk big enough for a board or card game? • Do you have access to an outdoor space if it is played outside? • What are the weather conditions like if it is being played outside?

Table 13.1 *Continued*

Consideration	Associated Questions
	• Are there other constraints, such as whether students need to be masked or physically distant from each other?
	• Does the game work better in person, or can players be apart?
	• What about a VR game's particular limitations or issues, such as motion sickness, disorientation, and space around the player? These issues may particularly affect women and younger players. Consider how to limit time on the device so that these types of issues are ameliorated.
	• Does the player have enough space for the necessary movement and play?
	• Do students need to share one VR headset or does a class of students each need their own headset?
	• Is the game dizzying or nausea-inducing for some students?
	• If students need to share equipment, how long will each student be able to play it for so that all the students can participate in the exercise?
	• How will shared equipment be sanitized between use?
	• What happens if a game gets ruined, destroyed, or ripped apart? For example, in the case of games such as *Pandemic: Legacy*, after each round of the game the players need to physically destroy part of the game.
	• If using a location-based AR game, what about physical limitations and obstacles such as traffic, hills, bad weather, and other problems that may affect the use of the game?
	• If using a location-based AR game, do you need to bring extra devices, such as mobile ones, and ensure that they can connect to networks as needed?
What is the play of the game?	• Does the gameplay match learning goals, contexts, and other considerations?
	• Is the gameplay too easy, too challenging, or on par with what the students can handle?
	• Is the gameplay and problem-solving the right level of complexity for the students?
	• Which design principles were used to create the gameplay?
	• What are the drawbacks and strengths of the game, and how can teachers explore these with the students?
	• What are the mechanics, aesthetics, and dynamics of the game?
	• How are values expressed through the game?
	• What types of biases are embedded in the game and through its play and communities?
	• Are there different modes or controls that can be adjusted (e.g., reading levels) that can support differing student needs?
	• How can students engage in design and creation through the game?
	• How is the gameplay connected to research-based best practices for learning?
	• Does the intent of the game match the learning outcomes?

Continued

Table 13.1 *Continued*

Consideration	Associated Questions
What are the activities around and within the game?	• What other activities might be used with the game? Games do not need to be standalone experiences. Teachers may want to pair the game with other learning activities such as reading textbooks or novels, along with interactive media such as websites and podcasts. • What types of activities and tasks does the player do in the game? • How will the game work with other activities and exercises outside of the game? • What gaps does the game have that could be filled through an exercise, extension activity, or supplement of some type? • Is the game complementary to another activity? • What are some connections to the game that students can further make through an activity, such as reading or discussion? • What are the skills that could be practiced through additional activities? • How will reflection be supported? Reflective exercises can include journaling, discussion, pair-and-shares, quiet meditations, and video testimonials. • How will students have options of activities to do, such as ones based on interests or play styles? • How might the game be integrated into the remote or physical classroom? Instead of just having students play a game, teachers may also show gameplay videos (videos of the game being played) or streamed live on Twitch to support the game's integration into the classroom, to point out different types of play strategies, or to discuss other's perspectives on playing the game.
What is the educator's role?	• What is the facility of the teacher with the game or learning topic? • Who are the educators or mentors supporting the game, and what is their expertise? • What do teachers need to do to contextualize or introduce the game to students before diving into a game? • How will the educator connect the game experience to the students' interests and needs? • How might teachers set the stage for the game by posing questions and prompts before and during the game play? How does the teacher factor into the play of the game? • How will the educator modify or adapt the game to students' needs? • Does the game come with an educators' guide or worksheets? • What type of training does the school, game, or district have? • What type of general professional development opportunities exist around using this game or games like it? • How will the educator guide the students through the process? • Will the teacher also play the game, or just host or facilitate it? • What fears or concerns might teachers (or their students) have about the game or topic? • Have language needs and tutorial issues been fully considered? Teachers may want to be mindful of vocabulary, directions, or game play that may be particularly difficult for students and should consider making a cheat sheet of useful terms or actions for students. • Can teachers create multiple saves of the game?

Table 13.1 *Continued*

Consideration	Associated Questions
What are the accessibility opportunities?	• Is the game accessible to all students? • Can the students play the game at home? • Is the game thematically accessible, in that it is about a topic that students can relate to, understand, and care about? • Can students with differing learning needs access further tutorials, in-game tutors, or types of scaffolding? • Can students get definitions of words they do not know? • Which languages would best support the learners? Does the game enable this language option? • Will the game read aloud any text or describe any visual images using both text and spoken aloud text? • If the game was ported or translated to a new time, place, or language, are cultural references updated and accessible? • Can students with different disabilities and abilities access the game, such as students that have different neurotypes, sensory processing needs, or different sight, sound, or movement abilities? Does the game use the correct terms and language around these differences (and can it be updated as necessary in the future)? • Is the game developmentally appropriate for the age group, as there may be certain capacities that have not yet been developed depending on the age group? • What other accessibility options might be considered? Teachers may consider games that have additional options for students who have a variety of needs, such as hearing, cognitive, health, or emotional needs. Finding games that have additional options will be more supportive for everyone, such as how including audio options for a game can help new readers, or speakers of different languages. For more information, see https://accessible.games/.
How inclusive is participation?	• Is the game encouraging an inclusive, equitable, caring, and compassionate community? • Does the game help create a community that models the types of respectful discourse, ethical interactions, and perspective-taking that we want students to embody? • How is the game moderated? Who are the moderators? • What are the policies and rules around gameplay, communication, and interaction? • What happens if a game player breaks the rules of the game and its community? How are rules enforced and problems reported? • Who feels like they belong and who feels empowered through the game? • How do intersectional identities interact with the game? • What types of systemic biases are embedded in the game and its communities? • How are you fostering a positive, supportive, harassment-free environment for playing the game? • If there is a built-in community in the game, how are you ensuring that all players are free from external harassment, or even with each other? • How are you ensuring inclusive dialogue around the game? • How are you supporting marginalized communities, game players, and games?

Continued

Table 13.1 *Continued*

Consideration	Associated Questions
	• Are there systemic or structural issues that constrain or exclude players? • What other design issues need to be considered? For further questions and guidelines, see www.adl.org/designinginclusivegames and https://fairplayalliance.org/wp-content/uploads/2020/12/FPA-Framework.pdf.
How does the game connect to the real world?	• Is the game accurately representing history, a system, or a governmental process? Is this even possible? • How are the fictive and real elements balanced in a game? • Is the game misrepresenting or misleading players, or furthering misconceptions or bias? • Is the game enabling real-world skills practice? • What types of knowledge is created or learned through the game and how is the game used to do this? • Is the game encouraging students to participate more directly in a civics process or problem, such as writing letters to representatives or talking to students in other nations? • How does the game help students get out in the real world and explore, or to connect to actual people, institutions, and organizations? • Does the game enable players to grapple with real ethical questions and issues? • How is the game helping students to partner with other classes or community organizations, or with each other?
What are the ethical challenges?	• What are the ethics of the game's play? • How does the player and gameplay affect how ethics are expressed through the game? • What are the ethical implications of learning with and through this game? • How does the game represent different cultures, backgrounds, or identities? How does this affect how players may play it, and how they may respond to it? • What types of values are embedded in the game's design and how are these expressed through the game? • What are the privacy, security, and sociocultural implications of the game? • Are students able to play privately or is the game too public? • Is the game upholding or maintaining social hierarchies or also enabling us to critique them? • Is the game further enabling all students to participate in our publics? • How are players involved in the design of the game? • How are players involved in the choice of playing the game? • How does the game help to facilitate ethical discussions around and through it? • Which ethical frameworks or approaches seem to connect to this game? Were any used in designing this game? Could students use any when playing the game? • How transparent is the game about its ethical implications? • What types of equity and justice issues are raised by this game?

Table 13.1 *Continued*

Consideration	Associated Questions
What are the assessment needs?	• What are the learning objectives, and how is the game supporting them (or not supporting them)? • How do we assess the ethics of one's behaviors, actions, or thoughts in the game? • Which methods do we use to assess learning? • To what extent should the assessment be formative or summative? • How can the game help to assess learning or behavior change? • How much assessment is already built into the game? • How do we test short-term and longer-term learning?

This table shares questions to ask (and attempt to answer) when using, choosing, and playing games for educational purposes. These questions may not pertain to every situation or context.

How Do We Choose and Design Activities Around a Game?

Once we have chosen a game, we also have to think about the other materials and activities we will use before, during, and after the game. Will we use the activities that come with the games, or will we create new activities? Daniels, a history teacher at a public school in Washington, DC, pairs the iCivics game *Branches of Power* with a food activity also created by iCivics. The activity involves splitting the class into three groups to work together on creating school lunches. You have the lead chefs, nutrition inspectors, and menu writers. Daniels has the students first do this food activity and then play the game afterward. Daniels explains, "It's like they are enacting how the different branches make decisions before they even get into the game. By the time they get into the game, they are already prepared for the lessons conveyed by the game."[11]

Farber also used this activity in his middle school social studies class in New Jersey, and explains that "students then transfer this [activity of making lunches] to thinking about the three branches of government, so that instead of making a menu, you are making laws" in the game.[12]

Other activities can happen after or even during a game. Darvasi describes the "Museum of Me" exercise he did alongside playing *What Remains of Edith Finch,* where he invited students to make their own "cabinets of curiosity" related to their identities (see more in chapter 7).[13] Teachers can also pair games with other games to reveal multiple perspectives on issues, as I do when I have students play games like *Loneliness, everyday the same dream, Gris,* and *The End of Us* to investigate how games can express feelings of sadness, helplessness, and disconnection.[14]

How do we know which activities to use to support game-based learning? Becker poses seven different questions we may want to ask when designing activities for game-based learning.

1. What is covered in the game and not covered in the game?
2. How does the game (coupled with any possible activities) provide an overview of the topic that needs to be taught, or how does it focus on one part of it?
3. How will the lessons be provided (single lesson, multiple)?
4. Are there any inaccuracies in the game that need to be addressed?
5. What are the different viewpoints that are in the game or beyond the game?
6. How will the gameplay be managed in and outside of the class?
7. Can the game be saved at any points and then shared?[15]

How Do We Assess the Learning?

Another concern for educators is whether the game is actually effective and meeting the pedagogical goals. How do we know whether students are actually learning through a game? How do we know if we are becoming more engaged ethical thinkers and civic participators?[16]

First, how do we assess civics and ethics knowledge and skills more generally, whether developed through a game or other educational intervention? "One of the key challenges in assessing ethics games is that we do not yet have clear, vetted, universal assessment techniques. This is not surprising, since every ethical moment or situation is different, and there is no objective checklist for how people should act, behave, share, or feel."

It is also particularly challenging to assess changes in behavior or practice over the longer term. How do we know that civics skills and proclivities are being developed for the future, such as longer-term attitudes, prosocial behavior changes, or civic participation? We cannot necessarily follow students to see if they vote, do volunteer work, or participate in town hall meetings over the course of their lives. We cannot continue to surveil them on social media, in their homes, or at their future workplaces to see if they are engaging in respectful discourse or sharing only vetted news information. We do not know if they will continue to develop a civic mindset, or if they have the necessary foundational skills and knowledge to participate effectively as part of a global society.

To assess character, then, researchers may aim to test knowledge of virtues or look at current behaviors, rather than investigate longer-term changes. In one study, the Jubilee Centre used a triangulation method to assess character in UK schools by investigating teachers' reports of student virtues, students' self-report of their own virtues, as well as measures of how students approach moral dilemmas.[17] We should also keep looking for effective ways to test longer-term changes in ethics and civics practices.

Third, assessment is always complicated, but it is particularly complex when it comes to games. A game may work under one set of circumstances but not another. It may reach one audience or one individual in a way that would not work in another community or country. Just as any educational intervention is affected by the teacher or mentor who supports it, games and their effectiveness are also affected by the ecosystem of their use, including the person providing the game and its assessment, among other factors.[18] Assessing games is complex because games are complex, and assessing ethics and civics is complex because they are complex—and we should revel in that complexity.

Simkins recommends three different questions to help guide the assessment of any game for learning. The questions are: (1) What are the game's learning goals? (2) What is the game's context (where it is played, who plays it, what is the ecosystem of play)? and (3) How is the game played (e.g., what are the mechanics, what are the game goals and how do they relate to learning goals, what is the gameplay like)?[19] Teachers will need to adapt any assessments to their unique game and the culture in which it is played.

Finally, what does it even mean to assess citizenship, ethics, or civics? We may need to rethink our myths around good citizenship. Mirra and Garcia argue that we should not get "bogged down by privileging adult perspectives on what youth should be doing as civic agents rather than asking young people what actually engages them or what kinds of civic learning opportunities they may already be experiencing."[20] We need to value and assess the skills that students bring, and the different ways that they already civically participate through games and beyond.

With a full understanding that any game is a complex ecosystem that needs to be assessed holistically and contextually, learning with games should still be assessed. The following are types of assessment that educators may want to use to better understand the strengths and limitations of a game, and what types of skills and concepts the students are learning.

Playtesting as Assessment

Playtesting is the process of testing a game with real players to see if it does what we expect it to do. To conduct playtesting we observe players playing the game, typically during many different stages of development (e.g., paper and digital prototypes, prealpha, alpha, and beta stages). We may note what players do and do *not* do when they play the game (e.g., when players are stuck, when players are smiling or laughing, when players are speaking to others, or whether players are wanting to play the game again). We may ask questions to players after their game play, such as about specific rules or interactions (see more about playtesting in chapter 12).

We may even think of playtesting as a type of cocreation of games with our players. For instance, Archer worked on a role-playing game that teaches Spanish language skills while also supporting the practice of life skills, like interviewing and resume creation. As he developed the game, he worked with students three or four times throughout the year to review it, and was able to adapt the game to be more relevant to student needs. While this type of assessment is useful as a formative assessment, such as to understand the game's general playability, this type of assessment does not typically serve as a summative assessment or rigorous assessment of learning.[21]

Game-Based Assessments

Games themselves can serve as assessments. They can function as both the intervention and as an assessment of learning from that intervention. Gibson and Webb argue that assessments of learning through games should move from summative-style assessments to ones that are "continual, diagnostic, and formative" and consider the "personal growth of the student, impact on social issues, and cultural importance."[22]

A well-designed game is always "assessing the player" to see if they are reaching the goals and making progress—such as by giving just-in-time, relevant feedback and nudges to help make sure this happens. That a player has (or has not) reached certain goals in a game could be indicative of a player's progress and learning needs.[23] Assessment and reassessment should be continually integrated into a game, as players should always know how they are progressing and whether they are meeting the game's goals. Games should also always be responding to players and giving them the feedback that they need to be successful—just like any educator would: "In other words, the act of playing and/or interrogating the game is a form of assessment."[24]

The game *Quest: Journey through the Lifespan* teaches about the stages of human development. It is divided into modules, where the player plays as different ages such as a baby, a teenager, and an older adult, and learns different concepts and theories related to that developmental stage. A module is only able to be completed if the player meets certain specific objectives in it, such as teaching a virtual peer or handling an NPC bully.[25] By completing the tasks in a module it suggests that the player has had to meet the learning objectives, like performing the relevant interaction or skill, or applying a necessary concept or theory. The game, in other words, continually assesses whether learning (and evidence of learning) is happening.

In-game artifacts can also be used to assess learning. In my location-based mobile game *Reliving the Revolution*, players worked together to figure out who fired the first shot at the Battle of Lexington while exploring the real-world Lexington Green (see chapter 5). At the end of the game, the players share evidence and deliberate what happened at the historic battle and put forth their version of the event, which serves as a type of assessment of the player's ability to evaluate, compare, and interpret evidence, engage in argumentation and discourse, and reflect on their learning.[26]

Out-of-Game Assessments

To assess the efficacy of a game in supporting learning, we can also use traditional quantitative and qualitative research methodologies and instruments, like classroom observations, surveys, interviews, focus groups, and ethnographies. If teachers are assessing student learning, the typical assessments that can be used with any social studies, ethics, or civics activity can also be used around games, such as essay prompts, exams, discussion forums, quizzes, journal entries, blog posts, wiki entries, presentations, videos and creative projects, or community outreach experiences. The Education Development Center (EDC) assessed *Mission US: For Crown or Colony*, a game where players explore Boston in the moments leading up to the American Revolution. To do this, they looked at students' analyses of an engraving by Paul Revere before and after the game, in addition to teacher and student interviews and classroom observations, to suggest that the game supported skills such as interpretation, argumentation, perspective-taking, and historical empathy.[27] Teachers should also expand the possibilities of what out-of-game assessments could be. They may want to, for instance, incorporate critical game-making, social media creations, and activities like moderation.[28] As we assess, we should consider all the different ways games can support civic engagement and ethical reflection.

14

We the Gamers

I tend my flowers, catch critters, and plant trees. I build bridges, place paths, and craft campsites. I visit the town square. I invite friends and create a village. I decide: How will I shape my world?

The game is *Animal Crossing: New Horizons*, a multiplayer world where players can design an island oasis, build a home, and visit others' lands. Through this social universe of island nations, players decide how they want to express themselves and with whom they want to connect. What type of community will they create? Who gets to come and stay? How will they govern their society? What values are reinforced and what norms are shared? Players can decide to work toward constructing a museum, and choose whether to contribute samples of fish and bugs, which can help to educate and serve the common good. They can send digital gifts and visit other players' islands to help celebrate real-world birthdays or milestones. Or players can hoard items, or decide only to visit islands where market prices are highest and they can sell turnips for a hefty profit.

Players can also use their islands to market and sell real-world brands, items, or ideas. For instance, players can develop digital knock-offs of designer clothes, or even recreate one's own real-life fashion collections. Players can even elect to engage virtually in real-world action, such as by participating in protests through the game. People for the Ethical Treatment of Animals (PETA) staged an in-game protest against the *Animal Crossing* museum, asking for the virtual tanks and exhibitions to be emptied and the digital critters to be freed. Players in Hong Kong have used the game to share criticisms of their government's policies—protesting in the game when they can't in person because it is banned.[1]

Animal Crossing: New Horizon helps us to connect and to take action, together. It allows us to make decisions and solve problems. It enables us to collaborate with friends and family, to teach others, and make a real-world impact. This is particularly compelling given that the game came out during the COVID-19 pandemic, a time when many people around the world did not have as many opportunities to do so. Through the game, we were able to continue to participate in public life. Through the game, we were able to imagine a new world. Through the game, we also found comfort in routine and ritual, and in the repetitive daily patterns of life. This *is* civics, in fact. In writing about *Animal Crossing: New Horizons*, Bogost explains that "civic life, after all, coheres not in abstract fantasies about politician-heroes, but in habitual practices that take place in real communities."[2]

We the Gamers. Karen Schrier, Oxford University Press. © Oxford University Press 2021.
DOI: 10.1093/oso/9780190926106.003.0014

We Are Connected

Animal Crossing: New Horizons, and the pandemic context in which it was released, helps to remind us that we are all connected. We are dependent on each other for our community, for our play, and for our future. We rely on each other and each other's decisions. What we do has consequences for our communities and for our human society as a whole. Our individual choices and our collective actions matter. For society to work, we all need to engage in decision-making and deliberation. We, the people, need to change our world, together.

It also reminds us that we are disconnected. We are apart, we are divided, and we are isolated. We are disconnected from our human truths: we are vulnerable, we are unequal, and we are unwise. As a society, we are unhealthy. It is clear that life, liberty, and the pursuit of happiness is not attainable for everyone.

Ethics and civics have *always* mattered, but perhaps now more than ever, it is becoming evident how *much* they matter. As I have explored in this book, we need to practice ethics and civics. We need to be more civically engaged, spend more time building character, and reflect on our values. We all need to be more involved in reimagining our rapidly changing, globally interdependent world.

Teaching ethics and civics is essential to our future. We need to teach ethics and civics for their own sakes, as well as to enhance civic participation, justice, care, and compassion; solve communal problems; and take societal action.[3] We need to teach ethics and civics to survive as a society.

But this doesn't just stop and start at our borders. We need to be global citizens who act, teach, learn, and grow together. We need to design a world where all students are educated and can flourish. We need to develop people who are inspired for lifelong inquiry and informed civic action. We need to "rebuild, reconcile, and recover."[4]

Delbanco refers to the COVID-19 pandemic by saying, "This is not only a public health crisis and an economic crisis … It's also a values crisis. It raises all kinds of deep human questions: What are our responsibilities to other people? Does representative democracy work?"[5] When another crisis occurs, how will we respond?

We need to answer these questions, together.[6]

Games May Help to Connect Us Further

Through games we are already practicing ethics and civics—by sharing knowledge, engaging in the habits of life, or taking real-world action. Games may help to connect us to each other and the community necessary for participating in ethical decision-making and civic engagement.

As I have described in this book:

- Games can help us to build knowledge of civic processes, institutions, and concepts, and ethics frameworks, values, and virtues.
- Games can help us to identify problems to solve, critique the information that we receive, and evaluate the actions that we take based on it.
- Games can help us to explore current issues. They can serve as arguments about, interpretations of, and perspectives on real-world topics and events.
- Games can help us to practice making ethical decisions, evaluating consequences, and reflecting on our choices.
- Games are communities and publics where we can engage civically. We can govern and shape our games, too, just like other communities.
- Games can help us to express ourselves and our views. They can help us to understand our roles in our communities and our responsibilities to each other.
- Games can help us to understand, respect, and care about other people, and their values and views. They can help us to consider new perspectives and include more voices in our solutions.
- Games can help us to connect with others to take action and make change—and to ensure that all of us are able to access this, equitably.
- Game playing *and* game designing may be acts of care, paths to justice, and chances to make change.

Through games, we can vote, protest, sign petitions, share values, tell stories, debate topics, deliberate policies, and solve real-world problems. We can play with ethics and civics, and see the playfulness already in them. We can be citizens. We can "citizen."

The Limits of Games

At the same time, games may not be the solution. Games may not solve our problems—and they may even create new ones. As in any community or experience, through games we can connect, care, and inspire, and we can also experience hate, harassment, and intolerance. Games can even be purposely designed or used to spur misinformation, misunderstandings, bias, or injustice. Even well-intentioned games may backfire. Games can reveal our flaws and expose the cruelty of humanity. They can show us the many obstacles that still exist in our world.

Games also bring up and highlight other ethical and systemic issues, such as privacy, inaccessibility and exclusion, racism, sexism, and other forms of inequality. These issues have always existed, and perhaps become more visible or even more magnified through games. For instance, let's pretend we are creating a game where players can vote—such as on an in-game policy or in a real-world election. This brings up further questions that need to be answered—and ones that we continue to grapple with as a society. How do we ensure a safe, fair, equitable vote on how we govern our society? For example:

- What are our responsibilities as voters?
- Who has access to the technological device or connectivity needed to participate and vote?
- How do we decide who is able or allowed to vote? What are the requirements for voting?
- How do we motivate people to vote?
- How will we ensure that votes be kept private, such that no one can match the vote to the person who voted?
- How do we ensure that our votes count, and that no other parties are able to see, halter, change, or delete any of the votes?
- Who gets to collect all the votes, and who communicates them to the public?
- What type of system should we use to weigh or count the votes—majority rule, representative, or something else?
- How does the public gain and maintain trust in this system of voting?
- How can these mechanisms be overturned? What are the vulnerable points in the process?[7]

Games, and how we design and use them, further our need to answer the deep-seated questions about who we are and how humanity should act. Who governs us? How should people participate in our governance? What types of behaviors and activities should be allowed in our society? How do we collectively decide how our society should function? These questions have always existed, but perhaps games can remind us that we need to further resolve them.

Teachers and students need to continually think about the ethics of games and their use. Like any other civic community, games may be inequitable and inhospitable. If games are not only closed to full participation, but perhaps actively deterring it, they are also part of the ethics and civics problems we need to solve. How do we design and govern game communities—and communities of all different types—to ensure that we can all live, work, interact, and play together?

How will we game? The choice is up to us.[8]

The Future of Ethics and Civics Games

How is the future going to play out?

Let's look to the past first.

The goal of public education has civically minded origins. In the United States, for example, to be a fully, democratically engaged society, we understood that we also needed to be an educated people. We, the people, rely on each other to make informed decisions, choose our representatives, care for our neighbors, and build our communities. We, the people, need knowledge growth alongside moral growth, and we need individuals alongside communities.[9]

Likewise, play has always been a way to engage with our world, to understand who we are, and to learn about how we could shape humanity. People have been expressing their identities, sharing perspectives, role-playing, caring for others, exploring, experimenting, and connecting through games well before even the advent of digital gaming. They have also been excluding others, competing with them, and escaping from them—because through play we can express and value all different facets of humanity, flaws and all.

Yet we have neglected this.[10] We have started to see education as transactional, and learning as tied to productivity rather than to living. Over the past few years crises like the COVID-19 pandemic, climate change, and socioeconomic inequalities have brought further into focus what we need to be successful as a society. Social studies, including ethics and civics, needs to be prioritized, alongside other fields, including STEM, languages, literature, and art, music, and other forms of humanistic expression. Bruni writes of the COVID-19 pandemic, "We need doctors right now ... We need research scientists. It falls to them to map every last wrinkle of this invader and find its Achilles' heel. But we also need Achilles. We need Homer. We need writers, philosophers, historians. They'll be the ones to chart the social, cultural, and political challenges of this pandemic—and of all the other dynamics that have pushed the United States so harrowingly close to the edge."[11]

Likewise, we may think that educating with games is old news or even "fake news." We may question why, after so many years, there has been no clear definitive proof that games are scalable, feasible, and effective ways to learn anything, let alone something as complex as civics and ethics. We may question why we can't just use games like a worksheet, or a video, or even a field trip that you can take for an hour or wedge into that time after the real work in school has been done. We may question why games are not more productive.

In my previous book, *Knowledge Games*, I looked at crowdsourcing games like *Foldit* and *EteRNA*. I showed how games may help us to build new societal knowledge, expanding knowledge production beyond universities and other knowledge-building centers, and giving it to the public, instead. I asked whether it followed that we now need to contribute (through games and other platforms) to be good citizens. Do we need to be producing something of value to be valuable parts of society?[12]

We have started to see education, citizenship, and play, as productive, rather than liberating. But we cannot simply conceive of games as machines or instruments to use to generate some quantifiable outcome. As teachers, will we use games to create people who will contribute, uphold, confirm, and sustain our public, or will we *also* use games to develop complex, complicated citizens who will inspire change, critique institutions, take action, and live meaningful lives? I hope it is also the latter.

So what is the future of games for ethics and civics?

Games help us to answer age-old questions about how to function as a society on a planet with limited resources, fragile communities, and unpredictable futures. Games can help us to see the flaws of our humble humanity and to view our old problems in new, revealing ways. Games can help us to recognize and reimagine our world.

Games can help us to see what has always really mattered. But we need to listen to them.

Like a good citizen, a good game interrogates. It uncovers. It challenges.

Cachinero-Sánchez explains that he would want his doctor to have read Chekhov, "because he's a fuller human being and he's going to treat *me* like a fuller human being."[13]

Likewise, if I were to choose, I would want my fellow citizens to have played *That Dragon, Cancer, Way, Kind Words, Minecraft, What Remains of Edith Finch, 1000 Cut Journey, When Rivers Were Trails, Red Dead Redemption,* and *Animal Crossing,* because then they are fuller human beings, too.

The question now is: Will we value games? Will we accept games fully for what they are—idiosyncratic, poetic, nuanced, and complicated—messy, just like us? Will we accept their foibles, our follies, and all?

We, the gamers, can play to overcome the unnecessary obstacles in our interconnected, strong yet vulnerable world. We the gamers can play to connect through our shared humanity, and our shared human flaws. We the gamers can play to remake, redo, revive. We, together, can "*citizen.*"[14]

We decide: How will we shape our world?

Example Lesson Outline 1

Objective

Help students critically evaluate evidence and information.

Chapter Connection

How do we read and evaluate information? (See more in chapter 10.)

Connections to US Standards

C3 Framework: Evaluating sources and using evidence.

Civics Assessment Framework: Civics skills; finding, explaining, and analyzing information, sources, perspectives and claims; and evaluating and critiquing positions on different issues.

Campaign for the Civic Mission of Schools: Intellectual skills; the ability to identify and analyze information.

US Common Core: Analyzing primary and secondary sources; distinguishing facts from opinions and evaluating claims.

Primary Question

Is the evidence accurate, reliable, and valid?

Secondary Questions

- How might we interpret and evaluate evidence?
- How do we check where something is from?
- Who created the evidence?
- How do we evaluate for bias?
- What types of biases are in this evidence?
- What is disinformation?
- What techniques are used by people to spread disinformation?

Additional Activity Ideas

A number of games and interactive resources may be useful for educators to use when teaching about these topics and questions (see Table A1.1). Educators can also use additional activities. They should adjust the activity depending on the topics covered in the class and the students' ages and reading level. The following are examples of activities that teachers could use.

Table A1.1 Possible games and interactive resources to use in lesson outline 1

Name of Game	Website	Chapters Discussed
Factitious	http://factitious.augamestudio.com/#/	10
Bad News	https://www.getbadnews.com/#intro	10
Fake Your Own (Re-) Election	https://senokos.itch.io/ fake-your-own-reelection	10
Civics! An American Musical	https://www.fablevisiongames.com/civics	5, 10, 12
Fake It To Make It	https://www.fakeittomakeitgame.com/	10
Balderdash	Board game	—
Newsfeed Defenders	https://www.icivics.org/games/ newsfeed-defenders	5, 10
Troll Factory	https://trollfactory.yle.fi/	10
Mission US	https://www.mission-us.org/	4,5,8,9,10,11
Constitutional Crisis	https://ithrivegames.org/ithrive-sim/ constitutional-crisis/	8
Harmony Square	https://harmonysquare.game/books/ default/	1, 10
Newsgames Website	http://journalismgames.org/	—
Games for Change games	http://www.gamesforchange.org/games/	—

Photoshopped or Not

To do this activity, the teacher explains what a Photoshopped image is and shows the class some examples. Then the teacher has the whole class evaluate an image, chart, or photo (images should be chosen depending on the age of the students and topics of the class). The teacher asks students to take turns commenting on the visual materials, such as colors used, captions used, the source of the image, or if there are any objects out of place. Each observation earns a student a point. Earning enough points gains the class access to discussing and finding out whether the image was Photoshopped or not.

Mixed-Up Files

In this activity, students need to help out a fictional character, Barney A. Whipplesnapper, who got his files all mixed up. Some of the files are from a historical archive, and some are for-geries. Students are placed in groups and each group gets a set of print outs (or digital copies) of historic-looking evidence in different files. The students need to figure out which evidence files are from the actual historical archive by comparing evidence, sourcing it, and searching in a library or online archive to ensure its accuracy.

Googler.com

This activity may be particularly useful in an online or remote learning environment. Students need to search for topics that interest them, such as currents events in their hometown or in the broader community. They need to find inaccuracies in either articles, social media, television reports, videos, or other media about that topic, and they will earn one point for each that they find, cross-reference, verify, and share with the class.

Escape the Evidence

Students work together to create their own game, where the players need to evaluate real-world evidence to play the game. For instance, students create an escape the room game where the players need to analyze evidence for clues, and solve other puzzles, to be able to exit the room and win the game. Then they have to play the games made by the other groups.

Discussion Questions

- What is the difference between validity and reliability?
- Why do we need to make sure that evidence is accurate?
- How might we judge evidence in a newspaper differently from that on social media, a textbook, or a scientific journal?
- What are some challenges with evaluating evidence?
- What is an author?
- How does authorship matter?
- What is disinformation and why is it problematic? Why might someone want to spread it?
- What are techniques that people may use to help spread disinformation? What can we do to counter these techniques?
- How do different social media platforms handle maintaining the accuracy of posts.

Tips and Hints

- Before students analyze information on their own, walk through the steps with the class together, and talk through how we might approach an evaluation.
- Provide a checklist or graphic organizer for evaluating evidence.
- Teachers may want to spend time considering with the class why "just googling it" may not be effective. Show students a search result to reveal possible pitfalls.
- If in a virtual or remote learning environment, make sure to explain that the useful information may not be the first result in an online search. Explain search algorithms and how that may affect what comes up first, rather than it being based on accuracy.

Example Lesson Outline 2

Objective

Help students understand themselves in relation to their community.

Chapter Connection

How do we understand ourselves and our emotions? (See chapter 7.)
How do we cultivate compassion and respect for others? (See chapter 8.)

Connections to US Standards

C3 Framework: Communicating conclusions and taking informed action.
Civics Assessment Framework: Civic dispositions; respecting individual worth and human dignity; assuming the personal, political, and economic responsibilities of a citizen.
Campaign for the Civic Mission of Schools: Dispositions; caring about others and equality and equity.
US Common Core: Working with and collaborating with people who have other perspectives.
CASEL: Social awareness, relationship skills, self-awareness.

Primary Question

Which roles do we play in our different communities?

Secondary Questions

- What is the role of a citizen?
- How can we express ourselves in our society?
- How are aspects of our identities reflected in our communities?
- What are our responsibilities to ourselves and to each other?
- Who represents us and how do we ensure we are represented?

Additional Activity Ideas

A number of games and interactive resources may be useful for educators to use when teaching about these topics and questions (see Table A2.1). Educators can also use additional activities. They should adjust the activity depending on the topics covered in the class and the students' ages and reading level. The following are examples of activities that teachers could use.

Table A2.1 Possible games and interactive resources to use in lesson outline 2

Name of Game	Website	Chapters Discussed
Buffalo: The Name Dropping Game	https://tiltfactor.org/game/buffalo/	1
Dys4ia	https://docubase.mit.edu/project/dys4ia/	8
A Normal Lost Phone	https://anormallostphone.com/	10
Life Is Strange series	https://lifeisstrange.square-enix-games.com/en-us	6,8,9,11,12
What Remains of Edith Finch	http://www.giantsparrow.com/games/finch/	7, 10, 13, 14
SweetxHeart	https://cattsmall.itch.io/sweetxheart	7
Offline	https://finngeergames.itch.io/	7
Gone Home	https://gonehome.game/	5, 12
Monster Prom	http://monsterprom.pizza/	7
iThrive game guides and curricula	https://ithrivegames.org/ithrive-curriculum/museum-of-me/	7
Guide to Making Games for Identity, Reducing Bias, and Perspective-Taking	https://www.adl.org/media/12529/download	12
Literary Safari list of Games	https://www.literarysafari.com/armmewithgames	—
Designing for Inclusive Games (a card deck of questions)	www.adl.org/designinginclusivegames	12, 13

The Students' Backpack

In this activity, students are placed into small groups. Each student in the group takes an object out of their bag, purse, tote, or backpack. Students then need to discuss how the object relates to their identity, and they take turns sharing stories about how they got their objects. The team then puts all the objects together and tries to figure out how to make a game with them—either as mechanics (actions that the player can take), obstacles, characters, goals, or topics.

This activity is adapted from the Game Developers' Bag exercise I created in the following guide: https://www.adl.org/media/12529/download.

A New Community

Students work in groups to create a brand-new society or human civilization. They have to name their community, explain its constitution, create its rules and laws, and explore what people like to eat, do, read, or watch. The students need to create artifacts for their community, perform skits, or make videos, and the other teams need to guess what the rules, norms, and features of the community are. This activity is adapted from one I did as a sixth grader in the Three Village School District in the United States.

Souvenir Shop

Have everyone in a class bring in a secret souvenir from their travels, such as one that reflects their interests. Put them in a pile in the room and mix them up and see if students can guess whose souvenir is whose. Think about having the students write or share a journal entry, poem, or riddle that is associated with the item, which needs to be matched with it by their peers.

Identity Game Jam

Students work together to create board games or digital games around the theme of identity. Students can make any game that helps them to express their own identities, or helps to express others' identities. I have created a free guide to doing this type of game jam, which can be accessed at https://www.adl.org/media/12529/download. Other tips for doing game jams can be found at https://www.adl.org/media/13011/download.

Identity in Action

Students can write letters, emails, or take some type of substantive action in their community based on their own interests, needs, and identities. For example, a student who is interested in sports may write to the school board about opening the gym for practice on the weekends. A person who likes the ocean may think about a doing a beach cleanup day, or taking part in an ocean-related citizen science project. A person who likes to cook may think about creating a special meal for first responders, or hosting a TikTok or YouTube tutorial on making cupcakes for a local cub troop.

Designing for Inclusion Cards

Have students think about how a game (or website, application, TV show, etc.) might have been designed differently to be more inclusive. What might we change to include or better represent all different identities, and to ensure that everyone belongs? Use the Designing Inclusive Games cards that I created to help students think through these design questions. The cards can be found at www.adl.org/designinginclusivegames.

Discussion Questions

- How do communities and their governance affect who gets included and who belongs?
- What does it mean to feel included or excluded?
- How should we shape society to better include everyone?
- What types of communities do we have in our local area? Online? Which communities do we belong to? Which do we wish we could belong to?
- What are the ways in which we express aspects of our identities through communities?

- How do people exercise and express themselves in their offline versus online communities?
- What are biases? How might they influence our attitudes and actions? How might biases be embedded in communities?
- All of these questions should be used sensitively and ethically, without causing trauma or harm.

Tips and Hints

- Remember that identity means a lot of different things—it can refer to our gender or sexual identity, race, ethnicity, religion, and nationality, as well as our interests, hobbies, and family structures. Provide a list or chart for students to fill out if that is helpful. There is an "identity molecule" diagram that teachers can use found at https://www.adl.org/media/12529/download.
- Make sure that the students feel comfortable discussing their identities, and do not pressure students into revealing anything too sensitive.
- Think about how using objects and personal souvenirs may help to support the sharing of oneself and one's identities.
- Help the students connect their own personal identities to that of the broader community.
- Ensure that the students understand that all different types of identities are welcome. If students do not feel welcome, be open to the feedback and work with students to make changes.
- If in a virtual environment, invite students to reflect on how their online or virtual identities in that environment may be different than their in-person identities would be.

Design Toolkit

A Toolkit for Designing Games or Activities for Civics and Ethics

I created a design toolkit to use for creating ethics and civics games. It is based on previous frameworks, design approaches, and research methodologies, and adapted for ethics and civics needs (see Table A3.1).[1] However, games do not need to be explicitly designed for ethics and civics to enable the practice of these skills. Figure A3.1 illustrates the three overriding questions identified in the table.

Table A3.1 A toolkit for designing ethics and civics games

Steps*	Summary	Associated Questions
Identify the goal	Designers need to identify the problem they want to solve or the goal they want the players to reach. This could include any change they want to make in their audience, such as perspectives, opinions, attitudes, or values. There are different types of goals. Games can have game goals; and we can also have pedagogical goals for the games we are making.	• What is the problem, purpose, or goal? • What are the changes you want to make and the goals you want the player to reach? • Are the changes realistic and measurable? • How do project goals align with game goals?
Research and brainstorm	In this step designers need to first get a lay of the land, understand what is already out there, where the gaps are, what should be taught, and how it has been taught in the past. This step includes doing research on possible problems and issues related to ethics and civics. This may also refer to doing brainstorming exercises as a team. Consider hosting brainstorming sessions with members of your audience and doing research with them, such as by doing focus groups or interviews.	• How has the topic or skill been taught already? • What is already out there? • Are there activities, texts, media, or other materials that are also used to teach these skills or content areas? • What is the landscape of problems and issues around this particular field? • How can you brainstorm topics and themes, as well as goals and outcomes?
Identify the audience	Designers need to specify their audience. Who are the players? What are their challenges and how do we ensure their participation? What are their networks? Designers may want to create and test concepts and engage with the audience during this phase.	• Who is the audience? • What are the specific curricular needs for the students? • What is the community that it needs to reach? • Is this for home-schoolers or middle-schoolers? Camp or kindergartners? • If it is for a school-based curriculum, what class would it work best in, and how does it fit their needs?

Continued

Table A3.1 *Continued*

Steps*	Summary	Associated Questions
		• What prior knowledge does your audience have, as well as what are their misconceptions? • Are there differences by state, country, or region? • Is the game accessible to students with different abilities and needs, including different neurotypes, motor abilities, or sight and hearing abilities? • What about different reading levels? • What types of scaffolding is needed for this audience?
Identify the actions and activities that support your goals	Designers need to think about the types of activities, skills, or tasks that would support the goals and changes you want to make. Chamberlin and Schell give some examples of activities, such as comparing or prioritizing values, solving problems, or building relationships (see https://docs.google.com/document/d/1ekXtk61kgCllF1j4Z2UFbeSp UhTfOQCWgiNMoe7-3Xk/edit).	• What are the actions and activities that support the goals and changes you want to make? • What are the types of activities that may help spur this change in real life that could be also used in the game? • Can a game inspire these types of practices to occur? • How does the game establish goals and make sure the player is moving toward them?
Develop and test the concept or idea	Designers can create a basic idea statement and concept of the game. They may want to test this concept by making a very raw prototype or written statement and share it with the audience before creating a more robust prototype.	• Does this concept meet the needs and interests of the audience? • Does this concept meet the educational goals and any other goals of the project? • What are the basic rules and gameplay?
Identify the obstacles, challenges, and opportunities	Designers need to consider the context for the game's use. This includes making sure that the method of delivery, platform, and type of game make sense—or if games are even the best way to support the learning.	• What are the obstacles, challenges, and opportunities in creating this game? • Is it for a classroom, after-school program, or home? • What are the technological limitations? • What is the ecology of its use—is there a community around or in the game? • Are the school administrators supportive, and are parents and families encouraging?

Table A3.1 *Continued*

Steps*	Summary	Associated Questions
		• What is the support system for using the game? • Do most schools have the computer, browser, or internet networking needs to support the game? • Which schools do not have the equipment or connectivity needed and does this game then contribute further to systemic inequities? • How much time, energy, and resources need to be taken by an educator to use it properly, and what other materials might be provided in support of the game (activities, lesson plans, tutorials, teacher's guide)?
Use research-based principles to design the game's experience	Designers should use research-based design principles for creating the game, while also considering the limitations of games.	• Which principles may be used to best drive knowledge building, skills practice, community, and action? • How might well-intentioned principles backfire? • What are the strengths and limitations of each principle (see chapters 4–12 and Appendix IV)?
Prototype, test, and retest the game	This step involves sketching out the game using raw materials or accessible digital tools. It also includes continually playtesting, testing, and retesting the game, and revising the prototype.	• Which materials should we use to prototype and playtest our game (e.g., paper, cardboard, card stock, tokens, dice, or a digital tool such as Word, Google Docs, Scratch, PowerPoint, PhotoShop, Twine, Balsamiq, Metaverse AR, Construct 2 or 3, Unreal Engine or Unity)? • What questions do we want to ask our playtesters about their experience? • What types of interactions do wc want to look for? • Which interactions are happening through our game—and which are missing?

Continued

Table A3.1 *Continued*

Steps*	Summary	Associated Questions
Reflect on ethics and evaluate for values	The game's design should continually be evaluated in terms of the values that are embedded in the design, and how the game expresses values. Additionally, the game needs to be evaluated for its commitment to accessibility, inclusivity, justice, and equity, among other factors. Use the cards at www.adl.org/designinginclusivegames for questions to guide the design process, as well as tools such as the AbleGamers Charity's Accessible Player Experience Cards at https://accessible.games/accessible-player-experiences/.	• Which values and biases are embedded in the design? • What assumptions are reproduced in the design? • How are values negotiated through play? • How are the characters, storylines, objects, and themes represented, and are they culturally appropriate? • How are players communicating through the game as well as around the game? • Are the players feeling safe, included, and cared for? • How does the game empower students?
Evaluate for education	Designers need to make sure their game is educationally effective. The team needs to ensure that it is designed for specific educational needs, such as meeting educational standards of a state, country, or region. If the game is for a school or classroom, educators and policymakers need to know how this game will fit into a specific educational or curricular need. This needs to be rigorously tested and evaluated throughout, alongside the playtesting and usability of the game.	• How does the game support the types of learning, skills, attitudes, and behaviors that are desired? • How do we know that learning is happening? • Does the game match standards? • Is the change that we want happening through the game (or through activities related to the game)? • What role does the game play in assessment? • How can educators modify and adapt the game, or integrate it into curricula? • How will the teacher be involved in its deployment and implementation? • How much expertise does a teacher or student need to be able to play the game?
Build the game, and continue testing it	This step involves the development process. If the game is digital or technical in nature, this may involve programming, art, and game design processes. As the game goes through the development process, the previous steps should be continually and iteratively considered and reflected upon.	• How will we develop the game, ethically and responsibly? • How does the game ensure learning, equity, and care? • How will the three core circles of design questions be approached? The three core circles of questions need to be continually reviewed in concert (see Figure A3.1).

Note that these steps are not necessarily in the order they should be completed; they also may be done concurrently and even iteratively. For more about design principles, please see Appendix IV.

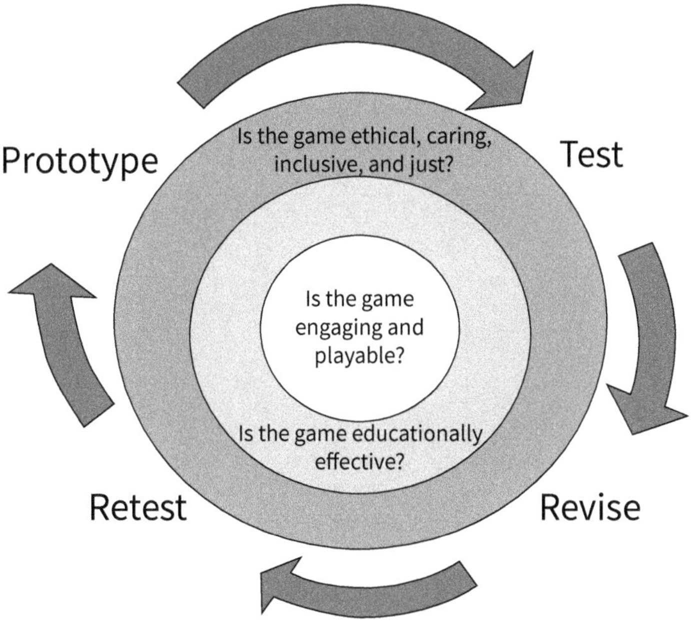

Figure A3.1 A diagram of the three core questions to ask when designing games for civics and ethics: (1) how are we designing for engagement and playability?, (2) how are we designing for educational effectiveness?, and (3) how are we designing for ethics, care, inclusion, and justice? Answering each of these questions requires iterative testing and revising. Image created by Kat Schrier.

Design Principles

List of Possible Design Principles

I created a set of design principles to use for designing a game for ethics and civics (see Table A4.1). I developed this set of principles based on my review of relevant literature and my past experience in designing games. I also looked at previous frameworks, design approaches, and research methodologies, while adapting them to ethics and civics needs.[1] Designers should consider this a set of optional possibilities to draw from, rather than principles that they must use. Depending on the goals, audience, and context, many of the design principles may not be necessary or appropriate to include.

Table A4.1 Design principles for making games for civics and ethics

Design principles	Description
Reading and literacy skills	Games may support reading text. Do not include so much text so as to overwhelm players and include options for different reading abilities. Make sure that the players need to actually read (and not just skip through) the text.
Critical inquiry and questioning	Players should be invited to ask questions. They may question sources, information, problems, and possibilities. They should be encouraged to think about alternative paths, solutions, and options, rather than just accepting the first. They should question assumptions.
Evaluating and interpreting information	Provide evidence and information that players can source, vet, and use. Give them opportunities to apply their findings.
Connection and connecting with others	Provide opportunities for players to connect with other people (and even characters), whether in the real world or virtual spaces. However, be mindful that many players need time to also learn things by themselves.
Modeling and exemplifying	Provide moral exemplars or role models, and examples for the player to observe and experience, so they can understand how to act. Games can serve as an exemplar themselves, as their stories can serve as morality tales. Their characters and players can serve as models who other players can observe.
Problem-solving	Provide opportunities for players to solve problems. However, these should be solvable (or at least approachable), and appropriately leveled to the student so that the problems are not too easy or too challenging.
Role-playing	Players may take on roles in games, which can help them in expressing and exploring their own identities, or another's identities. However, designers should ensure that this is not overwhelming for the player, and does not exploit or misappropriate certain roles or cultures.
Choices, decisions, and consequences	Provide opportunities to make choices and see both short-term and longer-term consequences. Choices and their consequences should be meaningful, impactful, and relevant. Players should also understand the limits of choice. When should choice-making be constrained?

Continued

Table A4.1 *Continued*

Design principles	Description
Communicating with others	Players may communicate verbally or nonverbally, as well as with other players or even other characters. However, designers need to find ways to make sure people are communicating ethically, and respectfully, as well as to encourage cross-cultural communication. Use frameworks like the FairPlay Alliance/ADL Framework to ensure inclusive communication: https://fairplayalliance.org/wp-content/uploads/2020/12/FPA-Framework.pdf
Relationship-building and community-building	Players should be able to form relationships—over time and authentically—with other players or even characters. Communities around and within games should be moderated and designed for respectful communication and interactions.
Transparency	Designers should ensure transparency in a number of ways, such as in revealing their own assumptions and decisions in making the game, and allowing players to be transparent about how they think through decisions. Transparency can also help a community develop, as players are more able to understand why a rule or norm has been established.
Perspective-taking	Players should be able to listen to and interact with the perspectives of other people, as this may help them to connect with them, or to understand their stories. However, perspective-taking can backfire, and can cause discomfort or even further stigma. Moreover, there are ethical issues with perspective-taking that should be explored further.
Simulating systems and situations	Players should be able to address issues and problems systemically, such that they can manipulate and interact with a dynamic system. However, players should not privilege this over other ways to see issues, such as through personal narratives, stories, and viscerally.
Exploration and experimentation	Players should be able to explore the game world and it stories and characters, as well as experiment with different views, identities, and ways of being. However, appropriate boundaries and constraints should be included.
Opportunities for reflection	Players need moments within and outside of the game where they can reflect and reconsider their decisions and choices. This could take the form of pauses or deliberations, or it could be a mindful, contemplative type of play.
Argumentation, deliberation, and discourse	Players should be given opportunities to engage in dialogue, deliberation, and discourse around viewpoints, issues, and problems. Players should be able to share arguments, as well as provide evidence that counters other's arguments. Games can also serve as a type of argument, such as about a particular view, process, or system.
Expressing and managing emotions	Players should be able to express their emotions and consider and use these emotions when they make decisions or evaluate choices, or when they connect with others. Players should also learn how to manage one's own emotions and identify other's emotions. However, players can also be overwhelmed by their emotions, and this can contribute to disconnection.
Practicing empathy and compassion	Players should have opportunities to practice empathy and compassion for other real people and societies, as well as virtual people, places, and creatures. However, empathy may not make players act ethically, and players may practice compassion in different or unexpected ways.

Table A4.1 *Continued*

Design principles	Description
Expressing and exploring identity	Players should have opportunities to reflect on and express their own identities as well as interact with other's identities. Players may be able to negotiate or even change positions with others and explore their identities. However, we need to be mindful of how we represent different identities and try on others' identities such that it isn't appropriative or even violent. We need to avoid also participating in digital Blackface, for instance. We need to question when it is problematic to enact others' identities, and when it is educationally useful.
Customization and personalization	Players should be able to customize (or change and adapt) an experience to what they are most interested in. However, designers should be mindful about which different options are allowed (as well as constraining the options so they are not overwhelming). The game should also adapt and alter to the player's needs, abilities, and interests. Designers should be ethical in how the game uses this data, such as by using informed consent and full transparency.
Active learning and responsibility	Players should feel like they are taking an active role in their learning, and managing resources, making decisions, and making an impact. They should have progressively more and more responsibility over aspects of the game. However, this type of responsibility needs to be scaffolded. Also, how are game players responsible for how they treat each other, how they treat themselves, and how they treat the game? How are designers responsible to their players and their games?
Exploring and expressing culture	Players should have the opportunity to explore different cultures, such as their norms, values, rituals, symbols, relationships, and languages. Designers should be mindful of not being culturally appropriative, misrepresenting cultures, stereotyping or tokenizing them. Fully including people who are experts in or people from a particular culture as codesigners of the game, or as members of the design team is one possible step.
Storytelling and story sharing	Players should have the opportunity to hear other's stories and personal accounts, as well as to share and express their own stories. Stories are one way to share and communicate, alongside other options, such as through data, systems, text, and mechanics.
Authenticity	When at all possible, designers should use authentic and realistic data, variables, information, sources, stories, people, and events. However, players should understand that the game is a representation of a view, argument, story, system, or world, and not an exact replica. As such, designers should be open and transparent about the balance between accuracy and imaginative play.
Real-world connections, data, people, and scenarios	Designers should use connections to the real-world as much as possible, such as real data, information, events, sources, communities, stories, problems, or issues. Games should also connect players to real people, communities, or issues, while being mindful of how in-game skills practice may (or may not) translate to real-world action.
Local and global issues	Players should have opportunities to see and solve issues and problems in their own communities. Players should also be able to see global themes and concerns, and connect with communities around the world. Designers should find ways to make the issues more personally relevant, or use issues that are already meaningful to players.

Continued

Table A4.1 *Continued*

Design principles	Description
Personal relevance and meaning	Topics, stories, themes, and problems should be made personally relevant to the players whenever possible. A game can be meaningful to a player in many different ways—such as being personally meaningful to their lives or meaningful in terms of the gameplay, or with a choice having a consequential impact on the game world. However, it's hard to predict how players will make connections with the game, so invite multiple entry points.
Agency	Agency is the feeling that your choices, moves, decisions, and views matter and that what you do in the game has an impact. You are the active agent in the game. However, games can use agency in different ways, such as by constraining it to show helplessness. Agency can backfire if players mistakenly think they would have the same agency in the real world.
Identify the right medium*	Designers should not use games, virtual reality, or mobile games just because they seem innovative, trendy, or new. Rather, they should be used only if it is the best way to support students' learning and the pedagogical goals.
Fun and engaging*	Make sure the game is appropriately fun and engaging, and well-designed to the needs of the player. What is fun for someone may not be fun for another person. Also, what is fun may be something challenging, surprising, or uncertain. Fun is not necessarily easy and something too easy may be boring or tedious.
Use clear goals and feedback*	The game's goals should be clear to the player, and how to achieve the goal should also be clear. Players should be given consistent, clear, and regular feedback as to how they are doing in reaching goals. Tying game goals to pedagogical goals is important.
Identify and challenge assumptions*	Designers should consider the assumptions and biases that are embedded in their creation. How can you reveal and communicate these to your players? How might these assumptions affect how players play, connect with each other, and connect with the world?
Reflect on the ethics of the creation*	Designers should also reflect on the ethics of their creation, including issues such as representation, privacy, and the inclusiveness of one's game world. What are the responsibilities of the game designer? What are the players' responsibilities?
Ensure full accessibility and participation*	Designers should consider how to ensure participation from their audience, such as designing for those who are marginalized, rather than for the majority. How are players able to access this game, and what challenges and obstacles might there be to equitable participation?

This repository should be considered a collection of possible principles to use when designing games for ethics and civics. A game can be successful without using all of them, or any of them, depending on the needs and goals of the game and its audience. Principles with an asterisk (*) are relevant to all different types of games, and not necessarily ethics and civics games. For additional information on the types of questions to ask as you design, see Designing Inclusive Games, a deck of question cards, at www.adl.org/designinginclusivegames.

Recommendations

Recommendations for Educators

Are you thinking about using games to teach civics and ethics?

- Make sure that games (whether analog, virtual reality, location-based or digital) are the best solution for the particular goals, needs, context, and audience. Games are complex and come in all different varieties. Their effectiveness depends on many factors, such as one's surroundings, the audience (and their prior knowledge and skills), the context of use, and ecosystem around the game.
- If you need help choosing a particular game for a particular need, see chapter 13 and Table 13.1.
- Teachers matter in the effectiveness of a game! An educator, guide, or mentor really affects how players can learn, feel cared for, and crystallize knowledge.
- Consider how to enhance player connections through the game—whether with each other, with themselves, with their communities, or with the world at large.
- Use a mix of stories, information, data, emotions, viewpoints, evidence, and systems to teach. No one way is better than another, and reasoning-related and emotion-related skills all matter.
- Consider how to relate the game to the students, their lives, and their interests. It can be personally meaningful to the students, as well as meaningful in the context of the classroom or other space. Let students choose their own games, too!
- The learning does not start and stop with the game—it's not a standalone experience. It should be paired usefully with other activities, tasks, curricula, and discussions.
- Educators need to consider logistical, practical, and technological constraints, such as whether you have the right computers, access, and materials, or enough time to support the game's play.
- Thinking of using a particular game? The first thing to do is to play the game a few times and learn all of its strengths and weaknesses, so that you can fill in any gaps and know what to expect when it's played in an educational space.
- Educators should consider digital and nondigital games, as all types of games can support different needs. Games can even be free—no materials required, just some players!
- Educators may want to consider making games or even codesigning them with students. Games can made out of recycled materials, or classroom art supplies, such as cardboard and construction paper, cards, or beads. Students can also use free programs to make their own digital creations, such as Twine 2 or Scratch.
- Educators should continually be reflecting on and revealing their assumptions, and questioning the ethics of a game. Adding players to a game may bring up ethical issues that are unexpected, but need to be articulated and managed.
- Problems may emerge as players play with each other, and connect. Consider how to maintain communities where all players feel safe, included, and supported.
- Don't be afraid to modify or adapt games to fit classroom and curricular needs, or even logistical constraints.

Recommendations for Game Designers and Developers

Are you thinking about designing games for civics and ethics?

- Consider using the design process in Appendix III and design principles in Appendix IV.
- Ask lots of questions and continue to reevaluate one's assumptions, biases, design decisions, and ethics.
- Reflect on how to ensure that your players have equitable access to your creation, and how they will feel a sense of safety and belonging in the communities within and around your game.
- Consider how to appropriately represent different views, communities, societies, cultures, perspectives, and identities, while being mindful of stereotypes and appropriation.
- Think through the strengths and limitations of games. Why are you creating games and not using another medium? Why is this the best way to teach what you want to teach?
- Don't forget about designing for fun, and thinking about how meaningful and personally relevant challenges can be highly engaging.
- Continually playtest and iterate through all aspects of the game, such as ensuring that it is changing what you want it to change, with the audience whom you want to change.
- Find ways to use authentic perspectives, locations, moments, events, and social issues, and connect players to real-world processes, stories, and needs.
- Think about how your game meets specific learning objectives, needs, and standards, so that your game will be useful to the most teachers and players.
- On the other hand, consider also designing for the most marginalized populations. How do we design for those who are marginalized rather than just those who are mainstream audience members?
- Educational goals and game goals should be intertwined, and game play should not just be plopped on top of the learning, but rather integrated more fully.
- Consider the types of connections that may be supported by games that are collaborative versus competitive, or in-person versus virtual.
- Try not to privilege digital and "next big thing" types of games over analog games, pen and paper games, or even in-person, material-free games. Keep it simple.
- Deeply connect with your audience and consider making them codesigners of the game in all different ways. Think about how to make the play meaningful to the player, both in terms of the player's own interests and background, as well as how their choices impact the game.
- Think about how to support players to do the actions that will help them make the change you want them to make—such as changes in behavior, attitudes, or knowledge. How can you make the game less didactic and more focused on doing, practicing, and acting?
- Do not just think about your own friends and communities. What are the needs for games in various countries, cultures, and communities?
- How can we better include different constituencies into the game design process?
- Use the Designing Inclusive Games card deck of questions at www.adl.org/designinginclusivegames to think through issues related to inclusion.
- Use the AbleGamers Charity Accessible Player Experience design patterns card deck and website at https://accessible.games/accessible-player-experiences/ to think through issues related to access.
- Use the Values @ Play framework and Grow-a-Game card deck at https://www.valuesatplay.org/grow-a-game-overview to think through how values are expressed through your game.

- Use the FairPlay Alliance and ADL Framework at https://fairplayalliance.org/wp-content/uploads/2020/12/FPA-Framework.pdf to think through community moderation and policies.

Recommendations for Activists and Community Organizers

Are you thinking about using games to support activism, social action, or community needs?

- Think about how to incorporate games into your workshops, interventions, or community activities.
- Games can be used to help connect people, help spur awareness and action, and help contribute real-world data, perspectives, opinions, and viewpoints.
- Think about using analog and location-based games that can take place in the community, or can be adapted to specific community needs.
- Community members may want to host game design events (game jams), with the thought that the game product may not be professional-level, but that the *process* itself may be meaningful.
- Community planning and collective problem-solving can be jumpstarted through a multiplayer game that relates to a specific problem or issue. It can give people a shared vocabulary and understanding of the perspectives involved.
- Playing itself can be a form of activism, resistance, and change. Think about how to support these types of activities, while keeping in mind the context of play.
- The ideas, perspectives, data, and outcomes from games may be unexpected. Keep players safe from known and surprising (dire) consequences based on their play, or what transpires through play.
- Use game design and game educator experts to support community activities. Partnering with different types of experts or organizations can be useful.
- Understand that player goals and community organizer goals may diverge. Players want to have a fun and meaningful experience, while organizers may want to fill a particular need. Ensure that these goals are complementary.
- Games come in all different varieties, and they can even be simple and quick. If you do not have a lot of time, or you need to support a remote experience or a large group, you can still use a game (or create a game) to fill a need.
- Remember that practical and emotional considerations (such as respecting the time volunteered by your game players, a need to eat and connect with others, and a need for safety and belongingness) are just as important as any other part of any game, action, event, or community intervention.

Recommendations for Researchers

Are you thinking about researching games for ethics and civics? Here are some areas for further investigation:

- What are the conditions under which perspective-taking, problem-solving, reflection, communication, exploration, choice-making, and systems thinking in a game are more effective or less ineffective, particularly when it comes to ethics and civics learning?
- How does the context of the game, educator, and other factors affect the game's effectiveness, particularly in relation to learning ethics and civics?
- How do we assess behavior change and skills practices over the long term?

- What are the best ways to support real-world action beyond the game, as well as longer-term attitudinal and behavioral changes?
- Which types of design patterns work best for different skills, audiences, and contexts?
- How do different gaming platforms and game types (virtual reality, digital games, analog games, location-based games) support the practice of different types of skills?
- How does one's identity, sense of self-efficacy, and belongingness affect how one learns and practices ethics and civics?
- How do we reshape institutions and systemic inequities to ensure greater access to play and civic engagement?
- How do players make ethical decisions in games as opposed to outside of games?
- How do relationships, empathy, and emotions, along with reasoning and critical thinking affect how people make ethical decisions in (and beyond) games?
- How can games shape civic attitudes and support civic engagement behaviors?
- How can we use games to not only teach ethics and civics, but to increase our societal knowledge and understanding of the nature of ethics and civics?

Notes

Chapter 1

1. SARS-CoV-2 stands for severe acute respiratory syndrome coronavirus 2, and is the virus that causes coronavirus disease 2019 (COVID-19); a popular meme during the spring of 2020 was "Though we are in this together, we are also unequal—same storm, different boats." See for instance P. Kirubakaran, "'We Are Not All in the Same Boat...' Covid Poster and Poem Win Internet; Here's Their Story," Republic World, May 6, 2020, https://www.republicworld.com/world-news/rest-of-the-world-news/we-are-not-all-in-the-same-boat-story-behind-viral-post-and-poem.html. See also E. Price-Haywood, J. Burton, D. Fort, and L. Seoane, "Hospitalization and Mortality among Black Patients and White Patients with Covid-19," *New England Journal of Medicine*, May 27, 2020, https://www.nejm.org/doi/full/10.1056/NEJMsa2011686?query=featured_coronavirus.

2. These inequities had been there all along. For instance, the global pandemic helped also to expose troubling systemic inequities such as differential access to healthcare among the Black, Hispanic, and Indigenous communities in the United States and Brazil. Who could stay quarantined was also based on systemic socioeconomic and racial and ethnicity patterns. These systemic injustices were also exemplified and exposed by reactions to the protests in spring 2020, to the pandemic quarantines, the pandemic itself, and police brutality, including the wrongful deaths of George Floyd, Breonna Taylor, Ahmaud Arbery, and many others. See more at Lisa Fitzpatrick, "Coronavirus and the Underserved: We Are Not All in This Together," *Forbes*, April 2, 2020, https://www.forbes.com/sites/lisafitzpatrick/2020/04/02/covid-19-and-the-underserved-we-are-not-all-in-this-together/#5eb58fdc5a71, and also António Guterres, "We Are All in This Together: Human Rights and COVID-19 Response and Recovery," United Nations, https://www.un.org/en/un-coronavirus-communications-team/we-are-all-together-human-rights-and-covid-19-response-and (accessed May 31, 2020). See also the inequities noted in Korbey, *Building Better Citizens: A New Civics Education for All* (Lanham, MD: Rowman & Littlefield, 2019) and Peter Levine and Kei Kawashima-Ginsberg, "The Republic Is (Still) at Risk—and Civics Is Part of the Solution" (Medford, MA: Jonathan M. Tisch College of Civic Life, Tufts University, 2017). For more about inequities in education more generally, see also Meira Levinson, "Diversity and Civic Education," in *Making Civics Count: Citizenship Education for a New Generation*, ed. David E. Campbell, Meira Levinson, and Frederick M. Hess (Cambridge, MA: Harvard University Press, 2012); Nicole Mirra, *Educating for Empathy* (New York: Teachers College Press, 2018). For the public being in crisis, see also J. Habermas, *The Structural Transformation of the Public Sphere* (Cambridge, MA: MIT Press, 1989).

3. Not totally dissipated, as many people still see the need to limit and confine game-playing rather than seeing it as part and parcel of being human. For more about the WHO decision see, for instance, WHO, *Addictive Behaviours: Gaming Disorder, 2018,* https://www.who.int/news-room/q-a-detail/addictive-behaviours-gaming-disorder (accessed December 28, 2020) explaining that the classification describes people who make gaming too much

of a priority in their lives over other so-called healthier activities—such as real-world socializing and going to school and work.

4. See, for instance ADL, July 2019, *Free to Play? Hate, Harassment, and Positive Social Experiences in Online Games*, https://www.adl.org/media/13139/download; ADL, November 2020, *Free to Play? Hate, Harassment, and Positive Social Experiences in Online Games 2020*, https://www.adl.org/free-to-play-2020#results (accessed January 12, 2021). I was a fellow at the ADL but did not work on this particular study. Note, ADL was formerly known as the Anti-Defamation League.

5. For instance, Riot CEO Nicolo Laurent said, "Let's stay physically apart—and take other public health steps such as hand hygiene—to help flatten the curve and #PlayApartTogether to help power through this crisis. For Rioters, playing games is more than just a game; it's a meaningful life pursuit. And now, for the billions of players around the world, playing games could help the pursuit of saving lives. Let's beat this COVID-19 boss battle together." See G. Torbet, "The World Health Organization Wants you to Stay Home and Play Video Games," Digital Trends, March 29, 2020, https://www.digitaltrends.com/gaming/who-video-games-playaparttogether/.

6. P. Suderman, "The World Health Organization Classified Video Game Addiction as a Disorder. Now It's Telling People to Play Video Games," *Reason Magazine*, March 31, 2020, https://reason.com/2020/03/31/the-world-health-organization-classified-video-game-addiction-as-a-disorder-now-its-telling-people-to-play-video-games/. See also Good Games Podcast, May 18, 2020, https://art19.com/shows/good-game-podcast/epi-sodes/26c80ab1-ce1a-48be-a3ee-8dbc9f266bea. It's also possible the public will go back to demonizing games once the pandemic is over. Moral panic over screentime during the pandemic has persisted. See, for instance, M. Richtel, "Children's Screen Time Has Soared in the Pandemic, Alarming Parents and Researchers," *New York Times*, January 16, 2021, https://www.nytimes.com/2021/01/16/health/covid-kids-tech-use.html. A moral panic is a feeling of fear spread over the public about a new technology or phenomenon, and its possible corruption or erosion of society, such as widespread fears about how television or games ("screens") may addict and corrupt youth.

7. Nintendo, *Animal Crossing: New Horizons*, 2020; Blizzard, *World of Warcraft*, 2004; Mojang Studios/Microsoft, *Minecraft*, 2011.

8. Alexandria Ocasio-Cortez and Ilhan Omar participated in this livestreamed event, meaning it was shared and broadcast live for people with internet-enabled computers to watch via a livestreaming platform called Twitch. Joshua Rivera, "AOC Played *Among Us* and Achieved What Most Politicians Fail at: Acting Normal," *The Guardian*, October 22, 2020, https://www.theguardian.com/games/2020/oct/22/alexandria-ocasio-cortez-ilhan-omar-among-us-twitch-stream-aoc; Alaa Elassar, "Joe Biden Has His Own Island on '*Animal Crossing*' Where You Can Learn About His Campaign," CNN, October 18, 2020, https://www.cnn.com/2020/10/18/business/biden-animal-crossing-island-trnd/index.html; Kristina Reymann-Schneider, "How Politicians Use Games for their Own Gains," *DW*, October 19, 2020, https://www.dw.com/en/how-politicians-use-video-games-for-their-own-gains/a-55286753. Gideon Dishon and Yasmin B. Kafai, "Connected Civic Gaming: Rethinking the Role of Video Games in Civic Education," *Interactive Learning Environments* (2019), p. 1–11, DOI: 10.1080/10494820.2019.1704791; M. Sicart, *The Ethics of Computer Games* (Cambridge, MA: MIT Press, 2009); K. Schrier, "Designing and Using Games to Teach Ethics and Ethical Thinking," in *Learning, Education & Games*

Vol. 1: Curricular and Design Considerations, ed. K. Schrier (Pittsburgh: ETC Press, 2014), p. 143–160.

9. See, for instance, the Learning, Education & Games book series: Schrier, *Learning, Education & Games Vol. 1*; Schrier (ed.), *Learning, Education & Games Vol. 2: Bringing Games into Educational Contexts* (Pittsburgh: ETC Press, 2016); and Schrier (ed.), *Learning, Education & Games Vol. 3: 100 Games to Use in the Classroom and Beyond* (Pittsburgh: ETC Press, 2019). For instance, the educational game *Quandary* almost doubled in usage in 2020 than over the same period in 2019, according to information shared during a meeting with Shannon Meneses and the *Quandary* team. Specifically, in December 2019 to December 2020, the number of users increased by 77% and gameplays increased by 17%.

10. iCivics, Toolkit, Spring 2020, https://www.icivics.org/toolkit?gclid=EAIaIQobChMItby0p-HK6QIVJYFaBR0EzAPFEAAYASADEgKSpPD_BwE.

11. Games such as *Plague Inc.* (a virus simulator) and *Pandemic* (a cooperative board game) skyrocketed in downloads and sales. See for instance Leslie Katz, "Coronavirus Leads to Sales Spike of *Plague Inc.*, a Game about Pandemics," CNET, January 25, 2020, https://www.cnet.com/news/coronavirus-leads-to-sales-spike-of-plague-inc-a-game-about-pandemics/.

12. M. Leacock, "No Single Player Can Win This Board Game: It's Called *Pandemic*," *New York Times*, March 25, 2020, https://www.nytimes.com/2020/03/25/opinion/pandemic-game-covid.html. As another example, the Tiltfactor Lab created *Pox: Save the People* (https://tiltfactor.org/game/pox/) and *ZombiePox* (https://tiltfactor.org/game/zombiepox/) to help stop the spread of disease. See also K. Andersen and M. May, "Playing Against the Virus," *The World*, March 8, 2013, https://www.pri.org/stories/2013-03-08/playing-against-virus

13. Players can change parameters to spur the pathogen on more rapidly. They are in development for a new version of the game where players play as the medical professionals and aim to contain a virus like Sars-CoV-2. See more at Ndemic Creations, *Plague Inc.*, https://www.ndemiccreations.com/en/ (accessed June 10, 2020). See also Ndemic Creations, *Plague Inc.: The Cure*, https://www.ndemiccreations.com/en/news/184-plague-inc-the-cure-is-out-now-for-ios-and-android (accessed November 11, 2020); E. Lofgren and N. Fefferman, "The Untapped Potential of Virtual Game Worlds to Shed Light on Real World Epidemics," *The Lancet*, 7(no. 9), 2007: 625–629; J. Elker, "*World of Warcraft* Experienced a Pandemic in 2005, Which May Help Coronavirus Researchers," *Seattle Times*, April 10, 2020, https://www.seattletimes.com/business/technology/world-of-warcraft-experienced-a-pandemic-in-2005-which-may-help-coronavirus-researchers/—about when *World of Warcraft* accidentally unleashed the Corrupted Blood plague.

14. H. Stevens, "Why Outbreaks Like Coronavirus Spread Exponentially and How to 'Flatten the Curve,'" *Washington Post*, March 14, 2020, https://www.washingtonpost.com/graphics/2020/world/corona-simulator/.

15. R. Ahuja, C. Huang, S. Kovach, and L. Woods, "Modeling the Spread of COVID-19 in UCLA Classrooms," May 12, 2020, https://stack.dailybruin.com/2020/05/12/covid-model/.

16. Marcel Salathe and Nicky Case, "'What Happens Next?' COVID-19 Futures, Explained with Playable Simulations," NCase, https://ncase.me/covid-19/ (accessed November 12, 2020).

17. Cait S. Kirby, September 7, 2020, https://caitkirby.com/downloads/Fall%202020.html. There is also a version about faculty perspectives, which can be found at Cait S. Kirby, October 1, 2020, https://caitkirby.com/downloads/October1st2020.html. The games were created in the summer of 2020, a few months prior to campuses reopening. When speaking to my students about the first game on September 9, 2020, they said the game was even more intense than what they are experiencing in person at a residential college in the northeast of the United States, but that it shared a perspective on what it was like if you are having underlying health conditions as a student, and in a more regimented residential situation.

18. UW Game Center, *Foldit*, https://fold.it/ (accessed June 10, 2020). In *Foldit*, players and computer work together to solve real-world "protein" puzzles. Human beings help manipulate 3-D versions of proteins to try to give a computer the algorithm or steps to being able to understand the structures of real protein. See also Carnegie Mellon University, *EteRNA*, https://eternagame.org/ (accessed June 10, 2020). In *EteRNA*, players develop new possible RNA protein molecules to solve real-world problems. See more about *EteRNA* in chapter 5. See more about both games in K. Schrier, *Knowledge Games: How Playing Games Can Solve Problems, Create Insight, and Make Change* (Baltimore: Johns Hopkins University Press, 2016).

19. This refers all types of analog and digital games, including virtual reality (VR) and augmented reality (AR) games. Games are yet another way to help support the practice of essential skills related to ethics and civics, in addition to (but not replacing) other instructional experiences such as lectures, case studies, books, films, worksheets, expository writing, debate, field trips, or maps. However, games are not simply analogous to a worksheet or a book; and they are more than a standalone tool.

20. W. A. Wines, "Seven Pillars of Business Ethics: Toward a Comprehensive Framework," *Journal of Business Ethics* 70 (2008): 483–499; R. Shafer-Landau, *The Fundamentals of Ethics* (New York: Oxford University Press, 2020).

21. N. Tierney, *Imagination and Ethical Ideals: Prospects for a Unified Philosophical and Psychological Understanding* (New York: SUNY Press, 1994).

22. S. Schwartz, "Are There Universal Aspects in the Structure and Contents of Human Values?" *Journal of Social Issues* 50 (1994): 19–45.

23. Shafer-Landau, *The Fundamentals of Ethics*; Jubilee Centre, *A Framework for Character Education in Schools*, 2017, https://www.jubileecentre.ac.uk/userfiles/jubileecentre/pdf/character-education/Framework%20for%20Character%20Education.pdf.

24. Gil de Zúñiga, Homero, Trevor Diehl, and Alberto Ardèvol-Abreu, "Assessing Civic Participation Around the World: How Evaluations of Journalists' Performance Leads to News Use and Civic Participation Across 22 Countries," *American Behavioral Scientist* 62, no. 8 (July 2018): 1116–1137.

25. This comes in part from the neo-Aristotelian model of virtue ethics, where a person does what a virtuous person would do. A virtuous person is someone who strives to be a moral exemplar, who can understand the messiness of moral decision making, and who gains moral wisdom and knowledge over time. We cannot have knowledge without wisdom. Education is a key component of virtue ethics, and it helps to cultivate virtues, which means that it's not just a habit of character, but also it is about having thoughts, motives, and intentions that strive to be good and virtuous. See more at Shafer-Landau, *The Fundamentals of Ethics*.

26. Quoted from Schrier, *Knowledge Games*, p. 192.

27. Yupanqui J. Munoz and Charbel N. El-Hani, "Student with a Thousand Faces: From the Ethics in Video Games to Becoming a Citizen," *Cultural Studies of Science Education* 7 (2012): 909–943, at 914. "Citizen" is a problematic word. Mirra and Garcia explain that "indeed, the term *citizen* itself becomes problematic when considering the tenuous status of undocumented immigrant students in this country who find their access to public services and voice in public life in constant limbo. While we use the terms *citizen* and *civic* in this chapter, we conceptualize them not as markers of legal status but as signifiers of the rights of individuals to participate fully in civic communities at local, national, and global levels regardless of age or legal residency. While we recognize citizenship as a concept that can complicate, challenge, or even transcend national borders, our primary focus here remains on civic engagement and disparities in the U.S. context." N. Mirra and A. Garcia, "Civic Participation Reimagined: Youth Interrogation and Innovation in the Multimodal Public Sphere," *Review of Research in Education* 41 (March 2017):136–158. See also, L. Ouellette, "Citizenship," in *Keywords for Media Studies*, ed. L. Ouellette and J. Gray (New York: NYU Press, 2017), https://keywords.nyupress.org/media-studies/essay/citizenship/.

28. One of the primary purposes of school, at least in the United States, has been to prepare ethically engaged people who can fully participate in civic life—to make citizens. David E.Campbell, "Introduction," in *Making Civics Count: Citizenship Education for a New Generation*, ed. D. E. Campbell, M. Levinson, and F. M. Hess (Cambridge, MA: Harvard Education Press, 2012), p. 1. Jubilee Centre, *A Framework for Character Education in Schools*, p. 1, explains that "the Schools should aim to develop confident and compassionate students, who are effective contributors to society, successful learners, and responsible citizens."

29. As I stated in *Knowledge Games*, p. 190. Also, to be responsibly engaging at any level of participation in the inner workings of one's society, whether governing, working, or representing a contingent, you need to be an ethical leader, citizen, and person.

30. Amber Coleman-Mortley also calls citizenship an act, rather than a status. See A. Coleman-Mortley, "How to Raise an Anti-Racist Kid," *New York Times*, June 24, 2020. However, again, "citizen" is a weighty word, and a status that is not equitably attainable. Who gets to be a citizen and who is deemed a citizen is unequitable and biased. Therefore, while I have tried to carefully realign how we should think of citizen as an act, not a status, we should still question the use of this word to describe these sets of behaviors, given its societal weight. Davisson and Gehm dive into the weight of this word. They explain that "the identity of citizen is both a status conferred by the state and a vision of self that must be adopted and acted on by members of that state in order that a society might sustain itself. The process of adopting the identity requires the ability to imagine oneself as a member of a community of individuals among whom there may be very little in common beyond a shared location. At its core, according to Lauren Berlant, "citizenship is a relation among strangers who learn to feel it as a common identity based on shared historical, legal, or familial connection to a geopolitical space." A. Davisson and D. Gehm, "Gaming Citizenship: Video Games as Lessons in Civic Life," *Journal of Contemporary Rhetoric* 4, no. 3–4 (2014): 39–57, citing Lauren Berlant, "Citizenship," in *Keywords for American Cultural Studies*, ed. Bruce Burgett and Glenn Hendler (New York: NYU Press, 2007), p. 37.

31. Davisson and Gehm, "Gaming Citizenship." Also, Davisson and Gehm point out that Robert Asen described citizenship as an act or process. They write, "Robert Asen, in his discourse theory of citizenship, proposes that 'rather than asking what counts as citizenship,

we should ask: how do people enact citizenship? Reorienting our framework from a question of what to a question of how usefully redirects our attention from acts to action.
Inquiring into the how of citizenship recognizes citizenship as a process." See also work
by Amber Coleman-Mortley, who explains that citizenship is an active process: https://
sharemylesson.com/blog/icivics-games and https://twitter.com/momofallcapes?lang=en.
The phrase repairing our world also relates to the concept of *Tikkun Olam* from Judaism,
which refers to behaving and acting in a way that improves the world.

32. See M. Ferrari and G. Potworowski, *Teaching for Wisdom: Cross-cultural Perspectives
on Fostering Wisdom* (New York: Springer, 2008) and B. B. Muhonja, *Radical Utu*
(Athens: Ohio University Press, 2020).

33. Quote at Jubilee Centre, *A Framework for Character Education in Schools.* The Jubilee
Centre likens flourishing to eudaimonia, an Aristotelian concept of engaging in the good
life, or a state of happiness through virtue. A good life is one that has intrinsic value (not instrumental value) in that it aims for good for its own sake. It is one that seeks self-sufficient
good, or one that is itself enough to make it good and valuable. And it is also one that is
distinctive, in that it engages with that which makes us human. See more about virtue
ethics and a virtuous life in Shafer-Landau, *The Fundamentals of Ethics.* See also the Jubilee
Centre, *A Framework for Character Education in Schools*, p. 1, which states that "human
flourishing is the widely accepted goal of life. To flourish is not only to be happy, but to
fulfil one's potential. Flourishing is the ultimate aim of character education."

34. Global Ethics Observatory, http://www.unesco.org/shs/ethics/geo/user/ (accessed June
14, 2020); H. ten Have, "Ethics Education: Global, Inspiring, Challenging," *International
Journal of Ethics Education* 1 (2016): 1–6.

35. See chapter 2 for more research on these trends. See also Korbey, *Building Better Citizens*;
Campbell, "Introduction"; J. Lerner, *Making Democracy Fun: How Game Design Can
Empower Citizens and Transform Politics* (Cambridge, MA: MIT Press, 2014); ADL,
"Eileen Hershenov's Testimony Before the House Judiciary Committee on Hate Crimes
and the Rise of White Nationalism," April 9, 2019, https://www.adl.org/news/article/
eileen-hershenovs-testimony-before-the-house-judiciary-committee-on-hate-crimes-
and.Though we cannot necessarily causally connect current educational policies and
practices to these trends, education has made a difference in closing gaps and raising proficiency. See more in Korbey, *Building Better Citizens*.

36. Campbell, "Introduction," p. 1.

37. J. Juul, *Half Real: Video Games between Real Rules and Fictional Worlds* (Cambridge,
MA: MIT Press, 2005), pp. 13. Jesper Juul defines games as having a "rule-based formal
system; with variable and quantifiable outcomes; where different outcomes are assigned
different values; where the player exerts effort in order to influence the outcome; the player
feels emotionally attached to the outcome; and the consequences of the activity are optional and negotiable." However, I tell my students that we can read, accept, and even embody a definition of a game, but as soon as we define games we should be seeking ways to
push on the boundaries of that definition, such as by finding examples that defy the definition, and inventing new forms that subvert it. See more about the contours of what counts
as a game in M. Consalvo and C. Paul, *Real Games* (Cambridge, MA: MIT Press, 2019).

38. What is deemed a real game and who is deemed a real gamer is also needing clarification and affects our identity as a game player or the identification as something as a game.
See more about this in Consalvo and Paul, *Real Games.* Real-world interactive games are

ones where participants interact with each other in shared physical environments, though they could be adapted for a remote learning environment. In digital games, most of the game play happens in a digital or virtual environment, where the goals, obstacles, and rewards are embedded in that environment. Online games enable some type of connectivity, such as among devices and players. A battle royale game is a multiplayer game where players compete to be the "last person standing," after surviving various obstacles—and each other.

39. Entertainment Software Association (ESA), *Essential Facts About the Games Industry*, May 2019, https://www.theesa.com/wp-content/uploads/2019/05/ESA_Essential_facts_2019_final.pdf. Also, only 21% of all gamers are under 18 years old.

40. See for instance B. Francis, "Unity Report Shows Massive Spike in Video Game Business Due to COVID-19," *Gamasutra*, June 10, 2020, https://www.gamasutra.com/view/news/364543/Unity_report_shows_massive_spike_in_video_game_business_due_to_COVID19.php?elq_mid=97698&elq_cid=12458567. See also, M. Hume, M. Klimentov, E. Favis, G. Park, and T. Amenabar, "The Biggest Questions Facing the Gaming World in 2021," *The Washington Post*, December 30, 2020, https://www.washingtonpost.com/video-games/2020/12/30/2021-video-game-outlook/.

41. K. Schrier, "Guiding Questions for Game-Based Learning," in *International Handbook of Information Technology in Primary and Secondary Education*, ed. D. Gibson (New York: Springer, 2018).

42. L. M. Takeuchi and S. Vaala, *Level Up Learning: A National Survey on Teaching with Digital Games* (New York: The Joan Ganz Cooney Center at Sesame Workshop, 2014), https://www.joanganzcooneycenter.org/wp-content/uploads/2014/10/jgcc_leveluplearning_final.pdf. This statistic is likely much higher now than it was in 2014, and certainly during the COVID-19 pandemic.

43. ESA, *Essential Facts About the Games Industry*, referring to video game content only (not hardware).

44. Metaari, *Global Game-Based Learning Market*, Serious Play Wire, https://seriousplaywire.com/metaari-game-based-learning/ (accessed November 12, 2020).

45. Words are important but I don't want it to obfuscate the variety and possibility of games, or predetermine how it is used, shaped, or modified. Serious games are those made not just for entertainment, but for the purpose of training (e.g., military, surgery); teaching (e.g., STEM, communication); increasing healthy behavior (e.g., tracking medications, enhancing exercise); or reporting on or solving real-world problems (e.g., crowdsourcing protein configurations, analyzing journalistic documents for *The Guardian*). "Games for change" is a term that has also been used, specifically in relation to games that aim to make social change, such as supporting greater understanding around climate change or immigration, or to teach civics, ethics, or other social-related skills. This term applies both to specific types of games as well as to the organization and movement that supports the use and creation of these types of games. Other useful terms include "engagement games," which refers to games that enable real-world processes, including all types of social action, such as "community planning and data collection, disaster preparedness, advocacy and fundraising ... skill and network building," as well as "social participation" games, which relate to using games to support collective or communal activities. See more in Schrier, *Knowledge Games*.

46. That said, this book is not focused on how we can turn school into a game or "gamify" a virtual class. Gamification relates to the application of game-like activities, such as rewards or points, to nongame environments, such as healthcare, workplaces, or schools. This would be like someone plopping game-like mechanics onto a school worksheet, such as providing points and badges for its completion, but not fully transforming the experience to be that of a game. In this case, the points and badges merely take the place of grades, rather than truly changing the way content is taught, skills are practiced, or communities emerge. However, whether a game is entirely a game or is playfully expanding the definitions of a game, "does not matter as much as whether it is useful, effective, and appropriate for the educational experience, needs, audience, and context. As such, what it means to be 'game-based learning' continues to evolve, and the role of ... [people and] technology in creating, offering, and experiencing games is also varied and evolving." Schrier, "Guiding Questions for Game-Based Learning," p. 4. See also the gamification definition in S. Deterding, M. Sicart, L. Nacke, K. O'Hara, and D. Dixon, "Gamification: Using Game Design Elements in Non-Gaming Contexts," Association of Computing Machinery CHI [Computer–Human Interaction] Conference on Human Factors in Computing Systems, May 7–12, 2011, Vancouver, BC, Canada. . For more about gamification in civic and government contexts, see J. T. Harviainen and L. Hassan, "Governmental Service Gamification: Central Principles," *International Journal of Innovation in the Digital Economy* 10, no. 3 (2019): 1–12.

47. Schrier, "Guiding Questions for Game-Based Learning"; P. Wouters, C. van Nimwegen, H. van Oostendorp, and E. D. van der Spek, "A Meta-Analysis of the Cognitive and Motivational Effects of Serious Games," *Journal of Educational Psychology* 105, no. 2 (2013): 249–265.; T. Sitzmann, "A Meta-Analytic Examination of the Instructional Effectiveness of Computer Based Simulation Games," *Personnel Psychology* 64 (May 2011): 489–528. For the inconsistency in the effectiveness in games and civics, see also Dishon and Kafai, "Connected Civic Gaming."

48. E. Middaugh, "The Social and Emotional Components of Gaming: A Response to 'The Challenge of Gaming for Democratic Education,'" *Democracy and Education* 24, no. 2 (2016):Article 8; J. Stoddard, A. M. Banks, C. Nemacheck, and E. Wenska, "The Challenges of Gaming for Democratic Education: The Case of iCivics," *Democracy and Education* 24, no. 2 (2016): Article 2.

49. K. Salen (ed.), *The Ecology of Games: Connecting Youth, Games, and Learning* (Cambridge, MA: MIT Press, 2007). The use of ecology throughout the book is inspired by this book.

50. Schrier, "Guiding Questions for Game-Based Learning," citing a Microsoft/SRI International grant for GlassLab Research and conducted by D. Clark, E. Tanner-Smith, and S. Killingsworth, *Digital Games, Design and Learning: A Systematic Review and Meta-Analysis (Executive Summary)* (Menlo Park: SRI International, 2014) and D. B. Clark, E. E. Tanner-Smith, and S. S. Killingsworth, "Digital Games, Design, and Learning: A Systematic Review and Meta-Analysis," *Review of Educational Research* 86, no. 1 (2016): 79–122.

51. Schrier, "Guiding Questions for Game-Based Learning." See also work on Spent by G. Roussos and J. F. Dovidio, "Playing Below the Poverty Line: Investigating an Online Game as a Way to Reduce Prejudice Toward the Poor," *Cyberpsychology: Journal of Psychosocial Research on Cyberspace* 10, no. 2 (2016): 1–24. For games and their messiness, see also C. Steinkuehler, "The Mangle of Play," *Games and Culture* 1, no. 3 (2006): 199–213.

52. C. Raphael, C. Bachen, K. M. Lynn, J. Baldwin-Philippi, and K. A. McKee, "Games for Civic Learning: A Conceptual Framework and Agenda for Research and Design," *Games and Culture* 5, no. 2 (2010): 199–235. Cited in Dishon and Kafai, "Connected Civic Gaming."

53. Likewise, S. S. Adams and J. Holden call this "civic engagement gameplay as play that is based upon civic content such as politics, economics, and society; play that encourages democratically oriented skills such as communication, negotiation, and problem-solving; play that fosters responsibility to cocreate the game; and play that provides advocacy opportunities." Sharman Siebenthal Adams and Jeremiah Holden, "Games Ethics and Engagement: Potential Consequences of Civic-Minded Game Design and Gameplay," in *Designing Games for Ethics: Models, Techniques and Frameworks*, ed. K. Schrier and D. Gibson (Hershey, PA: IGI Global, 2011).

54. Schrier, "Guiding Questions for Game-Based Learning," p. 3.

55. C. Weitze, "*Minecraft* with Second Graders," in Schrier, *Learning, Education, & Games Vol. 2*; "Gigantic Mechanic," *VoxPop*, https://www.voxpop.io/ (accessed November 11, 2020).

56. K. Schrier, "Introduction," in *Learning, Education, & Games Vol. 2*. See more at, Laura Kate Dale, *Acceptance*, 2015, https://laurakindie.itch.io/acceptance-jam-for-leelah-entry. This game may not be appropriate for younger students due to content about sexual assault and other forms of violence. See more at, M. Evans, "A Video Game Showed Me Who I Really Am," Polygon, April, 12, 2019, https://www.polygon.com/2019/4/12/18306040/acceptance-game-identity-gender

57. Schrier, "Guiding Questions for Game-Based Learning," p. 3, citing P. Darvasi, "Gone Home as an English Text," in Schrier, *Learning, Education, & Games Vol. 1*.

58. See work by B. Stokes, *Locally Played* (Cambridge, MA: MIT Press, 2020) and S. Schirra, "Playing for Impact: The Design of Civic Games for Community Engagement and Social Action," S.M. thesis, Massachusetts Institute of Technology, 2013.

59. See more about each of these in Schrier, *Learning, Education & Games Vol. 3*.

60. Schrier, "Guiding Questions for Game-Based Learning"; Valencia Abbott, personal interview, Spring 2019.

61. Dishon and Kafai, "Connected Civic Gaming"; M. Ito, K. Gutiérrez, S. Livingstone, B. Penuel, J. Rhodes, K. Salen, J. Schor, J. Sefton-Green, and S. Craig Watkins, *Connected Learning: An Agenda for Research and Design* (Irvine, CA: Digital Media and Learning Research Hub, 2019); M. Ito, E. Soep, N. Kliger-Vilenchik, S. Shresthova, L. Gamber-Thompson, and A. Zimmerman, "Learning Connected Civics: Narratives, Practices, and Infrastructures," *Curriculum Inquiry* 45 (2015): 10–29.

62. R. Carbo-Mascarell, *A Woman Goes to a Private Games Industry Party*, https://moreelen.itch.io/a-woman-goes-to-a-private-games-industry-party; C. Small, *SweetXHeart*, http://www.gamesforchange.org/game/sweetxheart/; see also games by P. Pedericini and J. Stiles, Mollendustria, such as, P. Pedericini, *Everyday the Same Dream*, https://www.molleindustria.org/everydaythesamedream/everydaythesamedream.html, or Porpentine, such as *Howling Dogs*, http://slimedaughter.com/games/twine/howlingdogs/.

63. K. Schrier, "EPIC: A Framework for Using Video Games for Ethics Education," *Journal of Moral Education* 44, no. 4 (2015): 393–424; Schrier, "Guiding Questions for Game-Based Learning"; and *Learning, Education, & Games Vol. 1*.

64. *Planet Planners*, http://www.lauravila.com/planet-planners. See more about ethical decision-making in games from: M. Sicart, *The Ethics of Computer Games* (Cambridge, MA: MIT Press, 2009); K. Schrier, "Designing and Using Games to Teach Ethics and Ethical

Thinking," in *Learning, Education & Games Vol. 1: Curricular and Design Considerations*, ed. K. Schrier (Pittsburgh, PA: ETC Press, 2014). M. Sicart, *Beyond Choices: The Design of Ethical Gameplay* (Cambridge, MA: MIT Press, 2013); K. Schrier and D. Gibson, eds., *Designing Games for Ethics: Models, Techniques, Frameworks* (Hershey, PA: IGI Global, 2010); K. Schrier and D. Gibson, eds., *Ethics and Game Design: Teaching Values through Play* (Hershey, PA: IGI Global, 2010); M. Flanagan and H. Nissenbaum, *Values at Play* (Cambridge, MA: MIT Press, 2014).

65. *Max*, https://www.amazon.com/Family-Pastimes-Max-Co-operative-Game/dp/B00000IUFD; *Bad News*, https://www.getbadnews.com/#intro; *Harmony Square*, https://www.harmonysquare.game/en/play; *Papers, Please*, https://papersplea.se/; *Parable of the Polygons*, https://ncase.me/polygons/.

66. This includes commercial, popular, and mainstream digital games, as well as short, in-person analog games. It includes below-the-radar indie games, student-designed games, and card games, as well as mobile, virtual reality, and augmented reality games. See more about the breadth of gaming and labeling games in M. Consalvo and C. Paul, *Real Games*. Also, as Dishon and Kafai explain, these categories are not dichotomous, but are useful for understanding the different ways games and play can contribute to our understanding of civics: "First, in light of the emphasis on the development of civic practices through youth's interest-driven pursuits, we distinguish between (i) games that enable players to learn about the civic sphere, focusing on civic knowledge, and (ii) games that aspire to facilitate opportunities for interactions simulative of civic participation. Second, we identify the relationship between the game context and civic ones, distinguishing between (i) games that focus on the development of players' reflection concerning civic issues, and (ii) those that strive to offer more concrete connections to the civic sphere. Importantly, rather than strict dichotomies, these distinctions are laid out in order to offer useful categories that tease out the diverse contributions video games can offer to civic education." Dishon and Kafai, "Connected Civic Gaming." See also Schrier, *Knowledge Games* and Schirra, "Playing for Impact."

67. An Indigenous people in what is now Canada and the United States. For more about the games listed: Elizabeth LaPensée (Design and Art), Exquisite Ghost (Music and Sound), in *Along the River of Spacetime*, https://www.spacetimeriver.com/ (accessed on November 12, 2020); American University Game Lab, *Factitious*, http://factitious.augamestudio.com/#/.

68. S. Biswas and P. Gestwicki, "*Buffalo*," in Schrier, *Learning, Education & Games Vol. 3*; see also Tiltfactor Lab, *Buffalo: The Name Dropping Game*, https://tiltfactor.org/game/buffalo/G. Kaufman and M. Flanagan, "A psychologically "embedded" approach to designing games for prosocial causes." *Cyberpsychology: Journal of Psychosocial Research on Cyberspace*, 9, no. 3, (2015): Article 1. doi: 10.5817/CP2015-3-5

69. Learning Games Network, *Quandary*, https://www.quandarygame.org/ ; Gigantic Mechanic, *The Migrant Trail*, https://theundocumented.com/. An open question around *The Migrant Trail* game is whether the two sides (migrants and border patrol officers) should be equated, or whether it is problematic to play a role such as that of oppressors in this game, so teachers should reflect on this game and its use further. See more about this in chapter 8. Information on *Quandary* and its usage was supported by the *Quandary* team and correspondence with them in winter, 2021. Quotation by the *Quandary* team, Winter 2021.

70. Aparna Khanna, researcher in India, personal interview, Spring 2019.

71. O. Jimenez, "*Keep Talking and Nobody Explodes*," in Schrier, *Learning, Education & Games Vol. 3*. There are also non-VR versions of this game. See more at Steel Crate Games, *Keep Talking and Nobody Explodes*, https://keeptalkinggame.com/, 2018.

72. Another module in *Mission US* is "A Cheyenne Odyssey," where players play as Little Fox, a Cheyenne boy in post–Civil War America, and there is a module around slavery as well. Some educators have boycotted these games because they feel these modules further stereotypes. Educators should reflect further on this game and the context of its use, and how to best represent different types of histories and identities through games. See more at WNET/Thirteen and Electric Funstuff, *Mission US*, https://www.mission-us.org/. See more in chapter 8.

73. L. Gillepsie, A. Chenoweth, and D. Frye, "*Time Trek*," in Schrier, *Learning, Education & Games Vol. 3*.

74. For instance, research suggests that games are not the bastions of aggressive behavior and violence that media reports may purport. A 2019 study from the Oxford Internet Institute, led by Andrew Przybylski, investigated information from parents and caretakers to help in evaluating the aggressiveness of the children in the study. The researchers also used specific ratings criteria to judge the violence in a particular game, rather than the subjective views of the players. They found no correlation between playing the games and aggressive behavior in teenagers, and even if they had found a correlation, it would not have meant that the games specifically caused the behavior to occur. A. K. Przybylski and N. Weinstein, "Violent Video Game Engagement Is Not Associated with Adolescents' Aggressive Behavior: Evidence from a Registered Report," Royal Society Open Science, February 3, 2019, https://royalsocietypublishing.org/doi/10.1098/rsos.171474. However, the connection between violence and games is not the focus of this book. All types of antisocial or potentially harmful behaviors may be happening online and through social media, such as the spread of disinformation, trolling, name calling, sexist and racist remarks, or trash talking, and sometimes these activities are happening in and through games and gaming communities just as they are on other platforms, offline communities, and societal interactions. Harmful and destructive behaviors are not limited to games but may be designed and algorithmically allowed, invited, and even propagated to foment, as on other online social media platforms and communities (e.g., Facebook, Twitter, Twitch, Discord). That said, we should avoid moral panics and consider instead the complexities of how these platforms enable community and care, as well as hate and cruelty. This is an opportunity for us to rethink about how we govern publics, whether in-person or through virtual worlds. Finally, the panacea comment is inspired by an interview with Kelli Dunlap and Susan Rivers, Spring 2019.

75. This idea is inspired by a talk by Bettina Love, available at https://www.youtube.com/watch?v=A3jrts4ekNQ&feature=youtu.be. She is describing how hip hop is creativity from Black and Brown people, and that it centers the history and culture of Black people and African Americans. It's not a perfect analogy, but it helps us to think about how games are already civics. Hip hop and other forms of Black and African American creativity are civics in action. This metaphor is—importantly—applied to how Black history, culture, and creativity are shared civically, in part through hip hop and other forms of art. Thus, the metaphor should not be inappropriately appropriated, as it is not fully able to be applied to how kids are generally civically engaging through games. However, I found it a useful and

inspiring concept for thinking about games moving forward, particularly in how we can reconceive games as civic spaces and youth as civically engaging already.

76. Mirra and Garcia, "Civic Participation Reimagined."

77. iCivics, https://www.icivics.org/.

78. This assertion is inspired by B. Roberg, *Videogames Have Always Been Queer* (New York: NYU Press, 2019).

79. Mirra and Garcia, "Civic Participation Reimagined." Mirra and Garcia cite work by Ito et al. and Jenkins et al.: "Ito et al. (2015) define connected civics as 'a form of learning fostered via participatory politics that emerges when young people achieve civic agency linked to their deeply felt interests, identities, and affinities' [p. 17] ....As Jenkins, Ito, and boyd (2015) note, 'Connected civics begins with an appreciation of how young people are developing political and civic capacity when they run their own *World of Warcraft* guilds, *Minecraft* servers, or fan conventions, a kind of "little p" politics that contrasts with the more adult-centered "big P" Politics. This kind of organizing may not be about the government, but it is about governance, and it involves trial by fire in experiencing what happens when you have power and authority' [p. 162]." See more at Ito et al., *Connected Learning*; Ito et al., "Learning Connected Civics"; H. Jenkins, M. Ito, and D. Boyd, *Participatory Culture in a Networked Era* (Cambridge: Polity, 2015).

80. "Ironically, it is how we have sought to account for what is remarkable about games by setting them apart (as play spaces, as stories) that is the largest roadblock to understanding what is powerful about them." T. M. Malaby, "Beyond Play: A New Approach to Games," *Games and Culture* 2, no. 2 (2007): 95–113. Cited by Adams and Holden, "Games Ethics and Engagement."

81. Schrier, *Knowledge Games*. Check it out—it's pretty good! The games I describe in this book, *We the Gamers*, do not *necessarily* seek to make real-world change or build brand new knowledge—though they may do so. Rather, the ethics and civics games in this book may enable practice of a skill, relay a perspective, or encourage curiosity. They may build knowledge of a specific civic institution or government structure. They may also support real-world action, collective problem-solving, and community engagement, but *they do not have to.*

82. Ian Bogost, "Reality Is Alright: A Review of Jane McGonigal's Book *Reality Is Broken*," http://bogost.com/blog/reality_is_broken/ (accessed May 5, 2015); Ian Bogost, "Fun," UX Week 2013 talk, http://vimeo.com/74943170 (accessed July 2, 2015).

83. B. Suits, *The Grasshopper: Games, Life, and Utopia* (Toronto, Ontario, University of Toronto Press, 1978), cited in K. Salen and E. Zimmerman, *Rules of Play: Design Fundamentals* (Cambridge, MA: MIT Press, 2003).

84. This is inspired in part by how we define citizens but also how we define games and gamers and how we define gaming and learning, because it affects who is included in games and the civic spaces of games. Also note that the term, "gamers" can be problematic in how it is used and applied. For example, the term may only be awarded to those who qualify as playing whatever is defined as a "hardcore" game in a community. This ignores the playful contributions and participations of the many others who play games. In this book, I acknowledge the problems surrounding this term. However, I use the term "gamer" to refer to anyone who plays any games of any type, which I would argue are all of us who live in this world. We are all gamers. See more in Consalvo and Paul, *Real Games*.

85. Schrier, *Knowledge Games*, citing Bogost, "Fun," and Suits, *The Grasshopper*; see also Suits, "Construction of a Definition," in *The Game Design Reader: A Rules of Play Anthology*, ed. Katie Salen and Eric Zimmerman (Cambridge, MA: MIT Press, 2005).

86. Ruha Benjamin writes, "Rather, positing decarceration as our overarching strategy, we would try to envision a continuum of alternatives to imprisonment—demilitarization of schools, revitalization of education at all levels, a health system that provides free physical and mental care to all, and a justice system based on reparation and reconciliation rather than retribution and vengeance.... How can innovation in terms of our political, cultural, and social norms work toward freedom? How might technoscience be appropriated and reimagined for more liberatory ends?" Ruha Benjamin, "Introduction," in *Captivating Technology* (Durham, NC: Duke University Press, 2019).

87. This phrase references a Black folk song, civil rights rallying statement, affirmation, and saying that was also popularized by a Pete Seeger song. For more information see N. Adams, "The Inspiring Force of 'We Shall Overcome,'" NPR, August 28, 2013, https://www.npr.org/2013/08/28/216482943/the-inspiring-force-of-we-shall-overcome. This line also refers to how games may help us to address our human flaws and foolishness through the "foolishness" of games. Ian Bogost explains that "the fool finds something new in a familiar situation and then shares it with us." He explains, "Instead of toeing the line, instead of maintaining the standard way of things, the fool asks, "What else is possible?"... and then actually caries out that other thing that's possible, even if it's outlandish." Bogost, "Fun."

88. "Play has always been a way that people learn about each other, connect, understand and share ideas, and contribute to humanity." K. Schrier, "Guiding Questions for Game-Based Learning," in *International Handbook of Information Technology in Primary and Secondary Education*, ed. D. Gibson (New York: Springer, 2018), p. 5; see also C. Raphael, C. Bachen, K. M. Lynn, J. Baldwin-Philippi, and K. A. McKee, "Games for Civic Learning: A Conceptual Framework and Agenda for Research and Design," *Games and Culture* 5, no. 2 (2010): 199–235.

89. Dishon and Kafai, "Connected Civic Gaming."

90. Ibid. With this in mind, although I describe specific games in this book, we should consider them as part of a connected approach to learning where the games themselves are part of an ecosystem. Also, games have been explicitly made for civics, historically. See more in Schirra, "Playing for Impact."

91. See more about ethically notable games at José Zagal, "Ethically Notable Videogames: Moral Dilemmas and Gameplay," 2009, http:// facsrv.cs.depaul.edu/~jzagal/Papers/ Zagal-EthicallyNotableVideogames.pdf.

92. Moreover, this book exposes my own biases. I am bounded by my own upbringing, education, expertise, and social networks. I am bounded by this particular sociopolitical moment. First, the examples and mindsets skew US/Northern North American. Second, an underlying assumption is that democratic participation matters and is meaningful. However, this is not the only way to be and the only way to act as a society. I have tried to incorporate examples from different countries and cultures of how games are being used designed and to teach and support participation of all different types. I have also tried to acknowledge how civic and ethics systems in different nations may intersect with game systems. However, this book is not comprehensive and is meant, rather, as a conversation

starter. New games, terms, standards, and practices are always being created, revised, and implemented. Let us evolve with them.

Chapter 2

1. For example, see Holly Korbey, *Building Better Citizens: A New Civics Education for All* (Lanham, MD: Rowman & Littlefield, 2019); Peter Levine and Kei Kawashima-Ginsberg, "The Republic Is (Still) at Risk—and Civics Is Part of the Solution" (Medford, MA: Jonathan M. Tisch College of Civic Life, Tufts University, 2017); Danielle Allen, "Here's One More Question Parents Should Think About During Back-to-School Season," *Washington Post*, September 5, 2019, https://www.washingtonpost.com/opinions/we-need-civics-education-in-schools-to-build-effective-democratic-citizens/2019/09/05/3280dea4-cfe6-11e9-b29b-a528dc82154a_story.html.

2. In 2012, 39 states required that every student have at least one class in American government or civics, though that number had increased to 44 states by 2018. Allen, "Here's One More Question Parents Should Think About," citing Michael Rebell, *Flunking Democracy* (Chicago: University of Chicago Press, 2018). Korbey, *Building Better Citizens*, explains that "about 90% get about a semester's worth of high school civics or government in order to graduate. Thirty-six states require at least one civics or government course for graduation; eight states require a full year" (p. 23). Emma Humphries explains that it used to be that all students in the United States had at least three courses in civics, and many states still do have at least one American government course. She recommends "more robust civic mandates [by state] . . . and having accountability measures tied to those, not because we want more tests, but because we know that what is tested is typically what is taught and what gets emphasized and what gets funded." Cited in Emma Humphries, personal interview, Spring 2020. See also Surbhi Godsay, Whitney Henderson, Peter Levine, and Josh Littenberg-Tobias, "State Civic Education Requirements," Center for Information and Research on Civic Learning and Engagement (CIRCLE) Fact Sheet, 2012, https://files.eric.ed.gov/fulltext/ED536256.pdf.

3. Supreme Court Justice Sandra Day O'Connor, speech at Games for Change, 2011, http://www.gamesforchange.org/resource/7th-annual-games-for-change-festival-day-1/.

4. Godsay et al., "State Civic Education Requirements."

5. Korbey, *Building Better Citizens*. See also Supreme Court Justice Sandra Day O'Connor, cited in Chris Baker, "Sandra Day O'Connor: Game Designer," *Wired*, June 4, 2008, https://www.wired.com/2008/06/justice-oconnor/; National Council for the Social Studies, C3 Framework, June 2017, https://www.socialstudies.org/sites/default/files/2017/Jun/c3-framework-for-social-studies-rev0617.pdf. See also Michael Hansen, Elizabeth Mann Levesque, Jon Valant, and Diana Quintero, "2018 Brown Center Report on American Education: Understanding the Social Studies Teacher World," Brookings Institute, June 27, 2018, https://www.brookings.edu/research/2018-brown-center-report-on-american-education-understanding-the-social-studies-teacher-workforce/ . C3 cites the "squeeze" that takes place when teachers need to fit everything in to ensure the material for a test is covered. They explain that "the loss of instructional time at the elementary level and the narrowing of instruction in response to multiple-choice, high-stakes testing has significantly impacted time, resources, and support for the social studies." Justice O'Connor explains that one of the unintended consequences of No

Child Left Behind in the United States was that there is less time in the classroom spent on history, civics, and ethics. As the story goes, government officials saw that United States kids were placing on the bottom of test scores among 20 different nations in science and mathematics. when other countries began to excel in scientific and mathematical fields, and when technology-related industries began to generate financial success, STEM began to be deemed as a top priority for schools. Likewise, STEM-focused college majors became more societally valued, and STEM experts became higher paid than those in other fields. Parents, communities, and corporations started to push technological and mathematical skills, and scientific reasoning. Federal money started to be used to incentivize those schools that raised their test scores in mathematics, science, and reading, so schools beefed up those programs and focused their content on teaching for those tests. As a result, schools also started to drop the courses that did not get rewarded, such as history, ethics, and civics. According to the Brookings Report, those students in states with history assessments spent 2.9 hours per week and those without assessments only spent 2.5 hours per week.

6. Street Law, "Civic Education in the 21st Century An Analytical and Methodological Global Overview," USAID/ENGAGE, 2018, https://www.streetlaw.org/assets/site_18/files/articles/2018/civic%20education%20in%20the%2021st%20century%20-%20final%20pdf.pdf.

7. Generation Citizen, "Generation Citizen: International Civic Education Analysis and Recommendations," 2016, https://generationcitizen.org/wp-content/uploads/2016/10/Internation-Civic-Education.pdf.

8. Ibid.

9. Ethics is not an existing part of the common core in the United States. Some of the common core standards relate to ethical thinking, such as analyzing evidence, but in public schools, ethics is not required to teach or assess.

10. Korbey, *Building Better Citizens*. Ethical thinking refers to "a type of literacy or constellation of skills and affective and thought processes related to determining how to act ethically and how to think through ethical scenarios. The skills, concepts, and processes related to ethical thinking could include, for example, perspective taking, consideration of another's emotions, interpretation of evidence, or reflection on one's personal ethics." Quoted from K. Schrier, *Knowledge Games: How Playing Games Can Solve Problems, Create Insight, and Make Change* (Baltimore: Johns Hopkins University Press, 2016), .p. 261.

11. Supreme Court Justice Sandra Day O'Connor, cited in Baker, "Sandra Day O'Connor."

12. Only 33% have confidence in the wisdom of the American people in making good decisions, and 35% of Millennials are losing faith in American democracy, and 25% were confident in the democratic system, cited in Levine and Kawashima-Ginsberg, "The Republic Is (Still) at Risk." Only 30% of US Millennials feel it is essential to live in a democracy, cited in Allen, "Here's One More Question Parents Should Think About."

13. See, for instance, Levine and Kawashima-Ginsberg, "The Republic Is (Still) at Risk," and K. Schrier, "Using Games to Solve Real-World Civic Problems: Early Insights and Design Principle," *Journal of Community Engagement and Higher Education* 10, no. 1 (2018): 21–35.

14. Sixty percent of rural young people live in "civic deserts," according to Levine and Kawashima-Ginsberg, "The Republic Is (Still) at Risk," and scores are lower for civic knowledge between white and Black eight graders and white and Hispanic eighth graders, in the National Assessment of Educational Progress, cited in Korbey, *Building Better Citizens*. "Urban schools with low-income, diverse students provide fewer and lower-quality civic

opportunities and affluent white students are twice as likely as those of average socioeconomic status to study the legislative process or participate in service activities and 150% more likely to do in-class debates," cited in Allen, "Here's One More Question Parents Should Think About."

15. Generation Citizen, "Generation Citizen," 2016, citing J. Torney-Purta, R. Lehmann, H. Oswald, and W. Schulz, "Citizenship and Education in Twenty-Eight Countries: Civic Knowledge and Engagement at Age Fourteen," Amsterdam, The Netherlands: International Association for the Evaluation of Educational Achievement, 2001, https://files.eric.ed.gov/fulltext/ED452116.pdf, Accessed on December 29, 2020. .

16. Korbey, *Building Better Citizens*.

17. Supreme Court Justice Sandra Day O'Connor, speech at Games for Change.

18. National Council for the Social Studies. "Revitalizing Civic Learning in Our Schools," position statement, 2013, https://www.socialstudies.org/positions/revitalizing_civic_learning#fn1, quoting para. 1. Note that this notion is from a United States perspective, and people in different countries may have other perspectives on the goals of education.

19. In Florida, where civics is mandated and tested, the percentage of those who pass the exam has risen from 61% to 70% and students are participating more frequently in their community, as cited in Levine and Kawashima-Ginsberg, "The Republic Is (Still) at Risk." See also Korbey, *Building Better Citizens*.

20. See, for instance, David E. Campbell, Meira Levinson, and Frederick M. Hess, *Making Civics Count: Citizenship Education for a New Generation* (Cambridge, MA: Harvard University Press, 2012); Korbey, *Building Better Citizens*; National Council for the Social Studies, "Revitalizing Civic Learning in Our Schools."

21. See, for instance, National Assessment Governing Board, US Department of Education, "Civics Framework for the 2018 National Assessment of Educational Progress," 2018, https://www.nagb.gov/content/nagb/assets/documents/publications/frameworks/civics/2018-civics-framework.pdf. The framework explains that for those people who are defined as "citizens" living in a constitutional democracy, however, this could give them the right to participate in the governing of that republic and the electing of representatives. For the United States, for instance, "without the participation of informed, effective, and responsible citizens, a democratic republic cannot and does not function, nor can it make progress toward its ideals. … Any increase in citizens' civic knowledge, skills, and participation strengthens our republic; any reduction in their knowledge, skills, and participation weakens it. Thus, civic education is central to American education and essential to the well-being of American constitutional democracy" (p. xiii).

22. O'Connor, speech at Games for Change. However, I do not mean to suggest that only legal citizens of a country should or deserve to be civically engaged or able to participate in the civic life of that place or of the world. Rather, I hope to encourage people who are denizens of all different types of communities—local, global, online, and offline—to be active participants in its culture and governance. Another definition to consider is that of Meira Levinson, "The Civic Empowerment Gap: Defining the Problem and Locating Solution," in *Handbook of Research on Civic Engagement in Youth*, ed. Lonnie Sherrod, Judith Torney-Purta, and Constance A. Flanagan (New York: Wiley, 2010), p. 319, where she states that a good citizen is one who "is knowledgeable about politics, history, government, and current events; they need to be skilled communicators, thinkers, deliberators, and actors; they need to be concerned about the common good in addition to their

own self-interest . . . they need to become involved in public or community affairs, through some combination of voting, protesting, contacting public officials, mobilizing others, contributing time or money to causes or campaigns, participating in community groups, and other appropriate actions."

23. Korbey, *Building Better Citizens*, citing rising loneliness around the world, with Generation Z reporting the highest rates of loneliness, with more than half feeling 10 of the 11 loneliness factors, and a Cigna Health study in 2018 that found few meaningful connections for many of the 20,000 respondents (see chapter 8) (see Cigna, "New Cigna Study Reveals Loneliness at Epidemic Levels in America," 2018, https://www.cigna.com/about-us/newsroom/news-and-views/press-releases/2018/new-cigna-study-reveals-loneliness-at-epidemic-levels-in-america, Accessed on December 29, 2020). Korbey and Levine and Kawashima-Ginsberg, "The Republic Is (Still) at Risk" also cite civic deserts where people have limited ways or places to connect with others—in rural, but also suburban and urban areas.

24. Cited in Kenneth T. Carano, "Global Citizenship: Teaching in an Interconnected World," in *No Reluctant Citizens: Teaching Civics in K-12 Classrooms*, ed. Jeremiah Clabough and Timothy Lintner (Charlotte, NC: Information Age Publishing, 2018), p. 216.

25. Inspired by the words of Amber Coleman-Mortley, iCivics, personal interview in Spring 2019.

26. See for instance, Ashley Finley, "The Joy of Learning: The Impact of Civic Engagement on Psychosocial Well-Being, AAUP, Diversity and Democracy," 2012, https://www.aacu.org/publications-research/periodicals/joy-learning-impact-civic-engagement-psychosocial-well-being; and Lynn E. Swaner, "Linking Engaged Learning, Student Mental Health and Well-Being, and Civic Development" (Washington, DC: Bringing Theory to Practice Project, 2005). Well-being is also related to belongingness (feeling like one belongs in a particular society or community), as cited in Schrier, "Using Games to Solve Real-World Civic Problems," p. 22.

27. For instance, see work by Joseph Kahne, E. Hodgin, and E. Eidman-Aadahl, "Redesigning Civic Education for the Digital Age: Participatory Politics and the Pursuit of Democratic Engagement," *Theory & Research in Social Education* 44, no. 1 (2016): 1–35; Joe O'Brien, Nick Lawrence, and Michael J. Berson, "Youth, Social Media, and Digital Civic Engagement, National Council for the Social Studies," December 2018, https://www.socialstudies.org/positions/youth-social-media-and-digital-civic-engagement#Kahne.

28. For instance, O'Brien, Lawrence, and Berson, "Youth, Social Media, and Digital Civic Engagement"; Henry Jenkins, Gabriel Peters-Lazaro, and Sangita Shresthova, *Popular Culture and the Civic Imagination: Case Studies of Creative Social Change* (New York, NY: NYU Press, 2020); Henry Jenkins, Katie Clinton, Ravi Parushotma, Alice Robison (Daer), and Margaret Weigel, "Confronting the Challenges of Participatory Culture: Media Education for the 21st Century," MacArthur Foundation Paper, 2006, https://www.macfound.org/media/article_pdfs/JENKINS_WHITE_PAPER.PDF.

29. Gabriele De Seta, "Wenming Bu Wenming: The Socialization of Incivility in Postdigital China," *International Journal of Communication* (May 2018), 2010–2030.

30. National Council for the Social Studies, C3 Framework.

31. Paul Bauman and Jan Brennan, "State Civic Education Policy: Framework and Gap Analysis Tool," 2017, https://www.ecs.org/wp-content/uploads/State-Civics-Education-Policy-Framework-and-gap-analysis-tool.pdf.

32. See for instance, World Economic Forum, "Want a Job in 2025? These Are the Sectors to Focus On," September 2016, https://www.weforum.org/agenda/2016/09/job-in-2025-skills-sectors-to-focus-on/, and World Economic Forum 2016 Jobs Report, 2016, http://reports.weforum.org/future-of-jobs-2016/.

33. For instance, we cannot just teach people how to create new artificially intelligent software, agents, or robots without also thinking about their ethical implications. We need to think about the ethics of data collection and interpretation, how algorithms are programmed, or about inequities in the access to technology globally. We need to ensure different types of people can participate in civic activities and policymaking when it comes to new technologies. In turn, we also need representatives who can understand scientific and technological issues, as well as their ethical implications, so that they can better lead.

34. See for instance, Korbey, *Building Better Citizens*.

35. See also the previous note from Levinson, "The Civic Empowerment Gap," on a "good citizen." The concept of citizenship varies greatly from country to country, and is defined and acquired differently depending on where someone lives and where they were born. One way to define it is the legal definition—for instance, in the United States, that you are an individual who was born in the country, or moved to the country and were naturalized in some way, such as by marrying a citizen, or a parent or self, gaining citizenship after a certain amount of time. Citizenship, however, can also refer to how a person participates in their community—whether that is hyperlocal or local, state-wide or regional, nationally, or even internationally, as a "citizen of the world." This type of citizenship involves a "commitment to and participation in a community's civic life," cited in National Assessment Governing Board, US Department of Education, Civics Framework for the 2018 National Assessment of Educational Progress, 2018, https://www.nagb.gov/content/nagb/assets/documents/publications/frameworks/civics/2018-civics-framework.pdf. It does not necessarily require legal citizenship, nor does it require someone to be in a particular place or location; rather, it is about an engagement in one's world, even if that world is a virtual one.

36. Bauman and Brennan, "State Civic Education Policy."

37. Ibid. See also statistics in Korbey, *Building Better Citizens*; and Levine and Kawashima-Ginsberg, "The Republic Is (Still) at Risk."

38. O'Connor, speech at Games for Change, 2011.

39. Generation Citizen, "Generation Citizen."

40. Ibid.; Torney-Purta et al., "Citizenship and Education in Twenty-eight Countries."

41. Generation Citizen, "Generation Citizen," citing J. Youniss, S. Bales, V. Christmas-Best, M. Diversi, M. McLaughlin, and R. Silbereisen, "Youth Civic Engagement in the Twenty-First Century." *Journal of Research on Adolescence* 12, no. 1 (2002): 121–148.

42. Karen Farkas, "86 Percent of College Students Say They Have Cheated. It's Easier Than Ever With Mobile Devices," Cleveland.com, January 11, 2019, https://www.cleveland.com/metro/2017/02/cheating_in_college_has_become.html. See also K. Schrier, "Designing Games for Moral Learning and Knowledge Building," *Games and Culture*, May 31, 2017. See also Angelo Antoci, Alexia Delfino, Fabio Paglieri, Fabrizio Panebianco, and Fabio Sabatini, "Civility vs. Incivility in Online Social Interactions: An Evolutionary Approach," *PLoS One* 11, no. 11 (2016), https://www.ncbi.nlm.nih.gov/pmc/articles/PMC5089744/. However, the term "incivility" can be used and applied problematically, being a way to oppress and marginalize those who are oppressed further, such as people of color; see for instance Karen Grigsby Bates, "When Civility is Used as a Cudgel Against

People of Color," NPR, March 14, 2019, https://www.npr.org/sections/codeswitch/2019/03/14/700897826/when-civility-is-used-as-a-cudgel-against-people-of-color; and Lynn Mie Itagaki, *Civil Racism* (Minneapolis: University of Minnesota Press, 2016). Civility's "uneasy history" in maintaining order and compliance and restraining difference is discussed in Sharika Thiranagama, Tobias Kelly, and Carlos Forment, "Introduction: Whose Civility?," *Anthropological Theory* 18, no. 2–3 (2018): 153–174. They argue that we should think of civility as a "worldly concept" in how people relate, respect, and care and "how we should all live together," for the good of the common (pp. 156–159).

43. Moral panics are discussed in Patrick M. Markey and Christopher J. Ferguson, "Teaching Us to Fear: The Violent Video game Moral Panic and the Politics of Game Research," *American Journal of Play*, Fall 2017, https://files.eric.ed.gov/fulltext/EJ1166785.pdf.

44. CIRCLE, "Young People Dramatically Increase Their Turnout to 31%, Shape 2018 Midterm Elections," 2018, https://civicyouth.org/young-people-dramatically-increase-their-turnout-31-percent-shape-2018-midterm-elections/; CIRCLE, "2016 Election Center," https://circle.tufts.edu/2016-election-center/, accessed on January 12, 2021.

45. For instance, see P. Hall, "Voting: Is it Just for Old People?" (MA thesis, University of Georgia, 2008); R. G. Niemi and M. Hanmer, "Voter Turnout Among College Students: New Data and a Rethinking of Traditional Theories," *Social Science Quarterly* 91, no. 2 (2010): 301–323. Also see CIRCLE, "An Estimated 24 Million Young People Voted in 2016 Election"; Schrier, "Using Games to Solve Real-World Civic Problems." Those aged 18 to 20 typically have a lower voter turnout than any other age group for public office elections in the United States.

46. Schrier, "Using Games to Solve Real-World Civic Problems," citing Hall, "Voting," and R. G. Niemi and M. Hanmer, "Voter Turnout Among College Students: New Data and a Rethinking of Traditional Theories," *Social Science Quarterly* 91, no. 2 (2010): 301–323. See also A. Jeffrey and S. Sargrad, "Strengthening Democracy with a Modern Civics Education," American Progress, 2019, https://www.americanprogress.org/issues/education-k-12/reports/2019/12/14/478750/strengthening-democracy-modern-civics-education/. See also, CIRCLE, "Election Week 2020: Young People Increase Turnout, Lead Biden to Victory," November 25, 2020, https://circle.tufts.edu/latest-research/election-week-2020.

47. Josh Lerner, *Making Democracy Fun* (Cambridge, MA: MIT Press, 2014), cites Colin Hay, *Why We Hate Politics* (Oxford: Polity, 2007), pp. 13, 21 and Robert D. Putnam, *Bowling Alone: The Collapse and Revival of American Community* (New York: Simon and Schuster, 2001).

48. Lerner, *Making Democracy Fun*. But note that this argument was pre-2020.

49. Civic engagement involves participation in communities such as "formal political activities such as voting and informal civic activities such as volunteering, working with others on community issues, and contributing to charity," quotation from J. Kahne, E. Middaugh, and C. Evans, "The Civic Potential of Video Games," 2009, https://clalliance.org/wp-content/uploads/files/Civic_Potential_of_Games.pdf, p. 4. According to this article, "disengaged" civically was defined as not participating in at least two electoral activities (voting in any election) or civic activities, such as signing petitions or attending a town hall), citing research from CIRCLE website at https://circle.tufts.edu/.

50. Personal interview, Steven Schrier, Spring 2019.

51. Schrier, "Using Games to Solve Real-World Civic Problems"; see also work by A. Syvertsen, L. Wray-Lake, C. Flanagan, D. W. Osgood, and L. Briddell, "Thirty Year Trends in U.S. Adolescents' Civic Engagement: A Story of Changing Participation and Educational Differences," *Journal of Research on Adolescence* 21, no. 3 (2011): 586–594 and J. Torney-Purta, C. Henry Barber, and W. Richardson, "Trust in Government-Related Institutions and Political Engagement Among Adolescents in Six Countries," *Acta Politica* 39 (2004): 380–406.

52. Lerner, *Making Democracy Fun.*

53. I started to attend the town meetings in my town because my neighbor invited me to participate to lobby for lowering the speed limit on our street, where our kids play outside. I then continued to attend the meetings to show support for a new referendum on enhancing diversity and inclusion in the town. For a taste of the town meetings and a community grappling with issues like racism amid the Black Lives Matter Protests, here are a few recorded meetings from summer 2020: https://www.youtube.com/watch?v=YFL-cDOXq2I and https://www.youtube.com/watch?v=MR49jm7Ylz4. Professor Steve Schrier has his community college students attend a local town meeting as one of the assignments in his college civics course.

54. Weber Shandwick, Powell Tate, and LRC Research, "Civility in America 2018: Civility at Work and in Our Public Schools," June 2018, https://www.webershandwick.com/wp-content/uploads/2018/06/Civility-in-America-VII-FINAL.pdf. This is an annual survey on American perceptions of civility in the United States.

55. In 2008, 65% of Americans shared that they believe civility is a major problem, and 29% thought it was a minor problem. In 2018, around 84% of Americans in the survey stated that they have experienced incivility, such as while shopping (39%), driving (39%), and on social media (38%). The respondents reported experiencing uncivil incidents an average of 10.6 times per week, which is up from 6.2 incidents per week in 2016. See Shandwick, Tate, and LRC Research, "Civility in America 2018." It would be interesting to see how this changed in 2020 and 2021, when many Americans shared stories of being harassed in stores or other public spaces for either wearing or not wearing masks, for instance.

56. About half of incidents per week in 2018 were from online media, but the number of offline incidents has also increased from just two years ago. Those who expect further deterioration in civility increased from 39% (2010) to 56% (2016). Cited in Shandwick, Tate, and LRC Research, "Civility in America 2018." See also Weber Shandwick, Powell Tate, and LRC Research, "Civility in America 2011," https://www.webershandwick.com/uploads/news/files/Civility_in_America_2011.pdf (accessed June 2, 2020). See also the complexities around the word "civility" expressed in an earlier note. In addition, we can also look at newer terms like "political civility." Peterson distinguishes civility from political civility. Civility relates to manners and everyday respect and courtesy, while political civility relates to civil conduct (genuine engagement and openness to others) and a desire for others to flourish. See more in, N. Snow, "Citizens' Relationships, Political Civility, and the Civic Virtue of Listening," Jubilee Centre for Character and Virtues, 2020, https://www.jubileecentre.ac.uk/userfiles/jubileecentre/pdf/insight-series/Snow%20-%20Citizens%20Relationships%20Political%20Civility%20and%20the%20Civic%20Virtue.pdf (Accessed on January 18, 2021). Snow writes, "When citizens understand themselves in terms of civic friendship, he believes, civility is nourished." This report cites A. Peterson, *Civility and Democratic Education.* (Singapore: Springer, 2019).

57. See ADL, "Online Hate and Harassment: The American Experience," https://www.adl.
org/onlineharassment (accessed June 2, 2020). Severe harassment includes "sexual harassment, stalking, physical threats, swatting, doxing and sustained harassment." A 2017 Pew
Research Center study found 18% of participants experienced severe harassment online.
See Pew Internet Research, "Online Harassment 2017,: July 2017, https://www.pewre-
search.org/internet/2017/07/11/online-harassment-2017/.
58. See ADL, "Online Hate and Harassment." While they may have been harassed for other
reasons too, this percentage of people believed they were specifically harassed because of
who they are, or who others perceive they are. When certain groups of people are more
often deterred because of who they are, games and other social spaces online are not necessarily appropriate, democratic, equitable, or beneficial.
59. ADL, *Free to Play: Hate, Harassment, and Positive Social Experiences in Online Games in
2020*, December 2020, https://www.adl.org/media/15349/download This is up from 2019,
where overall harassment was 74%. They also report that in 2020, "70 percent were called
offensive names in online multiplayer games, while 60 percent of gamers were the targets
of trolling, deliberate and malicious attempts to provoke them to react negatively . . . 68 percent of online multiplayer gamers experienced more severe forms of harassment, up from
65 percent in 2019." In the 2019 report, 67% experienced name-calling, 57% were targets
of trolling, 47% were directly harassed, 44% were threatened with physical violence, and
34% were stalked. See ADL, *Free to Play: Hate, Harassment, and Positive Social Experiences
in Online Games*, June 2019, https://www.adl.org/media/13139/download
60. According to the Southern Poverty Law Center (SPLC), hate groups in the United States
rose in numbers up 7% from 2017 to 2018. The year 2018 had the highest number of
hate groups since SPLC started to record the number in 1999. See SPLC, "The Year in
Hate: Rage Against Change," February 20, 2019, https://www.splcenter.org/fighting-hate/
intelligence-report/2019/year-hate-rage-against-change. See also FBI reports that hate
was at an a 16-year high in 2019, Adeel Hassan, "Hate-Crime Violence Hits 16-Year High,
F.B.I. Reports," *New York Times*, November 12, 2019, https://www.nytimes.com/2019/
11/12/us/hate-crimes-fbi-report.html. A hate crime is defined in the article as "criminal
offense against a person or property, motivated in whole or in part by an offender's bias
against a race, religion, disability, sexual orientation, ethnicity, gender, or gender identity." See also ADL, "Reports of Anti-Asian Assaults, Harassment and Hate Crimes Rise
as Coronavirus Spreads," May 27, 2020, https://www.adl.org/blog/reports-of-anti-asian-
assaults-harassment-and-hate-crimes-rise-as-coronavirus-spreads, about a rapidly developing series of incidences. See also FBI Reports, "Hate Crimes," 2018, https://ucr.fbi.gov/
hate-crime/2018
61. According to the ADL, hate crimes toward Jewish people and institutions have been
increasing more, year over year, than in most previous years. There was a 57% increase
between 2016 and 2017, which was the largest single rise in reported hate crimes since
1979. Meg Oliver, "Pittsburgh Shooting Highlights Rise in Hate Crimes Across the U.S.,"
CBS News, https://www.cbsnews.com/news/pittsburgh-shooting-highlights-rise-hate-
crimes-united-states/ (accessed June 2, 2018); the FBI 2018 hate crimes report had 60% of
reported hate crimes affecting Jewish individuals and institutions; see "2018 Hate Crime
Statistics," https://ucr.fbi.gov/hate-crime/2018/topic-pages/incidents-and-offenses. See
also J. Ogilvie, "An Increase in Hate Crimes Has Disproportionately Affected LA's Black
and Jewish Communities," LAist, January 23, 2020, https://laist.com/2020/01/23/an_

increase_in_hate_crimes_has_disproportionately_affected_las_black_and_jewish_com-munities.php.

62. For instance, see Wayne Journell, "Civic Education in a Post-Truth Society," in *No Reluctant Citizens: Teaching Civics in K-12 Classrooms*, ed. Clabough and Lintner, Charlotte, NC: Information Age Publishing, Inc., p. 113–129, which cites useful research on political homophily by C. H. Clark and P.G. Avery, "The Psychology of Controversial Issues Discussions: Challenges and Opportunities in a Polarized, Post-9/11 Society," in *Reassessing the Social Studies Curriculum: Promoting Critical Civic Engagement in a Politically Polarized, Post-9/11 World*, ed. W. Journell (Lanham, MD: Rowman & Littlefield, 2016), pp. 109–102; on echo chambers, E. Colleoni, A. Rozza, and A. Arvidsson, "Echo Chamber or Public Sphere? Predicting Political Orientation and Measuring Political Homophily in Twitter Using Big Data," *Journal of Communication* 64 (2014): 317–332; S. Jacobson, E. Myung, and S.L. Johnson, "Open Media or Echo Chamber: The Use of Links in Audience Discussions on the Facebook Pages of Partisan News Organizations," *Information, Communication, & Society* 19 (2016): 875–891; A. Mitchell, J. Gottfried, J. Kiley, and K. E. Matsa, "Political Polarization and Media Habits," Pew Research Center, October 21, 2014, https://www.journalism.org/2014/10/21/political-polarization-media-habits/; and a steady decline of Americans' interactions with people who are different than them, for instance, T. H. Sander and R. D. Putnam, "Still Bowling Alone? The Post-9/11 Split," *Journal of Democracy* 21 (2010): 9–16.

63. Pew Internet Research, "Online Harassment 2017," July 11, 2017, https://www.pewresearch.org/internet/2017/07/11/online-harassment-2017/.

64. See, for instance, Journell, "Civic Education in a Post-Truth Society"; Korbey, *Building Better Citizens*.

65. See, for instance, Journell, "Civic Education in a Post-Truth Society"; David M. J. Lazer, Matthew A. Baum, Yochai Benkler, Adam J. Berinsky, Kelly M. Kelly M. Greenhill, Filippo Menczer, Miriam J. Metzger, Brendan Nyhan, Gordon Pennycook, David Rothschild, Michael Schudson, Steven A. Sloman, Cass R. Sunstein, Emily A. Thorson, Duncan J. Watts, Jonathan L. Zittrain, "The Science of Fake News," *Science* 359, no. 6380 (2018): 1094–1096.

66. Cited in Lazer et al., "The Science of Fake News," p. 1094.

67. Studies cited in Lazer et al., "The Science of Fake News," include H. Allcott and M. Gentzkow, "Social Media and Fake News in the 2016 Election," *Journal of Economic Perspectives* 31, no. 211 (2017): 211–236; S. Vosoughi, D. Roy, and S. Aral, "The Spread of True and False News Online," *Science* 359, no. 6380 (2018): 1146–1151; O. Varol, E. Ferrara, C. Davis, F. Mencze, and A. Flammini, "Online Human-Bot Interactions: Detection, Estimation, and Characterization," in *Proceedings of the 11th AAAI Conference on Web and Social Media* (Montreal: Association for the Advancement of Artificial Intelligence, 2017), pp. 280–289; Senate Judiciary Committee, "Extremist Content and Russian Disinformation Online: Working with Tech to Find Solutions (Committee on the Judiciary, 2017)," www.judiciary.senate.gov/meetings/extremist-content-and-russian-disinformation-online-working-with-tech-to-find-solutions (accessed June 2, 2020). About bots, see *Wired* staff, "What Is a Bot?," *Wired*, 2018, https://www.wired.com/story/the-know-it-alls-what-is-a-bot/.

68. Rob Toews, "Deepfakes Are Going to Wreak Havoc on Society. We are Not Prepared," *Forbes*, May 25, 2020, https://www.forbes.com/sites/robtoews/2020/05/25/deepfakes-

are-going-to-wreak-havoc-on-society-we-are-not-prepared/. According to a Deeptrace report, there were 7,964 deepfake videos online and in nine months, that number went up to 14,678. See Giorgio Patrini, "Mapping the Deepfake Landscape," Deeptrace, July, 10, 2019, https://deeptracelabs.com/mapping-the-deepfake-landscape/.

69. See, for instance, Journell, "Civic Education in a Post-Truth Society."
70. Ibid.
71. For problem-solving, see K. Schrier, *Knowledge Games*. Having access to educational opportunities is also inequitable in general. Mirra and Garcia explain that "these inequalities exist in almost every aspect of American public life. In 2013, the Pew Research Center calculated the wealth of white American households to be 13 times the median wealth of African American households and 10 times the median wealth of Hispanic American households (Kochhar and Fry, 2014). Meanwhile, according to the 2010 Census, African American and Hispanic families are more than twice as likely as white families to be living below the federal poverty line (Macartney, Bishaw, and Fontenot, 2013). Scholars have exhaustively documented the discriminatory treatment that minoritized populations continue to experience in public systems of criminal justice (Alexander, 2010), health (Centers for Disease Control and Prevention, 2013), housing (Desmond, 2016), and education (Lipman, 2011)." N. Mirra and A. Garcia, "Civic Participation Reimagined: Youth Interrogation and Innovation in the Multimodal Public Sphere," *Review of Research in Education* 41 (March 2017): 136–158.
72. Bauman and Brennan, "State Civic Education Policy."
73. Korbey, *Building Better Citizens*, p. 25. See also Michael Hansen, Elizabeth Mann Levesque, Jon Valant, and Diana Quintero, "Brown Center Report on American Education: Understanding the Social Studies Teacher World," Brookings Institute, June 27, 2018, https://www.brookings.edu/research/2018-brown-center-report-on-american-education-understanding-the-social-studies-teacher-workforce/.
74. Korbey, *Building Better Citizens*, p. 25.
75. J. Kahne and E. Middaugh, "Democracy for Some: The Civic Opportunity Gap in High School," Circle Working Paper No. 59 (College Park, MD: Center for Information & Research on Civic Learning and Engagement, 2008). Bauman and Brennan, "State Civic Education Policy." Both Meira Levinson and the Education Commission of the United States use this term. See more in Korbey, *Building Better Citizens*, p. 25–27. Also see work by Meira Levinson, such as M. Levinson, "The Civic Achievement Gap" CIRCLE Working Paper No. 51 (College Park, MD: Center for Information & Research on Civic Learning and Engagement, 2007). However, there are other factors besides education. Rugh argues that home ownership changes affect voter turnout, for instance. See J. Rugh, "Why Black and Latino Home Ownership Matter to the Color Line and Multiracial Democracy," *Race and Social Problems* 12 (2020): 57–76.
76. Korbey, *Building Better Citizens*, p. 123.
77. CIRCLE, "Civic Deserts: 60% of Rural Millennials Lack Access to a Political Life," https://circle.tufts.edu/latest-research/civic-deserts-60-rural-millennials-lack-access-political-life, March 26, 2017. See more at M. Atwell, J. Bridgeland, and P. Levine, "Civic Deserts: America's Civic Health Challenge," CIRCLE Whitepaper, 2017, https://tischcollege.tufts.edu/research/civic-deserts-americas-civic-health-challenge. The term "civic desert" was coined by Kei Kawashima-Ginsberg and Felicia Sullivan to "describe places with few opportunities to participate in civic life," cited at https://tischcollege.tufts.edu/

research/civic-deserts-americas-civic-health-challenge, 2017, Accessed on December 29, 2020.

78. Mirra and Garcia explain that we also need to question the skills that matter in civic engagement, as these definitions are exclusionary. See Mirra and Garcia, "Civic Participation Reimagined."

79. B. Colyar, "6 Teens Organized a Protest. 10,000 People Showed Up," New York Magazine, June 17, 2020, https://www.thecut.com/2020/06/6-teens-organized-a-protest-10-000-people-showed-up.html.

80. S. Delgado, "K-Pop Fancams Got Political to Protect Black Lives Matter Protesters From Dallas Police," *Teen Vogue*, June 1, 2020, https://www.teenvogue.com/story/k-pop-fancams-protect-black-lives-matter-protestors-dallas-police. Stans refers to intense, devoted fans of particular pop cuture icons or celebrities. The word comes from an Eminem song.

81. T. Lorenz, K. Browing, and S. Frenkel, "TikTok Teens and K-Pop Stans ay They Sank Trump Rally," *New York Times*, June 21, 2020, https://www.nytimes.com/2020/06/21/style/tiktok-trump-rally-tulsa.html.

82. Mirra and Garcia, "Civic Participation Reimagined."

Chapter 3

1. See National Council for the Social Studies (NCSS), C3 Framework, June 2017, https://www.socialstudies.org/sites/default/files/2017/Jun/c3-framework-for-social-studies-rev0617.pdf.

2. Ibid.

3. For instance, 74% of K-8 teachers using games and 55% of teachers using games at least once a week in the classroom, according to L. M. Takeuchi and S. Vaala, "Level Up Learning: A National Survey on Teaching with Digital Games" (New York: The Joan Ganz Cooney Center at Sesame Workshop, October 2014), http://joanganzcoo neycenter.org/wp-content/uploads/2014/10/jgcc_leveluplearning_final.pdf.

4. For instance, based on my personal interviews with Amber Coleman-Mortley, iCivics, personal interview in Spring 2019.

5. Quote from Coleman-Mortley, ibid.

6. Michael Hansen, Elizabeth Mann Levesque, Jon Valant, and Diana Quintero, "Brown Center Report on American Education: Understanding the Social Studies Teacher World," Brookings Institute, June 27, 2018, https://www.brookings.edu/research/2018-brown-center-report-on-american-education-understanding-the-social-studies-teacher-workforce/, citing K. E. Vogler, "Comparing the Impact of Accountability Examinations on Mississippi and Tennessee Social Studies Teachers' Instructional Practices," *Educational Assessment* 13, no. 1 (2008): 1–32. L. Winstead, "The Impact of NCLB and Accountability on Social Studies: Teacher Experiences and Perceptions About Teaching Social Studies," *The Social Studies* 102, no. 5 (2011): 221–227.

7. Caitlin Daniels, personal interview, Spring 2019.

8. Trish Everett, personal interview, Spring 2019.

9. Valencia Abbott, personal interview, Spring 2019.

10. Quoted from an interview with two Generation Citizen employees, Brooke Wallace, and Sarah Andes, personal interview, Spring 2019. See also Generation Citizen Website, https://generationcitizen.org/ (accessed June 3, 2020).

11. "Standards are official state documents that itemize what must be taught … they influence curricula, textbooks, tests and other assessments, and education for teachers both before and during their teaching careers," cited in Surbhi Godsay, Whitney Henderson, Peter Levine, and Josh Littenberg-Tobias, "State Civic Education Requirements," CIRCLE Fact Sheet, 2012, https://files.eric.ed.gov/fulltext/ED536256.pdf, p. 2.

12. Quote from Coleman-Mortley, personal interview. On the other hand, we may want to design games for standards, as they are then more likely used in the classroom, or in other educational settings. But just because standards have deemed some areas of study as important does not mean that there aren't other areas that are also essential. For one thing, many important civics and ethics content and skill areas are missing from US state and national standards. What do standards and frameworks miss when it comes to the things that we want our students and adults to know and understand? Are there other skills that we want students to learn or situations that we want our society to be aware of? These needs are always changing and may not be the same for each community, so no one set of standards, textbook, or curriculum should dictate what they should be.

13. S. Godsay, W. Henderson, P. Levine, and J. Littenberg-Tobias, "Fact Sheet on Civic Learning," 2012, https://files.eric.ed.gov/fulltext/ED536256.pdf, Accessed on December 29, 2020.

14. Note that these are sample standards for the United States.

15. See NCSS, National Curriculum Standards for Social Studies, C3 Framework, 2013, https://www.socialstudies.org/c3. The framework aims to promote "civic competence" or the "the knowledge, intellectual processes, and democratic dispositions required of students to be active and engaged participants in public life." Their standards for social studies consider civics to be, at its core, the key mission of the discipline. Their curriculum standards include ten different themes that are also interrelated, including culture; civic ideals and practices; and power, authority, and governance. The civic ideals theme, for instance, includes such principles as "an understanding of civic ideals and practices is critical to full participation in society and is an essential component of education for citizenship, which is the central purpose of social studies," and "learning how to apply civic ideals as part of citizen action is essential to the exercise of democratic freedoms and the pursuit of the common good." The creators of this curriculum see this as a series of principles for guiding how social studies is taught, rather than dictating the specific content areas that need to be relayed. (See "National Curriculum Standards for Social Studies: Chapter 2—The Themes of Social Studies," https://www.socialstudies.org/standards/strands). The civics education standards for the NCSS was initially drawn from the Center for Civic Education. In general, the standards are focused on content rather than methods of inquiry or skills. The Center for Civic Education standards are broken down into K–4, 5–8 and 9–12 grade, include topics and questions such as:

   1. What is a government and what does it do, including themes of authority, and topics such as laws and rules? What is civic life?
   2. What are the foundations, values and principles of democracy in the United States?
   3. What is the constitution, and how do the different levels of government (state, local, national) and different branches work together?

4. How does the United States compare in relation to other governments and nations?
5. What does it mean to be a citizen and what are the responsibilities and duties of a citizen?

See Center for Civic Education, https://www.civiced.org/ (accessed June 3, 2020).

There are also additional standards and frameworks that influenced the C3 Framework, such as the civic action framework and the competencies by the Campaign for the Civic Mission of Schools, which can be found at National Curriculum Standards for Social Studies, "The Civic Mission of Schools," *Social Education* 69, no. 7 (December 2005): 414–416.

16. NCSS, C3 Framework, June 2017, https://www.socialstudies.org/sites/default/files/2017/Jun/c3-framework-for-social-studies-rev0617.pdf.
17. See NCSS, C3 Framework. Additionally, this component could include encouraging students to actively participate in real-world solutions or activities—such as going to city hall meetings and presenting case studies, spreading infographics through viral media, making posters for a march, creating a petition, reporting on local issues, or providing feedback on bullying policies, or engaging in everyday ethical questions.
18. See National Assessment Governing Board, US Department of Education, Civics Framework for the 2018 National Assessment of Educational Progress, 2018, https://www.nagb.gov/content/nagb/assets/documents/publications/frameworks/civics/2018-civics-framework.pdf. This framework is used to guide the creation of the National Assessment of Educational Progress (NAEP) civics exam. It also draws from the voluntary National Standards for Civics and Government, which was published in 1994 by the Center for Civic Education.
19. Ibid.
20. Ibid., p. xv.
21. Ibid.
22. Common Core standards, English/Language Arts, History/Social Studies, 11–12th grades, http://www.corestandards.org/ELA-Literacy/RH/11-12/ (accessed June 3, 2020) and Common Core standards, English/Language Arts, World History, 11–12th grades, http://www.corestandards.org/ELA-Literacy/WHST/11-12/ (accessed June 3, 2020).
23. Listed in Hansen et al., "Brown Center Report on American Education," citing Jonathan Gould (ed.), *Guardian of Democracy: The Civic Mission of Schools* (Philadelphia: Leonore Annenberg Institute for Civics of the Annenberg Public Policy Center at the University of Pennsylvania, 2011); L. Guilfoile and B. Delander, *Guidebook: Six Proven Practices for Effective Civic Learning* (Denver, Colorado: Education Commission of the States and National Center for Learning and Civic Engagement, 2014); and Peter Levine and Kei Kawashima-Ginsberg, "The Republic Is (Still) at Risk—and Civics Is Part of the Solution" (Jonathan M. Tisch College of Civic Life, Tufts University, 2017).
24. Quote at N. Mirra and A. Garcia, "Civic Participation Reimagined: Youth Interrogation and Innovation in the Multimodal Public Sphere," *Review of Research in Education* 41 (March 2017): 136–158.
25. Gideon Dishon and Yasmin B. Kafai, "Connected Civic Gaming: Rethinking the Role of Video Games in Civic Education," *Interactive Learning Environments* (2019), DOI: 10.1080/10494820.2019.1704791 and M. Ito, E. Soep, N. Kliger-Vilenchik, S. Shresthova, L. Gamber-Thompson, and A. Zimmerman, "Learning Connected Civics: Narratives, Practices, and Infrastructures," *Curriculum Inquiry* 45 (2015): 10–29.

26. See for instance B. Blevins, K. LeCompte, and T. Ellis, "Students at the Heart of Civic Learning: Best Practices in Implementing Action Civics," in *No Reluctant Citizens: Teaching Civics in K-12 Classrooms*, ed. Jeremiah Clabough and Timothy Lintner (Charlotte, NC: Information Age Publishing, Inc., 2018); Generation Citizen website, https://generationcitizen.org/ (accessed June 3, 2020). Paul Bauman and Jan Brennan, "State Civic Education Policy: Framework and Gap Analysis Tool," Education Commission of the States, 2017, https://www.ecs.org/wp-content/uploads/State-Civics-Education-Policy-Framework-and-gap-analysis-tool.pdf.

27. They call this "action civics," because it is about taking civics and practicing it in the real world. Brooke Wallace and Sarah Andes of Generation Citizen explain that it wants to innovate civics education from being taught by rote to "one in which students are engaged in learning about and exploring their roles and responsibilities as citizens. So, essentially they are connecting the role of government to their own everyday lives and … one way to do that is through asking people to brainstorm and come up with issues that they care about in their own communities, whether in their school, neighborhood, county, city or state level." To help students become more involved in their communities, teachers who use the Generation Citizen curriculum will include it twice a week for about 10–11 weeks (around 20 lessons). They often integrate it directly into social studies and government curricula. Past issues include things like police brutality, gun issues, bullying, and housing issues. Wallace and Andes explain that students are particularly tuned into their local communities, and notice issues before they are even in the news, such as "Massachusetts opioid abuse … Oklahoma students were identifying budget cuts and spending on like arts programs before the teachers striking national attention. And they are also talking about things like banning plastic straws in California or water access issues and overpopulation of turkeys on Staten Island." Quotes from Brooke Wallace and Sarah Andes, Generation Citizen, personal interview, Spring 2019.

28. In the previous bullet point: through the Generation Citizen curriculum, teachers encourage students to "show up and make personal contact, because that gets them more familiar with the civic processes and lowers the barriers to continuing to participate in the future. The goal is that the students begin participating in these types of action civics activities, because they are preparing for a lifetime of community and civic engagement. One of the most important goals is trying to reduce the fear, anxiety, and disengagement associated with civic and political participation." Wallace and Andes explain that "one thing that impacts and prevent students from getting engaged in politics in the future is the idea that we're just asking them to do things that they've not done before. … There's a level of fear associated with that for young people or even for adults. But political scientists have found that the most effective way to get a person to participate in the political process is by just asking them to participate." To further crystallize this, at the end of the semester, Generation Citizen also hosts something called "Civics Day," where youth can present their work and their future plans to local community leaders, teachers, and fellow student-activists. Quotes from Wallace and Andes, personal interview. In this bullet point, see more at ADL, "Curriculum Themes," 2020, http://adl-civics.bitesmedia.org/curriculum-themes; and ADL, "Strengthening Our Democracy: Civic Participation in the 21st Century," 2020, http://adl-civics.bitesmedia.org/. See also more about ADL's anti-bias framework at ADL, "Anti-Bias Approach to Civics," 2020, http://adl-civics.bitesmedia.org/anti-bias-approach-to-civics.

29. K. Schrier, "EPIC: A Framework for Using Video Games in Ethics Education," *Journal of Moral Education* 44, no. 4 (2015): 393–424.

30. Schrier, "EPIC."

31. See for example National Association of State Directors of Teacher Education and Certification (NASDTEC), "Model Code of Ethics for Educators," 2015, https://www.nasdtec.net/page/MCEE_Doc.

32. See also R. Gardiner, J. Cairns, and D. Lawton, *Education for Values: Moral, Ethics, and Citizenship in Contemporary Teaching* (London, UK and Sterling, VA: Kogan Page, 2000).

33. Common Core standards, English/Language Arts, History/Social Studies, 11–12th grades, http://www.corestandards.org/ELA-Literacy/RH/11-12/ (accessed June 3, 2020) and Common Core standards, English/Language Arts, World History, 11–12th grades, http://www.corestandards.org/ELA-Literacy/WHST/11-12/ (accessed June 3, 2020).

34. CASEL, CASEL Core Competences, 2020, https://casel.org/core-competencies/. See also how the CASEL Framework has been applied in different state standards at CASEL, An Examination of Frameworks for Social and Emotional Learning (SEL) Reflected in State K-12 Learning Standards, 2019, https://casel.org/wp-content/uploads/2020/04/in-state-K-12-leanring-standards.pdf

35. See, for instance, Levine and Kawashima-Ginsberg, "The Republic Is (Still) at Risk."

36. CASEL, CASEL Competencies, December 2019, https://casel.org/wp-content/uploads/2019/12/CASEL-Competencies.pdf. No framework is perfect, and this framework is one of many possible SEL frameworks, and SEL itself has been criticized. See more at Y. Zhao, "Another Education War? The Coming Debates Over Social and Emotional Learning," *Phi Delta Kappan*, April 27, 2020, https://kappanonline.org/another-education-war-social-emotional-learning-debates-zhao/

37. The Jubilee Center for Character & Virtues, University of Birmingham, "A Framework for Character Education in Schools," 2017, https://www.jubileecentre.ac.uk/527/character-education/framework.

38. It also includes civility, which has been problematized in the previous chapter's notes.

39. All quotations from the Jubilee Center for Character & Virtues, "A Framework for Character Education in Schools."

40. Schrier, "EPIC." The framework draws from moral action frameworks such as one by Narvaez and Rest, for instance D. Narvaez and D. Rest, "The Four Components of Acting Morally," in *Moral Behavior and Moral Development: An Introduction*, ed. W. Kurtines and J. Gewirtz (New York: McGraw-Hill, 1995), pp. 385–400.

41. D. Montgomery and M. Walker, "Enhancing Ethical Awareness," *Gifted Child Today* 35 (2012): 95–101.

42. This goal is essential to ethics education because it leads to greater personal and professional growth, and "awareness is a core aspect of ethics education, because it helps people become more cognizant of their ethical identity and moral orientation, which in turn often leads to more sound ethical decisions in the future," cited in Schrier, "EPIC," p. 404.

43. "To reason about emotions, and of emotions to enhance thinking," cited in Schrier, "EPIC," p. 404, quoting J. Mayer, P. Salovey, and D. Caruso, "Emotional Intelligence: Theory, Findings, and Implications," *Psychological Inquiry* 15 (2004): 197–215, p. 197. Daniel Goleman popularized the term "emotional intelligence"; see D. Goleman, *Emotional Intelligence* (New York: Bantam Books, 1995).

44. S. Krishnakumar and D. Rymph, "Uncomfortable Ethical Decisions: The Role of Emotions and Emotional Intelligence in Ethical Decision-Making," *Journal of Managerial Issues* XXIV (2012): 321–344.
45. Krishnakumar and Rymph, "Uncomfortable Ethical Decisions"; Schrier, "EPIC." They may even make better decisions, as emotions are an integral part of ethical decision-making, in that they affect interpreting and gathering information, and how decisions are made. Understanding our emotions and how they affect us can alter how we make decisions and how we use evidence to help us in making those decisions.
46. See for instance Schrier, "EPIC"; C. Gilligan, "Moral Orientation and Moral Development," in Women and Moral Theory, ed. E. F. Kittay and D. T. Meyers (Totowa, NJ: Rowman & Littlefield, 1987); N. Noddings, *Caring: A Feminine Approach to Ethics and Moral Education*, 2nd ed. (Berkeley: University of California Press, 2003).
47. Quoted in Schrier, "EPIC," p. 405.
48. "People need to be able to think through ethical issues and use the results in other capacities and situations," quoted in Schrier, "EPIC," p. 405, citing C. Lynn, "Teaching Ethics with an Integrated Online Curriculum," *Journal of Hospitality, Leisure, Sport & Tourism Education* 9 (2010): 124–130.
49. Schrier, "EPIC," p. 406.
50. Schrier, "EPIC," citing work by S. Merriam, "The Role of Cognitive Development in Mezirow's Transformational Learning Theory," *Adult Education Quarterly* 55 (2004): 60–68; J. Mezirow, "How Critical Reflection Triggers Transformational Learning," in *Fostering Critical Reflection in Adulthood* (San Fransicso: Jossey Bass, 1990), pp. 1–20; J. Dewey, *How We Think* (Chicago: Regnery, 1933). Reflecting on ethical issues and decisions and thinking through their consequences, as well as integrating how one's assumptions and information may have affected and influenced one's decision and its outcomes, is critical to ethics education. Merriam explains that being able to critically reflect on and critique one's assumptions, along with engaging in reflective discourse with others, is an important part of mature cognitive development. Although it seems as though reasoning and reflection are quite similar, reflection focuses on thinking through and interpreting one's beliefs and assumptions to gain further understanding or acceptance, whereas reasoning focuses on interpreting, sifting through, and analyzing causes and consequences, events, objects, people, situations, and scenarios. Merriam says that "having an experience is not enough to effect a transformation" (p. 62).
51. Schrier, "EPIC."
52. Quoted by C. H. Sommers, "How Moral Education is Finding Its Way Back Into America's Schools," in *Vice & Virtue in Everyday Life: Introductory Readings in Ethics*, ed. C. Sommers and F. Sommers (Belmont, CA: Wadsworth/Thomson Learning, 2004), p. 506.
53. See for instance R. Shafer-Landau, *The Fundamentals of Ethics* (New York: Oxford University Press, 2020).
54. For instance, M. Walker, "Universities and a Human Development Ethics: A Capabilities Approach to Curriculum," *European Journal of Education* 47 (2012): 448–461, 2012; M. Nussbaum, "Liberal Education and Global Community," *Liberal Education* 8 (2010): 145–151.
55. The content that could be taught in a civics or ethics class or educational setting varies widely across the globe—including different governments, policies, organizations, structures, and societal rules.

56. Moreover, not all governments, communities, and schools are created equal, and access to civic life is limited in even the most participatory democracy. For instance, see David E. Campbell, Meira Levinson, and Frederick M. Hess, *Making Civics Count: Citizenship Education for a New Generation* (Cambridge, MA: Harvard University Press, 2012); Korbey, *Building Better Citizens: A New Civics Education for All* (Lanham, MD: Rowman & Littlefield, 2019); NCSS, "Revitalizing Civic Learning in Our Schools."

57. See National Council of Social Studies (NCSS), "C3 (College, Career & Civic Life) Framework for Social Studies State Standards," https://www.socialstudies.org/sites/default/files/c3/c3-framework-for-social-studies-rev0617.pdf, 2017, Accessed on December 29, 2020.

58. First, I will discuss three overarching thematic questions that I believe drive teaching ethics and civics. These are based on the identified gaps, aforementioned frameworks, as well as best practices on teaching in these areas, such as from the Campaign for the Civic Mission of Schools, C3 Framework, EPIC Framework, Jubilee Centre Character Education Framework and the 10 Principles for Civics Learning. I also acknowledge that these themes, and the related questions and competencies that emerge are also relevant to all other disciplines as well—science, engineering, language arts, health, and music. In fact, these themes and skills are the foundation for all of human thought, analysis, creation, and expression. See 6 Pillars of Character at The Six Pillars of Character, https://charactercounts.org/character-counts-overview/six-pillars/.

59. This relates, for example, to the following United States standards and frameworks: College, Career, and Civic Life (C3) Framework for Social Studies State Standards: Civic and political institutions; processes, rules, and laws. Civics Assessment Framework: Civic Knowledge, including "what are civic life, politics, and government." Campaign for the Civic Mission of Schools: Content knowledge, and intellectual skills, such as analyzing information and evidence. (Individual games may relate to any of the skills, topics and knowledges areas, such as governmental structures or elections).

60. See Schrier, "EPIC."

61. Jubilee Centre for Character Education, "Schools of Virtue: Character Education in three Birmingham Schools," Research Report, 2017, https://www.jubileecentre.ac.uk/userfiles/jubileecentre/pdf/Research%20Reports/SchoolsOfVirtueResearchReport.pdf. They explain that virtue knowledge is an important part of character education.

62. "According to a 2014 report by Gallup Education, emotional engagement at school is the noncognitive factor that most directly correlates with academic achievement. Yet 45 percent of U.S. students are either 'not engaged' or are 'actively not engaged' in school," cited in Bauman and Brennan, "State Civic Education Policy," p. 1.

63. John Dewey, *Democracy and Education* (Teddington, Middlesex, UK: Echo Library, 2007), p. 259.

64. NCSS, C3 Framework.

65. It is one thing to learn skills in a classroom, virtual learning environment, or in an after-school space, but it's another to get connected with one's local and global communities and see how your actions can make real-world impact. These skills and practices are specifically cited in the C3 Framework, https://www.socialstudies.org/c3, and the 10 competencies, including work such as Levine and Kawashima-Ginsberg, "The Republic Is (Still) at Risk." See also Jeremiah Clabough and Timothy Lintner (eds.), *No Reluctant Citizens: Teaching Civics in K-12 Classrooms* (Charlotte, NC: Information Age Publishing, Inc., 2018.

66. See NCSS, "Revitalizing Civic Learning in Our Schools" and quoted in *Guardian of Democracy*, p. 6. See also Dishon and Kafai, "Connected Civic Gaming."

67. See for instance Blevins, LeCompte, and Ellis, "Students at the Heart of Civic Learning"; Generation Citizen website, https://generationcitizen.org/ (accessed June 3, 2020); Bauman and Brennan, "State Civic Education Policy."

68. See, for instance, the C3 Framework, CASEL Framework, Jubilee Character Education Framework and Levine and Kawashima-Ginsberg, "The Republic Is (Still) at Risk"; and *Guardian of Democracy*. "Complex societies are possible and durable only when people are emotionally invested in, and help, one another; we'd be living in smaller units and more solitary fashions if we weren't equipped for such collaboration; and human thriving within these societies guarantees future generations suited to them," cited in Frank Bruni, "A 'Disgusting' Professor Moves On," *New York Times*, March 19, 2019, https://www.nytimes.com/2019/03/19/opinion/nicholas-christakis-yale.html.

69. Dewey, *Democracy and Education*.

70. *Guardian of Democracy*.

71. Ibid., and CASEL Framework and C3 Framework.

72. See for example J. E. Zins (ed.), *Building Academic Success on Social and Emotional Learning: What Does the Research Say?* (New York: Teachers College Press, 2004); J. E. Zins and M. J. Elias, "Social and Emotional Learning: Promoting the Development of All Students," *Journal of Educational and Psychological Consultation* 17, no. 2–3 (2007): 233–255; J. Zins, M. Elias, and M. Greenberg, "Facilitating Success in School and in Life Through Social and Emotional Learning," *Perspectives in Education* 21, no. 4 (2003): 55–67.

73. See for instance Z. Xu and E. E. Jang, "The Role of Math Self-Efficacy in the Structural Model of Extracurricular Technology-Related Activities and Junior Elementary School Students' Mathematics Ability," *Computers in Human Behavior* 68 (2016): 547–555; L. Portnoy and K. Schrier, "Using Games to Support STEM Curiosity, Identity, and Self-Efficacy," *Journal of Games, Self, & Society* 1, no. 1 (2019): 66–96.

74. Henry Jenkins, Katie Clinton, Ravi Parushotma, Alice Robison (Daer), and Margaret Weigel, "Confronting the Challenges of Participatory Culture: Media Education for the 21st Century," MacArthur Foundation Paper, 2006, https://www.macfound.org/media/article_pdfs/JENKINS_WHITE_PAPER.PDF. See also, The Center for Collective Learning, https://centerforcollectivelearning.org/projects, accessed on January 20, 2021.

75. See for instance work by Gabriela Richard, Kishonna Gray, Shira Chess, and Yasmin Kafai, such as G. Richard, "Understanding Gender, Context, and Video Game Culture for the Development of Equitable Digital Games and Learning Environments" (PhD diss., New York University, 2013); G. Richard and K. L. Gray, "Gendered Play, Racialized Reality: Black Cyberfeminism, Inclusive communities of Practice, and the Intersections of Learning, Socialization, and Resilience in Online Gaming," *Frontiers: A Journal of Women Studies* 39, no. 1 (2018): 112–148; K. L. Gray, *Intersectional Tech: Black Users in Digital Gaming* (Baton Rouge: Louisiana State University Press, 2020); K. L. Gray, "Intersecting Oppressions and Online Communities: Examining the Experiences of Women of Color in Xbox Live," *Information, Communication, & Society* 15, no. 3 (2012): 411–428; Yasmin Kafai, Carrie Heeter, Jill Denner, and Jennifer Y. Sun, *Beyond Barbie and Mortal Combat* (Cambridge, MA: MIT Press, 2008); Shira Chess, *Ready Player Two*

(Minneapolis: University of Minnesota Press, 2017). See also Safiya Noble, *Algorithms of Oppression* (New York: NYU Press, 2018).

76. See the C3 Framework; *Guardian of Democracy*; Korbey, *Building Better Citizens*; and Clabough and Lintner, *No Reluctant Citizens*.

77. We need to be humanists, social scientists, and scientists. This is inspired by the director of the NCSS, Larry Paska, who spoke about the C3 Framework at the Social Studies Virtual Unconference, May 13, 2020, https://secondavenuelearning.com/socialstudiesunconference-resources/.

78. Jonathan Haber, *Critical Thinking* (Cambridge, MA: MIT Press, 2020), p. 22, citing work by John Dewey, such in *Democracy and Education*.

79. See for instance the C3 Framework; *Guardian of Democracy*; and Levine and Kawashima-Ginsberg, "The Republic Is (Still) at Risk."

80. See also Segregated by Design, https://www.segregatedbydesign.com/?fbclid=I-wAR3bM5F7FdV1w1Rc1flxqHyuKTg7wlb0puixrH5rszaUo72xl9oxoWP5gkc and events like "How Traditional Design Thinking Protects White Supremacy," 2020, https://www.eventbrite.com/e/how-traditional-design-thinking-protects-white-supremacy-encore-registration-109013446152?aff=eand&fbclid=IwAR3yEO1HVCHah2_cPeo_sLEiUb7P-GTETtY_y2EZmh64p8_xqmQ1Jfb29wsY.

81. Batelle for Kids, Partnership for 21st Century Learning, Framework for 21st Century Learning, https://www.battelleforkids.org/networks/p21 (accessed June 3, 2020), describes critical thinking among their 4Cs (Critical Thinking, Communication, Collaboration, and Creativity).

82. Critical thinking "involves thinking for ourselves by carefully examining the way that we make sense of the world." It is about asking questions, making decisions, solving problems, reflecting, and developing new ways of thinking about the world. Quotes and more in J. Chaffee, *Thinking Critically*, 12th ed. (Boston: Cengage Learning, 2018). Also, for a critique of critical thinking, see D. Boyd, You Think You Want Media Literacy, Do You?, Data & Society, March 9, 2018, https://points.datasociety.net/you-think-you-want-media-literacy-do-you-7cad6af18ec2.

83. Haber, *Critical Thinking*, citing a Foundation for Critical Thinking definition, p. 103.

84. The skills listed here are derived from Haber, *Critical Thinking* and Matthew Ventura, Emily Lai, and Kristen DiCerbo, "Skills for Today: What We Know About Teaching and Assessing Critical Thinking," Pearson, 2017, https://www.pearson.com/content/dam/one-dot-com/one-dot-com/global/Files/efficacy-and-research/skills-for-today/Critical-Thinking-FullReport.pdf.

85. Haber, *Critical Thinking*.

86. Ibid.

87. Ibid. describes these definitions more in depth, such as rhetoric.

88. This is derived in part from work by Dewey, Mezirow, and Merriam, as well as Haber, *Critical Thinking*.

89. Haber, *Critical Thinking*. Haber explains that it "is the ability to identify what information is needed, understand how the information is organized, identify the best sources of information for a given need, locate those sources, evaluate the sources critically, and share that information. It is the knowledge of commonly used research techniques" (p. 87).

90. Ventura, Lai, and DiCerbo, "Skills for Today."

91. Haber, *Critical Thinking*.

Chapter 4

1. I remember looking at a *Scholastic News* magazine in my social studies class, which listed the chances of becoming a United States president, giving it a one in at least 246 million chance of ever holding that position. There are limited statistics available, but this is one source, which should be further validated: "President of the United States, Odds of Getting In," https://www.shmoop.com/careers/president/odds-of-getting-in.html, Accessed on January 18, 2021.

2. See *Win the White House*, iCivics, https://www.icivics.org/games/win-white-house (accessed June 4, 2020). It says: "Do you want to be the next President of the United States? This refreshed version of *Win the White House* challenges you to build your campaign by: Building arguments to support timely issues that are relevant to you, Strategically raise funds to support your campaign, Keeping campaign momentum through targeted media campaigns and personal appearances, Polling local voters to see what issues resonate, You'll also meet our new campaign manager, named Ana, who will guide you through the process." iCivics is an organization that aims to create games and educational materials around civics and civic engagement; it was started by the Supreme Court Justice Sandra Day O'Connor in 2008 (see background information at https://www.icivics.org/our-story). In referring to the "knowledge that we need," I am drawing from the standards and frameworks shared in chapter 3, including the concepts, processes, terms, institutions, and approaches related to civics and ethics. "Knowledge" in this case refers to both an individual understanding and awareness of this information, as well as a collective "knowing" of this repository of information, which can be shared with the world through learning.

3. See *Executive Command*, iCivics, https://www.icivics.org/games/executive-command (accessed June 4, 2020). It says, "Ever wanted to be President for a day? In Executive Command, you can be President for four years! Try to accomplish what you set as your agenda while facing the challenges and responsibilities that crop up along the way. Being commander in chief and chief executive is no easy job! See how you do!"

4. Quote from Amber Coleman-Mortley, iCivics, personal interview in spring, 2019. She continues by saying, "where before a student might say, 'becoming a president or running for office is really huge or it's a really far off concept … When these experiences and processes are accessible, it becomes a lot more tangible and memorable. Civil service or an active civic life become experiences they can see themselves pursuing."

5. In reference to the representation in government—if we are living in a nation that has a representative government. Many do not. In reference to the quotation, it is by Emma Humphries, iCivics, personal interview in Spring 2019. She is referring to the game *Executive Command*.

6. For more information and quotations, see Megan Gately, Reagan Foundation, "The Brink of Nuclear War: Gaming in the Modern Museum, Games for Change," 2020, https://www.youtube.com/watch?v=9c7RaeTBfy8&list=PL1G85ERLMItAwgIJxb10QAwfOwYztOr-J4&index=21. See more at The Reagan Foundation, https://www.reaganfoundation.org/library-museum/permanent-exhibitions/.

7. National Council for the Social Studies (NCSS), C3 Framework, https://www.socialstudies.org/sites/default/files/c3/C3-Framework-for-Social-Studies.pdf, quote at p. 6; see also frameworks in chapter 3. "By focusing on inquiry, the framework emphasizes the disciplinary concepts and practices that support students as they develop

the capacity to know, analyze, explain, and argue about interdisciplinary challenges in our social world. It includes descriptions of the structure and tools of the disciplines, as well as the habits of mind common in those disciplines," as quoted in the C3 Framework, p. 6.

8. The specific state, region, or country needs to determine which information and knowledge is necessary for the audience (such as age group or grade) to know for full participation.

9. NCSS, C3 Framework, p. 31.

10. The goals in this chapter relate to the following standards: College, Career, and Civic Life (C3) Framework for Social Studies State Standards: civic and political institutions; processes, rules, and laws. Civics Assessment Framework: civic knowledge, including "what are civic life, politics, and government" Campaign for the Civic Mission of Schools. Content knowledge, and intellectual skills, such as analyzing information and evidence. United States Common Core: individual games may relate to any of the skills, and the topic and knowledge area is civics, governmental structures, and elections. Please also see Table 3.1 in chapter 3.

11. NCSS, C3 Framework, p. 31, and Jubilee Centre for Character Education, "Schools of Virtue: Character Education in Three Birmingham Schools," Research Report, 2017, https://www.jubileecentre.ac.uk/userfiles/jubileecentre/pdf/Research%20Reports/SchoolsOfVirtueResearchReport.pdf; and K. Schrier, "EPIC: A Framework for Using Video Games for Ethics Education," *Journal of Moral Education* 44, no. 4 (2015): 393–424. However, this book does not aim to dictate the specific real-world civics and ethics perspectives, processes, issues, and institutions that a student should learn. Rather, these should vary by locality, age group, and current needs, and should be decided through dialogues among educators, districts or local institutions, and professional organizations. The C3 framework explains that it "focuses on inquiry skills and key concepts, and guides—not prescribes—the choice of curricular content necessary for a rigorous social studies program" (p. 6). The framework does not aim to prescribe curricular content, but lays out conceptual knowledge that should be acquired. "Curricular content specifies the particular ideas to be taught and the grade levels at which to teach them; conceptual content is the bigger set of ideas that frame the curricular content. For example, rather than identify every form of governmental power, the C3 framework expects students in grades 6–8 to 'explain the powers and limits of the three branches of government, public officials, and bureaucracies at different levels in the United States and in other countries.' Similarly, rather than delineate every kind of map, the C3 framework expects students in grades 3–5 to 'create maps and other graphic representations of both familiar and unfamiliar places,'" p. 29. Moreover, the book also does not enforce one ethical perspective or set of virtues as being more "right" than others. Rather than tell people how to behave in a specific circumstance or environment, the curricula and frameworks give people a set of tools, skills, concepts, and virtues they can use to apply to a given context. See Jubilee Centre for Character Education, "Schools of Virtue," and R. Gardiner, J. Cairns, and D. Lawton, *Education for Values* (Sterling, VA: Kogan Page, 2000); Holly Korbey, *Building Better Citizens: A New Civics Education for All* (Lanham, MD: Rowman & Littlefield, 2019); and Jonathan Gould (ed.), *Guardian of Democracy: The Civic Mission of Schools* (Philadelphia: Leonore Annenberg Institute for Civics of the Annenberg Public Policy Center at the University of Pennsylvania, 2011).

12. Korbey, *Building Better Citizens*, xii, 47. The acquisition of procedural knowledge, and the practicing of the skills relevant to civics and ethics, are typically taught in tandem with this foundational declarative knowledge.

13. Ibid., p. 47, citing Daniel T. Willingham, "Critical Thinking: Why is it So Hard to Teach?" American Educator, Summer 2007, https://www.aft.org/sites/default/files/periodicals/Crit_Thinking.pdf.

14. Korbey, *Building Better Citizens*, p. 47, citing and quoting Willingham, "Critical Thinking: Why is it So Hard to Teach?" American Educator, Summer 2007, https://www.aft.org/sites/default/files/periodicals/Crit_Thinking.pdf.

15. Korbey, *Building Better Citizens*, p. 41–42, citing and quoting Diane Ravitch, "Deline and Fall of Teaching History," New York Times, November 17, 1985, https://www.nytimes.com/1985/11/17/magazine/decline-and-fall-of-teaching-history.html, who says, "If knowledge of the pat is in fact relevant to our ability to understand the present and to exercise freedom of mind—as totalitarian societies, both real and fictional, acknowledge by stringently controlling what may be studied or published, then there is cause for concern about many Americans' sense of history. The threat to our knowledge of the past comes ... from indifference and ignorance."

16. Gould, *Guardian of Democracy*.

17. Ibid., citing the most recent National Assessment of Educational Progress (NAEP) Civics Assessment, with more than two-thirds of all American studies scoring below proficient (2010).

18. Woodrow Wilson National Fellowship Foundation, "National Survey Finds Just 1 in 3 Americans Would Pass Citizenship Test," October 3, 2018, https://woodrow.org/news/national-survey-finds-just-1-in-3-americans-would-pass-citizenship-test/; Southern Poverty Law Center, "Teaching Hard History: American Slavery," 2018, https://www.splcenter.org/sites/default/files/tt_hard_history_american_slavery.pdf; Korbey, *Building Better Citizens*, explains that one-third of Americans would be able to pass a citizenship test, only 8% of high school seniors call identify slavery as the central cause of the Civil War, and two-thirds of young adults don't know what Auschwitz is and 22% have never heard of the Holocaust. She cites Woodrow Wilson, "National Survey," Southern Poverty Law Center, "Teaching Hard History," and Schoen Consulting, "Holocaust Knowledge and Awareness Study, Executive Summary," April 2018, https://www.jewishvirtuallibrary.org/jsource/images/holocaustknowledgestudy.pdf. They found that 11% of US adults and 22% of Millennials had not heard of the Holocaust or were not sure what it is. Some readers may also remember "Jaywalking" by Jay Leno, where he went on the street and asked people common civics-related questions, such as in this video from 2009, https://vimeo.com/5604554 (accessed September 12, 2020).

19. Korbey, *Building Better Citizens*, citing Ravitch, p. 41.

20. Gould, *Guardian of Democracy* and Peter Levine and Kei Kawashima-Ginsberg, "The Republic Is (Still) at Risk—and Civics Is Part of the Solution" (Medford, MA: Jonathan M. Tisch College of Civic Life, Tufts University, 2017).

21. Levine and Kawashima-Ginsberg, "The Republic Is (Still) at Risk" and Korbey, *Building Better Citizens*. Levin and Kawashima-Ginsberg explain that further engagement with the six civics practices that work helped, and this was further spurred by the passage of the Act. However, as mentioned earlier, we should not just focus on raising test scores, and other measures are needed to suggest greater civics or ethics engagement.

22. Levine and Kawashima-Ginsberg, "The Republic Is (Still) at Risk," p. 13.

23. Gideon Dishon and Yasmin B. Kafai, "Connected Civic Gaming: Rethinking the Role of Video Games in Civic Education," *Interactive Learning Environments* (2019), DOI: 10.1080/10494820.2019.1704791. E. Middaugh, "The Social and Emotional Components of Gaming: A Response to 'The Challenge of Gaming for Democratic Education,'" *Democracy and Education* 24, no. 2 (2016): Article 8.; E. A. Boyle, T. Hainey, T. M. Connolly, G. Gray, J. Earp, M. Ott, T. Lim, M. Ninaus, C. Ribeiro, and J. Pereira, "An Update to the Systematic Literature Review of Empirical Evidence of the Impacts and Outcomes of Computer Games and Serious Games," *Computers & Education* 94 (2016): 178–192; J. Stoddard, A. M. Banks, C. Nemacheck, and E. Wenska, "The Challenges of Gaming for Democratic Education: The Case of iCivics," *Democracy and Education* 24, no. 2 (2016): Article 2.

24. Gould, *Guardian of Democracy*.

25. See *Executive Command*, iCivics, https://www.icivics.org/games/executive-command.

26. K. Schrier, "Guiding Questions for Game-Based Learning," in *International Handbook of Information Technology in Primary and Secondary Education*, ed. D. Gibson (New York: Springer, 2018).

27. As explained by Christopher Harris, Director of the School Library System for the Genesee Valley Educational Partnership, personal interview, Spring 2019. See more at GMT Games/Z-Man Games, Inc., "1960: The Making of a President," 2007, https://boardgame-geek.com/boardgame/27708/1960-making-president. Likewise, teachers may use games such as the *Mission US* series to support historic understandings of current civic issues, like urban protests, workers' rights, social movements, and immigration (*Mission US: City of Immigrants* delves into these issues by using New York City and the early twentieth century as its anchor). However, note that some teachers are boycotting these modules because of some possibly problematic representations of different identities, and teachers should consider the use of these games with sensitivity and care depending on the context and ecosystem of their use. (See more in chapter 5.)

28. Annenberg Classroom/Filament Games, *That's Your Right*, https://games.annenbergclass-room.org/billofrights/index.html. The game requires teacher support as it is not immediately clear how to play or how to engage with the rights on the cards, and does not have enough scaffolding for those new to the game.

29. Dishon and Kafai, "Connected Civic Gaming"; C. Bachen, P. Hernández-Ramos, and C. Raphael, "Simulating Real Lives: Promoting Global Empathy and Interest in Learning through Simulation Games," in *Simulation & Gaming*, 43, no. 4 (2012): 437–460); for the source of the quotation, see also the icivics story at https://www.icivics.org/our-story, cited by Dishon and Kafai. K. Squire, "From Content to Context: Videogames as Designed Experience," *Educational Researcher* 35, no. 8 (2006): 19–29.

30. Schell Games, History Maker VR, https://www.schellgames.com/games/history-maker-vr (accessed June 4, 2020, when it was still in prototype phase according to the website). The VR tool features eight different US historic figures like Abraham Lincoln, Abigail Adams, and Sonia Sotomayor.

31. Levine and Kawashima-Ginsberg, "The Republic Is (Still) at Risk," p. 34, and citing research by D. W. Shaffer, *How Computer Games Help Children Learn* (London: Palgrave, 2006).

32. Lerner defines democracy as "the original Greek meaning of 'rule of the people.' This includes representative democracy, direct democracy, participatory democracy, and any other system that enables a group of people to govern itself. This is not limited to the

representative democracy of many Western governments, or even to government itself. Democracy can be just as valuable for governments deciding on policies as for organizations deciding on campaigns or friends deciding where to eat ... I understand democratic participation as any effort to influence or participate in decision-making about how a group of people is governed." J. Lerner, *Making Democracy Fun: How Game Design Can Empower and Transform Politics* (Cambridge, MA: MIT Press, 2014), p. 6.

33. Lerner, *Making Democracy Fun*, p. 3. He writes, "The legal regulations crated two compelling artificial conflicts ... Winners received a big monetary reward, but the results were uncertain and depended on reaching a certain score (number of votes)."

34. On the other hand, maybe we need to redefine what it means to have fun. The fun in games may not be that they are simplistic, frivolous, or extraneous. Rather, the fun could be that they are challenging, difficult, and even that they help us learn. Perhaps, "the fun in games is the work, the hard stuff, and the boundary pushing, rather than the 'spoonful of sugar' that's needed to take medicine or the chocolate in the 'chocolate-covered broccoli' metaphor." Ian Bogost asks, 'What if we arrive at fun ... by embracing the wretchedness of the circumstances themselves? ... What if, in a literal way, fun comes from impoverishment, from wretchedness? What if it is the broccoli without the chocolate?" K. Schrier, *Knowledge Games: How Playing Games Can Solve Problems, Create Insight, and Make Change* (Baltimore: Johns Hopkins University Press, 2016), p. 133, citing Ian Bogost, "Fun," UX Week 2013 talk, http://vimeo.com/74943170.

35. Quote by Neil Wrona, personal interview, Spring 2019. He explains that "they loved having to make those decisions and they could connect to what was really happening. And they're like, Oh man, I gotta really think about this.... The kids had to like talk it out and make decisions and have conversations with each other. Like, 'Oh, do you think that's a good idea? I think that's a good idea. Maybe we should do this. Okay, let's do that.' So that was a really, really cool and interesting dynamic to watch a happen because that's not something my students often do. They are not usually good collaborators."

36. Schrier, *Knowledge Games*, p. 54 citing R. Koster, *A Theory of Fun for Game Design*, Sebastopol, CA: O'Reilly Media, 2013. What counts as "fun" is not the same for everyone, although game designers often point out that fun is the most important aspect of a game. See, for instance, Koster, *A Theory of Fun for Game Design*. Likewise, Papert describes the concept of "hard fun" or the fun in rising above difficult obstacles, meeting challenges and solving unwieldy problems. Seymour Papert, "Hard Fun," http://www.papert.org/articles/HardFun.html (accessed April 12, 2019).

37. Ian Bogost, "Reality is Alright: A Review of Jane McGonigal's Book, *Reality is Broken*," http://bogost.com/writing/blog/reality_is_broken/ (accessed April 12, 2019).

38. Bogost, "Fun."

39. When players feel competent, autonomous, responsible, and worthy, which also relates to being motivated to learn, they are more compelled to acquire new knowledge and skills. When students "felt more connected to others, more competent, and had autonomy over their choices and behaviors." Quote from Schrier, "Guiding Questions," citing Richard M. Ryan and Edward L. Deci, "Intrinsic and Extrinsic Motivations," *Contemporary Educational Psychology* 25 (2000): 54–67.

40. Personal interview with Doris Rusch, Spring 2019.

41. Is fun the right word—or even excitement? Is it "fun" to play a game about a child dying, or about someone who is suffering from a mental or physical illness? Perhaps "fun" is really

about meaningfulness, or the pleasure of being fulfilled, immersed, and engaged. Fun is feeling that the game, and one's play of the game, matters—even if the game itself is not pleasurable.

42. Ryan and Deci, "Intrinsic and Extrinsic Motivations." Extrinsic and intrinsic motivation may both be useful for learning, and they often overlap more than we realize—how do we know whether we are truly motivated by something for our own interest, or whether external rewards have compelled our interests and drive for it? Schrier, *Knowledge Games*; quotes in J. T. Huck, E. A. Day, L. Lin, A. G. Jorgensen, J. Westlin, and J. H. Hardy, "The Role of Epistemic Curiosity in Game-Based Learning: Distinguishing Skill Acquisition from Adaptation," *Simulation & Gaming* 51, no. 2 (2020): 141–166.. First quotation, Huck et al., citing J. A. Litman, "Interest and Deprivation Factors of Epistemic Curiosity," *Personality and Individual Differences* 44 (2008): 1585–1595, p. 1586. Second quotation, R. P. Collins, J. A. Litman, and C. D. Spielberger, "The Measurement of Perceptual Curiosity," *Personality and Individual Differences* 36 (2004): 1127–1141 and D. E. Berlyne, "A Theory of Human Curiosity," *British Journal of Psychology* 45 (1954): 180–191.

43. Schrier, *Knowledge Games*; P. Wouters, C. van Nimwegen, H. van Oostendorp, and E. D. van der Spek, "A Meta-Analysis of the Cognitive and Motivational Effects of Serious Games," *Journal of Educational Psychology* 105, no. 2 (2013): 249. Although the relationship among motivation, engagement, and learning through games is complicated, and do not always enhance the other. Motivation is driven through carefully constructed goals, feedback, and rewards. But each type of player is motivated by different aspects of a game, and may be differentially motivated depending on other factors. In one study, by F. Crocco, K. Offenholley, C. and Hernandez, "A Proof-of-Concept Study of Game-Based Learning in Higher Education," *Simulation & Gaming* 47, no. 4 (2016): 403–422, they looked at the use of game-based lessons for a number of different types of courses, such as English, science and mathematics. They compared the game-based lessons to nongame lessons (control group) and found that the use of games correlated to greater enjoyment of the learning, which in turn related to higher-order thinking and deeper learning of the topics. This large, quantitative study suggested that games may motivate deeper curiosity and interest in a topic, and therefore, more learning of the topic. On the other hand, Wouters et al. investigated the use of digital games in the classroom versus traditional instruction methodologies (such as lectures, textbook reading, and skill and drill practice). They found that games were more effective in learning in terms of how they support cognitive development and retention of information, but that they did not enhance motivation to learn the topic. Thus, while games may help to motivate learning and curiosity, they do always do so consistently. We need to further refine how games are being used and designed to more effectively motivate learning.

44. Schrier, *Knowledge Games*. Deniz Eseryel, Victor Law, Dirk Ifenthaler, Xun Ge, and Raymond Miller, "An Investigation of the Interrelationships between Motivation, Engagement, and Complex Problem Solving in Game-based Learning," *Educational Technology & Society* 17, no. 1 (2014): 42–53. Being more engaged in an educational experience such as a game leads to greater learning outcomes. Eseryel et al. looked at *McLarin's Adventure*, a massively multiplayer online game (MMOG) designed to teach eighth and ninth graders and they found that giving the right balance of mastery and challenge for the player enhanced their motivation and engagement. But playing the game was not enough—players needed to feel like they were progressing in their ability to play the game,

and interaction with the interface, narrative, and social aspects of the game also helped to sustain the players' motivation. Deniz Eseryel, Xun Ge, Dirk Ifenthaler, and Victor Law, "Dynamic Modeling as a Cognitive Regulation Scaffold for Developing Complex Problem-Solving Skills in an Educational Massively Multiplayer Online Game Environment," *Journal of Educational Computing Research* 45, no. 3 (2011): 265–286. Teachers should consider asking students to share their favorite games or to come up with their own goals in a given goal, which matches their interests.

45. For more about the trolley problem see Judith Jarvis Thomson, "The Trolley Problem," *Yale Law Journal* 94, no. 6 (1985): 1395–1415. See also M. Schulzke, "Simulating Philosophy: Interpreting Video Games as Executable Thought Experiments," *Philosophy & Technology* 27 (2014):, 251–265 (2014); and M. Ryan, P. Formosa, S. Howarth, and D. Staines, "Measuring Morality in Videogames Research," *Ethics and Information Technology* 22 (2020): 55–68 (2020).

46. N. Martin, M. Draper, and A. Lamey, "*Justice*: A Role-Immersion Game for Teaching Political Philosophy," *Teaching Philosophy* 43, no. 3 (2020): 303–330.

47. Brendan Trombley, formerly of the Institute of Play, personal interview, Spring 2019.

48. Quoted in Emma Humphries, personal interview, Spring 2019.

49. Quoted in Christopher Harris, personal interview, Spring 2019; GMT Games, *A Distant Plain*, 2013, 2016, 2018, https://www.gmtgames.com/p-656-a-distant-plain-3rd-printing. aspx (accessed June 4, 2020).

50. Defined by I. Bogost, S. Ferrari, and B. Schweizer, *Newsgames: Journalism at Play* (Cambridge, MA: MIT Press, 2010). See also Alyssa Abkowitz, "Playing Around," *Columbia Journalism Review*, December 22, 2010, https://archives.cjr.org/critical_eye/ playing_around.php.

51. G. Frasca and Newsgaming, "September 12th: A Toy World," 2001, http://www.games-forchange.org/game/september-12th-a-toy-world/, which states that "*The New York Times* described September 12th as 'An Op-Ed composed not of words but of actions.'"

52. See Kirby, September 7, 2020, https://caitkirby.com/downloads/Fall%202020.html, and Salanthé and Case, "What Happens Next?," https://ncase.me/covid-19/.

53. See, for instance, N. Mirra and A. Garcia, "Civic Participation Reimagined: Youth Interrogation and Innovation in the Multimodal Public Sphere," *Review of Research in Education* 41 (March 2017): 136–158"; A. Davisson and D. Gehm, "Gaming Citizenship: Video Games as Lessons in Civic Life," *Journal of Contemporary Rhetoric* 4, no.3/4 (2014): 39–57, citing M. Schudson, *The Good Citizen: A History of American Civic Life* (New York: Simon and Schuster, 1998).

54. Davisson and Gehm, "Gaming Citizenship," p. 41, cite Bogost, who explains that engaging in a game is a type of ritual, with procedures that "'define the way things work: the methods, techniques, and logics that drive the operation of systems, from mechanical systems like engines to organizational systems like high schools to conceptual systems like religious faith.' The true rhetorical persuasiveness of the system comes with repeated exposure. Eventually, the gaming process itself becomes a ritual ... Over time, engaging a procedure begins to impact ways of thinking."

55. Mirra and Garcia, "Civic Participation Reimagined," citing P. Freire, *Pedagogy of the Oppressed* (New York: Seabury Press, 1970).

56. Christopher Harris, personal interview, Spring 2019. Emma Humphries of iCivics, an organization which makes educational games, acknowledges that "in the very early stages

and still to some extent we have had to fight that notion that if a student's having too much fun, they can't be learning … that the fun would distract from the learning … I mean, how absurd to think that if you're having fun, you can't be learning." As a result, teachers, administrators and even players may not take games seriously enough to use them to use them properly for instructional purposes, or even to use them at all. Quoted in Emma Humphries, personal interview, Spring 2019.

57. Quoted by Matthew Farber, a former social studies teacher at a middle school in New Jersey, personal interview, Spring 2019. Adding to the complexity is that the framing of games as being "fun" or "just entertainment," which may also affect how much people learn from them, and how they are used for educational purposes. Even if well-meaning adults are not the roadblocks, the students' myths about games can also prevail. First, students may not be as motivated by a game that is created for educational purposes. Part of it may not just be because it does not have the visuals, immersive storytelling, game play, or voice acting that a big-budget mainstream game may have. Part of it may be due to students' perceptions of educational games.

58. Framing a game as "fun" may alter how players approach these environments and treat them as "serious" learning. In one study, one portion of the participants were told to have fun while learning, and others were warned that what they would be doing was serious. Participants were also divided further into two groups: high and low importance. Some of the participants were told that what they were learning was of high importance, and the rest were not told this. Those participants who were in the "high importance and high fun" group ended up with a lower performance on learning than those in the "high importance and low fun" group. We may have expected that the "fun" framed group would be more motivating, and that this would therefore enhance our performance. However, what they found was that because people may expect that learning will be serious and not fun, being in the "fun group" ended up lowering their performance on the task. Or we could interpret this study as suggesting that if we frame a task as fun—and it's not fun—this may end up causing performance to be lower than if we had just admitted the task was no fun to begin with. Thus, educators need to set appropriate expectations, and perhaps even frame "fun games" as educational experiences, so that players take it seriously, even if it is quite fun. They also may be pleasantly surprised when it is more fun than they expected. Cited in E. Tory Higgins, *Beyond Pleasure and Pain: How Motivation Works* (New York: Oxford University Press, 2012).

59. J. T. Harviainen and L. Hassan, "Governmental Service Gamification: Central Principles," *International Journal of Innovation in the Digital Economy* 10, no. 3 (2019): 1–12. L. Hassan & J. Hamari, "Gameful Civic Engagement: A Review of the Literature on Gamification of e-Participation," *Government Inforation Quarterly* 37 no. 3, (2020): 1–21; J. Stenros, "The Game Definition Game: A Review," *Games and Culture* 12, no. 6, (2015): 499–520.

60. See, for instance, Schrier, "EPIC." See also Schrier, *Knowledge Games* and Schrier, "Guiding Questions," citing work by W. S. Ravyse, A. S. Blignaut, V. Leendertz, and A. Woolner, "Success Factors for Serious Games to Enhance Learning: A Systematic Review," *Virtual Reality* 21, no. 1 (2017): 31–58; F. Crocco, et al., "A Proof-of-Concept Study of Game-Based Learning in Higher Education"; M. P. J. Habgood and S. E. Ainsworth, "Motivating Children to Learn Effectively: Exploring the Value of Intrinsic Integration in Educational Games," *Journal of the Learning Sciences* 20, no. 2 (2011): 169–206.

61. G. A. Fine, "Frames and Games," in *The Game Design Reader*, ed. Katie Salen and Eric Zimmerman (Cambridge, MA: MIT Press, 2006), p. 579. In 2005 I tested players with a special glove that measured galvanic skin response (the Galvactivator, made at MIT) and found that players increased in this measurement when they were talking and interacting with other players, solving problems and more fully participating in the game (which was a mobile game that required collaboration among different players). But it is not clear whether galvanic skin response maps to engagement, or to just simply more movement, higher energy needs, and social interactions. Deeply engaged, but quiet reflection or puzzle-solving may not have raised this response. Also, what engages one player (such as social interactions) may not be the same as that which engages others. Thus, the connections among fun, engagement, motivation, and learning are complex, and bring up further questions (as described in K. Schrier, "A Comparison of Augmented Reality Games Using the Galvactivator to Measure Galvanic Skin Response," unpublished MIT/Harvard paper, 2005).

62. Quantic Foundry, 2017, GDC Talk, https://quanticfoundry.com/wp-content/uploads/2017/03/GDC-2017-Slides-Quantic-Foundry.pdf. For instance, some players are motivated by achievement, meaning that they want to collect all the hidden objects, level up their character to the highest level, or complete all the quests in a game, while others are most compelled by an immersive story (immersion motivation), or lots of explosions, noise and chaos (action motivation). Some people are interested in playing with others (social motivation), while others are not motivated by competition or community. Yee, Dicheneaut, and Quantic Foundry researched over 283K players to develop six player motivation types for video games. They found that different demographics of players are motivated by different types of game play, such as competition (leaderboards, rankings) and destruction (explosions, firing guns, car chases) being more of a factor for males and younger people, while others may even be demotivated if there are competitive elements. N. Yee, N. Dicheneaut, and Quantic Foundry, "Gamer Motivation Model," 2016, http://quanticfoundry.com/reports/. They also developed a separate gamer motivation model for board game players, which is similar to the video game model, but diverges in some key ways. See more at https://apps.quanticfoundry.com/surveys/start/tabletop/. Women and people above age 35 were more motivated by completion (collecting all the rewards, finishing missions) and fantasy (being in a new storyworld, acting in a role).

63. However, a game does not need to be polished, long, or even high-quality to be fun and motivating, though it may need to be fun and motivating for the particular person playing the game.

64. Quoted from personal interview with Ashley Penney, Spring 2019.

65. Mirra and Garcia, "Civic Participation Reimagined"

66. For instance, see work on constructivism and constructionism, such as J. Lave and E. Wenger, *Situated Learning: Legitimate Peripheral Participation* (Cambridge: Cambridge University Press, 1991); J. S. Brown, A. Collins, and P. Duguid, "Situated Cognition and the Culture of Learning," *Educational Researcher* 18, no. 1 (1989): 32–42; Papert, "Hard Fun"; B. Wilson, *Constructivist Learning Environments: Case studies in Instrumental Design* (Englewood Cliffs, NJ: Educational Technology Publications, 1996); and Y. Kafai and M. Resnick, *Constructionism in Practice: Designing, Thinking and Learning* (New York: Routledge, 1996). These all build on J. Piaget's learning theories.

67. Valencia Abbott, personal interview, Spring 2019; "Do I Have a Right?," iCivics, https://www.icivics.org/games/do-i-have-right (accessed June 4, 2020). It is described as "In *Do I Have a Right?* you can run your own firm of lawyers who specialize in constitutional law. Decide if potential clients have a right, match them with the best lawyer, and win their case. The more clients you serve and the more cases you win, the faster your law firm grows!"

68. Neil Wrona, personal interview, Spring 2019.

69. PolitiCraft, Inc, *PolitiCraft*, 2019, https://www.politicraft.org. For more about action civics, see chapter 4, and Levine and Kawashima-Ginsberg, "The Republic Is (Still) at Risk." They write that action civics refers to doing project-based and active learning experiences, such that, "students are encouraged to develop identities as citizens (with rights and responsibilities) and when they are encouraged to consider influencing institutional policies along with other options for addressing problems" (p. 5). See also Generation Citizen's curriculum, https://generationcitizen.org/our-programs/our-curriculum/ (accessed June 4, 2020).

70. Other cards include PowerPlay cards, such as a lawsuit card, which can be used to oppose or support other players, and End of Election Cycle cards, where players need to immediately do whatever action is on the card, such as shifting cards to the next player.

71. "How to Play *PolitiCraft*," 2016, https://vimeo.com/184565509. A similar quotation can also be found on a worksheet, "In-Class Activity: *PolitiCraft* Introduction + Let's Get to the Root," found at "Getting Started," https://www.politicraft.org/how-to-play-politicraft, (Accessed on January 18, 2021).

72. Teachers can have students use these cards to practice skills like communication, storytelling, problem identification and problem-solving, collaboration, ethical reasoning, improvisation, reading, and interpreting. The *PolitiCraft* team recommends activities on a number of worksheets shared at PolitiCraft, "Getting Started," https://www.politicraft.org/how-to-play-politicraft, (Accessed on January 18, 2021). The worksheet also references, J. Westheimer and J. Kahne, "What Kind of Citizen: The Politics of Educating for Democracy," *American Educational Research Journal*, 41, no. 2 (2004): 237–269. This section cites dialogue in the video, "How to Play *PolitiCraft*," 2016, https://vimeo.com/184565509.

73. The cards are aligned with the C3 civics framework explored in chapters 2 and 3, suggesting that the game was intentionally designed to teach the skills and processes associated with civics education.

74. See, for instance, Schrier, K., "Designing Digital Games to Teach History," in *Learning, Education and Games Vol. 1: Curricular and Design Considerations*, ed. K. Schrier (Pittsburgh: ETC Press, 2014). See also Channel 13, Mission US, https://www.mission-us.org/, and iCivics, https://www.icivics.org (accessed June 4, 2020).

75. Lisa Granshaw, "*Mass Effect* Trilogy: The 15 Toughest Story Decisions," SyFy.com, March 21, 2017, https://www.syfy.com/syfywire/mass-effect-trilogy-15-toughest-story-decisions. Note that my Shephard was a "she." Other people may have Sheps that are other genders.

76. See more in K. Schrier, "Ethical Thinking and Sustainability in Role-Play Participants: A Preliminary Study," *Simulation & Gaming* 46, no. 6 (2015): 673–696; K. Schrier, "Avatar Gender and Ethical Thinking In *Fable III*," *Bulletin of Science, Technology, and Society* 32, no. 5 (October 2012): 375–383.

77. This player's real-world experiences often affected his ethical decisions in the game, according to the player. See more in K. Schrier, "Emotion, Empathy and Ethical Thinking in *Fable III*," in *Emotion, Technology, and Games*, ed. S. Tettegah and W. Huang (New York: Elvesier); K. Schrier, "Ethical Thinking and Sustainability in Role-Play Participants: A Preliminary Study," *Simulation & Gaming* 46, no. 6 (2015): 673–696; and K. Schrier, K. "Ethical Thinking and Video Games: The Practice of Ethics in Fable III" (PhD diss., Columbia University, 2011).

78. See more in Schrier, "Emotion, Empathy and Ethical Thinking in *Fable III*"; Schrier, "Ethical Thinking and Sustainability in Role-Play Participants"; and Schrier, "Ethical Thinking and Video Games."

79. E. L. Felton and R. R. Sims, "Teaching Business Ethics: Targeted Outputs," *Journal of Business Ethics* 60 (2005): 377–391; T. G. Ryan and J. Bisson, "Can Ethics Be Taught?," *International Journal of Business and Social Science*,2 (2011): 44–52; K. Schrier, "Designing and Using Games to Teach Ethics and Ethical Thinking," in *Learning, Education and Games Vol. 1: Curricular and Design Considerations*, ed. K. Schrier (Pittsburgh: ETC Press, 2014). Fantastical environments may help make learning more meaningful, therefore, enhancing understanding, retention, and interest in the topic. On the other hand, if topics and skills are taught in a fantastic environment, is it harder to apply it to real-life contexts outside of the game? This is still an open question. See also, G. Kaufman, M. Flanagan, and M. Seidman. "Creating Stealth Game Interventions for Attitude and Behavior Change: An 'Embedded Design' Model." DIGRA 2015, Proceedings of the Digital Games Research Association (DiGRA), 2015, http://www.digra.org/digital-library/publications/creating-stealth-game-interventions-for-attitude-and-behavior-change-an-embedded-design-model/.

Chapter 5

1. Holly Korbey, *Building Better Citizens: A New Civics Education for All* (Lanham, MD: Rowman & Littlefield, 2019). The Parkland teens benefited from the Sandra Day O'Connor Law in 2010 being passed in Florida, which is why they had taken a civics course in middle school. See also V. Yee and A. Blinder, "National School Walkout," *New York Times*, 2018, https://www.nytimes.com/2018/03/14/us/school-walkout.html.

2. The six organizing activists are Nya Collins, 16; Jade Fuller, 15; Kennedy Green, 14; Emma Rose Smith, 15; Mikayla Smith, 16; and Zee Thomas, 15. See more in B. Colyar, "6 Teens Organized a Protest. 10,000 People Showed Up," *New York Magazine*, June 17, 2020, https://www.thecut.com/2020/06/6-teens-organized-a-protest-10-000-people-showed-up.html. And how young people are participating in their local governments to support social change, such as around Black Lives Matter, and anti-racism curricula in their schools. See for instance my own small town's board meeting, on June 22, 2020, via Zoom, https://www.youtube.com/watch?v=YFL cDOXq2I&feature=youtu.be.

3. Players can solve problems through the game by manipulating RNA molecules and creating brand new RNA designs. Other players will vote on different designs that they think work best. The *EteRNA* team then takes those RNA designs and synthesizes them in a lab. The team then again works with the players to do experiments with the molecules to test whether they do, in fact, solve the initial problem. The game platform regularly poses different RNA problems that it needs people to solve, and then invites players to submit

their real-time RNA solutions. Thus, Kim explains, they have found a way to "crowd-source the scientific method." For more information, see EteRNA.org/Carnegie Mellon University/Stanford University, EteRNA, https://eternagame.org/ (accessed June 5, 2020), and K. Schrier, *Knowledge Games: How Playing Games Can Solve Problems, Create Insight, and Make Change* (Baltimore: Johns Hopkins University Press, 2016). Quote by Do Soon Kim, Das Lab, Stanford University, EteRNA, "COVID-19 Vaccines from Scientific Crowdsourcing with Experiments in the Loop," webinar on April 24, 2020, https://www.youtube.com/watch?v=OX36TJQfaIA&feature=youtu.be.

4. EteRNA.org, "Special Announcement: Fight the Coronavirus with Eterna," March 18, 2020, https://eternagame.org/web/news/9804036/; Kim, "COVID-19 Vaccines from Scientific Crowdsourcing." They have created thermodynamically perfect riboswitches,

5. The campaign aims to "develop a COVID-19 vaccine by crowdsourcing scientific ideas ... including experiments." It aims to use the game platform to help create an mRNA vaccines for COVID-19 "for everyone, designed by everyone" through design puzzles related to the "RNA biology of coronaviruses, mRNA vaccines, RNA-based diagnostics, and antiviral strategies based on RNA." They also used games where players play "as the virus" to help predict the sequences of its RNA genome, especially as it mutates and new strains emerge. Quotes by Kim, "COVID-19 Vaccines from Scientific Crowdsourcing." See also EteRNA.org, "Special Announcement."

6. In Jesper Juul, *Half-Real: Video Games between Real Rules and Fictional Worlds* (Cambridge, MA: MIT Press, 2005), he argues that games are both inside and outside of everyday life. They "are 'half real,' in that they cross real and fictional worlds, and that 'to play a video game is therefore to interact with real rules while imagining a fictional world.'" Quote cited in Schrier, *Knowledge Games*, p. 47.

7. See, for instance, J. Lave and E. Wenger, *Situated Learning: Legitimate Peripheral Participation* (Cambridge: Cambridge University Press, 1991); J. S. Brown, A. Collins, and P. Duguid, "Situated Cognition and the Culture of Learning," *Educational Researcher* 18, no. 1 (1989): 32–42. For instance, Brown et al. consider the situated nature of learning, and how cognition is supported through first-hand experiences.

8. See David W. Shaffer's discussion of epistemic games in *How Computer Games Help Children Learn* (New York: Palgrave, 2006). See also Schrier, *Knowledge Games*; K. Schrier, "EPIC: A Framework for Using Video Games for Ethics Education," *Journal of Moral Education* 44, no. 4 (2015): 393–424; and K. Schrier, "Using Games to Solve Real-World Civic Problems: Early Insights and Design Principle," *Journal of Community Engagement and Higher Education* 10, no. 1 (2018): 21–35.

9. National Council for the Social Studies (NCSS), C3 Framework, p. 19.

10. John Dewey, *Democracy and Education* (London, UK and Sterling, VA: Echo Library, 2007)

11. Despite this, only a bit more than half of eligible American voters typically vote in elections (and it's often even lower for young people). People have also been less engaged in their local communities and are spending less time being engaged in civic activities. Jonathan Gould (ed.), *Guardian of Democracy: The Civic Mission of Schools* (Philadelphia: Leonore Annenberg Institute for Civics of the Annenberg Public Policy Center at the University of Pennsylvania, 2011), p. 14. The report explains that between 1973 and 1994, there was a 35% drop in number of people who had served in various local committees and attended local events, and 72% of Americans explained that they did not spend as much time on civic engagement. Voting numbers can also be found at the CIRCLE website at CIRCLE,

https://circle.tufts.edu/ (accessed June 5, 2020). Note that the 2020 election counts are still being calculated, but youth percentage in the United States 2020 presidential election is at around 52–55%. See, CIRCLE, "Election Week 2020: Young People Increase Turnout, Lead Biden to Victory," November 25, 2020, https://circle.tufts.edu/latest-research/election-week-2020.

12. Four of the proven practices in civics education described in the original *Guardians of Democracy* report also relate to taking action as well, including service learning, extracurricular activities, school governance, and simulations. Action civics is specifically cited in the expanded proven practices framework by Peter Levine and Kei Kawashima-Ginsberg, "The Republic Is (Still) at Risk—and Civics Is Part of the Solution" (Medford, MA: Jonathan M. Tisch College of Civic Life, Tufts University, 2017). They write that action civics refers to doing project-based and active learning experiences, such that "students are encouraged to develop identities as citizens (with rights and responsibilities) and when they are encouraged to consider influencing institutional policies along with other options for addressing problems" (p. 5). See also Generation Citizen's curriculum, https://generationcitizen.org/our-programs/our-curriculum/ (accessed June 4, 2020) and Gould, *Guardian of Democracy*. The quote comes from B. Blevins, K. LeCompte, and T. Ellis, "Students at the Heart of Civic Learning: Best Practices in Implementing Action Civics," in *No Reluctant Citizens: Teaching Civics in K-12 Classrooms*, ed. Jeremiah Clabough and Timothy Lintner (Charlotte, NC: Information Age Publishing, Inc., 2018), p. 83.

13. Blevins et al., "Students at the Heart of Civic Learning," p. 85 citing Meira Levinson, *No Citizen Left Behind* (Cambridge, MA: Harvard University Press, 2012), p. 224

14. Blevins et al., "Students at the Heart of Civic Learning," citing J. Westheimer and J. Kahne, "What Kind of Citizen? Politics of Educating for Democracy," *American Educational Research Journal* 41 (2004): 237–269. They explain that schools include a participatory citizen program that alongside other models.

15. The students need to get informed about their local governments by actually looking up where they live or finding out their voting record. Abbott hopes that the exercise of analyzing voting records will stick with students when they become of voting age. Valencia Abbott, personal interview, Spring 2019.

16. of J. Arthur, T. Harrison, E. Taylor-Collins, and F. Moller, "Habit of Service: The Factors that Sustain Service in Young People," The Jubilee Centre for Character & Virtues, 2017, https://www.jubileecentre.ac.uk/userfiles/jubileecentre/pdf/Research%20Reports/A_Habit_of_Service.pdf; Gould, *Guardian of Democracy*.

17. Quoted on page 5 of Arthur et al., "Habit of Service." The authors explain that service is "participating in meaningful action for the benefit of others" and includes activities "such as volunteering, campaigning, and fundraising" (p. 7). In regard to scaffolded civic engagement projects, see M. Janzen and C. Ford, "Scaffolding Civic Engagement Projects: A Study into the Effectiveness of Supported Small-Scale, Interrelated, Student-Designed Projects," *Transformative Dialogues: Teaching and Learning Journal* 13, no. 3 (2020): 9–29.

18. Quoted in Trish Everett, personal interview, Spring 2019.

19. Blevins et al., "Students at the Heart of Civic Learning"; Korbey, *Building Better Citizens*.

20. See for instance K. Schrier, "Guiding Questions for Game-Based Learning," in *International Handbook of Information Technology in Primary and Secondary Education*, ed. D. Gibson (New York: Springer, 2018); Schrier, *Knowledge Games*, and Schrier, *Learning, Education*

& Games Vols. 1, 2, and *3.* The remaining chapters will go into more detail about skills practice.

21. The Fullbright Company, *Gone Home,* https://gonehome.game/
22. The use of limited resources, such as real-time events, money, and time-based activities, adds further authenticity and relevancy to the content of a game, as well as urgency, which further encourages and motivates players. For example, in the iCivics' game, *Crisis of Nations,* a player needs to make real-time decisions about what types of steps their country will take and continue to play, otherwise they will automatically fail.
23. See for example, Shaffer, *How Computer Games Help Children Learn;* Schrier, *Knowledge Games.*
24. Brookings/Wilson Center, *Fiscal Ship,* http://fiscalship.org/ (accessed June 5, 2020); Wilson Center, *Budget Hero,* https://www.wilsoncenter.org/budget-hero (accessed June 5, 2020).
25. Schrier, *Knowledge Games;* Shaffer, *How Computer Games Help Children Learn.*
26. Shaffer, *How Computer Games Help Children Learn;* Schrier, *Knowledge Games;* Brown et al., "Situated Cognition and the Culture of Learning."
27. Shaffer, *How Computer Games Help Children Learn;* Schrier, *Knowledge Games;* Brown et al., "Situated Cognition and the Culture of Learning."
28. See more about the game in K. Schrier, "Revolutionizing History Education: Using Augmented Reality Games to Teach Histori(es)" (MIT thesis, 2005). Also see K. Schrier, "Using Augmented Reality Games to Teach 21st Century Skills," Siggraph '06: ACM Siggraph, 2006, p. 15–19. This type of game, which enables players to explore historic sites, may also help further historical empathy, or the taking on of a historic perspective or mindset. See more about historical empathy in K. Schrier, J. Diamond, and D. Langendoen, "Using Mission US: For Crown or Colony? To Develop Historical Empathy and Nurture Ethical Thinking," in *Ethics and Game Design: Teaching Values through Play,* ed. K. Schrier and D. Gibson (Hershey, PA: IGI Global, 2010). See also K. Schrier, "Designing and Using Games for History and Social Studies," in *Learning and Education Games Volume One: Curricular and Design Considerations,* ed. K. Schrier (Pittsburgh: ETC Press, 2014).
29. Stokes, *Locally Played* Talk, Games for Change, June 30, 2020. Likewise, in *Win the White House,* players are campaigning to be the candidate that wins the United States presidency. While the data in the game is not real, the tools and activities are modeled after real-world creations. The players need to work with media trend reports and state-by-state results to help them create strategies of what to do next to help them win the game. The electoral data and maps in the iCivics game *Win the White House* take on more personal significance because the players vie to win the electoral votes needed to become President of the United States. Players may also learn the terms and practices related to running an election (such as the Electoral College) because the game positions them as candidates on the election trail, and helps to meaningfully situate them in the sociocultural context of the electoral process.
30. Owen Gottlieb, personal interview, Spring 2019; Owen Gottlieb, Jennifer Ash, & Converjent, *Jewish Time Jump,* 2013, http://www.converjent.org/jewish-time-jump-new-york_page/ (accessed June 5, 2020). The game has been played in supplementary Jewish education programs. He goes on to say, "We have photographs from the same angle that we found in the archives. . . . we have images of Washington Square Park in 1909. We have images looking off the park in 1911." For more information, see O. Gottlieb, "Your iPhone

Cannot Escape History, and Neither Can You: Self-Reflexive Design for a Mobile History Learning Game," in *Mobile Learning: Perspectives on Practice and Policy*, ed. D. Herro, S. Arafeh, R. Ling, and C. Holden (Charlotte, NC: Information Age Publishing, 2018), pp. 247–264; O. Gottlieb, "Design-Based Research: Mobile Gaming for Learning Jewish History, Tikkun Olam, and Civics," in Methods for Studying Video Games and Religion, ed. V. Šisler, K. Radde-Antweiler, and X. Zeiler (New York: Routledge, 2017), pp. 83–100; O. Gottlieb, "New Design Principles for Mobile History Games," in *GLS 12 Conference Proceedings*, ed. S. Slater and A. Barany (Pittsburgh: ETC Press, 2017), pp. 211–219. Also, Gottlieb notes that *Jewish Time Jump* was inspired in part by *Reliving the Revolution* and also inspired by Jim Matthews, *Dow Day*, a mobile-based documentary game that places players in 1967 on the campus of University of Wisconsin during a protest of the Dow Chemical Corporation's creation of napalm and its use during the Vietnam War (see more at http://www.jimmathews.info/?page_id=404, accessed on January 5, 2021). Gottlieb also notes that the players also learn about the Uprising of the 30,000, the largest women-led strike in the United States.

31. Schrier, *Knowledge Games*.
32. Ralph Vituccio/Jaehee Cho/Stitchbridge, *Journey through the Camps*, 2018, https://medium.com/stitchbridgevr/a-vr-journey-through-the-concentration-camps-of-the-holocaust-d9c9fe7beed2; Rony Kahana, Na-Yeon Kim, Candace Li, M. D. Tauseef, Christophe Weidya, and Leona Yang, *Mind Field*, https://www.na-yeon.com/mind-field and http://mocking-birds.etc.cmu.edu/ (the game may not be accessible at this link, but was in 2019 when I first began researching the book; both games/experiences discussed during Ralph Vituccio, personal interview, Spring 2019); Alfred Twu, *Bay Area Regional Planner*, https://www.gamesofberkeley.com/bayarearegionalplannr-alfredtwu-atwregionalplanner.html (accessed June 5, 2020).
33. For instance, I write about the game *Way* in K. Schrier and D. Shaenfield, "Collaboration and Emotion in *Way*," in *Emotion, Technology, and Games*, ed. S. Tettegah and W. Huang (New York: Elvesier, 2015). Students can work together on a common and relatable problem that their community faces, which can help players connect more easily.
34. For instance, see Benjamin Stokes, *Locally Played* (Cambridge, MA: MIT Press, 2020). He describes games like *Macon Money*, which used a fictional currency and encouraged real-world connections in Macon, Georgia.
35. See more about these problem-solving real-world games in Schrier, *Knowledge Games*; and K. Schrier, "Designing Learning with Citizen Science and Games," *Emerging Learning Design Journal* 4, no. 1 (2018): Article 3; see more about *Reliving the Revolution* in Schrier, "Revolutionizing History Education." Also see Schrier, "Using Augmented Reality Games to Teach 21st Century Skills"; see more about real-world games in Stokes, *Locally Played* and E. Gordon and P. Mihailidis (eds.), *Civic Media: Technology, Design, Practice* (Cambridge, MA: MIT Press, 2016).
36. *Good Deeds*, https://www.thegoodcards.com/good-deeds/. Unfortunately, Mahalo no longer exists. A similar project is The Dalai Lama Center for Ethics, "Spark Change," https://thecenter.mit.edu/home/sparkchange/, (accessed on January 19, 2021).
37. *Kind Words*, Popcannibal, https://popcannibal.com/kindwords/.
38. See more at N. Mirra and A. Garcia, "Civic Participation Reimagined: Youth Interrogation and Innovation in the Multimodal Public Sphere," *Review of Research in Education* 41 (March 2017): 136–158, and M. H. Rafalow and K. S. Tekinbas, *Welcome to Sackboy*

Planet: Connected Learning Among LittleBigPlanet 2 Players (Irvine, CA: Digital Media and Learning Research Hub, 2014); K. Salen (ed.), *The Ecology of Games: Connecting Youth, Games, and Learning* (Cambridge, MA: MIT Press, 2008); Gideon Dishon and Yasmin B. Kafai, "Connected Civic Gaming: Rethinking the Role of Video Games in Civic Education," *Interactive Learning Environments* (2019), DOI: 10.1080/10494820.2019.1704791.

39. Schrier, "Using Games to Solve Real-World Civic Problems"; P. Mihailidis and R. Gerodimos, "Connecting Pedagogies of Civic Media: The literacies, Connected Civics, and Engagement in Daily Life," in *Civic Media: Technology, Design, Practice*, ed. E. Gordon and P. Mihailidis (Cambridge, MA: MIT Press, 2016); C. McDowell and M. Y. Chinchilla, "Partnering with Communities and Institutions," in *Civic Media*, ed. Gordon and Mihailidis; see also work by Eric Gordon, such as Eric Gordon and Gabriel Mugar, *Meaningful Inefficiencies* (New York: Oxford University Press, 2020).

40. Ralph Vituccio/Jaehee Cho/Stitchbridge, *Journey through the Camps*, 2018, https://medium.com/stitchbridgevr/a-vr-journey-through-the-concentration-camps-of-the-holocaust-d9c9fe7beed2 (accessed June 5, 2020); Rony Kahana, Na-Yeon Kim, Candace Li, MD Tauseef, Christophe Weidya, and Leona Yang, *Mind Field*, https://www.na-yeon.com/mind-field and http://mocking-birds.etc.cmu.edu/ (the game was accessible at this link in spring 2019). Both games discussed during Ralph Vituccio, personal interview, spring 2019; Alfred Twu, *Bay Area Regional Planner*, https://www.gamesofberkeley.com/bayarearegionalplannr-alfredtwu-atwregionalplanner.html (accessed June 5, 2020), discussed during Alfred Twu, personal interview, Spring 2019; and *Argument Wars*, iCivics, https://www.icivics.org/games/argument-wars (accessed June 5, 2020). They explain: "Ever tried to win a disagreement? In *Argument Wars*, you will try out your persuasive abilities by arguing a real Supreme Court case. The other lawyer is your competition. Whoever uses the strongest arguments wins!"

41. Leigh Hallisey, personal interview, Spring 2019. She cited FableVision, *Civics: An American Musical* (beta released at the time of writing this book), https://naomi-greenfield.squarespace.com/blog/?offset=1533308640872 (accessed June 5, 2020) and FableVision/Smithsonian, *Ripped Apart*, https://americanhistory.si.edu/ripped-apart (accessed June 5, 2020); also see EA/Maxis, *Sim City*, https://www.ea.com/games/simcity (accessed June 5, 2020); iCivics, *Counties Work*, https://www.icivics.org/games/counties-work (accessed June 5, 2020), which explains that to learn how to manage local government by playing a county official responding to citizen requests in *Counties Work*, you "Keep citizens happy and evaluate requests …See what county departments have solutions … Maintain a balanced budget by lowering or raising taxes …Work to keep your citizens safe when crisis strikes."

42. For instance, see Korbey, *Building Better Citizens*.

43. For instance, see Blevins et al., "Students at the Heart of Civic Learning"; Levinson, *No Citizen Left Behind*; J. Kahne and E. Middaugh, "Democracy for Some: The Civic Opportunity Gap in High School," CIRCLE Working Paper No. 59 (College Park, MD: CIRCLE, 2008).

44. J. Kahne and E. Middaugh, "Digital Media Shapes Youth Participation," *Phi Delta Kappan* 94, no. 3 (2012): 52–56; K. L. Gray, "Intersecting Oppressions and Online Communities: Examining the Experiences of Women of Color in Xbox Live," *Information, Communication & Society* 15, no. 3 (2012): 411–428; M. E. Ballard and K. M. Welch,

"Virtual Warfare: Cyberbullying and Cyber-Victimization in MMOG Play," *Games and Culture* 12, no. 5 (2017): 466–491.

45. "COVID Near You," Boston Children's Hospital/Harvard Medical Center, https://www. covidnearyou.org/#!/ (accessed June 5, 2020).

46. For instance, see work by Christian Fuchs, Tiziana Terranova, and Safiya Noble, *Algorithms of Oppression* (New York: NYU Press, 2018), and S. Zuboff, *The Age of Surveillance Capitalism* (New York: Public Affairs Press, 2020).

47. Yew Chiew Ping, "Commentary: Rating Citizens—Can China's Social Credit System Fix Its Trust Deficit?," Channel New Asia, 2018, https://www.channelnewsasia.com/news/ commentary/china-social-credit-system-public-deficit-trust-rating-citizens-10925002; Sara Bels, "When Fiction Becomes Reality: From Black Mirror to China's Social Credit Score," Blog, 2018, https://mastersofmedia.hum.uva.nl/blog/2018/09/23/when-fiction-becomes-reality-from-black-mirror-to-chinas-social-credit-score/.

48. Finally, will people do the deeds because they are intrinsically good or will they do it for the points? For more about citizenship participation in government, see G. Sgueo, *Games, Powers, & Democracies*, Milan, Italy: Bocconi University Press, 2018, and work by L. Hassan, "Governments Should Play Games: Towards a Framework for the Gamification of Civic Engagement Platforms," *Simulation & Gaming* 48, no. 2 (2017): 249–267.

49. Other issues include how data is attributed, the trustworthiness of the data collected, the transparency of how the platforms are designed or data is collected and used, and how data is reported and communicated to the public as well as those who are providing the data. See also the issue on ethics in citizen science, L. Rasmussen and Caren Cooper, "Citizen Science Ethics," *Citizen Science: Theory and Practice* 4, no. 1 (2019): 5. See also Schrier, *Knowledge Games*.

50. See also Schrier, *Knowledge Games*.

51. iNK Stories, *Revolution 1979: Black Friday*, https://1979revolutiongame.com/ (accessed June 5, 2020); Killer Snails, *BioDive* and *Scuba Adventure VR*, https://www.killersnails. com/ (accessed June 5, 2020); Fictional game elements can also be also applied to real-world locations to support learning, such as in the case of *Pokémon Go*. Niantic, *Pokémon Go*, https://pokemongolive.com/en/ (accessed June 5, 2020).

52. *Reliving the Revolution* (*RTR*) is one of the first educational augmented reality games (location-based) game, which I designed in the mid-aughts while a graduate student, using MIT's *Environmental Detectives* as a model. Note, the testimonials, while written by me, were based on the real testimonials from the Battle. For more information on the game, or how it was used, please see: Schrier, "Revolutionizing History Education." Also see Schrier, "Using Augmented Reality Games to Teach 21st Century Skills"; E. Klopfer, K. Squire, and H. Jenkins, H., "Environmental Detectives: PDAs as a Window Into a Virtual Simulated World," *Proceedings of IEEE International Workshop on Wireless and Mobile Technologies in Education* (*WMTE '02*) (2002): 95–98. The game's technology is no longer available but it used a phone (Palm Pilot), connected to a GPS device when it was played in 2005.

53. The character, Prince Estabrook, was a real life freed former slave who was a Minuteman solider in the Battle. Prince Estabrook was freed following his service in the military. See more at A. Hinkle, *Prince Estabrook, Slave and Soldier* (Lexington, MA: Pleasant Mountain Press, 2001). Players received slightly different evidence (or no evidence) based on who they are in their role. For instance, players who were a Loyalist might get more transparent

testimonials from British soldiers, but perhaps not from the Minutemen soldiers. However, using roles such as slaves or freed slaves should be handled sensitively so as not to further trauma, misconceptions, and oppression. The ADL counsels against students roleplaying in oppressor roles, for example.

54. Schrier, "Revolutionizing History Education," p. 140. The quotation goes on to say, "It's either that the Americans are the bad guys, and like of course it's going to be different depending on what side your country is on. The same with Iraq, people are going to in years to come when we read about that [War with Iraq] in textbooks it is going to be different."

55. Each time I ran the game, players came up with different hypotheses as to who fired the first shot, which were based on well-reasoned evidence and data that had been collected and digested by the group. We do not know who fired the first shot, but there are multiple theories. During the game, players hypothesized different possibilities such as two guns firing simultaneously or weapons misfiring due to the technologies of that time; the Minutemen having the greater motive to fire because they were not as well-trained and strict in terms of behavior as the British soldiers; or British soldiers firing because "they were angry the Minutemen were holding secret stores of guns and holding them up on the way to Concord." Schrier, "Revolutionizing History Education," pp. 79, 122.(I also wrote the game based on real-life testimonials from people who experienced the battle.)

56. Tools that are external to the game, but provide data, information, or perspectives that feed into the game can also be useful for students. These tools can help to enable students to survey or collect data in their communities and then use it to affect the game.

57. For example, take the drilling apparatuses in the mobile location-based game *Environmental Detectives*, which helps to measure groundwater samples in the real world. Although the oil spill that players are measuring are fictional, the game uses realistic processes and data to analyze. See more at Eric Klopfer, Environmental Detectives, http://web. mit.edu/mitstep/ar/ed.html. See also Klopfer and Squire, "Environmental Detectives."

58. Gordon explains that it is a "tool to facilitate planning processes, to be used ... with government organizations to support public engagement." Eric Gordon, personal interview, Spring 2019.

59. Quote from the Engagement Lab, *Community PlanIt*, 2011, https://elab.emerson.edu/ projects/community-planit. See also E. Gordon and J. Baldwin-Philippi, "Playful Civic Learning: Enabling Reflection and Lateral Trust in Game-Based Public Participation," *International Journal of Communication* 8 (2014): 759–786. The Engagement Lab website goes on to say that "at the same time, they learn about key issues related to the topic of the engagement process, connect with each other, and suggest solutions to problems. Each game culminates in a face-to-face community event, where players meet with each other and discuss the results of the process and next steps with curators of the game and other decision makers."

60. E. Gordon, personal interview, Spring 2019.

61. Dishon and Kafai, "Connected Civic Gaming"; Mirra and Garcia, "Civic Participation Reimagined."

62. See for instance, Bogost et al., *Newsgames*; work by E. Gordon, https://elab.emerson.edu/ projects/.

63. Aparna Khanna, personal interview, Spring 2019.

64. Eric Gordon, *Work Flow*, https://elab.emerson.edu/projects/games-for-social-change/work-flow.
65. Schrier, *Knowledge Games*.
66. Josh Archer, personal interview, Spring 2019.
67. As other personal examples, if there is a game about a health issue recently affecting a family member, or about a trauma that was personally experienced by the player, such as one related to assault or sexual harassment, racism and bias, or loss.
68. Interactivities Ink, *The Road Not Taken*, http://www.interactivitiesink.com/larps/trnt/ (accessed June 5, 2020).
69. Aaron Vanek, personal interview, Spring 2019.
70. Quotes from Alfred Twu, personal interview, Spring 2019. With Twu's game, *Bay Area Regional Planner*, players need to cooperatively work together. He has players role-play as different California regions, and poses authentic problems to the player, such as needing to deal with population growth, deciding whether to invest in water infrastructure and education, or how to handle special interest groups. They need to handle a housing crisis and negotiate different needs such as how to preserve different neighborhoods or balance out traffic. Twu explains that the game also helps to illustrate different real-world perspectives on housing, such as some who want more housing built, others who want more parking instead, some don't want tall buildings, and others who want more affordable housing. Twu explains that in the game, there's a card that says that "you don't want any tall buildings blocking your view … This actually came up one of our city council meeting in Berkeley where we were building something downtown. Some people were saying, oh no, it's going to block the view, but then there were other people who were in support of it because they were providing a large sum of money to affordable housing."
71. C. McDowell and M. Y. Chinchilla, "Partnering with Communities and Institutions," in *Civic Media*, ed. Gordon and Mihailidis.
72. We may not think about all the different ways that games could be designed, and the types of normate assumptions that game designers may make in how people can be able to access it. During the 2019 Super Bowl, for instance, Microsoft made an ad that showed how they were designing controllers and platforms for the realities of their many players. See work in disability studies, such as that of Sky LaRell Anderson, Sky LaRell Anderson and K. Schrier, "Disability and Video Games Journalism: A Discourse Analysis of Accessibility and Gaming Culture," *Unpublished manuscript*; and see Microsoft, Microsoft Xbox Adaptive Controller Super Bowl Ad, 2019, https://www.ispot.tv/ad/IS6b/microsoft-xbox-adaptive-controller-super-bowl-2019-we-all-win.
73. Elizabeth LaPensée, personal interview, Spring 2019.
74. Ibid. LaPensée explains that "While pipelines snake their way through Aki (Earth), thunderbirds walk among us. Winona LaDuke shares a Lakota version of the story which describes a black snake. Christi Belcourt cautions us to remember that snakes are not simply a representation of wrongs. There are snakes which help just as there is a snake which threatens to swallow the lands and waters whole. All life can be honored, and all greed must be recognized." The game also includes art work LaPensée created based on LaPensée's own photos that were taken "of the lands and waters damaged by oil infrastructure as well as the equipment and structures themselves … [and] which express the impact of oil industry on Indigenous lands and waters."

75. Elizabeth LaPensée, "*Thunderbird Strike*: Survivance in/of an Indigenous Video Game," *Video Game Art Reader* 2, no. 1 (2018): 28–37. "No, This Video Game is Not 'Eco-Terrorism,'" *The Verge*, Daniel Starkey, November 1, 2017, https://www.theverge.com/2017/11/1/16588166/game-ecoterrorism-politics-thunderbird; "*Thunderbird Strike*: Controversial Video Game Takes Aim at Oil Industry," CBC Unreserved, Rosanna Deerchild, November 5, 2017, http://www.cbc.ca/radio/unreserved/from-video-games-to-ya-novels-how-indigenous-art-is-evolving-1.4384041/thunderbird-strike-controversial-video-game-takes-aim-at-oil-industry-1.4384559; "Indigenous Game Designer Draws Fire for '*Thunderbird Strike*' Video Game," *Smoke Signals*, Danielle Frost, November 14, 2017, https://www.smokesignals.org/articles/2017/11/14/indigenous-game-designer-draws-fire-for-thunderbird-strike-video-game/. Even if, and especially if, those perspectives are necessary critiques on our current systems and inequities.

Chapter 6

1. CoCo & Co., *Way*, https://makeourway.com/ (accessed June 6, 2020). A player can move their avatar right or left, they can jump, they can lift one or both arms, and they can move their avatar's arm so it gestures to the right or left. They cannot make any sounds except for a "shout" which they can access through a limited array of emoticons (emojis) that they can click on their screen: happy, sad, or angry. Players play simultaneously, but from two separate locations. In this example, I am one of the players, and the other player is a stranger to me.

2. Players are fully interdependent with each other. Players need to let each other know where the platforms are (such as through their avatar's gestures). In *Way*, players can take turns jumping onto platforms and unlocking different parts of the puzzle for the other player, while pointing out to the other player where the platforms are located. The players cannot just say "hey, the platform is to your left"; they have to listen, watch, observe, and see what the other avatar is doing, and then gesture with their own avatar in different ways, hoping that the other player will understand what they are trying to communicate. Sometimes this works fluidly, and a more experienced player will be paired with a novice player, and be able to "teach" them where to go and what to do. The novice player may be confused at first, but eventually most of them will pick up on the cues, and act as they need to so they can both complete the puzzle. Sometimes, however, in a pairing, one of the players will become so frustrated that the other player does not understand what to do (or so guilty that the other player is relying on them, but they don't know what to do), that a player will exit the game (which ends up shutting down the game session for both participants). When I did research on the game, while many of the novice participants felt confused or uncertain at some points during their play, they also seemed to feel appreciative of the help from their coparticipant, and proud that they were able to complete the puzzle and support their partner in this journey. See also, K. Schrier and D. Shaenfield, "Collaboration and Emotion in *Way*," in *Emotion, Technology, and Games*, ed. S. Tettegah and W. Huang (New York, NY: Elvesier, 2015).

3. See, for instance, L. Vygotsky, *The Mind in Society* (Cambridge, MA: Harvard University Press, 1978); E. Bodrova, and D. J. Leong, *Tools of the Mind: The Vygotskian Approach to Early Childhood Education*, 2nd ed. (Columbus, OH: Merrill/Prentice Hall, 2007).

4. They will then begin behaving similarly, such that others now learn from it and enact the behaviors, and so forth. A. Bandura, *Social Learning Theory* (Englewood Cliffs, NJ: Prentice Hall, 1977).

5. W. Frey, "Teaching Virtue: Pedagogical Implications of Moral Psychology," *Science and Engineering Ethics* 16 (2010): 611–628.

6. For instance, see Bandura's work on modeling behavior (Bandura, *Social Learning Theory*); see also K. Schrier, "EPIC: A Framework for Using Video Games for Ethics Education," *Journal of Moral Education* 44, no. 4 (2015): 393–424; J. Belman and M. Flanagan, "Designing Games to Foster Empathy," *Cognitive Technology* 14 (2010): 5–15; K. Schrier, *Knowledge Games: How Playing Games Can Solve Problems, Create Insight, and Make Change* (Baltimore: Johns Hopkins University Press, 2016); work by P. Maclagan on business ethics such as "Conflicting Obligations, Moral Dilemmas and the Development of Judgment Through Business Ethics Education," *Business Ethics: A European Review* 21 (2012): 183–197.

7. J. Arthur, T. Harrison, E. Taylor-Collins, and F. Moller, *Habit of Service: The Factors that Sustain Service in Young People*, The Jubilee Centre for Character & Virtues, 2017, https://www.jubileecentre.ac.uk/userfiles/jubileecentre/pdf/Research%20Reports/A_Habit_of_Service.pdf.

8. National Council for the Social Studies (NCSS), C3 Framework, p 60.

9. For an example of Lave and Wenger's work, see Jean Lave and Etienne Wenger, *Situated Learning: Legitimate Peripheral Participation* (Cambridge, UK: Cambridge University Press, 1991). See also Schrier, *Knowledge Games*, p. 149.

10. Dewey, *Democracy and Education*, p. 261.

11. The public sphere is "a constellation of communicative spaces in society that permit the circulation of information, ideas, debates, ideally in an unfettered manner, and also the formation of political will." E. Colleoni, A. Rozza, and A. Arvidsson, "Echo Chamber or Public Sphere? Predicting Political Orientation and Measuring Political Homophily in Twitter Using Big Data," *Journal of Communication* 64 (2014): 317–332, citing P. Dahlgren, "The Internet, Public Spheres, and Political Communication: Dispersion and Deliberation," *Political Communication* 22, no. 2 (2005): 147–162. See also J. Habermas, *The Structural Transformation of the Public Sphere* (Cambridge, MA: MIT Press, [1962] 1989).

12. Mihailidis and Gerodimos, "Connecting Pedagogies"; McDowell and Chinchilla, "Partnering with Communities and Institutions." Examples of students learning through community involve helping students know the ins and outs of participating in local elections or how to behave and engage at a town hall meeting. This can also help support greater participation in civic communities, and more beneficial public participation.

13. J. Dewey, *Democracy and Education*, New York: Macmillan, 1916; N. Mirra and A. Garcia, "Civic Participation Reimagined: Youth Interrogation and Innovation in the Multimodal Public Sphere," *Review of Research in Education* 41 (March 2017): 136–158, citing H. Boyte, A Different Kind Of Politics: John Dewey and the Meaning of Citizenship in the 21st Century. *The Good Society*, 12, no. 2 (2003): 1–15. To be engaged in citizenship is to be part of a community.

14. For instance, see Nicole Mirra, *Empathy in Action* (New York: Teachers College Press, 2019).

15. See for instance Deniz Eseryel, Dirk Ifenthaler, and Xun Ge, "Towards Innovation in Complex Problem Solving Research: An Introduction to the Special Issue," *Education*

Technology Research and Development 61 (2013): 359–363; John D. Bransford, Ann L. Brown, and Rodney R. Cocking, *How People Learn: Brain, Mind, Experience, and School* (Washington, DC: National Academy Press, 1999); Schrier, *Knowledge Games.*

16. Schrier, *Knowledge Games,* describes different types of problems on pages 56–61. See also W. Hung, "Team-Based Complex Problem Solving: A Collective Cognition Perspective," *Educational Technology Research and Development* 61 (2013): 365–384; Detlef Schoder, Johannes Putzke, Panagiotis Takis Metaxas, Peter A. Gloor, and Kai Fischbach, "Information Systems for 'Wicked Problems'—Research at the Intersection of Social Media and Collective Intelligence," *Business & Information Systems Engineering* 6, no. 1 (2014): 3; J. Introne, R. Lauacher, G. Olson, and T. Malone, "Solving Wicked Social Problems with Socio-computational Systems," *Kunsliche Intelligenz* 27, no. 1 (2013): 45–52; for more about wicked problems see www.wickedproblems.com/1-wicked_problems. php. Wicked problems are ones that are "ill-structured, large-scale, systemic, complex dilemmas... Most are social and political problems are wicked problems ... such as health-care, global warming, and mental illness ... Wicked problems could be figuring out what to do about children who are struggling in school, ... or how to cure illnesses that have both social and scientific causes, such as heart disease," quoting Schrier, *Knowledge Games,* at p. 61. "Resolving wicked problems requires parallel discourse, multiple iterations, changes of beliefs, and unpredictable revisions." Quoted in Schoder et al., "Information Systems for 'Wicked Problems,'" p. 4; S. Wuchty, B. Jones, and B. Uzzi, "The Increasing Dominance of Teams in Production of Knowledge," *Science,* 316(5827), 2007, p. 1036–1039. Also, the sum abilities of the community is even greater than the sum of its individuals, because of synergistic interactions ;Schrier, *Knowledge Games.*

17. Jonathan Gould (ed.), *Guardian of Democracy: The Civic Mission of Schools* (Philadelphia: Leonore Annenberg Institute for Civics of the Annenberg Public Policy Center at the University of Pennsylvania, 2011), p. 23, citing the Center for Social and Emotional Education, "School Climate Guide for District Policymakers and Education Leaders," 2009, New York, NY: Center for Social and Emotional Education Report, https://www.nasmhpd.org/sites/default/files/School%20Climate%20Guide%20for%20 District%20Policymakers%20and%20Education%20Leaders.pdf: "As a matter of defi-nition, a school with a positive climate is one that promotes norms, values, and expec-tations that support people feeling socially, emotionally, and physically safe; supports a sense of unity and cohesion in the school as a community; promotes a culture of respect; and encourages students to consider themselves stakeholders in the school's success. The National School Climate Council perhaps defines school climate best: '[School climate is] the quality and character of school life based on patterns of people's experiences of school life and reflects norms, goals, values, interpersonal relationships, teaching, learning, lead-ership practices, and organizational structures.'"

18. Peter Levine and Kei Kawashima-Ginsberg, "The Republic Is (Still) at Risk—and Civics Is Part of the Solution" (Medford, MA: Jonathan M. Tisch College of Civic Life, Tufts University, 2017), p. 4. Discourse relates to spoken or written language or communication. It often relates to communication around civics and ethics, politics, or public matters.

19. Gould, *Guardian of Democracy.*

20. Colleoni et al., "Echo Chamber or Public Sphere?," citing Dahlgren, "The Internet, Public Spheres, and Political Communication." See also Habermas, *The Structural Transformation of the Public Sphere.*

21. Schrier, "EPIC"; quoting N. Noddings, "Moral Education and Caring," *Theory and Research in Education* 8 (2010): 145–151, p. 147.

22. Argumentation should not foster divisiveness, or stubbornness in one's own views, lack of understanding of each other's views, and fewer interconnections. Rather, dialogue and conversation should enable learning, education, and change. Students should have opportunities to share their own views, listen to other people's views, and even engage in discourse with those who do not agree with them as techniques for enhancing civic discourse. See, for instance, Wayne Journell, "Civic Education in a Post-Truth Society," in *No Reluctant Citizens: Teaching Civics in K-12 Classrooms*, ed. Jeremiah Clabough and Timothy Lintner (Charlotte, NC: Information Age Publishing, Inc., 2018); Holly Korbey, *Building Better Citizens: A New Civics Education for All* (Lanham, MD: Rowman & Littlefield, 2019); see also research on problem-solving in Schrier, *Knowledge Games*; P. Mihailidis and R. Gerodimos, "Connecting Pedagogies of Civic Media: The Literacies, Connected Civics, and Engagement in Daily Life," in *Civic Media: Technology, Design, Practice*, ed. E. Gordon and P. Mihailidis (Cambridge, MA: MIT Press, 2016); C. McDowell and M. Y. Chinchilla, "Partnering with Communities and Institutions," in *Civic Media*, ed. Gordon and Mihailidis; Mark Klein, Paolo Spada, and Raffaele Calabretta, "Enabling Deliberations in a Political Party Using Large-Scale Argumentation: A Preliminary Report." 10th International Conference on the Design of Cooperative Systems, 2012.

23. A. D. Galinsky and G. B. Moskowitz, "Perspective-Taking: Decreasing Stereotype Expression, Stereotype Accessibility, and In-Group Favoritism," *Journal of Personality and Social Psychology* 78, no. 4 (2000): 708–724; A. D. Galinsky, G. Ku, and C. S. Wang, "Perspective-Taking and Self–Other Overlap: Fostering Social Bonds and Facilitating Social Coordination," *Group Processes and Intergroup Relations* 8, no. 2 (2005): 109–124.; C. S. Wang, K. Tai, G. Ku, and A. D. Galinsky, "Perspective-Taking Increases Willingness to Engage in Intergroup Contact," *PLoS One* 9, no. 1 (2014): e85681; C. S. Wang, M. Lee, G. Ku, and A. K. Leung, "The Cultural Boundaries of Perspective-Taking: When and Why Perspective-Taking Reduces Stereotyping," *Personality and Social Psychology Bulletin* 44, no. 6 (2018): 928–943.

24. K. Schrier, "Designing Ourselves," ADL, 2019, https://www.adl.org/media/13011/download, p. xxviii, citing N. Goldstein, I. S. Vezich, and J. R. Shapiro, "Perceived Perspective Taking: When Others Walk in Our Shoes," *Journal of Personality and Social Psychology* 106, no. 6 (2014): 941–960.

25. Moreover, I will also discuss in Chapter 8 that fully listening to others' perspectives and views enhances perspective-taking and empathy, and enables people to more accurately understand and predict people's needs, mindsets, and actions.

26. See, for instance, C. Steinkuehler, K. Squire, and S. Barab (eds.), *Games, Learning, and Society: Learning and Meaning in the Digital Age* (New York: Cambridge University Press). See also Schrier, *Knowledge Games*; Kishonna Gray, *Intersectional Tech: Black Users in Digital Gaming* (Baton Rouge, LA: Louisiana State University, 2020), and T. L. Taylor, *Watch Me Play: Twitch and the Rise of Game Live Streaming* (Princeton, NJ: Princeton University Press, 2018). Players may also use other platforms to communicate and connect while playing games, such as using Twitch, Zoom, and Discord.

27. "Collaboration is the process of shared interaction, creation and completion, which leads to mutually beneficial outcomes) [and] cooperation (the mutually beneficial sharing of goals and tasks, but not necessarily involving direct interaction)." K. Schrier, *Learning,*

Education & Games: Bringing Games into Educational Contexts Vol. 2 (Pittsburgh: ETC Press, 2016); K. Schrier, "Using games to solve real-world civic problems: Early insights and design principles." *The Journal of Community Engagement and Higher Education*. Vol. 10, No. 1. (2018): 21–35.

28. iCivics, *Crisis of Nations*, https://www.icivics.org/games/crisis-nations. Countries can be controlled by other players in the multiplayer mode, or by the computer in the single-player mode.

29. See H. Jenkins, *Convergence Culture* (New York: NYU Press, 2006); ADL/FairPlay Alliance, Creating and Maintaining Community Guidelines for Online Games and Platforms, New York, NY: ADL, https://www.adl.org/media/15451/download, 2020. For instance, the hashtag on Twitter, #ACNH was popular in discussing strategies for *Animal Crossing: New Horizons*; and the *Life Is Strange* game group is on Facebook. See more at Phil Hornshaw, "What is Discord?" *Digital Trends*, May 8, 2020, https://www.digitaltrends.com/gaming/what-is-discord/.

30. For instance, see N. Yee, *The Proteus Paradox: How Online Games and Virtual Worlds Change Us—And How They Don't* (New Haven, CT: Yale University Press, 2014), as well as by Steinkuehler, Squire, and Barab, *Games, Learning, and Society*. Games have been invariably labeled as communities in a variety of ways. According to J. P. Gee and E.R. Hayes, "Nurturing Affinity Spaces and Game-Based Learning," *Cadernos de Letras*, 28, (2011): 19–38, games function as types of "affinity spaces" where people connect through a technologically supported platform to voluntarily share common knowledge, experiences, and interests learn together. Other ways of thinking about games as communities include communities of practice and participatory cultures. In reference to esports in the previous paragraph, see J. Seiner, "All-Girls School Welcomes its First Esports Teams," *AP News*, July 23, 2019, https://apnews.com/article/fe4f959c48c34cd28fb4cb98dacd93eb. See also, J. (G.) Collins, *Esports in Schools: Create a Supportive Gaming Community*, Washington, DC: International Society for Technology in Education, 2020). They also created their own league, the Mischief League, but it closed in March 2020. See more at G. Toppo, "Are Schools Ready for Competitive Video Gaming? By Including Girls and Downplaying First-Person Shooters, Cleveland Teacher Hopes to Chart New Course for 'Esports,'" *The 74*, https://www.the74million.org/article/are-schools-ready-for-competitive-video-gaming-by-including-girls-and-downplaying-first-person-shooters-cleveland-teacher-hopes-to-chart-new-course-for-esports/. Information for this section provided in part by G. Collins, Winter 2021. See also, Kristina Reymann-Schneider, "How Politicians Use Games for their Own Gains," *DW*, October 19, 2020, https://www.dw.com/en/how-politicians-use-video-games-for-their-own-gains/a-55286753.

31. Modeling is a key strategy for character education and ethics education. S. B. Simon, L. W. Howe, and H. Kirschenbaum, "The Values Clarification Approach," in *Vice & Virtue in Everyday Life: Introductory Readings in Ethics*, ed. C. Sommers and F. Sommers (Belmont, CA: Wadsworth/Thomson Learning, 2004), pp. 481–487; N. Noddings, *Caring: A Feminine Approach to Ethics and Moral Education*, 2nd ed. (Berkeley: University of California Press, 2003). For instance, in *Fable III*, a digital role-playing game, two different characters, Reaver and Page, model differing civic perspectives each time the player needs to make a major ethical decision for the fictional land of Albion. In one decision, the player needs to choose whether to build a school or reinstate child labor. Reaver explains that the Queen/King should build a factory, as "There is no greater waste than the idleness of

youth." Whereas Page explains that "the only way Bowerstone will climb out of the gutter is through education…. turn this factory into a school." After you make the choice you can actually see the result: you can explore either a new school or a factory, as well as see the differing financial and social results. One issue with this choice is that longer-term, education may in fact help out more financially and socially, though we never see this result. The school being built lowers funds while the factory raises it. Only shorter-term choices matter because the "coming darkness" ends up killing anyone who isn't protected (money, in this case, equals the protection of citizens, where one dollar is one citizen). It would have been better if the game could model shorter-term versus longer-term civic results dynamically. See more in K. Schrier, "Designing Role-playing Video Games for Ethical Thinking." *Educational Technology Research and Development*. 65, no. 4 (2017): 831–868.

32. Steinkuehler and Oh, "Apprenticeship in Massively Multiplayer Online Games."
33. C. A. Steinkuehler, "Massively Multiplayer Online Gaming as a Constellation of Literacy Practice," *E-Learning* 4, no. 3 (2007): 297–318; C. Steinkuehler and Y. Oh, "Apprenticeship in Massively Multiplayer Online Games," in Steinkuehler and Squire, *Games, Learning, and Society*.
34. D. Shaffer, *How Computer Games Help Children Learn* (New York, NY: Palgrave, 2006).
35. Shaffer, *How Computer Games Help Children Learn*; J. Lave and E. Wenger, *Situated Learning: Legitimate Peripheral Participation* (Cambridge: Cambridge University Press, 1991); B. Rogoff, "Social Interaction as Apprenticeship in Thinking: Guidance and Participation in Spatial Planning," in *Perspectives on Socially Shared Cognition*, ed. L. B. Resnick, J. M. Levine, and S. D. Teasley (Washington, DC: American Psychological Association, 1991); S. Barab and T. Duffy, "Practice Fields to Communities of Practice," in *Theoretical Foundations of Learning Environments*, ed. D.H. Jonassen and S.M. Land (Mahwah, NJ: Lawrence Erlbaum Associates, 2000, p. 25–55); Steinkuehler and Oh, "Apprenticeship in Massively Multiplayer Online Games."
36. C. Jung, "Role of Gamers' Communicative Ecology on Game Community Involvement and Self-Identification of Gamer," *Computers in Human Behavior* 104 (2020): 106164.
37. Y. Kafai and D. Fields, "The Ethics of Play and Participation in a Tween Virtual World: Continuity and Change in Cheating Practices and Perspectives in the Whyville Community," *Cognitive Development* 49 (2019): 33–42.
38. Personal interview, David Shaenfield, Spring 2019; iCivics, *Win the White House*, https://www.icivics.org/games/win-white-house.
39. Schrier, *Knowledge Games*, p. 105. "Many in-game and out-of-game practices acculturate users, such as problem-solving together on a quest, engaging in debates and other social events, or participating on fan sites and blogs."
40. Jung, "Role of Gamers' Communicative Ecology"; C. A. Steinkuehler and D. Williams, "Where Everybody Knows Your (Screen) Name: Online Games as Third Places," *Journal of Computer-Mediated Communication* 11, no. 4 (2006): 885–909; J. Kahne, E. Middaugh, and C. Evans, *The Civic Potential of Video Games* (Cambridge, MA: MIT Press, 2009); L. Molyneux, K. Vasudevan, and H. Gil de Zúñiga, "Gaming Social Capital: Exploring Civic Value in Multiplayer Video Games," *Journal of Computer-Mediated Communication* 20, no. 4 (2015): 381–399; C. Steinkuehler, "Massively Multiplayer Online Video Gaming as Participation in a Discourse," *Mind, Culture, and Activity* 13, no. 1 (2006): 38–52.
41. K. Schrier, "Designing and Using Games to Teach Ethics and Ethical Thinking," in *Learning, Education & Games: Curricular and Design Considerations Vol. 1*, ed. K.Schrier

(Pittsburgh: ETC Press, 2014); Schrier, "Designing Ourselves"; K. Schrier, "Emotion, Empathy and Ethical Thinking in *Fable III*," in *Emotion, Technology, and Games*, ed. S. Tettegah and W. Huang (New York: Elvesier, 2015); K. Schrier and D. Shaenfield, "Collaboration and Emotion in *Way*," in Tettegah and Huang, *Emotion, Technology, and Games*.

42. ADL, *Free to Play? Hate, Harassment, and Positive Social Experiences in Online Games 2020*, December 2020, https://www.adl.org/free-to-play-2020#results (accessed January 12, 2021). I was a fellow at the ADL from 2018–2019, but did not work on this particular study.

43. J. McGonigal, *Reality is Broken: Why Games Make Us Better and How They Can Change the World* (New York, NY: Penguin Press, 2011); Schrier, *Knowledge Games*.

44. Molyneux et al., "Gaming Social Capital"; Gordon and J. Philipp-Baldwin, "Playful Civic Learning: Enabling Reflection and Lateral Trust in Game-based Public Participation," *International Journal of Communication* 8 (2014): 759–786; Schrier, *Designing Ourselves*.

45. Molyneux et al., "Gaming Social Capital."

46. Susan Cain, *Quiet* (New York: Crown, 2012); deep practice in A. Newell and H. Simon, *Human Problem Solving* (Englewood Cliffs, NJ: Prentice Hall, 1972).

47. H. Song, J. Kim, K. Tenzek, and K.M. Lee, "The Effects of Competitiveness Upon Intrinsic Motivation in Exergames," *Computers in Human Behavior* 29 (2013): 702–1708.

48. Their definition of harassment included less severe behaviors such as offensive name-calling (27%), purposeful embarrassment (22%), and more severe behaviors such as physical threats (10%), sustained harassment (7%), stalking (7%), and sexual harassment (6%). Overall, of Americans, 18% had experienced any of the more severe behaviors in the list. See more in Pew Internet Research/M. Duggan, "Online Harassment 2017," July 11, 2017, https://www.pewresearch.org/internet/2017/07/11/online-harassment-2017/.

49. See ADL, "Online Hate and Harassment: The American Experience," 2019, https://www.adl.org/onlineharassment. See also ADL, "More Than One-Third of Americans Experience Severe Online Hate and Harassment," 2019, https://www.adl.org/news/press-releases/more-than-one-third-of-americans-experience-severe-online-hate-and-harassment.

50. See ADL, "Online Hate and Harassment." See also "Free to Play? Hate Harassment and Positive Social Experiences in Games," ADL, 2019, https://www.adl.org/media/13139/download; "Free to Play? Hate Harassment and Positive Social Experiences in Online Games 2020," ADL, December 2020, https://www.adl.org/media/15349/download. In the 2019 ADL report, of respondents surveyed, 67% experienced name-calling, 57% were targets of trolling, 47% were directly harassed, 44% were threatened with physical violence, and 34% were stalked. In the 2020 report, they state that, "70 percent were called offensive names in online multiplayer games, while 60 percent of gamers were the targets of trolling, deliberate and malicious attempts to provoke them to react negatively ... 68 percent of online multiplayer gamers experienced more severe forms of harassment, up from 65 percent in 2019... Forty-eight percent were directly harassed for a sustained period, and 53 percent were discriminated against by a stranger based on their identity. Fifty-one percent were threatened with physical violence, and 44 percent were stalked, their online presence was monitored in the game and the information gathered was used to threaten or harass them. The increase in stalking in online multiplayer games is the largest increase among the year-on-year harassment comparisons--a 10-point increase from 34 percent in 2019." In a 2020 ADL study, 75% of all players reported that their gameplay

was impacted in some way by harassment, such as by stopping playing or avoiding certain games. See also "Disruption and Harms in Gaming Framework," ADL/FairPlay Alliance, 2020, https://fairplayalliance.org/framework/. Trolling means that meaning players were the target of deliberate and malicious attempts to provoke and antagonize them into some form of negative reaction. Trash-talking is a social interaction, often among peers and players, where people jeer each other, possibly trying to intimidate or insult an opponent or teammate. While this may help to reinforce friendship and build camaraderie, it may also perpetuate harm, particularly when trash-talking includes hate speech or identity-based insults. The line between support and cruelty is very blurred. See also, S. Ortiz, "'You Can Say I Got Desensitized to It': How Men of Color Cope with Everyday Racism in Online Gaming," *Sociological Perspectives* 62, no.4 (2019): 572–588. In terms of standing up to bullies in online games, see, C. D'Anastasio, "BLM Supporters More Likely to Combat Hate in Videogames, Too," *Wired*, August 10, 2020, https://www.wired.com/story/blm-supporters-more-likely-combat-hate-videogames-survey/; L. Cary, J. Axt, A. Chasteen, "The Interplay of Individual Differences, Norms, and Group Identification in Predicting Prejudiced Behavior in Online Video Game Interactions," *Journal of Applied Social Psychology* 50, no. 11 (2020): 1–15. More research is needed to resolve the connection among gameplay, culture, and harm. Do games that have more prosocial game mechanics support more collaborative and community-minded interactions? Or is it a mix of the context, people, gameplay, and polities and moderation? These questions need to be considered further.

51. Gideon Dishon and Yasmin B. Kafai, "Connected Civic Gaming: Rethinking the Role of Video Games in Civic Education," *Interactive Learning Environments* (2019), DOI: 10.1080/10494820.2019.1704791; S. Chess and A. Shaw, "A Conspiracy of Fishes, or, How We Learned to Stop Worrying About #GamerGate and Embrace Hegemonic Masculinity," *Journal of Broadcasting & Electronic Media* 59, no. 1 (2015): 208–220; K. L Gray, "Intersecting Oppressions and Online Communities: Examining the Experiences of Women of Color in Xbox Live," *Information, Communication & Society* 15, no. 3 (2012): 411–428; A. Braithwaite, "It's About Ethics in Games Journalism? Gamergaters and Geek Masculinity," *Social Media+Society* 2, no. 4 (2016): 1–10; M. E. Ballard and K. M. Welch, "Virtual Warfare: Cyberbullying and Cyber-Victimization in MMOG Play," *Games and Culture* 12, no. 5 (2017): 466–491; ADL, "Free to Play? Hate Harassment and Positive Social Experiences in Online Games 2020," ADL, December 2020, https://www.adl.org/media/15349/download, they report that *DOTA 2, Call of Duty, League of Legends, Fortnite, Grand Theft Auto*, and *Valorant* were cited by players as the most hostile game environments in terms of harassment. Players may avoid acting as "upstanders" who stop others from engaging in harassing behavior.

52. People connect with people like themselves, such as in terms of their groups, whom they "friend" and converse with. People who are likeminded always tended to group together, but this has increased more recently, such as geographically. Moreover, conversations have moved online rather than just with families, neighbors, at places of worship, or at town halls, where people may have had some trust with each other, but perhaps differing views. For instance, see Journell, "Civic Education in a Post-Truth Society," which cites useful research on political homophily by C. H. Clark and P.G. Avery, "The Psychology of Controversial Issues Discussions: Challenges and Opportunities in a Polarized, Post-9/11 Society," in *Reassessing the Social Studies Curriculum: Promoting Critical Civic Engagement*

in a Politically Polarized, Post-9/11 World, ed. W. Journell (Lanham, MD: Rowman & Littlefield, 2016), pp. 109–120. See also research on echo chambers in Colleoni et al., "Echo Chamber or Public Sphere?"; S. Jacobson, E. Myung, and S. L. Johnson, "Open Media or Echo Chamber: The Use of Links in Audience Discussions on the Facebook Pages of Partisan News Organizations," *Information, Communication, & Society* 19 (2016): 875–891; A. Mitchell, J. Gottfried, J. Kiley, and K. E. Matsa, "Political Polarization and Media Habits," Pew Research Center, October 21, 2014, https://www.journalism.org/2014/10/21/political-polarization-media-habits/; and a steady decline of Americans' interactions with people who are different than them, for instance see T. H. Sander and R. D. Putnam, "Still Bowling Alone? The Post-9/11 Split," *Journal of Democracy* 21 (2010): 9–16; M. McPherson, L. Smith-Lovin, and J. M. Cook, "Birds of a Feather: Homophily in Social Networks," *Annual Review of Sociology* 27 (2001): 415–444.

53. R. Benjamin, "Introduction," in *Captivating Technology* (Durham, NC: Duke University Press, 2019); K. Gray, *Intersectional Tech: Black Users in Digital Gaming* (Baton Rouge: Louisiana State University Press, 2020).

54. For more about games as participatory cultures, bias and games, and about community moderation and games, see Yasmin Kafai, Carrie Heeter, Jill Denner, and Jennifer Y. Sun, *Beyond Barbie and Mortal Combat* (Cambridge, MA: MIT Press, 2008); Shira Chess, *Ready Player Two* (Minneapolis: University of Minnesota Press, 2017); K. L. Gray and D. J. Leonard, *Woke Gaming* (Seattle: University of Washington Press, 2018); Henry Jenkins, Katie Clinton, Ravi Parushotma, Alice Robison (Daer), and Margaret Weigel, "Confronting the Challenges of Participatory Culture: Media Education for the 21st Century," MacArthur Foundation Paper, 2006, https://www.macfound.org/media/article_pdfs/JENKINS_WHITE_PAPER.PDF; Jenkins, *Convergence Culture*; K. Schrier, "Reducing Bias through Gaming," *G/A/M/E*, 2019, https://www.gamejournal.it/07_schrier/.

55. A jigsaw method relates to designing an activity such that the students all need to rely on each other to complete it (like puzzle pieces that need to fit together to complete a puzzle). Students also learn from each other. See more at E. Aronson and S. Patnoe, *The Jigsaw Classroom: Building Cooperation in the Classroom*, 2nd ed. (New York: Addison Wesley Longman, 1997).

56. Alfred Twu, *Bay Area Regional Planner*, https://www.gamesofberkeley.com/bayarearegionalplannr-alfredtwu-atwregionalplanner.html (accessed June 5, 2020), discussed during Alfred Twu, personal interview, Spring 2019.

57. J. Quijano, "#BeFearless: Fear of Public Speaking," in *Learning, Education & Games: 100 Games to Use in the Classroom & Beyond (Vol. 3)*, ed. K. Schrier (Pittsburgh: ETC Press, 2019). At the writing of this book, Schell Game's *HistoryMaker VR* is only in the prototype stage, students need to recite speeches and hear them back, or export them for the students or teachers to evaluate. Schell Games, *History Maker VR*, https://www.schellgames.com/games/history-maker-vr (accessed June 4, 2020, when it was still in prototype phase according to the website).

58. O. Jimenez, O. "*Keep Talking and Nobody Explodes*," in *Learning, Education and Games Vol. 3*, ed. K. Schrier; *Keep Talking and No One Explodes*, Steel Crate Games, 2015, http://keeptalkinggame.com/.

59. Jiménez explains that the game needs to be managed properly, particularly because of the side effects and potential stressors associated with virtual reality. Students need to be able

to stop playing at any time, and to be aware of potential problems (such as motion sickness or headaches). Jimenez, "*Keep Talking and Nobody Explodes*"; R. Dormer, E. Cacali, and M. Senna, "Having a Blast with a Computer-Mediated Information Gap Task: *Keep Talking & Nobody Explodes* in the EFL," *The Language Teacher* 41, no. 31 (2017), http://www.jaltpublications.org/files/pdf-article/41.4tlt-wired.pdf

60. Matthew Farber, personal interview, Spring 2019.

61. K. Inkpen, K. S. Booth, M. Klawe, and R. Upitis, "Cooperative Learning in the Classroom: The Importance of a Collaborative Environment for Computer-Based Education," Technical Report 94–95 (Vancouver: Department of Computer Science, University of British Columbia, 1994).

62. Caitlin Daniels, personal interview, Spring 2019.

63. David Shaenfield, personal interview, Spring 2019.

64. David Shaenfield, personal interview, Summer 2020. He used the Flash game *Lasers*, which is no longer available, but other simple games can be effective, too. See more at D. Kuhn, W. Goh, K. Iordanous, and D. Shaenfield, "Arguing on the Computer: A Microgenetic Study of Developing Argument Skills in a Computer-Supported Environment," *Child Development* 79, no. 5 (2008): 1310–1328.

65. K. Salen, *Raising Good Gamers*, 2010, https://clalliance.org/publications/raising-good-gamers-envisioning-an-agenda-for-diversity-inclusion-and-fair-play/; ADL, "Encourage Inclusive and Safe Gaming During COVID-19," https://www.adl.org/blog/encourage-inclusive-and-safe-gaming-during-covid-19 (accessed September 29. 2020). See also work by AnyKey (https://www.anykey.org/en/inclusion-101), Love Has No Labels (https://lovehasnolabels.com/), AbleGamers Charity (https://ablegamers.org/), Take This (https://www.takethis.org/), and I Need Diverse Games (https://ineeddiversegames.org/). See also, ADL and FairPlay Alliance, Disruption and Harms in Online Gaming Framework, https://fairplayalliance.org/wp-content/uploads/2020/12/FPA-Framework.pdf, December 2020.

66. Yasmin B. Kafai, D. Fields, and E. Ellis, "The Ethics of Play and Participation in a Tween Virtual World: Continuity and Change in Cheating Practices and Perspectives in the Whyville Community," *Cognitive Development* 49 (2018): 1–17. See also, Y. Kafai, M. Cook, and D. Fields, "'Blacks Deserve Bodies, Too': Design and Discussion About Diversity and Race in a Tween Virtual World," *Games and Culture*, 5, no. 1 (2010), 43–63.

67. *Minecraft* is a "sandbox game that provides players with a wide range of materials and tools and a great deal of freedom to do whatever they want inside the game space." E. Bertozzi, "Using Games to Teach, Practice, and Encourage Interest in STEM Subjects," in *Learning, Education, & Games Vol. 1*, ed. Schrier; M. Shah, "*Minecraft*," in *Learning, Education, & Games Vol. 3*, ed. Schrier.

68. P. Anderson, "Campus Is Closed, So College Students Are Rebuilding their Schools in *Minecraft*," The Verge, March 31, 2020, https://www.theverge.com/2020/3/31/21200972/college-students-graduation-minecraft-coronavirus-school-closures. To find out more about the Dream SMP server election, and the political parties (including Politicians of Gaming (POG2020) and So We Are Gamers (SWAG2020)), check out, C. D'Anastasio, "In *Minecraft*'s Dream SMP," All the Server's A Stage, *Wired*, January 12, 2021, https://www.wired.com/story/minecraft-dream-smp-political-drama/ and "SWAG2020 vs. POG2020 Election," https://dreamteam.fandom.com/wiki/SWAG2020_vs_POG2020_Election (accessed on January 15, 2021). C. Michael, "Tommyinnit peaks at over 650,000 viewers in Dream SMP finale," January 20, 2021, https://dotesports.com/streaming/news/

tommyinnit-peaks-at-over-650000-viewers-in-dream-smp-finale. This was on the 2020 Inauguration Day in the United States.

69. See Shah, "*Minecraft*"; M. Shah and A. Foster, "Promoting Teachers' Identity Exploration: The Way Forward in Teacher *Education for Game-Based Learning*," Proceedings of the Society for Information Technology & Teacher Education International Conference (Waynesville, NC: Association for the Advancement of Computing in Education [AACE], 2018).; M. Shah and A. Foster, "Examining Game Design Features for Identity Exploration and Change," *Journal of Computers in Mathematics and Science Teaching* 35, no. 4 (2016): 369–384. Also based on Mamta Shah, personal interview, Spring 2019. Mojang Studios/Microsoft, *Minecraft*, https://www.minecraft.net/; see also https://minecraft.gamepedia.com/Minecraft_Wiki.

70. D. Anderson, J. Walker, Y. Kafai, and D. Lui, "The Gender and Race of Pixels: An Exploration of Intersectional Identity Representation and Construction within Minecraft and its Community," FDG'17, August 14–17, 2017, Hyannis, MA.

71. See *PolitiCraft*, 2019, https://www.politicraft.org (accessed June 4, 2020).

72. The game encourages players to step outside their own views and first actively listen to another's perspectives. It has students build on each other's arguments, while also stating their own. *Argument Wars*, iCivics, https://www.icivics.org/games/argument-wars (accessed June 6, 2020). The students need to look, for example, at the fourteenth amendment and also need to construct a statement that summarizes the argument's logic, such as "If segregation hurts Black students' education, then they are treated unequally."

Chapter 7

1. Epic Games, *Fortnite*, https://www.epicgames.com/fortnite/en-US/home (June 7, 2020); the toosie slide emote (based on a song by Drake) is an example of a quick dance emoji (see The Toosie Slide Emote Slides into *Fortnite*, May 29, 2020, https://www.epicgames.com/fortnite/en-US/news/the-toosie-slide-emote-slides-into-fortnite); see also Beano, https://www.beano.com/posts/7-best-fortnite-dances-in-real-life.

2. Ewan Moore, "'Fortnite' and Travis Scott Tore Up the Live Music Rulebook, According to Expert," May 4, 2020, https://www.ladbible.com/technology/gaming-is-travis-scotts-fortnite-show-the-future-of-live-music-20200504; J. Oller, "*Fortnite* Hosting: We the People In Game Fourth of July Discussion on Race," SyFy.com, 2020, ttps://www.syfy.com/syfywire/fortnite-we-the-people-race-discussion; J. Peters, "Epic Used Its Playbook for Forynite Events against Apple and Google," *The Verge*, August 18, 2010, https://www.theverge.com/2020/8/18/21373875/epic-games-fortnite-apple-google-ban-playbook-in-game-events. One of the race events in Fortnite was called the We the People event.

3. See more about social and emotional learning and skills at CASEL, CASEL Core Competences, 2020, https://casel.org/core-competencies/. Thousands of videos have been uploaded or shared of *Fortnite* players dancing. Millions of viewers have watched these, like, "Fortnite Dances In Real Life," June 23, 2018, https://www.youtube.com/watch?v=KHm_-832lYc, which has over two million views as of January 20, 2021.

4. "Identity is a lens by which people interact with others and the world. It is made up of many parts, including age, race, and profession." See K. Schrier, "ADL Mini-Guide to Identity, Bias, and Games," 2018, https://www.adl.org/media/12529/download. This refers to a number of different types of identity, including race and ethnicity, health state (physical

and mental), personal traits (courage, hard worker, connector), religion, parenting status, location, sexual identity and orientation, emotions, social relationships, national origin, and more.

5. For instance, see D. Hart, C. Richardson, and B. Wilkenfeld, "Civic Identity," in *Handbook of Identity Theory and Research*, ed. S. Schwartz, K. Luyckx, and V. Vignoles (New York: Springer, 2011); K. Schrier, "EPIC: A Framework for Using Video Games for Ethics Education," *Journal of Moral Education* 44, no. 4 (2015): 393–424; T. Krettenauer and S. Hertz, "What Develops in Moral Identities? A Critical Review," *Human Development* 58, no. 3 (2015): 137–153. See also The Jubilee Center for Character & Virtues, "A Framework for Character Education in Schools," 2017, https://www.jubileecentre.ac.uk/527/character-education/framework.

6. Quote in Y. Kafai, G. Richard, and B. Tynes, "The Need for Intersectional Perspectives and Inclusive Designs for Games," in *Diversifying Barbie and Mortal Combat*, ed. Y. Kafai, G. Richard, and B. Tynes (Pittsburgh: ETC Press, 2017), p. 7, and citing work by S. Noble and B. Tynes (eds.), *The Intersectional Internet: Race, Sex, Class, and Culture Online* (New York: Peter Lang); K. L. Gray, "Intersecting Oppressions and Online Communities: Examining the Experiences of Women of Color in Xbox Live," *Information, Communication & Society* 15, no. 3 (2012): 411–428; G. Richard, "Gender and Gameplay: Research and Future Directions," in *Playing with Virtuality: Theories and Methods of Computer Game Studies*, ed. B. Bigl and S. Stoppe (New York: Peter Lang, 2013), pp. 269–284; G. T. Richard, "Understanding Gender, Context and Video Game Culture for the Development of Equitable Digital Games and Learning Environments" (PhD diss., New York University, 2013); A. Shaw, "Do You Identify as a Gamer? Gender, Race, Sexuality, and Gamer Identity," *New Media & Society* 14, no. 1 (2012): 28–44. K. Crenshaw and Collins first coined the term "intersectionality" in 1989–1990. See more at K. Crenshaw, "Demarginalizing the Intersection of Race and Sex: A Black Feminist Critique of Antidiscrimination Doctrine, Feminist Theory, and Antiracist Politics," *University of Chicago Legal Forum* (1989): 139–167; K. Crenshaw, "Mapping the Margins: Intersectionality, Identity Politics, and Violence Against Women of Color," *Stanford Law Review* 43, no. 6 (1991): 1241–1299.

7. M. Komarraju and D. Nadler, "Self-Efficacy and Academic Achievement: Why Do Implicit Beliefs, Goals, and Effort Regulation Matter?" *Learning and Individual Differences* 25 (2013): 67–72.

8. References from this paragraph: see Z. Xu and E. E. Jang, "The Role of Math Self-Efficacy in the Structural Model of Extracurricular Technology-Related Activities and Junior Elementary School Students' Mathematics Ability," *Computers in Human Behavior* 68 (2016): 547–555; L. Portnoy and K. Schrier, "Using Games to Support STEM Curiosity, Identity, and Self-Efficacy," *Journal of Games, Self, & Society* 1, no. 1 (2019): 66–96; F. Shams, A. R. Mooghali, F. Tabebordbar, and N. Soleimanpour, "The Mediating Role of Academic Self-Efficacy in the Relationship Between Personality Traits and Mathematics Performance," *Procedia Social and Behavioral Sciences* 29 (2011): 1689–1692; S. Kim, M. Chang, N. Choi, J. Park, and H. Kim, "The Direct and Indirect Effects of Computer Uses on Student Success in Math," in *K-12 STEM Education: Breakthroughs in Research and Practice*, ed. M. Khosrow-Pour (Hershey, PA: IGI Global, 2018), pp. 322–340; S. Cheryan, A. Master, and A. Meltzoff, "Cultural Stereotypes as Gatekeepers: Increasing Girls' Interest in Computer Science and Engineering by Diversifying Stereotypes," *Frontiers of Psychology* 6, no. 49 (2015): 1–8; R. Delgado and J. Stefancic, *Critical Race Theory* (New York: NYU Press, 2001).

9. See, for instance, Wayne Journell, "Civic Education in a Post-Truth Society," in *No Reluctant Citizens: Teaching Civics in K-12 Classrooms*, ed. Jeremiah Clabough and Timothy Lintner (Charlotte, NC: Information Age Publishing, Inc., 2018); Holly Korbey, *Building Better Citizens: A New Civics Education for All* (Lanham, MD: Rowman & Littlefield, 2019); P. Mihailidis and R. Gerodimos, "Connecting Pedagogies of Civic Media: The Literacies, Connected Civics, and Engagement in Daily Life," in *Civic Media: Technology, Design, Practice*, ed. E. Gordon and P. Mihailidis (Cambridge, MA: MIT Press, 2016); C. McDowell and M. Y. Chinchilla, "Partnering with Communities and Institutions," *Civic Media*, ed. Gordon and Mihailidis.

10. To feel more motivated to civically participate, people need to feel they can express identities in a community and like their identities matter, belong, and are represented.

11. The Jubilee Centre for Character & Virtues, "A Framework for Character Education in Schools: The Building Blocks of Character," 2017, https://www.jubileecentre.ac.uk/527/character-education/framework. See also The Jubilee Centre, "A Framework for Character Education in Schools," 2017, https://www.jubileecentre.ac.uk/userfiles/jubileecentre/pdf/character-education/Framework%20for%20Character%20Education.pdf.

12. Eighty-four percent of Generation Z support equality according to Korbey, *Building Better Citizens*; K. Schrier, "Reducing Bias Through Gaming," G/A/M/E, 2019, https://www.gamejournal.it/07_schrier/; Schrier, "Using Games to Solve Real-World Civic Problems: Early Insights and Design Principle," *Journal of Community Engagement and Higher Education 10*, no. 1 (2018): 21–35. See also Pew Internet Research, "On the Cusp of Adulthood and Facing an Uncertain Future: What We Know About Gen Z So Far," https://www.pewsocialtrends.org/essay/on-the-cusp-of-adulthood-and-facing-an-uncertain-future-what-we-know-about-gen-z-so-far/.

13. J. Durlack, R. P. Weissberg, A. B. Dymnicki, R. D. Taylor, and K. B. Schellinger, "The Impact of Enhancing Students' Social and Emotional Learning: A Meta-Analysis of School-Based Universal Interventions," *Child Development* 82, no. 1 (2011): 405–432; R. Taylor, J. Durlack, E. Oberle, and R. Weissberg, "Promoting Positive Youth Development Through School-Based Social and Emotional Learning Interventions: A Meta-Analysis of Follow-Up Effects," *Child Development* 88, no. 4 (2017): 1156–1171.

14. CASEL, CASEL Core Competences, 2020, https://casel.org/core-competencies/. For more about SEL and CASEL see chapter 3.

15. For emotion in ethical decision-making, see Schrier, "EPIC"; K. Schrier, "Emotion, Empathy and Ethical Thinking in Role-Play Participants: A Preliminary Study," in *Emotion, Technology, and Games*, ed. S. Tettegah and W. Huang (New York: Elvesier, 2016); S. Krishnakumar, and D. Rymph, "Uncomfortable Ethical Decisions: The Role of Negative Emotions and Emotional Intelligence in Ethical Decision-Making," *Journal of Managerial Issues* 24 (2012): 321–344; N. Noddings, *Caring: A Feminine Approach to Ethics and Moral Education*, 2nd ed. (Berkeley: University of California Press, 2003); N. Noddings, "Moral Education and Caring," *Theory and Research in Education* 8 (2010): 145–151. Care, connectedness, and empathy are a core component of moral thinking and ethical practice. For emotions and SEL in developing a civic identity, see D. Donahue-Keegan, J. Karatas, V. Elcock-Price, and N. Weinberg, "Social-Emotional Competence: Vital to Cultivating Mindful Global Citizenship in Higher Education," in *Engaging Dissonance: Developing Mindful Global Citizenship in Higher Education (Innovations in Higher Education Teaching and Learning, Vol. 9*, ed. A. Lee and R. Williams (Bingley, UK: Emerald Publishing Limited,

2017), pp. 265–291. Ethical decision-making requires emotions, and it is an emotional process.

16. N. Noddings, "An Ethics of Care," in *Conduct & Character: Readings in Moral Theory*, ed. M. Timmons (Belmont, CA: Wadsworth/Thomson Learning, 2012), pp. 244–254,, quote at p. 244.

17. Ekman identifies six universal emotions that all human beings can access, express, and identify, regardless of their culture or which rules and norms may govern them. These include joy, fear, disgust, and sadness, and they matter in how people make decisions, solve problems, lead, or engage. P. Ekman, W. V. Friesen, M. O'Sullivan, A. Chan, I. Diacoyanni-Tarlatzis, K. Heider, R. Krause, W. A. LeCompte, T. Pitcairn, P. E. Ricci-Bitti, K. Scherer, M. Tomita, and A. Tzavaras, "Universals and Cultural Differences in the Judgments of Facial Expressions of Emotion," *Journal of Personality and Social Psychology* 53, no. 4 (1987): 712–717.

18. Emotions help us to empathize with others, show compassion, and to care for the issues and needs that others care about, so we can communally create a better society. Empathy is important in part because learning is social as we learned in the last chapter; it will be discussed further in chapter 8. Please see M. Farber and K. Schrier, "The Limits and Strengths of Using Digital Games as Empathy Machines," UNESCO Working Paper, 2017, http://unesdoc.unesco.org/images/0026/002619/261993E.pdf (accessed August 30, 2019). Empathy and compassion are different. Empathy refers to feeling what another is feeling or going through. Sympathy is recognizing what another is going through. Compassion is understanding someone else's feelings and wanting to reduce their suffering or pain. These are cited in K. Schrier, "Designing Ourselves," ADL, 2019, https://www.adl.org/media/13011/download, p. 13. However, although we all express and feel emotions, who is allowed to express emotion, which emotions are allowed, and how those emotions are interpreted is affected by sociocultural factors. People are continually grappling with an array of emotions and being able to identify, express, manage, and discuss these emotions both publicly and privately is integral to our humanity and our ability to be participants in society. How do emotions drive us as citizens? How does emotion, including anger, help us to speak up or to make change?

19. Beautiful Glitch, *Monster Prom*, http://monsterprom.pizza/. The game developers also used diversity consultants to ensure the authenticity of their characters. See more at S. Z., "Author and Diversity Consultant Quinn Titus Discusses 'Monster Prom' and Creating Diverse Games," 2020, https://geekdad.com/2020/02/author-and-diversity-consultant-quinn-titus-discusses-monster-prom-and-creating-diverse-games/. The game includes people who are trans and non-binary, though not all pronouns or identities are fully realized in this game. Another game that also enables multiple dating options and gender identities is Schell Games, *Mission: It's Complicated*, https://www.schellgames.com/games/mission-its-complicated/.

20. E. Anderson, J. Walker, Y. Kafai, and D. Lui, "The Gender and Race of Pixels: An Exploration of Intersectional Identity Representation and Construction within *Minecraft* and its Community," in *Proceedings of ACM Foundations of Digital Gaming*, DOI: 10.1145/123 4, Foundations of Digital Games (FDG) 17, Hyannis, MA. Gee describes the metagame as the communities surrounding games in James P. Gee, *What Videogames Have to Teach Us about Learning and Literacy*, (New York: Palgrave, 2003).

21. Richard, "Understanding Gender, Context, and Video Game Culture." T. L. Taylor, "Watch Me Play." People may also grapple with identities in online, maker, and livestreaming communities.

22. For instance, see Kafai et al., *Diversifying Barbie and Mortal Combat*; Schrier, *Designing Ourselves*; N. Yee, *Proteus Paradox* (New Haven, CT: Yale University Press, 2014); T. L. Taylor, *Watch Me Play* (Princeton, NJ: Princeton University Press). In the previous section, the example is based on a personal interview with Alyssa Shaenfield, winter 2021. The "Stars" did not win the SplatFest. Alyssa, however, earned the top rank of Super Star Queen. Nintendo, *Splatoon 2*, 2017. She was also able to buy and trade other clothes for her avatar to wear in the game's public square, where players can come together and interact.

23. Players may see some part of themselves performed through a game, which can enhance their self-efficacy and belongingness, and their ability to express themselves further through the game, as well as beyond the game. See Anderson et al., "The Gender and Race of Pixels."

24. Amber Coleman-Mortley, personal interview, Spring 2019.

25. Players may be able to select or alter a feature of the game. While both terms involve a player's experience being tailored to their own personal interests, customization is distinct from personalization, in that it involves the player actively adjusting the game to their own needs. Yet as I will discuss in the next section, this type of customization is limited. Whose body types, gender identities, pronouns, or characteristics are available affects how much someone can express their identities through a game. For instance, take hair textures, such as Type 4 hair. See more about *The Valley of Gods*, which the author, P. Martineau explains actually got this texture correct for once. P. Martineau, "The First Game to Actually Give a Damn About Natural Black Hair," The Outline, March 16, 2018, https://theoutline.com/post/3749/the-first-game-to-actually-give-a-damn-about-natural-black-hair?zd=2&zi=fgwxy7am. In another online game that I played with my daughter, the dolls with the white skin were available, but those with the black skin were "locked" unless you paid extra for the game. The design of the game and its option matters in how equitable and inclusive the expression of identities is.

26. iCivics, *Crisis of Nations*, https://www.icivics.org/games/crisis-nations (accessed June 8, 2020). It explains that "in *Crisis of Nations*, take the helm of your own country and work with others to solve international problems! As the leader of your own country, you'll have to make tough choices about how to use military, espionage, and economic resources to serve both the best interests of your own country and the larger global community. Navigate a shifting landscape of international allies and enemies as you declare war, broker peace, and increase prosperity at home." Nintendo, *Breath of the Wild*, 2017, https://www.zelda.com/breath-of-the-wild/; Lionhead Studios/Microsoft, *Fable* series, 2004–2009. As of this writing, *Fable 4* may still be in progress. In the original series, players could only choose between a limited set of male and female avatars, both white. Bethesda Softworks, *Skyrim*, 2011, https://elderscrolls.bethesda.net/en/; and BioWare/EA, *Dragon Age* series, 2009–2014, https://www.ea.com/games/dragon-age (accessed June 8, 2020). In *Dragon Age: Inquisition*, you can choose between being a human, elf, Qunari, or a dwarf, among other choices, such as gender and class (limited choices). iCivics, *Win the White House*, https://www.icivics.org/games/win-white-house; Learning Game Network, *Quandary*, https://www.quandarygame.org/; BioWare/EA, *Mass Effect* series, 2007–2017, https://

www.ea.com/games/mass-effect/mass-effect-andromeda; and Bethesda, *Fallout 3, 4, New Vegas*, 2008–2015, https://fallout.bethesda.net/en/.

27. In a sense, this involves the game listening to the player, observing how they approach problems in it, and adjusting as necessary.

28. Nintendo, *Super Mario Wii* (2012), uses a tutorial "frame," where players can keep asking to continue and gain more lives. My kids make good use of this.

29. Or even trying to manage mental health issues or learning disabilities. Certainly, as these types of games begin to be created and used for the purposes of identifying and adapting to various issues, needs and strengths and weaknesses of students, or even as a form of treatment or therapy, we need to carefully consider their ethical issues. For one thing, players should be able to opt in and opt out of this type of treatment, should be aware of what it entails, and should be able to maintain their privacy. There should be no unforeseeable harm done to the player, such as if their data is used, down the line, to adjust whether they get insured medically or get hired for a job. Finally, there would need to be some way that players can verify that they are actually the player—just as one might need to verify that they are the one who is crossing the border into another country, or voting in an election.

30. Catt Small, Phu Nguyen, Eden, and Arielle Martinez, *SweetXHeart*, https://cattsmall.itch.io/sweetxheart, 2019. The game provides a glimpse into individual interactions and their possibility for stress, but does not always fully grapple with bigger questions of systemic racism and a lack of agency within those systems. The scenarios do not show us the systemic results, and instead, just show us the short-term result. For instance, when you tell the boss not to call her a pet name, he agrees and apologizes. Her stress diminishes. She's able to ignore and avoid the catcallers. But what about the stress over time of continually having to navigate these situations—and not have them turn out in one's favor? A system may have helped to understand how larger forces affect personal choices. However, personal stories and individual perspectives are useful to share too—particularly as they may help us to connect emotionally.

31. The notion of games as civic communities builds on the previous concepts such as communities of practice, participatory cultures, or affinity spaces. Though these have different names and degrees of intimacy, the idea is that they are groups that are about sharing, learning and knowledge making, and that the cultural norms, values, and social interactions matter just as much as the fact that they are technologically mediated and part of a game, rather than a classroom, etc. See more in chapter 6, and K. Schrier, *Knowledge Games: How Playing Games Can Solve Problems, Create Insight, and Make Change* (Baltimore: Johns Hopkins University Press, 2016); S. C. Duncan and E. R. Hayes, "Expanding the Affinity Space: An Introduction," in *Learning in Video Game Affinity Spaces*, ed. E. R. Hayes and S. C. Duncan (New York: P. Lang, 2012), pp. 1–22; J. Gee and E. Hayes, "Nurturing Affinity Spaces and Game-Based Learning," in *Games, Learning, and Society: Learning and Meaning in the Digital Age*, ed. C. Steinkuehler, K. Squire, and S. A. Barab (Cambridge: Cambridge University Press, 2012), pp. 129–153; J. Lave, and E. Wenger, *Situated Learning: Legitimate Peripheral Participation* (New York: Cambridge University Press, 1991); K. Salen, "Toward an Ecology of Gaming," in *The Ecology of Games: Connecting Youth, Games, and Learning*, ed. K. Salen (Cambridge, MA: MIT Press, 2008), pp. 1–17. M. Ito, K. Gutierrez, S. Livingstone, B. Penuel, J. Rhodes, K. Salen, J. Schor, J. Sefton-Gree, and S. C. Watkins, *Connected Learning*, (Cambridge, MA: MIT Press, 2012); Y. Kafai

and Q. Burke, *Connected Gaming: What Making Video Games Can Teach Us about Learning and Literacy*, (Cambridge, MA: MIT Press, 2016), and Y. Kafai and D. Fields, *Connected Play: Tweens in a Virtual World* (Cambridge, MA: MIT Press, 2013) all also discuss the idea of connected learning and connected play.

32. For instance, playing as a character may support greater perspective-taking and engagement with its content and perspective-taking and role-playing will be discussed in greater detail in the next chapter. See for instance G. Simonovits, G. Kézdi, and P. Kardos, "Seeing the World Through the Other's Eyes: An Online Intervention Reducing Ethnic Prejudice," *American Political Science Review* 112, no. 1 (2018): 186–193; D. Banakou, P. Hanumanthu, and M. Slater, "Virtual Embodiment of White People in a Virtual Body Leads to a Sustained Reduction in their Implicit Racial Bias," *Frontiers in Human Neuroscience*, November 29, 2016, https://www.frontiersin.org/articles/10.3389/fnhum.2016.00601/full; G. S. Yang, B. Gibson, A. K. Lueke, L. R. Huesmann, and B. J. Bushman, "Effects of Avatar Race in Violent Video Games on Racial Attitudes and Aggression," *Social Psychological and Personality Science* 5, no. 6 (2014): 698–704.

33. See for instance work in Farber and Schrier, "The Limits and Strengths of Using Digital Games"; D. R. Johnson, "Transportation into a Story Increases Empathy, Prosocial Behavior, and Perceptual Bias Toward Fearful Expressions," *Personality and Individual Differences* 52, no. 2, 2012: 150–155, P. M. Bal and M. Veltkamp, Does Fiction Reading Influence Empathy?: An Experimental Investigation on the Role of Transportation, *PloS One* 8, no. 1, 2013: e55341. Though games are different than literature, research suggests that by feeling that this perspective is more familiar to them, because the characters that embody them become more familiar to them, players may more likely consider, accept and take on those perspectives.

34. People may be more open to befriending, interacting with, and taking on the perspective of those who are more similar to them—those in their in-group. They may feel more distant and less familiar with those they deem in an out-group—and also more biased against their views. This can be problematic because we need to connect with and listen to all different people to understand how to better move forward, equitably, fairly, and productively as a society. Moreover, when we see a person as a member of our in-group (rather than from an out-group), it helps us to practice empathy and compassion toward them, and helps us to listen and understand their views. Schrier, "Designing Ourselves"; Schrier, "Reducing Bias Through Gaming"; P. Darvasi, "Empathy, Perspective and Complicity: How Digital Games Can Support Peace Education and Conflict Resolution," 2016, https://unesdoc.unesco.org/ark:/48223/pf0000259928.

35. T. Vescio, G. B. Sechrist, and M. P. Paolucci, "Perspective Taking and Prejudice Reduction: The Mediational Role of Empathy Arousal and Situational Attributions," *European Journal of Social Psychology* 33, no. 4 (2003): 455–472; C. S. Wang, K. Tai, G. Ku, and A. D. Galinsky, "Perspective-Taking Increases Willingness to Engage in Intergroup Contact," *PLoS One* 9, no. 1 (2014): e85681; C. S. Wang, M. Lee, G. Ku, and A. K. Leung, "The Cultural Boundaries of Perspective-Taking: When and Why Perspective-Taking Reduces Stereotyping," *Personality and Social Psychology Bulletin* 44, no. 6 (2018): 928–943; A. D. Galinsky and G. B. Moskowitz, "Perspective-Taking: Decreasing Stereotype Expression, Stereotype Accessibility, and In-Group Favoritism," *Journal of Personality and Social Psychology* 78, no. 4 (2000): 708–724; Darvasi, "Empathy, Perspective, and Complicity."

36. Simonovits et al., "Seeing the World Through the Other's Eyes"; M. R. Nario-Redmond, D. Gospodinov, and A. Cobb, "The Unintended Negative Consequences of Disability Simulations," *Rehabilitation Psychology* 62, no. 3 (2017): 324–333; P. J. C. Adachi, G. Hodson, T. Willoughby, C. Blank, and A. Ha, "From Outgroups to Allied Forces: Effect of Intergroup Cooperation in Violent and Nonviolent Video Games on Boosting Favorable Outgroup Attitudes," *Journal of Experimental Psychology: General* 145, no. 3 (2016): 259–265; J.-L. Á. Castillo, C. P. Cámara, and A. J. Eguizábal, "Prejudice Reduction in University Programs for Older Adults," *Educational Gerontology* 37, no. 2 (2011): 164–190; Wang et al., "Perspective-Taking Increases Willingness to Engage in Intergroup Contact"; Wang et al., "The Cultural Boundaries of Perspective-Taking"; A. D. Galinsky, J. C. Magee, D. H. Gruenfeld, J. A. Whitson, and K. A. Liljenquist, "Power Reduces the Press of the Situation: Implications for Creativity, Conformity, and Dissonance," *Journal of Personality and Social Psychology* 95, no. 6 (2008): 1450–1466; J. F. Dovidio, L. Pagotto, and M. R. Hebl, "Implicit Attitudes and Discrimination Against People with Physical Disabilities," in *Disability and Aging Discrimination: Perspectives in Law and Psychology*, ed. R. L. Wiener and S. L. Willborn (New York, Springer, 2011), pp. 157–183; K. Crowley and M. Jacobs, "Building Islands of Expertise in Everyday Family Activity," in *Learning Conversations in Museums*, ed. G. Leinhardt, K. Crowley, and K. Knutson (Mahwah, NJ: Lawrence Erlbaum Associates, 2002), pp. 333–356; Banakou et al., "Virtual Embodiment of White People"; C. Steinkuehler and Y. Oh, "Apprenticeship in Massively Multiplayer Online Games," in *Games, Learning, and Society: Learning and Meaning in the Digital Age*, ed. C. Steinkuehler, K. Squire, and S. Barab (New York: Cambridge University Press, 2012); Yang et al., "Effects of Avatar Race in Violent Video Games"; Schrier, *Knowledge Games*; Elizabeth Behm-Morawitz, Hillary Pennell, and Ashton Gerding Speno, "The Effects of Virtual Racial Embodiment in a Gaming App on Reducing Prejudice," *Communication Monographs*, 83, no. 3 (2016): 396–418; T. F. Pettigrew and L. R. Tropp, "A Meta-Analytic Test of Intergroup Contact Theory," *Journal of Personality and Social Psychology* 90, no. 5 (2006): 751–783.

37. Finn Geer created this work. However, I collaborated with Finn Geer on this game by providing feedback and direction, and it was paid for by ADL. Quotation by J. Aviles, *Paths to Prejudice Reduction Utilizing Virtual Avatars and Agents*, Dissertation, Penn State, 2017, https://etda.libraries.psu.edu/files/ final_submissions/15444, p. 3.

38. Nonny de la Pena, *One Dark Night*, https://www.youtube.com/watch?v=1hW7WcwdnEg; SBS Australia, "Is Australia Racist? https://www.youtube.com/watch?v=qYWnPMhfO4k. The bias quotation is from ADL, "Education Glossary Terms," https://www.adl.org/education/resources/glossary-terms/education-glossary-terms, Accessed on January 16, 2021. The ADL distinguishes among bias, discrimination, stigma, stereotypes, and prejudice. Prejudice is "a systematically unfavorable attitude or belief toward a specific group of people." Stigma is "a mixture of 'stereotypic beliefs, prejudicial attitudes, and discriminatory actions' directed toward any specific group of people." Stereotypes are "automatic and (often) evaluative judgments of a specific group (e.g., a gender or racial group as being associated with particular characteristics)." And discrimination is "the 'operationalization' of these prejudices in the form of negative actions and behavior toward that group." Biases can be explicitly (deliberately) or implicitly (less consciously) applied. The quotations are taken from, K. Schrier, *Designing Ourselves: Identity, Bias, Empathy, and Game Design*, New York: ADL, June 2019, https://www.adl.org/media/13011/download, p. 19. G. Kaufman and M. Flanagan, "A psychologically "embedded" approach to designing

games for prosocial causes." *Cyberpsychology: Journal of Psychosocial Research on Cyberspace*, 9, no. 3, (2015): article 1. doi: 10.5817/CP2015-3-5. See more about *Awkward Moment* at Tiltfactor Lab, *Awkward Moment*, https://tiltfactor.org/game/awkward-moment/, accessed on January 19, 2021.

39. Chris Ip, "Changing Your Race in Virtual Reality," Engadget, September 28, 2017, https://www.engadget.com/2017/09/28/changing-your-race-in-virtual-reality/, about *1000 Cut Journey*, produced by Courtney Cogburn of Columbia University and Jeremy Bailenson of Stanford University. *Injustice* was created by a student team at the Entertainment Technology Center at Carnegie Mellon. See also, "LBS Faculty, Eugene Ohu wins $234,000 Grant for Virtual Reality Research," https://www.lbs.edu.ng/lbs-faculty-eugene-ohu-wins-234000-grant-for-virtual-reality-research/, Accessed on January 12, 2021. For example, through the game, a person who identifies as Yoruba may learn about the discrimination that someone who is Hausa or Igbo may face.

40. See more at Schrier, "Designing Ourselves," and Schrier, "Reducing Bias Through Gaming"; Simonovits et al., "Seeing the World Through the Other's Eyes"; Nario-Redmond et al., "The Unintended Negative Consequences of Disability Simulations"; Adachi et al., "From Outgroups to Allied Forces"; Castillo et al., "Prejudice Reduction in University Programs"; Wang et al., "The Cultural Boundaries of Perspective-Taking"; Galinsky et al., "Power Reduces the Press of the Situation"; Dovidio, Pagotto, and Hebl, "Implicit Attitudes and Discrimination Against People with Physical Disabilities"; Crowley and Jacobs, "Building Islands of Expertise in Everyday Family Activity"; Banakou et al., "Virtual Embodiment of White People"; Steinkuehler and Oh, "Apprenticeship in Massively Multiplayer Online Games"; Yang et al., "Effects of Avatar Race in Violent Video Games"; Schrier, *Knowledge Games*; Behm-Morawitz et al., "The Effects of Virtual Racial Embodiment"; Pettigrew and Tropp, "A Meta-Analytic Test of Intergroup Contact Theory"; Banakou et al., "Virtual Embodiment of White People."

41. For instance, see V. Lim-Fei, W. Huey Ming, and L. Ming Yew, "Serious Games to Develop Social and Emotional Learning in Students," in *Serious Games*, ed. T. Marsh, M. Ma, M. Oliveira, J. Baalsrud Hauge, and S. Göbel (New York: Springer, 2016).; Dunlap and Rivers, "Beyond Empathy"; M. J. Sutton and K. Allen, *Emotify! The Power of the Human Element in Game-Based Learning, Serious Games and Experiential Education*, EI Games (Independent Publisher), 2019.

42. Ekman et al., "Universals and Cultural Differences."

43. See more games at Literary Safari, *Arm Me with Games*, https://static1.squarespace.com/static/5be9b4aca2772c09d1c1d6ee/t/5c633f9615fcc055fd8e8f83/1550008215459/%23ArmMeWithGames.pdf (accessed September 14, 2020).

44. For instance, see Schrier, "EPIC"; Lim-Fei et al., "Serious Games to Develop Social and Emotional Learning in Students"; Dunlap and Rivers, "Beyond Empathy." See also Krishnakumar and Rymph, "Uncomfortable Ethical Decisions" and K. E. Gerdes, E. A. Segal, K. F. Jackson, and J. L. Mullins, "Teaching Empathy: A Framework Rooted in Social Cognitive Neuroscience and Social Justice," *Journal of Social Work Education* 47 (2011): 109–131. Gerdes et al. explain that "Using the medium of art can be a way to engage people in training or retraining the mirror neurons for affective sharing and the cognitive pathways for self-/other-awareness, mental flexibility, and emotion regulation" (p. 122).

45. *Nevermind: The Game*, https://nevermindgame.com/about/.

46. Chelsea Howe and Michael Molinari, *The End of Us*, 2011, https://www.the-end-of-us.com/. Games help us to confront difficult topics, experiences, and perspectives that we may not have access to in our everyday lives, as well as with our own vulnerabilities.

47. See J. Magnuson, *Loneliness*, https://www.necessarygames.com/my-games/loneliness/flash. Magnuson created this "notgame" for the children and adolescents in Korea who identify as being lonely, as well as "anyone who has ever felt lonely." For more about *Loneliness*, see Sky LaRell Anderson, "*Loneliness*," in *Learning, Education, and Games Vol. 3*, ed. Schrier. Students often comment that although the game is abstract in nature (it just uses squares on a screen), they feel sad, lonely, and even depressed through the experience. Practicing these emotion-related skills can help to support civic engagement and ethical decision-making.

48. See L. Portnoy and K. Schrier, "Using Games to Support STEM Curiosity, Identity, and Self-Efficacy," *Journal of Games, Self & Society* 1, no. 1 (March 2019): 66–96. Also see J. P. Ogle, K. H. Hyllegard, K. Rambo-Hernandez, and J. Park, "Building Middle School Girls' Self-Efficacy, Knowledge, and Interest in Math and Science Through the Integration of Fashion and STEM," *Journal of Family and Consumer Sciences* 109, no. 4 (2017): 33–40. R. Vacca, M. Bromley, J. Leyrer, M. Sprung, and B. Homer, "Designing Games for Emotional Health," in *Learning and Education Games Volume 1*, ed. Schrier; K. Dunlap and S. Rivers, "Beyond Empathy: Games to Foster Teens' Social and Emotional Skills," *Well Played* 7, no. 2 (2018): 132–159; K. Isbister, *How Games Move Us: Emotion By Design* (Cambridge, MA: MIT Press, 2016).

49. A. Foster and M. Shah, "Examining Game Design Features for Identity Exploration and Change," *Journal of Computers in Mathematics and Science Teaching* 35, no. 4 (2016): 369–384, Waynesville, NC: Association for the Advancement of Computing in Education (AACE); M. Shah, A. Foster, and A. Barany, "Projective Reflection: Facilitating Learning as Identity Exploration Through Game-Based Learning," in *Game-Based Learning: Theories, Strategies, and Performance Outcomes*, ed. Y. Baek (Hauppauge, NY: Nova, 2017).

50. Portnoy and Schrier, "Using Games to Support STEM Curiosity."

51. N. Akkuş Çakır, A. Gass, A. Foster, and F. J. Lee, "Development of a Game-Design Workshop to Promote Young Girls' Interest Towards Computing Through Identity Exploration," *Computers & Education* 108 (2017): 115–130.

52. J. Leonard, A. Buss, R. Gamboa, M. Mitchel, O. S. Fashola, T. Hubert, and S. Almughyirah, "Using Robotics and Game Design to Enhance Children's Self-Efficacy, STEM Attitudes and Computational Thinking Skills," *Journal of Science Education and Technology* 25, no. 6 (2016): 860–876.

53. N. Koval-Saifi and J. Plass, "*Antura and the Letters*: Impact and Technical Evaluation," 2018, Washington, DC: World Vision, Inc., https://allchildrenreading.org/wp-content/uploads/2019/07/Antura-Report-Final-Web.pdf; E. Guardiola and A. Czauderna, "Merging Gameplay and Learning in Educational Game Design: The Gameplay Loop Methodology in Antura and the Letters," 12th European Conference on Game Based Learning, 2018, https://www.researchgate.net/publication/328108441_Merging_Gameplay_and_Learning_in_Educational_Game_Design_The_Gameplay_Loop_Methodology_in_Antura_and_the_Letters; E. Guardiola, A. Czauderna, and Y. Samur, "Player-Centred Educational Game Design. The Case of Antura and the Letters," in *Digitalisierung des Bildungssystems: Aufgaben und Perspektiven für die LehrerInnenbildung*, ed. A Bresges & A. Habicher (Münster and New York, NY: Waxmann, 2019). Reports

and publications mentioning Antura, by external institutions and nongovernmental organizations: N. Koval-Saifi, and J. Plass, *Antura and the Letters: Impact and Technical Evaluation* (Washington, DC: World Vision and Foundation for Information Technology Education and Development, 2018), https://allchildrenreading.org/resources/antura-letters-impact-technical-evaluation/; J. Comings, *Assessing the Impact of Literacy Learning Games for Syrian Refugee Children: An Executive Overview of Antura and the Letters and Feed the Monster Impact Evaluations* (Washington, DC: World Vision and Foundation for Information Technology Education and Development, 2018), https://resource-centre.savethechildren.net/node/13365/pdf/eduapp4syria-ie-summary-2018.pdf; K. Y. T. Lim, J. Comings, R. Lee, M. D. Yuen, A. Hilmy, D. Chua, and B. H. Song, *Guide to Developing Digital Games for Early Grade Literacy for Developing Countries* (Quezon City, Philippines: Foundation for Information Technology Education and Development, Inc. and World Vision, Inc., 2018), https://allchildrenreading.org/wordpress/wp-content/uploads/2018/03/Gaming-Guidebook-web-2.pdf.

54. Emmanual Guardiola, personal interview, Spring 2019. The creators of *Antura and the Letters* want to help other displaced populations and are "working with NGOs in Afghanistan to create Pasto and Dari versions as well." They are also creating versions in ten additional languages.

55. Susana Ruiz, personal interview, spring 2019. She asks: how can we use games to enhance the skills of inclusivity and cultural understanding, while also making games themselves more inclusive?

56. See many accounts of people with different gender identities, sexual identities, and races/ethnicities, and discussions of #Gamergate, as well as research by Schrier, "Designing Ourselves," and Schrier, "Reducing Bias Through Gaming"; K. L. Gray and D. J. Leonard, *Woke Gaming* (Seattle: University of Washington Press, 2018); Kafai et al., *Diversifying Barbie and Mortal Combat*.

57. Schrier, *Designing Ourselves*, explains that "biases are even in the algorithms that drive online platforms, such as those behind Facebook and Twitter. This means that biases are embedded in platforms that rely on these algorithms, and their design affects everything from facial recognition to search results, as well as the types of content people see or the friends they make. The algorithms reflect broader social biases, which end up replicating and even furthering social inequity and systemic oppression."

58. *Parable of the Polygons* is an interactive simulation that helps to highlight how individual biases become propagated through systems. N. Case, *Parable of the Polygons*, https://ncase.me/polygons/ (accessed September 14, 2020). Games can also intentionally and unwittingly embed their own biases, with may intersect with individual and group biases. See also Gabriela T. Richard, "Video Games, Gender, Diversity, and Learning as Cultural Practice: Implications for Equitable Learning and Computing Participation Through Games," *Educational Technology* 57, no. 2 (2017): 36–43; Yasmin Kafai, Carrie Heeter, Jill Denner, and Jennifer Y. Sun, *Beyond Barbie and Mortal Combat* (Cambridge, MA: MIT Press, 2008); Shira Chess, *Ready Player Two* (Minneapolis: University of Minnesota Press, 2017); Gray and Leonard, *Woke Gaming*. See also Schrier, "Designing Ourselves"; Schrier, "Reducing Bias through Gaming"; Schrier, "Using Games to Solve Real-World Civic Problems"; Kafai et al., *Diversifying Barbie and Mortal Combat*.

59. The designers of *Valley of the Gods* tried to accurately represent type 4 hair (characterized by tightly coiled hair texture), a hair texture type that is rarely included in games. Martineau, "The First Game to Actually Give a Damn About Natural Black Hair."

60. Anderson et al., "The Gender and Race of Pixels."

61. See more in Schrier, "Designing Ourselves," and Schrier, "Reducing Bias Through Gaming"; Gray and Leonard, *Woke Gaming*; Kafai et al., *Diversifying Barbie and Mortal Combat*; Noble and Tynes, *The Intersectional Internet*; Gray, "Intersecting Oppressions and Online Communities"; Richard, "Gender and Gameplay"; Richard, "Understanding Gender, Context and Video Game Culture"; Shaw, "Do You Identify as a Gamer?"; Crenshaw, "Demarginalizing the Intersection of Race and Sex"; Crenshaw, "Mapping the Margins."

62. R. Benjamin, "Introduction," *Captivating Technology: Race, Carceral Technoscience, and Liberatory Imagination in Everyday Life*, (Durham, NC: Duke University Press, 2019); Anderson et al., "The Gender and Race of Pixels."

63. A. Davisson and D. Gehm, Gaming Citizenship: Video Games as Lessons in Civic Life, *Journal of Contemporary Rhetoric* 4, no. 3–4 (2014): 39–57; N. Mirra and A. Garcia, "Civic Participation Reimagined: Youth Interrogation and Innovation in the Multimodal Public Sphere," *Review of Research in Education* 41 (March 2017): 136–158; quotes from J. A. Banks, "Diversity, Group Identity, and Citizenship Education in a Global Age," *Educational Researcher* 37 (2008): 129–139.

64. See for instance, N. Yee, *Proteus Paradox* (New Haven, CT: Yale University Press, 2014). Are players taking on their own identity in a game, that of a character's or avatar's, or is there is some type of hybrid identity that results? Who is the player playing as? "If there is an avatar in the game, to what extent do players see themselves in their avatar (the digital representation that players control in a game), and to what extent does the avatar reflect back on the player?" Quoted in Farber and Schrier, "The Limits and Strengths of Using Digital Games." In Gee's notion of the projective identity, he argues there is a hybrid identity that is formed between the player's identity and the avatar's identity, where the player makes decisions based in part on how they think the avatar would make decisions. See J. Gee, *What Videogames have to Teach Us About Learning and Literacy* (New York: Palgrave, 2003). Foster and Shah build on this and describe a process of projective reflection, which extends the players' exploration of their projective identities, and which may lead to more permanent identity change. See A. Foster & M. Shah, "Knew Me and New Me: Facilitating Student Identity Exploration and Learning through Game Integration," *International Journal of Gaming and Computer-Mediated Simulations* 8, no. 3 (2016): 39–58. See also more about the complex intersections among games and identity at A. Foster and M. Shah, "Framing and Studying Learning and Identity in Virtual Learning Environments," *Journal of Experimental Education*, January 16, 2021, https://doi.org/10.1080/00220973.2021.1873092.

65. Banakou et al., "Virtual Embodiment of White People"; Yang et al., "Effects of Avatar Race in Violent Video Games."

66. G. Roussos and J. F. Dovidio, "Playing Below the Poverty Line: Investigating an Online Game as a Way to Reduce Prejudice Toward the Poor," *Cyberpsychology: Journal of Psychosocial Research on Cyberspace* 10, no. 2 (2016): 1–24. Following a play of a game, *Spent*, those who understood it already to be systemic were more likely to show

compassionate attitudes, but for those who didn't, they were more likely afterward to be less compassionate.

67. See Schrier, "Designing Ourselves"; Nario-Redmond et al., "The Unintended Negative Consequences of Disability Simulations"; Wang et al., "The Cultural Boundaries of Perspective-Taking"; Adachi et al., "From Outgroups to Allied Forces"; Castillo et al., "Prejudice Reduction in University Programs"; C. Sassenrath, S. D. Hodges, and S. Pfattheicher, "It's All About the Self: When Perspective Taking Backfires," *Current Directions in Psychological Science* 25, no. 6 (2016): 405–410; L. Quillian, "Measuring Racial Discrimination," *Contemporary Sociology* 35, no. 1 (2006): 88–90; L. Quillian, "Does Unconscious Racism Exist?" *Social Psychology Quarterly* 71, no. 1 (2008): 6–11; P. G. Devine, "Stereotypes and Prejudice: Their Automatic and Controlled Components," *Journal of Personality and Social Psychology* 56, no. 1 (1989): 5–18; T. Greitemeyer and D. O. Mügge, "Video Games Do Affect Social Outcomes: A Metaanalytic Review of the Effects of Violent and Prosocial Video Game Play," *Personality and Social Psychology Bulletin* 40 (2014): 578–589; Farber and Schrier, "The Limits and Strengths of Using Digital Games"; M. Flanagan, H. Nissenbaum, J. Belman, and J. Diamond, "A Method for Discovering Values in Digital Games," Digital Games Research Association (DIGRA) 2007 Conference Proceedings, Tokyo; M. Flanagan and H. Nissenbaum, *Values at Play in Digital Games* (Cambridge, MA: MIT Press, 2016); Schrier, "Reducing Bias Through Gaming"; Xuefei (Nancy) Deng, K. D. Joshi, and Robert D. Galliers, "The Duality of Empowerment and Marginalization in Microtask Crowdsourcing: Giving Voice to the Less Powerful Through Value Sensitive Design," *Management Information Systems (MIS) Quarterly* 40, no. 2 (2016): 279–302.

68. Vituccio explains further, "You feel the claustrophobia of the train cars. You hear the people talking about their experiences … You feel the humanity of it … you feel it, you feel the desperation, you feel the, you feel the hopelessness." Ralph Vituccio, personal interview, Spring 2019; Ralph Vituccio/Jaehee Cho/ Stitchbridge, *Journey through the Camps*, 2018, https://medium.com/stitchbridgevr/a-vr-journey-through-the-concentration-camps-of-the-holocaust-d9c9fe7beed2. *Journey through the Camps*, is an interactive virtual reality experience about the Holocaust that mixes realistic events, locations, and sounds with more fictionalized visuals. A question about this experience is whether we should recreate such horrific moments—are we ethically obligated to recreate them and relive them, or should we not recreate them as it is never going to be fully realistic or appropriately emotionally evocative?

69. Nario-Redmond et al., "The Unintended Negative Consequences of Disability Simulations." For more on these limitations, please see Farber and Schrier, "The Limits and Strengths of Using Digital Games"; Schrier, "Designing Ourselves."

70. For instance, when practicing ethical decision-making, people need to negotiate societal values, norms and morals, which requires social and emotional skills. L. Kohlberg, "Stage and Sequence: The Cognitive-Developmental Approach to Socialization," in *Handbook of Socialization Theory and Research*, ed. D. Goslin (Chicago: Rand McNally, 1969), pp. 347–480; Schrier, "EPIC"; Krishnakumar and Rymph, "Uncomfortable Ethical Decisions"; Noddings, *Caring*; N. Noddings, "Moral Education and Caring," *Theory and Research in Education* 8 (2003): 145–151; C. Gilligan, *In a Different Voice: Psychological Theory and Women's Development* (Cambridge, MA: Harvard University Press, 1982); C. Gilligan, "Moral Orientation and Moral Development," in *Woman and Moral Theory*, ed. E. F. Kittay

and D. T. Meyers (Totowa, NJ: Rowman & Littlefield, 1987), p. 19; Kohlberg, "Stage and Sequence"; Lim-Fei et al., "Serious Games to Develop Social and Emotional Learning in Students"; Dunlap and Rivers, "Beyond Empathy."

71. Emotions also affect how we make decisions, as well as how others view our decisions, and the extent to which we can even participate in the decision-making process.

72. In regard to inclusion generally, see Richard, "Video Games, Gender, Diversity." In regard to tips on letter writing in class, some ways to do this are to have students: (1) write to and respond to others in another school to ask them for advice about community problems or issues; take on new roles (such as ones from history or the community) and write letters as if they are that person; write letters using different emotions (fear, happiness, anger) and think about how the letter would change depending on the emotions they are feeling; write letters in response to fictional letters written by the teacher about community, school, or personal needs; talk in teams or as a class about how they might respond to community members or friends that need help; and anonymously put letters in a box and then have students respond to them (however, this last activity would need to be supported in a way that no personal information is shared and no one gets bullied or personally attacked because of any of the letters).

73. *Edith Finch* takes players on a first-person tour of the Finch family by exploring their home. The players can interact with many of the artifacts in the game, but not all of them. Darvasi explains that the game tells the "story of a young girl who goes back to her family home and searches for some answers about the family secrets, that she unearths by exploring the house and finding personal items that belonged to her various relatives who all met untimely demises in the house." The bedrooms each serve as a type of "museum" or even a mausoleum with fossilized artifacts and items that are related to the character that lived there, such as Walter's underground basement bunker, with items such as calendars, cans of peaches, and radio. The game is a focal point of a series of lessons that revolve around helping players better express and explore their identities. Rivers explains that unlike in other lessons, where the game is a prize, in this series of lessons the game is "a launch pad for conversations … We designed a unit that fully embedded game play and understanding of that game as well as building an understanding toward character development and narrative development and identity formation." Paul Darvasi, a teacher at a private all boys school in Toronto, taught the unit over the course of a month in his English language arts class (the pilot of this curriculum ran from November 2018 to January 2019). He would have students take turns playing the game on a big screen and then do activities and discussions around that part of the game, as a "jumping off point for deeper exploration into concepts around identity." The lessons and activities include one where the students need to create a social media posting for a character from Edith Finch, as well as a diary entry, to show the difference between what people may reveal about the identities in public versus in private. In another activity, using the interactive storytelling tool, Twine, students need to take a past story from their life and create two outcomes—one where they think about it more positively and one more negatively. As a final assignment, students make their own "Museum of Me," where they create an assemblage of art work of artifacts related to their identity and create an artist statement about why they chose the pieces they chose, and how they relate to their life. To create the assemblage, they could make a website, a Twine story, or a more hands-on art project of some type. Rivers of iThrive explains that a purpose of the curriculum was also to "show that commercially available games

could be used effectively in the classroom, and when embedded into traditional academic curriculum could meaningfully develop social emotional skills and deeply engage students in learning." When designing the unit, they really thought about how the game and the activities could work together to support their learning objectives. Just as the students were curating their own museums of their own artifacts, reflecting their identity, the curriculum designers also curated activities and lessons, together with the game, to meet their needs. Darvasi explains that the "artifacts in our life … especially with adolescence, say so much about us—the clothes that you wear are part of your external identity. The objects that you show, the status objects, the personal objects, all of these things are the outward markers of identity." All quotations by Paul Darvasi, personal interview, Spring 2019 and Susan Rivers, personal interview, Spring 2019. See also Giant Sparrow, *What Remains of Edith Finch*, http://www.giantsparrow.com/games/finch/. Teachers should be mindful of the difficult content in this game, and consider whether it is appropriate for a K-12 public school setting.

74. For instance, in Molly's bedroom there is a diary you can read, a broken starfish, and a gerbil, while Barbara's room has film reels, movie posters, and a comic book you can read. Paul Darvasi, personal interview, Spring 2019.

75. Some of the exercises helped them consider the identities of the characters in the game, such as one where they created a (public) social media posting and a (private) diary entry for a game character, which helped them to see how people might curate their public persona, and how it might differ from someone's private thoughts, fears, or insecurities. Paul Darvasi, personal interview, Spring 2019.

76. This unit was also used in a very different type of school in Georgia, where the teacher adjusted it for the students. They added, for instance, an additional option for the final project that allowed students to decorate a mask with relics of their identity (the mask serving as a metaphor for the types of ways we publicly present versus who we really are inside). Paul Darvasi, personal interview, Spring 2019.

77. Darvasi explains that, "I think [it] was really important for them to hear that because it's not unusual for boys to struggle with their fathers, and that the relationship can get better and can improve over time." Darvasi explained that although he had had these students for many years, through this unit, he learned more about them through this series of exercises: "I learned a lot about my students and these are some kids I've taught for two or three years and I learned a lot about them and saw them in different perspectives through this unit." Paul Darvasi, personal interview, Spring 2019.

78. All quotations, Paul Darvasi, personal interview, Spring 2019. He says, "they were able to articulate ideas and things that I think a little bit more clearly. I think the most, the most valuable element, they walked away with a, aside from the fact that they were able to take some steps into better communicating about themselves, speaking about themselves, which is really important for boys." See more in P. Darvasi and M. Farber, *Museum of Me Curriculum*, iThrive, 2020, https://ithrivegames.org/museum-of-me-sel-curriculum/.

79. C. Davison, "The Single Most Essential Requirement in Designing a Fall Online Course," May 11, 2020, https://www.hastac.org/blogs/cathy-davidson/2020/05/11/single-most-essential-requirement-designing-fall-online-course.

80. Gideon Dishon and Yasmin B. Kafai, "Connected Civic Gaming: Rethinking the Role of Video Games in Civic Education," *Interactive Learning Environments* (2019), DOI: 10.1080/10494820.2019.1704791.

81. Numinous, *That Dragon, Cancer*, 2016, http://www.thatdragoncancer.com/.

82. K. Schrier, "Would You Kindly Parent? Parenting, Caretaking, and Love in Games," in *Love and Affection in Games, A Design Primer*, ed. Lindsay Grace (New York: Taylor and Francis, 2020).

Chapter 8

1. While this project is not a game per se, it is an interactive experience. See more at, Rainforest Alliance, *Tree*, 2017, https://www.treeofficial.com/. Some of the sentences in this paragraph are taken from my blog post, K. Schrier, "Using Games to Inspire Empathy-Pros and Cons," *Gamasutra*, January 24, 2018, https://www.gamasutra.com/blogs/KarenSchrier/20180124/ 313566/Using_Games_to_Inspire_Empathy__Pros_and_Cons.php?utm_content=buffer-b7507&utm_medium=social&utm_source=twitter.com&utm_campaign=buffer

2. Chris Ip, "Changing Your Race in Virtual Reality," Engadget, September 28, 2017, https:// www.engadget.com/2017/09/28/changing-your-race-in-virtual-reality/, about *1000 Cut Journey*, produced by Courtney Cogburn of Columbia University and Jeremy Bailenson of Stanford University. See also, Courtney Cogburn and the Virtual Human Interaction Lab at Stanford University, *1000 Cut Journey*, 2018, https://vhil.stanford.edu/1000cut/, and C. D. Cogburn, J.N., Bailenson, E. Ogle, T. Asher, and T. Nichols, *1000 Cut Journey*. ACM (Association of Computer Machinery) SIGGRAPH 2018, 2018, DOI: https://doi. org/10.1145/3226552.3226575

3. Perspective-taking may benefit civics and ethics learning, as well as inspires the practice of empathy, respect, and cultural awareness, which in turn may also benefit learning. Castillo, Cámara, Eguizábal describes perspective-taking as the process of cognitively thinking through what one "cognitive approximation between the self and members of the stereotyped group and between the ingroup and the outgroup" (p. 168). J.-L. Á. Castillo, C. P. Cámara, and A. J. Eguizábal, "Prejudice Reduction in University Programs for Older Adults," *Educational Gerontology* 37, no. 2 (2011): 164–190. This book also delves into fostering cultural awareness, sensitivity, and humility through games, though with such limited time and space, I do not expand on it nearly enough.

4. Quote by J. Bailenson, in J. Bailenson, *Experience on Demand: What Virtual Reality Is* (New York: Norton, 2018), referring to Jamil Zaki, Stanford University researcher. Empathy has been debated a lot in terms of how t is used and applied, as it is often more broadly applied to many different types of experiences and actions, including understanding, allyship, care, and acceptance. Researchers have started to unpack the inconsistencies in how empathy is being used, measured, and talked about. For instance, see J. Hall and R. Schwartz, "Empathy Present and Future," *Journal of Social Psychology* 159, no. 3 (2019): 225–243.

5. "Empathy relates to a number of skills that are useful for connecting with others, reducing our negative judgments of others, and helping us better understand each other, such as perspective-taking, communication, listening, interpreting one's and another's emotions, caring about diverse voices, and having respect for others." Schrier, "Designing Ourselves." For more information about these areas, see M. Farber and K. Schrier, "The Limits and Strengths of Using Digital Games as Empathy Machines," UNESCO Working Paper, 2017, https://unesdoc.unesco.org/ark:/48223/pf0000261993_eng; iThrive Games, Empathy Design Kit, 2018, https://ithrivegames.org/wp-content/uploads/2020/05/Empathy_ DesignKit-1.pdf, Accessed on January 1, 2021; K. Schrier and M. Farber, "Open Questions

for Empathy and Games," Proceedings of Connected Learning Conference '18, Connected Learning 2018 (Pittsburgh: ETC Press, 2019); K. Schrier, "EPIC: A Framework for Using Video Games for Ethics Education," *Journal of Moral Education* 44, no. 4 (2015): 393–424; K. Schrier, "Using Games to Solve Real-World Civic Problems: Early Insights and Design Principles," *Journal of Community Engagement and Higher Education* 10, no. 1 (2018): 21–35; J. Haber, *Critical Thinking*, Cambridge, MA: MIT Press, 2020. The Jubilee Centre measures compassion as including a broader number of skills and practices than empathy. In this book I use the terms empathy and compassion more broadly than we should we use them if we are measuring change or identifying specific goals for a game. For more on compassion, see Jubilee Centre, Cultivating Compassion Teacher Handbook, https://www.jubileecentre.ac.uk/userfiles/jubileecentre/pdf/character-education/GratitudeAndCompassion/CultivatingCompassionTeacherHandbook.pdf (Accessed on January 21, 2021).

6. Vescio et al., "Perspective Taking and Prejudice Reduction"; Castillo et al., "Prejudice Reduction in University Programs"; Galinsky et al., "Perspective-Taking and Self–Other Overlap"; Galinsky and Ku, "The Effects of Perspective-Taking"; Wang et al., "The Cultural Boundaries of Perspective-Taking"; Wang et al., "Perspective-Taking Increases Willingness to Engage in Intergroup Contact"; L. R. Tropp and T. F. Pettigrew, "Differential Relationships Between Intergroup Contact and Affective and Cognitive Dimensions of Prejudice," *Personality and Social Psychology Bulletin* 31, no. 8 (2005): 1145–1158; T. F. Pettigrew and L. R. Tropp, "Allport's Intergroup Contact Hypothesis: Its History and Influence," in *On the Nature of Prejudice: Fifty Years after Allport*, ed. J. F. Dovidio, P. Glick, and L. A. Rudman (Oxford: Blackwell, 2005), pp. 262–277.

7. N. J. Goldstein, S. Vezich, and J. R. Shapiro, "Perceived Perspective-Taking: When Others Walk in Our Shoes," *Journal of Personality and Social Psychology* 106, no. 6 (2014): 941–960.

8. Haber, *Critical Thinking*. In addition to facilitating more honest discussions, empathy also turns out to be a powerful control for confirmation bias, the human mind's tendency to accept things that conform to what we already believe and reject things that do not, a flaw in our reasoning that makes us all vulnerable to misunderstanding and manipulation.

9. Haber, *Critical Thinking*.

10. J. Hubburb, "Elementary Civics Education and Diversity (and Inclusion)," in *No Reluctant Citizens*, ed. J. Clabough and T. Lintner (Charlotte, NC: Information Age Publishing, 2018), pp. 37–51, p. 39; Schrier, "Reducing Bias Through Gaming," *G/A/M/E*, 2019, https://www.gamejournal.it/07_schrier/; Castillo et al., "Prejudice Reduction in University Programs"; A. D. Galinsky and G. Ku, "The Effects of Perspective-Taking on Prejudice: The Moderating Role of Self-Evaluation," *Personality & Social Psychology Bulletin* 30, no. 5 (2004): 594–604; A. D. Galinsky and G. B. Moskowitz, "Perspective-Taking: Decreasing Stereotype Expression, Stereotype Accessibility, and In-Group Favoritism," *Journal of Personality and Social Psychology* 78, no. 4 (2000): 708–724; A. D. Galinsky, G. Ku, and C. S. Wang, "Perspective-Taking and Self–Other Overlap: Fostering Social Bonds and Facilitating Social Coordination," *Group Processes and Intergroup Relations* 8, no. 2 (2005): 109–124; A. D. Galinsky, J. C. Magee, D. H. Gruenfeld, J. A. Whitson, and K. A. Liljenquist, "Power Reduces the Press of the Situation: Implications for Creativity, Conformity, and Dissonance," *Journal of Personality and Social Psychology* 95, no. 6 (2008): 1450–1466;; C. S. Wang, M. Lee, G. Ku, and A. K. Leung, "The Cultural Boundaries of Perspective-Taking: When and Why Perspective-Taking Reduces Stereotyping," *Personality and Social Psychology Bulletin* 44, no. 6 (2018): 928–943; C. S. Wang, K. Tai, G. Ku, and A. D. Galinsky,

"Perspective-Taking Increases Willingness to Engage in Intergroup Contact," *PLoS One* 9, no. 1 (2014): e85681.

11. Castillo et al., "Prejudice Reduction in University Programs."

12. Perspective-taking can reduce biased attitudes and behaviors. T. Vescio, G. B. Sechrist, and M. P. Paolucci, "Perspective Taking and Prejudice Reduction: The Mediational Role of Empathy Arousal and Situational Attributions," *European Journal of Social Psychology* 33, no. 4 (2003): 455–472; Castillo et al., "Prejudice Reduction in University Programs"; Galinsky et al., "Perspective-Taking and Self–Other Overlap."

13. To be able to fully participate civically in the world, we need to be culturally adept. "Culture" should not just be a separate study, but should be integrated into all different disciplines, including science, art, and language arts. See Gideon Dishon and Yasmin B. Kafai, "Connected Civic Gaming: Rethinking the Role of Video Games in Civic Education," *Interactive Learning Environments* (2019), DOI: 10.1080/10494820.2019.1704791, https://www.tandfonline.com/doi/full/10.1080/10494820.2019.1704791; H. Jenkins, *Confronting the Challenges of Participatory Culture: Media Education for the 21st Century* (Cambridge, MA: MIT Press, 2009); D. Buckingham and C. Rodriguez-Hoyos, "Learning About Power and Citizenship in an Online Virtual World," *Comunicar* 20, no. 40 (2013): 49–58; M. Ito, S. Baumer, M. Bittanti, d. boyd, R. Cody, B. Herr Stephenson, H. A. Horst, P. G. Lange, D. Mahendran, K. Z. Martinez, C.J. Pascoe, D. Perkel, L. Robinson, C. Sims, and L. Tripp, *Hanging Out, Messing Around, and Geeking Out: Kids Living and Learning with New Media* (Cambridge, MA: MIT Press, 2013). In chapter 2, I problematized the word "civility," and it continues to be problematic. The term "respect" can also be problematized. By respect, I do not mean to imply that people should require acts of propriety or certain types of public behaviors based on their social standing. Unfortunately, the term "respect" may be used, like "civility," to control Black, Brown and other people of color in public spheres. Moreover, by giving "respect" to someone else, I also do not mean we should give credibility to hateful views, acts, or words. Rather, in using the word "respect," I mean to invoke that people should consider others' cultures, perspectives, and views as worthy of regard, evaluation, and care. We should regard each other as worthy human beings. However, we should not tolerate intolerance, and we should not respect hate. The term "respect for others" also relates to US civics standards regarding the respect for the dignity and humanity of others (see more in chapter 3).

14. Cultural factors affect voting and voter turnout. Culture affects all different forms of civic participation, such as in local, state, and national government. See, for instance, effects on voter turnout in the United States, Narren J. Brown, "Political Culture's Effect on Voter Turnout: The 2004 Election and Beyond" (MA thesis, Iowa State University, 2008). In Iran: A. Daghagheleh, "Ambivalent Voting Behavior: Ideology, Efficacy, and the Socioeconomic Dynamic of Voter Turnout in Iran, 1997–2005," *Sociological Forum* 33, no. 4 (2018): 1023–1044; in the Republic of Korea: Hee Yup Yoon, "The Impact of Socioeconomic Factors on Voter Turnout in the Republic of Korea: Empirical Research for the Results of 18th and 19th Presidential Elections," Martin School of Public Policy and Administration (MPA/MPP) Capstone Projects, 2017, https://uknowledge.uky.edu/mpampp_etds/297. For more on how culture affects how people vote, see Chujun Lin, R. Adolphs, and R. M. Alvarez, "Cultural Effects on the Association Between Election Outcomes and Face-Based Trait Inferences," *PloS One* 12, no. 7 (2017), DOI: 10.1371/journal.pone.0180837.

15. Law and culture affect each other in complicated ways, however. Attorney and law professor Steven Schrier, who teaches political science and business law at a large New York state community college, explains that "for most other cases, the law is a product of culture, religion, and what is moral and ethical at the time, and for the most part, law starts out as relatively [culturally] accepted." When culture and law do not go hand-in-hand, sometimes laws can create cultural divides. For instance, in the United States, "Abortions are not prohibited ... There was not a high level of cultural acceptance before the law, and it has remained divisive." At other times, changing laws may help drive further cultural acceptance. For instance, in the United States, "Laws at times ... will be ahead of the culture and will have initially little success in voluntary compliance. Like, smoking in certain places or wearing seatbelts or motorcycle helmets, those laws were initially unpopular and the cultural acceptance developed later, and you can see over time [in the United States] it has become less acceptable to smoke in public places. This cultural shift was mostly driven by the changes in the law." Quotes by Steven Schrier, personal interview, Spring 2019.

16. These terms refer to understanding one's own cultural identity and becoming aware of and accepting of others' cultures. The NEA (National Teacher's Association) defines cultural competence as "having an awareness of one's own cultural identity and views about difference, and the ability to learn and build on the varying cultural and community norms of students and their families. It is the ability to understand the within-group differences that make each student unique, while celebrating the between-group variations that make our country a tapestry." As seen on the NEA website, http://www.nea.org/home/39783.htm (accessed June 27, 2020).

17. Hubburb, "Elementary Civics Education and Diversity."

18. Ibid., p. 39 citing M. Tervalon and J. Murray-Garcia, "Cultural Humility Versus Cultural Competence: A Critical Distinction in Defining Physician Training Outcomes in Multicultural Education," *Journal of Health Care for the Poor and Undeserved* 9 (1998): 117–125(but altering it for a teacher-student context rather than doctor-patient); cultural humility is the "ability to maintain an interpersonal stance that is other-oriented (or open to the other) in relation to aspects of cultural identity that are most important to the [person]" (p. 2). Hook et al., cited in the APA Newsletter, "Reflections on Cultural Humility," 2013, https://www.apa.org/pi/families/resources/newsletter/2013/08/cultural-humility; J. N. Hook, D. E. Davis, J. Owen, E. L. Worthington Jr., and S. O. Utsey, "Cultural Humility: Measuring Openness to Culturally Diverse Clients," *Journal of Counseling Psychology* (2013), DOI: 10.1037/a0032595.

19. Hubburb, "Elementary Civics Education and Diversity." See also Hook et al., "Cultural Humility"; Tervalon and Murray-Garcia, "Cultural Humility Versus Cultural Competence."

20. Matthew Farber and I coauthored a working paper where we identified a number of elements of games that may support empathy. Some of these factors overlap with those that may also support the learning of civics and ethics, such as storytelling, roleplaying, or having agency. See Farber and Schrier, "The Limits and Strengths of Using Digital Games"; see also Schrier, "Reducing Bias Through Gaming"; Schrier, "Designing Ourselves." See also Candida Halton and Tina Cartwright, "Walking in a Patient's Shoes: An Evaluation Study of Immersive Learning Using a Digital Training Intervention," *Frontiers in Psychology* 9, no. 2124 (2018), DOI: 10.3389/fpsyg.2018.02124.

21. See more about role-playing games at S. Deterding and J. Zagal, *Role-Playing Game Studies* (New York: Routledge, 2018).

22. iThrive, *Lives in Balance*, https://ithrivegames.org/ithrive-sim/lives-in-balance/. See also another role-playing game, *Constitutional Crisis*, where players take on roles like government officials and journalists, evaluate information, and make decisions while engaged in a crisis. See more at: iThrive, *Constitutional Crisis*, https://ithrivegames.org/ithrive-sim/constitutional-crisis/

23. K. Schrier, J. Diamond, and D. Langendoen, "Using *Mission US*: For Crown or Colony? To Develop Historical Empathy and Nurture Ethical Thinking," in *Ethics and Game Design: Teaching Values Through Play*, ed. K. Schrier and D. Gibson (Hershey, PA: IGI Global, 2010), pp. 239–261; K. Schrier, "Using Augmented Reality Games to Teach 21st Century Skills," Proceedings of ACM Siggraph 2006, ACM Siggraph 2006, Boston, 2006.

24. Jennifer Worth, personal interview, Spring 2019; L. Morris and G. Wood, "A Model of Organizational Ethics Education," *European Business Review* 23 (2011): 274–286; K. E. Gerdes, E. A. Segal, K. F. Jackson, and J. L. Mullins, "Teaching Empathy: A Framework Rooted in Social Cognitive Neuroscience and Social Justice," *Journal of Social Work Education* 47 (2011): 109–131. N. Doorn and J. O. Kroesen, "Using and Developing Role Plays in Teaching Aimed at Preparing for Social Responsibility," *Science & Engineering Ethics* 19 (2013): 1513–1527; K. M. Brown, "Using Role Play to Integrate Ethics Into the Business Curriculum a Financial Management Example," *Journal of Business Ethics* 13 (1994): 105–110. In fact, role-play and role-playing games have traditionally been strategies for ethics and civics education, such as in the engineering and business ethics classroom, as they support "perspective-taking, self-/other-awareness, and emotional regulation," among other things.

25. Jenny Lim, "Social Studies Unconference," May 13, 2020, https://www.youtube.com/watch?v=UwHgONlOmz4&feature=youtu.be&t=95. Anachronistically, the students could also make Tweets or Instagram posts from those historical perspectives, too.

26. K. Schrier, "Designing Games for Real-World Moral Problem Solving," *Games & Culture*, May 31, 2017, DOI: 10.1177/1555412017711514.

27. G. Simonovits, G. Kézdi, and P. Kardos, "Seeing the World Through the Other's Eyes: An Online Intervention Reducing Ethnic Prejudice," *American Political Science Review* 112, no. 1 (2018): 186–193; cited by Schrier, "Reducing Bias Through Gaming." Quote from K. Schrier, *Designing Ourselves: Identity, Bias, Empathy, and Game Design*. New York: ADL, June 2019, https://www.adl.org/media/13011/download, p. 19.

28. D. Ham, *I Am a Man*, Civil Rights VR app, http://iamamanvr.logicgrip.com/. According to the blog post by C. Klocke, https://design.ncsu.edu/blog/2018/01/25/i-am-a-man-vr-civil-rights-app/, 2018, "One viewer described her response to this scene, "When I heard those words, I was startled. I thought, 'Me? I didn't do anything. I'm just standing here.' Then I realized that's how many African Americans probably feel—then and now. It made me feel, not just imagine, how someone in that situation feels. It was really powerful.'"

29. Akira Thompson, &maybetheywontkillyou, https://rainb.ro/amtwky. See also J. Boykin, "A Game Aims to Simulate the Exeprience of Everyday Racism. Does It Work?" 2016, http://globalcomment.com/a-game-aims-to-simulate-the-experience-of-everyday-racism-does-it-work/. *Injustice* was created by a student team at the Entertainment Technology Center at Carnegie Mellon. A question that we should consider also is how I should even discuss and use these games and experiences to talk about perspective-taking and bias in

this book. By including a series of three games about the experiences of Black males and Black communities, it suggests implicitly that the reader is not a Black person. It also suggests that Black people are an "other" to us, in that we would have to take on the perspectives of them to understand them. This is a problematic setup and I debated how to include these types of experiences without "othering" the perspectives of Black men. While it is important to have experiences where we spend time thinking about and understanding others' lives, we also need to make sure we are not unethically othering these lives, but rather embracing them further. How would I have described these experiences differently if I were a Black man? What types of bias am I fostering in the way I describe these and other games?

30. See work by Bernie DeKoven such as B. DeKoven and H. Gramazio, *The Infinite Playground* (Cambridge, MA: MIT Press, 2020). See also E. Zimmerman and T. Fullerton, PlayThink Talk, September 15, 2020, https://www.gameinnovationlab.com/playthink.

31. Pandemic, Z-Man Games, https://www.zmangames.com/en/games/pandemic/.

32. Darvasi, "Empathy, Perspective and Complicity." See also Schrier, "Designing Ourselves": "Seeing someone as being in one's 'in-group' or in an 'out-group' can be based on one's abilities, race, gender identity, religious affiliation, or even sports or fan interests."

33. K. Schrier, *Knowledge Games: How Playing Games Can Solve Problems, Create Insight, and Make Change* (Baltimore: Johns Hopkins University Press, 2016); P. J. C. Adachi, G. Hodson, T. Willoughby, C. Blank, and A. Ha, "From Outgroups to Allied Forces: Effect of Intergroup Cooperation in Violent and Nonviolent Video Games on Boosting Favorable Outgroup Attitudes," *Journal of Experimental Psychology: General* 145, no. 3 (2016): 259–265; T. Greitemeyer and D. O. Mügge, "Video Games Do Affect Social Outcomes: A Metaanalytic Review of the Effects of Violent and Prosocial Video Game Play," *Personality and Social Psychology Bulletin*, 40 (2014): 578–589. The more time spent together, the more likely we see someone as more like us and in our in-group.

34. CoCo & Co., *Way*, https://makeourway.com/ (accessed June 6, 2020); K. Schrier and D. Shaenfield, "Collaboration and Emotion in *Way*," in *Emotion, Technology, and Games*, ed. S. Tettegah and W. Huang (New York: Elsevier, 2015).

35. Schrier, "Designing Role-Playing Video Games for Ethical Ehinking."

36. K. Schrier, "Designing Role-playing Video Games for Ethical Thinking," *Education Technology Research Development* 65, no. 4 (2014): 831–868.

37. In-game collaborators do not even need to be humanoid. Players have noted their attachment to in-game objects, such as the Companion Cube in *Portal*. P. Darvasi explains that "an overidentification between player and avatar may 'collapse' the two identities and attenuate the critical distance necessary to contemplate the 'nonequivalent singularity' of the other." P. Darvasi, "Empathy, Perspective and Complicity: How Digital Games Can Support Peace Education and Conflict Resolution," 2016, https://unesdoc.unesco.org/ark:/48223/pf0000259928, citing C. Klimmt, D. Hefner, and P. Voderer, "The Video Game Experience as 'True' Identification: A Theory of Enjoyable Alterations of Players' Self-Perception," *Communication Theory* 19 (2009): 351–373; T. Smethurst and S. Craps, "Playing with Trauma: Interreactivity, Empathy, and Complicity in *The Walking Dead* Video Game," *Games and Culture* 10 (2015): 269–290; J. Newman, "The Myth of the Ergodic Videogame," *Game Studies* 2 (2002), http://www.gamestudies.org/0102/newman/. R. Simon, *A Pedagogy of Witnessing: Curatorial Practice and the Pursuit of Social Justice* (New York: SUNY Press, 2014) and J. Cohen, "Defining Identification: A Theoretical Look

at the Identification of Audiences with Media Characters," *Mass Communication & Society* 4 (2001): 245–264. This research on perspective-taking and embodiment is still forthcoming. For instance, I am working on a grant with collaborators and we are investigating whether a first-person perspective in a VR game elicits empathy and compassion, versus observing interactions with characters that embody those perspectives or identities.

38. Schrier, "EPIC," citing L. A. Floyd, F. Xu, R. Atkins, and C. Caldwell, "Ethical Outcomes and Business Ethics: Toward Improving Business Ethics Education," *Journal of Business Ethics* 117 (2013): 753–776. An entire book can be written just on the power of story to immerse, compel, and relay perspectives and share in our humanity. Some initial sources for finding out more about story, civics, ethics, and games, include J. Murray, *Hamlet on the Holodeck*, Revised (Cambridge, MA: MIT Press, 2017); H. Haste and A. Bermudez, "The Power of Story: Historical Narratives and the Construction of Civic Identity," in *Palgrave Handbook of Research in Historical Culture and Education*, ed. M. Carreteri, S. Berger, M. Grever (London: Palgrave Macmillan, 2017), p. 427–447, https://doi.org/10.1057/978-1-137-52908-4_23; S. Levesque, "Why Tell Stories? On the Importance of Teaching Narrative Thinking," *Canadian Issues* Fall, 5–11: (2014) and M. Gregory, *Shaped by Stories: The Ethical Power of Narratives* (Notre Dame, IN: Notre Dame Press, 2009). See also work by on *ZombiePox*, where using a fantastical setting helped players spread and retain more knowledge and information than the nonfantastical version of the game, Pox. G. Kaufman, M. Flanagan, and M. Seidman. "Creating Stealth Game Interventions for Attitude and Behavior Change: An 'Embedded Design' Model." DIGRA 2015, Proceedings of the Digital Games Research Association (DiGRA), 2015, http://www.digra.org/digital-library/publications/creating-stealth-game-interventions-for-attitude-and-behavior-change-an-embedded-design-model/.

39. K. Rajaratnam, *Go and Come Back,*, https://krajaratnam.itch.io/go-and-come-back.

40. *Mocking Birds*, Carnegie Mellon, http://mocking-birds.etc.cmu.edu/ (no longer available at this link).

41. This hearkens back to the need to truly listen. We can decide to directly confront the fact that her role was diminished, we can further query how she feels about it, or we can decide that her role is fine as it stands. The perspective that she shares is based on her life experiences: she explains that she was once seen as someone who was very capable, but after moving to the United States, she feels that people may judge her based on her English.

42. W. Cragg, "Teaching Business Ethics: The Role of Ethics in Business and in Business Education," *Journal of Business Ethics* 16 (1997): 231–245, p. 236. For more about story and ethics, see chapter 12 and see Schrier, "EPIC," citing Floyd et al., "Ethical Outcomes and Business Ethics." They can help "enable the practice of ethical reasoning and experimentation with different moral possibilities. Story allows access into other people's lives and opens us further to practicing empathy … story provides a context to how we view ethics, which helps us further understand ethical issues, our own ethical assumptions, and makes us more ethically self-aware." For instance, in *Life Is Strange*, players are playing as Max Caulfield, a high school student who is trying to help her best friend, Chloe Price. Throughout the game, the player (as Max) needs to make ethical choices that affect the story, such as which conversation responses to share with Kate, a girl who is thinking about committing suicide. The choices you make will impact whether you are able to help save her and keep her from committing suicide; it also impacts the rest of the game, such as how other people treat and view Max, how Max feels about herself, how Kate's parents and

friends respond to her, and whether Max can visit Kate at the hospital and continue to interact with her.

43. Darvasi, "Empathy, Perspective and Complicity."

44. The project was created using actual audio, video, and footage from events in Syria, but recreated so that the player can see the events unfold in real time.

45. Nonny de la Pena, *Project Syria*, quoted in a video on https://docubase.mit.edu/project/project-syria/.

46. E. Liu, "To Challenge Those in Power, Use Stories as a Weapon," Ted.com, March 28, 2017, https://ideas.ted.com/how-to-get-power/. Liu explains that civic power is "that capacity exercised by citizens in public, whether in elections or government or in social and economic arenas. Power in civic life takes many forms: force, wealth, state action, ideas, social norms, numbers. And it flows through many conduits: institutions, organizations, networks, laws and rules, narratives, and ideologies. Map these forms and conduits against each other, and you get what we think of as 'the power structure.'"

47. It helped to make change because it gave a more human perspective to pandemic preparations. Cait S. Kirby, September 7, 2020, https://caitkirby.com/downloads/Fall%202020.html.

48. See Dishon and Kafai, "Connected Civic Gaming"; Jenkins, *Confronting the Challenges of Participatory Culture*; Buckingham and Rodriguez-Hoyos, "Learning About Power and Citizenship"; Ito et al., *Hanging Out, Messing Around, and Geeking Out*.

49. LaPensée and Exquisite Ghost, *Along the River of Spacetime*, https://www.spacetimeriver.com/; Elizabeth LaPensée, personal interview, Spring 2019. By encouraging more stories and games from different cultures, we are also better able to include different cultural views in how we redesign our systems and make social change.

50. A. Davisson and D. Gehm, "Gaming Citizenship: Video Games as Lessons in Civic Life," *Journal of Contemporary Rhetoric* 4, no.3–4 (2014): 39–57, citing Ian Bogost, *Persuasive Games: The Expressive Power of Videogames* (Cambridge, MA: MIT Press, 2007), p. 64; James L. Hoban Jr., "Rhetorical Rituals of Rebirth," *Quarterly Journal of Speech* 66, no. 3 (1980): 275–288; Ian Bogost, *How to Do Things with Videogames* (Minneapolis: University of Minnesota Press, 2011), p. 61.

51. Susanna Ruiz, personal interview, Spring 2019. Take Action Games, *The Directing Game*, https://susanaruiz.org/takeactiongames-thedirectinggame, (accessed on January 23, 2021).

52. Eyal et al. found that exchanging perspectives with someone else through communication helps increase the accuracy. T. Eyal, M. Steffel, and N. Epley, "Perspective Mistaking: Accurately Understanding the Mind of Another Requires Getting Perspective, Not Taking Perspective," *Journal of Personality and Social Psychology* 114, no. 4 (2018): 547–571. Nario-Redmond et al. explain that "imagining oneself in the place of others—rather than taking the other's perspective—is less effective at inducing empathy and help." See Schrier, "Reducing Bias Through Gaming," citing M. R. Nario-Redmond, D. Gospodinov, and A. Cobb, "The Unintended Negative Consequences of Disability Simulations," *Rehabilitation Psychology* 62, no. 3 (2017): 324–333; Wang et al., "The Cultural Boundaries of Perspective-Taking."

53. F. Herrera, J. Bailenson, E. Weisz, E. Ogle, and J. Zaki, "Building Long-Term Empathy: A Large-Scale Comparison of Traditional and Virtual Reality Perspective-Taking," *PLOS One* 13, no. 10 (2018): e0204494.

54. Virtual reality perspective-taking increases cognitive empathy for specific others; see Austin van Loon, Jeremy Bailenson, Jamil Zaki, Joshua Bostick and Robb Willer, *PLoS ONE* 13, no. 8 (2018): pe0202442.

55. H. Farmer, A. Tajadura-Jiménez, and M. Tsakiris, "Beyond the Colour of My Skin: How Skin Colour Affects the Sense of Body-Ownership," *Conscious Cognition* 21, no. 3 (2012): 1242–1256; D. Banakou, P. Hamumanthu, and M. Slater, "Virtual Embodiment of White People in a Black Virtual Body Leads to a Sustained Reduction in Their Implicit Racial Bias," *Frontiers in Human Neuroscience* 10 (2016): 601; Béatrice S. Hasler, Bernhard Spanlang, and Mel Slater, "Virtual Race Transformation Reverses Racial In-Group Bias," *PLOS One* 12, no. 4 (2017): e0174965; Lara Maister, Mel Slater, Maria Sanchez-Vives, and Manos Tsakiris, "Changing Bodies Changes Minds: Owning Another Body Affects Social Cognition," *Trends in Cognitive Science* 19, no. 1 (2015): 6–12.

56. V. Groom, J. N. Bailenson, and C. Nass, "The Influence of Racial Embodiment on Racial Bias in Immersive Virtual Environments," *Social Influence* 4, no. 1 (2009): 1–18.

57. D. Olson and F. Harrell, " 'I Don't See Color': Characterizing Players' Racial Attitudes and Experiences via an Anti-Bias Simulation Videogame," Foundation of Digital Games (FDG) Conference, Virtual, 2020.

58. C. Sassenrath, S. D. Hodges, and S. Pfattheicher, "It's All About the Self: When Perspective Taking Backfires," *Current Directions in Psychological Science* 25, no. 6 (2016): 405–410.

59. See Schrier, "Reducing Bias Through Gaming"; Schrier, *Designing Ourselves*; Sassenrath, Hodges, and Pfattheicher, "It's All About the Self"; Nario-Redmond et al., "The Unintended Negative Consequences of Disability Simulations."

60. H. Rosin, "How Selective Empathy Can Chip Away at Civil Society," KQED, 2019, https://www.kqed.org/mindshift/53476/how-selective-empathy-can-chip-away-at-civil-society.

61. Aviles, "Paths to Prejudice Reduction Utilizing Virtual Avatars and Agents" (PhD diss., Pennsylvania State University, 2017), p. 3.

62. In our working paper, Farber and I also identified the limitations of using games for empathy. Farber and Schrier, "The Limits and Strengths of Using Digital Games."

63. Schrier, "Designing Ourselves"; Schrier, "Reducing Bias Through Gaming"; Greitemeyer and Mügge, "Video Games Do Affect Social Outcomes"; P. J. C. Adachi, G. Hodson, and M. R. Hoffarth, "Video Game Play and Intergroup Relations: Real World Implications for Prejudice and Discrimination," *Aggression and Violent Behavior* 25, Part B (2015): 227–236; T. Greitemeyer, "Playing Video Games Cooperatively Increases Empathic Concern," *Social Psychology* 44 (2013): 408–413.

64. The ADL recommends that these types of simulations not be used, because although they may be well-intentioned, they may "trivialize the experience of the victims and can leave students with the impression at the conclusion of the activity that they actually know what it was like to experience these injustices....They stereotype group behavior and distort historical reality by reducing groups of people and their experiences and actions to one-dimensional representations....They can put students in the position of defending and/or identifying with the oppressors." Schrier, "Designing Ourselves," p. 13.

65. Schrier, "Designing Ourselves."

66. See Victoria Grieve, "What Makes a Game Empathetic," *Serious Play*, June 25, 2020.

67. Perspective-taking may not help support understanding or empathy, and people may not be able to accurately predict another person's views, attitudes or mental state. Schrier, "Designing Ourselves."

68. Nario-Redmond et al., "The Unintended Negative Consequences of Disability Simulations"; Schrier, "Reducing Bias Through Gaming": "For instance, Gloor and Puhl (2016) looks at strategies for reducing weight bias and found that empathy-induction and perspective-taking conditions both enhanced more empathy for people with obesity than the other conditions, but may not reduce overall stigma about weight." J. L. Gloor and R. M. Puhl, "Empathy and Perspective-Taking: Examination and Comparison of Strategies to Reduce Weight Stigma," *Stigma and Health* 1, no. 4 (2016): 269–279.

69. C. D'Anastasio, "Why Video Games Can't Teach You Empathy," *Vice*, May 15, 2015, https://www.vice.com/en_us/article/mgbwpv/empathy-games-dont-exist. See, Anna Antropy, *Dys4ia*, https://freegames.org/dys4ia/, Accessed on January 21, 2021. The game relays Antropy's experiences with hormone replacement therapy and gender dysphoria.

70. See Grieve, "What Makes a Game Empathetic." I learned about this exhibit from this talk by Grieve.

71. D'Anastasio, "Why Video Games Can't Teach You Empathy."

72. Emily Roxworthy quotes Lisa Nakamura as saying, "their performances online use[d] race and gender as amusing prostheses to be donned and shed without 'real life' consequences . . . these identity tourists often [take] their virtual experiences as other-gendered and other-raced avatars as a kind of lived truth." E. Roxworthy, "Revitalizing Japanese American Internment: Critical Empathy and Role-Play in the Musical *Allegiance* and the Video Game *Drama in the Delta*," *Theatre Journal* 66, no. 1 (2014): 93–115, quoting Lisa Nakamura, *Cybertypes: Race, Identity, and Ethnicity on the Internet* (New York: Routledge, 2002), pp. 13–14.. See also J. Kung, "Should Your Avatar's Skin Match Yours," https://www.npr.org/sections/codeswitch/2019/08/31/430057317/should-your-avatars-skin-match-yours, 2019 (accessed September 15, 2020). In the section above this one, see P. Bloom, *Against Empathy: The Case for Rational Compassion* (New York, Ecco, 2016); S. Illing, "The Case Against Empathy," *Vox*, January 16, 2019, https://www.vox.com/conversations/2017/1/19/14266230/empathy-morality-ethics-psychology-compassion-paul-bloom; and B. Ruberg, "Empathy and Its Alternatives: Deconstructing the Rhetoric of 'Empathy,'" *Video Games, Communication, Culture, and Critique* 13, no. 1 (2020), with the quotation from page 67. The problematic application and usage of empathy to games may disproportionately negatively affect players and designers who are from marginalization populations or communities, like the Queer community. In terms of empathy being misapplied to games or overused, or inaccurately used in research, see J. Hall and R. Schwartz, "Empathy Present and Future," *Journal of Social Psychology* 159, no. 3 (2019): 225–243; L. Polansky, "Empathy is Not Enough, Part 1," March 27, 2019, https://rhizome.org/editorial/2019/mar/27/empathy-is-not-enough-part-1/. See also, M. Brice, "empathy machine," June 30 2016, http://www.mattiebrice.com/empathy-machine/. Some of the citations on empathy are thanks to N.P. Houe.

73. See G. Mortley's quotation in T. Parker-Pope, "How to Raise an Anti-Racist Kid," *New York Times*, June 24, 2020, https://www.nytimes.com/2020/06/24/well/family/how-to-raise-an-anti-racist-kid.html. This is problematic if the game player is not Black themselves, as they are painting themselves in a performative, inauthentic way. (Note that Mortley is the daughter of one of my interviewees, Amber Coleman-Mortley.) See also Roxworthy, *Revitalizing Japanese American Internment*, which cites Saidiya Hartman, *Scenes of Subjection: Terror, Slavery, and Self-Making in Nineteenth-Century America* (New York: Oxford University Press, 1997), p. 7: "empathy is a projection of

oneself into another in order to better understand the other," and the racial violence of slavery's legacy in American culture is reproduced in "the slipping on of blackness or an empathic identification in which one substitutes the self for the other."

74. Aaron Vanek explains that "the personality makeup of the person, the real person infects the character and vice versa." Aaron Vanek, personal interview, spring 2019. Role-playing can be detrimental if a player's role bleeds into their real life and has devastating real-world consequences.

75. Elizabeth LaPensée, "Collaboration for Inclusive Games," #ResistJam, March 3–11, 2017, https://www.youtube.com/watch?v=VqXFzxtGzXg; Elizabeth LaPensée, "Why Cultural Collaboration Matters," IndieCade, Culver City, CA, October 9–12, 2014, https://vimeo. com/112193585; Elizabeth LaPensée, personal interview, Spring 2019.

76. See Schrier, "Designing Inclusive Games."

77. "Second School District Halts Use of WNET *Mission US* Games," November 2017, https://current.org/2017/11/second-school-district-halts-use-of-wnets-mission-us-games/. We also need to question whether we as a culture deem these types of games as being ethical to play and learn with.

78. Ruiz explains that "game makers (both independent and working in the industry), game scholars, and game educators must work at making this an inclusive practice and culture; this is not easy, if we're not paying attention or we're not supporting those who need it when they need it, bad things can happen.... if we want to make games that comment on or teach ethics, then the design team needs to value—in fact, prioritize—social and emotional learning, activism, inclusion, community building, equity, etc. This is an opportunity to not only create good games but create a culture and an industry around games that is willing and capable of being reflexive and ethical." Quoted by Susanna Ruiz, personal interview, Spring 2019.

79. Davisson and Gehm, *Gaming Citizenship*; N. Mirra and A. Garcia, "Civic Participation Reimagined: Youth Interrogation and Innovation in the Multimodal Public Sphere," *Review of Research in Education* 41 (March 2017): 136–158; R. Benjamin, "Introduction," *Captivating Technology: Race, Carceral Technoscience, and Liberatory Imagination in Everyday Life*, Durham, NC: Duke University Press, 2019. For instance, Mirra and Garcia explain that what counts as a "good citizen" in the United States is culturally constructed and constricting.

80. Benjamin, "Introduction."

81. Schrier, Diamond, and Langendoen, "Using *Mission US*"; K. Schrier, "Designing and Using Games to Teach Ethics and Ethical Thinking," in *Learning, Education and Games Vol. 1: Curricular and Design Considerations*, ed. K. Schrier (Pittsburgh: ETC Press, 2014).

82. See Schrier, "Designing Inclusive Games."

83. WNET/Channel 13, Electric Funstuff, *Mission US*, https://www.mission-us.org/.

84. For instance, a historic figure such as Paul Revere may explain that the British soldiers are escalating threats, whereas a loyalist may complain about the secret meetings hosted by the colonists. The player needs to begin to decide which views they ascribe to, and which characters they will align with, as a result. Schrier, Diamond, and Langendoen, "Using *Mission US*."

85. Likewise, in an exercise done outside the game, provided by *Mission US*, students may read a report from the *Boston Gazette and County Journal* from 1770 that describes "[British] Captain Preston with a party of men with charged bayonets, came from the

main guard to the Commissioner's house the soldiers pushing their bayonets, crying, Make way! They took place by the custom-house, and continuing to push, to drive the people off, pricked some in several places; on which [the crowd] were clamorous, and, it is said threw snow balls. On this, the Captain commanded them to fire." They may also read Captain Preston's deposition, which describes, "On this a general attack was made on the men by a great number of heavy clubs and snowballs being thrown at them, by which all our lives were in imminent danger. Some persons at the same time called out, 'damn your bloods-why don't you fire.'" See WNET/Channel 13, https://cdn.mission-us.org/uploads/document/document_file/194/part4-documentactivity1.pdf.

86. This deposition was held after the massacre, where people ask them what they think happened, and who initiated the massacre (who was to blame). Students can use what they saw to make their interpretation, as well as the views that they have been hearing all along in the game.

87. For instance, students can share the viewpoints they heard throughout the game and categorize and classify them. They can also share what they saw at the massacre, compare how it was different from other student's experiences, and then explain how they interpreted it. They can then reflect on what they shared in their disposition.

88. Jennifer Worth, personal interview, Spring 2019.

89. See D. Sefton, "Second School District Halts Use of WNETs' Mission US Game," Current, November 2017, https://current.org/2017/11/second-school-district-halts-use-of-wnets-mission-us-games/. When and if teachers decide to use any game, they should also have students take a step back and deliberate why the game was designed and how it was designed, and how this affected our interpretations of the world.

90. Quotations by Vít Šisler, personal interview, Spring 2019. The game was originally released in Czech but now is in other languages, including English. Attentat 1942, Charles Games, Charles University and the Czech Academy of Sciences, 2017.

91. " A sequel to Attentat 1942 is planned called Svoboda 1945, which will deal with the aftermath of World War II in Czechoslovakia, the expulsion of Sudeten Germans from Czechoslovakia, and the rise of Communism to power. The game should be released in 2020. Vít Šisler, personal interview, Spring 2019.

92. Farber and Schrier, "The Limits and Strengths of Using Digital Games"; Schrier, "Designing Ourselves"; Schrier, "EPIC."

93. The migrant group experiences different hardships that have to be managed by the player, such as snake bites or losing food to wild animals. By playing this mini-game, the players learn a perspective (though fictionalized) on the difficulties of migrating to the United States through the Mexico-US border. In the two mini-games, very distinct and diametrically opposed actions are rewarded (escaping from border patrol and finding migrants who have escaped). Gigantic Mechanic, The Migrant Trail, https://theundocumented.com/, a game made by Gigantic Mechanic to act as a companion to a documentary on migration.

94. For instance, a teacher in Westchester had Black students play the role of slaves and get punished by the White students in their class, who are playing the role of slaveowners. J. Chung, "Westchester School That Held Mock Slave Auction Makes Deal With NY AG, Agrees To Changes," May 29, 2019, https://gothamist.com/news/westchester-school-that-held-mock-slave-auction-makes-deal-with-ny-ag-agrees-to-changes. See also "Slavery Simulation Homework Assigment at Oxford School Draws Ire," 2020,

https://www.ctinsider.com/local/newstimes/article/Slavery-simulation-homework-assignment-at-15322281.php?origin=facebook&fbclid=IwAR2kIyq2UWEpj3C2AX-klrJWQiPq-mT7neTdvy7kZ32GuysPyjLEdx8ERD4c.

95. *The Road Not Taken*, Interactivities Ink, 2008, https://library.interactiveliterature.org/brands/interactivities-ink/projects/16-the-road-not-taken. A. Vanek, Personal Interview, Spring 2019. He also explains that, "A rising trend in larps is also asking players to check in with each other; not just the larp facilitator, who cannot be everywhere at once. Some larps have on-site counselors (not actual licensed therapists, just someone to decompress with)." Note, it is acknowledged that the poem by R. Frost, "The Road Not Taken," has a different meaning than how the phrase is popularly applied and used in this game.

96. P. Hourdequin, "Osaki ni Shitsurei Shima-su!!," in *Learning, Education & Games Vol. 3*, ed. Schrier. The game shows how people might make respectful requests in professional environments, such as the workplace.

97. LaPensée, "Collaboration for Inclusive Games"; LaPensée, "Why Cultural Collaboration Matters."

98. For instance, *Mission US*'s module "A Cheyenne Odyssey," stemmed from a partnership with the Northern Cheyenne Tribe. The website explains that, "Northern Cheyenne Tribe at Chief Dull Knife College, a tribally managed institution on the Northern Cheyenne reservation in Montana. President Richard Littlebear and his colleagues consulted on educational content, scripting, design, and casting for the game, and all actors voicing the roles of the Northern Cheyenne characters are Northern Cheyenne themselves" (https://www.mission-us.org/about/our-team/credits/credits-a-cheyenne-odyssey/). However, even this game's representation of the Cheyenne was critiqued, so we need to be continually mindful of our creations and our use of games over time.

99. LaPensée, Elizabeth, *When Rivers Were Trails*, https://indianlandtenure.itch.io/when-rivers-were-trails. *When Rivers Were Trails* is a 2-D adventure game created through a collaboration with the Indian Land Tenure Foundation, including Nichlas Emmons, the creative director of the Indian Land Tenure Foundation, and Michigan State University's Games for Entertainment and Learning Lab.

100. Elizabeth LaPensée, "Video Games Encourage Indigenous Cultural Expression," *The Conversation*, March 2017, https://theconversation.com/video-games-encourage-indigenous-cultural-expression-74138.

101. Elizabeth LaPensée, personal interview, Spring 2019. At the time of the interview, the game had been played with 300 youths in public schools so far.

Chapter 9

1. In *Before the Storm* players play as Chloe, a character from *Life Is Strange*. The game is a prequel and takes place prior to the original game, but in the same high school context. Square Enix, Dontnod, *Life Is Strange*, 2015; Square Enix, Dontnod, *Life Is Strange 2*, 2019; Deck Nine, *Life Is Strange: Before the Storm*, 2017; https://lifeisstrange.square-enix-games.com/en-us? See more in, K. Schrier and D. Shaenfield, *Life is Strange* (Dontnod Entertainment, 2015–Present); S. Bacon, ed., *Transmedia Cultures: A Companion*. (New York: Peter Lang, 2021). In addition to the examples shared in the text, the episodes also end with a sharing of the percentages of players overall who chose each of the choices. This serves as an additional way for players to reflect on their choices as

compared to the collective choices, and they may even find choices that they never even encountered based on how they played the game.

2. See the C3 Framework; Jonathan Gould, ed., *Guardian of Democracy: The Civic Mission of Schools* (Philadelphia: Leonore Annenberg Institute for Civics of the Annenberg Public Policy Center at the University of Pennsylvania, 2011); Holly Korbey, *Building Better Citizens: A New Civics Education for All* (Lanham, MD: Rowman & Littlefield, 2019); and J. Clabough and T. Lintner, *No Reluctant Citizens: Teaching Civics in K-12 Classrooms* (Charlotte, NC: Information Age Publishing, Inc., 2018); Jonathan Haber, *Critical Thinking* (Cambridge, MA: MIT Press, 2020).

3. Haber, *Critical Thinking*. However, we cannot just question everything. Rather we need to be aware of our biases and limitations. We also cannot always question how we can arrive at the truth. See more in T. Wan, "danah boyd: How Critical Thinking and Media Literacy Efforts Are 'Backfiring' Today," *EdSurge*, March 7, 2018, https://www.edsurge.com/news/2018-03-07-danah-boyd-how-critical-thinking-and-media-literacy-efforts-are-backfiring-today and D. Boyd, "What Hath We Wrought?," SXSW EDU, Austin, TX, 2018, https://points.datasociety.net/you-think-you-want-media-literacy-do-you-7cad6af18ec2.

4. David Shaenfield, personal interview, Spring 2019. For more on argumentation and critical thinking see Haber, *Critical Thinking*.

5. Ibid., p. 122, citing J. Dewey, *Democracy and Education* (New York, NY): Macmillan, 1916. S. Merriam, "The Role of Cognitive Development in Mezirow's Transformational Learning Theory," *Adult Education Quarterly* 55 (2004): 60–68, p. 62; L. Morris and G. Wood, "A Model of Organizational Ethics Education," *European Business Review* 23 (2011): 274–286.

6. To distinguish reasoning from reflection: "Reflection focuses on thinking through and interpreting one's beliefs and assumptions to gain further understanding or acceptance, whereas reasoning focuses on interpreting, sifting through, and analyzing causes and consequences, events, objects, people, situations, and scenarios." Quote by K. Schrier, "EPIC: A Framework for Using Video Games for Ethics Education," *Journal of Moral Education* 44, no. 4 (2015): 393–424, p. 406, citing J. Mezirow, "How Critical Reflection Triggers Transformational Learning," in *Fostering Critical Reflection in Adulthood* (San Francisco: Jossey Bass, 1990), pp. 1–20; J. Mezirow, *Transformative Dimensions of Adult Learning* (San Francisco: Jossey-Bass, 1991); J. Dewey, *How We Think* (Chicago, IL: Regnery, 1933); J. M. Paxton, L. Ungar, and J. D. Greene, "Reflection and Reasoning in Moral Judgment," *Cognitive Science* 36, no. 1 (2012): 163–177. Dewey explains that reflection involves "'assessing the grounds [justification] of one's beliefs,' the process of rationally examining the assumptions by which we have been justifying our convictions," in Mezirow, "How Critical Reflection Triggers Transformational Learning," p. 5, citing Dewey, *How We Think*, p. 9.

7. D. Montgomery and M. Walker, "Enhancing Ethical Awareness," *Gifted Child Today* 35 (2012): 95–101.

8. Merriam, "The Role of Cognitive Development"; Mezirow, "How Critical Reflection Triggers Transformational Learning"; K. Schrier, "Would You Kindly Parent? Parenting, Caretaking, and Love in Games," in *Love and Affection in Games, A Design Primer*, ed. Lindsay Grace (New York: Taylor and Francis, 2020); K. Schrier and D. Shaenfield, "Developing Identity Through Playable Transmedia Experiences," in *Transmedia Reader*, ed. S. Bacon (forthcoming). Thus reflecting on our actions, and then continually revising our choices going forward, is important.

9. Games may have different goals, but goals are fundamental to what a game is. Charlotte Weitze describes that game goals as "objectives ... what we strive for." They are a reason why we have decided to play and continue playing, and they are what we hope to achieve when we complete our game. A game may have multiple mini-goals, steps, tasks, activities, or even realizations that are needed to be met before a player can fully complete or win a game. Goals can also take many forms. There can be activities that a player needs to do (such as talking to another player, or reading a note), storylines that need to be experienced (such as reaching a particular plot point), or even approaches or attitudinal changes that a player needs to do (such as finding a new way to solve a problem, or being more open to other viewpoints). The end-goal of the game is just that—the final objective or outcome. Though games may have different end-goals and mini-goals, or may provide different pathways and obstacles on the way to the goals, all games have goals, as they are fundamental to what a game is. Quotes from C. Weitz, "Developing Goals and Objectives for Gameplay and Learning," in *Learning, Education and Games Vol. 1: Curricular and Design Considerations*, ed. K. Schrier (Pittsburgh: ETC Press, 2014). See also T. Fullerton, *Game Design Workshop*, 4th ed. (Burlington, MA: Morgan Kaufmann Publishers, 2018).

10. A. W. Dorn, S. Webb, and Sylvain Pâquet, "From Wargaming to Peacegaming: Digital Simulations with Peacekeeper Roles Needed," *International Peacekeeping* 27, no. 2 (2020): 289–310.

11. Entertainment Technology Center, Carnegie Mellon, *Decisions that Matter*, https://www.cmu.edu/dietrich/news/news-stories/2015/may/decisions-that-matter.html.

12. 11 Bit Studios, *This War of Mine*, 2014, https://www.epicgames.com/store/en-US/product/this-war-of-mine/home.

13. S. Papert, *Mindstorms: Children, Computers, and Powerful Ideas* (New York: Basic Books, 1980) talks about microworlds in and Barab talks about practice fields in S. A. Barab and T. Duffy, "From Practice Fields to Communities of Practice," in *Theoretical Foundations of Learning Environments*, ed. D. Jonassen and S. M. Land (Mahwah, NJ: Lawrence Erlbaum, 2000), pp. 25–56.

14. "Players themselves can interact within those systems, affecting how ethics and values are negotiated and experienced." Quotes at Schrier, "EPIC," p. 401; M. Sicart, *Ethics and Computer Games* (Cambridge, MA: MIT Press, 2009). A power of games, then, may be in how they enable players to experiment with, reflect on, and revisit ethical decisions in a system. Even if players do not entirely make decisions based on how they would in real life, being able to explore a system, grapple with its constraints and rules, and even transgress in an ethical play space helps players to explore the boundaries of their own moral systems. This may then help them to consider how their morality intersects with other people's and other systems, and where it disconnects, dissects, and diverges.

15. Gideon Dishon and Yasmin B. Kafai, "Connected Civic Gaming: Rethinking the Role of Video Games in Civic Education," *Interactive Learning Environments* (2019), DOI: 10.1080/10494820.2019.1704791.

16. Schrier, "EPIC"; K. Schrier, "How Do We Teach Ethics and Empathy Through Games?," in *Ethics in Digital Game Cultures*, ed. M. Groen, N. Kiel, A. Tillann, and André Weßel (New York: Springer, 2020). K. Schrier, "Designing and Using Games to Teach Ethics and Ethical Thinking," in *Learning, Education and Games Vol. 1*, ed. Schrier; J. Melenson, "The Axis of Good and Evil," in *Designing Games for Ethics: Models, Techniques, and Frameworks*, ed. K. Schrier and D. Gibson (Hershey, PA: IGI Global, 2011), pp. 57–71.

A morality system is a system that accounts for one's moral or ethical choices in the game. For instance, if you are making so-called good choices, your meter may move closer to a "good" measure, meaning that your character and the world they live in may be altered based on the morality outcomes. Games use a variety of morality systems, such as renegade versus paragon in *Mass Effect*, karma points in *Fallout*, and a bounties system in *Red Dead Redemption*. A nonplayer character or NPC is a virtual character in the game that is controlled by the game or computer and not by another human.

17. Sarah Ertelt, "Evolving Apocalyptic Narratives and the Ethics of *Fallout*," October 11, 2017, https://www.prindlepost.org/2017/10/evolving-apocalyptic-narratives-ethics-fallout/.

18. In *Fallout 4,* how a player interacts with others (such as helping or not), and the resulting personality or role that is shaped, affects how a companion NPC treats the player and whether they are a potential romantic partner. Sicart, *Ethics and Computer Games*; J. P. Zagal, "Ethically Notable Videogames: Moral Dilemmas and Gameplay," *Proceedings of the 2009 Digital Games Research Association International Conference (DiGRA)*, London, 2009, Vol. 5, http://www.digra.org/digital-library/publications/ethically-notable-videogames-moral-dilemmas-and-gameplay/; ; J. P. Zagal, "Ethical Reasoning and Reflection as Supported by Single-Player Videogames," in *Designing Games for Ethics: Models, Techniques and Frameworks*, ed. Schrier and Gibson, pp. 19–35; J. Stevenson, "A Framework for Classification and Criticism of Ethical Games," in *Designing Games for Ethics: Models, Techniques and Frameworks*, ed. Schrier and Gibson, pp. 36–55.

19. Schrier, "EPIC," quote at 410.

20. Schrier, "EPIC"; K. Schrier, *The Weird Humanity of I Have No Mouth and I Must Scream. Well-Played* (Pittsburgh: ETC Press, 2014). CyberDreams/NightDive Studios, "I Have No Mouth and I Must Scream," https://store.steampowered.com/app/245390/I_Have_No_Mouth_and_I_Must_Scream/ (accessed June 11, 2020).

21. Ian Bogost, *Persuasive Games: The Expressive Power of Videogames* (Cambridge, MA: MIT Press, 2007), p. ix.

22. Schrier, "EPIC," citing J. Singal, "A Foreign Video Game Concept: Making Red Tape Fun," *Boston Globe*, August 17, 2013, https://www.bostonglobe.com/arts/2013/08/17/video-game-about-immigration-bureaucracy-awesome/vZeSFIheJmot75tQ64oWDP/story.html, and Bogost, *Persuasive Games*. For more about how a player might work the system and story of a game, see Sicart, *Ethics and Computer Games*; M. Sicart, "The Banality of Simulated Evil: Designing Ethical Gameplay," *Ethics and Information Technology* 1, no. 3 (2009): 191–202; M. Sicart, "Values Between Systems," in *Ethics and Game Design*, ed. K. Schrier (Hershey, PA: IGI Global, 2010), pp. 1–15; M. Sicart, *Beyond Choices: The Design of Ethical Gameplay* (Cambridge, MA: MIT Press, 2013). For more about *Papers, Please* and ethics, see Paul Formosa, Malcolm Ryan, and Dan Staines, *Ethics and Information Technology* 18, no. 3 (2016): 211–225; and V. H. H. Chen and W. J. D. Koek, "Understanding Flow, Identification with Game Characters and Players' Attitudes," Foundations of Digital Games (FDG), virtual, (2020).

23. A. Davisson and D. Gehm, "Gaming Citizenship: Video Games as Lessons in Civic Life," *Journal of Contemporary Rhetoric* 4, no.3–4 (2014): 39–57, citing Bogost, *Persuasive Games*, 64; James L. Hoban Jr., "Rhetorical Rituals of Rebirth," *Quarterly Journal of Speech* 66, no. 3 (1980): 275–288; Ian Bogost, *How to Do Things with Videogames* (Minneapolis: University of Minnesota Press, 2011), p. 61.

24. Schön, *The Reflective Practitioner*; K. Schrier and D. Shaenfield, "Collaboration and Emotion in *Way*," in *Emotion, Technology, and Games*, ed. S. Tettegah and W. Huang (New York: Elvesier, 2015).

25. D. Schön, *The Reflective Practitioner* (New York: Basic Books, 1983); Schrier and Shaenfield, "Developing Identity Through Playable Transmedia Experiences."

26. Montgomery and Walker, "Enhancing Ethical Awareness"; Schrier and Shaenfield, Developing Identity through Playable Transmedia Experiences." Stopping at the bench is optional. They can reflect back on how the story and town has evolved due to their decisions.

27. Kim McAuliffe, *Play the Mirror*, http://mirrorga.me/, 2016. The game may not be playable anymore depending on the browser used, but I hope it still works!

28. Schrier, "Guiding Questions for Game-Based Learning," in *International Handbook of Information Technology in Primary and Secondary Education*, ed. D. Gibson (New York: Springer, 2018); J. Groff, J. McCall, P. Darvasi, and Z. Gilbert, "Using Games in the Classroom," in *Learning, Education, and Games Vol. 2: Bringing Games into Educational Contexts*, ed. K. Schrier (Pittsburgh: ETC Press, 2016).

29. Schrier, "Guiding Questions"; K. Becker, "Choosing and Using Games in the Classroom," in *International Handbook of Information Technology in Primary and Secondary Education*, ed. Gibson

30. K. Schrier, "Designing Role-Playing Video Games for Ethical Thinking," *Education Technology Research Development* 65, no. 4 (2014): 831–868; K. Schrier, "Emotion, Empathy and Ethical Thinking in *Fable III*," in *Emotion, Technology, and Games*, ed. S. Tettegah and W. Huang (New York: Elvesier, 2016).

31. Players need to make choices with outcomes that matter (in that they have a measurable and consequential effect on the gameplay, game world, or character or role of the player, or some effect on the player themselves, or are personally relevant to the player in some way). Sicart, *Ethics and Computer Games*; Zagal, "Ethically Notable Videogames"; Zagal, "Ethical Reasoning and Reflection"; Schrier, "Designing and Using Games." In reference to games with fantastical approaches, see G. Kaufman, M. Flanagan, and M. Seidman. "Creating Stealth Game Interventions for Attitude and Behavior Change: An 'Embedded Design' Model." DIGRA 2015, Proceedings of the Digital Games Research Association (DiGRA), 2015, http://www.digra.org/digital-library/publications/creating-stealth-game-interventions-for-attitude-and-behavior-change-an-embedded-design-model/.

32. Quote by Dishon and Kafai, "Connected Civic Gaming," citing N. Carpentier, "Beyond the Ladder of Participation: An Analytical Toolkit for the Critical Analysis of Participatory Media Processes," *Javnost-The Public* 23, no. 1 (2016): 70–88.

33. See also an article on life in authoritarian states at T. Pepinsky, "Life in Totalitarian States is Mostly Boring and Tolerable," *Vox*, Jan. 9 2017, https://www.vox.com/the-big-idea/2017/1/9/14207302/authoritarian-states-boring-tolerable-fascism-trump.

34. However, if you play as a female avatar in *Fallout 3* and get the black widow perk as the first perk before you go to megaton, you can persuade the bomber to defuse the bomb which obviates the choice of having to shoot the sheriff.

35. Bogost, *Persuasive Games*. On the other hand, Chan argues that having so-called obviously good and bad decisions and moral alignments in a game is important, because it reinforces the fact that some perspectives are more immoral than others. Intolerant, racist,

or otherwise problematic perspectives are not morally ambiguous but in fact, immoral and to be denounced, and not considered or regarded further. See more at K. Chan, "Games Need to Return to Black and White Morality," *Polygon*, August 3, 2020, https://www.polygon.com/2020/8/3/21352437/games-morality-last-of-of-us-bioshock-good-bad.

36. "*The Walking Dead* game series, which takes place in a post-apocalyptic world, is based on *The Walking Dead* comic book series. The player, as the main avatar, makes dialogue choices, such as whom to save from zombie attacks, which have a short-term effect on the story, but also affect one's relationships with other characters (NPCs) and how the NPCs view the avatar. The story, so far, has ended up in the same narrative result, even if the mini-choices differ." Schrier, "EPIC."

37. Even if they were able to procedurally generate all of the outcomes, we wouldn't know how relevant, specific, and meaningful those outcomes would be. Also, game developers may approximate these outcomes, but it is still resource taxing.

38. The consequences of the decision do not get fully realized, sometimes, until the end of a game. This type of less obvious or longer-term feedback may relate to the player eventually gaining access to particular storylines, gameplay or new goals; gaining ability to make certain dialogue choices or persuade other characters; developing stronger or weaker relationships with particular characters or groups; or even getting one ending to a game rather than another.

39. In *Bioshock*, players can decide whether to extract "Eve" (the game's version of magic energy or "mana") from the Little Sisters, or to forgo it. But players will not see the results of this choice until the very end of the game. If they never extract the Eve, they have a different ending to the overall game than if they ever did once extract it. K. Schrier, "*BioShock* as the Infinite Parent: Parenting and Play in the *BioShock* series," in *New Perspectives on BioShock*, ed. Jessica Aldred and Felan Parker (Montreal: McGill-Queen's University Press, 2018).

40. (Games may struggle in that the choices and outcomes are not realistic or nuanced enough to deeply promote the practice of critical thinking.) Alternatively, it's not necessarily the case that it's poor design to only have one or two ultimate endings. Having limited endings could also suggest to the player that while their ethical decisions matter in that it expresses who they are and their own identity, they may not have ultimate control over the final consequences of their actions. Systemic pressures and constraints may keep us from fully controlling our future. These games suggest that we think of all the times that outcomes were inevitable no matter what paths we chose, even if we, as the player of our lives, were changed along that path.

41. D. Staines, M. Consalvo, A. Stangeby, and S. Pedraça, "State of Play: Video Games and Moral Engagement," *Journal of Gaming & Virtual Worlds* 11, no. 3 (2019): 271–288; Zagal, "Ethically Notable Videogames"; Zagal, "Ethical Reasoning and Reflection"; D. Rusch, *Making Deep Games: Designing Games with Meaning and Purpose* (New York: CRC Press, 2016).

42. Jordan Magnuson, *Loneliness*, https://www.necessarygames.com/my-games/gametrekking-omnibus; Heiden, *Girl with the Gray Hair Awakens*, https://heiden.itch.io/the-girl-with-the-gray-hair-awakens; J. Rohrer, *Passage* (may be unplayable); Porpentine, *Howling Dogs*, http://slimedaughter.com/games/twine/howlingdogs/; InnerSloth, *Among Us*, https://store.steampowered.com/app/945360/Among_Us/; *Werewolf* (party game); K. Schrier, *Trade Off*, learn more about it in M. Flanagan and H. Nissenbaum, *Values at Play* (Cambridge, MA: MIT Press, 2014); R. Carbo-Mascarell, *A Woman Goes to a Game*

Industry Party, https://moreelen.itch.io/a-woman-goes-to-a-private-games-industry-party; Beautiful Glitch, *Monster Prom*, https://store.steampowered.com/app/743450/Monster_Prom/; V. Hart and N. Case, *Parable of the Polygons, https://ncase.me/polygons/*; A. Antropy, *Queers in Love at the End of the World*, https://w.itch.io/end-of-the-world.

43. Schrier, "Designing Role-Playing Video Games"; Schrier, "Emotion, Empathy and Ethical Thinking in *Fable III*."

44. J. Villareale, C. Biemer, M. S. El-Nasr, and J. Zhu, *Reflection in Game-Based Learning: A Survey of Programming Games* (Virtual: Foundations of Digital Games (FDG) Conference, 2020). They also note a number of good works on reflection in games, including X. Lin, C. Hmelo, C. Kinzer, and T. Secules, "Designing Technology to Support Reflection," *Educational Technology Research and Development* 47, no. 3 (1999): 43–62; R. Fieck and G. Fitzpatrick, "Reflecting on Reflection: Framing a Design Landscape. In Proceedings of the 22nd Conference of the Computer Human Interaction Special Interest Group of Australia on Computer-Human Interaction," *ACM* OZCHI Computer Human Interaction Special Interest Group of Australia on Computer-Human Interaction (2010): 216–223.

45. Staines et al., "State of Play," quote at p. 284.

46. Villareale et al., *Reflection in Game-Based Learning*.

47. Dishon and Kafai, "Connected Civic Gaming," citing G. Dishon, "Fulfilling the Rousseauian Fantasy: Video Games and Well-Regulated Freedom," *Philosophy of Education Archive* (2016): 113–121, https://educationjournal.web.illinois.edu/archive/index.php/pes/article/view/5248.pdf.

48. When someone else seems to be driving unpredictably—in and out of a lane, or cutting people off—do we hang back?

49. Scalable Cooperation, MIT Media Lab, http://moralmachine.mit.edu/ (accessed June 11, 2020).

50. Thus all of these decisions have to already have been programmed into the car for it to function; every permutation of every scenario needs a preplanned decision so that the car knows what to do just as we might know. We may initially think that we predict all scenarios and program for it, because traffic rules are well-established. But traffic is not a perfect system, and it is affected by human error, random events (e.g., animal crossings), and even systemic biases. Can we really program a car to drive perfectly accurately? Think, for instance, of how often GPS-provided or mobile device-provided directions are wrong.

51. Sometimes students are resistant to this type of activity, because they think that self-driving cars do not need to be able to answer these questions, or that these questions will not ever come up. We may respond by saying that the car is programmed to follow the rules, and to know how to turn left or right, drive straight, or hit the brakes. But driving is not just about following traffic laws.

52. In a remote classroom, I can share my screen using a video conferencing application, and I can invite live discussion and polling, too. I did this in my Fall 2020 course, for instance.

53. Before they decide, they share their strategies and why they made their decisions. For many of the decision points, the students are split in what to do and their opinions on it widely vary. Once the students vote, by raising their hand, I ask them to divulge why they made their decision. What is most exciting about using this is that each student has a different perspective on what to do and why to do it—and this experience helps to foster that for the students. Students will give viewpoints such as basing it on human potential (wanting to save younger people, for instance), or the ability to save greater numbers of

people. Students also grapple with the ethics of having cars make this decision at all. We discuss that cars, if they are truly self-driving, need to be preprogrammed with all possibilities, even if they seem totally unlikely to ever occur in real life. Sometimes the choice is whether to kill the people inside the car or the ones who are following the law (for instance, deciding whether to cross the street at the right moment). In these cases, students will often ignore the fact that the car that a person bought actively tried to kill them—and therefore, we discuss how technology should differentially protect given who bought or who used it. We are able to go from individual and personal ethics, to societal consequences, to the overlapping perspectives of technological, personal and societal ethics.

54. E. Awad, S. Dsouza, R. Kim, J. Schulz, J. Henrich, A. Shariff, J.-F. Bonnefon, and I. Rahwan, "The Moral Machine Experiment," *Nature* 563 (2018): 59–64; R. Noothigattu, S. Gaikwad, E. Awad, S. Dsouza, I. Rahwan, P. Ravikumar, and A. D. Procaccia, A Voting-Based System for Ethical Decision Making, Thirty-Second AAAI Conference on Artificial Intelligence (AAAI-18) (New Orleans, 2017); A. Shariff, J. F. Bonnefon, and I. Rahwan, Psychological Roadblocks to the Adoption of Self-Driving Vehicles. *Nature Human Behaviour* 1 (2017): 694–696. J. F. Bonnefon, A. Shariff, and I. Rahwan, "The Social Dilemma of Autonomous Vehicles," *Science* 352, no. 6293 (2016): 1573–1576

55. Awad et al., "The Moral Machine Experiment." The participants of Moral Machine are actually helping us to better understand moral decision-making in general, and perhaps, even to help codesign a moral decision-making algorithm for self-driving cars. We can see some of these differences in cultural values play out in the policies and actions taken by different governments in the 2020 pandemic, for instance, such as around lockdown policies, ventilator use, or who is prioritized with mitigation and medical techniques.

56. Ibid.

57. Ibid. It also suggests that autonomous car makers and policymakers may not be able to create an algorithm or set of laws that is universal to all cultures' ethics. Teachers can use this to explore cultural differences in decision-making with their students.

58. To apply ethics and civics to real-world decisions is useful, even if it is not something a student has ever faced, because it contextualizes the decisions, and helps to make them matter more. Likewise, while the content of the Moral Machine car decisions may not seem realistic (how often are two cartoon cats, five athletes, and one child crossing the street at the same time?), the application of these choices, and the connection to a real-world problem (how to program self-driving cars), help to make it seem more meaningful.

59. Any choices within and around the game should have appropriate and relevant outcomes and feedback. In the *Fable* series, players make ethical choices (such as whether to sacrifice a friend or villagers or whether to continue to protect their mentor, Walter), and depending on their decisions, they will experience different interactions with other characters, different storylines, and even their avatar may change in appearance, going from more devilish and bumpy, to more angelic and smooth. The in-game consequences of that decision could be some type of direct or explicit feedback, such as rewards or penalties (e.g., tokens, increases or decreases in scores, greater or lower Karma ratings), or clear reminders (such as text that says that a "character will remember this," such as in *The Walking Dead* [Telltale] game or *Life Is Strange*). Schrier, "EPIC." Feedback can also take the form of clear audio cues that signify completion, rewards, penalties, errors, or hints. Or consequences could be revealed in a more complex way, in that players need to

participate and experience a system of choices and consequences that have varying, dynamic effects on the game, both in the long term and in the short run. Also see J. Peacock, L. N. Harkrider, Z. Bagdasarov, S. Connelly, J. F. Johnson, C. E. Thiel, A. E. MacDougall, M. D. Mumford, and L. D. Devenport, "Effects of Alternative Outcome Scenarios and Structured Outcome Evaluation on Case-Based Ethics Instruction," *Science & Engineering Ethics* 19 (2012): 1283–1303.

60. *Undertale*, Toby Fox, 2015, http://store.steampowered.com/app/391540/Undertale/. For more about *Undertale*, seeF. Geer and F. Matthew, "*Undertale*," in *Learning, Education & Games, Vol. 3*, ed. Schrier.

61. C. Lynn, "Teaching Ethics with an Integrated Online Curriculum," *Journal of Hospitality, Leisure, Sport, & Tourism Education* 9 (2010): 124–130; W. A. Wines, "Seven Pillars of Business Ethics: Toward a Comprehensive Framework," *Journal of Business Ethics* 79 (2008): 483–499; P. Maclagan, "Varieties of Moral Issue and Dilemma: A Framework for the Analysis of Case Material in Business Education," *Journal of Business Ethics* 48 (2003): 21–32. P. Maclagan, "Conflicting Obligations, Moral Dilemmas and the Development of Judgement Through Business Ethics Education," *Business Ethics: A European Review* 21 (2012): 183–197; R. S. Upchurch, "A Conceptual Foundation for Ethical Decision Making: A Stakeholder Perspective in the Lodging Industry (U.S.A.)," *Journal of Business Ethics* 17 (1998): 1349–1361.

62. Geer and Matthew, "*Undertale*."

63. Schön, *The Reflective Practitioner*.

64. E. Smith, Teaching Critical Reflection," *Teaching in Higher Education* 16 (2011): 211–223, p. 211. Trish Everett, Personal Interview, Spring 2019.

65. Students can also reflect outside of the game with other students, to compare and discuss how they played their game and what happened during their deposition. K. Schrier, J. Diamond, and D. Langendoen, "Using *Mission US*: For Crown or Colony? To Develop Historical Empathy and Nurture Ethical Thinking," in *Ethics and Game Design: Teaching Values through Play*, ed. Schrier and Gibson, pp. 239–261. .

66. K. Schrier, *Using Augmented Reality Games to Teach 21st Century Skills* (Boston: Educators Program, 2006).

67. Some games purposely remove pauses so that players need to make decisions under pressure—and without any reflection.

68. Tracy Fullerton/USC, *Walden*, 2015/2016, https://www.waldengame.com/ (accessed June 11, 2020). *Walden* was created by a University of Southern California team led by Fullerton.

69. M. Chen and N. Zdeb, "*Walden*, a Game," in *Learning, Education & Games, Vol. 3*, ed. Schrier.

70. Ibid.

71. Teacher's guide at https://static1.squarespace.com/static/5972908bf7e0ab1a5fe04927/t/5d2a5803710e6a0001052567/1563056137304/WALDEN_CURRICULUM_ALL.pdf.

72. Chen and Zdeb, "*Walden*, a Game." See also T. Fullerton, "*Walden*: Reflection," in *How to Play Video Games*, ed. N. Hunteman and M. Payne (New York: NYU Press, 2018); B. Peterson, "Can a Video Game Capture the Magic of *Walden*? Henry David Thoreau's Famed Retreat Gets Pixelated," *The Smithsonian*, March 2017, https://www.smithsonianmag.com/artsculture/can-video-game-capture-magic-walden180962125/; R. Pogrebin, "In *Walden* Video Game, the Challenge Is Stillness," *New York Times*,

February 24, 2017, https://www.nytimes.com/2017/02/24/arts/henry-david-thoreau-video-game.html. A teachers' guide is found at https://www.waldengame.com/educators.

Chapter 10

1. JoLT/American University Game Lab, *Factitious*, 2017/2018/2020, http://factitious. augamestudio.com/#/ (accessed June 11, 2020). For instance, one tip explains that the article was from a satire source and that "the use of loaded words like 'insane' should tip you off this is not a neutral news article. Note also that the sources are named, but the story doesn't why they are quoted. Are they state officials? Lawyers?" Correct answers also earn points for the player. The game has three different difficulty levels, depending on the age of the participants (college [hard], high school [medium], or middle school [easy]). Players start at easy and as they successfully complete choices, they continue through different rounds until they reach the harder levels. The game is tough: most of the students who have played the game in my classes have not been able to figure out which news is fake or real 100% of the time.

2. A classroom edition of *Factitious* is in the works.

3. Lindsay Grace and Robert Hone, "Factitious News Game: Polling Fact from Fake," Games for Change, New York, NY: 2018; B. Hone, "How the *Factitious* News Game Helps People Learn to Detect Fake News," September 19, 2018, https://medium.com/@bobhone. designer/how-the-factitious-news-game-helps-people-learn-to-detect-fake-news-3a8165a22600. The thought is that if we can understand the mechanisms by which disinformation is more easily believed or spread, we can create better tools and education to counter this.

4. This book was written with the assumption that the United States will still be a democracy when you read this.

5. Ashley Penney, personal interviews, Spring 2019; Neil Wrona, personal interview, Spring 2019.

6. In the last chapter I outline a number of critical thinking skills, including information literacy and evaluation and skills.

7. See D. Buckingham, *Media Education: Literacy, Learning and Contemporary Culture*, Cambridge, UK: Polity, 2003; Paul Mihailidis, *Media Literacy & The Emerging Citizen: Youth, Engagement and Participation in Digital Culture* (New York: Peter Lang Publishing, 2014); Laura Stein and Anita Prewett, "Media Literacy Education in the Social Studies: Teacher Perceptions and Curricular Challenges," *Teacher Education Quarterly* (Winter 2009): 131–148; Jeff Share and Elizabeth Thoman, "Teaching Democracy: A Media Literacy Approach," National Association for Media Literacy Education, 2014, https://namle.net/2014/11/01/teaching-democracy-a-media-literacy-approach; Robert Kubey, "Media Literacy and the Teaching of Civics and Social Studies at the Dawn of the 21st Century," *American Behavioral Scientist* 48, no.1 (2004): 69–77; Frank W. Baker, *Media Literacy in the K12 Classroom* (Washington, DC: International Society for Technology in Education, 2012).

8. Wayne Journell, "Civic Education in a Post-Truth Society," *No Reluctant Citizens: Teaching Civics in K-12 Classrooms*, ed. Jeremiah Clabough and Timothy Lintner (Charlotte,

NC: Information Age Publishing, Inc, 2018), p. 113–129, which cites useful research on political homophily by C. H. Clark and P. G. Avery, "The Psychology of Controversial Issues Discussions: Challenges and Opportunities in a Polarized, Post-9/11 Society," in *Reassessing the Social Studies Curriculum: Promoting Critical Civic Engagement in a Politically Polarized, Post-9/11 World*, ed. W. Journell (Lanham, MD: Rowman & Littlefield, 2016), pp. 109–120.

9. Students need to figure out what is truth in a world that may be "post-truth," from Journell, "Civic Education in a Post-Truth Society"; see also W. Journell, *Unpacking Fake News: An Educator's Guide to Navigating the Media with Students* (New York: Teachers College Press, 2019); J. Kahne and B. Bowyer, "Educating for Democracy in a Partisan Age: Confronting the Challenges of Motivated Reasoning and Misinformation," *American Educational Research Journal* 54 (2017): 3–34; Joseph Kahne and Benjamin Bowyer, "Can Media Literacy Education Increase Digital Engagement in Politics?," *Learning, Media and Technology* 44, no. 2 (2019): 211–224. See also Holly Korbey, *Building Better Citizens: New Civics Education for All* (Lanham, MD: Rowman & Littlefield, 2019).

10. Clark and Avery, "The Psychology of Controversial Issues Discussions"; Journell, "Civic Education in a Post-Truth Society"; R. Putnam, Bowling Alone: The Collapse and Revival of America Community, (New York: Simon & Schuster), 2000.

11. For instance, see Journell, "Civic Education in a Post-Truth Society," which cites useful research on political homophily by Clark and Avery, "The Psychology of Controversial Issues Discussions"; echo chambers, E. Colleoni, A. Rozza, and A. Arvidsson, "Echo Chamber or Public Sphere? Predicting Political Orientation and Measuring Political Homophily in Twitter Using Big Data," *Journal of Communication* 64 (2014): 317–332; S. Jacobson, E. Myung, and S. L. Johnson, "Open Media or Echo Chamber: The Use of Links in Audience Discussions on the Facebook Pages of Partisan News Organizations," *Information, Communication, & Society* 19 (2016): 875–891; A. Mitchell, J. Gottfried, J. Kiley, and K. E. Matsa, "Political Polarization and Media Habits," Pew Research Center, October 21, 2014, https://www.journalism.org/2014/10/21/political-polarization-media-habits/; and a steady decline of Americans' interactions with people who are different than them, for instance, T. H. Sander and R. D. Putnam, "Still Bowling Alone? The Post-9/11 Split," *Journal of Democracy* 21 (2010): 9–16; C. T. Nguyen, "The Problem of Living Inside Echo Chambers," September 11, 2019, https://theconversation.com/the-problem-of-living-inside-echo-chambers-110486; K. H. Jamieson and J. N. Cappella, *Echo Chamber* (New York: Oxford University Press, 2008); T. Nguyen, *Echo Chambers and Epistemic Bubbles* (Cambridge: Cambridge University Press, 2018); S. Flaxman, S. Goel, and J. M. Rao, "Filter Bubbles, Echo Chambers, and Online News," *Public Opinion Quarterly* 80, Special Issue (2016): 298–320; David M. J. Lazer, Matthew A. Baum, Yochai Benkler, Adam J. Berinsky, Kelly M. Greenhill, Filippo Menczer, Miriam J. Metzger, Brendan Nyhan, Gordon Pennycook, David Rothschild, Michael Schudson, Steven A. Sloman, Cass R. Sunstein, Emily A. Thorson, Duncan J. Watts, and Jonathan L. Zittrain, "The Science of Fake News," *Science* 359, no. 6380 (2018): 1094–1096.

12. Lazer et al., "The Science of Fake News." I do also wonder if the rapid change in who can write, share, distribute, and convey the news, science, and other professional institutions has disrupted this. In my previous book, *Knowledge Games*, I talk about how science

became professionalized from being mostly amateurs, to being mostly vetted scientists, and how the use of citizen science and crowdsourcing, as well as games, has disrupted this. It seems like a democratization of knowledge, which means more people have access to creating it and sharing it. But perhaps the very thing that helps us to democratize knowledge also upends knowledge because we can no longer trust any knowledge. How do we make decisions if we cannot trust where our knowledge comes from because the very institution of knowledge is overturned? See K. Schrier, *Knowledge Games: How Playing Games Can Solve Problems, Create Insight, and Make Change* (Baltimore: Johns Hopkins University Press, 2016).

13. S. Wineburg, *Historical Thinking and Other Unnatural Acts: Charting the Future of Teaching the Past* (Philadelphia: Temple University Press, 2001); S. Wineburg, D. Martin, and C. Monte-Sano, *Reading Like a Historian: Teaching Literacy in Middle and High School History Classrooms* (New York: Teachers College Press, 2011).

14. National Council for Social Studies (NCSS), "Position on Media Literacy," *Social Education* 80, no. 3 (2016): 183–185; Journell, "Civic Education in a Post-Truth Society."

15. Journell, "Civic Education in a Post-Truth Society"; Mihailidis, *Media Literacy & The Emerging Citizen*; Stein and Prewett, "Media Literacy Education in the Social Studies"; Share and Thoman, "Teaching Democracy"; Kubey, "Media Literacy and the Teaching of Civics"; Baker, *Media Literacy in the K12 Classroom*.

16. And 40% even argued that the image provided sound evidence.

17. Kahne and Bowyer, "Educating for Democracy in a Partisan Age"; Journell, "Civic Education in a Post-Truth Society."

18. M. S. Crocco, *Teaching The Levees: A Curriculum for Democratic Dialogue and Civic Engagement* (New York: Teachers College Press, 2007); M. Crocco, A. Halvorsen, R. Jacobsen, and A. Segall, "Teaching with Evidence," *Phi Delta Kappan* 98, no. 7 (2017): 67–71; Journell, "Civic Education in a Post-Truth Society."

19. Kahne and Bowyer, "Educating for Democracy in a Partisan Age," cited in Journell, "Civic Education in a Post-Truth Society."

20. Journell, "Civic Education in a Post-Truth Society," citing W. Journell, M. W. Beeson, and C. A. Ayers, "Learning to Think Politically: Toward More Complete Disciplinary Knowledge in Civics and Government Courses," *Theory & Research in Social Education* 43, no. 1 (2015): 28–67.

21. See for instance, Civilopedia, https://civilization.fandom.com/wiki/Civilopedia (accessed June 11, 2020).

22. But these games are quite long and may not be appropriate for a classroom context (though *Civilization* has been modified for classroom use by Kurt Squire and others. See for instance K. D. Squire, "Replaying History: Learning World History Through Playing *Civilization III*" (PhD diss., Indiana University, 2004).

23. iCivics, *Race to Ratify*, https://www.icivics.org/games/race-to-ratify.

24. K. Schrier, "Using Augmented Reality Games to Teach 21st Century Skills," *Proceedings of ACM Siggraph 2006*, Boston. In *Factitious*, players need to decide whether an article is real or fake, or built on false premises or information.

25. Jennifer Worth, personal interview, Spring 2019, in reference to Mark C. Barnes, *Reacting to the Past*, https://reacting.barnard.edu/, created by Mark C. Barnes, professor of history at Barnard College.

26. The students need to put the principles in action and play out the partisan perspectives related to different civic issues, such as the role of church in government or who gets to be a citizen.

27. Jennifer Worth, personal interview, Spring 2019. For instance, one student may take on the role of The Archbishop of Paris, and will need to share different perspectives than a more radical revolutionary.

28. Gideon Dishon and Yasmin B. Kafai, "Connected Civic Gaming: Rethinking the Role of Video Games in Civic Education," *Interactive Learning Environments* (2019), DOI: 10.1080/10494820.2019.1704791.

29. The journey of a Syrian migrant through her WhatsApp thread, *LeMonde*, https://www.lemonde.fr/international/visuel/2015/12/18/dans-le-telephone-d-une-migrante-syrienne_4834834_3210.html#/ (accessed June 11, 2020); K. Gray, "Real-Time Syrian Refugee Game, Bury Me, My Love, Is Now On Switch and Your Should Play It," *Kotaku*, January 12, 2019, https://kotaku.com/real-time-syrian-refugee-game-bury-me-my-love-is-now-o-1831704781; PixelHunt, Figs, ARTE France, *Bury Me, My Love*, 2017, http://burymemylove.arte.tv/.

30. See for instance E. Zimmerman, *Gaming Literacy, The Video Game Theory Reader*, 2007, https://llk.media.mit.edu/courses/readings/Zimmerman-Gaming-Literacy.pdf.

31. I. Bogost, *Persuasive Games* (Cambridge, MA: MIT Press, 2007); I. Bogost, S. Ferrari, and B. Schweizer, *Newsgames* (Cambridge, MA: MIT Press, 2011).

32. Inspired by the quotation "In doing so, they stop being a mere viewer, and much more of a witness." C. Malmo, "A New Virtual Reality Tool Brings the Daily Trauma of the Syrian Civil War to Life," *Vice*, 2014, https://www.vice.com/en_us/article/jp5jx3/virtual-reality-is-bringing-the-syrian-war-to-life.

33. A. J. Katz, "Here's the Median Age of the Typical Cable News Viewer," *Ad Week*, January 19, 2018, https://www.adweek.com/tvnewser/heres-the-median-age-of-the-typical-cable-news-viewer/355379/. The median age of the cable news watcher was in their sixties, for instance, suggesting that the audience is not representative of the world at large.

34. C. Baker, B. Moore, and M. Lacher, *New York Times Voting Suppression* Game, November 3, 2016, https://www.nytimes.com/interactive/2016/11/01/opinion/voting-suppression-videogame.html?mtrref=www.google.com. It is called an "op-documentary."

35. See more about games as procedural rhetoric in Bogost, *Persuasive Games*. See also Bogost et al., *Newsgames*.

36. Darvasi used Twine for the narrative writing. See more in chapter 7. Based on personal interview with Paul Darvasi, Spring 2019.

37. See more in chapter 7.

38. These types of harmful discussions in games may not even be intentionally spurred on by the games or the players. When we bring people into a public sphere or community like a game, we need to imagine the range of possible human interactions that may occur—including those that are inhumane. We need to design and enforce boundaries in games to ensure these types of activities are not propagated. ADL, December 2020, *Free to Play? Hate, Harassment, and Positive Social Experiences in Online Games 2020*, https://www.adl.org/free-to-play-2020#results (accessed January 12, 2021); ADL, 2020, *This is Not a Game: How Steam Harbors Extremists*, https://www.adl.org/steamextremism (accessed on January 18, 2021); G. Kaufman, M. Flanagan, and M. Seidman. "Creating Stealth Game Interventions for Attitude and Behavior Change: An 'Embedded Design' Model." DIGRA 2015, Proceedings

of the Digital Games Research Association (DiGRA), 2015, http://www.digra.org/digital-library/publications/creating-stealth-game-interventions-for-attitude-and-behavior-change-an-embedded-design-model/; DROG/University of Cambridge, *Harmony Square*, 2020; Yle, *Troll Factory*, 2020; Yle, "Yle's *Troll Factory* game was chosen as the best digital project to engage young people," July 5, 2020, https://yle.fi/aihe/artikkeli/2020/05/07/yles-troll-factory-game-was-chosen-as-the-best-digital-project-to-engage-young; J. Roozenbeek and S. van der Linden, "Breaking *Harmony Square*: A game that "inoculates" against political misinformation," *MisInformation Review*, November 6, 2020, https://misinforeview.hks.harvard.edu/article/breaking-harmony-square-a-game-that-inoculates-against-political-misinformation/. We cannot let alternate fictions override vetted truths or to be used to spread harmful inaccuracies. See also, A. Barron, "QAnon is an Alternate Reality, But it's No Game," The *New Yorker* Radio Hour, January 15, 2021, https://www.wnycstudios.org/podcasts/tnyradiohour/segments/qanon-alternate-reality-its-no-game; R. Berkowitz, A Game Designer's Analysis of QAnon: Playing with Reality, *Medium*, September 30, 2020, https://medium.com/curiouserinstitute/a-game-designers-analysis-of-qanon-580972548be5. Some of the questions in this section are also inspired by conversations with people like Elizabeth Newbury. An important additional research question is to what extent games may be used to enhance distrust in others and others' evidence. What are the factors that enhance the spread of disinformation? Will you join me in investigating this?

39. As described in chapter 8, please also consider the cultural context and ramifications of *Mission US*. However, regardless of whether it is culturally relevant for a classroom or learning purpose, I feel that the game is a useful as an example of showing and using words in context.
40. iCivics, *Executive Command*, https://www.icivics.org/games/executive-command. *Executive Command* is a game where players play as the president of the United States and need to make domestic and international policy decisions.
41. Neil Wrona, personal interview, Spring 2019.
42. Teachers may want to use games to reveal the techniques of persuasion and mechanics, in an effort to then show how to spread and halt the spread of disinformation.
43. Senokos Games, *Fake Your Own Election*, 2020, https://senokos.itch.io/fake-your-own-reelection.
44. Associated Press, https://www.euronews.com/tag/2020-belarusian-presidential-election; Belarus: "Opposition Protesters Maintain Pressure on Lukashenko," *EuroNews*, September 13, 2020, https://www.euronews.com/2020/09/13/belarus-opposition-protesters-maintain-pressure-on-lukashenko.
45. GOP Arcade, *Thoughts and Prayers: The Game*, https://www.thoughtsandprayersthegame.com/.
46. This lesson also inevitably occurs after a gun violence incident in schools or public areas, and therefore I approach this game with sensitivity given the social context.
47. *Newsfeed Defenders*, iCivics, https://www.icivics.org/games/newsfeed-defenders. Amber Coleman-Mortley, personal interview, Spring 2019.
48. Amanda Warner, *Fake It to Make It*, https://www.fakeittomakeitgame.com/. A question is whether practicing how to *spread* false information (in a safe, bounded game environment) helps the player to know what to look out for in the future.
49. DROG/Cambridge University, *Bad News*, 2018, https://www.getbadnews.com/#intro; see teachers' guide at https://www.getbadnews.com/wp-content/uploads/2019/03/Bad-News-Game-info-sheet-for-educators-English.pdf.

Chapter 11

1. But this time, the problem you need to solve is not how to stop a plague, but how to spread it far and wide and infect people around the world. *Plague Inc.*, Ndemic, 2012, https://www. ndemiccreations.com/en/22-plague-inc.

2. Players need to continually adjust the parameters of this system such that the virus continues to spread—such that no one can cure the organism and enough people (hosts) stay alive long enough to transmit the disease to others before their hosts perish.

3. M. Kelly, "Designing Game-Based Writing Projects to Foster Critical Ethical Reasoning in the English Classroom: A Case Study Using *Plague Inc*: Evolved, Simulation & Gaming," September 3, 2020, https://journals.sagepub.com/doi/abs/10.1177/1046878120953592.

4. *Plague Inc.*, Ndemic, 2012, https://www.ndemiccreations.com/en/22-plague-inc. The interface is even similar to the many COVID-19 trackers, so much so that you may have to remind students that it is a game, tracking a fictional plague, because it seems to celebrate deaths as victories in a tally rather than real human losses. A COVID-19 version will be coming out after the writing of this book. See K. Orland, "*Plague Inc.* Maker: Don't Use our Game for Coronavirus Modeling," *Ars Technica*, January 27, 2020, https://arstechnica.com/gaming/2020/01/plague-inc-maker-dont-use-our-game-for-coronavirus-modeling/, Accessed on January 1, 2021 ; S. Totilo, When a Gaming Fantasy is Eerily Close to Reality, *New York Times*, April 8, 2020, https://www.nytimes. com/2020/04/08/arts/plague-inc-video-game-gaming-coronavirus-covid-pandemic. html. A new mode of the game lets a player save the world from the plague rather than spur it on, and players will control government responses to the plague, healthcare systems, and public services. See S. Feder, "The *Plague Inc.* Creators Made a New Version of the Game that Lets Users Save the Planet from a Pandemic Instead of Destroying It," *Business Insider*, March 25, 2020, https://www.businessinsider.com/plague-inc-creates-new-version-lets-people-save-planet-coronavirus-2020-3 and B. Stephen, "The Creators of *Plague Inc.* Are Adding a New Game Mode That Lets You Stop an Outbreak," *The Verge*, March 24, 2020, https://www.theverge.com/2020/3/24/21192420/ plague-inc-who-donation-coronavirus. See also, "*Plague, Inc.: The Cure* is Now Out for IOS and Android," November 11, 2020, https://www.ndemiccreations.com/en/news/ 184-plague-inc-the-cure-is-out-now-for-ios-and-android

5. See more in K. Schrier, *Knowledge Games: How Playing Games Can Solve Problems, Create Insight, and Make Change* (Baltimore: Johns Hopkins University Press, 2016).

6. X. Briggs, *Democracy as Problem Solving: Civic Capacity in Communities Across the Globe* (Cambridge, MA: MIT Press, 2008). Moreover, Nussbaum argues that a "citizen of the world" type of problem-solving is one that does not aim to solve it to make the most money, or achieve the most, but to solve it in a way that we all flourish. How do we educate so that we can solve problems less for profit, but for eudaimonia? See M. Nussbaum, *Education for Profit/Education for Freedom* (Kolkata, India: Institute of Development Studies, March 2008). How can we create new models and systems where people are rewarded for their caring and fulfilling work, rather than using it to oppress and create social hierarchies and further social problems?

7. D. Jonassen, "Toward a Design Theory of Problem Solving," *Educational Technology and Research Development* 48, no. 4 (2000): 63–84.

8. Schrier, *Knowledge Games*, p. 53.

9. Jonassen, "Toward a Design Theory of Problem Solving"; Newell and Simon, *Human Problem Solving* (Englewood Cliffs, NJ: Prentice Hall, 1972).

10. Jonassen and Hung explain that "In everyday life and professional workplaces, people expend their greatest intellectual effort solving problems." D. H. Jonassen and W. Hung, "All Problems are Not Equal: Implications for Problem-Based Learning," *Interdisciplinary Journal of Problem-Based Learning* 2, no. 2 (2008): 6–28.

11. Schrier, *Knowledge Games*; Jonassen and Hung, "All Problems are Not Equal."

12. Wicked problem are problems with no clear solutions, or even ever fully solved, can take a long time and solutions not right or wrong, straddle disciplinary boundaries. Schrier, *Knowledge Games*, describes different types of problems on pages 56–61. See also W. Hung, "Team-Based Complex Problem Solving: A Collective Cognition Perspective," *Educational Technology Research and Development*, 61 (2013): 365–384; Detlef Schoder, Johannes Putzke, Panagiotis Takis Metaxas, Peter A. Gloor, and Kai Fischbach, "Information Systems for 'Wicked Problems'—Research at the Intersection of Social Media and Collective Intelligence," *Business & Information Systems Engineering* 6, no. 1 (2014): 3; J. Introne, R. Lauacher, G. Olson, and T. Malone, "Solving Wicked Social Problems with Socio-computational Systems," *Kunsliche Intelligenz* 27, no. 1 (2013): 45–52; for more about wicked problems see www.wickedproblems.com/1-wicked_problems. php. Wicked problems are ones that are "ill-structured, large-scale, systemic, complex dilemmas," ... Most are social and political problems are wicked problems ... such as healthcare, global warming, and mental illness ... Wicked problems could be figuring out what to do about children who are struggling in school ... or how to cure illnesses that have both social and scientific causes, such as heart disease," quoting Schrier, *Knowledge Games*, p. 61. "Resolving wicked problems requires parallel discourse, multiple iterations, changes of beliefs, and unpredictable revisions." Quoted in Schoder et al., "Information Systems for 'Wicked Problems'", p. 4; S. Wuchty, B. Jones, and B. Uzzi, "The Increasing Dominance of Teams in Production of Knowledge," *Science* 316, no. 5827 (2007): 1036–1039.

13. These were some of the problems mentioned in the graduation speech by President Barak Obama; *New York Times*, May 16, 2020, https://www.nytimes.com/2020/05/16/us/obama-graduation-speech-transcript.html.

14. Being able to understand a system and solve problems involves a number of overlapping cognitive processes and skills, some of which are discussed in other chapters, such as having domain knowledge, system knowledge (knowledge of the variables and components of a system), procedural knowledge (how to adjust variables in a system), experiential knowledge (knowledge of past solutions), and strategic knowledge (how to gather and evaluate information used to make a solution). Jonassen and Hung, "All Problems are Not Equal"; Matthew Ventura, Emily Lai, and Kristen DiCerbo, "Skills for Today: What We Know About Teaching and Assessing Critical Thinking," Pearson, 2017, https://www.pearson.com/content/dam/one-dot-com/one-dot-com/global/Files/efficacy-and-research/skills-for-today/Critical-Thinking-FullReport.pdf, citing D. H. Jonassen and W. Hung, "Learning to Troubleshoot: A New Theory-Based Design Architecture," *Educational Psychology Review* 18 (2006): 77–114.

15. Ventura et al., "Skills for Today."

16. Systems thinking has been seen as both a methodology and an orientation toward thinking, and has been seen as something interdisciplinary, multiperspectival, holistic, appreciative of complexity, and a "conceptual framework and model for thinking

about and learning about systems of all kinds—scientific, organizational, personal, and public … [that] highlights the crucial relationship between systems (the basic unit of how the natural world works) and thinking (the process of constructing mental models of real-world phenomena and evolving them based on feedback to better approximate reality." Quote from D. Cabrera and L. Cabrera, "What Is Systems Thinking?," in *Learning, Design, and Technology*, ed. M. Spector, B. Lockee, and M. Childress (New York: Springer, 2019).

17. For example, Toni (https://twitter.com/TSand83) explains in a video how we can give everyone the right to vote in the United States, but people (such as Black people) may still be systemically denied the right by intimidation, by additional laws around voting ID cards, and other systemic issues, like racism. Toni explains that "we need to change the system of attitudes" to make real lasting change. We need to totally redesign systems from the ground up. See more at https://twitter.com/ChuckModi1/status/1275646998243311617 (accessed June 25, 2020).

18. Cabrera and Cabrera, "What Is Systems Thinking?"

19. Jennifer Worth, personal interview, Spring 2019. "Maybe it is because we had a super charismatic leader, or maybe it is because someone just didn't show up that day because they had the measles."

20. The problem, then, is defined by a game's rules, boundaries, and constraints. Quote at Jonassen, "Toward a Design Theory of Problem Solving"; Schrier, *Knowledge Games*.

21. K. Schrier, "Guiding Questions for Game-Based Learning," in *International Handbook of Information Technology in Primary and Secondary Education*, ed. D. Gibson (New York: Springer, 2018).

22. A. Shaenfield, personal interview, Summer 2020.

23. Schrier, *Knowledge Games*; Schrier, "Guiding Questions."

24. Jonassen, "Toward a Design Theory of Problem Solving"; Jonassen and Hung, "All Problems are Not Equal"; T. Fullerton, *Game Design Workshop*, 4th ed. (Burlington, MA: Morgan Kaufmann Publishers, 2018).

25. Sungrazer Studio, *Resilience*, 2019/2020, https://www.sungrazerstudio.com/. The game presents the types of problems that an international humanitarian organization might face, and enables players to decide how they might solve them.

26. A famous example is giving students a candle, book of matches, and box of thumbtacks, and then asking them to attach the candle to a corkboard. Many participants did not think to empty the thumbtack box and use it as a stand for the candle, which could be attached to the wall. Rather, they were fixated on the box as being a way of holding the tacks, rather than as also a stand. See Newell and Simon, *Human Problem Solving*.

27. Proctor used this module in his college classes, such as first-year seminars or upper-level courses, where players need to take on roles from an Athenian context, which helps them to break away from their own present-day responses. Mark C. Carnes, Josiah Ober, and Naomi J. Norman, *Threshold of Democracy*, 4th edition (New York: Norton, 2015). Civic problems include questions such as, "Will Athens retain a political system where all decisions are made by an Assembly of 6,000 or so citizens? Will leaders continue to be chosen by random lottery? Will citizenship be broadened to include slaves who fought for the democracy and foreign-born metics who paid taxes in its support?"

28. Nicholas Proctor, personal interview, Spring 2019. He explains that "the roles become multifaceted and [players will] see that there are some things that they personally agree

with. And there are others that they really strongly disagree with . . . It's also good that they have to fully express and understand ideas that they don't agree with."

29. Players may also have their own unique goals or responsibilities, which are hidden from the other players.

30. D. Shaffer, *How Computer Games Help Children Learn* (New York: Palgrave, 2006); Schrier, *Knowledge Games.*

31. " 'Players enter and explore within a game world, which is a deliberately designed system based on a set of rules, assumptions, and values' and which is further influenced by the addition of human players, their game play, the communities that emerge, and their own unique activities." Quoted in Schrier, *Knowledge Games*, p. 39. "A game can simulate, for example, an ethical system or a key ethical issue, and enable a player to try out different possibilities related to it. In a sense, this is similar to a case, in that it allows the participant to play out different scenarios and experience changes, results or outcomes. Participants may not make specific choices, per se, but may act, express, or behave in ways that affect the game's system. Games and simulations go beyond a story or case, however, because it can algorithmically incorporate many factors, and model an issue from many perspectives. A simulation is also more scalable than a nondigital case, such that the data and outcomes could be analyzed and implemented anywhere, and shared among participants . . . A player can then experiment with this model iteratively to learn more about it, to enhance their ethical awareness, understanding of issues or frameworks, or to better reason through scenarios. A simulation does not necessarily need to have a realistic or real-world counterpart (for example, a fantasy role-playing game could simulate a currency or ethics system that has no direct connection to the real world), but the simulation strategy can be used in tandem with strategy 10 (application to real-world issues) for enhanced impact." See K. Schrier, "EPIC: A Framework for Using Video Games for Ethics Education," *Journal of Moral Education* 44, no. 4 (2015): 393–424. See also K. R. Fleischmann, R. W. Robbins, and W. A. Wallace, "Information Ethics Education for a Multicultural World," *Journal of Information Systems Education* 22 (2011): 191–201.

32. Quoted in Schrier, *Knowledge Games*, p. 39. Likewise, Harviainen explains that "we see not just direct consequences of actions but how they affect a business relationship or an organization, a community, a municipality or country. [Through play we also] learn to read that system and compare it with other existing systems including the ones we have in real life." J. Tuomas Harviainen, personal interview, Spring 2019, referencing also I. Bogost, *Persuasive Games: The Expressive Power of Videogames* (Cambridge, MA: MIT Press, 2007).

33. O. Gottlieb, I. Schreiber, and K. Murdoch-Kitt, *Lost & Found*, 2017, accessed on March 3, 2021 https://scholarworks.rit.edu/other/904/; O. Gottlieb and I. Schreiber, *Lost & Found: Order in the Court——The Party Game*, 2017, accessed on March 3, 2021 https://scholarworks.rit.edu/other/903/; O. Gottlieb and I. Schreiber, *Lost & Found: New Harvest*, 2020. See more about the game at O. Gottlieb and I. Schreiber, "Acts of Meaning, Resource Diagrams, and Essential Learning Behaviors: The Design Evolution of Lost & Found," *International Journal of Designs for Learning* 11, no. 1 (2020): 151–164; Owen Gottlieb and Ian Schreiber, "Designing Analog Learning Games: Genre Affordances, Limitations, and Multi-Game Approaches," in *Rerolling Boardgames: Essays on Themes, Systems, Experiences, and Ideologies*, ed. Douglas Brown and Esther MacCallum Stewart (Jefferson, NC: McFarland & Company, 2020), pp. 195–211); O. Gottlieb, "Re-Playing Maimonides'

Codes: Designing Games to Teach Religious Legal Systems," *Teaching Theology & Religion* 21, no. 4 (2018): 246–259; O. Gottlieb, Finding *Lost & Found*: Designer's Notes from the Process of Creating a Jewish Game for Learning, *gamevironments* 7, 2017: 42–65. See also, *Lost & Found: New Harvest*, https://www.thegamecrafter.com/games/lost-found:-new-harvest, accessed on January 5, 2021.

34. K. Salen and E. Zimmerman, *Rules of Play* (Cambridge, MA: MIT Press, 2004); Schrier, "Guiding Questions."

35. Players can decide which widgets to make, such as batteries, toasters, or coffee makers, or how to spend their resources—cash and super cash. For example, you can use your cash to decide which part of the system to level up so that they are incrementally more and more efficient, or to unlock new widgets to produce. You can also decide to wait to collect enough cash to unlock something with longer-term benefits. See more in Kolibri Games, *Idle Factory Tycoon*, https://www.idlefactorytycoon.com/, Accessed on January 23, 2021.

36. On the other hand, it's sometimes hard to see the direct results of your decisions—such as whether it was good to open another workstation, upgrade a material, or unlock a skill point—because the system is constantly dynamically changing over time and cash is constantly being generated. The system-level feedback obscures some of the individual decisions you make because you cannot compare your series of decisions to another series of decisions, unless you were able to "stop time" and compare the resulting systems. Teachers may also want to use games like these to talk about broader systems, like economic and labor systems and their systemic problems.

37. Mollendustria, https://www.molleindustria.org/demsocsim/; A. Robertson, "Run an America Full of Talking Animals in *Democratic Socialism Simulator*," The Verge, March 1, 2020, https://www.theverge.com/2020/3/1/21155909/democratic-socialism-simulator-review-game-2020-election

38. Josh Archer, personal interview, Spring 2019. Archer is a creator of analog role-playing games.

39. Vi Hart and Nicky Case, *Parable of the Polygons*, https://ncase.me/polygons/.

40. Shaffer, *How Computer Games Help Children Learn*, 2006.

41. Though we can argue that scientific problems are also civic in nature too and civic problems require scientific expertise alongside other types of experiences.

42. D. Brabham, *Crowdsourcing* (Cambridge, MA: MIT Press, 2013).

43. One of the Audubon projects involves identifying birds in one's backyard, as with the Audubon's Holiday bird count, one of the longest running citizen science projects. See History of the Christmas Bird Count, Audubon Society; Cornell Lab of Ornithology, https://www.audubon.org/conservation/history-christmas-bird-count; for a crowdsourcing app on the weather, see https://mping.nssl.noaa.gov/; for Gravestone crowdsourcing, see https://billiongraves.com/ or https://www.findagrave.com/.

44. D. McKinley, *Design Principles for Crowdsourcing Cultural Heritage*, 2015, http://nonprofitcrowd.org/crowdsourcing-heuristics. In another series of projects, people help to analyze cultural heritage sites. E. Ridge (ed.), *Crowdsourcing our Cultural Heritage* (Farnham, UK: Ashgate Publishing, 2014); M. Ridge, "On the Internet, Nobody Knows You're a Historian: Exploring Resistance to Crowdsourced Resources Among Historians," paper presented at the Digital Humanities Conference, Hamburg, July 16–20, 2012; F. Romeo and L. Blaser, "Bringing Citizen Scientists and Historians Together," paper presented at the Museums and the

Web 2011, Philadelphia; G. Rockwell, "Crowdsourcing the Humanities: Social Research and Collaboration," in *Collaborative Research in the Digital Humanities*, ed. M. Deegan and W. McCarty (Farnham, UK: Ashgate, 2012), pp. 135–154; D. Paraschakis, "Crowdsourcing Cultural Heritage Metadata Through Social Media Gaming" (Master thesis, Malmo University, 2013; J. Oosterman, A. Nottamkandeth, C. Dijkshoorn, A. Bozzon, G.-J. Houben, and L. Aroyo, "Crowdsourcing Knowledge-Intensive Tasks," in *Cultural Heritage, Proceedings of the 2014 ACM Conference on Web Science*, pp. 267–268.

45. D. Brabham, "Crowdsourcing the Public Participation Process for Planning Projects," *Planning Theory* 8, no. 3 (2009): 242–262; Brabham, *Crowdsourcing*; moving the crowd at iStockphoto: the composition of the crowd and motivations for participation in a crowd-sourcing application by Daren C. Brabham, *First Monday* 13, no. 6, June 2, 2008, https://firstmonday.org/ojs/index.php/fm/article/download/2159/1969.

46. The AAVSO stands for the American Association of Variable Star Observers. See more in M. Jordan Raddick, G. Bracey, P. L. Gay, C. J. Lintott, C. Cardamone, P. Murray, K. Schawinski, A. Szalay, and J. Vandenberg, "Galaxy Zoo: Motivations of Citizen Scientists," *Astronomy Education Review* 12, no. 1 (2013), DOI:10.3847/AER2011021; A. Wiggins, "Crowdsourcing Scientific Work: A Comparative Study of Technologies, Processes, and Outcomes in Citizen Science." (PhD diss., Syracuse University, 2012); "Community Science: American Eel Research," New York Department of Environmental Conservation, https://www.dec.ny.gov/lands/49580.html (accessed on January 1, 2021); see Črtomir Podlipnik, Marko Jukić, N. Nikitina, S. Pleško, L. Gilardoni, G. Tomšič, Ž. Pevec, B. Laba, M. Manzyuk, and T. Kočar, "COVID.SI," https://covid.si/en/ (accessed June 13, 2020).

47. These games aim to bring players and computational power together, in a dynamic system, such that they can optimize the strengths of each to better solve complex issues. I call these games knowledge games because they develop new knowledge through the playing of the game. These types of games are only just beginning to emerge, but could be applied to creating both scientific and social scientific knowledge. Students playing these games, therefore, could be able to work on real-world civics and ethics problems. See more in Schrier, *Knowledge Games*.

48. P. Landwehr, M. Spraragen, B. Ranganathan, K. M. Carley, and M. Zyda, "Games, Social Simulations, and Data—Integration for Policy Decisions: The SUDAN Game," *Simulation & Gaming* 44, no. 1 (2013): 151–177.

49. University of Washington Center for Game Science, *Foldit*, https://fold.it/.

50. Carnegie Mellon University, *EteRNA*, https://eternagame.org/home/.

51. For instance, see *EteRNA*, March 18, 2020, https://eternagame.org/news/9804036.

52. For more about confirmation bias, see U. Peters, "What Is the Function of Confirmation Bias?," *Erkenn* (2020), https://doi.org/10.1007/s10670-020-00252-1, https://link.springer.com/article/10.1007/s10670-020-00252-1 and Rich Ling, "Confirmation Bias in the Era of Mobile News Consumption: The Social and Psychological Dimensions," *Digital Journalism* 8, no. 5 (2020): 596–604.

53. David Shaenfield, personal interview, Spring 2019.

54. Ibid.

55. "A heuristic is a shortcut that your mind in the sense of the cognitive heuristic," quote from David Shaenfield, Personal interview, spring 2019.

56. Saarella, *The Stranded Game*, http://strandedgame.net/teacher.html (accessed June 13, 2020).

57. If they don't have enough food or shelter, for instance. However, as a result, that means that a player can go an entire turn without harvesting food or building a shelter, and only lose some happiness. It's also not always clear how to gain happiness or find what they need to find on the island.

58. Schrier, *Knowledge Games*; Schrier, "Guiding Questions."

59. See more at Steven T. Wright, "Why the Makers of *Plague Inc.* Are Building a Mode Where You Destroy the Virus," Gamasutra, May 4, 2020, https://www.gamasutra.com/view/news/361998/Why_the_makers_of_Plague_Inc_are_building_a_mode_where_you_destroy_the_virus.php.

60. Schrier, "Guiding Questions"; G. Roussos and J. F. Dovidio, "Playing Below the Poverty Line: Investigating an Online Game as a Way to Reduce Prejudice Toward the Poor," *Cyberpsychology: Journal of Psychosocial Research on Cyberspace* 10, no. 2 (2016): 1–24; M. Farber and K. Schrier, "The Limits and Strengths of Using Digital Games as Empathy Machines," UNESCO Working Paper, 2017, https://unesdoc.unesco.org/ark:/48223/pf0000261993_eng. Example decisions include things such as whether to pitch in to help out a sick colleague or pay to attend a concert.

61. Roussos and Dovidio, "Playing Below the Poverty Line."

62. After playing this game, which presented a series of choices, people who thought that poverty resulted from a series of bad choices, and then felt even less empathetic to those who do not have money. People who believed in the idea of a meritocracy were more likely to believe that any lack of money was the result of poor choices rather than systemic oppression. Roussos and Dovidio, "Playing Below the Poverty Line"; Farber and Schrier, "The Limits and Strengths of Using Digital Games."

63. Research on financial insecurity reveals that it is difficult and even impossible to rise above poverty and financially insecure situations because of systemic issues, such as racism, fewer educational opportunities, lower wages, most of which are out of an individual person's control.

64. Perhaps because it did not confirm the bias that players have had about poverty being under the control of a person. We may also need players to *feel* the consequences of their choices—such as how our lives and the lives of those around us might be systemically affected if we cannot fix an appliance or give our kid a pair of sneakers.

65. Some of these crowdsourcing activities also have some game-like features (rewards, badges, points) even if they are not, altogether, games. We could call this process gamification, which involves using game-like features and applying them to nongame contexts, such as a crowdsourcing app or website. Schrier, *Knowledge Games*; Schrier, "Guiding Questions."

66. L. Hassan, "Governments Should Play Games: Towards a Framework for the Gamification of Civic Engagement Platforms," *Simulation & Gaming* 48, no. 2 (2017): 249–267, citing X-L. Jin, Z, Zhou, M. K. O. Lee, ad C. M.K. Cheung, "Why Users Keep Answering Questions in Online Question Answering Communities: A Theoretical and Empirical Investigation," *International Journal of Information Management*, 33, no.1, 2013: 93–104; and J. Lee, and S. Kim, "Active Citizen e-Participation in Local Governance: Do Individual Social Capital and e-Participation Management Matter?" *2014 47th Hawaii International Conference on System Sciences (HICSS), Hawaii, IEEE* (2014): 2044–2053.

67. L. Hassan and J. Hamari, "Gamification of E-Participation: A Literature Review," *Proceedings of the 52nd Hawaii International Conference on System Sciences* (2019): 3077.

68. Or to have a voting mindset. J. T. Harviainen and L. Hassan, "Governmental Service Gamification: Central Principles," *International Journal of Innovation in the Digital Economy* 10, no. 3 (2019): 1–12.

69. However, because these apps are location-specific and not accessible from my current location, it is unclear whether these are complete games, where the participants are playing a game where they happen to respond, report, or contribute; or whether the apps are gamifying what is really just a crowdsourcing activity. EuroCities, *Traffic Agent*, 2016.

70. United Nations World Food Programme, *Free Rice*, http://freerice.com/#/english-vocabulary/1498. I argue that the game is poorly designed and not effective as a game about solving hunger.

71. Even though it may actually help to solve a real-world hunger problem (because it gives rice away), we may wonder why they aren't giving away the rice already if they have it for people to eat. Why wait for a game to do that? On the other hand, it has given away so much rice. It's difficult to weigh the game's effectiveness. (This question is inspired by a perspective from Olivia Montoya, https://metaparadox.itch.io/.) Likewise, with *Spent*, it did actually raise quite a bit of money to better support nonprofits that aim to reduce poverty and it brought about more awareness to the issue.

72. For much more on these ethical issues, see K. Schrier, "The Ethics of Citizen Science Gaming: Perspectives from STS," Meeting of the Society for the Social Studies of Science (4S), Boston. 2017; K. Schrier, "Designing Learning with Citizen Science and Games," *Journal of Emerging Learning Design* 4, no. 1 (2017): 19–26.; and Schrier, *Knowledge Games.*

73. Schrier, *Knowledge Games.*

74. What is the purpose of the company making the game? Kavya Pearlman, "XR and Ethics," Games for Change talk, June 25, 2020.

75. Inspired by Kent Bye, "XR and Ethics," Games for Change talk, June 25, 2020. Privacy laws are also different in different countries. For instance, in the United States, digital companies cannot store private personal information of youth under the age of 13. European GDPR include additional considerations and data protections for digital experiences.

76. J. Stefanska, P. Magnuszewski, J. Sendzimir, P. Romaniuk, T. Taillieu, A. Dubel, Z. Flachner, and P. Balogh, "A Gaming Exercise to Explore Problem-Solving Versus Relational Activities for River Floodplain Management," *Environmental Policy & Governance* 21, no. 6 (2011): 454–471.; K. Schrier, "Using Games to Solve Real-World Civic Problems: Early Insights and Design Principles," *Journal of Community Engagement and Higher Education* 10, no. 1 (2018): 21–35.

77. "For instance, we could use a simulation to look at the conditions of a lake over time. Participants could to try out different parameters (such as adding pollutants, changing weather conditions, or taking away predators of lake inhabitant populations), and then can then experience any consequences, without having to actually affect a real lake and cause possible dangers." Schrier, "EPIC." K. Schrier, "Ethical Thinking and Sustainability in Role-Play Participants: A Preliminary Study," *Simulation & Gaming* 46, no. 6 (2015): 673–696

78. This has implications for environmental policy and education. Schrier, "Ethical Thinking and Sustainability."

79. Christopher Harris, personal interview, Spring 2019.

80. In *Papers, Please*, a player acts as an immigration officer for an ambiguous Eastern European country, and needs to detect issues with passports and other documentation based on current rules and regulations. The officer's performance results in financial compensation, which has repercussions for one's in-game family; not following the rules could end in termination. At points in the game, players can decide to break the rules to help certain immigrants enter the country, with potentially destructive consequences. Schrier, "EPIC."

81. Players can make no more than two mistakes on whether to accept or deny a person in each round, and after that they are terminated, which affects the officer's ability to take care of their family. You also have to inspect passports to see if the photo inside matches their image.

82. "Through the playing of the game and its rules, players begin to understand the game's ethical system, and experience its brutal arbitrariness, as well as the suffocating nature of the bureaucracy surrounding immigration." Schrier, "EPIC," referencing J. Singal, "A Foreign Video Game Concept: Making Red Tape Fun," *Boston Globe*, August 17, 2013, https://www.bostonglobe.com/arts/2013/08/17/video-game-about-immigration-bureaucracy-awesome/vZeSFIheJmot75tQ64oWDP/story.html.

83. In fact, the interactions with a ruleset or system of rules is one of the ways that games differ from other types of media. Games involve rules, goals, mechanics, and other elements. "Games 'mount claims through procedural rhetorics,' Games make arguments about its meaning through the ways in which people play it. Unlike books or television, games are making arguments through 'rule-based representations and interactions' and not just text or images." Through a game, players get the opportunity to interact with a dynamic system or model, rather than something static. However, this goes beyond just being able to interact with a system in that through the very act of being in and navigating rules, players are embodying an argument about the world, and how ethics, ethical systems and issues function in it. Thus, "Even if no obvious ethical choice or behavior is required, and there is no clear-cut consequence of a choice, the very rules of play that a player must navigate can lend themselves to making claims." An integral part of this is that the player can break rules, as well as follow them. Quotes from I. Bogost, *Persuasive Games* (Cambridge, MA: MIT Press, 2007), p. ix and Schrier, "EPIC."

84. Killer Snails, *BioDive*, https://www.killersnails.com/products/biodive-virtual-reality.

85. While the problems should be structured, they should also have some variety and complexity such that the player needs to continue to test and retest their hypotheses and possible solutions, given different scenarios. W. Frey, "Teaching Virtue: Pedagogical Implications of Moral Psychology," *Science & Engineering Ethics* 16 (2010): 611–628.

86. K. Schrier, J. Diamond, and D. Langendoen, "Using *Mission US: For Crown or Colony?* To Develop Historical Empathy and Nurture Ethical Thinking," in *Ethics and Game Design: Teaching Values through Play*, ed. K. Schrier and D. Gibson (Hershey, PA: IGI Global, 2010), pp. 239–261; K. Schrier, "Designing and Using Games to Teach Ethics and Ethical Thinking," in *Learning, Education and Games Vol. 1: Curricular and Design Considerations*, ed K. Schrier (Pittsburgh: ETC Press, 2014).

87. Players may be able to share, compare, and verify solutions through games. They can interact with other characters or real players, either inside or outside the game, and compare possible hypotheses, outcomes, and solutions. I. Guy, A. Perer, T. Daniel, O. Greenshpan, and I. Turbahn, "Guess Who? Enriching the Social Graph Through a Crowdsourcing

Game," in *Proceedings of the SIGCHI Conference on Human Factors in Computing Systems* (2011), pp. 1373–1382. In *Mission US*, players may interpret events different, and can share those interpretations with their classmates. Schrier et al., "Using *Mission US*."

88. Learning Game Networks, *Quandary*, https://www.quandarygame.org/play.

89. The Quandary team explains, in a personal correspondence, "In *Quandary*, however, there is no one right answer, just as with life's thorniest ethical quandaries." Additional information by Shannon Meneses and Scot Osterweil, personal interview, Spring 2019. Quotation by Scot Osterweil, personal interview, Spring 2019.

90. Or they may get the same number of points but have different solutions because they supported their solutions with relevant evidence, even if they came to distinct conclusions about how best to proceed in Braxos. Learning Games Network, *Quandary*, https://www.quandarygame.org/. The *Quandary* team provides resources for teachers to use, like lesson plans and a tool to design characters. For teacher resources and guides see, "*Quandary* Educator Resources," https://quandarygame.org/resources, accessed on January 17, 2021. A disclosure is that I joined the advisory board of *Quandary* in Fall 2020, after writing most of this book. Some of the information in this example has been inspired by conversations with the advisory board.

91. J. Tuomas Harviainen, personal interview, Spring 2019. He says, "And that's a huge message also to the citizens that if you play this, you can actually affect political processes and improve things in your community."

92. Bloomberg Cities, "How Helsinki Uses a Board Game to Promote Public Participation," January 17, 2018, https://medium.com/@BloombergCities/how-helsinki-uses-a-board-game-to-promote-public-participation-39d580380280.

93. iCivics, *Represent Me*, https://www.icivics.org/games/represent-me.

94. University of Southern California (USC), Annenberg Center, *Redistricting Game*, http://www.redistrictinggame.org/; http://www.redistrictinggame.org/game/launch-game.php.

95. Is a game using shallow gamification, or more deep and meaningful engagement?

96. Suggestions from Lim on role-playing include focusing on intellectual understanding of a characters' desires, rather than performing as them or acting like them. For instance, avoid tokenistic or stereotypical performances, do not recreate or cause trauma (such as having people perform as slave/master pairs). She also suggests having people switch roles so they can experience a breadth of perspectives. Find out more at Jenny Lim and Greg Trefry, "Social Studies Unconference," May 13, 2020, https://www.youtube.com/watch?v=UwH-gONlOmz4&feature=youtu.be&t=95. See also materials from Ed Zinn, "How to—and How Not to—Do Role Plays," September 15, 2019, https://www.zinnedproject.org/news/how-to-teach-role-plays/.

97. Lim also shares that the historical distance of the problem helps the students take more risks, while also understanding how it applies to today's issues, and encourages students to argue and ask questions. Find out more at Lim and Trefry, "Social Studies Unconference." Also see Vox Pop, "Role-Playing Our Way through History," Games for Change 2020, Virtual, https://www.youtube.com/watch?v=IRofIuJUqyM&feature=youtu.be.

98. Gigantic Mechanic, *Vox Pop*, 2021, https://www.voxpop.io/. The game launches in 2021. I played an early prototype of a remote version of the game. Find out more at Lim and Trefry, "Social Studies Unconference." All quotes from Jenny Lim and Greg Trefry.

Chapter 12

1. Lin-Manuel Miranda is the creator of the *Hamilton* musical. FableVision, an interactive studio in Boston, was inspired by the popularity of *Hamilton*, as well as the immersiveness of games, and came up with a new game, *Civics! An American Musical*. This game, targeted toward middle school students, is funded by the Library of Congress, and plans to be released in FableVision, *Civics! An American Musical*, https://civics.fablevisiongames.com/, 2020.

2. Leigh Hallisey, Creative Director of FableVision, Spring 2020. And once all the components are chosen, the musical gets performed through the game and even rated by the "critics . . . based on the choices that you made and how well you represented the time period," Hallisey explains. Hallisey hopes that students in the classrooms will also "put on the musicals and record them and put them online." Hallisey also explains that the topics that are included in the game are ones that appeal to the age group of the game's audience (middle school in the United States).

3. Hallisey, personal interview, Spring 2019. In *Knowledge Games*, I talk about how seeing the "real" documents and written word were considered more authentic than printed (and now digital formats) because you could see the expressiveness of the script or the pressure of the ink point, which helped to establish it as more acceptable knowledge. K. Schrier, *Knowledge Games: How Playing Games Can Solve Problems, Create Insight, and Make Change* (Baltimore: Johns Hopkins University Press, 2016).

4. Quoted by Hallisey, personal interview, Spring 2019. "Kids become more civically engaged, more knowledgeable citizens." The game may also be engaging students in learning about the past and getting them excited about how they can participate as citizens beyond the classroom. Hallisey's hope is that the game will "capture that energy and excitement that kids have about *Hamilton* to spark their interest in history and underscore that it shouldn't be viewed in isolation, but rather look for connections between the past, what's happening today, and how they can get involved in shaping the future."

5. See for instance H. Jenkins, G. Peters-Lazaro, and S. Shresthova, *Popular Culture and the Civic Imagination: Case Studies of Creative Social Change* (New York: NYU Press, 2020).

6. D. Jonassen, "Toward a Design Theory of Problem Solving," *Educational Technology and Research Development* 48, no. 4 (2000): 63–84.

7. Ibid.

8. Schrier, *Knowledge Games*, p. 43.

9. Matthew Ventura, Emily Lai, and Kristen DiCerbo, "Skills for Today: What We Know About Teaching and Assessing Critical Thinking," Pearson, 2017, https://www.pearson.com/content/dam/one-dot-com/one-dot-com/global/Files/efficacy-and-research/skills-for-today/Critical-Thinking-FullReport.pdf.

10. C. E. Hmelo, D. L. Holton, and J. L. Kolodner, "Designing to Learn About Complex Systems," *Journal of the Learning Sciences* 9, no. 3 (2000): 247–298; J. L. Kolodner, "Facilitating the Learning of Design Practices: Lessons Learned from an Inquiry into Science Education," *Journal of Industrial Teacher Education* 39, no. 3 (2002): 9–40; J. L. Koldner, P. J. Camp, D. Crismond, B. Fasse, J. Gray, J. Holbrook, S. Puntambekar, and M. Ryan, "Problem-Based Learning Meets Case-Based Reasoning in the Middle School Science Classroom: Putting Learning by Design TM Into Practice," *Journal of the Learning Sciences* 12, no. 4 (2003): 495–547.

11. I. Bogost, *Persuasive Games* (Cambridge, MA: MIT Press, 2007); A. Davisson and D. Gehm, "Gaming Citizenship: Video Games as Lessons in Civic Life," *Journal of Contemporary Rhetoric* 4, no.3–4 (2014): 39–57. See also chapters 3 and 11 of this book.

12. R. Benjamin, "Introduction," in *Captivating Technology* (Durham, NC: Duke University Press, 2019).

13. Take for instance how the 1619 project helps to address our assumptions and biases with how the United States presents history. It realigns it with a central focus on slavery and its legacy. See more at the Pulitzer Center, https://pulitzercenter.org/lesson-plan-grouping/1619-project-curriculum (accessed on January 1, 2020). How can we do something similar with games and revealing our civics and ethical systems?

14. Lindsay Portnoy, personal interview, Spring 2019. See alsoL. Portnoy, *Designed to Learn* (Alexandria, VA: Association for Supervision and Curriculum Development [ASCD], 2019).

15. The process of creation can also help us to construct knowledge, externalize it, and connect to others. See for instance K. A. Peppler, E. Halverson, and Y. B. Kafai (eds.), *Makeology: Makerspaces as Learning Environments (Volume 1)* (New York: Routledge, 2016); Y. B. Kafai, K. A. Peppler, and R. Chapman (eds.), *The Computer Clubhouse: Constructionism and Creativity in Youth Communities* (New York: Teachers College Press, 2009); Y. B. Kafai and Q. Burke, "Constructionist Gaming: Understanding the Benefits of Making Games for Learning," *Educational Psychologist* 50, no. 4 (2015): 313–334; D. Fields, V. Vasudevan, and Y. B. Kafai, "The Programmers' Collective: Fostering Participatory Culture in a High School Scratch Mashup Coding Workshop," *Interactive Learning Environments* 23, no. 5 (2015): 1–21.

16. Schrier, "Designing Ourselves."

17. "Designing civic games requires a complex thought process concerning civic issues, as designers consider how these can be expressed via gameplay." Quotes by Gideon Dishon and Yasmin B. Kafai, "Connected Civic Gaming: Rethinking the Role of Video Games in Civic Education," *Interactive Learning Environments* (2019), DOI: 10.1080/10494820.2019.1704791. See also work they cite by H. Jenkins, *Confronting the Challenges of Participatory Culture: Media Education for the 21st Century* (Cambridge, MA: MIT Press, 2009); Bogost, *Persuasive Games*; M. Flanagan, *Critical Play: Radical Game Design* (Cambridge, MA: MIT Press, 2009); M. Flanagan and H. Nissenbaum, *Values at Play in Digital Games* (Cambridge, MA: MIT Press, 2014); Kafai and Burke, "Constructionist Gaming." Dishon and Kafai also describe how Owens "explored how modding Civilization supports engagement with issues such as the development of social and historical movements."T. Owens, "Modding the History of Science: Values at Play in Modder Discussions of Sid Meier's Civilization," *Simulation & Gaming* 42, no. 4 (2011): 481–495.

18. Quotes by Scot Osterweil, personal interview, Spring 2019.

19. T. Fullerton and B. Upton, The USC Game Innovation Lab, https://www.gameinnovation-lab.com/playthink/2018/9/7/brian-upton-at-playthink, October 16, 2018, citing Brian Upton, *Siuational Game Design* (Boca Raton, FL: CRC Press, 2017). The game is inclusive of the player's state of mind, and what they bring to the game, like their prior experiences, expectations, or their emotions. They are playing a game that is not necessarily the game that was designed, but, explains Upton, "it is the game that they think that they have in their head . . . sometimes it lines up with what was designed and something it doesn't." He also explains that when we go to design a game, we should think about "who do you

want the player to be while they play your game . . . all games are role-playing games in some way . . . every game encourages you to be" someone or something. He asks: What constraints, actions, and rules can I provide to the player to help encourage the player to be performing as this person? If students are unsure how to proceed when engaged in a design activity like a game jam, teachers can show them the variety of games in this book, which may help students imagine and visualize possible new types of games and experiences to create.

20. The participants reported feeling safer from threats and uncertainties after (M = 4.51, SD = .695) versus before (M = 4.21, SD = .983), t(84) = -2.656, p = .009. Tiredness and feeling good emotionally, as reported by the participants, did not change. Participants enjoyed working with others. One participant noted, "I feel more understood and supported. It was a healing experience and we made a healing game." One participant explained that "our game encouraged being vulnerable with your friends, so we [game jam team members] all learned a bit more about each other." Another participant noted that "My teammates were not neurotypical and that opened up a conversation on something I was not familiar or experienced with." Part of what helped was doing the identity exercises, but the process of designing with others was also helpful. One participant explained that "I think other people are more relatable to me than I would have guessed by appearance. I was worried I would not relate well to other members, but I had a lot in common." See more in K. Schrier, "Designing Ourselves."

21. While not all games tell stories, there are a number of ways that games can tell stories. They can express stories in similar ways as other media, such as through a series of events, or plots, as well as exposition, dialogue, characters, and action. Story can also emerge from the way that the player interacts with the environment. For instance, in *Gone Home* (Fullbright Company), players need to explore a virtual home with objects and artifacts that a player can pick up and inspect, such as videotapes, notes, or locker doors. The player begins to actively reveal the story by meaningfully exploring this environment, interacting with narrative scraps, and piecing together clues about a family's past. Story also can come from how players play the game, such as the obstacles, and how they overcome them to reach the goal. Game players can also reveal narrative through their solving of a particular problem in a particular way or in how the goals are met and how the game is played, moment to moment. For more about story, see chapter 8.

22. W. Frey, "Teaching Virtue: Pedagogical Implications of Moral Psychology," *Science & Engineering Ethics* 16 (2010): 611–628, 2010.

23. K. Schrier, "EPIC: A Framework for Using Video Games for Ethics Education," *Journal of Moral Education* 44, no. 4 (2015): 393–424; K. Schrier, "*BioShock* as the Infinite Parent: Parenting and Play in the BioShock Series," in *New Perspectives on BioShock*, ed. Jessica Aldred and Felan Parker (Montreal, QC: McGill-Queen's University Press, 2018); R. Travis, "BioShock in the Cave: Ethical Education in Plato and in Video Games," In *Ethics and Game Design: Teaching Values through Play*, ed. K. Schrier and D. Gibson (Hershey, PA: IGI Global, 2010), pp. 86–101; L. Cuddy, *BioShock and Philosophy: Irrational Game, Rational Book* (New York: Wiley, 2015). See also *Hades*, Supergiant Games, 2020, https://store.steampowered.com/app/1145360/Hades/; Cardboard Computer, LLC/Annapurna Interactive, *Kentucky Route Zero*, 2013, http://kentuckyroutezero.com/.

24. Story helps to transport an audience to another realm, where people feel immersed, empowered, and that the stakes are higher because they are "really there experiencing the

events." Quote by S. T. Murphy, L. B. Frank, M. B. Moran, and P. Patnoe-Woodley, "Involved, Transported, or Emotional? Exploring the Determinants of Change in Knowledge, Attitudes, and Behavior in Entertainment-Education," *Journal of Communication* 61, no. 3 (2011): 407–431, p. 411. Samuel Taylor Coleridge coined the phrase in 1817. This suspension "refers to a reader's (or audience's) willingness to accept the author's vision of a time, place, world, or characters that, were they not in a work of fiction, would be unbelievable … even if it makes no sense within our own world" See K. Schrier, E. Torner, and J. Hammer, "Worldbuilding in Role-Playing Games," in *Role-Playing Game Studies: Transmedia Foundations*, ed. S. Deterding and J. Zagal (New York: Routledge, 2018). See more about story in chapter 8.

25. S. T. Murphy, L. B. Frank, M. B. Moran, and P. Patnoe-Woodley, "Involved, Transported, or Emotional? Exploring the Determinants of Change in Knowledge, Attitudes, and Behavior in Entertainment-Education," *Journal of Communication* 61, no. 3 (2011): 407–431, p. 411; G. Kaufman, M. Flanagan, and M. Seidman. "Creating Stealth Game Interventions for Attitude and Behavior Change: An 'Embedded Design' Model." DiGRA 2015, Proceedings of the Digital Games Research Association (DiGRA), 2015, http://www.digra.org/digital-library/publications/creating-stealth-game-interventions-for-attitude-and-behavior-change-an-embedded-design-model/.

26. In regard to my daughter and *Mario Maker 2*, the process of sharing the game with the public also helped her to identify as someone who is a creator. It helped her to design for the imaginary audience, and to think about what they might like, and craft her level to better suit them. It also made her more confident in making other things, like writing a mini-book in her third grade class. (Her golden mushroom level is also her most played and "liked" level thus far). Molecule Media, *Dreams*, 2020, https://indreams.me/. See also Roblox Corporation, *Roblox*, 2006, https://www.roblox.com/

27. Schrier, "EPIC," citing L. A. Floyd, F. Xu, R. Atkins, and C. Caldwell, "Ethical Outcomes and Business Ethics: Toward Improving Business Ethics Education," *Journal of Business Ethics* 117 (2013): 753–776. They can help "enable the practice of ethical reasoning and experimentation with different moral possibilities. Story allows access into other people's lives and opens us further to practicing empathy … story provides a context to how we view ethics, which helps us further understand ethical issues, our own ethical assumptions, and makes us more ethically self-aware." For instance, in *Life Is Strange*, players are playing as Max Caulfield, a high school student who is trying to help her best friend, Chloe Price. Throughout the game, the player (as Max) needs to make ethical choices that affect the story, such as which conversation responses to share with Kate, a girl who is thinking about committing suicide. The choices you make will impact whether you are able to help save her and keep her from committing suicide; it also impacts the rest of the game, such as how other people treat and view Max, how Max feels about herself, how Kate's parents and friends respond to her, and whether Max can visit Kate at the hospital and continue to interact with her.

28. See Kristine Jørgensen and Faltin Karlsen (eds.), *Transgression in Games and Play* (Cambridge, MA: MIT Press, 2019); Schrier, "*BioShock* as the Infinite Parent."

29. M. Consalvo, *Cheating* (Cambridge, MA: MIT Press, 2007).

30. Dishon and Kafai, "Connected Civic Gaming."

31. M. Flanagan and Nissenbaum, *Values at Play in Digital Games* (Cambridge: MIT Press, 2014); Xuefei (Nancy) Deng, K. D. Joshi, and Robert D. Galliers, "Microtask

Crowdsourcing Can Both Empower and Marginalise Workers," *LSE Business Review* (April 15, 2016), http://eprints.lse.ac.uk/73616/1/blogs.lse.ac.uk-Microtask%20crowd-sourcing%20can%20both%20empower%20and%20marginalise%20workers.pdf.   See also Christopher Paul, *The Toxic Meritocracy of Games* (Minneapolis, MN: University of Minnesota Press, 2018); regarding different gender and sexual identities, races or ethnicities, or sizes and shapes, which could possibly contribute to toxic communi-ties and antisocial interactions of all types. Biases are also embedded in design itself—whether a learning experience, game, or anything that a human has created. Games embed biases of all types; games may show biased representations of people, cultures, or how systemic bias influences and is influenced by people and policies. For more about this, see Benjamin, *Captivating Technology*. See also Consalvo, *Cheating*, who explains that we should "design understanding to look below the hood of the game and understand how it works; what values, misconceptions, or biases it may express or mag-nify; or how students may cheat, hack, bully, or otherwise transgress in the game. They may not know how to question or interrogate the game with students even if they have a lot of experience with a particular game." Think about how rapidly the culture changes, and how much media seems "dated" because of these cultural shifts. Take favorite US shows from just a few decades ago: sitcoms like *Friends*, *Frasier*, and *Seinfeld*, while still lauded, are also now seen as culturally problematic, whether due to racism, homo-phobia, or lack of compassion for others. Even during the writing of my books, cultural changes led to writing norm changes. During *Knowledge Games*, the norm went from writing s/he to be inclusive, to they, to be inclusive. During the writing of this book, the norm around writing the word "Black" went from having the "b" be lowercase to up-percase to help signify the cultural importance of Black identity. We don't always know what changes will occur, and even in this book there will be cultural anachronisms in just a few years in the future.

32. G. Yang, B. Gibson, A. Lueke, L. Huesmann, and B. Bushman, "Effects of Avatar Race in Violent Video Games on Racial Attitudes and Aggression," *Social Psychological and Personality Science* 5, no. 6 (2014): 698–704.

33. For instance, see accusations of racism and sexism against the creators of *Cards Against Humanity*: N. Carpenter, "Former Employees Accuse *Cards Against Humanity* of a Racist and Sexist Office Culture," *Polygon*, June 23, 2020, https://www.polygon.com/2020/6/23/21300435/cards-against-humanity-max-temkin-report; T. Lorenz and K. Browning, "Dozens of Women in Gaming Speak Out About Sexism and Harassment," *New York Times*, June 23, 2020, https://www.nytimes.com/2020/06/23/style/women-gaming-streaming-harassment-sexism-twitch.html; L. Plunkett, "Riot Games Executive Says George Floyd Was Murdered By Police Because Of His 'Criminal Lifestyle' [UPDATE]," *Kotaku*, June 10, 2020, https://kotaku.com/riot-games-executive-says-george-floyd-was-murdered-by-1843987857?fbclid=IwAR1xjNaKk7W3F8jcOr3i1j6rpcvLEZvqXb4iZ7spFEMy-Zn4MXmb5WZCfLo0; C. Hall and S. Polo, "The Game and Comics Industries Are Grappling with Widespread Allegations of Harassment and Abuse," *Polygon*, June 25, 2020,   https://www.polygon.com/2020/6/25/21302341/video-game-tabletop-game-comics-allegations-harassment-abuse-racism-metoo?fbclid=IwAR1LrF5ltZqOvyp-39kKiEid31h1j4Sqb6bhDeuQLk7E-3bUh7pM_ImAgA6k. Researchers have also pointed out bias, exclusion, and marginalization in design and development communities. See also ADL, *Free to Play? Hate, Harassment, and Positive Social Experiences in Online Games*

2020, December 2020, https://www.adl.org/free-to-play-2020#results (accessed January 12, 2021)

34. See more in chapter 8. These include the misuse or exploitation of one's roles or avatars, inappropriate or even illegal interactions with other players, or even using the game in a way that it misrepresents the designers' intentions so drastically that it damages other players.

35. While the purpose of this book is not to grapple with all of the ethics of games, as we could write a whole separate book on this, it is important to consider the ethics of our use and play. See more in Schrier, *Knowledge Games*; M. Sicart, *Ethics of Computer Games* (Cambridge, MA: MIT Press, 2009).

36. Sabrina Culyba, personal interview, Spring 2019. Culyba explains that "if you're specifically aiming to leave people different after your game, to behave differently or to think differently, and you're not telling them that this is your purpose, is that okay? How much of the message is opt-in versus subterfuge? I personally prefer designing where the players are partners, where you're trying to facilitate a change that players are interested in achieving for themselves." It is okay to try to change someone? Is that manipulation?

37. See for instance this workshop on design thinking and white supremacy. It says, "White supremacy and its values have been constructed into our societal structures and norms—including those found in design." Quote by Creative Reaction Lab, https://www.creativereactionlab.com/, on the workshop website, https://www.eventbrite.com/e/how-traditional-design-thinking-protects-white-supremacy-encore-registration-109013446152?aff=eand&fbclid=IwAR3yEO1HVCHah2_cPeo_sLEiUb7PGTETtY_y2EZmh64p8_xqmQ1Jfb29wsY (accessed June 28, 2020).

38. Doris Rusch, personal interview, spring 2019. Rusch explains that "When it comes to personal development or emotional well-being or personal transformation, I find this approach really problematic … How can we empower players more to seek out what their desire for transformation in a game actually is … I think there is a really large underexplored area of what we can do when we get people sensitive to their own needs and desires and give them a playground to explore different ways of acting and being that are more congruent with who they want to become and stimulate change on that level."

39. Some games are intentionally problematic, such as ones that are created to spur racial and ethnic stereotypes and foster hate, or ones that are created to purposely foster real-world violence, such as terrorism propaganda games serving as hate speech or terrorist propaganda. This is distinct from games and gaming platforms that can be used for hate, when it is not intentionally its purpose. See more at J. Ebner, "Dark Ops: Isis, the Far-Right and the Gamification of Terror," *Financial Times*, February 14, 2020, https://www.ft.com/content/bf7b158e-4cc0-11ea-95a0-43d18ec715f5 .

40. Giant Bomb: In this white supremacy propaganda first-person shooter, the player is given the disgusting task of killing racial stereotypes; see https://www.giantbomb.com/ethnic-cleansing/3030–29306/ (accessed June 12, 2020); R. Khosravi, "Neo-Nazis Are Making their Own Video Games and They're Just as Horrifying as You'd Think," *Mic*, May 22, 2017, https://mic.com/articles/174705/neo-nazis-are-making-their-own-video-games-and-they-re-just-as-horrifying-as-you-d-think#.3Yba2q8Zz; J. Funk, "Flash Game Makes Players Beat Up Tropes vs. Women Creator," *Escapist Magazine*, July 6, 2012, http://www.escapistmagazine.com/news/view/118310-Flash-Game-Makes-Players-Beat-Up-Tropes-vs-Women-Creator; A. Zimmerman, " 'Rape Day' Game Where You Play as a 'Dangerous Rapist' Pulled After Backlash," *The Daily Beast*, March 8, 2019, https://www.thedailybeast.

com/rape-day-game-where-you-play-as-a-dangerous-rapist-pulled-from-steam-after-backlash. See also ADL, "Free to Play? Hate, Harassment, and Positive Social Experiences in Online Games 2020," https://www.adl.org/free-to-play-2020#results (accessed January 12, 2021), which cites evidence of white supremacist discourse and other forms of hate in games (see also chapter 6 and 10). It also notes that, "None of the open responses mentioned recruitment or explicit attempts to indoctrinate players. Instead, the responses seem to indicate the continued normalization of white supremacist rhetoric and ideas in online multiplayer games, a trend we continue to see in all digital spaces. That does not mean that recruitment or indoctrination to extremist movements is absent in online multiplayer games, simply that this survey does not presently show evidence of that behavior"; See also, R. Kowert, "State of the Research: Toxicity in Games and Gaming Cultures," September 23, 2020, https://www.youtube.com/watch?v=ZiS_akCFk_4&feature=youtu.be. For moral panic responses to games, and moving beyond it, see R. Kowert and T. Quandt, *The Video Game Debate: Unravelling the Physical, Social, and Psychological Effects of Video Games*, New York: Routledge, 2016. About design, see also, I. Perrson, "Good Design Is Invisible. But So Is Design That Harms," UX Design, January 12, 2021, https://uxdesign.cc/good-design-is-invisible-but-so-is-design-that-harms-1ca98569b2f3

41. Numinous, *That Dragon, Cancer*; see more in chapter 7. See also K. Schrier, "Would You Kindly Parent? Parenting, Caretaking, and Love in Games," in *Love and Affection in Games, A Design Primer*, ed. Lindsay Grace (New York: Taylor and Francis, 2020).

42. R. Broderick, "Someone Made a Video Game About Sandy Hook Where You Play as Adam Lanza and Shoot Children," *BuzzFeed News*, November 20, 2013, https://www.buzzfeednews.com/article/ryanhatesthis/someone-made-a-video-game-about-sandy-hook-where-you-play-as.

43. For instance, see a Change.org petition at https://www.change.org/p/the-slaying-of-sandy-hook-elementary-online-game (accessed June 27, 2020).

44. Joshua A. Fisher, personal interview, Spring 2019; Ralph Vituccio, personal interview, Spring 2019.

45. Ralph Vituccio, personal interview, Spring 2019.

46. Schrier, "Designing Ourselves."

47. Matthew Farber, personal interview, Spring 2019. He explains: "Don't worry if the games you make or projects or podcasts are not even great ... They should be the ones making it. So even if it's like a half-baked scratch game, you're learning."

48. Schrier, "Designing Ourselves."

49. Jessica Hammer, personal interview, Spring 2019. The players play in pairs (siblings, or married couples) and they need to make different types of ethical decisions throughout the game. One type of decision relates to how to respond to different events or choices that impact the pair, such as whether a secular couple should baptize their children for safety's sake. Jessica Hammer, one of the designers of the game (along with Moyra Turkington), explains that in one example, which takes place after Kristallnacht, two characters discover that the shop next door to their bookstore has been destroyed. See more at: https://unrulydesigns.com/rosenstrasse/ (accessed on January 5, 2021).

50. Jessica Hammer, personal interview, Spring 2019. "The players have to deal with someone who is more vulnerable than they are ... and they have to decide ... are we going to help her clean up the next morning with everyone watching and facing that decision and thinking about how much am I willing to take a risk? How much am I willing to express

compassion? How much am I willing to show up? … We have actually had people say at the end of the game things like, 'I was so angry when this character came to my character who didn't help me. They didn't do anything to help me the whole game. And then I felt guilty because I didn't do anything the whole game to help anyone else. I kept turning away from people who needed me, even though, as a player, I know it wouldn't have made a difference.' So it's this idea people seeing the opportunity to stand up or to protest, to resist, but also thinking about those daily decisions that you make about whether or not you go with the flow." Moreover, Hammer explains that the game deliberately "masks the consequences" until the end of the game where the players are scored by a facilitator, learn the results, and then engage in a post-game discussion about the consequences and how it was shaped by their decisions. Hammer explains that, in reference to the players trying something new, "And that's one of the opportunities of doing this is that you can try on the identity and try things you might not try in real life." Through playing the game, however, people start to question things like what makes a good activist.

51. Jessica Hammer, personal interview, Spring 2019 explains that someone playing might "try on an identity and try things [they] might not try in real life … Why not try … and play a character who would protest?' "

52. I held a design charette at ADL in fall 2018 with the following people: Seth Bleecker, Sharang Biswas, Jason Engerman, Joan Getman, Ailsa Gilliam, Elaine Gomez, Steven Hodas, Daniel Kelley, Heidi McDonald, David Or, Lindsay Portnoy, Zhenzhen Qi, and Mamta Shah.

53. The Global Game Jam organization, which coordinates game design events around the world. As mentioned earlier, a game jam, often a weekend-long, intensive, game creation event—involves lots of people working together to create a game under rapid and often, sweaty, circumstances. The games are often not polished or fully finished, but may provide a glimpse at the creative way of approaching a particular theme. Past Global Game game jam themes have been things like "Transmission," "Waves," and "What Home Means to You." Game jams are starting to be hosted for social and emotional-related topics. See more at https://globalgamejam.org/.

54. Games for Change, Student Challenge Events, http://www.gamesforchange.org/studentchallenge/events/. For instance, Games for Change is a community and movement that supports the use and design of games for social change and impact. They organized a student game challenges for teens, including one in January 2019 at the NYC Public Library, which related to the theme of gender equity, diversity and inclusion.

55. See the games made at the Emotions and Feelings jam held in August 2020 at https://itch.io/jam/emotional-jam-friendship. Five games made from the #ResistJam game jam were analyzed and researchers found that three supported potential for civic learning. The five #ResistJam games were analyzed in reference to learning democracy and politics. See more at M. Laumer and M. Kabaum, "Code of Resistance. On the Potential of Digital Games and Game Jams for Civic Education." *gamevironments* 13, (2020): 420–456. Available at http://www.gamevironments.uni-bremen.de. For more about the Global Game Jam, see Global Game Jam, "About," https://globalgamejam.org/about (accesed on January 18, 2021).

56. Schrier, "The ADL Mini-Guide to Identity, Bias, and Games," https://www.adl.org/media/12529/download, 2018. The guide was created to be used during a game jam. At the ADL game jam I co-organized, participants were asked to create a game that expressed identity in some way. This could include: "Expressing your own identity through a game, Making a

game that helps others understand parts of a personal or social group identity, Designing a game that shows how identity affects an individual's views, biases and perceptions of others and the world. Helping players learn about and share experiences that shaped their own identity, as well as their views of other people." The guide states, "Your mission is to make games related to identity, including identity expression, formation, and experimentation, which help players understand the different parts of their own identity, as well as others' identities." The game jam was first piloted at Marist College in Poughkeepsie, New York in September 2018. Then, the game jam events were held in October and November of 2018 at eight different locations around the United States, including Atlanta, Seattle, Austin, and New York City, as well as online through GameJolt.com. In fact, the process of making a game that is specifically related to perspective-taking, bias reduction, or empathy topics may even help students build skills in this area. In 2018–2019, I helped create a series of game jams; I worked with the ADL, an advocacy group for "stopping the defamation of the Jewish people, and to secure justice and fair treatment to all. The game jam was also run in Israel in 2019. The game jam took place over a Saturday night to a Sunday night, for a total of 13 hours, which is shorter than most game jams. Over 200 people participated in all of the game jams. See more in Schrier, *Designing Ourselves*.

57. Can we use game design to support identity exploration, perspective-taking, reduce bias, and enhance connection, compassion, and empathy? Overall, the participants ranged from high school students to experienced game development professionals. Almost half of the participants (who responded to a survey) had never been to a game jam prior to the event. Over 50 games were created at the events and of those made at the October and November game jams 38% of them were explicitly related to perspective-taking or bias in some way. For example, *aCutely aware* was a digital game about an interracial relationship and *Identity Crisis* is a game that asks players to make ethical choices when they only have "two days to live." So while a total of over 50 games have been created at these game jam events, the actual games themselves may not be effective at reducing bias or enhancing perspective-taking, but the event—and the game design process that they engaged in—may be effective. To understand the process, I researched the individuals (who were 18 and over and agreed to participate) at the event and looked at the extent to which they may have changed their attitudes toward games, toward their own identity, and their perspective-taking, empathic concern, and handling conflicts. The participant teams were randomly organized into three conditions: (1) control condition: participating in the event with the theme, as they would typically participate; (2) Guide condition: in addition to getting the theme, these participants also received a (paper) guide that could help support designing games for identity theme, as well as designing for empathy and learning more generally. The guide includes possible design steps to take; brainstorming exercises; design principles to use; research-based findings; guiding questions; and tips, hints, and resources; (3) educator condition: these participants were given a guide, and they also had an ADL anti-bias educator join the team and participate fully in the entire game jam and game design process. See more in Schrier, "Designing Ourselves."

58. Schrier, "Designing Ourselves."

59. One participant noted, "Our game encouraged being vulnerable with your friends, so we [game jam team members] all learned a bit more about each other." Another explained, "I think other people are more relatable to me than I would have guessed by appearance. I was worried I would not relate well to other members, but I had a lot in common." Participants

also started to become more aware and accepting of other's worldviews and perspectives. One participant explained that, "I got to explore the perspectives of those who I wouldn't necessarily agree with throughout the process of creating this game." Being able to engage in design seemed to support also engaging in civil discourse—feeling more vulnerable and more trusting with collaborators helped them to share viewpoints and listen in ways that they typically might not. Participants' own estimation of their identity also changed, as they self-reported that they saw themselves as game developers after the event (significantly more) than before the event. They also became more aware of their own identities and how that shapes their lives and how others perceive them. One participant said about their identity, "That I may have more privilege than others because of who I am and acknowledge that I am based on my race, social status, and culture." Participants began to ethically question their creations and how they represent identity through a game. One participant explained, "Trying to bring awareness of racial or gender bias seemed to have easy pitfalls of accidentally making a game that is racist or sexist. We had to check our intentions several times to avoid these." See more in Schrier, "Designing Ourselves."

60. Part of the fun was the theme itself, which 88% of participants felt comfortable or very comfortable with. For instance, one participant said that "the focus on hatred, empathy, and identity allowed for the creation of games with substance." Making a game about a meaningful topic deeply engaged the participants because they felt like their creations mattered. This was reflected in the event itself, which also felt supportive, inclusive, and caring. One participant noted, "I feel more understood and supported. It was a healing experience and we made a healing game." See more in Schrier, "Designing Ourselves."

61. However, participants did not all enjoy the theme and some were initially resistant or hesitant. A game jam may be a way of reaching those types of participants, who may feel these types of topics are frivolous or unnecessary. Twelve percent of the participants were not comfortable with the theme, suggesting that even in an event where the participation is an opt-in, participants may be uncomfortable designing for social issues. For instance, one participant said, "I don't really care about 'fighting for' identity or bias, but if they make for compelling pieces to a game I'll take advantage of them as best as possible." Perhaps games and game design may be one way to reach and even inspire students with all different viewpoints and attitudes toward civic and ethics issues. See more in Schrier, "Designing Ourselves."

62. See more in Schrier, "Designing Ourselves." This section suggests also that one way to possibly reduce hateful designs (or hateful uses of designs) is by teaching and reaching students *through* design. How can we empower antiracist approaches to design by enabling the practice of antiracism *through* design?

63. For instance, one participant explained, "It was helpful to have more knowledge on the team of what to think about when creating a game. Staying aware of certain topics ... Also just having another brain with different perspectives during design discussions ended up being very helpful." Another mentioned that the ADL facilitator "was incredibly intelligent, and [their] insight was really helpful with forming the emotional beats of the game." This describes the integral role that a teacher can play even if they do not have a design background or games expertise. Participants were significantly more likely to report an interest in making games about bias and identity—if they were in the Educator condition. Participants overall were significantly higher in overall means on a self-reported response to whether games can increase empathy, and lower on means on the question of whether

games can increase biases and hate, after the game jam. Participants also seemed to find it effective in having an anti-bias educator on their team, suggesting that the teacher, mentor, or classroom resource is an integral part of the process. This anti-bias educator was not well-versed in game design or development, but served as a subject matter expert, who questioned assumptions and provided just-in-time information to use to help in designing the game. Schrier, "Designing Ourselves."

64. However, one bias measurement did change in the Educator condition, which was the use of one's cultural background to perceive others. We did not see changes, possibly because the sample sizes were too small, we used a limited likert scale, we used the wrong measures, because it was a short event, or because the event was not focused enough on perspective-taking skill development. Further consideration should be taken to how to better practice, emphasize, and measure these skills throughout a design activity. Schrier, "Designing Ourselves."

65. A program run by Elana Shneyer and the organization BetaNYC. See more about the series of hackathons at N. Hidalgo, "Making History: The First Hackathon Inside the Historic New York City Hall," May 2, 2019, https://beta.nyc/2019/05/02/first-city-hall-hackathon/ . To do this: First, they needed to identify the problem. Next, they researched their audiences, the problem, and the context. Finally, they proposed a possible solution and prototyped it.

66. This group ended up winning the challenge. See more at https://beta.nyc/2019/05/02/first-city-hall-hackathon/ (accessed June 27, 2020).

67. Full disclosure: I acted as a judge for the event and I was inspired by their passion, rigor, and creativity. They were practicing a type of citizenship through games and in doing so, helping to solve real-world problems. As they designed, students shared compelling stories about their own lives, and how that inspired their designs. They also researched all the steps involved in the problems and solutions they identified.

68. The ethics around who can access the game, and how it is accessed, needs to be considered just as much as the design itself. Games may both replicate and propagate societal biases, and may themselves affect and be affected by these biases. These can in turn influence the inclusivity of a game and its surrounding community, and whether all people feel like they belong as a player of a game, or as a member of the game, which is a type of identity in and of itself. See also Schrier, "Designing Inclusive Games." When designing a game for an audience in another country or culture, developers need to think not only about changing the language, but also perhaps the target audience, storyline and dialogue, gameplay, art, and even how the game is shared and distributed. They also need to think about how the game can become part of the ecosystem of the local community, so it actually gets played, used, talked about, shared, and distributed. How can they ensure that everyone belongs and that the game is logistically, technically, physically, economically, socially, and emotionally accessible? Just as the ethics of others' designs, and our game play, need to be considered, the ethics of our own designs also need to be reflected on more deeply.

69. See more at Fullerton, *Game Design Workshop*; Schrier, "Designing Inclusive Games." Also, games evolve based on the relationships that form among designer, player, and the game, as well as the game community that forms within and around the game.

70. Sue Spiegel and Marla Felton, Common Circles, personal interview, Spring 2019.

71. The participants started with a number of activities, such as doing get-to-know-you and identity exercises and an introduction to game design.

72. The nondigital card game could also be turned into a digital card game as well. Each card features a different celebrity, including famous entertainers, artists, politicians, scientists, social advocates, and writers, such as Beyonce, Fred Rogers, P!nk, Colin Powell, Kazuo Ishiguro, Lin Manuel Miranda, Nikola Tesla, Lorraine Hansberry, or Michael Jordan. Each card lists biographical stats about the person, including their date and place of birth, race, gender identity, and professional role, as well as different "fun facts" about them. For instance, Lorraine Hansberry is a Black woman, born in 1930 in Chicago, who was a playwright and screenwriter. Her facts include writing an opera, winning many awards, including best play, being an activist, and teaching at Frederick Douglass School. This game was further developed by Common Circles and can be played in a number of different ways. For instance, in one mode of the game, players get dealt a hand of 5–7 different cards. One celebrity card is placed face up on the table. Participants need to pick which person in their hand would have the most things in common with the celebrity card in the middle of the table. In another mode, players need to find the celebrity card that they think has the most in common with themselves, and try to see if they can get more commonalities than their competitors. In a more collaborative mode, players try to work together to create a chain of all the cards that they are dealt by finding a matching characteristic or fact about each one.

73. Thirty-five participants took a survey after the event and based on the self-reported results, according to Sue Spiegel and Marla Felton, Common Circles, personal interview, Spring 2019, and their personal notes. They understood the factors that make up their identity (88%) and the factors that make up others' identity (88%).

74. Sue Spiegel and Marla Felton, Common Circles, personal interview, Spring 2019. They also understand unconscious bias better, such as understanding what it means (88%), understanding their own (83%) and that everyone has it (86%).

75. One teacher noted that "at first, the students were uncomfortable. By the end of the time they were all great contributors and even connected with other students … They learned how to really work through difficult situations." Eighty-six percent said that they feel more comfortable having conversations about identity and bias, and 83% are more comfortable engaging with people from other backgrounds. 71% felt that their game and app design knowledge increased. All participants would be interested in this type of workshop and felt that it was a great way to learn about challenging topics (97%) and an engaging way to learn about identity and bias (91%). Sue Spiegel and Marla Felton, Common Circles, personal interview, Spring 2019.

76. Sue Spiegel and Marla Felton, Common Circles, personal interview, Spring 2019. While the assessment did not include a pre- and post- measure or comparison to a control condition, where participants did not receive a workshop or received a different type of workshop, the results suggest that this type of intervention could be effective. Overall, the students started to reflect on their decisions and interactions. One student explained that she was "recognizing that I was stereotyping people and I had a whole lot of unconscious biases that I was not aware of. I got to meet people that I had never met before and I got to hear their stories." Thus, incorporating collaborative game design as part of an anti-bias workshop may have helped facilitate a more inclusive and welcoming environment for learning and growing.

77. SheroHub is an organization that creates educational games that aim to raise awareness of domestic violence and help people become more aware of the factors, situations, and

communication practices that are signs of abusive relationships. One out of three women in the United States are in or have been in an abusive relationship (and one in seven men). Research suggests that intervention helps, such as a friend standing up and supporting a person who they observe may be in a problematic relationship. Prevention of people getting into these types of relationships is more effective than trying to rehabilitate batterers. Therefore, Ailsa Gilliam, CEO of SheroHub, LLC, created a visual novel-format game called *SheroHub*, which enables middle and high school students (targeted to ages 12 to 19) to explore different relationships and learn the subtle signs of domestic abuse. SheroHub also encourages empathy toward victims of domestic and dating violence. She explains that the game uses storytelling to show "all the different types of abuse such as verbal abuse, emotional abuse, intimidation, physical or financial abuse … You also learn about the cycles of abuse and how it may manifest through following 8 different characters stories." The use of a game in this scenario is "less threatening," particularly given the difficult and uncomfortable content. The player explores various character stories, making choices on how to interact with the characters and how to progress the story. The game provides resources and guidance on how to identify the subtle warning signs of domestic violence as well as giving tangible strategies and approaches for the community to support a victim. The pervasiveness of domestic violence and abusive relationships in our society suggests that it is imperative to find innovative ways to teach awareness of this issue, as well as the skills to identify signs, manage communications, and safely stand up when faced with this type of relationship (or that of a friend). Ailsa Gilliam, personal interview, Spring 2019. See more in A. Gilliam, *A Formative Evaluation of a Video Game to Educate on Gender-Based Violence in Low-and Middle-Income Countries*, A Thesis in the Field of International Relations, for the Degree of Master of Liberal Arts in Extension Studies, Harvard University, March 2021 (I read an unpublished version of this manuscript).

78. Personal interview, Ailsa Gilliam, Spring 2019, citing a report, Institut Haitien de l'Enfance (IHE) et ICF. 2018. *Enquete Mortalité, Morbidité et Utilisation des Services* (EMMUS-VI 2016–2017) Pétion-Ville, Haiti, et Rockville, Maryland, USA: IHE et ICF. She explains that "one in three women internationally are suffering from domestic violence, but it is probably a lot higher in Haiti," though she acknowledges it is hard to find accurate data on it. Her hope is that if we start to educate teens and young adults on "how they could live differently despite what they might have seen their parents doing … then the chances of achieving equality and improving society are far greater," which is why she is also creating a Haitian version of the game for teens as well as for the adults in the garment factories, who have already asked for this type of resource." See more in A. Gilliam, *A Formative Evaluation of a Video Game to Educate on Gender-Based Violence in Low-and Middle-Income Countries*.

79. Gilliam explains that "studies show that it's very important to deliver something that's culturally relevant and responsive to the needs of the population." Personal interview, Ailsa Gilliam, Spring 2019. See more in the previous note.

80. Personal interview, Ailsa Gilliam, Spring 2019.

81. Personal interview, Ailsa Gilliam, Spring 2019.

82. It could be done over time and use points, such as one that integrates *Classcraft*, an online system for managing student progress, though it would need to be meaningfully applied to the learning tasks. Classcraft Studio, https://www.classcraft.com/. This is not a recommendation, but simply an example. Tools for creating quick digital prototypes of games

could include: Scratch, Twine 2, GameMaker, GameSalad, Unity, Unreal Engine, ARIS, Metaverse AR, and Godot. Students could also use modding tools, and modify existing games (like using Garry's Mod). Games do not need to be digital, however. Which tool or approach to use depends on student and teacher needs, experience levels, and other factors.

83. S. Martyniuk, "*Monster Mash*, a Bomb Game," in *Learning, Education & Games Vol. 3: 100 Games to Use in the Classroom and Beyond*, ed. K. Schrier (Pittsburgh: ETC Press, 2019).

84. Thomas Kunze, the founder of Games Institute Austria, personal interview, Spring 2019.

85. This approach relied on the social infrastructure that was already in place, where girls would travel somewhere and "actually exchange games and bring them back to their home community." Jessica Hammer, personal interview, Spring 2019. See more at Jessica Hammer, "Context, Constraints, and Community: Designing Games for Girls in Rural Ethiopia," 2015, https://www.youtube.com/watch?v=9e7Wti8MaX0. See K. Schrier, *Trade Off*, in M. Flanagan and H. Nissenbaum, *Values at Play* (Cambridge, MA: MIT Press, 2014).

Chapter 13

1. There are many different ways to teach and approach learning, including social, cognitive, and constructivist approaches, as well as instructional theories for using technologies in the classroom. While covering the intricacies of all of these different approaches is not the aim of this book, for an overview of different game-based pedagogies and learning approaches, as well as an in-depth look at how to choose and use games in the classroom, readers may want to check out K. Becker, "Choosing and Using Games in the Classroom," in *International Handbook of Information Technology in Primary and Secondary Education*, ed. D. Gibson (New York: Springer, 2018). See also M. Farber, *Gamify Your Classroom: A Field Guide to Game-Based Learning* (New York: Peter Lang Publishing, 2015).

2. E. Zimmerman talk with T. Fullerton, University of Southern California (USC) Playthink, September 15, 2020, https://www.gameinnovationlab.com/playthink/2019/9/3/bonnie-ruberg-at-playthink-91019-8b8cx (accessed September 20, 2020).

3. Gigantic Mechanic, *The Migrant Trail*, https://theundocumented.com/ and iCivics, Immigration Nation, https://www.icivics.org/games/immigration-nation; the Pixel Hunt, Arte France, Figs, *Bury Me My Love*, http://burymemylove.arte.tv/; BBC, Syrian Journey, https://www.bbc.com/news/world-middle-east-32057601; *The Guardian, Refugee Choices*; https://www.theguardian.com/global-development/ng-interactive/2014/jan/refugee-choices-interactive.

4. Lindsay Portnoy, personal interview, Spring 2019.

5. Katrin Becker argues that using a game that is already specifically created for an educational purpose (such as a serious game) may be easier than one that is meant for other purposes, and needs to be adapted more significantly to support a specific curricular need. However, she also argues that commercial off-the-shelf (COTS) games may be useful in that they may have rich engaging stories, worlds, and activities. See Becker, "Choosing and Using Games in the Classroom." Becker outlines a four-pillar approach of questions to ask when choosing a game for the classroom.

6. For instance, J. Groff, J. McCall, P. Darvasi, and Z. Gilbert, "Using Games in the Classroom," in *Learning, Education, and Games Vol. 2: Bringing Games into Educational Contexts*, ed. K. Schrier (Pittsburgh: ETC Press, 2016).

7. This is because games are highly complex systems and are being put into other highly complex systems. The dynamics among them are sometimes unpredictable, and there are many different overlapping factors that can affect whether a game works or not. Teachers need to continue testing and retesting, and reflecting and revising, even after they get it right and find one effective way to use a game.

8. Educators should then continue to adapt its use based on their observations, student response and perceived learning, and whether it continues to be viable, practically, for a particular curricular need, goal, or context. The games also may be free and online, only available on a particular console, or downloadable from a platform such as Steam or the Apple store. For a reference to a number of games and how they may be used in the classroom, please see Schrier, *Learning, Education & Games Vol. 3*. This reference is free to download from the ETC Press site.

9. Gideon Dishon and Yasmin B. Kafai, "Connected Civic Gaming: Rethinking the Role of Video Games in Civic Education," *Interactive Learning Environments* (2019), DOI: 10.1080/10494820.2019.1704791. See also more factors in Becker, "Choosing and Using Games in the Classroom." This passage is inspired also by Lindsay Portnoy, personal interview, Spring 2019.

10. This table of questions was created using Becker's model and the EPIC framework as an inspiration. The EPIC framework, described in more detail in chapter 3, may be helpful for finding the right games. See K. Schrier, "EPIC: A Framework for Using Video Games for Ethics Education," *Journal of Moral Education* 44, no. 4 (2015): 393–424. Other frameworks may also be helpful, such as curricular frameworks like the C3 framework, also described in chapter 3 (NCSS, C3 framework). See more in Becker, "Choosing and Using Games in the Classroom."

11. Caitlin Daniels, personal interview, Spring 2019. iCivics, *Branches of Power*, https://www.icivics.org/games/branches-power. In *Branches of Power*, players learn about the different parts of the United States government, including the Legislative, Executive and Judicial Branches. Before even having the students play this game, Daniels first uses an exercise created by iCivics called "Separation of Powers: What's for Lunch?" The students need to work together to decide on a healthy lunch menu. To do this, they have to role-play the responsibilities that each of the branches have, where one group, acting like the executive branch needs to make a plan, and another group, acting like the judicial branch, has to decide whether certain foods fit the rules. Daniels' school hosts over one-third of the middle school students in Washington, DC proper. The explanation of the activity was conveyed by Matthew Farber, personal interview, Spring 2019.

12. Matthew Farber, personal interview, Spring 2019.

13. Paul Darvasi and Matthew Farber worked with Susan Rivers of iThrive, and created a curriculum ("Museum of Me") around the game *What Remains of Edith Finch*. See more in P. Darvasi and M. Farber, iThrive, 2020, https://ithrivegames.org/museum-of-me-sel-curriculum/.

14. J. Magnoson, *Loneliness*, https://www.necessarygames.com/my-games/gametrekking-omnibus; Mollendustria, *everyday the same dream*, https://www.molleindustria.org/everydaythesamedream/everydaythesamedream.html; dikaffe, *End of Us*, https://www.the-end-of-us.com/; Nomada Studio, *Gris*, 2018, https://nomada.studio/. Other games that may be useful to check out are Z. Quinn, *Depression Quest*, http://www.depressionquest.com/, 2013 and Jo-Mei Games, *Sea of Solitude*, https://www.ea.com/games/

sea-of-solitude, 2019. As another example, one of the activities that the *Mission US* team provides is based on Paul Revere's engraving, which they recommend the teacher use in class on *Mission US: For Crown or Colony*. The students can then interpret his engraving and compare the perspectives of Nat (game character), Paul Revere (historic figure), and the student-player. This can also lead to questions about the use of propaganda more generally, as well as activities such as a creation of their own colored pencil drawing (similar to Revere's engraving) of what happened at the Boston Massacre. Students can then share and discuss their creations. For instance, with, players can play a different module each day, and may do some in-class activities before and after each module. The game centers on Nat Wheeler, a printer's apprentice, who is collecting items and going on quests that take him to different historic figures, such as Paul Revere. During one of the final modules, the player, as Nat, interacts with a scene at King Street, the site of the massacre. Each player gets a different randomized series of scenes from the event that may show the differing perspectives on what happened (such as whether a snowball thrown by Minuteman incited the event or whether the British soldiers were threatening with bayonets). The teacher can use this module to help students discuss what may have happened at the battle, and why there are differing views on what happened. See more in WNET/Channel 13, *Mission US: For Crown or Colony*, https://www.mission-us.org/ and materials at https://cdn.mission-us.org/uploads/document/document_file/1117/Mission1-ALL-EDUCATOR-MATERIALS.pdf (accessed June 9, 2020). See also K. Schrier, J. Diamond, and D. Langendoen, "Using *Mission US*: For Crown or Colony? to Develop Historical Empathy and Nurture Ethical Thinking," in *Ethics and Game Design: Teaching Values Through Play*, ed. K. Schrier and D. Gibson (Hershey, PA: IGI Global, 2010), pp. 239–261.

15. Becker, "Choosing and Using Games in the Classroom."

16. For further information, see D. Simkins, "Assessing Video Games for Learning," *Learning, Education & Games Vol 1: Curricular and Design Considerations*, ed. K. Schrier (Pittsburgh: ETC Press, 2014); D. Gibson and M. Webb, "Assessment as, for and of 21st Century Learning," in *International Summit on ICT in Education* (Torun: EDUsummIT, 2013), p. 17; US Department of Education, "Learning Powered by Technology: Transforming American Education," Educational Technology, 2010, https://www.ed.gov/sites/default/files/netp2010.pdf.

17. K. Schrier, "Designing and Using Games to Teach Ethics and Ethical Thinking," in *Learning, Education & Games Vol. 1*, ed. K. Schrier (Pittsburh, PA: ETC Press, 2014), p. 151. See the Jubilee Centre, *Character Education in UK Schools*, 2015, https://www.jubileecentre.ac.uk/userfiles/jubileecentre/pdf/Research%20Reports/Character_Education_in_UK_Schools.pdf. How might games help us to measure behavioral change in the longer-term?

18. Sometimes they work and sometimes they fail—not even because of the game by itself—but also because of their context and how they are played. See more in Simkins, "Assessing Video Games for Learning"; Gibson and Webb, "Assessment as, for and of 21st Century Learning."

19. Simkins, "Assessing Video Games for Learning"; K. Schrier, "Guiding Questions for Game-Based Learning," in *International Handbook of Information Technology in Primary and Secondary Education*, ed. D. Gibson (New York: Springer, 2018). Metrics that teachers may want are whether a player reached all of the game's goals and completed it, whether players were proficient on in-game or out-of-game quizzes, or whether the game spurred real-world attitudinal change or action.

20. N. Mirra and A. Garcia, "Civic Participation Reimagined: Youth Interrogation and Innovation in the Multimodal Public Sphere," *Review of Research in Education* 41 (March 2017): 136–158.

21. We try to step away from the play and see if players understand everything from the instructions to how to win. You want to make sure that the game is fun and engaging, and challenging in the right ways. Archer asked them questions such as, "Are you having fun? Is this something that is interesting to you? If you could change anything about the game, what would that be? Or, are there aspects that stand out as being the best parts or as being the worst part?" Josh Archer, personal interview, Spring 2019. See more about playtesting in T. Fullerton, *Game Design Workshop* (Boca Raton, FL: A K Peters/CRC Press, 2018).

22. *When* a person assesses learning through a game, and *how* those assessments are used, matters. Gibson and Webb, "Assessment as, for and of 21st Century Learning," p. 17. Moreover, there are different types of assessments. Quantitative methodologies focus on measuring with a goal of replicating, verifying, and comparing results across and between students. Simkins describes some possible quantitative methodologies such as pre- and post-game examinations or eye tracking of what students are doing in a game. Qualitative methodologies "involve collecting data on what people are doing within their context ... [could] involve a very close read of the actions, speech, practices, and behaviors ... [and the] environment, social, cultural, and physical" context. Simkins, "Assessing Video Games for Learning," p. 279. The Department of Education also suggests the benefit of collecting and making use of student-learning data in real time so that educators and schools can make more effective, data-driven decisions and can better support differentiated learning, accessibility and greater feedback, inclusion, and transparency. US Department of Education, "Learning Powered by Technology."

23. Schrier, "Guiding Questions." Some ways that games can support students and assess them in partnership with their play may be to "investigate students' decisions in a game, comment on peer students' game creations, and/or respond to a prompt through the creation of a game or interactive project." See also Gibson and Webb, "Assessment as, for and of 21st Century Learning."

24. Schrier, "Guiding Questions," p. 15.

25. McGraw-Hill, *Quest: Journey through the Lifespan*, https://www.youtube.com/watch?v=Rcf9ACZcuV8 (accessed June 9, 2020), and McGraw-Hill, *Quest: Journey through the Lifespan*, 2020, https://www.mheducation.com/highered/connect/quest.html.

26. Likewise, a virtual world, *River City*, assessed student engagement in communication skills and scientific inquiry skills within the context of the game (multiuser virtual environment) itself. US Department of Education, "Learning Powered by Technology"; See more about *River City* in C. Dede, "Immersive Interfaces for Engagement and Learning," *Science* 323 (2009): 66–69; Schrier, *Reliving the Revolution* (game), 2005; see more in K. Schrier, *Revolutionizing History Education Using Augmented Reality games to Teach Histor(ies)* (Master thesis, MIT, 2005).

27. Schrier et al., "Using *Mission US*."

28. Dishon and Kafai, "Connected Civic Gaming." In chapter 12, and appendices III and IV, teachers can find out more about designing activities and games for and with their students.

Chapter 14

1. Nintendo, *Animal Crossing*, 2020; Katie Deighton, "*Animal Crossing* Is Emerging as a Media Channel for Brands in Lockdown," *The Drum*, April 21, 2020, https://www.thedrum.com/news/2020/04/21/animal-crossing-emerging-media-channel-brands-lockdown; S. Lim, "Ads We Like: Singapore's Sentosa Island Creates Branded Island on *Animal Crossing*," *The Drum*, May 8, 2020, https://www.thedrum.com/news/2020/05/08/ads-we-singapores-sentosa-island-creates-branded-island-animal-crossing; Imogen Watson, "Peta Storms *Animal Crossing* to Protest Treatment of Digital Animals," *The Drum*, May 22, 2020, https://www.thedrum.com/news/2020/05/22/peta-storms-animal-crossing-protest-treatment-digital-animals. See also, B. Gilbert, "Some *Animal Crossing* players in China are using the game to protest government policies, and now the Chinese government is banning the game," *Business Insider*, April 10, 2020, https://www.businessinsider.com/animal-crossing-new-horizons-nintendo-switch-banned-in-china-protests-2020-4. See also, D. Gilbert, "Hong Kong Gamers Protested Inside Animal Crossing, Now China Wants to Ban It," April 10, 2020, https://www.vice.com/en/article/epg3qp/hong-kong-gamers-protested-inside-animal-crossing-now-china-wants-to-ban-it. Where the game is currently banned, they have imported versions of the game and used it to protest their government's policies. Offline protests are banned.

2. I. Bogost, "The Quiet Revolution of *Animal Crossing*," *The Atlantic*, April 15, 2020, https://www.theatlantic.com/family/archive/2020/04/animal-crossing-isnt-escapist-its-political/610012/. He also cites Naomi Clark's work, where she posits *Animal Crossing* as "a nostalgic fantasy for the Japanese *furusato*, a pastoral hometown." (N. Clark, Why Tom Nook symbolizes village debt in 18th century Japan, YouTube video, 2020, https://www.youtube.com/watch?v=BgEnbXPZX4s). Clark explains that "it was the perfect idyllic village," complete with catching dragonflies and fishing. Bogost, citing Clark, explains that "the size and economies of these villages were too modest even to sustain their basic familial and mercantile needs, so the villages would take on collective debt—to pay for fishing nets and supplies, say. But nobody would ever pay back the debt, Clark explained. They didn't have the money! Instead, it would bind the locals to their village—you owed something to the collective, so how could you ever leave? And so the community would persist, a tableau of georgic calm sealed inside the bottle of a company town."

3. Coleman-Mortley of iCivics explains that "civic education can teach civil discourse; provide context for one's opinions and responsibilities in the context of the wider world; and highlight tangible examples of government operations." Amber Coleman-Mortley, personal interview, Spring 2019, and A. Coleman-Mortley, Let's Fix Civic Education, Mom of All Capes Blog, 2017, https://www.momofallcapes.com/blog/lets-fix-civic-education, Accessed on December 31, 2020.

4. See Muñoz and Hani's description of citizen in Yupanqui Muñoz and Charbel El-Hani, "The Student with a Thousand Faces: From the Ethics in Video Games to Becoming a Citizen," *Cultural Studies of Science Education* 7 (2012), DOI: 10.1007/s11422-012-9444-9. The quotation is from Amanda Gorman, "The Hill We Climb," 2021, recited on January 20, 2021 at the US Presidential Inauguration.

5. Andrew Delbanco, quoted in F. Bruni, "The End of Colleges as We Know It?," *New York Times*, June 4, 2020, https://www.nytimes.com/2020/06/04/opinion/sunday/coronavirus-college-humanities.html.

6. Yet when we need civics and ethics education the most, it is being undermined and undervalued. Such as through fewer liberal arts programs in colleges and universities, changing economic models for universities, less of a focus on social studies in K–12, and less overall funding for education, in addition to growing anti-elitist and anti-education attitudes in the United States and beyond. People see education as about productiveness for capital, rather than as a necessary part of citizenship and democratic engagement. See M. Nussbaum, *Not for Profit* (Princeton, NJ: Princeton University Press, 2010).
7. Parts of this list are inspired by César Hidalgo; see more at peopledemocracy.com.
8. But while we may mention that one way to spur participation in civic life and ethical thinking may be through play, and that gaming may help to achieve more democratic interactions and support, it may also do the opposite. Moreover, the game-like, us-versus-them aspects of the political process may even further its divisiveness, with each wanting to take compete against the other, rather than finding common ground.
9. Dewey writes, "All education which develops power to share effectively in social life is moral." J. Dewey, *Democracy and Education* (London, UK and Sterling, Virginia: Echo Library, 2007), p. 263.
10. We have lost sight of the purpose of learning and the purpose of games.
11. Bruni, "The End of Colleges as We Know It?"
12. When we "citizen" through games, must we participate in knowledge-making and value-making? Inspired by a quotation in K. Schrier, *Knowledge Games: How Playing Games Can Solve Problems, Create Insight, and Make Change* (Baltimore: Johns Hopkins University Press, 2016), p. 193.
13. Cachinero-Sánchez quoted by Bruni, "The End of Colleges as We Know It?"
14. I use the title of this book, *We the Gamers*, with a suggestion and understanding that I mean all of us game players—all of us who play, game, or live our lives playfully. But I realize that the term "gamer" has a problematic and exclusionary connotation and history, as I described in chapter 1. I hope readers can reconsider the term in a more expansive, lyrical way to mean everyone who plays games and plays—which is to say, all of us.

Appendix III

1. This framework is inspired by design approaches, interviews, and frameworks, such as Tracy Fullerton's approach to game design: T. Fullerton, *Game Design Workshop* (Boca Raton, FL: CRC Press, 2019); the transformational games framework design model (Sabrina Culyba), S. Culyba, *The Transformational Games Framework* (Pittsburgh: ETC Press, 2018); Jesse Schell and Barbara Chamberlin, "How to Make Games That Matter: A Framework for Making Games that Matter," presented at Connected Learning Summit 2018, https:// docs. google.com/document/d/1ekXtk61kgCllF1j4Z2UFbeSpUhTfOQCWgiNMoe7-3Xk/edit; K. Schrier, "Guiding Questions for Game-Based Learning," 2018, https://www.research-gate.net/publication/325357728_Guiding_Questions_ for_Game-Based_Learning; approaches to iterative design by Zimmerman and Salen, E. Zimmerman and K. Salen, *Rules of Play* (Cambridge, MA: MIT Press, 2004) and Sharp and Macklin, J. Sharp and C. Macklin, *Iterate: Ten Lessons in Design and Failure* (Cambridge, MA: MIT Press, 2019). See more at K. Schrier, *Designing Ourselves*, 2019, https://www.adl.org/media/13011/download; Schrier, EPIC; Schrier, "ADL Guide to Identity, Bias & Games," 2018, https:// www.adl.org/media/12529/download; Mary Flanagan and her Tiltfactor Lab, along with

Helen Nissenbaum, "The Values @ Play Framework," https://www.valuesatplay.org/grow-a-game-overview; K. Dunlap and Susan Rivers, personal interview, Spring 2019; Barbara Chamberlin, Jesus Trespalacios, and Rachel Gallagher, "The Learning Games Design Model: Immersion, Collaboration, and Outcomes-Driven Development," International Journal of Game-Based Learning, 2, no. 3 (2012): 87–110; M. Farber and K. Schrier, "The Limits and Strengths of Using Digital Games as Empathy Machines," UNESCO Working Paper, 2017, https://d1c337161ud3pr.cloudfront.net/files%2Fd61c7672-81d3-4ae0-8cc0-b14f53d1ab01_Working%20Paper%205.pdf.

Appendix IV

1. These principles are inspired in part by my work with ADL, iThrive's work, my work with Matthew Farber on the strengths and weaknesses of empathy games, my interviews with designers and teachers, and my own work with civics and ethics games. To see the full list of literature that these principles are based on, see more in Schrier, "Designing Ourselves," 2019, https://www.adl.org/media/13011/download; K. Schrier, "EPIC: A Framework for Using Video Games for Ethics Education," *Journal of Moral Education* 44, no. 4 (2015): 393–424; K. Schrier, "Designing Games for Real-World Moral Problem Solving," *Games & Culture*, 14, no. 4 (2019): 306–343; Schrier, "Using Games to Solve Real-World Civic Problems: Early Insights and Design Principle," *Journal of Community Engagement and Higher Education* 10, no. 1 (2018): 21–35; M. Farber and K. Schrier, "The Limits and Strengths of Using Digital Games as Empathy Machines," UNESCO Working Paper, 2017, https://d27gr4u-vgxfbqz.cloudfront.net/files%2Fd61c7672-81d3-4ae0-8cc0-b14f53d1ab01_Working%20Paper%205.pdf. See also, iThrive Games, "iThrive Game Design Kits," https://ithrivegames.org/resources/game-design-kits/ (Accessed on January 18, 2021). This list is also inspired by the frameworks and approaches that I used in creating the design toolkit, which can be found in the footnotes for Appendix III.

Index

For the benefit of digital users, indexed terms that span two pages (e.g., 52–53) may, on occasion, appear on only one of those pages.

Tables and figures are indicated by *t* and *f* following the page number

&maybetheywontkillyou (game), 121–22
1000 Cut Journey (game), 117, 118*f*, 125–26

A Distant Plain (game), 57–58
A Woman Goes to a Private Games Industry Party (game), 11, 150
AbleGamers Charity, 95, 239*t*, 250*t*
accessibility, 26–28, 204, 213*t*
action civics, 34, 35, 62–63, 62*f*, 66
activities
   designing activities, 219–20
   using activities around games, 61, 213*t*, 219–20
ADL
   civics curricula, 35
   game jams, 195, 202–3
   reports and studies, 25, 89, 91, 95
   role-playing, 126, 134
agency, 183, 245*t*
Along the River of Spacetime (game), 13, 13*f*, 125
alternate reality games (ARGs), 10
Among Us (game), 4, 14, 87, 150
Animal Crossing: New Horizons (game), 4, 11, 113, 161–62, 224
anti-bias workshops, 205
Antropy, A., 127
Antura and the Letters (game), 8–9, 107
Archer, J., 176, 221
Argument Wars (game), 72, 97–98, 98*f*
Argumentation, 46, 86, 142–43, 146, 192–193, 245*t*
assessment
   of games and design, 221–22
   of learning, 151, 213*t*, 220–23
Attentat 1942 (game), 131–32, 132*f*
audience
   designing for an audience, 192–196, 206, 239*t*, 245*t*
   identifying the audience, 213*t*, 239*t*
augmented reality (AR) games, 8, 14, 70, 74–75, 154

Bad News (game), 11–12, 165–66, 169–70, 170*f*, 232
Baldwin-Philippi, J., 76–77, 89–90
Bandura, Albert, 83–84

Bay Area Regional Planner (game), 70–71, 78–79, 79*f*, 93
belongingness, 21, 28, 101, 111–16, 251, 252
Benjamin, Ruha, 92–93, 108, 129, 193–94
Bias
   become aware of biases, 13, 15, 37–38, 45, 70–71, 118
   cognitive bias, 46, 141–42, 168, 175, 181
   definition of, 105
   in design, 92–93, 107–8
   and identity, 104–5, 109
   perspective-taking and, 118–19, 120–21, 125
   systemic bias, 11–12, 212, 213*t*
BioShock (series), 145, 150, 195
Black Lives Matter (protests), 28, 65, 99, 128, 155
Bogost, Ian, 16, 55, 125, 146, 224
Branches of Power (game), 176, 219
Budget Hero (game), 69
Buffalo (game), 13, 236
Bury Me, My Love (game), 162–63, 212

C3 Framework, 22, 31–32, 41*t*, 66, 84
Campaign for the Civic Mission of Schools, 33, 41*t*, 43–44
Case, N., 5, 58
CASEL Framework, 36, 41*t*, 44–45, 101–2
change
   as games for change, 9, 198, 202, 211–12, 232
   as real-world change, 10, 65–66, 67–72, 183–84
in character
   education, 19, 20, 35, 37
   in games, 69, 88, 89, 90, 92–93, 99–100, 103, 104–5, 121, 122–24, 130, 175
   of a person, 6, 16, 38, 43, 53, 59, 67, 101
cheating, 88–89, 95–96, 196–97
choices
   and consequences, 145–46
   in ethics, 141–42
   in games, 141, 143–46, 151–53
CIRCLE, 23–24, 27
citizen
   definition of, 6–7, 84–85
   problematized term, 6–7, 59, 72, 109

citizen science, 76, 178, 237
citizenship
  assessing, 221
  developing skills of, 6–7, 32, 59, 66, 72, 101,
    125, 194
civic communities, 11, 44, 87, 100–101,
  117, 227
Civic Education Study (IEA), 23
civic empowerment gap, 27, 72
Civics Assessment framework, 32, 33, 41t
Civics! An American Musical (game), 72,
  161–62, 191
civility
  incivility, 24–25, 226
  political civility, 24–25
  problems with the term, 24–25
Civilization (game series), 54, 161–62
Coleman-Mortley, A., 29, 30–31, 51, 103, 169
Collaboration, 83, 97, 122–23, 129
commercial off-the-shelf games (COTs), 211–12
Common Circles, 205, 206f
Common Core (US), 31, 33, 35, 41t
Common Threads (game), 205, 206f
communication
  in games, 83, 87–98, 245t
  skills, 83–86
community
  civic communities, 11, 44, 87, 100–101
  in games, 83, 87–98, 239t, 245t
  problems with, 90–93
  volunteering in, 6, 20, 23–24, 26–28, 41t, 84,
    100, 179t, 220
Community PlanIt (game), 71
compassion
  competition, 90–91, 93, 97
  definition, 119
  with games, 71, 89–90, 109, 110,
    122–23, 130–37
  perspective-taking and, 119, 125–28
  skills, 11, 37, 38, 40–42t, 44, 84, 101, 102
confirmation bias, 119, 159, 181
connected civics, 17, 34–35
connected civic gaming, 34–35
Consalvo, Mia, 196
Constitution (US), 53, 54, 55, 61–62, 161–62
constraints, 77–78, 143–44, 146, 192–93, 196–97,
  202, 203–4, 213t
Counties Work (game), 76
COVID-19
  pandemic, 3–6, 225, 228
  projects about, 5, 65, 72–73, 157, 169–70,
    171–72, 178, 180
creativity, 16, 45–46, 47, 195–196, 200–1, 207–8
Crisis of Nations (game), 87, 103
critical design, 204–7

critical inquiry
  definition of, 11–12, 45–47
  in games, 143–47
  skills, 11–12, 39, 45–47, 141–43, 148, 245–246t
critical thinking
  definition of, 11–12, 45–47
  in games, 143–47
  skills, 11–12, 39, 45–47, 141–43, 148, 245–246t
cultural awareness, 45, 119–120
cultural competency, 119–120
cultural humility, 119–120
culture
  cultural norms, 91, 99, 120, 135
  how it affects laws, 107–8, 119–20
  respect of cultures, 119–120, 124–125
curiosity, 56–57, 137
curricular needs, 29–47, 211, 213t, 239t
customization, 97, 103, 113, 245t

Darvasi, Paul, 10, 113–14, 165, 219
Davisson, A., 7, 59, 125, 146
debriefing, 134–35, 151, 190
decision-making
  and consequences, 145–46
  in games, 141, 143–46, 151–53
  skills, 141–42
deliberation, 13–14, 45–47, 76–77, 88–89, 93–94
Democratic Socialism Simulator (game), 176
Design
  for accessibility, 26–28, 204, 213t
  of activities, 219–20
  biases in, 92–93, 107–8
  definition of, 192–94
  game design, generally, 194–97
  principles, 245
  toolkit, 239
design thinking, 192–196, 198
Dewey, J., 43, 44, 45, 66, 84–85, 143
dialogue
  dialogue choices, 123–24, 145
  dialogues and discourse, 7, 28, 44–45, 76–77,
    85–86, 92, 94–97, 245t
dialogues, 7, 28, 44–45, 76–77, 85–86, 92,
  94–97, 245t
Discord, 87, 91, 96, 103, 152
discourse
  civil discourse, 7, 28, 44–45, 76–77, 85–86, 92,
    94–97, 245t
  limitations, 90–93
discrimination, 107, 121–22
Dishon, G., 17, 34–35, 54, 91, 144–45
disinformation, 11–12, 26, 157–58, 160–61, 169
distance learning, 4–5, 21, 190, 211, 213t
Do I Have a Right? (game), 10–11, 61–62, 63
Dreams (game), 196

echo chambers, 92, 159–161
ecology of use, 9–10, 15–16, 134, 199–200, 213*t*,
    221, 239*t*
ecosystem of use, 9–10, 15–16, 134, 199–200, 213*t*,
    221, 239*t*
educational games, 8–9, 59, 211–12
election, 10, 23–24, 26, 51–52, 59–61, 96, 161,
    163–164, 168, 174, 226–227
Electoral College, The, 10–11, 39, 43, 54, 60–61, 195
emotions
    with empathy, 119
    with identity, 100–6
    overwhelming, 109–10, 114–16, 199
    SEL and education, 33, 34, 35, 36, 37–38, 44–45,
        100, 101–2, 106–7, 112–13
empathy
    definition, 119
    with games, 71, 89–90, 109, 110, 122–23, 130–37
    historical empathy, 130, 201, 298
    perspective-taking and, 119, 125–28
    skills, 11, 37, 38, 40–42*t*, 44, 84, 101, 102
Entertainment Software Association (ESA), 8
EPIC (Ethics Practice and Implementation
    Categorization) Framework, 37–38
EteRNA (game), 5, 65, 72, 181, 228
ethical thinking, 22, 23, 36, 37–38, 64
ethically notable games, 17–18, 150
eudaimonia, 60
Executive Command (game), 51, 52*f*, 54, 55,
    154, 167
experimentation, 47, 102–4, 146–147, 195–196,
    200, 245*t*
experts, 41*t*, 57–58, 68*t*, 70–71, 79, 93, 129,
    135, 188–89
exploration, 47, 105, 109, 144, 194–197,
    200, 245*t*

Fable III (game), 64, 89, 122, 150, 154, 185
Facebook, 21, 24–25, 26, 87, 91, 142, 159–60
Factitious (game), 13, 157, 158*f*, 162, 232*t*
Fake It to Make It (game), 169, 232*t*
fake news, 157, 169–170, 172*f*
Fake Your Own Election (game), 168, 232*t*
Fall Guys (game), 96, 103, 163
Fallout (game series), 87, 103, 143–44, 145, 149,
    196, 211–12
Farber, Matt, 59, 94, 200, 219
Fiscal Ship (game), 69
flourish, 7, 37, 60, 101, 149, 172, 193
Foldit, 5, 181, 228
Fortnite (game), 4, 10, 87, 91, 99–100, 103, 211–12
Free Rice (game), 184, 189
Fullerton, T., 155*f*, 195
Fun, 54
functional fixedness, 175
game jam, 106, 195, 202–3, 237, 251

gamer, 8
games for change (type of game), 9, 198, 202,
    211–12, 232
Games for Change (organization), 202, 232*t*
Gamification, 9, 72–73, 183
Garcia, A., 16, 27–28, 71–72, 84, 221
Gee, James Paul, 87, 308, 319, 325
Gehm, D., 7, 59, 125, 146
Generation Citizen, 30, 35
gerrymandering, 43, 188–89
Gilliam, A., 205–7
Global Game Jam, 106, 202
Gone Home, 69, 236
Gordon, Eric, 76–77, 89–90
governance, 6, 28, 34, 43–44, 53, 65–66, 84–85,
    227, 237
Grand Theft Auto (game series), 4
Gray, K., 92–93, 108
Gris (game), 105, 219
*Guardian of Democracy: The Civic Mission of
    Schools,* 33–34, 54, 86

Haber, J., 45
hackathon, 202–4
Hallisey, L., 191
Hammer, J., 201, 201*f*, 207–8
Happy Farm (game), 185
harassment, 7, 11, 24–25, 26, 91–92, 107–8,
    197–98, 217–218*t*
Harmony Square (game), 11–12, 165–66
Harris, C., 57–58, 185
Harviainen, J.T., 60, 183, 188
Hassan, L., 60, 183
hate, 7, 11, 24–25, 26, 91–92, 107–8, 197–98,
    217–218*t*
HistoryMaker VR (game), 54
Holocaust, The, 53, 70–71, 109–10,
    199–200, 201
humanity, 55–56, 63, 105, 124, 227, 228, 229
Humphries, E., 51, 57

I am a Man (VR experience), 121–22
iCivics, 4–5, 10–11, 11*f*, 51, 52*f*, 55, 57, 60–62, 72,
    87, 98*f*, 103, 167, 169, 188–89, 219
identity
    and bias, 104–5, 109
    and emotions, 100–6
    and games, 102–5, 111–16
Idle Factory Tycoon (game), 176–77
immigration, 185–86, 212
Immigration Nation, 10, 212
incivility, 24–25, 226
information literacy, 157, 159–60,
    164–66, 168–70
Injustice (game), 105, 121–22, 126
Instagram, 65, 91, 159–60

interpretation, 11–12, 45, 69, 74, 125, 130–31, 147–48, 164, 165, 168–70, 178
iThrive Games, 121, 232t
Ito, Mizuko (Mimi), 34–35

Jewish Time Jump (game), 10, 70, 71f, 162
jigsaw method, 93
Jonassen, David, 174, 192
Journey through the Camps (game), 70–71, 109–10, 110f, 199–200
Jubilee Centre, The, 7, 37, 41t, 101, 220–23
Justice (game), 56–57

Kafai, Y., 17, 34–35, 54, 91, 144–45
Kahne, J., 27, 66, 160–61
Kantian ethics, 38, 43, 56–57
Kawashima- Ginsberg, K., 66, 86
Keep Talking and Nobody Explodes (game), 14, 93–94
Khanna, A., 14, 77
Killer Snails, 73–74
Kind Words (game), 71, 111–13, 112f, 229
Kirby, C., 5, 10, 58, 124
Knowledge Games (book), 16, 59, 228
knowledge games, 181
Korbey, Holly, 27, 53
Koster, Raph, 55

LaPensée, E., 13f, 79–80, 125, 129, 135–37, 136f
larp (live action role-playing game), 8, 78, 128, 134–35
Lasers (game), 94–95
Lave, Jean, 84–85
League of Legends, 91
Lerner, J., 24, 55
lesson plans, 231, 235
Levine, P., 66, 86
Levinson, M., 27
Life is Strange (series), 141, 145, 147, 150, 176, 236t
listening, 36, 44, 76–77, 86, 88–89, 93, 94–95, 97–98, 102, 143, 155, 158–59
literacy
    information literacy, 157, 159–61, 164–66, 168–70
    media literacy, 34, 45, 51, 157–58, 159–61, 163–64
    reading, 111–13, 158–59, 161–62, 165, 166–67
    writing, 32, 69, 111–13, 154–56, 158–59, 161–62, 165–66
Loneliness (game), 14, 106, 150, 219
Lost & Found (series), 176, 177f
Love, Bettina, 16, 28

Macon Money (game), 10, 69
Mass Effect (game series), 63, 103, 145, 161–62
Massively Multiplayer Online (MMO), 84–85, 96

media literacy, 34, 45, 51, 157–58, 159–61, 163–64
Middaugh, E., 27
Mind Field (game), 70–71, 123–24
Minecraft (game), 4, 9, 10, 16, 96–97, 103, 108, 211–12
Mirra, N, 16, 27–28, 71–72, 84, 221
Mission US (game), 14, 63, 129, 130–31, 154, 166–67, 223, 232t
Monster Prom, 104, 236t
Moral Machine, 151–52
moral panic, 23, 131
Motivation, 56–57
Museum of Me (curriculum), 113–14, 219

Nakamura, L, 128
National Assessment Governing Board, 32
National Council for the Social Studies, 22, 31–32
NAEP (National Assessment of Educational Progress) Assessment, 23, 26–28
Nevermind (game), 105
NewsFeed Defenders (game), 169, 232t
Noddings, N., 86, 102
non-playing characters (NPCs), 64, 87, 104, 126, 144, 145, 187, 222

O'Connor, Sandra Day, 20, 21, 23, 54
Offline, 104, 236t
online learning, 4–5, 21, 190, 211, 213t
Oregon Trail (game), 133, 164
Osaki Ni Shitsurei Shima- su! (game), 135
Overwatch (game), 10, 87, 91

Pandemic (board game), 5, 197
Pandemic: Legacy (board game), 197, 213t
Papers, Please (game), 11–12, 146, 185–86
Parable of the Polygons, 11–12, 150, 176
partisan bubbles, 25–26, 92
personalization, 103–4, 133, 159–60, 245t
perspective-taking, 118–19, 120–21, 125
Plague, Inc. (game), 5, 171–72
Planet Planners (game), 11–12
Play to Cure: Genes in Space (game), 164–65
playtesting, 204–7, 221–22, 239t
Pokémon Go (game), 10, 70, 199–200
political homophily, 92, 159–60
PolitiCraft: An Action Civics Card Game (game), 62–63, 62f, 97, 186
practical needs, 57–58, 211, 213t
prejudice, 13, 121–22, 124
privacy, 73, 184, 213t, 226–27, 245t
problems
    games and, 174–90, 245t
    and skills, 172–74
    types of, 85–86, 172–73
problem-solving
    games and, 174–90, 245t

and skills, 172–74
types of, 85–86, 172–73
public sphere, 17, 84–85, 86, 87, 88–89, 92, 144–45, 196, 211

Quandary (game), 13–14, 103, 187–88, 187f, 211–12
Quest: Journey through the Lifespan (game), 222

Race to Ratify (game), 161–62
racism, 3, 26, 33, 72–73, 117, 123–24, 131, 226–27
Reacting to the Past (game series), 121, 162, 174, 175–76
reading, 111–13, 158–59, 161–62, 165, 166–67
reasoning, 11–12, 22, 38, 46, 142–43, 159–60
Red Dead Redemption (series), 87, 145, 164, 211–12, 229
reflection
    in education, generally, 143
    in games, generally, 146–47, 150–56
reflection-in-action, 147, 154
reflection-on-action, 147, 154
Reliving the Revolution, 70, 74–75, 154, 162, 222
remote learning, 4–5, 21, 190, 211, 213t
Resilience (game), 175
respect, 6–8, 11, 32, 36, 37, 38, 44–45, 101, 119–120, 124–25
Revolution 1979: Black Friday (game), 73–74, 75, 162
Roblox (game), 128, 196
role-playing
    games, 57–58, 77–78, 121–22, 134–35, 145, 147, 153, 162, 221
    historical roles, 121–22, 130–32, 189
    use of in general, 120–21
role model, 83–84, 88, 114, 142
Rosenstrasse (game), 201, 201f
Ruiz, S., 125, 129
Rusch, D., 55–56, 198

Salen, Katie, 95
scaffolding learning, 69, 76–77, 113, 213t
Schrier, Steven, 24, 188–89
Scratch, 239t
SeeClickFix, 178, 180t
self-determination theory, 56
self-efficacy, 36, 44–45, 100–1, 106–7, 165–66, 252t
September 7, 2020 (game), 5, 10, 58, 124
September 12 (game), 58
serious games, 8–9, 59, 211–12
service learning, 34, 43–44, 67
Shaenfield, David, 88–89, 94–95, 142–43, 181
Shaffer, David, 65–66
Shah, Mamta, 96–97, 102
Shaw, A., 108
SheroHub (game), 205–7, 207f
Sicart, Miguel, 144–45

SimCity, 54, 69, 76
slavery, 14, 53, 126, 129, 131, 134
social and emotional learning (SEL), 33, 34, 35, 36, 37–38, 44–45, 100, 101–2, 106–7, 112–13
social impact games, 9, 198, 202, 211–12, 232
social justice, 16, 34–35, 45, 225
Spent (game), 109, 182–83
stigma, 4, 111, 126, 127, 148
Stokes, B., 68t, 69
story, 69, 97, 105, 195–96, 247t
storytelling, 125, 195–96, 204–7, 247t
Suits, Bernard, 16–17
Super Mario Bros. (series), 99–100, 103–4, 143–44, 174–75
surveillance, 72–73, 220
survival gap, 3
SweetXHeart (game), 11, 12f, 104, 236t
systems
    games and, 174–90, 245t
    and skills, 11–12, 41t, 172–74
systems thinking, 11–12, 41t, 173–74, 185

The Directing Game (game), 125
That Dragon, Cancer, 10, 115, 115f, 199, 229
That's Your Right (game), 54
The End of Us (game), 106, 219
The Migrant Trail (game), 14, 133–34, 212
The Redistricting Game, 188–89
The Republic is (Still) at Risk, 33–34
The Road Not Taken (game), 78, 134–35
The Slaying of Sandy Hook Elementary (game), 199
The Sims (game), 4
The SUDAN Game (game), 181
The Walking Dead (Telltale) (game), 148–49
Thoughts and Prayers (game), 168
Thunderbird Strike (game), 79–80
TikTok, 28, 65
Time Trek (game), 10, 14, 15f
toxicity, 11, 24–25
Trade Off (game), 150, 207–8
Traffic Agent (application), 180t, 184
transgress, 147, 185–86, 196–97, 198–99, 200–1
transparency, 169, 184, 193–94, 213t, 245t
Tree (VR experience), 117
Troll Factory (game), 165–66
Twine, 5, 10, 114, 239t
Twitch, 4, 87, 91, 96, 99–100, 103, 197, 213t
Twitter, 26, 28, 65, 91, 142, 197
Twu, Alfred, 78–79, 79f

Undertale (game), 145, 153, 196
Utu, 7

Valorant (game), 163
Vanek, A., 78, 128, 134–35

virtual classroom, 4–5, 21, 190, 211, 213*t*
virtual worlds, 95–96
virtue ethics, 55
Vituccio, R., 109–10, 110*f*, 199–200
Volunteering, 6, 20, 23–24, 26–28, 41*t*, 84,
     110*f*, 100, 179*t*, 220
Voter Suppression Trail (game), 164
voting, 6, 10, 23–24, 30, 54, 61, 66–67, 72–73, 100,
     121, 146, 164, 226–27
VoxPop (game), 10, 11, 121, 189–90, 189*f*

Walden (game), 154–56, 155*f*
Way (game), 83, 97, 122, 147, 229
Wenger, E., 84–85
What Happens Next? (online interactive), 5, 58
What Remains of Edith Finch (game), 113–14, 229, 236

When Rivers Were Trails (game), 135–37, 136*f*
Whyville (game), 88–89, 95–96
wicked problems, 85–86, 173
Win the White House (game), 10–11, 51, 59, 60–61,
     63, 88–89, 103, 111, 164–65
Workflow (game), 77
World Health Organization (WHO), 3–4, 169–70
World of Warcraft, 4, 10, 87, 88
writing, 32, 69, 111–13, 154–56, 158–59,
     161–62, 165–66

Youth Participatory Action Research
     (YPAR), 34
YouTube, 91, 103, 108, 237

Zoom, 87, 190